Circumplex Models
of
Personality and Emotions

Circumplex Models of Personality and Emotions

Robert Plutchik & Hope R. Conte, Editors

American Psychological Association
Washington, DC

Published by
American Psychological Association
750 First Street, NE
Washington, DC 20002

Copies may be ordered from
APA Order Department
P.O. Box 92984
Washington, DC 20090-2984

In the UK and Europe, copies may be ordered from
American Psychological Association
3 Henrietta Street
Covent Garden, London
WC2E 8LU England

Typeset in Goudy by PRO-Image Corporation, Techna-Type Div., York, PA

Printer: Data Reproductions Corporation, Rochester Hills, MI
Jacket Designer: Anne Masters Design, Washington, DC
Technical/Production Editor: Edward B. Meidenbauer

Library of Congress Cataloging-in-Publication Data
Circumplex models of personality and emotions/edited by Robert Plutchik and Hope R.
Conte.
    p.   cm.
    Includes bibliographical references and index.
    ISBN 1-55798-380-1 (alk. paper).
    1. Personality and emotions.   2. Interpersonal relations.
3. Psychometrics. I. Plutchik, Robert. II. Conte, Hope R., 1929-.
BF698.9.E45C57   1997
155.2—dc20
                                                   96-33333
                                                   CIP

British Library Cataloguing-in-Publication Data
A CIP record is available from the British Library.

Printed in the United States of America
First edition

CONTENTS

PART II: THE CIRCUMPLEX IN RELATION TO EMOTIONS

PART III: APPLICATIONS OF THE CIRCUMPLEX MODEL TO CLINICAL ISSUES

CONTRIBUTORS

John Birtchnell, MD, Senior Lecturer and Consultant Psychiatrist, Institute of Psychiatry, London, England.

John M. Bynner, PhD, Professor of Social Psychology, Director of the Social Statistics Research Unit, City University, London, England.

D. Christopher Dryer, PhD, Research Staff Member at the IBM Almaden Research Center, Almaden, California.

Gene A. Fisher, PhD, Associate Professor of Sociology, University of Massachusetts at Amherst, Amherst, Massachusetts.

Lewis R. Goldberg, PhD, Professor of Psychology, Department of Psychology, University of Oregon, and Research Scientist, Oregon Research Institute, Eugene, Oregon.

Michael B. Gurtman, PhD, Professor of Psychology, Department of Psychology, University of Wisconsin-Parkside, Kenosha, Wisconsin.

Steven Hagemoser, MA, Graduate student, Department of Psychology, University of Kentucky, Lexington, Kentucky.

William P. Henry, PhD, Associate Professor of Psychology, Department of Psychology, University of Utah, Salt Lake City, Utah.

Leonard M. Horowitz, PhD, Professor of Psychology, Department of Psychology, Stanford University, Stanford, California.

Donald J. Kiesler, PhD, Professor and Director of Clinical Psychology, Department of Psychology, Virginia Commonwealth University, Richmond, Virginia.

Elena N. Krasnoperova, BA, third-year doctoral student, Department of Psychology, Stanford University, California.

Maurice Lorr, PhD, Professor of Psychology, Life Cycle Institute, Catholic University of America, Washington, DC.

James K. Madison, PhD, Coordinator for Program Development, Eating Disorders Program, University of Nebraska Medical Center, Omaha, Nebraska.

Clarence C. McCormick, Eugene, Oregon.

Rauni Myllyniemi, PhD, Associate Professor of Social Psychology, University of Helsinki, Finland.

Robert Plutchik, PhD, Professor Emeritus of Psychiatry, Department of Psychiatry, Albert Einstein College of Medicine, Bronx, New York.

David M. Romney, PhD, Professor of Clinical Psychology, University of Calgary, Calgary, Alberta, Canada.

James Rounds, PhD, Associate Professor of Educational Psychology and Psychology, Chair and Director of Training for Counselling Psychology, University of Illinois at Urbana-Champaign; Clinical and Research Associate, Department of Psychology, Roswell Memorial Park Institute, Buffalo, New York.

James A. Russell, PhD, Professor of Psychology, Department of Psychology, University of British Columbia, Vancouver, British Columbia, Canada.

Earl S. Schaefer, PhD, Professor Emeritus of Psychology, Department of Maternal and Child Health, School of Public Health, University of North Carolina, Chapel Hill, North Carolina.

James A. Schmidt, PhD, Assistant Professor of Psychology, Department of Psychology, Western Illinois University, Macomb, Illinois.

Stephen Soldz, PhD, Director of Research, Boston Institute for Psychotherapsy and Assistant Clinical Professor of Psychology, Harvard Medical School, Cambridge, Massachusetts.

Terence J. G. Tracey, PhD, Professor of Educational Psychology and Psychology, Department of Educational Psychology, University of Illinois at Urbana-Champaign, Illinois.

Krista K. Trobst, PhD Candidate in Clinical Psychology, University of British Columbia, Vancouver, British Columbia, Canada.

Christopher C. Wagner, PhD, Postdoctoral Fellow in Psychology, Department of Psychiatry, Medical College of Virginia, Virginia Commonwealth University, Richmond, Virginia.

Thomas A. Widiger, PhD, Professor of Psychology, Department of Psychology, University of Kentucky, Lexington, Kentucky.

Jerry S. Wiggins, PhD, Professor of Psychology, Department of Psychology, University of British Columbia, Vancouver, British Columbia, Canada.

INTRODUCTION

CIRCUMPLEX MODELS OF PERSONALITY AND EMOTIONS

ROBERT PLUTCHIK and HOPE R. CONTE

During the past few decades two major approaches have been used in an effort to define the structure of personality traits and emotions. One is based on the use of factor analytic techniques with the aim of identifying a relatively small number of basic or underlying dimensions. The other approach focuses on determining the similarity structure of all traits and emotions; the underlying assumption of this approach is that a relatively seamless circular ordering or circumplex is a parsimonious description of the relations among traits and among emotions.

The study of personality structure as it is understood today began with the efforts of Cattell, Eysenck, and Guilford in the 1940s. The factor analytic procedures they and their many followers used, based on the criterion of simple structure, led to the conclusion that anywhere from 4 to 16 basic dimensions were needed to describe the structure of personality. In recent years, the view has gained favor that all personality traits may be described as belonging to one or another of five broad dimensions of personality—the Five Factor Model. Considerable support for this model exists. The five basic factors have been called *extroversion*, *agreeableness*, *conscientiousness*, *emotional stability*, and *openness to experience*. Some investigators have preferred to use the terms *culture* or *intellect*, for *openness*, *neuroticism* for *emotional stability*, and *behavioral control* for *conscientiousness*.

Less well known is an alternative structural model that has been applied to both personality and emotions. This model stems from the early work of Guttman in psychometrics, Leary and Wiggins in personality, and Plutchik and Lorr in emotions. These various investigators have demonstrated that the descriptive language of traits and emotions, two domains that show considerable overlap both in terminology and meaning, can be organized conceptually and mathematically by means of a circular model. Such a model has the property of similarity of adjacent elements (traits or emotions) and increasing dissimilarity of elements that are further removed on the circle. Another one of its properties is the bipolarity of opposite elements on the circle. These properties can be defined in terms of patterns of correlations as well as by means of other mathematical procedures. Contributors to these ideas have emphasized that the circumplex applies primarily to the interpersonal aspects of personality and not necessarily to the intellectual and cultural dimensions.

During the past 30 years the circumplex model has been applied to an increasing number of conceptual domains by investigators. In addition to emotions and personality, these applications include the study of facial expressions, the development of new kinds of psychometric instruments, the interpretation of clinical phenomena, and the understanding of vocational choices. To date, no one has provided a single forum for presenting the variety of circumplex models that are currently in existence. Therefore, this book will attempt to remedy this situation. The 26 contributors represent a significant proportion of those who are currently contributing new data and theory based on the circumplex concept.

In order to provide some coherence to the contributions, the editors requested each author or set of authors to respond directly or indirectly to a number of questions. These included, "How should a circumplex be defined and measured?" "In what ways is a circumplex useful?" "How are circumplex models related to factor analytic models?" "What are some research or clinical implications of the circumplex?"

As we began to read through the chapters it became evident that each varied in its focus of interest, but that they could be grouped into three major sections. Part One is concerned mainly with showing the application of the circumplex idea to personality theory and description. Part Two tends to relate the circumplex model to emotions and interpersonal interactions. Part Three is largely concerned with the application of the circumplex model to clinical issues; for example, the diagnosis of personality disorders, the role of the circumplex in psychotherapy, and the circumplex as a basis for psychometric test development. It should be emphasized, however, that these three sections are not sharply divided, and that some overlap exists in all chapters. The groupings were made primarily to recognize a major theme in each contribution. These sections are followed by a detailed Epilogue, which addresses important issues raised by the book's contributors. In the following overview of the book, we provide a brief description of the contributions of each chapter in the three sections.

PART ONE: THE CIRCUMPLEX IN RELATION TO PERSONALITY

The eight chapters of Part One are concerned with showing how the circumplex concept contributes to personality theory. The chapters describe the practical techniques for identifying the presence of a circumplex, mathematical methods for describing circumplex parameters as well as tests that are derived from the circumplex idea. A key concept frequently noted is that the circumplex reflects many characteristics of interpersonal relations.

Robert Plutchik

In the introductory chapter of this section, Plutchik has two aims. He first attempts to demonstrate that the study of emotions and the study of personality are aspects of the same basic domain of interpersonal relations. Several reasons are given. First, there is extensive overlap of the language describing emotions and personality; second, there is considerable overlap of functions of both; and third, the circumplex model describes the structure of both very well. Plutchik's second aim is to summarize the history of attempts to apply the circumplex model to these two domains and to then provide an overview of his psychoevolutionary theory of emotions. In this theory, interpersonal personality traits are interpreted as derivative of the more basic emotions, in the same sense in which most colors are derived from mixtures of the primary ones. The theory also implies that several other domains are derivatives of emotions including personality disorders and ego defenses. Several studies are described that reveal circumplex structures for emotions, personality traits, personality disorders, and ego defenses. These observations support the generality of the model for interpersonal relations.

Maurice Lorr

Lorr is a pioneer in the application of the circumplex model to affects, personality, and psychotherapy, and he provides an overview of the development of the concept of the interpersonal circumplex. He describes the different ways one can test for the presence of a circumplex structure and how different approaches have led to quite similar findings. Over the years, Lorr has developed several psychometric instruments for measuring moods, interpersonal proclivities, and psychotic syndromes. Several of these instruments are described and empirical data are presented to show their essential circumplex structures.

Jerry S. Wiggins and Krista K. Trobst

Wiggins and Trobst point out that the circumplex idea has been applied in recent years to affects, diagnoses, facial expressions, and vocational choice. They hold that all such circumplexes reflect interpersonal processes, which in turn express the basic interpersonal relations of status and love. Previous research by Wiggins has established scales for defining interpersonal space by means of the circumplex. Such scales may provide a trait profile that takes into consideration the correlations among traits. As an extension of these ideas, Wiggins and Trobst describe the development of a new scale for measuring individual dispositions toward social support of others. The scale, called the Supportive Actions Scale, was shown to form a circumplex and a goodness of fit measure confirms its circumplex nature. Relations between trait measures and social support style measures were moderate. The properties of this scale suggest that it may be used to assign individuals to types and also may provide a theoretical basis for evaluating the general adequacy of other inventories designed to measure the same general concept.

Michael B. Gurtman

Gurtman emphasizes that the circumplex provides a nomological net for a trait construct by describing its relations to other traits. He calls this process *construct elucidation*. As useful as the circumplex model is, Gurtman believes that it applies primarily to the interpersonal and emotional domains. He goes further and claims that the circumplex better represents interpersonal and affective traits than does the simple structure approach of factor analyses as illustrated, for example, by the Five Factor Model. One of the reasons for this statement is that the existence of factor loadings on two or more factors is typical of the interpersonal domain, which is a characteristic more clearly understood within a circumplex model than a linear one.

Gurtman's chapter analyzes previously published data from several different investigators who have used the California Q-Set item pool and methodology. He finds that the majority of the items of the Q-Set load on more than one factor, as is typical of the circumplex. Of equal importance, Gurtman describes several interesting ideas about circular mathematics as well as an iconic method of representation for showing a trait's characteristics. From both a mathematical and content viewpoint, the circumplex reveals a trait's location, its relation to other traits, and its "bandwidth," or degree of overlap with adjoining traits. He concludes that the application of circumplex ideas to existing data may reveal many insights about personality.

Clarence C. McCormick and Lewis R. Goldberg

McCormick and Goldberg point out that most psychological variables have strong associations with at least two factors derived from a simple structure approach to factor analysis. This fact raises questions about the meaning of total scores obtained on tests that are based on the idea of factorially univocal dimensions. The circumplex deals with systematically overlapping categories and requires complex numbers and circular statistics to adequately represent their interactions.

McCormick and Goldberg illustrate some of these ideas by analyzing data collected using the Interpersonal Checklist based on the Leary system. They show that items selected for endorsement by any one research participant form a circumplex distribution and that the averages of all members of a sample also form a circumplex distribution. Circumplex analyses of items may be used to identify deviant participants from a sample as well as to identify ambiguous items from an item pool. These authors emphasize the importance of using both factor-analytic and circumplex types of analyses of test data.

Earl S. Schaefer

Schaefer believes that a spatial plot of the interrelations of a set of measures is a more economical presentation of relationships among concepts than is a verbal description, a matrix of intercorrelations, or a list of factor loadings. The circumplex is one such spatial plot and it is often found in studies of social and emotional behaviors. Schaefer reviews some of his and others' early research on the description of a mother's behavior toward her child, which generally found a two-dimensional circumplex order of the various subscales. Children's reports of their parents' behaviors also led to a two-dimensional circular order. Circumplex structures have also been found through factor analysis of items describing spouses' perceptions of their mates' behavior toward themselves, women's descriptions of their mothers' behavior toward themselves, and teacher ratings of 13-year-old children. An early study also revealed that diagnostic constructs also showed a circumplex ordering.

Later research demonstrated that the addition of items descriptive of the domain of academic competence led to a more general model of personality and adaptive behavior, a model that approximates a sphere. In general, the circular and spherical models for interpersonal relationships reveal that love, acceptance, control, and involvement are key elements of all relationships.

John Birtchnell

Birtchnell presents his interpersonal model as an octagon rather than as a circle. He prefers to think of the axes as reflecting the dimensions of upper–lower and distant–close. He assumes that interpersonal behavior is not based on flight *from* something but on a move *toward* something. Unlike motivational states such as hunger, interpersonal goals can be met only by interaction with other people.

From a conceptual point of view, Birtchnell provides a description of personality traits associated with each of the four main positions of the octagon; that is, closeness, distance, upperness, and lowerness. He notes that there are both positive and maladaptive forms of the octant positions. For example, positive closeness is associated with intimacy, informality, affection, and free communication. Negative closeness is associated with fear of desertion, increased attempts to attract attention, and anxiety when alone.

Birtchnell argues that each of the *DSM-IV* personality disorders can be described in terms of the negative forms of the eight octants. For example, he sees the paranoid personality disorder as a disorder of distance. Patients with this disorder are preoccupied with issues of power and rank and often reveal grandiose fantasies. In contrast narcissism is a disorder associated with upperness. Such patients believe they are superior and are entitled to special treatment. Their fears concern the images of being small and insignificant. Birtchnell's elaboration of the circumplex is an interesting attempt to show its relevance to clinical issues, but empirical support is yet to be obtained.

Terence J. Tracey and James Rounds

In the final chapter of Part One, Tracey and Rounds review their work on evaluating vocational interests using the circumplex model. The major focus is on Holland's theory that postulates six types of vocational personality and work environments: realistic, investigative, artistic, social, enterprising, and conventional (RIASEC). These are arranged around a hexagonal structure, with proximity related to degree of similarity.

Holland's circular structure is examined across a wide variety of studies. Meta-analyses showed that the model fit the specifications of three different circular models more adequately and in a more parsimonious manner than did an alternative cluster model. The authors also examine two basic approaches to thinking about structural issues in vocational and personality psychology: the factor list approach and the circumplex approach. The latter places emphasis less on the specific underlying dimensions and more on the circular structure itself. Results showed that both approaches accounted equally well for the six RIASEC types. However, in view of the essentially arbitrary nature of the underlying dimensions, the authors believe it more valid to focus on the circular structure itself.

With respect to generalizability, a large number of studies based on U.S. samples showed Holland's model to be adequate to describe the relations among the RIASEC interest scales, and no differences were found in this structure across gender, age, or instruments. However, the structure was not invariant across cultures.

In their final section, Tracey and Rounds summarize their recent work that suggests that the specific number of interest types is arbitrary and may be either greater or less than six. In addition, they demonstrate that by adding the dimension of prestige to Holland's circular arrangement of types, a spherical structure is formed that is posited to have considerable heuristic value.

PART TWO: THE CIRCUMPLEX IN RELATION TO EMOTIONS

In Part Two, the authors focus attention on how the circumplex idea applies to emotions. These chapters generally interpret emotions as aspects of interpersonal interactions. They reveal that the language of emotions and of personality traits are closely related and that both can be represented by a circular structure. And the authors also provide experimental data showing the applicability of the circumplex idea to emotions.

James A. Russell

In this chapter, Russell states that a fairly complete description of emotions requires that at least six properties be presented. The first requires a specific instance of the emotion category. The second recognizes that emotions vary in degree of intensity and that the language of emotions reflects this fact. The third characteristic of emotions is that their relations may be described by a circumplex. The fourth is that emotions may be described in terms of certain broad dimensions, such as hedonic value and arousal. The fifth is that emotions reflect scripts—that is, prototypic sequences of connected events. The sixth is that emotion categories are illustrations of fuzzy concepts.

The circumplex represents a kind of fuzzy logic by not placing emotions in separate categories but by identifying their varying degrees of overlap. The circumplex is a way of describing a continuously varying reality, something that is characteristic of emotions. Russell goes on to summarize the history of circumplex descriptions of emotions. He points out that the circumplex does not depend on a specific language because it has been replicated in different languages. It also has been found with judgments of facial expressions even in 2-year-old children and in individuals with extensive brain damage. Different analytic techniques have also yielded support for a circumplex.

Donald J. Kiesler, James A. Schmidt, and Christopher C. Wagner

In this chapter, Kiesler, Schmidt, and Wagner focus on the impact messages that exist between two interacting individuals. These include feelings, action tendencies, and fantasies. The messages imply claims of one person on another that relate to issues of control and affiliation. Interpersonal acts (messages) tend to elicit restricted classes of reactions from others. The theory of complementarity is described in which it is hypothesized that dominant behaviors tend to elicit submissive ones, friendly behaviors tend to elicit friendly ones, and hostile behaviors tend to elicit hostile ones. These ideas are summarized by means of a circumplex model.

The chapter describes the development of the Impact Message Inventory, a self-report inventory designed to measure the typical, automatic, relatively preconscious sets of emotional and other covert reactions each person has to others. A recent 56-item version of the Impact Message Inventory was factor analyzed and was shown to have a circumplex structure. The primary axes were interpreted to be dominance and affiliation, and the elements of the circumplex fell quite close to their predicted locations.

In the final section of the chapter, Kiesler and his coauthors argue that the Impact Message Inventory measures certain covert elements of complex emotional reactions. They state that the most important type of event that produces emotional reactions is interpersonal behavior. They further claim that interpersonal behavior is best described by means of a circumplex model. They essentially reconceptualize impact message theory within the framework of contemporary emotion theories. They conclude by emphasizing that tests of the theory of interpersonal complementarity must include the covert elements of the chain of interpersonal events as well as the overt ones.

Gene A. Fisher

The chapter by Fisher describes a study of self-reported moods rated diurnally by college students. His analyses of these data demonstrate that a circumplex model, one that is highly correlated with that reported by other investigators, fits the data well. He considers moods as a bridge between emotions and personality traits, and shows that the same model applies to both. However, it was necessary to reduce social desirability bias in order to obtain the clearest expression of the circumplex.

Fisher raises the question of why the language of emotions and personality traits tend to have a circular structure. He hypothesizes that the circumplex is a reflection of the semantic differential dimensions of evaluation and activation. This idea is in turn based on the concept that emotions, as subjective experiences, are readouts of various states of the organism. It is also based on the assumption that emotion reflects a degree of discrepancy between desired behaviors and what actually happens as a consequence of environmental inputs.

Rauni Myllyniemi

In the last chapter of this section, Myllyniemi explores the idea of what it is about interpersonal behavior that generates a circular pattern of interrelations of traits and affects elements. She provides an emotion-based interpretation of this observation, suggesting that interpersonal behavior is largely centered around emotional security orientations. Emotional orientations are considered to be control processes that involve the recognition of harmful and beneficial events, the motivation to rid oneself of harm, and the actions necessary to carry out this goal. She proposes that each element of the interpersonal circle has both a social meaning and an emotional meaning. For example, the affiliation–hostility axis implies such emotions as affectionate, warm, bitter, and hurt.

Myllyniemi then describes several of her studies that have dealt with the interpersonal circle. One concerned similarity judgments of language adjectives. Factor analysis of the correlation matrix demonstrated a clear circumplex. A second study was concerned with the similarity structure of drawn face diagrams and photographs of posed expressions. Multidimensional scaling led to two-dimensional circumplex structures. Myllyniemi concludes by suggesting an evolutionary interpretation of the social and emotional orientations.

PART THREE: APPLICATIONS OF THE CIRCUMPLEX MODEL TO CLINICAL ISSUES

The six chapters of Part Three focus attention on the role of the circumplex model in helping to understand clinical issues. Several chapters show how the circumplex applies to a description of personality disorders. Another chapter shows how the circumplex has helped in the construction of several psychometric instruments for the measurement of personality and interpersonal relations. Several chapters demonstrate the usefulness of the circumplex model in a psychotherapeutic context.

Thomas A. Widiger and Steven Hagemoser

Widiger and Hagemoser review theoretical and empirical attempts to apply the interpersonal circumplex to *DSM* personality disorders. They conclude that maladaptive interpersonal relatedness does appear to be a major component for some of the personality disorders and that the manner of this relatedness may be understood with respect to the interpersonal circumplex. It appears that some of the personality disorders, most notably borderline but also others such as schizotypal and compulsive, involve aspects of personality that are primarily interpersonal in nature. The authors, therefore, compare the success of the interpersonal circumplex in describing and understanding personality disorders to the alternative Five Factor Model of personality.

Costa and McCrae's (1989) assessment of the relationship of the Five Factor Model to the interpersonal circumplex leads them to argue that these two models of personality enhance one another, inasmuch as the Five Factor Model provides a larger context in which to orient the interpersonal circumplex, and the interpersonal circumplex provides a useful elaboration of two aspects of the Five Factor Model: extroversion and agreeableness and their combinations. Widiger and Hagemoser illustrate this formulation with respect to the dimensions of neuroticism, conscientiousness, and openness. The authors conclude that the interpersonal circumplex and the Five Factor Model of personality complement rather than contradict one another.

David M. Romney and John M. Bynner

Romney and Bynner present a brief overview of the models that have been used by personality theorists to investigate the structure of personality characteristics. These include the hierarchical model produced by exploratory factor analysis, Louis Guttman's work on the radex representation as an alternative to factors, and K. Joreskog's confirmatory factor analysis and his subsequent use of structural equation modeling. For interpersonal personality traits, and, by extension, for personality disorders related to these traits, the authors believe the circumplex model to be the strongest rival to the traditional hierarchical structure. Thus they applied structural equation modeling to data from two complementary studies to test Wiggins' theory that interpersonal personality disorders could be arranged around a circle similar to that earlier proposed by Leary for interpersonal traits.

Results indicated that the circumplex model provided a good fit for five (histrionic, dependent, schizoid, paranoid, and narcissistic) of the ten *DSM-III-R* personality disorders and for seven of these disorders that were originally proposed by Wiggins. Further analyses indicated that a quasi-simplex model was the most appropriate for depicting the relationships among antisocial, borderline, avoidant, passive–aggressive, and compulsive disorders.

Leonard M. Horowitz and D. Christopher Dryer

Horowitz and Dryer summarize their thinking about the organization and nature of interpersonal problems. Their chapter begins by describing the Inventory of Interpersonal Problems and a number of its applications. These problems are representative of those that individuals bring to psychotherapy. They have been empirically demonstrated to be circumplical in structure and are interpreted to correspond to combinations of two underlying factors: affiliation–nurturance and control–dominance. The Inventory of Interpersonal Problems has been used to describe graphically the problems of individual patients, to study the psychotherapeutic process, and to compare different instruments and clarify what a given instrument is measuring.

Horowitz and Dryer present a model of interpersonal behavior that contains four principal postulates: (a) interpersonal behaviors can be described in terms of the two dimensions of affiliation, ranging from hostile to friendly behavior, and dominance, ranging from yielding to dominating behaviors; (b) an interpersonal behavior invites a complementary reaction, and the relationship between the two is also characterized in terms of the circumplex; (c) noncomplementarity creates an interpersonal tension between partners; and (d) people learn complete interpersonal sequences rather than isolated, individual responses to particular stimuli. Empirical evidence is provided to illustrate each of these postulates.

In the final section of their chapter, the authors examine the nature of interpersonal goals. They emphasize that interpersonal problems are a function of frustrated interpersonal goals. To understand a person's interpersonal problems, it is necessary first to assess that person's interpersonal goals or wishes and to determine whether his or her partner's behavior is in accordance with them. The Inventory of Interpersonal Goals fulfills this function. The authors discuss its construction, development, and application and provide evidence to show that like interpersonal behaviors and problems, interpersonal goals can be described succinctly in terms of a two-dimensional circumplex.

William P. Henry

Henry summarizes his recent research using Benjamin's Structural Analysis of Social Behavior (Benjamin, 1993), a circumplex system that measures interpersonal actions toward another person, interpersonal actions from another person, and behavior by the self toward the self. This research provides evidence to buttress his belief that the circumplex model is useful not only for description but for explanation and prediction as well.

Henry describes a methodology for using the Structural Analysis of Social Behavior model in the description of the dynamics of a patient's interpersonal problems and in the subsequent measurement of the outcome of treatment. He goes on to show how the use of this model has enabled him, along with Benjamin, to generate a theoretical model of abnormal personality that proposes a qualitative definition for differentiating abnormal from normal personality. This is in contrast to earlier circumplex-based definitions in which pathology was seen quantitatively as a matter of degree of the expression of certain traits. Further uses of this circumplex model are described. These include the development of new instruments to test the underlying theory and to assess current interpersonal wishes, fears, and power tactics. The fact that all these instruments yield data in the same metric facilitates the integration of diverse clinical information and provides for congruence of problem, treatment, and outcome data. Henry concludes by demonstrating ways in which he believes the circumplex provides a basis for the integration of theories of psychopathology and psychotherapy that are as diverse as cognitive, behavioral, and psychodynamic.

Stephen Soldz

Soldz focuses on areas that exemplify the use of the interpersonal circumplex as a structural model in clinical research. The first example given involves the investigation of patient behaviors during group psychotherapy. A principle components analysis of scores on an instrument to measure process in groups clearly demonstrated the interpersonal circumplex dimensions when two components were extracted. The results are important inasmuch as they provide evidence that interpersonal behavior in a therapeutic group setting can be represented in circumplex space, even when the instrument used to measure this behavior was not designed explicitly on circumplex principles.

The second area of focus was the ability of the interpersonal circumplex to depict the relationships among the *DSM III-R* personality disorders. Interpretable relations were found, and results support the essential identity of the interpersonal circumplex space with that marked by the extraversion and agreeableness factors of the Five Factor Model. However, many of the disorders—for example, borderline and paranoid—were not distinguishable from each other, and there were gaps at both poles of the affiliation dimension. Including the other Five Factor Model dimensions improved the structural representation of the personality disorders.

Soldz describes the development and psychometric properties of the IIP-SC, a very brief measure of the circumplex representation of interpersonal problems and useful when time constraints preclude the use of longer instruments. It measures treatment responses as well as the longer version from which it was derived and provides useful information about the structural placement of an individual in circumplex space.

James K. Madison

Madison focuses on applying a circumplex model of personality to the diagnosis and treatment of individuals with eating disorders. Employing the interpersonal circumplex articulated by Wiggins and general descriptors of eating disorders, Madison formulates hypotheses about the interpersonal style of such individuals. The Interpersonal Adjective Scales, developed to operationalize Wiggins' model, were used to validate the expectations, derived from the literature, that these individuals would present with a largely hostile interpersonal style.

The results obtained from a number of different empirical analyses indicated that eating-disordered clients are not homogeneous in their interpersonal styles; there are two distinct and highly dissimilar subgroups. One group is, in fact, distant and hostile. The other is nurturant and overly values contact with people. Interpersonal theory and the two-dimensional circumplex are used to postulate therapeutic strategies for these two groups.

EPILOGUE

In an epilogue we address a number of important conceptual issues that have been raised by the various contributors. The first issue is concerned with how one identifies and measures the circumplex. A large number of methods are described, and various inconsistencies are noted in the precise labeling of circumplex structures. However, there is also evidence that suggests that the circular order of personality traits and emotions appears to be fairly reliable over different samples of individuals and analytic procedures.

The second issue deals with the question of the meaning of axes, regardless of whether they are based on traditional factor analytic methods or on circumplex analyses. Over the years there has been both agreement and disagreement on the labels to be given to basic dimensions of personality. However, from the circumplex point of view axes are arbitrary reference points that simply help us plot the positions of the variables relative to one another. An investigator may choose to use or ignore the labels, but all relationships among the variables are expressed through the circular network.

The third issue is concerned with the exploration of the implications of the circumplex for test construction and for measurement. A number of circumplex-based tests are reviewed briefly, and then two examples are given of how the circumplex model has created new ways to characterize and describe test items and how a reanalysis of existing data may show circumplex patterns that have not been previously recognized. Item analyses based on the circumplex concept have been shown to help identify both deviant raters and ambiguous items.

The fourth issue deals with the relation between the circumplex model and the Five Factor Model. A brief history of the bases of these concepts is presented and the point is made that in the interpersonal domain most items used in personality and affect studies are factorially complex, with substantial loadings on two or more factors. This has been demonstrated in a number of studies. Recent work has shown that several of the Five Factor dimensions, when considered two at a time, demonstrate strong circumplex properties. This is particularly true for the axes of extroversion, agreeableness, and emotional stability, all of which are related primarily to interpersonal relations. The conclusion is reached that the Five Factor Model and the circumplex model are complementary and that one's particular research interest should determine the use of one model or the other.

The final issue discussed in the epilogue concerns some uses of the circumplex model. We point out that the many contributors to the volume have shown the usefulness of the circumplex for understanding personality traits, personality disorders, emotions, psychiatric symptoms, psychotherapy interactions, adaptive functioning, vocational preferences, and goal setting. The model has encouraged the development of new tests and scales as well as new mathematical ways to describe circular configurations. Finally, the circumplex model has led to the development of many testable hypotheses about interpersonal interactions and psychotherapeutic interventions. We believe the ideas presented in this book will provide the basis for much future theory and research.

REFERENCES

Benjamin, L. S. (1993). *Interpersonal diagnosis and treatment of personality disorders.* New York: Guilford.

Costa, H. R., & McCrae, R. R. (1989). *The NEO-PI/FFI manual supplement.* Odessa, FL: Psychological Assessment Resources.

I

THE CIRCUMPLEX IN
RELATION TO
PERSONALITY

1

THE CIRCUMPLEX AS A GENERAL MODEL OF THE STRUCTURE OF EMOTIONS AND PERSONALITY

ROBERT PLUTCHIK

Although the domains of personality and emotions traditionally have been considered and taught as two distinct conceptual areas, there are several reasons for considering them as part of the same domain of interpersonal relations.

THE OVERLAP OF LANGUAGE

The first reason concerns the remarkable overlap of words used to describe emotions and personality. For example, Storm and Storm (1987) asked several hundred children and adults to list every emotion word they could think of. They also were asked to label the feelings of characters in clips from commercial television shows. This procedure resulted in a list of more than 500 terms that were grouped into various categories. Of great interest is the fact that many of the terms refer to words commonly used to describe personality. Thus, words such as *gloomy, resentful,* or *calm* can describe personality traits as well as emotional feelings. In a similar study, Clore, Ortony, and Foss (1987) asked college students to rate a long list of presumed emotion words taken from the writings of other psychologists and to indicate their degree of certainty that each word was or was not an emotion word. Considerable disagreement was found among the participants. One reason for the inconsistencies was that the simple presentation of a word does not identify a temporal context. Thus, the word *good* on the list may be interpreted as a feeling or as a personality trait. In the same way, the word *aggressive* could describe a transitory feeling or a personality disposition.

Language is a complex structure that has evolved over a period of thousands of years. As different historical elements interact, a multiplicity of meanings may become attached to a word. In addition, if a word becomes used in a scientific or technical context, it is often given a new meaning. To illustrate these points, consider the word *anxiety*. Webster's International Unabridged Dictionary provides three definitions: (a) "a painful uneasiness of the mind"; (b) "a pathological state of restlessness and agitation"; and (c) "an expectancy of danger without adequate ground explained as a transformed emotion derived from repressed libido." The same word can be defined as a transient state or may be said to describe a long-lasting condition. Emotional states usually are thought of as relatively transient feelings evoked by a situation, whereas traits usually are considered to be stable patterns of behavior that are manifested in a variety of situations. Someone may feel anxiety in anticipation of an examination, and at the other end of the continuum are people for whom anxiety is a constant part of their lives.

The distinction between states and traits is largely arbitrary (Allen & Potkay, 1981). Often the same adjective checklist can be used to measure both states and traits by a simple change in instructions. If the research participants are asked to describe how they feel *now*, or within the past few days or so, we are asking about emotional states or moods. If, however, they are asked to describe how they *usually* feel, we are asking about personality traits. Whether we call a condition an emotion or a personality trait is generally a matter of time frame. McCrae and Costa (1994) have summarized the evidence that indicates that personality traits are quite stable over long periods of time. Test–retest correlations over long time intervals (years) are generally in the range of .60 to .80, and the generalizations apply to both genders and all races.

The idea that time frame determines a term's designation applies to animals as well. In his early paper describing his work with chimpanzees, Hebb (1946) pointed out that the same behavior might be labeled fear, nervousness, or shyness, depending on a number of factors. In each case, the immediate behavior is some form of avoidance, but in the case of fear it is strong, clearly related to an identifiable stimulus, and not a common occurrence in that animal. Nervousness refers to a long-term characteristic of an animal and usually is recognized by a low startle threshold. Shyness implies that the animal tends to avoid strangers. It is thus evident that the same behavior may be interpreted as a transient emotional state or a personality trait, depending on information about the stimulus condition, the details of the behavior, and a knowledge of the organism's typical past behavior.

FUNCTIONAL SIGNIFICANCE OF EMOTIONS AND TRAITS

The second reason for considering emotions and personality traits as part of the same broad conceptual domain is that there is an overlap of functions. Although the question is not asked as often as it should be, one can reasonably inquire about the functions of emotions. One can also ask, "What functions do personality traits have?"

The Function of Emotions

Although Darwin presented a functional view of emotions in his book, *The Expression of the Emotions in Man and Animal*, published in 1872, his ideas were largely ignored by psychologists until a decade after World War II. Since that time an evolutionary, ethological approach to emotions has become increasingly recognized, and many investigators have contributed ideas to this viewpoint (Plutchik, 1980a).

Evolutionary theory as applied to emotions assumes that the natural environment creates survival problems for all organisms that must be successfully dealt with if these organisms are to survive. Problems include appropriate responses to prey and predators, to caregivers and care solicitors, and to potential mates. From this point of view emotions may be conceptualized as basic adaptive patterns that can be identified at all phylogenetic levels. These adaptive patterns, examples of which are agonistic behavior, sexual behavior, and investigative behavior, are adaptations that have been maintained in functionally equivalent form through all phylogenetic levels. Emotions are fundamentally communication processes in the service of individual and genetic survival. Emotional behaviors act as signals of intentions of future action that function to influence the interpersonal relations of the interacting individuals. By appropriate reactions to emergency events in the environment (by flight or fight, for example), the chances of individual survival are increased (Plutchik, 1994).

Nesse (1991) described emotions as strategies for negotiating interpersonal relationships:

> Friendship and love maintain good relationships, even through rough periods. Anger prevents exploitation. . . . Anxiety and guilt . . . motivate people to fulfill their commitments, to abide by the social contract, and to stay loyal to their friends. (p. 33)

An important illustration of the functional significance of emotions may be seen from the study of infants. From an evolutionary point of view, the newborn is most vulnerable to the dangers of the environment. This reality is the basic reason behind the various signals, displays, communication patterns, and behaviors found in immature organisms that are present at or shortly after birth. These various behaviors have effects that increase the chances of survival in the newborn by influencing the behavior of the caretakers. And because the problems of survival exist from the moment of birth, certain mechanisms must exist both in the child and the caretaker to help ensure survival. If young infants had to wait until they learned how to attract their parents' attention and support, and if the parents had to learn how to provide it, the chances of species survival would be small. Communication patterns have to work the first time they are used. From this viewpoint, emotions may be thought of in part as communication signals emitted by the infant to caretakers that help increase the chances of survival. Emotions are not disruptive, maladaptive states, but rather act to stabilize the internal state of the organism. They represent transitory adjustment reactions that function to return the organism to a stable, effective relationship with its environment when that relationship is disrupted.

A similar point is made by Dix (1991) in a discussion of parenting. Emotions, he argued, are

> barometers for relationships because they reflect parents' assessments of how well interactions . . . with children are proceeding . . . negative emotions are perturbations that realign a system . . . positive emotions motivate attunement to children, facilitate responsiveness to the children's wants and needs, and enable parents and children to coordinate their interactions to the benefit of both. (p. 19)

A final example of the functional significance of emotions may be taken from the work of ethnologists who have studied primate vocalizations. For example, Seyforth, Cheney, and Marler (1980) have shown that vervet monkey alarm calls function to designate different classes of external danger related to specific types of predators: Animals on the ground respond to leopard alarms by running into trees, to eagle alarms by looking up, and to snake alarms by looking down.

These examples, which can be elaborated (Plutchik, 1994), indicate that emotional signals or displays are related to important events in the life of each animal: events such as threats, attacks, alarms, courtships, mating, social contact, isolation or separation, greetings, appeasement, dominance, submission, and play. They influence a large variety of interpersonal relations. Emotions may be conceptualized as homeostatic devices designed to maintain a relatively steady (or "normal") state in the face of interpersonal challenges. Emotions represent transitory adjustment reactions that function to return the organism to a stable, effective relationship with its immediate interpersonal environment when that relationship is disrupted.

The Function of Personality Traits

The psychoanalysts have had the most to say about the functional significance of personality traits. For example, Fenichel (1946), a major synthesizer of psychoanalytic ideas, has described character (personality) as the precipitates of instinctual conflict. His view is that the conflict of emotions leads to fixations and a "freezing" of emotional tendencies. Such a process transforms transient emotional reactions into persistent personality traits. Rapaport (1950) noted that children show their emotions in transient ways, but in later life anxiety is continuous in the anxious person, the pessimist is permanently melancholy, and the cheerful person consistently buoyant.

In a recent work, another psychoanalyst, Spezzano (1993), has argued that an explicit theory of affects is embedded in psychoanalytic writing, and that, in fact, psychoanalysis is primarily a theory of affect. Among the points he makes is the idea that psychopathology is always an attempt at affect regulation. This implies that psychopathology, which generally means in this context character neuroses or personality disorders, has a function—the function is the regulation of interpersonal relations. We use love to keep others invested in our personal agendas. We use intimidation to inhibit interactions that would be painful or threatening or to gain power over others. Psychoanalytic interpretation is concerned with the patient's affects, particularly with how patients deceive themselves about their own affects. And self-deception has an obvious function—to mitigate the pain of recognizing our own limitations.

Nonpsychoanalytic writers also have contributed to the concept of the functional value of personality traits. Millon (1994), for example, has pointed out that personality refers to an individual's lifelong style of relating to others, to coping with problems, and to expressing emotions. These relatively stable patterns of thinking and interacting have the overall function of using, controlling, or adapting to external forces. The expression of personality traits tends to evoke reciprocal and often predictable responses from others that influence whether an individual's problems will decrease or stabilize.

Millon (1994) has implied that chronic emotional patterns (that is, personality traits) such as anxiousness, depression, or self-criticism, serve a variety of goals; they produce such secondary gains as eliciting nurturance from others; they excuse the avoidance of responsibilities; they rationalize poor performance; or they justify the expression of anger toward others. He raises the question of what it is that turns a transient emotion into a chronic personality trait and suggests that this occurs because "the range of experiences to which people are exposed throughout their lives is both limited and repetitive" (p. 287).

Applying this analysis to chronic sadness or melancholy as a trait, it is generally recognized that the most common precipitating event for sadness is a loss of something or someone important to the individual. This loss often results in characteristic facial expressions and vocalizations (such as crying or distress signals). Such distress signals typically produce an empathic response in adults who are exposed to them, a feeling often followed by some attempt at helpful actions. Chronic depression as a trait thus may be considered to be an extreme and persistent distress signal that continually functions to solicit help from others. This may be true regardless of whether the individual is aware of this function.

Cantor and Harlow (1994) suggested that the function of the trait of social anxiety is to solve the problem of insecurity by allowing an individual to accept the lead of other people in social situations. People with social anxiety use their anxiety to avoid attention from others, which in turn removes performance pressure.

An alternative analysis of the function of anxiousness as a trait is given by Trower and Gilbert (1989). They point out that most mammals and especially primates live in social groups that are organized and stabilized by means of dominance hierarchies. The fact that each individual in a group enacts a role that defines his or her position within the hierarchy functions to maintain cohesiveness of the group. If someone else of higher dominance status threatens another group member, escape from the group is rarely possible because survival generally depends on the group's support. The result is usually some form of submissive ritual or gesture that allows the threatened individual to remain in the group. Social anxiety may have evolved as a method for maintaining group cohesion. According to this hypothesis, the socially anxious person has an appraisal and coping style that focuses on threats and loss of status in a hostile and competitive world.

To take one final example of the function of a personality trait, we may consider the trait of aggressiveness. Novaco (1976) has noted a number of useful functions of aggressiveness in humans. First, it increases the intensity with which we act to accomplish our goals. Aggressiveness is associated with a sense of power that may facilitate the attainment of personal goals. Second, aggressive individuals tend to intimidate others and give the impression of a strong, threatening presence. Aggressive expressions often increase a person's ability to gain resources and survive in the face of threat. Third, aggressiveness reduces feelings of vulnerability and may even prevent feelings of helplessness from reaching levels of conscious awareness. And fourth, aggressive individuals are often central in establishing a dominance or hierarchical structure within a group. Such a social structure acts to stabilize relations among members of a group and thus maintains group cohesion, a property that contributes to the survival of members of the group.

These various ideas suggest that both emotions and personality traits have similar functions—that is, to regulate social relations—and that traits are fundamentally persistent expressions of emotional tendencies and that both are aspects of the same conceptual domain.

THE STRUCTURE OF EMOTIONS AS REPRESENTED BY THE CIRCUMPLEX

In this section I will briefly trace the history of attempts that have been made to use a circular or circumplex model to describe the relations among emotions. A parallel and overlapping effort also has been made to show that a circumplex model describes the relations among personality traits.

In 1921, McDougall commented on a parallel between emotions and colors. He wrote

> The color sensations present, like the emotions, an indefinitely great variety of qualities shading into one another by imperceptible gradations; but this fact does not prevent us regarding all these many delicate varieties as reducible by analysis to a few simple primary qualities from which they are formed by fusion, or blending, in all proportions . . . the same is true of the emotions. (p. 114)

This simple parallel between emotions and colors suggests that an emotion circle may be constructed based on the assumption of basic emotions that is analogous to the color circle. In 1941, Schlosberg reported on a study in which he asked research participants to judge the emotions posed in the 72 Frois–Wittmann pictures of facial expressions. They were to use only six broad categories: love, happiness, mirth; surprise; fear, suffering; anger, determination; disgust; and contempt. Schlosberg found that the overlap of judgments led to a circular scale somewhat like the color wheel. He suggested that two axes or dimensions could account for this circular surface of facial expressions. He called one axis pleasantness–unpleasantness and the other attention–rejection. In 1954, Schlosberg added an intensity dimension as a third axis to produce a cone–shaped model.

In 1958, I proposed a similar cone–shaped model to describe the relations among emotions and suggested that there are eight basic bipolar emotions: joy versus sorrow; anger versus fear; acceptance versus disgust; and surprise versus expectancy. The implications of this model have been elaborated in several books (1962; 1980a; 1994) and in a number of papers (1970; 1980b; 1983; 1989; 1990; 1993; 1994; 1995).

In another attempt made to study the circular structure of emotions, Block (1957) asked a group of female college students to describe a series of 15 emotions using 20 semantic differential scales applied to each emotion. The scales were 7-point bipolar scales defined at each end by such terms as good–bad, high–low, active–passive, and tense–relaxed. The mean rating for each emotion was obtained on each scale to produce a profile of semantic differential terms to describe each emotion. Later, I intercorrelated the profiles to produce a matrix of all possible pairs of correlations, which was then factor analyzed. Two factors accounted for most of the variance, and a circular order was obtained that had the following sequence: pride, anticipation, elation, love, contentment, sympathy, nostalgia, boredom, grief, guilt, humiliation, worry, envy, fear, and anger. Some of the bipolarities that were found included elation versus grief, contentment versus worry, and love versus boredom. The results obtained from the men and women were almost identical, and similar results were obtained from a group of Norwegian students.

In a further study of the circumplex structure of emotions, I used a modified paired-comparison method (Plutchik, 1980a). Three emotion words that were clearly not synonyms were chosen as reference words. Judges were asked to rate the relative similarity of 146 emotion words to each of the three reference words using an 11-point bipolar scale ranging from *opposite* (−5), through *no relation* (0), to *the same* (+5). The mean similarity ratings were converted to angular locations on a circle based on the idea that *no relation* corresponds to a 90° divergence on a circle whereas *opposite* corresponds to 180°. The resulting circle for a subset of 40 emotion terms is shown in Figure 1.

It is worth noting that all areas of the circle are represented, although with somewhat different densities. Words that are similar in meaning are found near one another whereas opposite terms such as *accepting* and *hostile* (or *assertive* and *withdrawn*) are almost 180° apart. The circumplex also helps clarify the somewhat ambiguous language of emotions. For example, the terms *stubborn*, *resentful*, and *suspicious* have much closer connotations than is commonly recognized.

In order to determine the validity of this emotion circle, an independent method based on the semantic differential was used to locate the same terms on a circle. Five judges rated the connotative meanings of each of the same 40 emotion terms on 20 7-point semantic differential scales. The correlations among emotion profiles were factor analyzed and the factor loadings used to plot the data from which the angular placements of each emotion word was obtained. These angular placements were then compared with the angular placements obtained with the paired comparison method. The product–moment correlation was +.90, indicating that the two sets of orderings on the circle were almost identical.

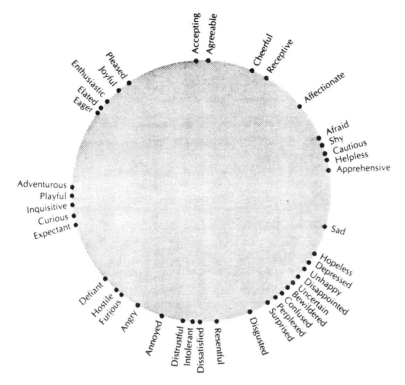

Figure 1. A circumplex structure of emotion concepts based on similarity scaling and on the semantic differential. From Plutchik 1980a, copyright HarperCollins. Reprinted with permission.

Other methods also have been used to obtain a circumplex for emotions (Russell, 1989). Differences in the sequence of terms found is partly related to the method and partly to the sample of terms chosen.

THE STRUCTURE OF PERSONALITY TRAITS AS REPRESENTED BY THE CIRCUMPLEX

In 1903, Wundt proposed that the four temperaments described by the Greeks could be thought of in bipolar terms with the *phlegmatic type* (controlled, persistent, calm) being opposed to the *choleric type* (exhibitionistic, hotheaded, active), and the *sanguine type* (sociable, easygoing, contented) opposed to the *melancholic type* (anxious, suspicious, serious; Eysenck, 1970). This idea had little impact on American psychology until Cattell (1946) carried out a series of factor analytic studies based on 171 terms selected from Allport and Odbert's (1936) list of traits. Cattell's work produced 36 clusters, which were described by bipolar labels and named the *standard reduced personality sphere.* In 1951, Freedman, Leary, Ossorio, and Coffey presented a circular model of what they called *interpersonal purposes.* They hypothesized that there are 16 modes of interpersonal interaction described by such words as *dominating, rejecting, trusting,* and *loving.* According to their model these 16 modes of interaction may be represented as segments around a circle with "normal" modes of interaction conceived as represented by the center of the circle, with the periphery representing more extreme types of interpersonal behavior. LaForge and Suczek (1955) reported that the average correlations among ratings of traits tended to decrease as more distant variables were correlated.

Another circular model of personality was described by Stern (1958) and used as the basis for a psychometric test of personality. Respondents were asked to indicate their likes and dislikes for a large number of activities such as "driving fast," "flirting," "leading a well-ordered life," and "taking care of someone who is ill." The responses were scored on 30 scales, ordered in the form of a circumplex, with *outgoing* opposite *withdrawn, independent* opposite *dependent,* and *aggressive* opposite *timid.*

At about the same time Schaefer (1959, 1961) reported the results of several studies of the social–emotional behavior of mothers toward their children. He correlated ratings of parent–child interactions and then factor analyzed the resulting matrix of correlations. He found that two factors accounted for most of the variance, that they could be used to plot the location of each variable in a two-dimensional space, and that the pattern was close to a circle. In this circumplex *expression of affection* was opposite *ignoring, strictness* was opposite *equalitarianism,* and *autonomy* was opposite *intrusiveness.*

In his papers Schaefer referred to the circular ordering of variables as a circumplex, a term taken from the work of Guttman (1954). It refers to the geometric implications of a correlation matrix in which the correlations systematically increase and then decrease. If the correlations range gradually from high positive to high negative, then a factor analysis of the data usually will reveal a circular ordering of the variables in a two-dimensional space.

In 1963, Lorr and McNair reported the development of an *interpersonal behavior circle.* They had constructed an inventory of statements describing various kinds of interpersonal behaviors that was used by clinicians to rate both patients and non-patients. Correlations then were obtained among the items of the inventory, and the correlation matrix was factor analyzed. Plots of the factor loadings of all items on the first two factors revealed a circular ordering of clusters of items. Based on these findings and a replication (Lorr & McNair, 1965), they constructed their interpersonal behavior circle, with 14 sectors in the following order: sociability, affection, nurturance, agreeableness, deference, submission, abasement, inhibition, detachment, mistrust, hostility, recognition, dominance, and exhibition.

In 1965, Rinn reviewed the literature suggesting that the emotional domain, the interpersonal domain, and the attitude domain all could be conceptualized by means of circumplex structures. He pointed out that the many dichotomies that have been proposed for describing interpersonal behavior may be conceptualized as different aspects of the circumplex. In other words, so-called basic dimensions such as dominance–submission, hostility–love, control–autonomy, and extraverted–introverted may be thought of simply as different aspects of the generalized circumplex of interpersonal behaviors. Because in a circle no one axis is any more fundamental than any other, so-called "basic dimensions" are entirely arbitrary.

A year later, Schaefer and I (Schaefer & Plutchik, 1966) asked clinicians to judge the extent to which a patient who was given a diagnostic label such as paranoid, depressed, manic, and so on, would show each of a number of traits and emotions. Ratings for all pairs of traits were intercorrelated and factor analyzed, and factor loadings for the traits were plotted. An approximate circumplex was found.

In the next few years, several studies reported circumplex orders for data related to personality (Bayley, 1968; Conte & Plutchik, 1981; Gerjuoy & Aaronson, 1970; Rimmer, 1974). The study by Conte and Plutchik produced the circumplex shown in Figure 2.

In this circumplex the traits are fairly uniformly distributed around the circle. Those that are opposite make good sense (e.g., anxious versus self-confident, accepting versus stubborn; quarrelsome versus peaceful), whereas those that are close on the circle are clearly of similar meaning.

From the 1980s to the present there has been an increasing number of publications that demonstrate the application of the circumplex idea to various domains of interpersonal behavior. These include normal personality, personality disorders, family relations, psychotherapy, vocational psychology, and social interactions (Kiesler, 1983; Olson, 1993; Wiggins, 1979, 1982). Many of these contributors are represented in this book.

In summary, in this part of the chapter I have tried to demonstrate the intimate connection between emotions and personality. I have emphasized the overlap of language and the role of the temporal dimension as an ambiguous way of distinguishing emotions from personality. I have shown that both emotions and personality traits have similar functional roles; that is, they influence and attempt to regulate social interactions. And finally, I have reviewed some of the literature demonstrating that a circular or circumplex model is appropriate as a description of the interrelations of both emotions and personality traits. It thus seems reasonable to conclude that emotions and personality traits are aspects of the same conceptual domain—that is, the domain of interpersonal relations.

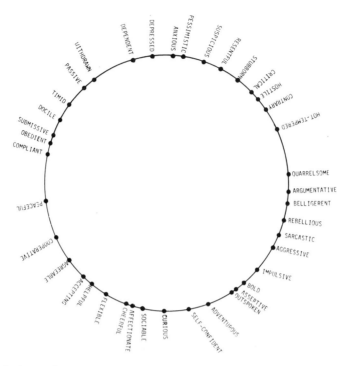

Figure 2. A circumplex structure of personality traits based on similarity scaling and on the semantic differential. From Conte and Plutchik, 1981. Reprinted with permission.

SOME IMPLICATIONS OF THE CIRCUMPLEX MODEL

Although not every investigator may agree on the following points, there are some important ideas about the circumplex model that should be made explicit.

1. The circumplex is a reflection of certain types of relations or interactions. These include the idea of *similarity* and *polarity*. If the elements being considered vary in degree of similarity to one another (as do emotions, personality traits, and diagnoses) and show polarities (e.g., joy versus sorrow, dominance versus submissiveness, antisocial versus avoidant), then a circle as an analogue model may possibly be used to represent these relations. Statistically, a set of correlations among these elements should show systematic increases and decreases in the degree of correlation between the elements, depending on their degree of conceptual closeness and their degree of polarity. Polar opposites are represented by a -1.0 correlation, independent or unrelated elements are repre-

sented by a 0.0 correlation; and similar elements are represented by positive correlations.

    To summarize what has been said, it is important to
recognize that there are a number of different methods that
can be used to determine the precise location of the elements
of the circumplex. Any two uncorrelated variables can be
used as axes and the relative location of all other variables
can be estimated. Factor analysis can be used to determine
two major independent axes and then the factor loadings of
all other variables can be plotted on these axes. It is also
possible to use direct similarity scaling to estimate locations
of elements on the circumplex (Conte & Plutchik, 1981) and
to use multidimensional scaling as well (Paddock & Nowicki,
1986). Other statistical methods have also been used (Russell, 1989) and new ones will probably be invented.

2. The idea of a circumplex does not imply that the elements
   of the circle need to be arranged with equidistant spacing. It
   does not imply that there needs to be any specific number of
   categories around the circumference of the circle (4, 6, 8, or
   16). And the circumplex model does not per se specify any
   particular set of axes as fundamental or basic. In a true circle,
   there are no special axes. The statistical determination of
   basic axes, based on factor analysis, for example, may be a
   reflection of the initial sample of items or variables chosen
   for analysis, or may reflect the relative frequency of overlapping terms describing emotions or personality, or may express
   theoretical proclivities of an investigator.

3. The circumplex as applied to personality primarily describes
   the interpersonal aspects of personality, not everything that
   investigators over the years have labeled personality. The circumplex probably does not apply well or at all to physical
   characteristics of a person, to perjorative terms, to intellectual abilities, to aptitudes, or to cognitive styles, all of which
   have been considered at one time or another to be aspects
   of personality.

4. The concept of polarity inherent in the circumplex model
   implies the idea of conflict between opposing elements. Conflict is inherent in interpersonal relations. Conflicts reflect
   such basic processes as approaching versus avoiding, taking
   in versus expelling, attaching versus disconnecting, and attacking versus retreating. These polarities may be thought of
   as control systems that regulate social interactions (Horowitz
   & Stinson, 1995).

IMPLICATIONS OF A GENERAL MODEL OF EMOTIONS

The circumplex represents only one aspect of a more general approach to a conceptualization of emotions. Table 1 represents some basic propositions of my psychoevolutionary theory of emotion. Within this theory the circumplex is seen as a cross-section of a three-dimensional cone-shaped model of emotions. All these propositions have been elaborated in other publications (e.g., Plutchik, 1993). In this chapter, in which the focus is on the circumplex as a model of interpersonal relations, I will discuss only the last proposition—in other words, emotions are related to a number of derivative conceptual domains.

The term *derivative* is used in three different senses. In an evolutionary sense it is used to indicate that human attributes are derived from those of lower animals; for example, the sneer of a human being is believed to be derived from the snarl of a lower primate. In a developmental sense it is used to describe the fact that certain adult characteristics are derived from certain infantile ones; for example, resentfulness as a trait being derived from early experiences of punishment. The third sense in which the term is used refers to the idea that certain conceptual domains are derived from other more basic domains. An example of this would be the concept that personality traits are derived from mixtures of emotions in the same way that most colors are derived from mixtures of primary hues. The concept of derivatives as described in the following pages refers primarily to the latter use of the term.

In a number of studies, I have shown that the language of mixed emotions is identical to the language of personality traits (Plutchik, 1980a). Hostility has been judged to be composed of anger and disgust; sociability is thought to be a blend of joy and acceptance; and guilt is judged to be a combination of joy and fear. Emotional components have been identified for hundreds of personality traits. It has been argued that the reason per-

TABLE 1
Basic Propositions of a Psychoevolutionary Theory of Emotions

1. Emotions are communication and survival mechanisms based on evolutionary adaptations.
2. Emotions influence and attempt to regulate interpersonal relations.
3. Emotions have a genetic basis.
4. Emotions are hypothetical constructs inferred from various classes of evidence.
5. Emotions are complex chains of events with behavioral, negative feedback loops that function to stabilize social interactions.
6. The relations among emotions can be represented by a three-dimensional structural model. A cross-section through the model produces a circumplex.
7. Emotions are related to a number of derivative conceptual domains.

sonality traits can be described by means of the circumplex is that they are derived from emotions that have a circumplex structure (Conte & Plutchik, 1981). And the reason emotions have a circumplex structure is that social interactions invariably imply conflict and polarities.

The concept of derivatives has been extended to several other conceptual domains. The idea is illustrated in Table 2. To illustrate this point, when someone is made fearful on many repeated occasions he or she is likely to exhibit a personality trait that would be called *timidity* (or any of a number of related terms such as shyness, withdrawal, or meekness). If the trait of timidity is excessive and seriously interferes with a person's life, an Axis II diagnostic label such as *passive* might be attributed to the individual. This is based on the idea that personality disorders may be interpreted as exaggerations of normal personality traits.

If these ideas are correct then it is reasonable to argue that the derivative domains (such as personality) have some properties in common with those of the basic domain (that is, emotions). This would imply that personality disorders and ego defenses, as well as personality and emotions, have circumplex structures. This point has been made by many others; for example, Wiggins (1982), Strack, Lorr, and Campbell (1990), and several contributors to the present volume (e.g., Lorr, chapter 2; Schaefer, chapter 6; Fisher, chapter 11; and Widiger and Hagemoser, chapter 13).

THE CIRCUMPLEX MODEL AS APPLIED TO PERSONALITY DISORDERS

In order to demonstrate the application of the circumplex to personality disorders, the following study was carried out (Plutchik & Conte, 1994). A modified paired-comparison procedure (Plutchik & Conte, 1985)

TABLE 2
Emotions And Their Derivatives

Subjective language	Personality trait language	Diagnostic language	Ego defense language
Fear	Timid	Passive	Repression
Anger	Quarrelsome	Antisocial	Displacement
Joy	Sociable	Manic	Reaction–formation
Sadness	Gloomy	Depressed	Compensation
Acceptance	Trusting	Histrionic	Denial
Disgust	Hostile	Paranoid	Projection
Expectation	Curious	Obsessive–compulsive	Intellectualization
Surprise	Indecisive	Borderline	Regression

was used. Sixteen experienced clinicians were asked to rate the degree of similarity or dissimilarity of the 11 *DSM-III-R* Axis II personality disorders plus the proposed categories of sadistic personality disorder and self-defeating personality disorder. A category for dysthymia as another possible personality disorder was added also. The clinicians rated each of the 14 disorders against three reference disorders using a 7-point bipolar scale. The reference disorders represented the three diagnostic clusters, A, B, and C listed in *DSM-III-R*, and were schizotypal, narcissistic, and dependent.

However, in the present study, it was decided not to use single diagnostic terms such as antisocial, narcissistic, or schizoid, simply because such terms in isolation may have somewhat different meanings to different clinicians. Instead, we prepared a brief descriptive paragraph for each personality diagnosis based explicitly on the criteria given in *DSM-III-R*.

In the study, the condensed descriptions of each personality diagnosis were compared with the three reference descriptions. In other words, no personality disorder labels were used; descriptive paragraphs were compared against one another. In the method used, ratings ranged from -3, indicating the two diagnostic descriptions were perceived as opposite in meaning; through 0, meaning there was no relation between them; to $+3$, indicating the two descriptions were perceived as identical. The similarity ratings, therefore, represented subjective judgments that corresponded to implied correlation coefficients between the diagnostic labels. For example, a rating of $+3$ corresponded to perceived identity and a correlation of 1.00. A similarity rating of 0 implied a correlation of .00 (no relation), and a rating of -3 implied a correlation of -1.00 or maximum dissimilarity—in other words, it is descriptive of perceived opposites (Stone & Coles, 1970).

The average similarity ratings for the diagnostic descriptions relative to each reference description were transformed into angular placements on a circle. Figure 3 shows the placement of each of the personality disorders on a circle or circumplex. Paranoid, schizotypal, and schizoid are sequential and clearly form the eccentric cluster. The remaining grouping of terms show important differences from the *DSM-III-R* clusters.

The erratic or dramatic cluster as defined in *DSM-III-R* is not confirmed. For example, borderline and histrionic are not found in this segment of the circle. It is interesting to note, however, that sadistic fits nicely with narcissistic and antisocial. This cluster seems to be centered around aspects of aggression. We therefore believe that this cluster or segment of the circle should more properly be labeled the aggressive cluster.

The traditional anxious cluster purportedly consisting of avoidant, dependent, obsessive–compulsive, and passive–aggressive, is also not confirmed. Our findings indicate that the avoidant and dependent diagnoses are highly similar to one another and are similar to self-defeating and dysthymic disorders. We suggested calling this empirical grouping the anxious–depressed cluster. From our empirical data, the passive–aggressive

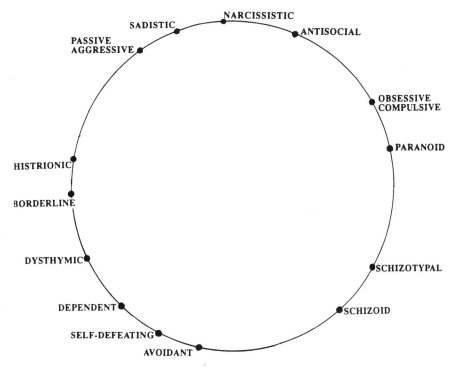

Figure 3. A circumplex structure of personality disorders based on a paired-comparison technique.

and obsessive–compulsive disorders appear to be quite dissimilar to the anxious–depressed grouping.

Of some interest is the fact that the histrionic and borderline diagnoses are near each other on the circumplex and also near the dysthymic diagnosis. If one were trying to identify a cluster into which they fit, it would be the anxious–depressed cluster. The presence of strong features of both anxiety and depression in these two diagnoses supports this placement.

In terms of opposition of personality disorders, we find that the aggressive cluster is opposite the anxious–depressed cluster. We also see that the eccentric cluster is opposite the histrionic and borderline diagnoses.

The modified method of paired comparisons used in this study has revealed an empirical circumplex for the personality disorders. It shows the traditional clusters to some degree but with some important differences. The so-called erratic cluster seems clearly to be related to problems of handling aggression, and we believe they should be relabeled as such. The anxious cluster is seen to include the newly proposed disorder of self-defeating personality. It also includes the dysthymic personality, even though dysthymia is not included at present in Axis II. It is even likely that the borderline and histrionic diagnoses should be considered as part of the anxious cluster but only if this cluster is expanded to include depressive symptoms as well. We therefore have called this cluster the anxious–depressed cluster.

These findings help us understand that some degree of comorbidity exists for all personality disorders and that there is a gradual transition from one personality disorder to another in terms of similarity. Strictly speaking, this implies that clusters are somewhat arbitrary and are based on arbitrary selection of boundaries. The circumplex concept implies that all personality disorders, those we now recognize and those that may be clinically labeled in the future, can be represented by placements on a circle varying in degree of closeness.

Another implication of these findings is that the concept of comorbidity is a narrow way of describing the more fundamental similarity structure of personality disorders. Comorbidity applies only to pairs of overlapping disorders. The concept of the circumplex implies that most personality disorders overlap in different ways and to different degrees. For example, an opposite placement of two disorders on the circumplex implies that they will almost never be mistaken for one another, which might be called a kind of negative comorbidity.

Finally, we believe that these findings have relevance to the issue of whether personality disorders should be thought of in terms of discrete categories or in terms of dimensions. The present data suggest that personality disorders are not discrete categories and that various kinds of overlap and comorbidity exist for all disorders. All disorders vary in degree of similarity to one another, and in this sense there is a dimension of similarity that relates all personality disorders. In addition, for any single diagnostic label there are different numbers of symptoms that can be used to define it. This implies a dimension of intensity for each diagnosis, even though many clinicians prefer to use an arbitrary criterion to decide when a diagnosis is said to exist. The selection of patients for psychotherapy research should be based on a recognition of the arbitrary nature of single diagnoses and on the need to provide a meaningful profile for each individual of all personality disorders.

Another study carried out with one of my colleagues also provided data that could be used to establish an initial approximation to a circumplex order for diagnoses in preadolescent psychiatric patients (Pfeffer & Plutchik, 1989). DSM-III-R diagnoses were obtained on 106 preadolescent psychiatric inpatients, 101 preadolescent psychiatric outpatients, and 101 nonpatient preadolescents. Examination of the data revealed that for a given diagnosis such as conduct disorder there are varying frequencies of other diagnoses that were given to the children. For example, of those 66 children who were diagnosed as having a conduct disorder, 51.1% were also diagnosed as having a borderline personality disorder, 39.4% as having a specific development disorder, 22.7% as having an attention deficit disorder, and 21.1% as having a dysthymic disorder. The same type of overlap analyses was done for each disorder. The approximation to a circumplex structure is shown in Figure 4. This model is meant to represent the relative positions on a similarity scale of the different diagnoses, but not their absolute positions. Such a circumplex reveals which diagnoses are most difficult to differentiate from one another, as well as those that are easy to distinguish.

Table 3 presents a summary of nine circumplex models that have been applied to personality disorders. In each case, different methods of data acquisition and different analysis, judges, and patient samples were used. The table lists the relative sequence of personality disorders around the circumplex. From the actual published figures, an estimate of the exact angular location of each diagnosis was made.

Despite the differences in methodology many commonalities may be seen. Starting with paranoid as an arbitrary reference point, almost all studies have found that narcissistic and antisocial diagnoses are close to it on the circumplex; borderline is usually found somewhere in the middle of the list, whereas dependent, self-defeating and avoidant are generally found near the schizoid or schizotypal diagnoses. For example, narcissistic has a mean location of 45°; histrionic has a mean location of 117°; and schizoid

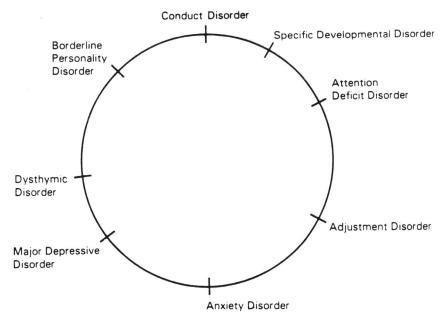

Figure 4. An approximation to a circumplex for preadolescent psychiatric disorders based on a confusion matrix. From Pfeffer and Plutchik, 1989. Reprinted with permission.

TABLE 3
A Summary of Angular Circumplex Locations of Personality Disorders

Plutchik and Platman (1977)	Angle (in degrees)	Wiggins (1982)	Angle (in degrees)
Paranoid	0	Paranoid	0
Sociopathic	82	Narcissistic	45
Cyclothymic	130	Compulsive	90
Histrionic	156	Hypomanic	140
Well–adjusted	187	Histrionic	180
Compulsive	283	Dependent	220
Passive–aggressive	320	Passive–aggressive	270
Schizoid	340	Schizoid	315

Plutchik and Conte (1985)	Angle (in degrees)	Millon (1987)	Angle (in degrees)
Paranoid	0	Paranoid	0
Antisocial	40	Narcissistic	27
Narcissistic	53	Histrionic	58
Borderline	65	Passive–aggressive	81
Histrionic	115	Borderline	103
Well adjusted	180	Self–defeating	128
Dependent	216	Dependent	153
Compulsive	300	Avoidant	193
Avoidant	327	Schizotypal	221
Passive–aggressive	330	Schizoid	245
Schizotypal	333	Compulsive	275
Schizoid	335	Aggressive	305
		Antisocial	335

Romney and Bynner (1989)	Angle (in degrees)	Pincus and Wiggins (1990)	Angle (in degrees)
Paranoid	0	Paranoid	0
Narcissistic	32	Antisocial	22
Compulsive	90	Narcissistic	78
Hypomanic	147	Histrionic	106
Histrionic	180	Dependent	236
Dependent	203	Avoidant	274
Passive–aggressive	270	Schizoid	310
Schizoid	330		

Sim and Romney (1990)	Angle (in degrees)	Strack, Lorr, and Campbell (1990)	Angle (in degrees)
Paranoid	0	Paranoid	0
Narcissistic	12	Narcissistic	30
Histrionic	40	Aggressive	40
Hypomanic	54	Histrionic	60
Compulsive	112	Antisocial	70
Dependent	172	Passive–aggressive	104
Borderline	185	Borderline	150
Schizotypal	202	Self-defeating	190
Avoidant	233	Avoidant	210
Schizoid	254	Schizotypal	211
Passive–aggressive	281	Schizoid	232
Antisocial	350	Dependent	240
		Compulsive	306

Plutchik and Conte (1994)	Angle (in degrees)
Paranoid	0
Obsessive–compulsive	20
Antisocial	60
Narcissistic	85
Sadistic	102
Passive–aggressive	117
Histrionic	160
Borderline	170
Dysthymic	192
Dependent	210
Self-defeating	225
Avoidant	240
Schizoid	292
Schizotypal	312

has a mean location of 295°. Despite some differences among studies, there appears to be good agreement on the sector of the circumplex in which each diagnosis is located. These findings support the value of a circumplex analysis of personality disorder diagnoses and demonstrate both the similarity and polarity structure of such diagnoses.

THE CIRCUMPLEX MODEL AS APPLIED TO EGO DEFENSES

The concept of ego defenses has been acknowledged as one of the most important contributions of psychoanalysis. Ego defenses are recognized as relevant to drives, affects, social relations, development, personality, adaptation, and psychotherapy. In a recent paper (Plutchik, 1995) I presented a theory of defenses that examined and elaborated on these connections; I will present a brief outline of this model.

Overlap of Meaning of Ego Defenses

A careful reading of the literature on ego defenses leads to the conclusion that there is a considerable overlap of meaning of many defenses. For example, the terms *internalization, identification, introjection,* and *incorporation* are used interchangeably and inconsistently. So too are such concepts as *isolation, rationalization, ritual, undoing,* and *magical thinking* (Vaillant, 1971). In addition to the similarity of meaning of many defenses, the literature also suggests that some defenses are polar opposites. For example, *acting out* is seen as the opposite of *repression,* whereas *projection* is the opposite of *identification.* It thus appears that the similarity and polarity relations among defenses allows the application of a circumplex model to ego defenses.

The definitions of the different ego defenses each seem to have a theme. For example, displacement is generally defined as the discharge of anger toward individuals who are less dangerous than the "real" object of the anger. Projection is associated with the hostile rejection of other individuals because they are believed to possess the person's own unacceptable or dangerous traits or feelings. Compensation refers to the attempt to find substitutes for real or imagined losses or inadequacies.

What is implied by each of these examples is that the defense is a reaction to a complex, mixed emotional state that involves a particular emotion plus anxiety. Thus, for example, displacement involves anger mixed with anxiety over the expression of anger. Projection involves disgust with (or rejection of) self mixed with anxiety over the self-hatred. Compensation involves sadness about a loss and anxiety over whether the lost object can be regained. Denial involves a person's uncritical acceptance or falsification of his or her perception of a potentially dangerous or unpleasant object mixed with anxiety over the expression of such feelings. And regression involves the desire for help with dangerous events mixed with anxiety over the need for help. All these events are unconscious. These observations suggest that emotions are involved intimately in the conceptual system of ego defenses.

Structure of Ego Defenses

From the point of view of the present theory, all ego defenses have a basic underlying structure. For each defense there is a set of associated personality traits, a social need, a characteristic method, and a purpose or function. This idea is shown in Table 4 and is elaborated in part from the description provided by Kellerman (1979).

TABLE 4
The Underlying Structure of Ego Defenses

Ego defense	Associated traits	Social needs	Method	Function
Repression	Timid Passive Lethargic Obedient	Need to avoid or withdraw from social relationships	Forget painful events	To maintain passivity and avoid decisions and anxiety
Displacement	Aggressive Provocative Cynical	Need to find scapegoats who will absorb hostility	Attack a symbol or substitute for source of frustration	To express anger without fear of retaliation
Reaction formation	Altruistic Puritanical Conscientious Moralistic	Need to show good (or correct) behavior	Reverse feelings of interest to their opposite	To hide interest in bad and especially sexual behavior
Compensation	Boastful Daydreamer Worried about inadequacies	Need to be recognized, admired, and applauded	Exaggerate positive aspects of self	To improve a perceived weakness or replace a loss
Denial	Uncritical Trusting Suggestable Gullible Romantic	Need to avoid conflict in social relationships	Interpret threats and problems as benign	To maintain feeling of being liked or loved
Projection	Critical Fault finding Blaming	Need to identify imperfections in others	Blame or be hypercritical	To decrease feelings of inferiority, shame, or personal imperfections
Intellectualization	Obsessional Domineering Possessive	Need to control all social relationships	Find a rational justification for all acts	To prevent the expression of sudden or unacceptable impulses
Regression	Impulsive Restless Undercontrolled	Need to act out all impulses	Express impulsive and immature behaviors	To achieve acceptance of impulsive acts

Note. Reprinted from "A Theory of Ego Defenses," by R. Plutchik, 1995, in H. R. Conte and R. Plutchik, *Ego Defenses: Theory and Measurement*. New York: John Wiley & Sons. Reprinted by permission.

THE CIRCUMPLEX AS A GENERAL MODEL

Let us consider several examples of these hypotheses. People who frequently use displacement tend to be aggressive, provocative, or cynical. Their need is to find scapegoats to whom hostility can be safely directed. The method used is to attack a substitute for the source of the frustration, and the function of displacement is to express anger without fear of retaliation.

To take another example, people who use denial a lot are likely to be suggestible, trustful, and gullible. Their need is to avoid conflict with others in social relationships. The method they use, in contrast to the individual who uses repression, is to interpret social problems as benign, trival, or even desirable. The function of this unconscious strategy is to maintain the feeling of being liked or loved. From this description, it is evident that denial and repression have certain similarities. Both imply a need to avoid pain or conflict in social relationships. In fact, all ego defenses function in the regulation of social relationships. This implies that the circumplex may be a descriptive model of the similarity and polarity relations among defenses.

In order to examine this hypothesis, a study dealing with the relative similarity of a set of 16 defenses was carried out. Experienced psychiatrists were asked to make paired-comparison ratings of these defenses in terms of degree of similarity. The details of the method are described by Plutchik, Kellerman, and Conte (1979).

The results of the analyses reveal an approximate circumplex showing the degree of similarity of all defenses, as well as polarities. Thus, denial, repression, and undoing are considered to be relatively similar in meaning, just as intellectualization, rationalization, and isolation are similar in meaning. The cluster of projection, displacement, and acting out are also found near one another and thus represent similar methods by which the ego defends itself. This is shown in Figure 5.

Polarities may also be seen in Figure 5. *Displacement* is opposite the defenses of *fantasy* and *introjection; sublimation* is opposite *regression* and *reaction formation;* and *acting out* is opposite *repression.* These are all relations that make clinical sense. On the basis of this model a psychometric test has been developed and widely used (Conte & Apter, 1995).

CONCLUSION

The circumplex is a way of analogically describing the relations among elements or variables that are characterized by similarity and polarity dimensions. Inherent in this analogue is the implication of conflict between opposing elements. Social relationships can be described in these terms and therefore can be represented conceptually by means of a circumplex model. Such a model applies to a variety of interpersonal domains,

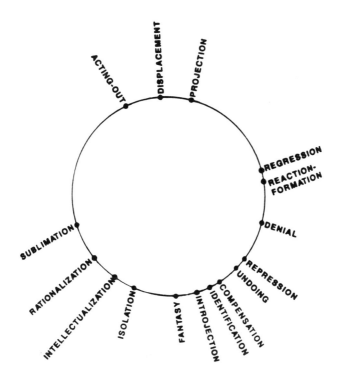

Figure 5. Similarity scaling of 16 ego defenses by a paired-comparison technique. From Plutchik, Kellerman, and Conte, 1979. Reprinted with permission.

including emotions, personality traits, personality disorders, and ego de-fenses. It also applies to facial expressions (Myllyniemi, chapter 12, this volume), to clinical syndromes (Widiger & Hagemoser, chapter 13, this volume), and to psychotherapy (Henry, chapter 16, this volume), as several of the authors of this book demonstrate. The model has implications for test construction as well (Plutchik, 1989) and eventually may be proven to be a general model of the structure of interpersonal relations.

REFERENCES

Allen, B., & Potkay, C. R. (1981). On the arbitrary distinction between states and traits. *Journal of Personality and Social Pathology, 4,* 916–928.

Allport, G. W., & Odbert, H. S. (1936). Trait names: A psychological study. *Psychological Monographs, 47* (211).

Bayley, N. (1968). Behavioral correlates of mental growth: Birth to thirty-six years. *American Psychologist, 23,* 1–17.

Block, J. (1957). Studies in the phenomenology of emotions. *Journal of Abnormal and Social Psychology, 54,* 358–363.

Cantor, N., & Harlow, R. E. (1994). Personality, strategic behavior, and daily-life problem solving. *Current Directions in Psychological Science, 3,* 169–172.

Cattell, R. B. (1946). *The description and measurement of personality.* New York: Harcourt Brace.

Clore, G. L., Ortony, A., & Foss, M. A. (1987). The psychological foundations of the affective lexicon. *Journal of Personality and Social Psychology, 53,* 751–766.

Conte, H. R., & Apter, A. (1995). The Life Style Index: A self-report measure of ego defenses. In H. R. Conte & R. Plutchik (Eds.), *Ego defenses: Theory and measurement* (pp. 179–201). New York: Wiley.

Conte, H. R., & Plutchik, R. (1981). A circumplex model for interpersonal personality traits. *Journal of Personality and Social Psychology, 40,* 701–711.

Darwin, C. (1872/1965). *The expression of the emotions in man and animals.* London: Murray, 1872. Reprinted by University of Chicago Press, 1965.

Dix, T. (1991). The affective organization of parenting: Adaptive and maladaptive processes. *Psychological Bulletin, 110,* 3–25.

Eysenck, H. J. (1970). A dimensional system of psychodiagnostics. In A. R. Mahrer (Ed.), *New approaches to personality classification.* New York: Columbia University Press.

Fenichel, O. (1946). *The psychoanalytic theory of neurosis.* Boston: Routledge & Kegan Paul.

Freedman, M. D., Leary, T. F., Ossorio, A. G., & Coffey, H. S. (1951). The interpersonal dimension of personality. *Journal of Personality, 20,* 143–161.

Gerjuoy, H., & Aaronson, B. S. (1970). Multidimensional scaling of terms used to describe personality. *Psychological Reports, 26,* 3–8.

Guttman, L. A. (1954). A new approach to factor analysis. The radex. In P. F. Lazarsfeld (Ed.), *Mathematical thinking in the social sciences* (pp. 238–248). New York: Free Press.

Hebb, D. O. (1946). Emotion in man and animal: An analysis of the intuitive processes of recognition. *Psychological Review, 53,* 88–106.

Horowitz, M. J., & Stinson, C. H. (1995). Defenses as aspects of person schemas and control processes. In H. R. Conte & R. Plutchik (Eds.), *Ego defenses: Theory and measurement* (pp. 79–97). New York: Wiley.

Kellerman, H. (1979). *Group therapy and personality: Intersecting structures.* New York: Grune & Stratton.

Kiesler, D. J. (1983). The 1982 interpersonal circle: A taxonomy for complementarity in human transactions. *Psychological Review, 90,* 185–214.

LaForge, R., & Suczek, R. F. (1955). The interpersonal dimension of personality: III. An interpersonal check list. *Journal of Personality, 24,* 94–112.

Lorr, M., & McNair, D. M. (1963). An interpersonal behavior circle. *Journal of Abnormal and Social Psychology, 67,* 68–75.

Lorr, M., & McNair, D. M. (1965). Expansion of the interpersonal behavior circle. *Journal of Personality and Social Psychology, 2,* 823-830.

McCrae, R. R., & Costa, P. T., Jr. (1994). The stability of personality: Observations and evaluations. *Current Directions in Psychological Science, 3,* 173–175.

McDougall, W. (1921). *An introduction to social psychology.* Boston: Luce.

Millon, T. (1987). *Manual for the MCMI-II* (2nd ed.) Minneapolis, MN: National Computer Systems.

Millon, T. (1994). Personality disorders: Conceptual distinctions and classification issues. In P. J. Costa & T. A. Widiger (Eds.), *Personality disorders and the five-factor model of personality* (pp. 279–301). Washington, DC: American Psychological Association.

Nesse, R. M. (1991). Psychiatry. In M. Maxwell (Ed.), *The sociobiological imagination.* Albany: State University of New York Press.

Novaco, R. W. (1976). The functions and regulation of the arousal of anger. *American Journal of Psychiatry, 133,* 1124–1128.

Olson, D. H. (1993). Circumplex model of marital and family systems: Assessing family functioning. In F. Walsh (Ed.), *Normal family processes* (pp. 104–136). New York: Guilford Press.

Paddock, J. R., & Nowicki, S. (1986). The complexity of Leary's interpersonal circle. A multidimensional scaling perspective. *Journal of Personality Assessment, 50,* 279–289.

Pfeffer, C. R., & Plutchik, R. (1989). Co-occurrence of psychiatric disorders in child psychiatric patients and nonpatients: A circumplex model. *Comprehensive Psychiatry, 30,* 275–282.

Pincus, A. L., & Wiggins, J. S. (1990). Interpersonal problems and conceptions of personality disorders. *Journal of Personality Disorders, 4,* 342–352.

Plutchik, R. (1958). Outlines of a new theory of emotions. *Transactions of the New York Academy of Sciences, 20,* 394–403.

Plutchik, R. (1962). *The emotions: Facts, theories and a new model.* New York: Random House.

Plutchik, R. (1970). Emotions, evolution and adaptive processes. In M. Arnold (Ed.), *Feelings and emotions.* New York: Academic Press.

Plutchik, R. (1980a). *Emotion: A psychoevolutionary synthesis.* New York: Harper & Row.

Plutchik, R. (1980b). A general, psychoevolutionary theory of emotion. In R. Plutchik & H. Kellerman (Eds.), *Emotion: Theory, research and experience* (Vol. 1). *Theories of emotion* (pp. 3–34). New York: Academic Press.

Plutchik, R. (1983). Emotions in early development: A psychoevolutionary approach. In R. Plutchik & H. Kellerman (Eds.), *Emotion: Theory, research and experience* (Vol. 2). *Emotions in early development* (pp. 221–258). New York: Academic Press.

Plutchik, R. (1989). Measuring emotions and their derivatives. In R. Plutchik & H. Kellerman (Eds.), *Emotion: Theory, research and experience* (Vol. 4). *The measurement of emotions* (pp. 1–36). San Diego, CA: Academic Press.

Plutchik, R. (1990). Emotions and psychotherapy: A psychoevolutionary perspective. In R. Plutchik & H. Kellerman (Eds.), *Emotion: Theory, research and experience* (Vol. 5). *Emotion, psychopathology, and psychotherapy* (pp. 3–42). New York: Academic Press.

Plutchik, R. (1991). Emotions and evolution. In K. T. Strongman (Ed.), *International review of studies on emotion* (pp. 37–58). New York: John Wiley.

Plutchik, R. (1993). Emotions and their vicissitudes: Emotions and psychopathology. In M. Lewis & J. M. Haviland (Eds.), *Handbook of emotions* (pp. 53–66). New York: Guilford Press.

Plutchik, R. (1994). *The psychology and biology of emotion.* New York: Harper Collins.

Plutchik, R. (1995). A theory of ego defenses. In H. R. Conte & R. Plutchik (Eds.), *Ego defenses: Theory and measurement* (pp. 13–37). New York: Wiley.

Plutchik, R., & Conte, H. R. (1985). Quantitative assessment of personality disorders. In R. Nickols, J. O. Cavenar, Jr., & H. K. H. Brodie (Eds.), *Psychiatry* (Vol. 7) pp. 1–13. Philadelphia, PA: J. B. Lippincott.

Plutchik, R., & Conte, H. R. (1994, June). *The circumplex structure of personality disorders: An empirical study.* Paper presented at the annual meeting of the Society for Psychotherapy Research, York, England.

Plutchik, R., Kellerman, H., & Conte, H. R. (1979). A structural theory of ego defenses and emotions. In C. E. Izard (Ed.), *Emotions in personality and psychopathology* (pp. 229–257). New York: Plenum Press.

Plutchik, R., & Platman, S. R. (1977). Personality connotations of psychiatric diagnoses. *Journal of Nervous and Mental Disease, 165,* 418–422.

Rapaport, D. (1950). *Emotions and memory.* New York: International Universities Press.

Rimmer, A. (1974). Radex of the language of emotion. *Israel Annals of Psychiatry and Related Disciplines, 12,* 238–241.

Rinn, J. L. (1965). Structure of phenomenal domains. *Psychological Review, 72,* 445–466.

Romney, D. M., & Bynner, J. M. (1989). Evaluation of a circumplex model of DSM-III personality disorders. *Journal of Research in Personality, 23,* 525–538.

Russell, J. (1989). Measures of emotion. In R. Plutchik & H. Kellerman (Eds.), *Emotion: Theory, research and experience* (Vol. 4). *The measurement of emotions* (pp. 83–112). New York: Academic Press.

Schaefer, E. S. (1959). A circumplex model for maternal behavior. *Journal of Abnormal and Social Psychology, 59,* 226–235.

Schaefer, E. S. (1961). Converging conceptual models for maternal behavior and for child behavior. In J. Glidewell (Ed.), *Parental attitudes and child behavior* (pp. 124–146). Springfield, IL: C. C. Thomas.

Schaefer, E. S., & Plutchik, R. (1966). Interrelationships of emotions, traits, and diagnostic constructs. *Psychological Reports, 18,* 399–410.

Schlosberg, H. (1941). A scale for the judgment of facial expressions. *Journal of Experimental Psychology, 29,* 497–510.

Schlosberg, H. (1954). Three dimensions of emotion. *Psychological Review, 61,* 81–88.

Seyforth, R. M., Cheney, D. L., & Marler, P. (1980). Monkey responses to three different alarm calls: Evidence of predator classification and semantic communication. *Science, 210,* 801–803.

Sim, J. P., & Romney, D. M. (1990). The relationship between a circumplex model of interpersonal behaviors and personality disorders. *Journal of Personality Disorders, 4,* 329–341.

Spezzano, C. (1993). *Affect in psychoanalysis: A clinical synthesis.* Hillsdale, NJ: Analytic Press.

Stern, G. G. (1958). *Activities Index.* Syracuse, NY: Syracuse University Psychological Research Center.

Stone, L. A., & Coles, G. J. (1970). Correlation similarity: The basis for a new revised method of similarity analysis. *Studia Psychologica, 12,* 258–265.

Storm, C., & Storm, T. (1987). A taxonomic study of the vocabulary of emotions. *Journal of Personality and Social Psychology, 53,* 805–816.

Strack, S., Lorr, M., & Campbell, L. (1990). An evaluation of Millon's circular model of personality disorders. *Journal of Personality Disorders, 4,* 353–361.

Trower, P., & Gilbert, P. (1989). New theoretical conceptions of social anxiety and social phobia. *Clinical Psychology Review, 9,* 19–35.

Vaillant, G. E. (1971). Theoretical hierarchy of adaptive ego mechanisms. *Archives of General Psychiatry, 24,* 107–118.

Wiggins, J. S. (1979). A psychological taxonomy of trait-descriptive terms: The interpersonal domain. *Journal of Personality and Social Psychology, 37,* 395–412.

Wiggins, J. S. (1982). Circumplex models of interpersonal behavior in clinical psychology. In P. C. Kendall & J. N. Butcher (Eds.), *Handbook of research methods in clinical psychology* (pp. 183–221). New York: Wiley.

2

THE CIRCUMPLEX MODEL APPLIED TO INTERPERSONAL BEHAVIOR, AFFECT, AND PSYCHOTIC SYNDROMES

MAURICE LORR

The circumplex model was first drawn to my attention about 1953. I was asked to review a funding request by Louis Guttman to the Office of Naval Research. The topic concerned "a new approach to factor analysis: The radex." Initial applications of the model by Guttman were to mental test data on measures of addition, multiplication, and division. The model also was applied to verbal ability tests such as letter grouping, letter series, sentences, and vocabulary. This chapter seeks to review some of the studies in which the circumplex model was applied to interpersonal behavior, mood states, and psychotic behaviors.

A circumplex was defined as a set of qualitatively different traits in a given domain that have an order without beginning or end (Guttman, 1954). The circumplex was viewed as a type of correlation structure and referred to a geometric representation of the matrix. The differences among variables are reducible to differences in two dimensions or planes with a constant radius. The variables optimally are uniformly and equally spaced along the circle circumference. To establish the presence of a circumplex in a matrix, a principal component analysis or a multidimensional scaling analysis can be applied. Two components are present usually, but if a general factor is also found it can be removed by ipsatizing the profile scores prior to the analysis (Horowitz, Rosenberg, Baer, Ureño, & Villaseñor, 1988).

The best known circumplex is found in the interpersonal circle first proposed by Freedman, Leary, Ossorio, and Coffey (1951). It was later expanded and modified by LaForge and Suczek (1955) and by Leary (1957). In their initial study Lorr and McNair (1963) looked for and found evidence of a circular order and for a sinusoidal function among the category intercorrelations of items in their Interpersonal Behavior Inventory (IBI). In a subsequent series of studies (Lorr & McNair, 1965) they identified two axes interpreted as dominance versus submission and nurturance versus hostility. In their analyses of the Interpersonal Checklist (ICL; LaForge & Suczek, 1955), it became evident that the ICL contained no measures of affiliation (sociability), a major aspect of the interpersonal circle.

Wiggins' (1979) studies were the most extensive in the literature, exploring the well-known interpersonal circumplex. He contended that the ICL lacked bipolarity in its trait adjectives. This reasoning led to selection of eight adjectives to define eight interpersonal adjective clusters (Wiggins, Trapnell, & Phillips, 1988). Their 64-item short form (called IAS-R) was shown to represent two factors of the circumplex. Trapnell and Wiggins (1990) subsequently showed that the two dimensions correspond closely to the extraversion and agreeableness dimensions of the Five Factor Model developed by McCrae and Costa (1987).

The eight IAS-R adjective clusters define four bipolar vectors: dominance versus submission, calculating versus unassuming, cold versus agreeable, and introverted versus extraverted. Lorr and Strack (1990) hypothesized that four bipolar lower-order factors could account for the correlations among the adjectives. A principal component analysis of their intercorrelations demonstrated the existence of these four dimensions within the interpersonal circumplex. These findings suggest that the interpersonal circumplex and this dimensional conception of the interpersonal circle are complementary viewpoints—one supplements the other.

The Five Factor Model has received growing support. The five factors are labeled *extraversion, agreeableness, neuroticism* (versus emotional stability), *conscientiousness,* and *openness to experience.* The use of simple structure as a criterion for factor rotation tends to maximize convergent correlations and to minimize divergent correlations between scales. In perfect simple structure there are no interstitial variables. Saucier (1992) proposed a squared factor loading index (SQLI). It constitutes a measure of adherence to simple structure. Of the ten possible two-dimensional spaces among the five main factors taken, the space defined by factors extraversion, agreeableness, and emotional stability are most prone to interstitial correlations. Conscientiousness and openness are characterized by a clearer simple structure. The interpersonal circumplex (Trapnell & Wiggins, 1990) corresponds to extraversion and agreeableness.

Conte and Plutchik (1981) used two independent methods to test the hypothesis that a circumplex model could represent interpersonal personality traits terms. First, they derived a representative sample of trait terms. Second, they analyzed these traits in terms of their degree of similarity to test for a circular configuration. Third, they used the semantic differential technique (Osgood, Suci, & Tannenbaum, 1957) to test the validity of the first method. Results supported the validity of the circumplex model.

Fisher, Heise, Bohrnstedt, and Lucke (1985) sought evidence for extending the circumplex model of personality trait language to self-reported moods. It remains uncertain whether the circular organization of trait and state terms also reflect the way people actually behave or feel. They sought to replicate the interpersonal trait circumplex with self-reported state measures. Asymptotically the average of behavioral states approached the measure of a trait. Respondents were asked to rate three adjectives on a 5-point scale. A principal component analysis of the correlation matrix of average ratings showed two components that accounted for 46% and 27% of the variance. Thus Fisher and colleagues concluded that the circumplex model represents a valid theoretical construct. It does not arise from an illusion of implicit personality theory.

BENJAMIN'S THREE CIRCUMPLEXES

Another application of the circumplex is found in Benjamin's (1974) Structural Analysis of Social Behavior (SASB). The SASB is based on three circular orders, two of which are interpersonal and the third of which characterizes intrapsychic experiences. The model classifies behavior in terms of its *focus*. When the focus is on the other person, the contrast, on the vertical axis of the circle, is control versus giving autonomy. The focus in the second circle is on the response of the *self* to the other person. It reflects the prototypic subordinate or childlike role. The third surface reflects introjective behavior. Here the vertical axis represents self-control versus self-emancipation. The horizontal axis in all three cases represents affection and moves from friendly and loving to hostile and attacking. Benjamin has demonstrated the presence of two factors that define each circle (1994).

In other studies Benjamin and her colleagues turned to the development of a cluster form of the SASB (Benjamin, 1993). The items of each circle were grouped into eight clusters much the way Wiggins grouped his adjectives into eight interpersonal adjective scales (IAS-R). Each of the three circles could be defined by eight clusters. Each cluster has a bipolar opposite. In focus on other the clusters are freeing versus controlling, affirming versus belittling, loving versus rejecting, and protecting versus neglecting. These clusters represent the vertical and the horizontal axes of the circle. In focus on self the eight clusters and their opposites are asserting versus submitting, disclosing versus appeasing, approaching versus withdrawing, and trusting versus walling off. The third set of introject clusters consist of expressing self versus restraining self, accepting self versus rejecting self, cherishing self versus rejecting self, and protecting self versus self-neglecting. It is our hypothesis in this chapter that a factor analysis of the correlations among *items* of these sets will yield four factors. A factor analysis of the intercorrelations among the eight clusters of scores should disclose the two factors that define each circumplex.

Earlier Schaefer (1961) developed a conceptual model for maternal behavior similar to Benjamin's focus on the other. The two factors of the circumplex were love versus hostility and autonomy versus control. The two intermediate bipolar vectors were protect versus ignore and affirm versus belittle. It seems evident that this circumplex developed by Schaefer and his colleagues is consistent with Benjamin's elaboration as reported in her book on personality disorders (1993).

A NEW VIEW OF DOMINANCE–SUBMISSION

It is important to emphasize the SASB view that the opposite of dominance is to give autonomy. Submission is indirectly the complement of dominance. Lorr (1991) proposed a redefinition of the personality dimension of dominance–submission. On both theoretical and empirical grounds the opposite of directive (dominant) behavior is nondirective behavior when peer–peer relations are symmetric. However, submission or compliance is complementary to a parent or superordinate's controlling behavior. But when dyadic relations are asymmetric, the dyads differ in status, prestige, or influence. The higher-status person initiates action and takes the superordinate dominant role. The lower-status person takes the subordinate role. Nearly all inventories reflect peer–peer interactions. The SASB scales are primarily concerned either with subordinate or superordinate relations. They do not reflect peer–peer (equal status) relations as in conventional inventories.

To demonstrate this view of dominance, use was made of scores on the directive scale of the Interpersonal Style Inventory (ISI; Lorr & Youniss, 1986) and the dominance scale of the Personality Research Form (PRF; Jackson, 1967). Both scales consist of 20 statements, of which half are keyed as *true* and half are keyed as *false*. A scale score consists of the sum of true-keyed items, marked T, and the sum of false-keyed items, marked F. It was predicted that the true-keyed items would correlate negatively at significant levels with the false-keyed items. In a sample of 216 college students, the true- and false-keyed items of the dominance scale correlated −0.64. The true- and false-keyed items of directive correlated −0.70 in the ISI. In another sample of 327 high school students, the half-scale scores of the PRF dominance correlated −0.63, and the ISI half-scale scores of directive correlated −0.65. Thus directiveness and nondirectiveness are substantially but negatively correlated with each other. These relations imply that one is the opposite of the other in peer–peer relations.

CIRCULAR MODELS OF AFFECT

In 1962 Plutchik formulated a comprehensive theory of primary emotions that he viewed as adaptive devices that have played a role in individual survival. The basic prototypic dimensions of adaptive behavior and the emotions that are related to them are as follows: (a) incorporation (acceptance), (b) rejection (disgust), (c) destruction (anger), (d) protection (fear), (e) reproduction (joy), (f) deprivation (sorrow), (g) orientation (surprise); and exploration (expectation). The model presents the eight emotions in a circular order.

Russell (1980) also has proposed a circular model of affect. Supportive evidence was obtained by scaling 28 affect adjectives in several different ways. These included multidimensional scaling procedures based on perceived similarity among adjectives. A unidimensional scaling procedure was applied that hypothesized a pleasure–displeasure and an arousal dimension. A third procedure involved a principal components analysis of self-reports of the research participant's own current affective state. The circular order he found was defined by two dimensions. The vertical axis contrasted arousal with sleep and fatigue, whereas the horizontal axis contrasted pleasure with misery.

Lorr and Lingoes (1995) undertook another approach to establishing the existence of a circular order for mood or affect by first studying the bipolarity of moods. Osgood and his associates (1957) had developed a semantic differential that interpreted language in terms of three dimensions of meaning. These dimensions are evaluation (good–bad, happy–sad), potency (large–small, strong–weak), and activity (fast–slow, active–passive). Some theorists argued that the differentials should not be bipolar. Bentler (1969) conducted a study in which he demonstrated that semantic space was approximately bipolar. Lorr, McNair, and Fisher (1982) administered the Profile of Mood States (McNair, Lorr, & Droppleman, 1971) to a large sample of psychiatric patients. After extreme bias score was partialled out of the 72 adjective ratings, the ratings were intercorrelated and analyzed by the method of principal components. Five bipolar mood states were clearly demonstrated.

A circular order of moods was hypothesized and tested in Lorr and Lingoe's (1995) unpublished study using nine adjective scale scores. The scales were designed to be measures of nine moods: cheerful, energetic, aroused, angry, tense–anxious, thoughtful, dejected, tired–inert, and composed. The scale intercorrelations ($N = 200$) were converted into distances. Next with the help of Lingoes, the Lingoes–Guttman nonmetric factor analysis (1967) was applied to the data. Two dimensions proved to be sufficient to fit the data. Kruskal's normalized stress index of $<.05$ was interpreted as "good." The plot indicated that the first factor contrasted *cheerful* and *energetic* with *depression* and *tension*. The second factor contrasted *aroused* with *tired* and *inert*. The factor coordinates are given in Table 1. Thus these moods do fit into a circular order much as Russell (1980) found.

CIRCULAR ORDER OF PSYCHOTIC SYNDROMES

A hierarchical model of higher-order psychotic syndromes has often been suggested. Some of these proposals are summarized in *Syndromes of Psychosis* (Lorr, Klett, & McNair, 1963). However, such a model is better suited to an all-positively correlated set of variables. Variables of personality and psychopathology are much more likely to be bipolar. The search for a psychotic syndrome circle was sought in the 75 scales of the *Inpatient Multidimensional Psychiatic Scales* (IMPS; Lorr, Klett, McNair, & Lasky, 1963). Eight of the ten scales within IMPS can be shown to be ordered in a circular sequence. The scale intercorrelations are presented in Table 2.

To test for the anticipated two-dimensional framework, the table was analyzed by the method of principal components. Two components, with associated eigenvalues of 3.5 and 2.6, accounted for 76% of the variance. The third component's eigenvalue was only 0.67. The first dimension, as presented in Table 3, contrasts excitement, grandiosity, and paranoid pro-

TABLE 1
Lingoes–Guttman Smallest Space Coordinates

Variable	Dimension	
	I	II
Cheerful	−95.3	−37.7
Energetic	−100.0	−36.1
Aroused	−14.8	−100.0
Angry	90.3	−63.8
Tense	97.1	−42.7
Thoughtful	93.9	−89.2
Dejected	100.0	−6.1
Tired–inert	51.1	76.9
Composed	−91.0	−18.9

Note. Adapted from *A Circular Affect Order*, by Lorr and L. C. Lingoes, 1995, unpublished manuscript.

TABLE 2
Correlations Among Eight Syndromes Based on IMPS Normative Sample

	EXC	GRN	PAR	DEP	RTD	DIS	MTR	CNP
Excitement	*							
Grandiose expansiveness	.44	*						
Paranoid projection	.27	.38	*					
Anxious depression	−.12	−.05	.16	*				
Retardation and apathy	−.37	−.13	−.12	.14	*			
Disorientation	−.04	−.02	−.06	−.11	36	*		
Motor disturbances	.28	.10	.18	−.03	.34	.34	*	
Conceptual disorganization	.46	.31	.29	−.14	.15	.30	.51	*

Note. IMPS=Impatient Multidimensional Psychiatric Scales. Reprinted from Lorr, Klett, McNair, and Lasky (1963).

jection with retardation. The second dimension contrasts motor distur-bances and conceptual disorganization with anxious depression.

CONCLUSION

This chapter has provided a brief historical introduction to the con-cept of the circumplex model as first conceived by Guttman (1954) and documents its even earlier use by Freedman and colleagues (1951) and LaForge and Suczek (1955). The circular conception was also used by Leary

TABLE 3
Varimax Factors for IMPS Psychotic Syndromes

Syndrome	Factor	
	I	II
Excitement	.74	.38
Grandiosity	.87	.00
Paranoid projection	.33	.03
Anxious depression	−.53	−.69
Retardation	−.72	.04
Disorientation	−.19	.31
Motor disturbances	−.29	.89
Conceptual disorganization	.34	.85

Note. IMPS=Impatient Multidimensional Psychiatric Scales. Reprinted from Lorr, Klett, McNair, and Lasky (1963).

and colleagues (1957) and Lorr and McNair (1963, 1965). It then showed how Wiggins' later (1979) and more extensive studies of the interpersonal circumplex demonstrate how its dimensions for depicting interpersonal behavior may be considered complementary to the dimensions of the Five Factor Model (McCrae & Costa, 1987).

Additional studies indicating the value of the circumplex model in conceptualizing the relations among interpersonal personality traits are also described (Benjamin, 1974; Conte & Plutchik, 1981; Lorr & Youniss, 1986). Finally, the chapter documents the usefulness of circular models of affect (Lorr, McNair, & Fisher, 1982; Lorr & Lingoes, 1995; Russell, 1980) and provides evidence for its possible utility in depicting psychotic syndromes.

REFERENCES

Benjamin, L. S. (1974). Structural analysis of social behavior. *Psychological Review, 81*, 392–425.

Benjamin, L. S. (1993). *Interpersonal diagnosis and treatment of personality disorders.* New York: Guilford Press.

Benjamin, L. S. (1994). SASB: A bridge between personality theory and clinical psychology. *Psychological Inquiry, 5*, 273–316.

Bentler, D. M. (1969). Semantic space is (approximately) bipolar. *Journal of Psychology, 71*, 33–40.

Conte, H. R., & Plutchik, R. (1981). A circumplex model for personality traits. *Journal of Personality and Social Psychology, 40*, 701–711.

Fisher, G. D., Heise, D. R., Bohrnstedt, G. W., & Lucke, J. I. (1985). Evidence for extending the circumplex model of personality trait language to self-reported moods. *Journal of Personality and Social Psychology, 49*, 233–242.

Freedman, M. B., Leary, T., Ossorio, A. G., & Coffey, H. S. (1951). The interpersonal dimension of personality. *Journal of Personality, 20*, 143–161.

Guttman, L. (1954). A new approach to factor analysis: The radex. In Paul F. Lazerfeld (Ed.), *Mathematical thinking in the social sciences* (pp. 258–348). Glencoe, IL: Free Press.

Horowitz, L. M., Rosenberg, S. E., Baer, B. A., Ureño, G., & Villaseñor, V. S. (1988). Inventory of Interpersonal Problems: Psychometric properties and clinical applications. *Journal of Clinical and Consulting Psychology, 56*, 885–892.

Jackson, D. N. (1967). *Personality research form manual.* Goshen, NY: Research Psychologist Press.

LaForge, R. S., & Suczek, R. F. (1955). The interpersonal dimension of personality. An interpersonal checklist. *Journal of Personality, 24*, 94–112.

Leary, T. (1957). *Interpersonal diagnosis of personality: A functional theory and methodology for personality evaluation.* New York: Ronald Press.

Lingoes, J. C., & Guttman, L. (1967). Nonmetric factor analysis: A rank reducing alternative to linear factor analysis. *Multivariate Behavioral Research, 2,* 485–505.

Lorr, M. (1991). A redefinition of dominance. *Personality and Individual Differences, 12,* 807–879.

Lorr, M., Klett, C. J., & McNair, D. M. (1963). *Syndromes of psychosis.* New York: Macmillan.

Lorr, M., Klett, C. J., McNair, D. M., & Lasky, J. J. (1963). *The inpatient multidimensional psychiatric scale.* Palo Alto, CA: Consulting Psychologist Press.

Lorr, M., & Lingoes, J. C. (1995). *A circular affect order.* Unpublished manuscript.

Lorr, M., & McNair, D. M. (1963). An interpersonal behavior circle. *Journal of Abnormal and Social Psychology, 67,* 68–75.

Lorr, M., & McNair, D. M. (1965). Expansion of the interpersonal behavior circle. *Journal of Personality and Social Psychology, 2,* 823–830.

Lorr, M., McNair, D. M., & Fisher, S. (1982). Evidence for bipolar mood states. *Journal of Personality Assessment, 46,* 432–436.

Lorr, M., & Strack, S. (1990). Wiggins Interpersonal Adjective Scales: A dimensional view. *Personality and Individual Differences, 11,* 423–425.

Lorr, M., & Youniss, R. (1986). *Interpersonal Style Inventory (ISI) manual.* Los Angeles: Western Psychological Services.

McCrae, R. R., & Costa, P. T., Jr. (1987). Validation of the Five-Factor Model of personality across instruments and observers. *Journal of Personality and Social Psychology, 52,* 81–90.

McNair, D. M., Lorr, M., & Droppleman, L. F. (1971). *The profile of mood states.* Los Angeles: Educational and Industrial Testing Service.

Osgood, C. E., Suci, G. J., & Tannenbaum, P. H. (1957). *The measurement of meaning.* Urbana: University of Illinois Press.

Plutchik, R. (1962). *The emotions: Facts, theories and a new model.* New York: Random House.

Russell, J. A. (1980). A circumplex model of affect. *Journal of Personality and Social Psychology, 39,* 1161–1178.

Saucier, G. (1992). Bench marks: Integrating affective and interpersonal circles within the big five personality factors. *Journal of Personality and Social Psychology, 62,* 1025–1035.

Schaefer, E. S. (1961). Converging conceptual models for maternal behavior and for child behavior. In J. C. Glidwell (Ed.), *Parental attitudes and child behavior.* Springfield, IL: Charles C. Thomas.

Trapnell, P. D., & Wiggins, J. S. (1990). Extension of the interpersonal adjective scales to include the big five dimensions of personality. *Journal of Personality and Social Psychology, 59,* 1–10.

Wiggins, J. S. (1979). A psychological taxonomy of trait-descriptive terms: The interpersonal domain. *Journal of Personality and Social Psychology, 37,* 395–412.

Wiggins, J. S., Trapnell, P., & Phillips, N. (1988). Psychometric and geometric characteristics of the revised Interpersonal Adjective Scales (IAS-R). *Multivariate Behavioral Research, 23,* 517–530.

3

WHEN IS A CIRCUMPLEX AN "INTERPERSONAL CIRCUMPLEX"? THE CASE OF SUPPORTIVE ACTIONS

JERRY S. WIGGINS and KRISTA K. TROBST

The circumplex model has come a long way since its unheralded inception as a schematic representation of the empirical interrelations found among tests of mental abilities (Guttman, 1954). The checkered history of both the geometric model and of its substantive applications is itself an interesting story, but more recent developments and their implications for the future are even more striking. Consider, for example, the year of 1992 in which circumplex models were the topic of a presidential address to the Psychometric Society (Browne, 1992), were judged to have held their own as the "basic dimensions" of personality research (Wiggins & Pincus, 1992) and were applied to all possible combinations of the Big Five dimensions of personality by distinguished proponents of the simple structure tradition (Hofstee, De Raad, & Goldberg, 1992).

The variety and scope of many of the circumplex applications in this book attest to the continuing vitality of the model but also raise some questions concerning the boundary conditions of its applications. In some circumstances, the fit between the circumplex model and many constructs from classical and contemporary interpersonal theory has been so close that one can hardly distinguish the theory from the model (Wiggins, Phillips, & Trapnell, 1989). In other circumstances, however, when circumplex structures are obtained for affects, psychiatric diagnoses, face diagrams, or the axes of neuroticism and extraversion, the relation between interpersonal theory and the obtained circumplex structure may be less clear.

To assert that a circumplex is an *interpersonal* circumplex requires both an empirically demonstrated circumplex structure *and* a plausible substantive rationale for placing an interpersonal interpretation on the measures that gave rise to the circumplex. The circumstances under which interpersonal interpretations of a circumplex may or may not be appropriate are often quite evident. For example, the demonstrated utility of the circumplex model in capturing similarity ratings among physically specifiable visual or auditory stimuli (Shepard, 1978) would hardly lead one to speculate about the interpersonal nature of the underlying circumplex coordinates. Conversely, although the circumplex structures obtained by Myllyniemi (chapter 12, this volume) for her face diagrams may have been less than optimal due to certain technical problems in measurement, her well-articulated facet theory provides a convincing argument for interpreting the obtained structures as interpersonal in nature. A circumplex is an *interpersonal* circumplex when there are good reasons to interpret it as such.

We hasten to add that "good reasons" will vary, of course, from investigator to investigator, depending on his or her conceptual approaches to interpersonal behavior. However, our purpose here is not to arrogate usage of the term *interpersonal* but rather to emphasize that circumplex structures are useful only to the extent that one can place *interpretations* on them, whether the context of interpretation be clinical practice or basic research. Such interpretations require (a) a general theory of, or a set of orienting attitudes toward, interpersonal behavior as applied to circumplex dimensions and (b) a sensitivity to several parameters of measurement that may particularize interpretations in a given setting. To illustrate these points, we will first provide the outlines of a theory of interpersonal behavior as applied to the circumplex and then enumerate some of the parameters that affect interpretations in different settings.

THEORETICAL ORIENTATION

On a highly abstract level, we have found the metaconcepts[1] of *agency* and *communion* (Bakan, 1966) to be useful as conceptual coordinates for characterizing (a) philosophical world views (Wiggins, 1991); (b) the common challenges provided by all societies (Redfield, 1960); (c) the cultural bases of social behavior among societies (Triandis, 1995); (d) the division of labor (Parsons & Bales, 1955) and solution of reproductive problems (Buss, 1991) within societies; (e) the narrative themes in myth, stories,

---

[1]Concepts used to discuss, describe, or analyze other concepts.

and individual lives (McAdams, 1993); (f) theories of personality in general (Wiggins, 1991); and (g) the dynamics of interpersonal behavior in particular (see Wiggins & Trapnell, 1996).

On a somewhat less abstract level, the concept of *interpersonal situation* (Sullivan, 1953) is employed to designate a complex field in which past and present bidirectional interpersonal influences are embedded in an equally influential sociocultural matrix. The key notion here is that of *social exchange* (Foa & Foa, 1974) in which members of a dyad negotiate preferred definitions of interpersonal situations in terms of the resources of status (agency) and love (communion). Successful negotiations of interpersonal transactions satisfy agentic needs for self-esteem and communal needs for security, thereby avoiding the debilitating effects of agentic and communal anxiety, respectively (Wiggins & Trapnell, 1996).

Foa (1965) provided a facet analysis of interpersonal variables that decomposed them into: (a) object (self and other), (b) resource (love and status), and (c) directionality [giving (+) and taking away (−)]. The class of interpersonal variables that has figured most prominently in personality assessment is that of interpersonal traits—individuals' characteristic patterns of social exchange that recur within and across interpersonal situations. For example, an individual who is characteristically warm, nurturant, and helpful may seek situations in which he or she may give (+) resources (love and status) to those in need (others). Such an individual will (correctly) regard himself or herself as generally liked in helping situations [love (+)] but not feel more important than others being helped [status (−)]. The individual's preferred definition of interpersonal situations would be

self [love (+1); status (−1)] and other [love (+1); status (+1)]

This pattern of social exchange defines the interpersonal variable we call *warm–agreeable*, and it is one of eight such variables that differ from one another in values of the facets just described. Table 1 presents the facet composition of the remaining interpersonal variables. Note that each variable differs from its preceding variable by only one facet element. For example, arrogant–calculating behavior (BC) differs from assured–dominant behavior (PA) in the denial of love to other. Note that the first and last listed variables also differ by only one element. The difference between gregarious–extraverted behavior (NO) and assured–dominant behavior (PA) is that the latter denies status to other.

To the extent that the hypothesized values assigned to these eight variables are in fact true, the empirical interrelations among measures of these variables will necessarily form a circumplex (Wiggins & Trapnell, 1996). The two principal components that give rise to this circumplex (dominance–agency and nurturance–communion) define the universe of

TABLE 1
Facet Composition of Interpersonal Variables

Octant	IAS Scale	Social Outcome			
		Self		Other	
		Status	Love	Love	Status
PA	Assured–Dominant	+1	+1	+1	−1
BC	Arrogant–Calculating	+1	+1	−1	−1
DE	Cold–hearted	+1	−1	−1	−1
FG	Aloof–Introverted	−1	−1	−1	−1
HI	Unassured–Submissive	−1	−1	−1	+1
JK	Unassuming–Ingenous	−1	−1	+1	+1
LM	Warm–Agreeable	−1	+1	+1	+1
NO	Gregarious–Extraverted	+1	+1	+1	+1

Note. IAS = Interpersonal Adjective Scales.

content of interpersonal space, which, in principle, could involve any dyadic interactions that have social (status) and emotional (love) implications for both participants (self and other).

The Interpersonal Adjective Scales (IAS; Wiggins, 1995) form a well-structured circumplex representation of interpersonal space, within which it is possible to locate items, scales, or persons with considerable geometric precision. Figure 1 presents the IAS profile of a warm–agreeable woman of the type just described. The circular profile of interpersonal variables is divided into eight equal octants of 45° that are designated by both letters (PA, BC, DE . . .) and descriptive labels (assured–dominant, arrogant–calculating, cold–hearted . . .) in a counterclockwise direction.[2]

The profile illustrated has a characteristic configuration in which the defining octant [warm–agreeable (LM)] has the highest elevation, followed by moderately elevated adjacent octants (NO and JK) and diminishing to the opposite octant (DE). The mean of these eight vector scores is the *angular location* of this profile, and the distance of the mean vector from the center of the circle is referred to as *vector length*. As can be seen in Figure 1, the average angular location of this profile is 356°, which falls close to the midpoint of the warm–agreeable category that ranges from 337° to 22°. The vector length of this profile (indicated by a black mark on the vector) is 60, in a metric with a mean of 50 and a standard deviation

---

[2]These letters were employed originally by Freedman, Leary, Ossario, and Coffey (1951) to designate 16 interpersonal variables that were ordered in a counter-clockwise direction from the top of the circle: (A) dominant, (B) arrogant, (C) calculating . . . (P) assured. Contemporary workers have tended to combine these sixteenths into octants: (PA) assured-dominant, (BC) arrogant-calculating, . . . (NO) gregarious-extraverted. The names of these octant variables have changed over time, but the letters have been preserved to designate sectors of the circle: for example, PA (67°-112°), BC (112°-157°), . . . NO (23°-67°).

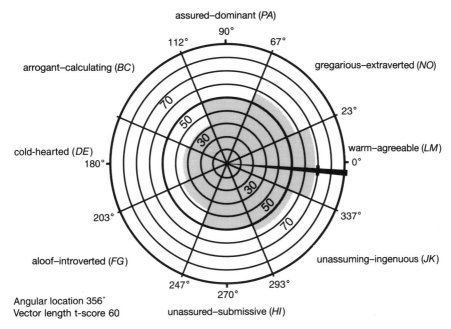

Figure 1. Interpersonal Adjective Scales profile of a warm–agreeable woman.

of 10. Vector length may be interpreted as the intensity with which an interpersonal pattern is expressed.

Were we to interpret this profile, we would characterize the woman placed within this category as a moderately intense (vector length) and somewhat prototypical (angular location near center of sector) warm–agreeable "type" who is disposed to be warm, nurturant, sympathetic, and caring in social transactions and who is inclined to provide material or emotional benefits to others who are in trouble, who need help, who are ill, or who are otherwise in need of care and support (Wiggins, 1995).

MEASUREMENT PARAMETERS

As a first approximation, we distinguish among five of what are likely many more parameters that may qualify or particularize circumplex interpretations.

Contexts

For lack of a better word, we have used the term context to designate the variety of instructions to respondents that have been employed to assess different interpersonal constructs for different purposes (Wiggins & Trapnell, 1996). The most frequent context of measurement has been that which assesses single acts or dispositions (Wiggins, in press) that involve social exchange among two or more participants. The two dimensions of dominance and nurturance that define this standard universe of content have figured prominently in both the lexical research tradition that emphasizes the meaning of trait terms (Saucier, 1992) and the Five Factor Model tradition that emphasizes the attribution of trait terms to self and others (McCrae & Costa, 1989). The Interpersonal Adjective Scales were developed to serve as markers of the space defined by the coordinates of dominance and nurturance.

In principle, there are many subuniverses of interpersonal content that focus on different constructs in different measurement contexts. For example, when respondents are instructed to indicate the extent to which they find their interpersonal transactions to be distressing, a subuniverse of interpersonal problems is defined (Horowitz, Rosenberg, Baer, Ureño, & Villaseñor, 1988) that is well captured by a circumplex model (Alden, Wiggins, & Pincus, 1990). An extensive conceptual rationale has been provided for the interpretation of this circumplex as interpersonal (e.g., Gurtman, 1994; Horowitz, Weckler, & Doren, 1983; Pincus & Wiggins, 1990).

Other examples can be cited of circumplex structures that are perhaps less obviously related to standard interpersonal space. For example, in the realm of vocational interests, there is little doubt that Holland's (1985b) Vocational Preference Inventory forms a well-ordered circumplex (Tracey & Rounds, 1993; Trapnell, 1989). An interpersonal interpretation of this space is not implausible (Hogan, 1983; Tracey & Rounds, 1993) if one incorporates Holland's (1985a) well-established theory of the relation between vocational interests and personality into a more general theory of interpersonal behavior.

Perspectives

Interpersonal reports, ratings, or reactions can be obtained from the perspectives of self, other, third party, or from combined levels, such as, "I think he thinks I deceive him" (Laing, Phillipson, & Lee, 1966). Kiesler's (1987) Impact Message Inventory provides an especially subtle interpersonal perspective. Respondents are asked to indicate, on a four-place scale, the covert feelings, action tendencies, and perceptions of evoking messages that they experience in the course of their interactions with a particular significant other. Despite the subtlety, the octant version of this inventory has a quite respectable circumplex structure (Kiesler & Schmidt, 1991). Judgments of personality from different perspectives differ from one another and present different problems of measurement "accuracy." Although many of these problems are daunting, a major investigator in this area remains impressed ". . . not because judgments are perfect, but because in the face of enormous difficulties it seems remarkable they manage to have any accuracy at all" (Funder, 1989, p. 12).

Roles

Although sociological in nature, the institutions and conventions of society facilitate, constrain, and generally affect the course of interpersonal relationships so strongly that they may be legitimately considered causal factors to be reckoned with (Searle, 1995). On a worldwide basis, the operation of agentic and communal institutions among societies is characterized by the distinction between individualistic and collectivistic cultures (Triandis, 1995). Within cultures, one may identify agentic and communal situations (Moskowitz, 1994) in which institutionalized conventions are manifest in roles based on friendship, marriage, or kinship (e.g., father–son), social organization (e.g., employer–employee), vocation (e.g., psychotherapist–patient), and a variety of other role definitions that may facilitate or constrain the exchange of love and status.

Levels of Measurement

The level of measurement in interpersonal assessment ranges from the microanalytic analysis of stimulus–response behavioral sequences in ongoing transactions to the macroanalytic analysis of global patterns that endure over time and situation. The originators of the interpersonal system observed microanalytic patterns of exchange in group psychotherapy (Freedman, Leary, Ossorio, & Coffey, 1951) and more recently, Gifford (1991, 1994) mapped the circumplex with microanalytic units of nonverbal behavior observed in group interactions. The principal macroanalytic unit of measurement has been the global interpersonal disposition, as self-reported (trait) and as perceived by others (reflex) (Leary, 1957).

Levels of Interpretation

The interpersonal circumplex has been interpreted in three different ways that reflect varying assumptions about the quantitative and qualitative properties of a circumplex and that have proven useful for different purposes. The three kinds of interpretations might be designated as *intuitive*, *ordinal*, and *metric*.

1. On a nonquantitative level, one may consider a circumplex to be a convenient pictoral representation of concepts from interpersonal theory, such as the *change*, *direction*, or *intensity*

of a patient's characteristic mode of self-presentation during the course of psychotherapy. There is strong precedent for this intuitive type of reasoning in the early work of Lewin (see Cartwright, 1959) and the visual and psychological appeal of the circumplex renders it an especially heuristic device for brainstorming about interpersonal transactions (Wiggins, 1996).

2. On a quantitative level, making minimal assumptions, one may test for a specific pattern of ordering among a set of observed variables without reference to the magnitude of their intercorrelations, their angular locations, or their distances from the center of the circle (Guttman, 1954).

3. One also may interpret a circumplex as a formal geometric model of the interrelations among indicants of constructs derived from an explicit theory of interpersonal behavior (Wiggins, Phillips, & Trapnell, 1989). This level involves strong metric assumptions that are required to establish the construct validity of interpretations placed on the results of empirical investigations.

Reporting Circumplex Findings

A description of the results of a given interpersonal assessment should include a specification of content, perspective, roles, level of measurement, and level of interpretation. Thus the statement, "The circumplex version of the Inventory of Interpersonal Problems was used to assess spouse perceptions of problematic interpersonal dispositions" is complete and informs the reader that

> The circumplex version of the Inventory of Interpersonal Problems [*level of interpretation: metric*] was used to assess spouse [*role: spouse*] perceptions [*perspective: other*] of problematic [*context: problems*] interpersonal dispositions [*measurement level: macroanalytic*].

SOCIAL SUPPORT AS INTERPERSONAL TRANSACTIONS

Interpersonal interpretations of social support transactions have been surprisingly absent in the literature of that topic. This is so despite the strong precedent for the application of interpersonal theory to a conceptual analysis of social support in the classic paper of Cobb (1976), which is better known for its review of the empirical evidence demonstrating that support is protective against the health consequences of life stress. Cobb (1976) defined social support as "information leading the subject to believe that he is cared for and loved, esteemed, and a member of a network of mutual obligations" (p. 300). Cobb discusses, in addition to the social resources of *love* (emotional support) and *status* (esteem support), the material resources of *goods*, *services*, and *information*. In that respect, his formulations are strikingly similar to those of Foa and Foa (1974), which provide the social exchange foundation of the dyadic–interactional perspective (Wiggins & Trapnell, 1996). However, with respect to material resources, Cobb (1976) argued that they

> are not of themselves information of any of the major classes mentioned above. This does not mean that the deferential manner of the intern may not provide esteem support or that the tender care of the nurses may not communicate emotional support. It is only to say that the services themselves do not in themselves constitute such support. . . . (p. 301)

Although we agree with Cobb that the provision of the social resources of love and status is paramount in social support contexts, we also believe that the provision of material resources (i.e., goods, services, information, and money) serves an important function and should not be overlooked. To the extent that the provision of a material resource addresses a need of the recipient and thereby facilitates his or her coping with the problem at hand, this material provision should be deemed a supportive action. From an interpersonal perspective, however, the provision of material resources also may act as a medium through which interpersonal messages about love and status (social resources) can be communicated. Thus, the same act may take on different interpersonal significance depending on the manner in which it is presented. The lending of money may provide an opportunity for the nurturant individual to communicate his or her love and esteem for the recipient, or it may provide the arrogant–calculating individual with an opportunity to communicate his or her relative superiority and worthiness.

The IAS profile we described earlier (Figure 1) came from a woman who was prototypically warm–agreeable. When asked by a friend or family member to provide support, this woman would be likely to define the interpersonal situation as one in which she would provide love and status to the person in need while minimizing her own status. Most social scientists would characterize this transaction as *social support* and would likely judge the concrete behaviors involved to be *helpful* (as opposed to *unhelpful*).

Clearly, it would seem a good idea to seek help and support from helpful and supportive persons, but not all of us are fortunate enough to have friends or family members who would fit this specification, and, indeed, the proportion of warm–agreeable people may be close to one out of eight! There are, of course, closely related types of people such as the adjacent categories of unassuming–ingenuous and gregarious–extraverted, both of whom grant love and status to others (see Table 1). But the unassuming–ingenuous type's denial of both love and status to self may result in idle deference and the gregarious–extraverted type's granting of status to self may diminish somewhat the status granted to others. The arrogant–calculating, cold–hearted, and aloof–introverted types are out of the question because they deny both love and status. The assured–dominant type offers love while denying the importance of others and the unassured–submissive type grudgingly grants others status while denying love.

We are emphasizing the apparently neglected point that there will be individual differences in response to others in need of support that reflect the potential providers' characteristic patterns of social exchange in other interpersonal situations.[3] As such, we would anticipate that individual differences in supportive actions would be well captured by a circumplex model. The measurement parameters under consideration here are context (helping and supporting others), perspective (self), roles (friends and relatives), measurement (macro), and interpretation (metric). Of these, the parameter of context might be most influential because, as discussed, there would appear to be definite constraints on what generally counts as helping behavior in our society.

THE SUPPORTIVE ACTIONS SCALE

Earlier work conducted by the second author Trobst examined characteristics of providers as determinants of support provision. Part of this research involved preliminary construction of a scale (Supportive Actions Scale; SAS) assessing the amount and kinds of support providers believed they would offer to a friend in need (Trobst, 1991; Trobst, Collins, & Embree, 1994). Dakof and Taylor's (1990) comprehensive list of support received by people with cancer provided a definition of the universe of content (Loevinger, 1957) of supportive actions and served as a guide for the generation of 31 items. Principal components were extracted from an intercorrelation matrix of the 31 SAS items, yielding an oblique three-factor solution that appeared to represent stylistic differences in the types of support providers expect to deliver. Closer inspection of these factors suggested clear theoretical placement within the interpersonal circumplex space. Specifically, Factor I (encouraging–emotional actions) assessed relatively *nurturant* types of support; Factor II (directive actions) represented *dominant* supportive actions; and Factor III (avoidant actions) contained behaviors best characterized as *submissive* (negative dominance) tendencies. These

---

[3]Although not considered here, individual differences in characteristic patterns of social exchange among potential recipients of support may be of equal importance in establishing the eventual definition of an interpersonal situation.

findings suggested a circumplex structure with some apparent gaps in coverage. Encouraged by this result we attempted to construct a full circumplex model of supportive actions.

In our first study, three judges (the two authors and Paul Trapnell) generated provisional items for mapping eight sectors of the interpersonal circle. This pool of 139 items was administered to 169 University of British Columbia undergraduate students, with instructions to report how they typically respond when a friend or family member needs support. A 7-place Likert format was employed that ranged from 1 ("definitely would not do this") to 7 ("definitely would do this"). A circumplex-generating program was employed to establish eight preliminary octant clusters and to evaluate the angular location and variance contribution of all items. The circumplex structure that emerged was less than optimal with respect to equal spacing among octants.

In our second study, items with low communality values ($\leq .10$) were deleted and additional items were generated to form a pool of 140 items, which was administered to 444 undergraduate subjects. Angular location and communality values were taken into account in selecting items for eight circumplex scales. Principal component analysis of the intercorrelations among these scales (see Table 2) indicated two circumplex components accounting for 35.4% and 29.4% of the variance, respectively, and a relatively small general factor (Wiggins, Steiger, & Gaelick, 1981) accounting for 14.8% of the variance on which none of the variables had their defining loading. As can be seen from Figure 2, the obtained circumplex structure is well formed (Trobst & Wiggins, 1995), and it compares favorably with some of the better solutions reported in the literature, as we will discuss later.

Table 3 provides representative items for each of the Supportive Actions Scale–Circumplex (SAS-C) octants and illustrates the interpersonal

TABLE 2
Intercorrelation Matrix of Supportive Actions Scale—Circumplex Octants

	PA	BC	DE	FG	HI	JK	LM	NO
PA	1.00							
BC	.6032	1.00						
DE	.1067	.5026	1.00					
FG	−.2475	.1038	.4910	1.00				
HI	−.4117	−.2788	.1766	.5196	1.00			
JK	−.1813	−.3419	−.2590	.0073	.4114	1.00		
LM	.1989	−.2642	−.4916	−.4273	−.0297	.3888	1.00	
NO	.4965	.0844	−.3286	−.5274	−.3227	.1122	.6675	1.00

Note. $N = 444$. PA = directive; BC = arrogant; DE = critical; FG = distancing; HI = avoidant; JK = deferential; LM = nurturant; NO = engaging.

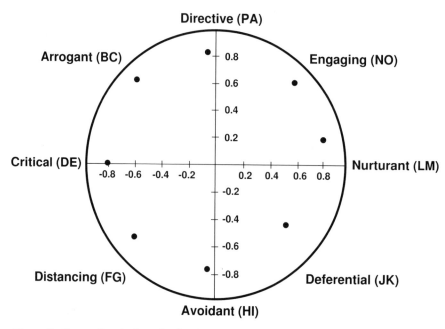

Figure 2. Supportive Actions Scale circumplex structure (*N* = 444).

TABLE 3
Illustrative Supportive Actions Scale—Circumplex

Scale	Location[a]	Sample Item
Directive (PA)	90°	"Give advice"
		"Tell them to let me deal with things"
Arrogant (BC)	135°	"Persuade them to change their behavior"
		"Emphasize how well qualified I am to help"
Critical (DE)	180°	"Remind them that people sometimes get what they deserve"
		"Remind them that whining doesn't help"
Distancing (FG)	225°	"Try to keep them from leaning on me too much"
		"Remain detached while listening to their problem"
Avoidant (HI)	270°	"Avoid being directive"
		"Be afraid to express my point of view on the problem"
Deferential (JK)	315°	"Not argue with them"
		"Just listen quietly"
Nurturant (LM)	0°	"Give them a hug"
		"Just try to be there"
Engaging (NO)	45°	"Get them to talk more about their problem"
		"Check up on them frequently"

[a]Midpoint of scale indicated in upper-left-hand corner

nature of the circumplex of supportive actions. Although highly in accord with theory, the item content of some of these octants may seem surprising in light of the context of responding to a friend or family member in need of support. It is perhaps not surprising that some individuals "give advice" (directive; PA) or that others "give them a hug" (nurturant; LM), but though in accord with theoretical expectations, it is a bit surprising that some individuals "remind them that whining doesn't help" (critical; DE) and that others "try to keep them from leaning on me too much" (distancing; FG). The fact that some individuals could behave in such clearly inappropriate ways in response to a loved one's distress has been the source of perplexity and speculation among social support researchers for some time, and the possible explanation that unhelpful actions result from ignorance of appropriate behavior has proven to be incorrect (Lehman, Ellard, & Wortman, 1986). From our perspective such unhelpful actions reflect the prepotency of dispositional traits despite strong contextual pressures to respond otherwise.

Although we anticipate that this instrument will provide a novel and useful tool for research on social support when the final version becomes available,[4] our purpose here is to illustrate the somewhat more subtle properties of this instrument that are specific to the social support context and to show how this type of measurement differs from the traditional measurement of interpersonal dispositions. Toward this end, we must look more closely at the substantive and psychometric properties that underlie the SAS circumplex structure illustrated in Figure 2.

SOCIAL SUPPORT CIRCUMPLEXES: CAVEATS AND CONJECTURES

In characterizing an individual's general interpersonal dispositions, his or her granting or withholding of love and status to both self and others are of equal concern. Perhaps not surprising, however, in the somewhat narrowed context of supportive actions, greater weight is placed on the tendency of an individual to grant or withhold love and status to the other. This shift of emphasis to the recipient appears to have the effect of increasing the perceived similarity among interpersonal types with respect to the two dimensions of (a) denying versus granting status and (b) granting love and status versus denying love and status. From the "other" columns in Table 1 it can be seen that directive (PA) and arrogant (BC) types *deny* status and that avoidant (HI) and deferential (JK) types *grant* status. In a similar way, nurturant (LM) and engaging (NO) types *grant* love and status

---

[4]A revised version of SAS-C with exemplary psychometric properties is now available from the second author.

and critical (DE) and distancing (FG) types deny love and status. This merging of type categories based on similar patterns of assigning resources to others is apparent in some, but not all, of the findings we will now consider.

Generation and Selection of Items

We found it relatively easy to generate items for each of the hypothesized circumplex octants of the SAS-C. During the item selection process, however, we encountered a number of instances of octant misplacement (relative to theoretical expectation) that reflected a difficulty in discriminating between adjacent octants. In particular, difficulty was experienced in discriminating between the nurturant (LM) and engaging (NO) hypothesized octants. Items generated for one of these octants would often appear in the other, and a conceptual rationale for our initial misplacement was not immediately forthcoming. The correlation between nurturant and engaging in the current version of the SAS-C octant scales is .67, which is higher than the average correlation between circumplex octants that one usually obtains. Some difficulty also was experienced in achieving an optimal separtion between items in the arrogant (BC) and directive (PA) hypothesized octants, as indicated by the correlation of .60 between current octant versions of these two scales. Moreover, it appeared to be even more difficult to rationalize certain octant placements than it was in the case of nuturant and engaging. Finally, although we had generated approximately equal numbers of items for each octant (17 to 18), only five items were found to be located within the deferential (JK) octant; the majority of the hypothesized deferential items were located in the avoidant (HI) octant space. As a consequence, although the eventual location of the deferential octant scale in the current SAS-C space is close to optimal, the communality value of this octant is low (see Figure 2), probably reflecting the fact that this octant contains only five items (alpha = .64).

The title of the present section forewarned the reader about conjectures, and we will now indulge in some unsubstantiated post hoc speculation. It would seem that one kind of effective social support might be judged to lie somewhere within the stronger portion of the nurturant sector (LM). To actually be of help, provision of a clear message of love and status might require more than simply giving off nurturant vibes. In this circumstance, a nurturant person might endorse stronger LM items and, in fact, the majority of LM items that survived had locations greater than 360°. By similar reasoning, the engaging person (NO), to be effective, might have to be more than simply cheerful, outgoing, and vivacious; in this context, he or she might endorse warmer items in the NO sector. Under these circumstances, items in the two octants would tend to be associated closely. These same conditions also would make it difficult to write deferential (JK) items that were strong enough to approach the effective social support of the nurturant (LM) category, and such items might be more closely associated with the avoidant (HI) category.

Depending on the circumstances, another kind of effective social support might be judged to lie within the directive sector of the circle. Many of us have experienced circumstances in which we asked a friend for their (presumably good) advice about a distressing problem. There would seem to be a bit of arrogance associated with taking charge of a friend's life circumstances, and although the purely directive individual (PA) has learned to finesse such a role, the arrogant supporter (BC) enjoys it a bit too much. Because neither type of supporter grants status to the other, it might be difficult to discriminate the communal aims of the former (PA) from the noncommunal aims of the latter (BC).

First-Order Factors Underlying the Supportive Actions Scale Circumplex Structure

When the items of an eight-variable interpersonal circumplex are subjected to a factor analysis, the expectation is that there will be four bipolar factors accounting for about half of the common variance among items (Lorr & Strack, 1990). For example, we have found that the four first-order factors underlying the IAS circumplex are the expected bipolar contrasts of dominant versus submissive, arrogant versus unassuming, cold versus warm, and introverted versus extraverted.

When the items of the present SAS circumplex were subjected to a principal components analysis, the variance accounted for by the first four components was only 38%, and the factors, although interpretable, were primarily unipolar combinations of octant variables. The first factor was loaded primarily by nurturant and engaging (LM and NO), the second factor primarily by directive (PA), arrogant (BC), and critical (DE), the third factor primarily by avoidant (HI) and deferential (JK), and the fourth factor primarily by distancing (FG). This suggests that, on the item level, the three shadow factors of encouraging–emotional (LM–NO), directive (PA–BC), and avoidant (HI–JK) found in the original SAS study (Trobst, 1991) underlie the current SAS circumplex even though only five of the items from the original study survived item selection for the current version.

Estimating Population Correlation Coefficients

Circumplexity in a given data set also may be evaluated by a straightforward and computationally simple procedure that estimates a matrix of population correlations coefficients, of which obtained correlation coefficients are presumed to be samples, and then tests the goodness of fit of the two matrices (Wiggins et al., 1981). The estimated population correlation coefficients are used to form an ideal circulant correlation matrix in which correlations within the same diagonals are exactly equal to each other and in which successive minor diagonals decrease and increase in accord with a circulant pattern. The mean squared residual between the obtained matrix of SAS-C intercorrelations and the ideal circulant matrix of estimated population intercorrelations was 0.0058; the mean squared residual value for the best empirical circumplex solution among the 18 examples considered by Wiggins and collleagues (1981, p. 273) was 0.0053. On psychometric grounds, the SAS circumplex is among the better available in the literature.

Additional information about circumplexity is sometimes provided by the six principal components of the estimated population intercorrelations that remain after extraction of the two circumplex components (Wiggins et al., 1981). For example, a general component accounting for 14% of the variance was present, as was a specificity component that indicated deviations from equal positive loadings on that general component. In the original factor analysis of the obtained SAS-C intercorrelations, an apparent general component had unexpectedly higher loadings on the avoidant (HI) and deferential (JK) octants. To determine whether or not this was a general component, we ipsatized all items with respect to each research participant's average item score and refactored the adjusted intercorrelation matrix. The complete disappearance of the third principal component under these circumstances confirmed that it was a general factor. One might speculate that this somewhat unusual general factor reflects stylistic tendencies to deal actively with another's need for support as opposed to avoiding the issue passively. In any event, this issue is primarily an academic one, because ipsatization has only a slight effect on the circumplex structure of the SAS-C scales.

Correlations of Supportive Actions Scale Octants With Interpersonal Adjective Scale Octants

From the findings discussed thus far, it should be clear that the SAS-C is not completely isomorphic with standard dispositional space as measured by the IAS, nor should it be. We administered the IAS to our sample of 444 participants and determined that the average correlation between SAS-C and IAS octant scales was .37, with a range from .22 to .56. More important, we found that the relations (both positive and negative) between supportive styles and dispositional measures were much stronger for communal variables than for agentic variables. IAS-LM was correlated .56 with SAS-LM and −.50 with SAS-DE; IAS-DE was correlated .47 with SAS-DE and −.38 with SAS-LM. This suggests that the behavior of warm–agreeable individuals in support situations is more predictable (both positively and negatively) than is that of assured–dominant individuals. This is not surprising if one considers other contexts, such as the evaluation of leadership potential, in which information concerning communal dispositions might be somewhat less valuable than information concerning agentic propensities.

It is not possible to specify precisely the extent to which comparable octants from trait dispositional space and the space of specialized contexts should be correlated with each other (Wiggins & Trapnell, 1996). The correlations between octants from the IAS and octants from the circumplex version of the Inventory of Interpersonal Problems (IIP-C) are a case in point. In a sample of 974 participants, the average correlation between comparable IAS and IIP-C octants was .46 and the range of correlations was between .36 and .58 (Alden et al., 1990). The range of IAS versus IIP-C octant correlations was similar to that of IAS versus SAS-C correlations, and the average octant correlation of IAS with IIP-C was slightly higher (.46 as opposed to .37).

On the assumption of a continuity between normal trait dispositions and their problematic manifestations, one clearly would expect correlations between the intensity of trait expression and the psychopathology of that expression (Pincus, 1994). But the context of psychopathology itself, in largely unknown ways, may involve constraints on measurement. For example, the essentially problematic nature of exaggerated aloof–introverted behavior (FG) would seem to be considerably more obvious than that of exaggerated warm–agreeable behavior (LM), which, in its normal manifestations, is singularly related to good adjustment (see Wiggins, 1995, p. 26). It is also the case that the substantial general complaint or neuroticism factor of IIP (Gurtman, 1995) has no counterpart in the standard interpersonal space of IAS. These and other differences between trait-dispositional and problematic interpersonal spaces are likely to affect the magnitude of correlations between the two instruments.

PARAMETERS OF SOCIAL SUPPORT MEASUREMENT

As stated earlier, at least five parameters may qualify circumplex interpretation. These will now be examined with reference to the Supportive Actions Scale Circumplex (SAS).

Context

Although interpersonal measures of trait dispositions require the specification of resource exchanges for both self and other, the context of supportive actions appears to be focused more on the granting or withholding of love or status to the other. Our early SAS findings suggested that supportive actions may reflect the underlying clusters of encouraging–emotional actions, directive actions, and avoidant actions that may be specific to the context of social support. Nonetheless, we hypothesized that supportive actions would reflect individuals' characteristic trait dispositions in other contexts and therefore would form a circumplex, which they did.

Perspective

The effectiveness of supportive actions may be viewed differently from the perspectives of provider and recipient (Lehman & Hemphill, 1990) and these perspectives, in turn, may be influenced by the personality characteristics of both participants. Although we have not yet begun to explore this obviously complex interpersonal situation, a few intriguing findings from a study employing the preliminary version of the SAS-C may serve as an illustration. Hemphill (1996) examined the personality characteristics of both individuals with chronic fatigue syndrome and their support providers, as well as both provider and recipient reports of the supportive actions providers performed throughout the course of the illness. In one analysis, lower scores on recipients' self-reported agreeableness (Big Five measure) were associated significantly with recipients' increased reports of receiving critical (DE) and distancing (FG) actions from providers on SAS-C. Also, providers who indicated that their friend's or family member's chronic fatigue had resulted from psychological factors (rather than from environmental, genetic, or viral factors) were reported by recipients as providing critical (DE) and avoidant (HI) actions and as *not* providing engaging (NO) support as measured by the SAS-C.

Role

The press of a friend or relative in need of social support may place certain types of individuals (e.g., critical, distancing, avoidant) in a most uncharacteristic situation, involving role demands (e.g., supportive cousin) that are contrary to their typical ways of behavior. Other types of individuals (e.g., nurturant, engaging, deferential) are more likely to view helping behavior as part and parcel of role enactments in existing relationships with friends and relatives. In our culture, a friend "in need" is so widely considered to be one "indeed" that it is unlikely critical, distancing, or avoidant individuals would blatantly insist on their preferred definitions of the interpersonal situation from the outset (at least those in our sample of presumably normal research participants did not). Nevertheless, the self-admitted preferences of these individuals are likely to be expressed eventually in ways that are perceived as both role-incongruent and unhelpful by their friends and relatives.

Measurement

Macroanalytic measurement of broad, enduring dispositions was opted for in order to test the hypothesis that such dispositions could be meaningfully located in traditional interpersonal space. Measurement on this level does not preclude and, in fact, may facilitate subsequent microanalytic investigations. The SAS circumplex provides a taxonomy of supportive actions that may be applied to individual acts in ongoing interpersonal transactions. Thus, individual differences in supportive styles among psychotherapists could be studied in relation to such variables as rated quality of therapeutic alliance.

Interpretation

The geometric and substantive properties of SAS-C suggest that the instrument may be employed justifiably in such diverse enterprises as the assignment of persons to typological categories (Wiggins et al., 1989) and the classification of scales (or items) from other inventories (Wiggins & Broughton, 1991). The issue of the basic or optimal level of interpretation (Rosch, Mervis, Gray, Johnson, & Boyes-Braem, 1976) has yet to be determined for SAS-C. The number of categories employed for circumplex interpretation has ranged from 4 (e.g., Carson, 1969) to 36 (Benjamin, 1974), and Wiggins (1980) has made the case for an 8-category system being closest to a basic level for standard dispositional space. For reasons described in the preceding section, we would hold out the possibility that a 4-category system of the kind illustrated in Figure 3 may approach an optimal level of category richness and distinctiveness for the current version of SAS-C. Note that the categories shown in the figure slice the circumplex pie into sectors that differ from traditional quadrant analysis in which octants are split according to the primary axes of interpersonal behavior. Regardless of whether one wishes to interpret the support types captured by the SAS-C as dispositionally driven, the SAS-C scales provide a conceptual and measureable basis for categorizing supportive actions that may be of interest to social psychologists and other social support researchers.

CONCLUSION

As we have argued, there are both substantive and psychometric issues raised by the question of whether the circumplex of supportive actions is an interpersonal circumplex. With respect to the former, we have argued that there are good theoretical reasons for expecting interpretable individ-

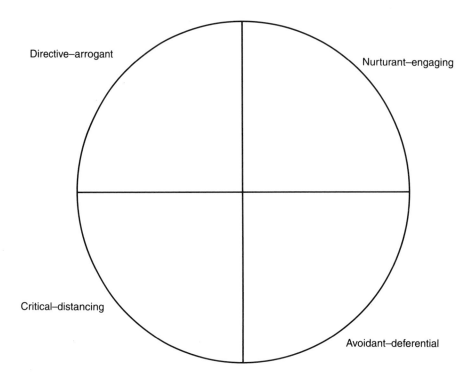

Figure 3. Quadrant representation of Supportive Actions Scale—Circumplex.

ual differences in the manner in which persons repond to the press provided by significant others in need of help and support. To the extent that a social support situation is interpersonal, it will entail dyadic exchanges of love and status and it seems intuitive that social support transactions exemplify such exchanges (Cobb, 1976). Individual differences in needs for these resources will operate much as they do in other interpersonal situations and will reflect the characteristic ways in which persons respond across interpersonal situations (i.e., interpersonal traits). But these characteristic ways of responding might be expected to be modulated by the context of social support itself, just as we might expect modulations in other contexts such as a press for leadership or a press for competition.

With respect to the psychometric considerations raised by the issue at hand, the SAS-C was found to form a well-structured circumplex that is highly compatible with the substantive issues just discussed. The ordering of supportive styles (directive, arrogant, etc.) was in accord with our facet-based theory of resource exchange, and the correlations of these styles with independent trait measures (IAS) were as expected. Our additional psycho-metric explorations of possible modulating effects of the support context itself were more exploratory in nature and were meant to suggest procedures that others might wish to employ in the ever expanding application of circumplex models to new domains.

REFERENCES

Alden, L. E., Wiggins, J. S., & Pincus, A. L. (1990). Construction of circumplex scales for the Inventory of Interpersonal Problems. *Journal of Personality Assessment, 55*, 521–536.

Bakan, D. (1966). *The duality of human existence: Isolation and communion in Western man.* Boston: Beacon.

Benjamin, L. S. (1974). Structural analysis of social behavior. *Psychological Review, 8*, 392–425.

Browne, M. W. (1992). Circumplex models for correlation matrices. *Psychometrika, 57*, 469–497.

Buss, D. M. (1991). Evolutionary personality psychology. In M. R. Rosenzweig & L. W. Porter (Eds.), *Annual review of psychology* (Vol. 41, pp. 459–491). Palo Alto, CA: Annual Reviews.

Carson, R. C. (1969). *Interaction concepts of personality.* Chicago: Aldine.

Cartwright, D. (1959). Lewinian theory as a contemporary systematic framework. In S. Koch (Ed.), *Psychology: A study of science* (Vol. 2, pp. 7–91). New York: McGraw-Hill.

Cobb, S. (1976). Social support as a moderator of life stress. *Psychosomatic Medicine, 38*, 300–314.

Dakof, G. A., & Taylor, S. E. (1990). Victims' perceptions of social support: What is helpful from whom? *Journal of Personality and Social Psychology, 36*, 752–766.

Foa, U. G. (1965). New developments in facet design and analysis. *Psychological Review, 72*, 262–274.

Foa, U. G., & Foa, E. B. (1974). *Societal structures of the mind.* Springfield, IL: Charles C. Thomas.

Freedman, M. B., Leary, T. F., Ossorio, A. G., & Coffey, H. S. (1951). The interpersonal dimension of personality. *Journal of Personality, 20*, 143–161.

Funder, D. C. (1989). Accuracy in personality judgment and the dancing bear. In D. M. Buss and N. Cantor (Eds.), *Personality psychology: Recent trends and emerging directions* (pp. 210–223). New York: Springer.

Gifford, R. (1991). Mapping nonverbal behavior on the Interpersonal Circle. *Journal of Personality and Social Psychology, 61*, 279–288.

Gifford, R. (1994). A lens framework for understanding the encoding and decoding of interpersonal dispositions in nonverbal behavior. *Journal of Personality and Social Psychology, 66*, 398–412.

Gurtman, M. B. (1994). The circumplex as a tool for studying normal and abnormal personality: A methodological primer. In S. Strack & M. Lorr (Eds.), *Differentiating normal and abnormal personality* (pp. 243–263). New York: Springer.

Gurtman, M. B. (1995). Personality structure and interpersonal problems: A theoretically-guided item analysis of the Inventory of Interpersonal Problems. *Journal of Personality Assessment, 3,* 343–361.

Guttman, L. (1954). A new approach to factor analysis: The radex. In P. R. Lazarsfeld (Ed.), *Mathematical thinking in the social sciences* (pp. 258–348). Glencoe, IL: Free Press.

Hemphill, K. J. (1996). *Supportive and unsupportive processes within the stress and coping context.* Unpublished manuscript. Department of Psychology, University of British Columbia, Vancouver.

Hofstee, W. K. B., De Raad, B., & Goldberg, L. R. (1992). Integration of the Big Five and circumplex approaches to trait structure. *Journal of Personality and Social Psychology, 63,* 146–163.

Hogan, R. (1983). A socioanalytic theory of personality. In M. M. Page (Ed.), *1982 Nebraska symposium on motivation: Personality—current theory and research* (pp. 58–89). Lincoln: University of Nebraska Press.

Holland, J. L. (1985a). *Making vocational choices: A theory of vocational personalities and work environments* (2nd ed.). Englewood Cliffs, NJ: Prentice-Hall.

Holland, J. L. (1985b). *Professional manual for the Vocational Preference Inventory.* Odessa, FL: Psychological Assessment Resources.

Horowitz, L. M., Rosenberg, S. E., Baer, B. A., Ureño, G., & Villaseñor, V. S. (1988). Inventory of Interpersonal Problems: Psychometric properties and clinical applications. *Journal of Consulting and Clinical Psychology, 56,* 885–892.

Horowitz, L. M., Weckler, D. A., & Doren, R. (1983). Interpersonal problems and symptoms: A cognitive approach. In P. Kendall (Ed.), *Advances in cognitive–behavioral research and therapy* (pp. 81–125). London: Academic Press.

Kiesler, D. J. (1987). *Manual for the Impact Message Inventory: Research edition.* Palo Alto, CA: Consulting Psychologists Press.

Kiesler, D. J., & Schmidt, J. A. (1991). *The Impact Message Inventory: Form IIA Octant Scale Version.* Richmond: Virginia Commonwealth University.

Laing, R. D., Phillipson, H., & Lee, A. R. (1966). *Interpersonal perception: A theory and method of research.* New York: Springer.

Leary, T. (1957). *Interpersonal diagnosis of personality: A functional theory and methodology for personality evaluation.* New York: Ronald Press.

Lehman, D. R., Ellard, J. H., & Wortman, C. B. (1986). Social support for the bereaved: Recipients' and providers' perspectives on what is helpful. *Journal of Consulting and Clinical Psychology, 54,* 438–446.

Lehman, D. R., & Hemphill, K. J. (1990). Recipient's perceptions of support attempts and attributions for support attempts that fail. *Journal of Social and Personal Relationships, 7,* 563–574.

Loevinger, J. (1957). Objective tests as instruments of psychological theory. *Psychological Reports, 3,* 635–694 (Monograph No. 9).

Lorr, M., & Strack, S. (1990). Wiggins' Interpersonal Adjective Scales: A dimensional analysis. *Personality and Individual Differences, 11,* 423–425.

McAdams, D. P. (1993). *The stories we live by: Personal myths and the making of self.* New York: William Morrow.

McCrae, R. R., & Costa, P. T., Jr. (1989). The structure of interpersonal traits: Wiggins' circumplex and the Five-Factor Model. *Journal of Personality and Social Psychology, 56,* 586–595.

Moskowitz, D. S. (1994). Cross-situational generality and the interpersonal circumplex. *Journal of Personality and Social Psychology, 66,* 921–933.

Parsons, T., & Bales, R. F. (1955). *Family, socialization, and interaction process.* Glencoe, IL: Free Press.

Pincus, A. L. (1994). The interpersonal circumplex and the interpersonal theory: Perspectives on personality and its pathology. In S. Strack & M. Lorr (Eds.), *Differentiating normal and abnormal personality* (pp. 114–136). Glencoe, IL: Free Press.

Pincus, A. L., & Wiggins, J. S. (1990). Interpersonal problems and conceptions of personality disorders. *Journal of Personality Disorders, 4,* 342–352.

Redfield, R. (1960). How society operates. In H. L. Shapiro (Ed.), *Man, culture and society* (pp. 345–368). New York: Oxford University Press.

Rosch, E., Mervis, C. B., Gray, W. D., Johnson, D. M., & Boyes-Braem, P. (1976). Basic objects in natural categories. *Cognitive Psychology, 8,* 382–439.

Saucier, G. (1992). Benchmarks: Integrating affective and interpersonal circles with the Big Five personality factors. *Journal of Personality and Social Psychology, 62,* 1025–1035.

Searle, J. R. (1995). *The construction of social reality.* New York: Free Press.

Shepard, R. N. (1978). The circumplex and related topological manifolds in the study of perception. In S. Shye (Ed.), *Theory construction and data analysis in the behavioral sciences* (pp. 29–80). San Francisco: Jossey-Bass.

Sullivan, H. S. (1953). *The interpersonal theory of psychiatry.* New York: Norton.

Tracey, T. J., & Rounds, J. (1993). Evaluating Holland's and Gati's vocational-interest models: A structural meta-analysis. *Psychological Bulletin, 113,* 229–246.

Trapnell, P. D. (1989). *Structural validity in the measurement of Holland's vocational typology: A measure of Holland's types scaled to an explicit circumplex model.* Unpublished Master's thesis, Vancouver, University of British Columbia.

Triandis, H. C. (1995). *Individualism and collectivism.* Boulder, CO: Westview Press.

Trobst, K. K. (1991). *Determinants of support provision: Interaction of provider and recipient factors*. Unpublished Master's thesis, University of British Columbia, Vancouver.

Trobst, K. K., Collins, R. L., & Embree, J. M. (1994). The role of emotion in social support provision: Gender, empathy and expressions of distress. *Journal of Social and Personal Relationships, 11,* 45–62.

Trobst, K. K., & Wiggins, J. S. (1995, August). *A circumplex measure of stylistic differences in social support provision*. Poster presented at the annual convention of the American Psychological Association, New York.

Wiggins, J. S. (1980). Circumplex models of interpersonal behavior. In L. Wheeler (Ed.), *Review of personality and social psychology* (Vol. 1, pp. 265–293). Beverly Hills, CA: Sage.

Wiggins, J. S. (1991). Agency and communion as conceptual coordinates for the understanding and measurement of interpersonal behavior. In W. Grove & D. Cicchetti (Eds.), *Thinking clearly about psychology: Essays in honor of Paul E. Meehl* (Vol. 2, pp. 89–113). Minneapolis: University of Minnesota Press.

Wiggins, J. S. (1995). *Interpersonal Adjective Scales: Professional manual.* Odessa, FL: Psychological Assessment Resources.

Wiggins, J. S. (1996). An informal history of the interpersonal circumplex tradition. *Journal of Personality Assessment, 66*(2), 217–233.

Wiggins, J. S. (in press). In defense of traits. In R. Hogan, J. A. Johnson, & S. R. Briggs (Eds.), *Handbook of personality psychology.* San Diego, CA: Academic Press.

Wiggins, J. S., & Broughton, R. (1991). A geometric taxonomy of personality scales. *European Journal of Personality, 5,* 343–365.

Wiggins, J. S., Phillips, N., & Trapnell, P. (1989). Circular reasoning about interpersonal behavior: Evidence concerning some untested assumptions underlying diagnostic classification. *Journal of Personality and Social Psychology, 56,* 296–305.

Wiggins, J. S., & Pincus, A. L. (1992). Personality: Structure and assessment. In M. R. Rosenzweig & L. R. Porter (Eds.), *Annual review of psychology* (Vol. 43, pp. 473–504). Palo Alto, CA: Annual Reviews.

Wiggins, J. S., Steiger, J. H., & Gaelick, L. (1981). Evaluating circumplexity in personality data. *Multivariate Behavioral Research, 16,* 263–289.

Wiggins, J. S., & Trapnell, P. D. (1996). A dyadic–interactional perspective on the Five-Factor Model. In J. S. Wiggins (Ed.), *The Five-Factor Model of personality: Theoretical perspectives* (pp. 88–162). New York: Guilford Press.

4

STUDYING PERSONALITY TRAITS: THE CIRCULAR WAY

MICHAEL B. GURTMAN

Much of contemporary research in personality psychology is aimed at furthering understanding of particular traits (e.g., Machiavellianism, extraversion, narcissism, self-monitoring). At the heart of it, this process involves the grand enterprise of *construct validation* (Cronbach & Meehl, 1955)—that is, developing a nomological net for a trait construct by establishing its connections to other traits and then to observables. The process then defines the trait implicitly by its pattern of connections—its place—within the systematized organization of the net.

Of the various nets that may be woven, perhaps most useful from a scientific standpoint may be a net that integrates the trait within an established, comprehensive model of personality. Models such as the Big Five or Five Factor Model (e.g., Goldberg, 1993; McCrae & John, 1992) and the circumplex (e.g., Wiggins, 1979) essentially provide encompassing nets for particular domains of personality and thus platforms for studying the descriptive characteristics of different trait concepts and measures.

The purpose of this chapter is to show how circumplex, or circular, models of personality could serve the broad purpose of construct elucidation. Circumplex structure appears to characterize two domains of special interest to personality psychologists: the interpersonal (e.g., Wiggins, 1979)

I gratefully acknowledge the valuable input of Terence Tracey.

and the affective (e.g., Plutchik, 1989; Russell, 1980). I believe that analyzing interpersonal and affective traits "the circular way"—in harmony
with the special geometric implications of the model—is likely to yield
greater understanding about their descriptive features than would adoption
of other orienting perspectives.

I first will define the circumplex and relate this model to its principal
alternative, the Big Five or Five-Factor Model (e.g., Saucier, 1992). There
is now an emerging view that the common factor spaces for interpersonal
traits and for affective traits are better represented by the circumplex than
by the simple-structure alternative (e.g., Hofstee, de Raad, & Goldberg,
1992; Johnson & Ostendorf, 1993; Meyer & Shack, 1989; Saucier, 1992).
Second, I will show how the key descriptive features of a trait—its thematic quality, breadth, and factorial saturation—can be obtained from the
fundamentally geometric methods of analysis that derive from the circumplex. In turn, these methods lend themselves to concise, yet informative,
meta-iconic (Wainer & Thissen, 1981) representations of a trait's place
within its net. Third, I will apply the methods to published data from a
number of studies, demonstrating how these analytic tools can illuminate
and bring context to the particular traits of interest. Several articles now
directly afford the opportunity for this kind of secondary analysis, in that
they present the raw materials in the form of trait correlations with established circumplex measures of personality (e.g., Buss & Chiodo, 1991;
Gifford, 1991; Gifford & O'Connor, 1987; Horowitz, Rosenberg, & Bartholomew, 1993; Moskowitz, 1994). Yet, if the interpersonal and affective
domains conform generally to the circumplex model, then it should be
possible to extract the circumplex factor space from any comprehensive
measure of personality, and hence do similar, opportunistic analyses from
suitably reconfigured measures. In this chapter, I will explore this possibility
with the California Q-Set (CQ; Block, 1961/1978), a widely used and re-
spected approach to personality description. If circumplex analyses are fea-
sible from subsets of CQ item content, then this opens up an extensive
literature for what is essentially a domain-centered reanalysis of personality
research data. Moreover, it would suggest that other comprehensive personality measures would be amenable to similar analysis with comparable
payoff.

Before proceeding, however, it may be useful to have a brief overview
of the California Q-Set (Block, 1961/1978). Unlike conventional measures
of personality, the CQ offers a person-centered approach (Ozer, 1993) to
description that relies on the Q-sort technique. It consists of 100 statements (e.g., "has a rapid personal tempo; behaves and acts quickly," "tends
to project his own feelings and motivations onto others") that together are
intended to provide a basic language for formulating an individual's personality (Block, 1961/1978, p. 138). The CQ is usually completed by expert
judges (observers), with the statements sorted into a fixed distribution of

nine categories (from "extremely uncharacteristic" [1] to "extremely characteristic" [9]). A recent volume edited by Funder, Parke, Tomlinson-Keasey, and Widaman (1993) provides a showcase for the CQ method, revealing it to be a versatile tool for the intensive study of personality.[1]

McCrae, Costa, and Busch (1986) and Lanning (1994) have conducted exploratory factor analyses of the CQ. Both studies demonstrated that the basic five factors of personality can be recovered from the CQ item set. Lanning's data are especially valuable in that they are based on a very large sample (940 research participants) assessed by expert judges during 1- to 3-day periods of observation. The factor loadings reported in Lanning's article will be the foundation for several analyses done later in this chapter.

THE CIRCUMPLEX AND ITS RELATION TO THE FIVE-FACTOR MODEL

The term *circumplex* was first introduced by Guttman (1954), who used it to refer to a particular kind of nonrestrictive correlation pattern having a distinct circular ordering (see also Browne, 1992). This characteristic pattern (see, e.g., Browne, 1992; Wiggins, Steiger, & Gaelick, 1981) also has been called a *circulant* or *circular* matrix.

The more familiar concept of the circumplex—as simply a circular arrangement of traits (e.g., Conte & Plutchik, 1981; Hofstee et al., 1992; Saucier, 1992; Wiggins, 1979, 1982)—is the consequence of factor analyzing this matrix (e.g., Wiggins et al., 1981). Thus, it is possible to redefine this geometric circumplex as a particular, descriptive factor model. This model, of course, is a circle, which, as a geometric figure, has three properties: two-dimensionality, fixed radius, and continuous form. The two-dimensionality criterion is met to the extent that differences between traits in a given domain can be reduced to differences in two dimensions (factors). In practice, this would require that two factors account for a sizable proportion of the common variance (e.g., Wiggins, 1979; Wiggins et al., 1981). Fixed radius is achieved when traits have equal projections in this two-factor space—they fall an equal distance from the center of the figure. In the language of factor analysis, all traits have equal communality (h^2) with the two factors. The circle's radius, then, is given by the square root of any trait's communality (h) or vector length.

The circumplex and simple structure (i.e., Big Five) models of trait organization are essentially contrasted by the third criterion: whether trait

---

[1]The astute reader may recognize that the title of this piece alludes to Block's (1993) opening chapter ("Studying Personality the Long Way") in the Funder and colleagues (1993) volume. His title, in turn, alludes to an earlier work by R. W. White. My apologies to all concerned!

projections are distributed uniformly, directionally, throughout the two-factor space (circumplex), or are tightly clustered near the factor axes (simple structure). Several studies (Hofstee et al., 1992; Johnson & Ostendorf, 1993; Saucier, 1992) have addressed this question specifically. In each, the investigators looked at the loading patterns of adjective trait terms identified as markers for the Big Five factors of personality—Extraversion (I), Agreeableness (II), Conscientiousness (III), Neuroticism or Emotional (in)stability (IV), and Intellect or Openness to experience (V). The results were consistent in suggesting two conclusions. First, the majority of marker trait terms are not univocal (Goldberg, 1993) for a given factor (i.e., most have sizable, secondary loadings on another factor); this finding makes it possible (but does not guarantee) circumplex structures within the Big Five. Second, some pairings of Big Five factors produce trait distributions in the two-factor space that are quasi-uniform—that is, characteristic of the circumplex. Saucier's (1992) study is especially clear in showing that those Big Five factors that are typically identified as marking the interpersonal (I, II) and affective (I, IV) domains of personality (e.g., John, 1990; McCrae & Costa, 1989; Meyer & Shack, 1989) appear to possess quasi-circumplex structure in their distribution characteristics. Saucier's analysis yielded three circumplex spaces: an interpersonal circumplex pairing Extraversion (I) and Agreeableness (II) (cf. Wiggins, 1979), an affective circumplex combining Extraversion (I) and Neuroticism (IV), (cf. Russell, 1980; Watson & Tellegen, 1985); and a third, unlabeled circumplex consisting of Agreeableness (II) and Neuroticism (IV).

CIRCUMPLEX STRUCTURE IN THE CALIFORNIA Q-SET?

If the interpersonal and affective domains are circumplexical, then it should be possible to recover this structure from any comprehensive set of personality descriptors. In this section, I will examine this possibility directly, using the 100 items of the California Q-Set item pool. For this project, I will rely on the factor loadings published in Lanning's (1994) analysis. As noted earlier, they are based on expert Q-sorts of 940 individuals observed over 1- to 3-day periods. This section also will serve as an exercise in how such domains could be constituted and evaluated.

The first question is whether items (Q-Set statements) are generally univocal (conform to simple structure) or include blended loadings more characteristic of a circumplex (e.g., Hofstee et al., 1992).[2] An item was considered to load on a factor if its correlation with the factor (sign ignored) exceeded .30. By this criterion, 40 items had single (univocal) load-

---

[2]Note that a circumplex pattern would be characterized by both univocal and blended loadings, depending on the item's position on the circle (on-axis versus off-axis).

ings, 43 had double loadings, 14 had triple loadings, and 2 loaded on 4 factors (1 item did not load on any of the dimensions). Thus, the majority of items loaded on more than one factor, consistent with a circumplex rendering.

In order to select items for the interpersonal and affective domains, I calculated the vector length (projections) of each CQ item in the planes, or two-dimensional spaces, that theoretically constituted those domains; three such planes were fabricated (interpersonal: I/II; affective: I/IV; and mixed: II/IV). In standard fashion, the vector length was calculated as the square root of the sum of the squared factor loadings (e.g., Mardia, 1972). Items were considered members of the domain if vector length exceeded .30. It is noteworthy that, by this criterion, only 15% of the items did not fall in at least one of the three planes; moreover, each domain encompassed a majority of the CQ items: 62% in the interpersonal plane, 68% in the affective plane, and 75% in the mixed plane.

There are two critical tests for CQ versions of the affective and interpersonal circumplexes; by reflection, they also test the generality of the theoretical models themselves. First, are the items, when projected to equal length, distributed uniformly around an imaginary circle (circumplex) or do they instead show significant gaps in coverage—that is, form discontinuous groupings? Second, how well does the observed continuum of traits (i.e., the continuum of meaning) correspond to established models (e.g., the Wiggins circumplex)? The first question addresses the *structural* integrity of the derived circumplex; the second its *substantive* validity (e.g., Gurtman, 1994).

The initial set of figures show the circular plots for the three CQ-rendered domains. Figure 1 depicts the interpersonal domain; Figure 2, the affective; and Figure 3 the mixed (agreeableness–neuroticism) domain.[3] Each figure shows how member items are distributed when projected to unit length. These circular plots are similar to those presented originally in Hofstee and colleagues (1992; see also Goldberg, 1993; Gurtman, 1993). Even without quantitative verification, it is apparent that, for each domain, the item distributions are more consistent with the circumplex than with a simple-structure model. The affective circumplex is somewhat less developed (uniformly populated) than the other two, perhaps reflecting gaps in the affective space (e.g., Meyer & Shack, 1989) or in CQ item sampling.

---

[3]In order to make the interpersonal circumplex comparable to others in the literature, I rotated the Extraversion–Agreeableness factors of Lanning's (1994) solution in order to produce a Dominance and Love coordinate system (e.g., Wiggins, 1979). I did this by first identifying seven CQ items that seemed to be markers for seven of the eight octants of Wiggins' (1979) model; I could not find a clear marker for the unassuming–ingenuous (JK) octant. Then I rotated the original factors for maximum concordance to the theoretical positions of those items. The rotation was 28° clockwise from the original axes, which is consistent with how the circumplex and Big Five models are assumed to differ in their dimensional orientations for the interpersonal space (e.g., John, 1990; McCrae & Costa, 1989).

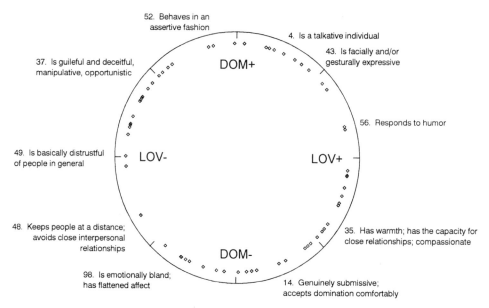

Figure 1. Interpersonal circumplex constructed from California Q-Set items. *Note:* Sample items highlighted. DOM = Dominance, LOV = Love. Modified and reproduced by special permission of the Publisher, Consulting Psychologists Press, Inc., Palo Alto, CA 94303, from *The Q-Sort Method in Personality Assessment and Psychiatric Research* by Jack Block, PhD. Copyright 1961 by Charles C. Thomas. All rights reserved. Further reproduction is prohibited without the publisher's written consent.

The substantive correspondence of these circumplexes to those appearing in the literature is also quite good; to aid in the interpretation, I have highlighted several items in each plot. Although I will ask the reader to make the detailed comparisons, the Figure 1 circumplex of the interpersonal domain bears an obvious resemblance to the Wiggins (1979, 1982) and Kiesler (1983) circles. The affective circumplex of Figure 2 also seems to conform generally to other articulated Neuroticism–Extraversion structures, including the well-known models of Eysenck (e.g., Eysenck & Eysenck, 1985), Russell (1980), and Watson and Tellegen (1985). Until recently, the third circumplex (Figure 3), which crosses Agreeableness and Neuroticism, has been largely neglected; Saucier's (1992) octangonal model (p. 1032), which is based on analysis of an adjective set, has some likeness to it.

Although circumplex structure is often easily discerned in a general sense, it is also useful to index the degree to which that ideal is approximated in a given circular distribution. In theory, perfect circumplex structure implies a uniform item density around the circumference of the imaginary circle. (In turn, this implies that the underlying population of traits

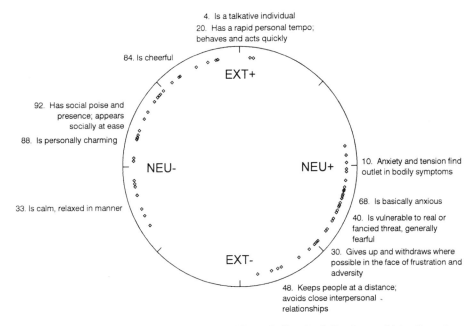

Figure 2. Affective circumplex constructed from California Q-Set items. *Note*: Sample items highlighted. EXT = Extraversion, LOV = Love, NEU = Neuroticism. Modified and reproduced by special permission of the Publisher, Consulting Psychologists Press, Inc., Palo Alto, CA 94303, from *The Q-Sort Method in Personality Assessment and Psychiatric Research* by Jack Block, PhD. Copyright 1961 by Charles C. Thomas. All rights reserved. Further reproduction is prohibited without the publisher's written consent.

has a uniform distribution.) The *probability plot* is a graphic device that can be of special value in addressing this point (Wainer & Thissen, 1981; Wilkinson, 1990). Probability plots, or P-plots, display empirical distributions (e.g., items' angular positions on the circle) against their expected values given a specific theoretical model, such as uniform distribution. Figure 4 shows the (uniform distribution) probability plots for the three domains. If items are from a perfectly uniform circular distribution, then their plotted values would fall along a straight line running diagonally. Deviations from this line indicate poor fit. As can be seen clearly, the interpersonal and Agreeableness–Neuroticism circumplexes have close fit to the uniformity model; the affective circumplex conforms somewhat less well.

It is also possible to test statistically the fit of a circular item distribution to the uniform probability criterion. In a recent volume, Upton and Fingleton (1989, chap. 9) reviewed various gap tests for evaluating this property (see also Fisher, Heise, Bohrnstedt, & Lucke, 1985; and Mardia, 1972). If *n* items are uniformly distributed around a circle, then the angular

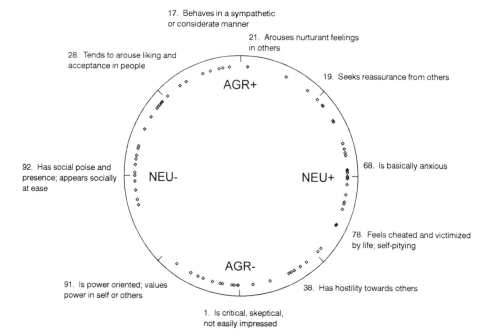

Figure 3. Affective–Neuroticism circumplex from California Q-Set items. *Note*: Sample items highlighted. AGR = Agreeableness, NEU = Neuroticism. Modified and reproduced by special permission of the Publisher, Consulting Psychologists Press, Inc., Palo Alto, CA 94303, from *The Q-Sort Method in Personality Assessment and Psychiatric Research* by Jack Block, PhD. Copyright 1961 by Charles C. Thomas. All rights reserved. Further reproduction is prohibited without the publisher's written consent.

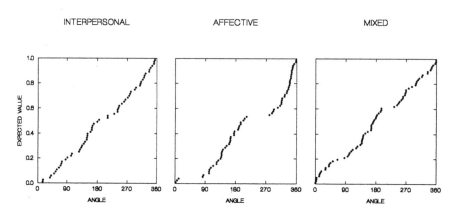

Figure 4. Probability plots of the items of the three CQ-circumplexes. Items' angular positions plotted against the expected values assuming a uniform distribution; Mixed refers to Agreeableness–Neuroticism circumplex.

distances (or gaps) between nearest neighbors will be a constant, equal to $360°/n$. Gap tests evaluate departures from this ideal of equal spacing. When distributions have major empty spaces coupled with dense areas, the null hypothesis is likely to be rejected.

Rao's gap test, described in detail by Upton and Fingleton (1989, pp. 246–247), is based on the sum of the absolute deviations of each gap, G_i, from the expected value of $360°/n$. The resultant G-value is approximately normally distributed when $n > 50$, and hence can be tested for significance through computation of a z-value. Applying this test, item distributions for the interpersonal ($z = -0.47$) and Agreeableness–Neuroticism ($z = 0.15$) circumplexes were not found to be significantly deviant from chance, assuming a uniform distribution; however, the z-value for the Affective circumplex ($z = 3.90$) was significant ($p < .001$), confirming that this space had relatively poorer fit to the circumplex ideal.

THE CIRCUMPLEX AS AN ANALYTIC FRAMEWORK: SOME PRINCIPLES

In the previous section, I showed that it is possible to fabricate three circumplex or quasi-circumplex structures from the California Q-Set of personality descriptors. These structures are circular representations of the interpersonal and affective trait domains. In this section, I will show how these representations can provide a framework for a trait analytic approach that meets the descriptive aims of construct validation. The approach exploits the special geometric features of these nomological nets, leading to understanding that can be expressed in the basic currency of the circumplex model. From this perspective, there are three key descriptive features of a particular trait or, more precisely, its respective measure—thematic quality, breadth of coverage, and factorial saturation. These or similar issues have been touched on in some of my previous work (see Gurtman, 1992a, 1992b, 1993, 1994).

I use the term thematic quality, to refer to a trait's predominant descriptive content, which, in a circumplex medium, reduces to its specific blend of the two factors that define that common space. For example, in the interpersonal circumplex, traits vary in their mix of Dominance and Love (e.g., Leary, 1957; Wiggins, 1979); a trait such as social introversion theoretically is composed of equal parts of negative Dominance and negative Love (e.g., Kiesler, 1983). Ultimately, however, it is more desirable to express a trait's factorial composition in the native language of the circle—that is, in a polar coordinate system (e.g., Gurtman, 1992a, 1993; Wiggins & Broughton, 1991). (The trigonometric formulas for converting rectangular coordinates to polar coordinates are given in a number of places—e.g., Gurtman, 1991; Mardia, 1972; Wiggins & Broughton, 1991).

A trait's descriptive character is then revealed by its location on the circular continuum, specifically its angular displacement (in degrees, counterclockwise) from an arbitrary starting point. Hence, a trait's thematic quality, and consequently its resemblance to other traits, can be inferred from its angular location on the circle. Figure 5 shows the standard polar coordinate system for the three circumplex factor spaces.

Fixing a trait's position on the circle essentially involves estimating its directional central tendency (Mardia, 1972). Consider the example of Figure 6, specifically developed to show how this could be done with the kind of data typically reported in a Q-sort study.[4] The figure identifies by their respective angular positions the Q-set items that most highly characterize a particular trait. Think of each item as a vector of unit length, differing only in angular orientation or direction (θ_i). The trait's point location on the circle, then, is the mean directional trend of the items, that is, the angle, θ_R, of the resultant vector obtained when the six item vectors are added together. This angle is that of the *circular mean* (Mardia, 1972), which in this example is 91°. In a geometric sense, this vector is

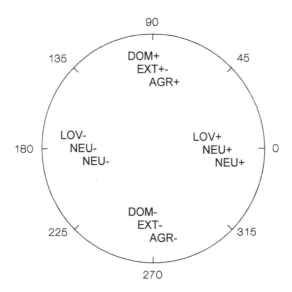

Figure 5. The polar coordinate system for the three circumplexes. Staggered labels identify each circumplex's major axes. Shown, top to bottom, are the interpersonal, affective, and mixed circles. AGR = Agreeableness, DOM = Dominance, EXT = Extraversion, LOV = Love, NEU = Neuroticism.

---

[4]The data for this example were taken from the validity section of the California Psychological Inventory manual (CPI; Gough & Heilbrun, 1987). The items highlighted in the figure are the six CQ items correlating most highly with the CPI Dominance (Do) scale, based on Q-sort assessments done by staff members at the Institute for Personality Assessment and Research.

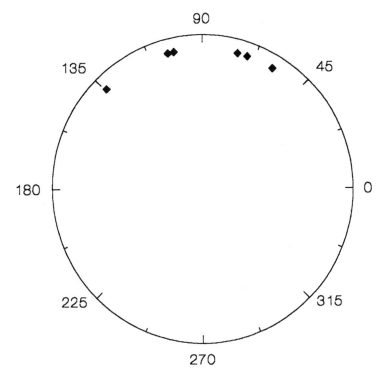

Figure 6. An example of a circular plot.

the best dimension to summarize the set of items, in that it maximizes the quantity:

$$\Sigma \, cos \, (\theta_R - \theta_i)$$

where θ_i is the angle of item, i. This property may be related to the maximum loading criterion in factor analysis. In a perfect, two-factor space, these cosine terms geometrically define a variable's loading (i.e., correlation) with any dimension in the same plane (e.g., Comrey, 1973) Analogously, the circular mean specifies the angular orientation of the dimension that maximizes the item's loadings in the circumplex space.

Another descriptive trait feature is its *breadth of coverage* or, in the inverse, its *cohesiveness*. Some traits logically cover a broad expanse of territory, and others are relatively narrow in their inclusiveness. This distinction, generally referred to as *fidelity versus bandwidth* (e.g., Cronbach, 1990), is familiar to most personality psychologists.

The circumplex may be especially well-suited for gauging a trait's scope of coverage, because it naturally offers a horizontal view (Goldberg,

1993) of personality trait organization. A trait's breadth of coverage, then, is shown by the dispersion of its referents (items) on the circular continuum; this reflects how much territory the trait covers in the domain of interest (interpersonal, affective). Facet traits (e.g., Costa & McCrae, 1992) are probably relatively narrow in coverage. The trait categories of the Wiggins's (1979) interpersonal circumplex (e.g., Arrogant–Calculating) are examples of octant-wide traits, each theoretically covering 45°. The broadest possible traits cover 90° sectors (or quadrants).[5] The personality factors of the Big Five (e.g., Extraversion, Agreeableness) are examples; they are superordinate traits that make 90° sweeps of the circle (e.g., Costa & McCrae, 1992; Goldberg, 1993).

Of the various ways of quantifying a trait's circular breadth, the circular variance (Mardia, 1972) is a logical choice. Like its analogue, the (linear) standard deviation, it is a measure of dispersion from the central tendency. As applied here, the circular variance would indicate how spread out the trait's referents are from the mean directional tendency and would serve as a circular equivalent to an internal reliability estimate.

As Mardia (1972, p. 22) has shown, the circular variance, S, can be written as:

$$S = 1 - \Sigma \cos(\theta_R - \theta_i)/n$$

where n refers to the number of items, θ_R is the angle of the circular mean, and θ_i is the angle of item, i. If, once again, the term, $\cos(\theta_R - \theta_i)$, is interpreted as a given item's loading on the trait dimension, then the circular variance is an inverse measure of the "average" item loading. For $S = 0$, the average loading is 1, meaning that all items are at the same point on the circumplex. For $S = 1$, items are maximally dispersed, and hence, have no shared directional orientation in the circumplex space. For the example of Figure 6, the average item loading is .905, and hence S is .095.

By taking the arc-cosine of the average loading, dispersion is converted back to degrees and thus expresses the variance as an interval around the mean. So, if $S = .5$, the interval around the mean is a plus or minus 60° [i.e., arc-cosine (.5)]. Assuming a normal distribution around the mean, this interval would encompass 68% of the trait items, a characteristic the same as that of the ordinary standard deviation. In the present example, the circular variance, expressed in degrees, is 25°.

An effective, yet simple, means of conveying the summary information about a trait's coverage on the circle is through an iconic representation of the circular plot. As illustrated in Figure 7, the icon provides a

---

[5]Beyond 90°, some elements would be correlated negatively, and hence the trait would not be cohesive at all points.

Circular Plot

Iconic Representation

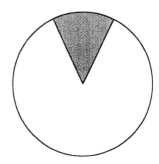

Figure 7. A circular plot and its iconic representation.

concise, easily understood graphic depiction of the trait's predominant content.

The final trait characteristic that I would like to develop is factorial saturation, which reflects the amount of variance the trait shares with the circular domain in which it is being projected. This fundamentally concerns to what extent the trait belongs to the particular domain. In an early article (Gurtman, 1991), I showed that certain traits (e.g., Machiavellianism) have greater interpersonalness than do others; in the same way, it could be argued that some traits are more affective than others. A simple way of estimating this feature is by the average vector length of the trait's CQ referent items in a given circular space. Recall that an item's vector length is the square root of its communality; it is also then the item's multiple correlation, R, with the two factors that comprise the circular domain. Saturation, measured in this way, is the average referent-domain correlation.

TRAIT ANALYSIS: SOME ILLUSTRATIVE EXAMPLES

In this section, I will apply these structural methods of analysis to previously published California Q-Set data. In each case, the data were simply the CQ items that the investigators reported to be most descriptive (by means or correlations) of a particular trait or attribute. Through these secondary analyses, I hope to show how the circumplex model can enhance our understanding by bringing context and order to CQ research findings. I chose the featured studies in part because their reported conceptual analyses (Ozer, 1993) were in themselves compelling.

The first analysis is of the "optimally adjusted personality." Block's (1961/1978) introduction to the Q-sort method provides the relevant Q-Set descriptions (Appendix D of his book), which are the composite sorts of a panel of expert psychologists. Block lists both positively and negatively defining CQ items.

Table 1 shows the results of the circumplex analyses done on this concept. The table's innovative feature is the column showing iconic representations of the trait's characteristics. These icons concisely depict the trait's central tendency (circular mean) and breadth of coverage (circular variance) in the context of a specific circular domain.

As the table reveals, these consensual descriptions of adjustment and its antithesis are generally cohesive in, and relevant to, each of the circumplex spaces. For example, with regard to the interpersonal circle (Kiesler, 1983; Wiggins, 1979), optimal adjustment is centered at a point of warm–agreeableness (346°), and maladjustment is at hostile–aloofness (213°); it is important to note, then, that these concepts are *not* polar opposites interpersonally, because they are not fully 180° apart. However, as might be expected (e.g., Costa & McCrae, 1992), for describing adjustment, the two circles that implicate Neuroticism seem to be the best performing, with the Agreeableness–Neuroticism domain especially useful. When projected in this space, the two adjustment constructs are relatively cohesive (i.e., have relatively low dispersion) and have high content saturation (i.e., high vector length). The signature blend for optimal adjustment (at 154°) is an almost equal measure of low neuroticism and high

TABLE 1
Descriptive Analysis of Optimally Adjusted Personality in Three
Circumplex Domains

Trait	Circumplex	Circular mean (degrees)	Circular variance	Circular variance (degrees)	Mean vector length
Positive Adjustment	Interpersonal	346°	.646	70°	.374
	Affective	186°	.130	30°	.341
	Mixed	154°	.256	42°	.481
Negative Adjustment	Interpersonal	213°	.255	42°	.433
	Affective	336°	.188	36°	.573
	Mixed	336°	.149	32°	.587

Note. Based on results reported in Block (1961/1978), Appendix D.

agreeableness; the converse describes the defining point for maladjustment (at 336°).

Wink's exemplary research on adult development and the trait of narcissism (e.g., Wink, 1991a, 1991b, 1992a, 1992b) is the source of data for the second illustration. As part of his investigation of the life course of adult women, Wink (1991a) employed the CQ item set to develop a prototypic description of the narcissist. Following object-relations theory, he distinguished between narcissism, conceptualized as *self-directedness*, and its opposite orientation pattern, *object directedness*. An expert panel of personality psychologists supplied Q-sort descriptions; 13 positive items served to define self-directedness, and 13 negative items defined object-directedness. To differentiate the constructs further, Wink conducted factor analyses of the item sets (see also Wink, 1992a). These yielded three narcissism factors: Hypersensitivity, Willfulness, and Autonomy–intellectual ambition, and two object directedness factors: Straightforwardness–dependability and Givingness.

Table 2 presents the results of the circumplex analyses conducted on those CQ items defining narcissism and object-directedness, respectively. In discussing the results, I will restrict my focus to the interpersonal domain. As the table shows, the results place narcissism at 162°, which indicates that, as reflected in the expert's prototypes and the CQ item set, this construct is a slightly dominant form of hostility (e.g., Kiesler, 1983; Wiggins, 1979). Other researchers (e.g., Bradlee & Emmons, 1992; Buss & Chiodo, 1991; Gurtman, 1992a; Soldz, Budman, Demby, & Merry, 1993; Wiggins & Pincus, 1989) also have used the interpersonal circumplex to study nar-

TABLE 2

Descriptive Analysis of Self-Directness (Narcissism) and Object-Directness in Three Circumplex Domains

Trait	Circumplex	Circular mean (degrees)	Circular variance	Circular variance (degrees)	Mean vector length
Self-directness	Interpersonal	162°	.225	39°	.411
	Affective	55°	.781	77°	.353
	Mixed	289°	.285	44°	.526
Oject-directness	Interpersonal	321°	.102	26°	.516
	Affective	206°	.308	46°	.350
	Mixed	119°	.139	31°	.610

Note. Based on results reported in Wink (1991a).

cissism, whether as a normal trait or diagnosable personality disorder. In general, the varieties of narcissism are characterized by particular blends of Dominance and Hostility, and so tend to be between 90° (more dominance) and 180° (more hostility) on the circle. So-called healthy forms of narcissism (e.g., Emmons, 1987), that reflect aspects of assertiveness, social facility, and self-confidence, emphasize Dominance and are found near 90°; pathological versions of narcissism are closer to 180° and include more antisocial features, such as antagonistic attitudes, exploitativeness, and lack of empathy. As a overall composite, then, Wink's narcissist is closer to the pathological than the healthy.

It is not surprising that Wink's (1991a) factor analysis of the prototype yielded distinctions that closely follow the contour of the circumplex. As shown in Figure 8, the projections (central tendencies) of Autonomy (138°), Willfulness (130°), and Hypersensitivity (198°) on the circumplex indicate that these forms of narcissism are differentiated in their mix of Dominance and Hostility. Hypersensitivity is an obvious marker for pathological narcissism; autonomy and (perhaps) Willfulness are more healthy variants. Wink's (1992b) article on the "two faces of narcissism" suggests that measures of "covert narcissism" and "overt narcissism" also would be differentiated by their Dominant–Hostile blend, with overt aspects of the narcissism complex closer to Dominance (i.e., 90°). Finally, note from the figure that the two other-directedness factors—Straightforwardness (316°) and Givingness (325°)—are relatively close (hence similar) in interpersonal space.

The last example is from the work of Funder, a champion of the Q-sort method in personality research. In a study on social acuity, Funder and Harris (1986) used the CQ as part of a battery of measures intended to assess the coherence of the construct across different data sources. They

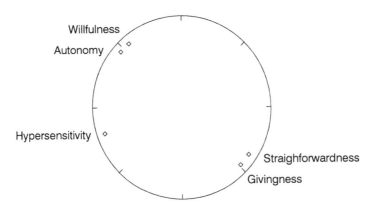

Figure 8. Projections of Winks' (1991a) self-directedness and object-directedness factors on the CQ-interpersonal circumplex.

defined social acuity as "the ability and inclination to perceive the psychological state of others and to guide one's behavior in accordance with that perception" (p. 530). Among their data sources were three well-known measures of interpersonal sensitivity: the Self-Monitoring Scale (Snyder, 1974); the Profile of Nonverbal Sensitivity (Rosenthal, Hall, DiMatteo, Rogers, & Archer, 1979), which is an ability test; and the Empathy Scale (Hogan, 1969). These measures, diverse either in method or origin, were compared to each other, and to participant's Q-sort descriptions furnished by both self and acquaintances (informants).

Funder and Harris were interested in determining to what extent the various measures of acuity were coherent—that is, converged on some common construct. To address this question, they examined the various correlations between measures. Here I will take the alternative, circumplex approach to examine the same issue. In this case, convergence (or construct calibration, Gurtman, 1992a) is defined mainly in terms of proximity on the circumplex, which in turn reflects convergence defined specifically within particular domains of personality (interpersonal, affective). This approach, it should be noted, provides an important advantage over simple correlational methods: it *references* similarity to specific, descriptive categories (i.e., personality domains).[6]

The present analysis is predicated on the composite informant Q-sorts. For each measure (henceforth self-monitoring, nonverbal sensitivity, and empathy), I identified the CQ items that correlated most highly with that measure (consult Tables 4, 5, and 6 in Funder & Harris, 1986).

Table 3 summarizes the results of the circumplex analyses conducted on the basis of these data. Each social acuity measure is referenced to three domains—interpersonal, affective, and Agreeableness–Neuroticism. The table clearly indicates convergence between Self-Monitoring and Empathy; in each circle, their resultant angular positions are very close. Nonverbal Sensitivity, however, is consistently less coherent with the other measures of acuity. The degree of convergence can be quantified readily by the cosine-difference correlation (Gurtman, 1992a, 1993; also Fisher et al., 1985), which is the cosine of the angular discrepancy. As a correlation coefficient, it ranges from 1 (complete convergence—i.e., 0° discrepancy between positions on the circle) through 0 (orthogonal, 90° apart) to −1 (polar opposite, 180° apart). The cosine-difference correlations for Self-Monitoring and Empathy are .97 (interpersonal), .99 (affective), and .98 (Agreeableness–Neuroticism). Nonverbal Sensitivity has its highest convergence with another measure in the Agreeableness–Neuroticism circle (.83, with Em-

---

[6]Another advantage, difficult to explain in a limited space, is that the approach also minimizes differences that result from methodological variance. Consider the correlations of a given trait measure with, for example, the eight octants of a circumplex standard (e.g., Wiggins, 1979). Methodological variance mainly would affect the magnitude, not the pattern, of the measure's correlations around the circumplex. Location is determined by the pattern of correlations.

TABLE 3
Descriptive Analysis of Three Measures of Social Acuity in Three
Circumplex Domains

Measure	Circumplex	Circular mean (degrees)	Circular variance	Circular variance (degrees)	Mean vector length
Self-monitoring	Interpersonal	45°	.118	28°	.519
	Affective	134°	.058	20°	.605
	Mixed	164°	.109	27°	.453
Nonverbal sensitivity	Interpersonal	335°	.331	48°	.454
	Affective	203°	.437	56°	.318
	Mixed	118°	.222	39°	.542
Empathy	Interpersonal	31°	.384	52°	.519
	Affective	142°	.376	51°	.465
	Mixed	151°	.386	52°	.440

Note. Based on results reported in Funder and Harris (1986).

pathy), and its least convergence in the affective space. In all three circles, Nonverbal Sensitivity is closer to Empathy than it is to Self-Monitoring (mean $r = .63$ versus .47).

CONCLUSION

The purpose of this chapter is to show how the circumplex can provide an integrative nomological net for researchers seeking greater understanding and delineation of personality traits. The circumplex adds an additional level of complexity (e.g., Guttman, 1954) to factor models of personality, a complexity that is in greater harmony with the actual multifaceted structure of personality traits than is the traditional, simple-structure view (e.g., Goldberg, 1993; Johnson & Ostendorf, 1993). In the case of interpersonal and affective traits, the circumplex may provide a defining domain-space for investigating traits' descriptive characteristics.

Circumplex structures can be created, as in the exemplary test development projects of Wiggins (1979) and Kiesler (1983). However, these structures also can be discovered (e.g., Wiggins & Broughton, 1991) through a careful analysis of existing measures. Indeed, this chapter demonstrated how the California Q-Set (CQ) could yield structurally and substantively valid circles for data analysis. Two recent studies, by Piedmont, McCrae, and Costa (1991) and Wiggins and Broughton (1991), suggest that the Adjective Check List Scales (ACL; Gough & Heilbrun, 1983) also may be especially friendly grounds for circumplex excavations.

In a manner perhaps foreseen by Hofstee and colleagues (1992), this chapter focused simultaneously on three personality circles rather than simply one. The interpersonal and affective circles are generally known to personality researchers; however, the circle that is generated from the confluence of agreeableness and neuroticism has only recently (e.g., Saucier, 1992) been considered. Yet, as shown here, in many instances it may serve as a better space for capturing a trait's essential characteristics than the venerable interpersonal and affective circles.

When circumplex structures are recovered from existing measures, such as the CQ or the ACL, this opens the possibility for secondary analyses of previously published or archival data. For the adventurous researcher, the CQ's extensive literature offers rich opportunity for this kind of domain-centered exploratory analysis and reframing. The methods developed here for analyzing CQ data were specifically designed to take advantage of the kinds of descriptive data typically available from published reports (e.g., Ozer, 1993). Hence, this chapter also serves as an invitation for researchers to apply the circumplex coding system to other CQ data. Ultimately, we will need to show that the trait implications from using the CQ circle (or ACL circle, for that matter) are convergent with those derived from standard circles and factor spaces. I strongly suspect that they are, but for now I leave this question to those who wish to explore this approach further.

REFERENCES

Block, J. (1961/1978). *The Q-Sort Method in personality assessment and psychiatric research*. Palo Alto, CA: Consulting Psychologists Press.

Block, J. (1993). Studying personality the long way. In D. C. Funder, R. D. Parke, C. Tomlinson-Keasey, & K. Widaman (Eds.), *Studying lives through time: Personality and development* (pp. 9–41). Washington, DC: American Psychological Association.

Bradlee, P. M., & Emmons, R. A. (1992). Locating narcissism within the interpersonal circumplex and the Five-Factor Model. *Personality and Individual Differences, 13*, 821–830.

Browne, M. W. (1992). Circumplex models for correlation matrices. *Psychometrika, 57*, 469–497.

Buss, D. M., & Chiodo, L. M. (1991). Narcissistic acts in everyday life. *Journal of Personality, 59*, 179–215.

Comrey, A. L. (1973). *A first course in factor analysis*. New York: Academic Press.

Conte, H. R., & Plutchik, R. (1981). A circumplex model for interpersonal personality traits. *Journal of Personality and Social Psychology, 40*, 701–711.

Costa, P. T., Jr., & McCrae, R. R. (1992). Normal personality assessment in clinical practice: The NEO Personality Inventory. *Psychological Assessment, 4*, 5–13.

Cronbach, L. J. (1990). *Essentials of psychological testing* (5th ed.). New York: Harper & Row.

Cronbach, L. J., & Meehl, P. E. (1955). Construct validity in psychological tests. *Psychological Bulletin, 52,* 281–302.

Emmons, R. A. (1987). Narcissism: Theory and measurement. *Journal of Personality and Social Psychology, 52,* 11–17.

Eysenck, H. J., & Eysenck, M. W. (1985). *Personality and individual differences: A natural science approach.* New York: Plenum Press.

Fisher, G. A., Heise, D. R., Bohrnstedt, G. W., & Lucke, J. F. (1985). Evidence for extending the circumplex model of personality trait language to self-reported moods. *Journal of Personality and Social Psychology, 49,* 233–242.

Funder, D. C., & Harris, M. J. (1986). On the several facets of personality assessment: The case of social acuity. *Journal of Personality, 54,* 528–550.

Funder, D. C., Parke, R. D., Tomlinson-Keasey, C., & Widaman, K. (1993). *Studying lives through time: Personality and development.* Washington, DC: American Psychological Association.

Gifford, R. (1991). Mapping nonverbal behavior on the interpersonal circle. *Journal of Personality and Social Psychology, 61,* 279–288.

Gifford, R., & O'Connor, B. (1987). The interpersonal circumplex as a behavior map. *Journal of Personality and Social Psychology, 52,* 1019–1026.

Goldberg, L. R. (1993). The structure of personality traits: Vertical and horizontal aspects. In D. C. Funder, R. D. Parke, C. Tomlinson-Keasey, & K. Widaman (Eds.), *Studying lives through time: Personality and development* (pp. 169–188). Washington, DC: American Psychological Association.

Gough, H. G., & Heilbrun, A. B. (1983). *The Adjective Check List manual.* Palo Alto, CA: Consulting Psychologists Press.

Gough, H. G., & Heilbrun, A. B. (1987). *Administrator's guide for the California Psychological Inventory.* Palo Alto, CA: Consulting Psychologists Press.

Gurtman, M. B. (1991). Evaluating the interpersonalness of personality scales. *Personality and Social Psychology Bulletin, 17,* 670–677.

Gurtman, M. B. (1992a). Construct validity of interpersonal personality measures: The interpersonal circumplex as a nomological net. *Journal of Personality and Social Psychology, 63,* 105–118.

Gurtman, M. B. (1992b). Trust, distrust, and interpersonal problems: A circumplex analysis. *Journal of Personality and Social Psychology, 62,* 989–1002.

Gurtman, M. B. (1993). Constructing personality tests to meet a structural criterion: Application of the interpersonal circumplex. *Journal of Personality, 61,* 237–263.

Gurtman, M. B. (1994). The circumplex as a tool for studying normal and abnormal personality: A methodological primer. In S. Strack & M. Lorr (Eds.), *Differentiating normal and abnormal personality* (pp. 243–263). New York: Springer.

Guttman, L. (1954). A new approach to factor analysis: The radex. In P. F. Lazarsfeld (Ed.), *Mathematical thinking in the social sciences* (pp. 258–348). Glencoe, IL: Free Press.

Hofstee, W. K. B., de Raad, B., & Goldberg, L. R. (1992). Integration of the Big Five and circumplex approaches to trait structure. *Journal of Personality and Social Psychology, 63,* 146–163.

Hogan, R. (1969). Development of an empathy scale. *Journal of Consulting and Clinical Psychology, 33,* 307–316.

Horowitz, L. M., Rosenberg, S. E., & Bartholomew, K. (1993). Interpersonal problems, attachment styles, and outcome in brief dynamic psychotherapy. *Journal of Consulting and Clinical Psychology, 61,* 549–560.

John, O. P. (1990). The "Big Five" factor taxonomy: Dimensions of personality in the natural language and in questionnaires. In L. A. Pervin (Ed.), *Handbook of personality theory and research* (pp. 66–100). New York: Guilford Press.

Johnson, J. A., & Ostendorf, F. (1993). Clarification of the Five-Factor Model with the abridged Big Five dimensional circumplex. *Journal of Personality and Social Psychology, 65,* 563–576.

Kiesler, D. J. (1983). The 1982 interpersonal circle: A taxonomy for complementarity in human transactions. *Psychological Review, 90,* 185–214.

Lanning, K. (1994). Dimensionality of observer ratings on the California Adult Q-Set. *Journal of Personality and Social Psychology, 67,* 151–160.

Leary, T. (1957). *Interpersonal diagnosis of personality: A functional theory and methodology for personality evaluation.* New York: Ronald Press.

Mardia, K. V. (1972). *Statistics of directional data.* New York: Academic Press.

McCrae, R. R., & Costa, P. T., Jr. (1989). The structure of interpersonal traits: Wiggins's circumplex and the Five-Factor Model. *Journal of Personality and Social Psychology, 56,* 586–595.

McCrae, R. R., Costa, P. T., Jr., & Busch, C. M. (1986). Evaluating comprehensiveness in personality systems: The California Q-Set and the Five-Factor Model. *Journal of Personality, 54,* 430–446.

McCrae, R. R., & John, O. P. (1992). An introduction to the Five-Factor Model and its applications. *Journal of Personality, 60,* 175–215.

Meyer, G. J., & Shack, J. R. (1989). Structural convergence of mood and personality: Evidence for old and new directions. *Journal of Personality and Social Psychology, 57,* 691–706.

Moskowitz, D. S. (1994). Cross-situational generality and the interpersonal circumplex. *Journal of Personality and Social Psychology, 66,* 921–933.

Ozer, D. J. (1993). The Q-Sort Method and the study of personality development. In D. C. Funder, R. D. Parke, C. Tomlinson-Keasey, & K. Widaman (Eds.), *Studying lives through time: Personality and development* (pp. 147–168). Washington, DC: American Psychological Association.

Piedmont, R. L., McCrae, R. R., & Costa, P. T., Jr. (1991). Adjective check list scales and the Five-Factor Model. *Journal of Personality and Social Psychology, 60,* 630–637.

Plutchik, R. (1989). Measuring emotions and their derivatives. In R. Plutchik & H. Kellerman (Eds.), *The measurement of emotions* (Vol. 4, pp. 1–35). New York: Academic Press.

Rosenthal, R., Hall, J. A., DiMatteo, M. R., Rogers, P. L., & Archer, D. (1979). *Sensitivity to nonverbal communication: The PONS test.* Baltimore: Johns Hopkins University Press.

Russell, J. A. (1980). A circumplex model of affect. *Journal of Personality and Social Psychology, 39,* 1161–1178.

Saucier, G. (1992). Benchmarks: Integrating affective and interpersonal circles with the Big-Five personality factors. *Journal of Personality and Social Psychology, 62,* 1025–1035.

Snyder, M. (1974). Self-monitoring and expressive behavior. *Journal of Personality and Social Psychology, 30,* 526–537.

Soldz, S., Budman, S., Demby, A., & Merry, J. (1993). Representation of personality disorders in circumplex and Five-Factor space: Explorations with a clinical sample. *Psychological Assessment, 5,* 41–52.

Upton, G. J. G., & Fingleton, B. (1989). *Spatial data analysis by example (Vol. 2: Categorical and directional data).* New York: Wiley.

Wainer, H., & Thissen, D. (1981). Graphical data analysis. *Annual Review of Psychology, 32,* 191–241.

Watson, D., & Tellegen, A. (1985). Toward a consensual structure of mood. *Psychological Bulletin, 98,* 219–235.

Wiggins, J. S. (1979). A psychological taxonomy of trait-descriptive terms: The interpersonal domain. *Journal of Personality and Social Psychology, 37,* 395–412.

Wiggins, J. S. (1982). Circumplex models of interpersonal behavior in clinical psychology. In P. C. Kendall & J. N. Butcher (Eds.), *Handbook of research methods in clinical psychology* (pp. 183–221). New York: Wiley.

Wiggins, J. S., & Broughton, R. (1991). A geometric taxonomy of personality scales. *European Journal of Personality, 5,* 343–365.

Wiggins, J. S., & Pincus, A. L. (1989). Conceptions of personality disorders and dimensions of personality. *Psychological Assessment: A Journal of Consulting and Clinical Psychology, 1,* 305–316.

Wiggins, J. S., Steiger, J. H., & Gaelick, L. (1981). Evaluating circumplexity in personality data. *Multivariate Behavioral Research, 16,* 263–289.

Wilkinson, L. (1990). *SYSTAT: The system for statistics.* Evanston, IL: SYSTAT.

Wink, P. (1991a). Self- and object-directedness in adult women. *Journal of Personality, 59,* 769–791.

Wink, P. (1991b). Two faces of narcissism. *Journal of Personality and Social Psychology, 61,* 590–597.

Wink, P. (1992a). Three narcissism scales for the California Q-Set. *Journal of Personality Assessment, 58,* 51–66.

Wink, P. (1992b). Three types of narcissism in women from college to mid-life. *Journal of Personality, 60,* 7–30.

5

TWO AT A TIME IS BETTER THAN ONE AT A TIME: EXPLOITING THE HORIZONTAL ASPECTS OF FACTOR REPRESENTATIONS

CLARENCE C. McCORMICK and LEWIS R. GOLDBERG

A factor matrix can be examined from two different points of view: The vertical or hierarchical view is focused on the columns of the matrix and the horizontal view is focused on its rows. The two viewpoints have different implications for the construction, scoring, and interpretation of psychological tests (Goldberg, 1993). In this chapter, we explain some of these differences, stressing the advantages of the horizontal viewpoint. We contrast linear and circulinear psychometric models and describe some concepts advanced by Guttman (1954) and Stevens (1951). We discuss some basic issues in circulinear psychometrics and provide a brief explanation of some of the major circular statistical techniques. We show the advantages of item-level analyses of personality scales, using the Interpersonal Checklist (ICL) as an example. Finally, we compare the findings on the structure of the ICL derived from external analyses (e.g., self-descriptions using ICL items) with those derived from internal analyses (e.g., judgments of semantic similarity obtained via two quite different procedures). Our goal is

Support for the second author was provided by Grant MH-49227 from the National Institute of Mental Health, U.S. Public Health Service. The authors are grateful to G. Rolfe LaForge, Daniel Levitin, Robert R. McCrae, Gerard Saucier, and Jerry S. Wiggins for their thoughtful suggestions.

to provoke further discussion of alternative methodologies for structural analyses of personality concepts in order to accelerate the systematic development of personality psychology as a cumulative science.

THE VERTICAL VIEWPOINT

The long dominant point of view in factor analysis has been vertical; in this view each factor is interpreted in terms of those variables that are highly associated with it. In an ideal situation, some variables are strongly associated with each factor and with no others, so that the pattern of factor loadings includes many that are near zero and some that are near unity; such an ideal has been termed *simple structure* by Thurstone (1947), and most modern factor rotation algorithms such as varimax serve to approximate this ideal as closely as the data permit. In a perfectly simple-structured world, the vertical viewpoint would be all one would need, because those variables highly associated with each of the factors would have essentially zero loadings on all of the other factors. Unfortunately, real life is messier, and most psychological variables have strong associations with at least two factors.

If the variables are items, those with high loadings on any one factor are typically combined to form a scale. Such scales are construed as summary variables in components analysis and as latent variables in classical factor analysis (Goldberg & Digman, 1994). In either case, the use of such a procedure is based on the assumption that the salient items for any given factor exhibit no intrinsic order among themselves; rather, the items are considered to be equivalent and interchangeable units (like the inch marks on a yardstick). Such a practice is consistent with classical psychometric theory. Scale scores then can be obtained by simply counting the number of responses in the keyed direction for each of the resulting scales. These scores are used to compare research participants with one another or with some normative sample. Scale scores are assumed to indicate how much of the attribute is exhibited by the individuals; and the individuals can be ranked according to their scores, with higher scores indicating more of the attribute.

Unfortunately, such a practice implicitly requires one to accept some strong assumptions: (a) aside from unreliability, all of the items selected for each scale measure *only* that one attribute (the unidimensionality assumption); (b) the item intercorrelations are all approximately equal; and (c) all of the item variances are approximately equal (Wherry, 1984). In practice, these assumptions are typically unrealistic, as has long been recognized (e.g., McNemar, 1946). Indeed, most items are at least two-dimensional (factorially complex) rather than one-dimensional (factorially univocal); that is, most items have been found to exhibit important secondary loadings on one or more factors other than the primary factor. Such findings have been demonstrated in studies that go back to the early use of factor analysis (e.g., Guilford & Guilford, 1936; Mosier, 1937).

If the assumptions are not met, similar total scores obtained by individuals can be achieved by endorsing quite different subsets of items, with the result that the meaning of the score can be ambiguous (e.g., Briggs & Cheek, 1986). Comparing and contrasting individuals on the basis of their total scores will involve some systematic error of an unknown extent. With different scales, each of which purports to measure the same construct but consists of somewhat different sets of items, the rank order of individuals can change radically (e.g., Butt & Fiske, 1968).

THE HORIZONTAL VIEWPOINT

In contrast to the vertical focus, in which the meaning of each factor is derived from reading down the column of factor loadings, the horizontal focus forces an analysis of each item in terms of its pattern of loadings across all of the factors. In a perfectly simple-structured world, each item would be associated with one and only one factor, and all of its loadings on other factors would be near zero. In the real world, most items are factorially complex rather than factorially univocal, and most items have substantial loadings on two or more factors. That is, an item (the basic, indivisible unit of psychological measurement) is in fact a multidimensional package, rather than the unidimensional variable that is assumed by current psychometric procedures.

Most items, then, can be conceptualized as blends of at least a pair of factors. If one examines the bivariate frequency distribution (scatterplot) for any two factors and includes all of the items with their highest loadings on that particular pair of factors (Hofstee, de Raad, & Goldberg, 1992), the items typically are scattered throughout the bivariate space rather than being densely packed in a few regions. With the items projected onto a unit circle, most of them tend to be distributed over the arcs between the poles, and only a few items tend to be clustered tightly around the poles.

Examination of the circular plots typically reveals that items located close together on the circle tend to be roughly synonymous in their meanings, and the degree of synonymity tends to decline with increasing arc distance between the items. When the arc distance between the items is about 90°, the meanings of the items tend to appear to be independent. As the arc distance increases toward 180°, the meanings of the items tend to display increased antonymity. One way of thinking about this configuration is that the items are organized relative to the degree of their shared connotations. If any one item is taken as the focus of interest, its shared connotations with other items range in two different directions (clockwise and counterclockwise) from that focal item. With each item taken as the center of a set of items with which it shares connotations, we can interpret the angular location of the central item as an index of the meaning of the item set.

LINEAR VERSUS CIRCULINEAR CONTINUA

In the history of psychological measurement, there have been two major contributors to our understanding of the nature of circular data structures: Louis Guttman and S. S. Stevens.

Guttman's Model

Guttman (1954) noted that variables can exhibit two different types of order. First, some variables can be ordered along a continuum of differences in degree. He labeled this continuum a simplex—a contraction of the phrase "simple order of complexity" (p. 260). Variables can be rank ordered along this continuum "from 'least' to 'most'" (p. 260). Such a ranking requires that the observations exhibit the property of ordered transitivity (if $a > b$ and $b > c$, then $a > c$), which is a property of the real number system. Second, other variables can be ordered around a circular continuum according to differences in kind. Guttman coined the term *circumplex* (a contraction of the phrase "circular continuum of complexity") as a label for this type of continuum, which is characterized by an order among the variables that is not of such a nature that there is a ranking from highest to lowest nor from least to most of any property; rather, this order "has no beginning and no end, namely, a circular order" (p. 260). Clearly, transitivity is not a property of variables exhibiting a circular order.

According to Guttman, the postulated circular order among the different kinds of variables is determined by a "law of neighboring," which can be operationalized by a set of correlation coefficients (Guttman, 1954) or any other similarity coefficients (Shepard, 1978). This law of neighboring can serve as a criterion by which one can recognize a circumplex; if any one variable is taken as a focus, its correlations with its nearest neighbors should be the highest of the set, and the correlations should gradually diminish as one moves clockwise or counterclockwise away from the focus, becoming increasingly negative up to the point 180° from the focus and then increasing again as one returns to the original variable.

If the intercorrelations conform to the circumplex model, they can be arranged to exhibit the properties of a circulant matrix (Davis, 1979): For an ideal matrix, the row and column sums will be equal, the values in each diagonal will be equal, and these values will decrease in magnitude from the main diagonal to a minimum and then rise again to the off-diagonal corner cells. Empirical matrices, of course, only approximate this ideal. Lorr and McNair (1963) have pointed out that if the values of the correlations in each of the rows of an empirical circumplex matrix are plotted on the same graph, one will obtain a series of approximate overlapping (out-of-phase) sine waves.

The circumplex topologically is a one-dimensional representation, just as is a straight line, although both require an embedding plane for their spatial representation (Shepard, 1978). Although it seems natural to conceive of a circular structure as determined by the coordinates of two orthogonal dimensions, the use of such bipolar dimensions is not essential for the structuring and interpretation of a configuration of similarity relations such as correlation coefficients (Shepard, 1978; Torgerson, 1986). The necessary and sufficient information is the set of intercorrelations among the variables. Factor analysis may be used to embed the variables in a dimensional space, but the dimensions then may be removed and ignored without affecting the interpretation of the configuration. As Plutchik (1980) has noted, "In a circumplex there are no preferred positions or axes except by the accident of poor sampling of tests or items . . . because in a circle any change of axes leaves all the relationships between parts of the circle invariant" (p. 196).

Guttman (1954) combined the simplex and circumplex into a bivariate model, which he labeled a *radex* (for "radial order of complexity"). The circumplex model also can be generalized to variables that are distributed over the surface of a sphere or a higher dimensional hypersphere such as a four-dimensional torus (Degerman, 1972).

Stevens' Model

The same distinction that Guttman made between the simplex and circumplex representations was made independently by Stevens (1975) for psychophysical variables. Stevens distinguished between *prothetic* continua, which can be used to represent differences in degree, magnitude, or intensity and that answer the question "how much?"; and *metathetic* continua, which can be used to represent differences of kind or quality, and that answer questions such as "what kind?" and "where?" Examples of prothetic continua are those for loudness and brightness; examples of metathetic continua are those for auditory pitch, color hues, and inclination or direction (angles).

One then might consider the circumplex as a model for variables that are ordered around metathetic continua and the simplex as a model for variables that are ordered along prothetic continua. As Krantz, Luce, Suppes, and Tversky (1971) have pointed out:

While direct comparisons of intervals can be attained in many ways, there is a sharp distinction between cases for which the ordering has the properties of intervals on a straight line (sensation continuum, conditional probability, utility continuum) and cases for which more complex structures are needed to provide a representation. (p. 140)

This is so, they noted, because for many paired comparisons "... it is extremely doubtful that the individual objects ... are appropriately represented along a single continuum" (p. 140).

Stevens never pursued in any detail the implications of measuring metathetic variables. His empirical research was focused on developing scales for sensory intensities, and his theoretical discussions of scale types were focused on the real number system (Stevens, 1951), which are the appropriate numbers for the study of prothetic variables.

CIRCULINEAR PSYCHOMETRICS

One major assumption of current psychometric theory is that items, and the scales produced from them, are unidimensional. In practice this means that current psychometric theory assumes that psychological test scores can be mapped to points on the "real number line," and thus provide at least ordinal-scale information on the individuals who obtain the scores. This is the reason for the importance of, and concern over, the unidimensionality assumption. Indeed, most of psychometric theory has been developed using the algebra of the real number system with its associated property of ordered transitivity.

However, it seems clear that most psychological test items are multidimensional. This means that the item and scale scores should not be mapped to points on the real number line; rather, they need to be mapped to points in two-dimensional (or more) space, as we ordinarily do when we plot the variables of a factor analysis. In turn, this means that the quantities involved are not those indexed by the numbers of the real number system; rather, they are the quantities that are expressed as ordered pairs (or triplets, or more) of numbers. As Guttman (1954) has noted, these quantities do *not* possess the property of ordered transitivity; that is, points in space cannot be given the simple order of points on a line (Halberg & Devlin, 1967).

One result of this difference between real number points and points in space is that these latter quantities require the use of a somewhat different arithmetic from that of the real numbers (Ross, 1938). These quantities require the use of vector algebra or the procedures of analytic geometry and trigonometry; a mathematician would say that they are quantities from the complex number system. The notation for complex numbers can take different forms: Complex numbers can be represented algebraically as an ordered pair of numbers (e.g., x, y), as a vector $[x \; y]$, as polar coordinates such as "r, θ" (where r is a vector length and θ is an angle), or as a complex number such as "$a + bi$" (where i is the square root of -1 and a and b are real numbers), whatever is the most convenient. The use of this arithmetic can be seen in the scoring of the Interpersonal Checklist (ICL) (LaForge, Leary, Naboisek, Coffey, & Freedman, 1954) and the Interpersonal Adjective Scales (IAS) (Wiggins, Trapnell, & Phillips, 1988).

Treating circumplex scale scores as if they were real numbers can lead to the calculation of means that are in considerable error (e.g., Batschelet, 1981; Mardia, 1972; Ross, 1938; Schlosberg, 1941; Woodworth & Schlosberg, 1954). If the means are in error, so then are all the statistics that involve the mean, such as deviation scores, variances, standard deviations, standard scores, correlation coefficients, reliability estimates, and the like. For example, the circular locations (in degrees) of the items in the Warm–Agreeable scale of the IAS (Wiggins, Trapnell, & Phillips, 1988, Table 1, p. 521) are 348.6, 356.0, 359.7, 360.0, 4.1, 5.6, 6.2, and 8.6. Using regular, real number arithmetic the mean of these values is 181.1°, which is dramatically incorrect because it lies on the opposite side of the circle from the set of numbers. Using the arithmetic of the complex number system, the average is 1.1°, which is the correct measure of central tendency for the set of observations in this interval. The problem stems from the fact that "... the usual linear measures depend heavily on the choice of the zero direction and are therefore inappropriate for circular distributions" (Mardia, 1972, p. 18).

These considerations point to a need for psychometricians to develop an extension to current test theory based on the complex number system. As the popularity of circumplex models increase, this need will intensify. Although this is not the place to provide a primer on circulinear psychometrics, it is necessary to provide some discussion of the basic concepts and some examples of their potential uses.

The location of an observation on a circulinear continuum is indexed by θ, and ρ represents the distance of the observation from the origin, which is referred to as its vector length. If the observations have been normalized to the unit circle, then each ρ will equal 1.0. The subset of items that are endorsed by an individual can be represented by a circulinear distribution over an arc of the continuum. The θ values can be added, using vector algebra or trigonometric operations, and their sum provides an ordered pair of numbers that indicate the mean location of, and the vector length for, the subset. The empirical vector length (R) will equal the number of observations in the subset (N) if *all* of the observations lie at the same location and thus have the same θ. If the observations are instead distributed over some interval, the θ values will differ, and R will be smaller than N. Thus, the vector length provides information about the variability of the set of observations. The index R divided by N, called the mean vector length (r), is the circulinear analogue to the familiar linear standard deviation.

Figure 1 illustrates these operations. The figure shows four observations, labeled A, B, C, and D, located on a circulinear continuum. The observations are all considered to be of the same vector length and thus are located on the circumference of a unit circle. If these observations represent four different test items, and one were to add them together to form a scale according to the procedures of classical test theory, they would sum to a score of +4.

However, because we know that these variables are related to each other in a circulinear fashion, one needs to add them using trigonometric operations. From an analytical viewpoint, this means that one must take into account the directional differences among the observations, as well as their vector lengths (which in this case are all unity). That is, we need to add together the four sines and the four cosines to obtain their two sums, rather than just the item unit weights. From a graphic viewpoint, this amounts to placing the four observations end-to-end, which can be done

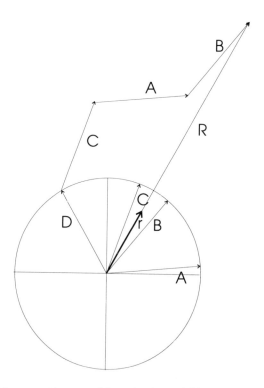

Figure 1. The trigonometric sum of four circular variables.

in any order. We have chosen to illustrate this property by using the arbitrary order $D + C + A + B$.

As can be seen in Figure 1, the concatenation of the vectors must maintain the directions of the variables as given within the unit circle; the endpoint of the last variable (B) extends beyond the unit circle, in a location that is near the center of the four observations, were they all extended to this same distance from the origin. The line connecting the endpoint with the origin, which is the trigonometric sum of the four vectors, is called the resultant, and it is labeled R in Figure 1. The resultant vector indicates the mean direction of the set of observations. The length of the resultant vector in Figure 1 is not 4 but rather is 3.044. It is smaller than the sum obtained by simply adding together the units because the directional information is included in its calculation. If all of the observations were in the same location, they all would lie on the resultant, and their sum would be a vector of length 4. The vector length, therefore, supplies information about the variability of the circular locations of the observations.

When the vector length R is divided by N (the number of observations), the result is another vector, called the mean vector length, which is always in the same direction as the resultant but ending within the original circle; the mean vector length is the circulinear analogue of the familiar linear standard deviation. In Figure 1, $R/N = 3/4$ or .75, and this vector is darkened and labeled r. Assuming a von Mises distribution for these four observations, their mean vector length corresponds to a circular standard deviation of 40.5° (their range is $120° - 5° = 115°$).

When one uses the algebra of complex numbers, the mean of the items is itself a complex number. One aspect of the mean location can be interpreted as the typical kind or type for the subset of observations. The other aspect, the mean vector length, can be interpreted as a measure of variability within the subset. Neither of these numbers provides any information that can answer the question "how much?" and therefore neither of them is an estimate of magnitude or intensity.

Nevertheless, an intensity aspect is often postulated for measures of psychological traits and states. Some people appear to be more dominant, more friendly, more anxious, or more happy than others, and one would like to be able to measure how much they differ. For this purpose, prothetic and metathetic measures must be combined. One model for accomplishing this goal is Guttman's (1954) radex, an example of which has been provided by the Interpersonal Checklist (ICL; LaForge & Suczek, 1955); the circular continuum was divided into 16 intervals (arcs), and the items located within each interval were ordered along a simplex continuum divided into four linear intervals (e.g., *dictatorial* is the extreme member and *good leader* a moderate member of the *Managerial* simplex).

Another example has been provided by Plutchik's (1980) structural model for adjectives describing emotional states. Partly in analogy with the color solid, Plutchik organized the emotion terms into an eight-interval circumplex (analogous to hues) and then postulated a unipolar dimension of intensity (analogous to brightness) along which the terms also are ordered. Based on the mean ratings from 30 research participants on an 11-point scale of intensity, the emotion terms were grouped into three intervals. The resulting structural model then is a three-dimensional hemisphere (or cone), with three circumplexes appearing at different latitudes corresponding to their intensity. If all of the terms are projected into the plane at the base of the hemisphere, the model corresponds to Guttman's radex.

Circular Statistics: A Brief History

In the early 1950s, R. Fisher (1953) and Gumbel, Greenwood, and Durand (1953) introduced the basic distributions for data that are located on the surface of a sphere and around the circumference of a circle, respectively. These articles were followed by substantial research that developed the appropriate descriptive and inferential statistical techniques for use with circulinear and spherical distributions. These procedures now have been presented in several textbooks, including those by Mardia (1972), Zar (1974), Batschelet (1981), Upton and Fingleton (1989), and N. Fisher (1993) for circular data; and Mardia (1972), Watson (1983), and N. Fisher, Lewis, and Embleton (1987) for spherical data.

Some psychologists have begun to use these circular statistics. For example, in their textbook on multidimensional scaling, Schiffman, Reynolds, and Young (1981) included a chapter on the use of circulinear statistics for the interpretation of individual differences. More recently, G. Fisher, Heise, Bohrnstedt, and Lucke (1985) used Kuiper's test (the circular analogue of the familiar Kolmogorov–Smirnov significance test) to compare two circular item distributions. These investigators also applied a circular correlation coefficient to assess agreement between two different procedures used to locate the same set of adjectives on a circulinear continuum. Gurtman (1993) has proposed the use of periodic regression techniques to fit cosine waves to circular data; he also has used the circulinear Rayleigh test to compare simple structure and circumplex models (Gurtman, 1994). And Levitin (1994) used the Rayleigh test as a measure of goodness-of-fit in a study of people's memories for musical pitch. We expect that interest in the use of these procedures will increase as investigators learn of their usefulness for psychological measurement.

TO LEARN ABOUT SCALES, ANALYZE THEIR ITEMS

Guttman (1954, 1957) postulated that many psychological variables can be represented by their locations on a circulinear continuum in a particular order given by the law of neighboring. In the ideal case, this order is assumed to be invariant. In fact, when the empirically obtained scale scores of circumplex instruments have been intercorrelated and factored, it typically has been shown that the circular order of the scales is quite similar across different samples of individuals (e.g., Paddock & Nowicki, 1986; Rounds & Tracey, 1993; Wiggins et al., 1988). This useful information is not available when the factors are interpreted one at a time; it only becomes available when the factors are examined two or three at a time.

However, the scale intercorrelations themselves do not indicate any particular law of neighboring that might have produced the obtained configurations. Scale intercorrelations reflect the mean locations of the items included in those scales, and typically the scales show rather large intervals between their locations. These large intervals make it difficult to infer much about the nature of the circular continuum that underlies the intercorrelations. The situation is quite different when the items themselves are analyzed: The intervals between the items are much more likely to be small, and the increased density around the circulinear continuum encourages the examination of systematic similarities and differences in the meanings of the items.

Moreover, if any one item is selected as a focal point, items located close to it normally will tend to have similar meanings, and those located in a clockwise direction will have discriminably different connotations from the set located in a counterclockwise direction. Such directional differences in locations can help investigators understand the differences between personality scales with the same or similar labels.

As an example, consider the findings of Butt and Fiske (1968), who compared scales, all of which purported to measure the concept of *dominance*. The Dominance scale of Gough, McClosky, and Meehl (1951) and the Dominance scale of Cattell, Saunders, and Stice (1957) correlate only about .35. When Butt and Fiske compared the two sets of items, they found that most of those on Gough's scale emphasized a friendly, socially oriented style of leadership, whereas most of those on Cattell's scale emphasized an egotistic, forceful, pugnacious style of leadership. Although some of the items included in the two scales were quite similar in their meanings, the central tendencies of the item locations in each of the two scales reflect two somewhat different denotations of the meaning of the trait of dominance. As Butt and Fiske noted, using the two scales to select highly dominant individuals ". . . would result in two very distinct groups of people" (1968, p. 513). It is clear that the failure to differentiate between these two identically labeled scales by different investigators can impede the systematic accumulation of findings and thus can interfere with the development of personality psychology as a cumulative science.

Familiarity with the Big Five factor structure and its circumplex operationalization in the AB5C structure of Hofstee and colleagues (1992) helps to elucidate these directional differences between the two item sets, both of which lie in the plane formed by Factor I (Surgency or Extraversion) and Factor II (Agreeableness): Items located in the clockwise direction from dominance turn out to be blends of Agreeableness (e.g., friendliness) and Extraversion, whereas items located in the counterclockwise direction are blends of Disagreeableness (e.g., hostility) and Extraversion. Thus, we can see that the two item sets each can be related to a common concept (dominance) and yet be discriminably different from each other.

This simple example has an important implication—namely, that the common practice of examining the relations among different scales is not as informative as examining the relations among the items in these scales. That is, a taxonomy that makes explicit the horizontal relations among the variables generally will prove to be more useful than the simple-structure oriented vertical representations typically provided in many scale-level analyses.

DISCOVERING SOME OF THE LAWS OF NEIGHBORING

These arguments can be investigated empirically through the use of those procedures that have been developed to scale sets of items for similarity in meaning (e.g., Conte & Plutchik, 1981; Deese, 1965; McCormick & Kavanagh, 1981; Miller, 1969; Russell, 1980; Schlosberg, 1952). These procedures can produce circulinear distributions that provide information about each item's location or central tendency and the amount of variability around that mean. The mean of each item's distribution across a sample of research participants can be used as an index of the average meaning of that item. Such information is crucial for test construction and interpretation in order to make sure that both the test constructor and the test respondents are construing the meaning of the item in the same way. The circulinear standard deviation provides an index of the amount of agreement within the sample of respondents about the meaning of the item. Items that elicit large standard deviations in their locations exhibit interpretive ambiguity (Goldberg, 1963), and therefore are poor candidates for inclusion in any measure. Items with small standard deviations are more useful because individual differences in their interpretations are minimized.

There are two general classes of procedures for scaling items in terms of the similarities and differences in their meanings; these procedures have been labeled *external* and *internal* by Wiggins (1973). The essence of all internal procedures is that participants *directly* assess the degree of similarity among pairs of items by methods such as paired-comparisons or sorting. In external analyses, participants rate the extent to which each of the items are characteristic of themselves or others, and the similarities among the items are derived *indirectly* from analyses of these ratings. In general, the structures derived from internal and external procedures are quite similar (e.g., Peabody & Goldberg, 1989), and both procedures provide similar information about item locations or central tendencies. However, whereas internal procedures tend to be far more labor-intensive than external procedures, they alone provide information about each item's circulinear standard deviation or interpretive ambiguity.

THE STRUCTURE OF THE INTERPERSONAL CHECKLIST

We will now illustrate these points by some analyses of the Interpersonal Checklist (ICL), developed by LaForge and Suczek (1955). The ICL was intended to operationalize one aspect (self- and other descriptions) of a complex theoretical system devised for the study and measurement of interpersonal behavior (Freedman, Leary, Ossorio, & Coffey, 1951; Leary, 1957). It is necessary to summarize some of the details of the test construction procedures and some of the subsequent research with the ICL so that the results presented here can be understood and appreciated.

The Interpersonal Checklist

The authors of the Interpersonal System (Freedman et al., 1951) proposed that interpersonal behavior could be organized on the basis of two independent dimensions: love–hate and dominance–submissiveness. They also postulated that brief descriptions of interpersonal behaviors could be written so as to provide blends in varying degrees of the meanings of pairs of the four poles of the two dimensions. A circular ordering of the variables was required in order to express the idea that "the theoretical degree of relationship between any two variables is a decreasing function of their separation on the perimeter of the circle" (LaForge & Suczek, 1955, p. 96). Thus, highly correlated variables should be located near to one another, and their logical opposites should appear on the opposite side of the circle. The circular continuum was divided into 16 intervals or scales, which are collapsed into eight scales for convenience in scoring and in graphing the resulting scores. In addition, each of the intervals was divided into four levels to accommodate ratings of the intensity of the interpersonal behaviors. The intensity dimension was defined as varying between normal, well-adjusted behaviors and abnormal extremes. Thus, although the ICL often has been referred to as a *circumplex*, it would be more accurate to apply Guttman's term *radex* to this model.

The ICL, in the course of its development, went through three major revisions. Each item originally had been located in one of the 16 sectors by the ratings of five psychologists regarding its similarity of meaning relative to their definitions of the sectors, as summarized by the sector labels. However, the use of these item classifications resulted in research participants endorsing more items on the right (friendly) side of the circle than on the left (hostile) side. Participants had been expected to exhibit more balance in their endorsements around the circular structure, with abnormal rigidity being indexed by the endorsement of the more extreme (intense) terms in each sector.

In order to obtain a more balanced pattern of endorsements, a rule was established that "intensity 1 words should be answered *yes* by about 90 per cent . . . intensity 2 by about 67 per cent, intensity 3 by about 33 per cent, and intensity 4 by about 10 per cent" of the participants (LaForge & Suczek, 1955, p. 102). The original intensity scale thus estimated some mixture of intensity and endorsement frequency (popularity or social desirability). This correction forced the authors to locate moderately intense as well as highly popular items in each sector of the circle. As we shall see, this procedure for allocating items to the eight scales (sectors of the circle) appears to have been responsible for some of the problems found in subsequent research. Interestingly, the item *intensity* weights were not used in the scoring of the ICL; rather, the total number of item endorsements on each scale was used as an indicator of how much of the attribute characterizes each individual.

ICL Factor Analyses

An unpublished study (McCormick, 1976) provides the data for some analyses of the ICL. Self-descriptions were obtained from 763 middle-class men and women, the median age of whom was 41 years. The protocols were scored for the eight scales according to the instructions given in an early ICL manual (Leary, 1956) by counting the number of items in each scale that the participant had endorsed. A principal components analysis of the eight scale scores produced one general and two bipolar factors. The factor plot for the two bipolar factors, which is presented in Figure 2, is quite similar to the findings from other analyses of the ICL scales by Rinn (1965) and Paddock and Nowicki (1986). As Figure 2 indicates, the scales are located in the circular order postulated for them by the ICL authors.

Nonetheless, in this analysis and those by Rinn (1965) and Paddock and Nowicki (1986), the intervals between adjacent scales are not equal,

Figure 2. Factor plot for the Interpersonal Checklist scales in their original locations.

and instead the scales form two somewhat separate clusters, essentially op-posite one another on the circle, with large gaps between the clusters. This characteristic has been interpreted as indicating that the ICL authors had inadequately sampled the interpersonal trait domain, "having nothing rel-evant to extrovertive social participation and emotional lability" (Stern, 1970, p. 64).

An analysis of the ICL items serves to clarify the problematical scale structure displayed in Figure 2. For the item factor analysis, each partici-pant's response distribution was standard-scored, thus eliminating individ-ual differences in endorsement frequency and the resulting general factor. The first two unrotated factors were used in order to calculate the angular locations of the items. The 128 items were found to cover most of the circular continuum, although some of the sectors were populated more densely than others. The numbers of items found in each of the sectors were Managerial (20), Competitive (8), Aggressive (25), Skeptical (14), Modest (22), Docile (15), Cooperative (11), and Responsible (13).

The items then were listed in their circular order and partitioned into eight sectors (scales); scale scores again were obtained by simply counting the number of items endorsed. The intercorrelations were factored, and one general and two bipolar factors were obtained. A factor plot for the two bipolar factors is presented in Figure 3.

Compared to Figure 2, the configuration in Figure 3 more nearly approximates an ideal circumplex. The scales no longer form two clear clusters on opposite sides of the circle, thus affirming that the two large gaps found between the two sets of scales in the analyses based on the test authors' scoring procedure was not a result of an item sampling problem, as inferred by Stern (1970). Rather, the gaps result from the ICL authors' allocation of the items to the eight sectors of the circle, which was based on their theoretical expectation that participants should exhibit some endorsements in each of the sectors.

In contrast, when scales were constructed empirically, the intervals between the scales were more nearly equal. The Cooperative and Responsible scales, which were located only about 5° apart in Figure 2, are separated by a more satisfying 28° in Figure 3. The average differences from the ideal of 45° for the scale locations in Figure 2 is 23°, as compared to 13° for the scale locations in Figure 3. These improvements in the configuration stem from relocating the items from those postulated by the ICL

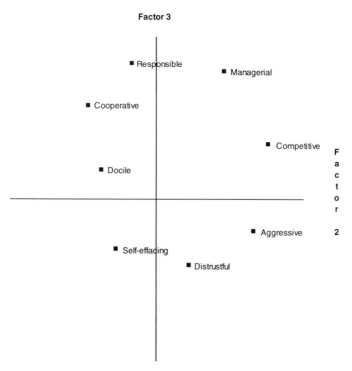

Figure 3. Factor plot for the Interpersonal Checklist scales in their revised locations.

authors to the order determined from the item factor analysis. The results provide support for the implication we drew from the analyses of Butt and Fiske (1968): For the purposes of test construction, it is more useful and informative to examine item rather than scale relations.

Wiggins (1979) drew the same conclusion in constructing his Interpersonal Adjective Scales (IAS). When he originally attempted to replicate the test-construction procedures used by the ICL authors, Wiggins found that "we partially succeeded in replicating the Leary system with trait-descriptive adjectives, but in doing so we carried over the faults of the system as well" (1979, p. 402). When he used the item locations obtained empirically from participants' self-descriptions, he demonstrated in four separate cross-validation samples that the IAS scale locations formed nearly perfect circumplex structures.

EXTERNAL ANALYSES OF INTERPERSONAL CHECKLIST ITEMS

The items selected for endorsement by any one individual form a circulinear distribution. In general, the distribution will range over some relatively limited arc of the circle. Circular statistical techniques can be used to evaluate the similarities and differences in an individual's item endorsement patterns obtained under different conditions (e.g., self and peer, husband and wife, self and ideal, self before and after treatment, patient and therapist). In addition, one can compare the various trigonometric moments of these circular distributions (e.g., the circulinear mean, circulinear variance, skew). When the mean locations of different individuals are trigonometrically averaged across all the members of some sample, these means also form a circulinear distribution. Therefore, one also can compare the average distributions (or their moments) of samples of participants (e.g., men versus women, hysterics versus compulsives, extraverts versus introverts) using circulinear statistical procedures.

The calculations of some circular statistics for the item responses from one fairly typical participant in the study by McCormick (1976) are presented in Table 1. The responses have been grouped into the eight revised class intervals, and this participant's frequency distribution can be found in the column headed f. The basic statistics describing the distribution are presented below the line. Although his endorsements ranged over about 270° of the continuum, 87% of his responses were located in three of the eight octants, ranging over 135°. The distribution is somewhat skewed toward the Dominant pole of the configuration.

The mean of the distribution (θ) is about 26°, a location that would classify his self-presentation as primarily a responsible person. The vector length (R) is the statistic used most often in statistical inference. The mean

TABLE 1
Calculation of the Mean Angle, Standard Deviation, and 95% Confidence Interval From a Circulinear-Grouped Frequency Distribution

Class-interval	sin	cos	f	sin × f	cos × f
Managerial (PA)	1.000	0.000	13	13.000	0.000
Competitive (BC)	0.707	−0.707	1	.707	−0.707
Aggressive (DE)	0.000	−1.000	0	0.000	0.000
Distrustful (FG)	−0.707	−0.707	0	0.000	0.000
Self-effacing (HI)	−1.000	0.000	1	−1.000	0.000
Docile (JK)	−0.707	0.707	6	−4.242	4.242
Cooperative (LM)	0.000	1.000	26	0.000	26.000
Responsible (NO)	.707	0.707	16	11.312	11.312
Sum			63	19.777	40.847

Notes. κ can be obtained from a table in Batschelet (1981), Fisher (1993), or Mardia (1972).
N = the sum of the values in the "f" column = 63.
Σsin = the sum of the values in the "sin × f" column = 19.777. Σcos = the sum of the values in the "cos × f" column = 40.847.
R = vector length = $[(\Sigma\text{sin})^2 + (\Sigma\text{cos})^2]^{.5}$ = 45.383.
r = mean vector length = R/N = .720.
Standard deviation, in radians = $[2(1 - r)]^{.5}$ = $[2(1 - .720)]^{.5}$ = .748. Standard deviation, in degrees = .748 $(180°/\pi)$ = 42.9°.
Standard error = $[1.96/(R \times \kappa)^{.5}]$ × $(180°/\pi)$ = 11.4°. θ = mean angle = arctan $(\Sigma\text{sin} / \Sigma\text{cos})$ = 25.8°.
95% confidence interval = 25.8° ± 11.4° = 14.4° to 37.2°.

vector length (r) and the mean (θ) are the maximum-likelihood estimators of the population parameters. The standard deviation of the distribution is provided in terms of both radian and angular measures; the descriptive meaning of the latter seems to be grasped more easily by most people. The standard deviation of one participant's frequency distribution typically is found to be, as for this individual, about 43°, or almost one octant of the circular continuum.

Both the vector length and the mean vector length can be used to calculate a 95% confidence interval for the mean angle. To do this requires the value of κ, an estimate of the scaling parameter of the von Mises distribution, which serves in circular statistics as the analogue of the linear normal distribution; it is obtained most easily from a table that provides equivalences between the mean vector length (r) and κ. The 95% confidence interval for this individual's mean angle is ± 11.4°, and so the expectation for the mean angle ranges from 14° to 37°.

The means of the individuals in a sample of research participants also form a distribution around a circulinear continuum. These distributions can be examined for goodness-of-fit with statistical procedures analogous to the familiar Kolmogorov–Smirnov test; or differences between their trigonometric moments can be evaluated statistically. The distributions of the individual means for the men and for the women separately and for the total sample from McCormick (1976) are presented in Table 2. The indi-

TABLE 2
Circulinear-Grouped Frequency Distributions of the Locations (Mean
Angles) of the 763 Research Participants

Class-interval	Men	Women	Total
Managerial (PA)	128	133	261
Competitive (BC)	9	8	17
Aggressive (DE)	5	2	7
Distrustful (FG)	6	4	10
Self-effacing (HI)	1	9	10
Docile (JK)	4	24	28
Cooperative (LM)	13	50	63
Responsible (NO)	84	283	367
N	250	513	763
R	195.0	402.4	587.9
r	.78	.78	.77
Standard deviation	37.1°	38.0°	38.9°
κ	2.6	2.6	2.5
θ	72.2°	50.4°	57.5°
Standard error	± 4.9°	± 3.4°	± 3.2°

vidual means are much more tightly distributed over the continuum than are the item endorsements of any one individual (Table 1). The distribution of men has its mode in the Managerial category, with the next largest frequency in the adjacent Responsible category; the distribution of women has its mode in the Responsible category, with its next highest frequency in the Managerial category.

The circulinear standard deviations are all two to three times smaller than those typically found for individual endorsement distributions; that is, as is usual, the means are much more stable than individual observations. The difference between the means for men and women is about 19°, which is statistically significant as can be seen by comparing the two confidence intervals. In fact, when a two-sample test (Watson & Williams, 1956) is applied to the data, the difference is found to be significant beyond the .001 level.

INTERNAL ANALYSES OF THE INTERPERSONAL CHECKLIST ITEMS

One problem with using external analyses to select items for a circumplex structure is that such analyses do not supply any information regarding the relative ambiguity of the items, and thus they do not permit the test constructor to select items that exhibit the least ambiguity. For this purpose, we need internal analyses, which serve to scale items for similarity of meaning. One such procedure, used by Schlosberg (1941) and Woodworth and Schlosberg (1954), may be particularly appropriate for scaling personality test items to a circumplex pattern. The procedure can produce a circulinear frequency distribution from which estimates of an item's average meaning and the degree of agreement around that average can be obtained. The procedure was used by McCormick and Kavanagh (1981) to scale the items of the ICL.

The scaling procedure was fairly simple. Eight separate bins were labeled with the ICL moderate-level category labels: Cooperative, Responsible, Managerial, Competitive, Aggressive, Distrustful, Self-effacing, and Docile. The bins were presented in random orders to 104 college students who were instructed to sort each of the 128 ICL items (also randomized for each participant) into the bin with whose label it was most similar in meaning. It was expected that when the bins were reordered to accord with the circular sequence postulated by the ICL authors (Leary, 1956), the frequency distributions for most of the items would be unimodal, and when the item frequency distributions were arranged in order by their modes, they would form a quasi-circulant matrix as described by Guttman (1954). However, this scaling procedure puts no constraints on the resulting frequency distributions, which can emerge as either linear or circular and as either unimodal or multimodal.

Table 3 presents the frequency distributions for eight of the 128 ICL items, one from each of the eight circular segments; the distributions for the other items are generally quite similar. The matrix of frequencies does exhibit the properties of an empirical circulinear structure. For example, the values in the diagonal entries first decrease and then increase again toward the northeast and southwest corners; indeed, if relative, rather than raw, frequencies had been used, the resulting matrix of proportions would resemble a correlation matrix, displaying the typical correlational pattern associated with a circumplex.

The circulinear means and standard deviations of these distributions were calculated by the same procedures illustrated in Table 1. The center of any one of the class intervals is arbitrarily selected as the point of zero degrees; to maintain comparability with the ICL model, the Cooperative interval was selected as this initial point in these analyses. The circulinear means (θ) of the items are presented below the frequency distributions. The item mean locations range over the entire circle in the sequence postulated by the test authors. Just as was found with the external analyses, the 128 items were distributed around the entire circle, and there were similar relative densities across the eight class intervals. As before, examination of the items' content indicated that items located close to one another were nearly synonymous.

The item locations obtained from the similarity-scaling distributions can be compared to those given in an early ICL manual (Leary, 1956). Just

TABLE 3

Some Item Frequency Distributions, With Their Mean Angular Locations
and Standard Deviations

Item Numbers

Class-interval	3	72	43	112	50	54	27	63
Managerial (AP)	77	22	1	1	0	8	5	22
Competitive (BC)	2	41	6	7	1	1	2	0
Aggressive (DE)	1	20	57	17	6	0	0	0
Distrustful (FG)	0	15	25	73	11	0	0	0
Self-effacing (HI)	0	3	9	6	55	5	8	12
Docile (JK)	2	0	1	0	29	34	17	10
Cooperative (LM)	0	2	5	0	2	34	47	11
Responsible (NO)	22	1	0	0	0	19	29	49
r	.90	.66	.74	.86	.80	.68	.75	.62
θ	81°	146°	197°	215°	276°	354°	5°	35°
Standard deviation	26°	47°	41°	30°	36°	46°	41°	50°

Note. $N = 104$. Item   3: Able to give orders.
  72: Shrewd and calculating.
  43: Irritable.
112: Distrusts everybody.
  50: Lacks self-confidence.
  54: Very respectful to authority.
  27: Friendly.
  63: Enjoys taking care of others.

as with the item factor analysis, about one third of the items were found to be seriously misplaced, relative to the meanings attributed to the items by the participants. (For the items shown in Table 3, the modal categories agreed with the authors' placements, but this was not true for some of the other items.) New scales were developed according to the locations provided by this scaling procedure. When these new scales were analyzed in the original sample of self-descriptions, the results were much the same as those found using the scales developed on the basis of the item factor analysis. Indeed, the factor plot of the new scales was virtually identical to that shown in Figure 3. The differences between the empirical scale locations and the 45° ideal were 23° for the original ICL scales, 13° for the scales derived from the external item factor locations, and only 8° from these internal analyses. Thus, the findings based on this quite different procedure support the contention that item sampling was not the cause of the large gaps found when the original ICL scale scores are analyzed (Figure 2), but rather the problem appears to stem from the allocation of the items to the scales. The congruence in the findings from the external and the internal analyses, each using a different sample of research participants, indicate that individuals tend to interpret the items for their self-descriptions very much in accord with the meanings used by the participants in the similarity-scaling task.

The similarity-scaling distributions also help to clarify individual differences in interpretations of the items. For example, one can see in the frequency distribution for item 3 ("able to give orders") that 77 of the 104 participants (74% of the sample) agreed that the item was most similar in meaning to the label *Managerial*, whereas 22 participants (21%) agreed that it was most similar to the label for the adjacent interval (*Responsible*). Thus, these analyses reveal some individual differences in the interpretation of an item between two discriminable, but related, concepts. The three participants who saw the item as most similar to Competitive and Aggressive seem to possess relatively idiosyncratic connotations for the item, but even these categories are located in the two intervals adjacent to Managerial in the opposite direction from Responsible.

There were also two participants who seemed to disagree completely with the majority interpretation; they placed the item in the Docile category on the opposite side of the circle. Because it is difficult to see how "able to give orders" could be interpreted as most similar in meaning to Docile, it is likely that these two participants either did not know the meaning of the word *docile* or that they were responding in a quasi-random fashion in order to finish the task as quickly as possible. In either case, the responses from such participants probably should be omitted from the analyses.

Just as one can use these internal analyses to cull deviant individuals from one's sample, the similarity-scaling data also can be used to cull ambiguous items from the initial item pool. An index of the degree of agreement among the participants for each item is provided by the circulinear standard deviations of the distributions. Highly ambiguous items have large standard deviations, whereas clear items have small ones. The standard deviations of the eight example items are presented in the last line of Table 3. For these particular items, the standard deviations range from 26° to 50°, values that indicate very good to excellent agreement among the participants on their meanings.

Table 4 presents a frequency distribution for the mean vector lengths (r) of all 128 ICL items. The angular equivalents of the mean vector lengths (circular standard deviations) are also shown. Table 4 indicates that 63% of the items obtained rs of .70 or higher (corresponding to standard deviations of 44° or less). In the literature on circular statistics, these are considered to be usefully compact distributions. Given that a test developer would include at least a few items to represent each interval and that their trigonometric sum would be used to index their central value, it seems reasonable to include items with standard deviations as large as 52° (r = .50). Using this standard, 93% of the ICL items would be judged acceptable for use in a personality inventory.

TABLE 4
Grouped Frequency Distribution of the Mean Vector Lengths for the 128 Interpersonal Checklist Items Obtained From the Similarity-Scaling Procedure

Class Interval		Raw Frequency	Relative Frequency	Cumulative Frequency
Length	Degrees			
.90–.99	8°–26°	15	12	12
.80–.89	27°–36°	27	21	33
.70–.79	37°–44°	39	30	63
.60–.69	45°–52°	23	18	81
.50–.59	52°–57°	15	12	93
.40–.49	58°–62°	7	5	98
.30–.39	63°–67°	1	1	99
.20–.29	68°–72°	1	1	100
.10–.19	73°–76°	0	0	100
.00–.09	77°–81°	0	0	100
Sum		128		

When r is less than .45 (corresponding to a standard deviation greater than 60°), the distributions are generally considered to be much less useful for statistical inference (N. Fisher, 1993). About 7% of the ICL items exhibit such large standard deviations. These items appear to be too ambiguous in meaning to be useful, and their presence in the checklist contributes to error in the use of the instrument. The distributions and circulinear statistics for the seven items with the largest standard deviations are presented in Table 5. The last line of the table shows that the standard deviations range from 60° to 69° (r = .28 to .45). The frequency distributions for these items are either bipolar or nearly rectangular, with some judgments appearing in every category.

As an example of a highly ambiguous item, consider Item 74 (self-seeking). The ICL authors located this item in the Aggressive sector; however, the modal category in the similarity-scaling data was Competitive, with 54% of the participants locating the item in that interval. However, 26% of the participants placed the item in the Self-effacing category, almost opposite the Competitive category and an octant away from the Aggressive category, and the remaining 20% of the participants spread their judgments over the other six intervals. It would seem that many participants did not understand the meaning of either *self-effacing*, *self-seeking*, or both. However, because the distribution for Item 50 (lacks self-confidence) was appropriate, with a clear mode (53%) in the Self-effacing category and with another 38% of the participants placing the item in the adjacent

TABLE 5
Frequency Distributions of the Seven Interpersonal Checklist Items With the Largest Standard Deviations

	Item Numbers						
Class-interval	74	8	15	96	13	17	70
Managerial (AP)	5	9	4	19	8	3	12
Competitive (BC)	56	28	4	1	3	4	31
Aggressive (DE)	3	23	14	3	14	20	5
Distrustful (FG)	3	23	56	5	5	2	1
Self-effacing (HI)	27	3	0	26	5	18	13
Docile (JK)	3	8	2	14	3	0	0
Cooperative (LM)	1	7	5	12	23	4	7
Responsible (NO)	6	3	19	24	43	53	35
r	.40	.43	.40	.31	.45	.28	.43
θ	155°	172°	210°	355°	40°	54°	85°
Standard deviation	63°	61°	63°	67°	60°	69°	61°

Note. $N = 104$. Item 74: Self-seeking.
        8: Can be indifferent to others.
      15: Able to doubt others.
      96: Overprotective of others.
      13: Can complain if necessary.
      17: Able to criticize self.
      70: Proud and self-satisfied.

categories (Docile and Distrustful), it seems reasonable to infer that the item itself, not the interval label, was particularly ambiguous.

COMPARING THE FINDINGS FROM EXTERNAL AND INTERNAL ANALYSES

The Pearson product-moment correlation, which is based on the general linear model, should not be used with circular variables. A circulinear analogue of the Pearson correlation has been provided by N. Fisher (1993), and it should be used instead. When the circulinear correlation was used to assess the amount of agreement between the 128 angular item locations obtained in the item factor analysis and those obtained from the similarity-scaling task, the coefficient was .74; when the nine most ambiguous items were omitted from the analysis, the correlation rose to a healthy .87. Given the substantial differences between the external and internal procedures, the fact that different research samples were used with each task, and the lack of any efforts to develop particularly unambiguous items, this value seems remarkably high.

It is widely accepted that most items are inherently unreliable (e.g., Comrey, 1962). However, if the findings based on ICL items can be generalized to typical items included in other current personality inventories, it would suggest that such items may be more reliable than first appears, if only their two-dimensional properties are taken into account. McCormick and Kavanagh (1981) also scaled the ICL items, using a somewhat different procedure and another separate sample of research participants ($N = 142$). The ICL authors (Freedman et al., 1951) had postulated two bipolar dimensions—love–hate and dominance–submission—as the basis for the circular order of the ICL items. McCormick and Kavanagh (1981) used these bipolar dimensions as 9-point scales, anchored by a set of adverbs (neutral, mild, moderate, strong, extreme). The participants judged the degree of similarity of the items to the polar terms defining each dimension. The participants scaled each item twice, once for each of the dimensions. The items were presented to each participant in random order.

The means of the resulting response distributions were used as the coordinates in the two-dimensional space formed by the two, presumably orthogonal, dimensions; indeed, the two sets of means correlated only −.09, which is not significantly different from zero, even with a sample size as large as 142. The coordinates of the items were used to calculate their angular locations in the two-dimensional space. When these angles were correlated with those obtained by the similarity-sorting procedure, the circulinear correlation for the entire set of 128 items was .79, which rose to .84 when the nine most ambiguous items were omitted. Thus, the circular order of the items appears to be quite reliable over three different samples and three different analytic procedures.

CONCLUSION

In this chapter, we have contrasted two general approaches to the analysis of personality structure, the vertical (or hierarchical) and the horizontal, and we have provided arguments in favor of the horizontal viewpoint. Our major premise is that personality attributes are inherently multidimensional, and therefore we will learn more from an analysis of two or more dimensions together than from analyses of any one of them alone. When one examines attributes two at a time, it is often useful to project them onto a unit circle in order to discriminate among them as finely as possible. In this context, we showed that some of the major concepts proposed by Guttman (1954)—his simplex, circumplex, and radex structures—can be integrated with Stevens' (1951) distinction between prothetic and metathetic continua. These ideas, in addition to those provided by recent developments in circular statistics, form the basis for an extension of classical test theory to incorporate circulinear psychometric techniques.

As examples of these ideas and techniques, we used some analyses of the scales and items from the Interpersonal Checklist (ICL), perhaps the most widely studied instrument developed to conform with a circular structure. We showed how anomalies at the scale level can be resolved by analyses of the items, and we compared two general approaches to such analyses. As an example of the external approach, we analyzed the self-ratings of 763 adult participants in order to locate each of the 128 ICL items in a circular representation. We showed that when new ICL scales were developed from these empirical locations, they provided a circumplex structure that was far closer to the ideal than that based on the original scales provided by the test authors. As a comparison with these external data, we used two varieties of internal analyses: (a) a semantic-sorting task and (b) similarity ratings against each of the two bipolar dimensions assumed to underlie the circumplex structure. Perhaps the most striking finding from these analyses was the substantial similarity in the item locations among the three types of representations.

We see a number of important implications from these findings. Although much the same representations can be obtained from either external or internal analyses, only the more labor-intensive internal procedures provide evidence about the appropriateness of each individual's judgments (thus permitting the investigator to omit highly deviant research participants) and about the relative interpretive ambiguity of the items themselves (thus permitting the test developer to cull highly ambiguous items). Does the richness of the data that can be derived from internal analyses overcome their inherent costs in participant time and effort? We suspect that different investigators will project different cost–benefit ratios as they plan their research. In an ideal situation, both types of procedures will be included in at least some future studies so that their findings can be compared (e.g., Peabody & Goldberg, 1989).

REFERENCES

Batschelet, E. (1981). *Circular statistics in biology.* New York: Academic Press.

Briggs, S. R., & Cheek, J. M. (1986). The role of factor analysis in the development and evaluation of personality scales. *Journal of Personality, 54,* 106–148.

Butt, D. S., & Fiske, D. W. (1968). Comparison of strategies in developing scales for dominance. *Psychological Bulletin, 70,* 505–519.

Cattell, R. B., Saunders, D. R., & Stice, G. (1957). *The Sixteen Personality Factors Questionnaire* (Rev. ed. with 1961 supplement). Champaign, IL: Institute for Personality and Aptitude Testing.

Comrey, A. L. (1962). Factored homogeneous item dimensions: A strategy for personality research. In S. Messick & J. Ross (Eds.), *Measurement in personality and cognition* (pp. 11–26). New York: Wiley.

Conte, H. R., & Plutchik, R. (1981). A circumplex model for interpersonal personality traits. *Journal of Personality and Social Psychology, 40,* 701–711.

Davis, P. J. (1979). *Circulant matrices.* New York: Wiley.

Deese, J. (1965). *The structure of associations in language and thought.* Baltimore: Johns Hopkins University Press.

Degerman, R. (1972). The geometric representation of some simple structures. In R. N. Shepard, A. K. Romney, & S. B. Nerlove (Eds.), *Multidimensional scaling: Theory and applications in the behavioral sciences* (Vol. 1). New York: Seminar.

Fisher, G. A., Heise, D. R., Bohrnstedt, G. W., & Lucke, J. F. (1985). Evidence for extending the circumplex model of personality trait language to self-reported moods. *Journal of Personality and Social Psychology, 49,* 233–242.

Fisher, N. I. (1993). *Statistical analysis of circular data.* New York: Cambridge University Press.

Fisher, N. I., Lewis, T. I., & Embleton, B. J. J. (1987). *Statistical analysis of spherical data.* New York: Cambridge University Press.

Fisher, R. (1953). Dispersion on a sphere. *Proceedings of the Royal Society of London, Series A, 217,* 295–305.

Freedman, M. B., Leary, T. F., Ossorio, A. G., & Coffey, H. S. (1951). The interpersonal dimension of personality. *Journal of Personality, 20,* 143–161.

Goldberg, L. R. (1963). A model of item ambiguity in personality assessment. *Educational and Psychological Measurement, 23,* 467–492.

Goldberg, L. R. (1993). The structure of personality traits: Vertical and horizontal aspects. In D. C. Funder, R. D. Parke, C. Tomlinson-Keasey, & K. Widaman (Eds.), *Studying lives through time: Personality and development* (pp. 169–188). Washington, DC: American Psychological Association.

Goldberg, L. R., & Digman, J. M. (1994). Revealing structure in the data: Principles of exploratory factor analysis. In S. Strack & M. Lorr (Eds.), *Differentiating normal and abnormal personality* (pp. 216–242). New York: Springer.

Gough, H. G., McClosky, H., & Meehl, P. (1951). A personality scale of dominance. *Journal of Abnormal and Social Psychology, 46,* 360–366.

Guilford, J. P., & Guilford, R. R. (1936). Personality factors S, E, and M, and their measurement. *Journal of Psychology, 2,* 109–127.

Gumbel, E. J., Greenwood, J. A., & Durand, D. (1953). The circular normal distribution: Theory and tables. *Journal of the American Statistical Association, 48,* 131–152.

Gurtman, M. B. (1993). Constructing personality tests to meet a structural criterion: Application of the interpersonal circumplex. *Journal of Personality, 61,* 237–263.

Gurtman, M. B. (1994). The circumplex as a tool for studying normal and abnormal personality: A methodological primer. In S. Strack & M. Lorr (Eds.), *Differentiating normal and abnormal personality* (pp. 243–263). New York: Springer.

Guttman, L. (1954). A new approach to factor analysis: The radex. In P. F. Lazarsfeld (Ed.), *Mathematical thinking in the social sciences* (pp. 258–348). Glencoe, IL: Free Press.

Guttman, L. (1957). Empirical verification of the radex structure of mental abilities and personality traits. *Educational and Psychological Measurement, 17,* 391–407.

Halberg, C. J. A., Jr., & Devlin, J. F. (1967). *Elementary functions.* Atlanta, GA: Scott, Foresman.

Hofstee, W. K. B., de Raad, B., & Goldberg, L. R. (1992). Integration of the Big Five and circumplex approaches to trait structure. *Journal of Personality and Social Psychology, 63,* 146–163.

Krantz, D. H., Luce, R. D., Suppes, P., & Tversky, A. (1971). *Foundations of measurement. Vol. I. Additive and polynomial representations.* San Diego, CA: Academic Press.

LaForge, R., Leary, T. F., Naboisek, H., Coffey, H. S., & Freedman, M. B. (1954). The interpersonal dimension of personality: II. An objective study of repression. *Journal of Personality, 23,* 129–153.

LaForge, R., & Suczek, R. F. (1955). The interpersonal dimension of personality: III. An Interpersonal Check List. *Journal of Personality, 24,* 94–112.

Leary, T. (1956). *Multilevel measurement of interpersonal behavior.* Berkeley, CA: Psychological Consultation Service.

Leary, T. (1957). *Interpersonal diagnosis of personality: A functional theory and methodology for personality evaluation.* New York: Ronald Press.

Levitin, D. J. (1994). Absolute memory for musical pitch: Evidence from the production of learned memories. *Perception and Psychophysics, 56,* 414–423.

Lorr, M., & McNair, D. M. (1963). An interpersonal behavior circle. *Journal of Abnormal and Social Psychology, 67,* 68–75.

Mardia, K. V. (1972). *Statistics of directional data.* New York: Academic Press.

McCormick, C. C. (1976). [Item factor analysis of the Interpersonal Checklist]. Unpublished raw data.

McCormick, C. C., & Kavanagh, J. A. (1981). Scaling Interpersonal Checklist items to a circular model. *Applied Psychological Measurement, 5,* 421–447.

McNemar, Q. (1946). Opinion–attitude methodology. *Psychological Bulletin, 43,* 289–374.

Miller, G. A. (1969). A psychological method to investigate verbal concepts. *Journal of Mathematical Psychology, 6,* 169–191.

Mosier, C. L. (1937). A factor analysis of certain neurotic symptoms. *Psychometrika, 2,* 263–286.

Paddock, J. R., & Nowicki, S., Jr. (1986). An examination of the Leary circumplex through the Interpersonal Check List. *Journal of Research in Personality, 20,* 107–144.

Peabody, D., & Goldberg, L. R. (1989). Some determinants of factor structures from personality-trait descriptors. *Journal of Personality and Social Psychology, 57,* 552–567.

Plutchik, R. (1980). *Emotion: A psychoevolutionary synthesis.* New York: Harper & Row.

Rinn, J. L. (1965). Structure of phenomenal domains. *Psychological Review, 72,* 445–466.

Ross, R. T. (1938). A statistic for circular scales. *Journal of Educational Psychology, 29,* 384–389.

Rounds, J., & Tracey, T. J. (1993). Prediger's dimensional representation of Holland's RIASEC circumplex. *Journal of Applied Psychology, 78,* 875–890.

Russell, J. A. (1980). A circumplex model of affect. *Journal of Personality and Social Psychology, 39,* 1161–1178.

Schiffman, S. S., Reynolds, M. L., & Young, F. W. (1981). *Introduction to multidimensional scaling.* New York: Academic Press.

Schlosberg, H. (1941). A scale for the judgment of facial expressions. *Journal of Experimental Psychology, 29,* 497–510.

Schlosberg, H. (1952). The description of facial expressions in terms of two dimensions. *Journal of Experimental Psychology, 41,* 229–237.

Shepard, R. N. (1978). The circumplex and related topological manifolds in the study of perception. In S. Shye (Ed.), *Theory construction and data analysis in the behavioral sciences* (pp. 29–80). San Francisco: Jossey-Bass.

Stern, G. G. (1970). *People in context.* New York: Wiley.

Stevens, S. S. (1951). Mathematics, measurement, and psycho-physics. In S. S. Stevens (Ed.), *Handbook of experimental psychology* (pp. 1–49). New York: Wiley.

Stevens, S. S. (1975). *Psychophysics.* New York: Wiley.

Thurstone, L. L. (1947). *Multiple factor analysis.* Chicago: University of Chicago Press.

Torgerson, W. S. (1986). Scaling and psychometrika: Spatial and alternative representations of similarity data. *Psychometrika, 51,* 57–63.

Upton, G. J. G., & Fingleton, B. (1989). *Spatial data analysis by example: Categorical and directional data* (Vol. 2). New York: Wiley.

Watson, G. S. (1983). *Statistics on spheres.* New York: Wiley.

Watson, G. S., & Williams, E. J. (1956). On the construction of significance tests on the circle and the sphere. *Biometrika, 43,* 344–352.

Wherry, R. J., Sr. (1984). *Contributions to correlational analysis.* Orlando, FL: Academic Press.

Wiggins, J. S. (1973). *Personality and prediction: Principles of personality assessment.* Reading, MA: Addison-Wesley.

Wiggins, J. S. (1979). A psychological taxonomy of trait-descriptive terms: The interpersonal domain. *Journal of Personality and Social Psychology, 37,* 395–412.

Wiggins, J. S., Trapnell, P., & Phillips, N. (1988). Psychometric and geometric characteristics of the Revised Interpersonal Adjective Scales (IAS-R). *Multivariate Behavioral Research, 23,* 517–530.

Woodworth, R. S., & Schlosberg, H. (1954). *Experimental psychology* (Rev. ed.). New York: Henry Holt.

Zar, J. H. (1974). *Biostatistical analysis.* Englewood Cliffs, NJ: Prentice-Hall.

6

INTEGRATION OF CONFIGURATIONAL AND FACTORIAL MODELS FOR FAMILY RELATIONSHIPS AND CHILD BEHAVIOR

EARL S. SCHAEFER

A major goal of this chapter is to persuade students and researchers that systematic use of relatively simple methods can contribute substantially to analysis and integration of psychological domains. The development of parsimonious conceptual models requires a recurring process of analysis and synthesis, differentiation and integration, of relevant concepts. Different researchers often focus on either detailed analysis or integrating synthesis, yet both are essential in developing adequate models for personality research. A precondition for developing an integrating synthesis or conceptual model is definition of a meaningful realm of discourse that provides a basis for developing concepts. Thurstone's (1947) discussion of a domain is paralleled by Guttman's (1954) discussion of a universe as a basis for conceptual integration. The concept of domain implies a limited and specific focus—for example, social and emotional or interpersonal behavior. The concept of a universe implies a more comprehensive realm—for example, the realm of personality or adaptive behavior. Anal-

I gratefully acknowledge that my professor, Maurice Lorr, taught me factor analysis and referred me to Guttman's paper on the circumplex. I also gratefully acknowledge my collaborators in conceptualization and measurement—Richard Q. Bell, Leo Droppelman, and May Aaronson at the National Institute of Mental Health; Alex Kalverboer at the University of Groningen, the Netherlands; and Marianna Edgerton and Charles K. Burnett at the University of North Carolina at Chapel Hill.

133

yses of the domain of social and emotional behavior reveal a two-dimensional circumplex model. However, combined analyses of social and emotional behavior and academic competence reveal a three-dimensional spherical configuration that integrates personality research.

METHODS FOR CONCEPTUALIZATION, MEASUREMENT, AND INTEGRATION

The Process of Conceptualization and Measurement

The definition of a domain guides selection of a sample of concepts and of behaviors to be included in a conceptual model. Schaefer, Bell, and Bayley (1959) developed scales for many maternal individual characteristics as well as material behaviors directed toward the child. In developing a model for maternal behavior (Schaefer, 1959), only a mother's behaviors *toward* her child were included. In developing a circumplex model for child behavior, initially only social and emotional or interpersonal behaviors were included (Schafer, 1961). In a more comprehensive conceptualization of the child's classroom behavior, concepts for a child's academic competence were added that yielded a spherical model for adaptive behavior.

The development of homogeneous scales consisting of sets of trait actions or prototypical behaviors often yields efficient measures for empirical research. Selecting traits to be measured may be guided both by the research literature on the domain and by expert judgment of the relevance of each trait. From a collection of observable behaviors that are relevant for a domain, a scale for a trait may be developed from a group of similar or related behaviors. Scales also can be developed for constructs by writing a set of related trait actions (Furfey, 1926). In research on various domains, my colleagues and I developed sets of 20 to 64 traits, each defined by between five and ten specific behaviors. Self-report scales typically require a larger sample of specific behaviors—in other words, ten or more—than ratings by observers—in other words, five or more—to achieve internal consistency reliability. Of course, the higher the reliability of measures to be integrated by a conceptual model, the more stable their location within a configuration or factor structure.

Behavior items should be short, simple descriptions of observable behaviors that have adequate distributions and variability for the samples to be studied. The items to be included in a scale should describe related or similar behaviors that are substantially intercorrelated. Reliability of a scale for a specific sample is influenced both by the number and intercorrelations of the items and by the variability of the trait within the sample to which it is applied. Poor distributions and low variability of pathological behavior items, when applied to population samples, often result in low scale reliability and poor measurement within the normal range of behavior.

Although an individual researcher could carry out the process of concept and scale development for a specified domain, I have found that a research partnership or team is both productive and enjoyable. Consensus in definition of a domain, in selecting traits relevant for the domain, and in selecting and writing specific behaviors that define a trait results in rapid development of concepts and of reliable scales for measurement of the concepts. A systematic team approach to concept and scale development provides a basis for subsequent development of a conceptual model for a domain. A conceptual model derived from less systematically developed sets of behavior items or scales is often incomplete or unclear.

Methods for Developing a Conceptual Model From Scale Intercorrelations

The process of hierarchical integration, which begins with developing items that are integrated by scales, typically has been continued by factor analysis of scale intercorrelations. Thurstone's (1947) plots of factor loadings for two- and three-factor analyses yielded configurations that revealed the similarity of scales. Thurstone's (1947) goal in plotting a configuration was to rotate factors to simple structure—in other words, interpretable factors. In contrast, Guttman's (1954) radex theory emphasized a goal of organizing an order of neighboring among variables determined by intercorrelations that reveal their shared variance. Guttman emphasized the order of neighboring or configuration that integrates a set of related measures as contrasted to Thurstone's emphasis on identification of relatively independent dimensions.

A simple method for developing an order of neighboring is to place each measure included in a correlation matrix adjacent to the measure with which it is most highly correlated. Frequently an A, B, C, D order can be generated, which reveals systematic changes in degree of correlation among measures.

A circumplex ordering also can be generated from a correlation matrix for a domain by plotting correlations of each measure with two measures that have zero or low correlations with one another. This method is similar to plotting factor loadings for a two-dimensional factor analysis. Although a factor analysis would yield more precise locations, a plot of the correlations of all measures with two relatively independent measures will yield a similar order of neighboring. Reorganization of the correlation matrix based on an order of neighboring typically reveals a highly ordered set of intercorrelations.

Multidimensional scaling analysis (Kruskal & Wish, 1977; Shepard, Romney, & Nerlove, 1972) provides a direct way of generating values for a spatial plot of a conceptual domain. For a two-dimensional plot of three bipolar dimensions, it is necessary to invert negative measures. For example, a high negative correlation between altruism and hostility, after inversion of the negative scale, reveals that altruism and low hostility are similar or related measures that are plotted in the same sector of a configuration. A multidimensional scaling analysis of a three-dimensional space, after inversion of negative measures, can be plotted on a flat surface. A spatial plot of interrelationships of measures is a more economical presentation of relationships among concepts than a verbal description, intercorrelations, or factor loadings.

The process of conceptualization, measurement, and integration of a domain yields a hierarchical analysis of specific behaviors, traits, dimensions, and an ordered configuration. The process of abstraction from observable behaviors, to verbal description, to quantitative measures, to statistical analyses of intercorrelations, and to spatial representation of relationships among measures yields a parsimonious integration of a conceptual domain. Conceptual models derived from these processes provide a basis for further research, for integration of empirical studies, and for theoretical analyses. Salient concepts and measures selected to sample sectors of the domain can provide marker variables for inclusion in studies of more comprehensive sets of concepts for an extended domain. For example, research that complemented a circular configuration of social and emotional behaviors with scales for intelligence and motivation yielded a spherical model for the universe of adaptive behavior.

DEVELOPMENT OF HIERARCHICAL CONFIGURATIONAL MODELS

Development of Circumplex and Spherical Models for Maternal Behavior

Quantification of notes on maternal behavior from the Berkeley Growth Study resulted in the development of the Maternal Behavior Research Instrument (Schaefer et al., 1959). The concepts and behaviors of this method were influenced by work on the Parent Attitude Research Instrument (Schaefer & Bell, 1958), by knowledge of research on parent behavior, and by the extensive notes on Bayley's (1933) observations of maternal behavior during testing sessions with their infants during the first 3 years. Three raters, after reading the set of observations on each of 56 mothers, rated 32 concepts, each of which were defined by several specific trait actions. After eliminating trait–actions that were not rated or showed little variability and reliability, the several trait–actions for each concept were summed for each of the three raters. Interrater reliabilities for the three combined ratings varied from .89 for the scale of ignoring the child to .76 for intrusiveness.

The 18 scales that describe behaviors of mothers toward their children were included in the development of the circumplex model for maternal behavior. Guttman's (1954) paper on radex theory suggested the development of an order of neighboring for the 18 scales as determined by their intercorrelations. A plot of the correlations of all scales with the scales of autonomy and positive evaluation initially revealed a circular ordering. The two-dimensional ordering was confirmed by a factor analysis (Schaefer, 1959). The empirical order was generalized by the hypothetical circumplex of 14 maternal behavior concepts (shown in Figure 1). A circumplex organization of ratings derived from interviews with a sample of the same mothers during their children's adolescence were also rated and organized into an identical two-dimensional circumplex order.

Becker (1964) subsequently proposed a three-dimensional model of warmth versus hostility, permissiveness versus strictness, and calm detachment versus anxious emotional involvement. Schaefer's (1965b) factor analysis of children's reports of parent behavior (Schaefer, 1965a) revealed

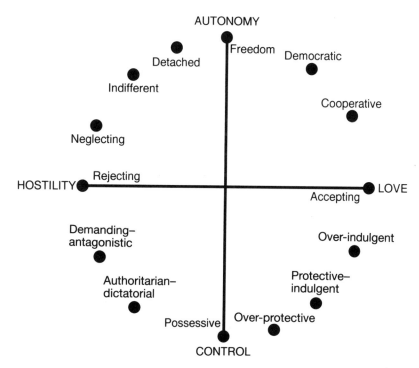

Figure 1. Circumplex model of maternal behavior. From "A circumplex model for maternal behavior," Earl S. Schaefer, 1959, *Journal of Abnormal and Social Psychology, 59*, 232. Copyright by the American Psychological Association. Reprinted with permission.

CONFIGURATIONAL AND FACTORIAL MODELS   137

a two-dimensional circular order of neighboring among scales from encouraging sociability and independent thinking, to positive evaluation and expression of affection, to protectiveness and possessiveness, to intrusiveness, to nagging and negative evaluation, to neglect and ignoring. The factor analysis also identified a third dimension of lax versus firm control that suggested a spherical model for parental behavior.

Development of a Two-Dimensional Circumplex Model for Marital and Adult Parent–Child Relationships

Research on husband–wife relationships provided further evidence of a two-dimensional circular ordering of interpersonal behavior. Factor analysis of items describing spouses' perceptions of their mates' behavior toward themselves (Schaefer & Edgerton, 1979) revealed two major dimensions of autonomy versus control and relatedness versus hostile detachment (Schaefer & Burnett, 1987). Factor analyses of brief scales for different sectors of this two-dimensional space in a second sample revealed an order of neighboring from relatedness, to acceptance, to autonomy for positive scales and from hostile detachment, to hostile control, to control for negative scales.

Factor analysis of an augmented version of the Autonomy and Relatedness Inventory (Schaefer, Edgerton, & Burnett, 1992) confirmed a two-dimensional circumplex organization of (a) self disclosure, affection, and relatedness versus hostile detachment and withdrawal of relationship, (b) autonomy and respect for privacy versus control and hostile control. Listening and acceptance shared variance with both factors of autonomy versus control and relatedness versus hostile detachment.

Women's descriptions of their mother's behavior toward themselves also yielded a circumplex order. In reports of relationships between adults, acceptance is correlated with both autonomy and relatedness reflecting interpersonal needs for both loving involvement and for independence and individuality. These needs vary during childhood from an infancy need for loving involvement to an adolescent need for autonomy. Although an optimal parent–child relationship during infancy is involvement with acceptance, with increasing maturity, both adolescents and adults value autonomy as well as loving involvement. Loving acceptance as opposed to hostile rejection is a major dimension throughout the life span.

Development of a Circumplex Model for Child Behavior

The two-dimensional circumplex model for maternal behavior motivated the search for a parallel model for child social and emotional behavior. Initially correlations among teacher ratings of 13-year-old children (McDonough, 1929) and of nursery school children (Richards & Simons,

1941) were organized into a two-dimensional circumplex model (Schaefer, 1961). Both studies reveal a dimension of kindness–sympathy and a second dimension of gregariousness–sociability versus self-consciousness–social apprehensiveness, with other traits sharing variance with both dimensions. The studies were generalized by a circumplex model for social and emotional behavior (Figure 2).

This model is similar to previous two-dimensional conceptualizations of personality, including the four temperaments (Allport, 1937), the interpersonal circle (Leary, 1957) and Osgood, Suci, and Tannenbaum's (1957) two principle dimensions for the description of persons. Schaefer (1961) concluded that studies using different methods and conceptual schemes yield similar circumplex organizations of social and emotional behavior. Further evidence for the circumplex model was provided by Becker and Krug's (1964) organization of a number of empirical studies of child behavior.

The Classroom Behavior Checklist was developed by Schaefer and Leo Droppelman (1962) for teacher ratings of child social and emotional behavior. Seventeen scales, consisting of five to nine specific behaviors,

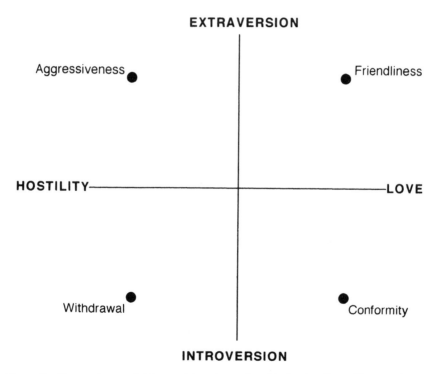

Figure 2. Circumplex model for social and emotional behavior. From "Converging conceptual models for maternal behavior and child behavior," Earl S. Schaefer, 1961. In John C. Glidwell (Ed.), *Parental Attitudes and Child Behavior*, 137. Copyright by Charles C. Thomas, Springfield, IL, 1961. Reprinted with permission.

yielded mean internal consistency reliabilities of .86 for boys and .77 for girls. Plots of factor loadings revealed a two-dimensional circumplex order. The two major dimensions of consideration versus cruelty–resentfulness and of verbal expressiveness–gregariousness versus withdrawal–self-consciousness replicated the circumplex framework of earlier studies.

Development of a Circumplex Model for Diagnostic Constructs

Robert Plutchik suggested we collaborate in a systematic study of the relationships of diagnostic constructs to emotions and traits. The selection of trait concepts was guided by a circumplex organization of trait terms used to integrate data on child behavior in the Berkeley Growth Study (Schaefer & Bayley, 1963). Plutchik (1962) selected a set of emotion terms from his studies and together we selected a set of diagnostic constructs. Experienced clinicians were asked to rate the extent to which each diagnostic construct implied the presence of each of the sample of traits and emotions. Intercorrelations of diagnostic constructs across the ratings of traits and emotions and of the traits and emotions across the set of diagnostic constructs were factor analyzed on the basis of data from two independent sets of clinicians. These analyses yielded replicated two-dimensional circumplex orders for traits and emotions and for diagnostic constructs. The circumplex ordering integrated the traits and emotions and confirmed earlier circumplex models for social and emotional behavior. The two-dimensional circumplex ordering of diagnostic constructs derived from their implications for traits is shown in Figure 3. The results supported ". . . the hypothesis that emotion, trait, and diagnostic signs form a conceptually differentiated but highly integrated system of interconnected signs" (Schaefer & Plutchik, 1966, p. 409).

Multifactor Analyses of Child Adaptive Behavior

The Classroom Behavior Inventory was revised and extended for use in the Netherlands with Alex Kalvenboer (Schaefer, Droppelman, & Kalverboer, 1965). Scales were added to obtain data on hyperkinetic, distractible behavior. The 29 scales of 5 to 11 specific behaviors had a median internal consistency reliability of .81, with a range from .68 to .94. A rotated factor analysis of the scale scores replicated factors of hostility and extroversion and revealed a third factor of hyperactivity and distractibility versus conscientiousness. An orthographic projection of the three factors revealed a spherical configuration with a sector of maladjustment that differentiated hostile from hyperactive behavior.

Schaefer, Aaronson, and Burgoon (1967) extended the conceptual scheme to provide a more detailed analysis of classroom behavior. Sixty-

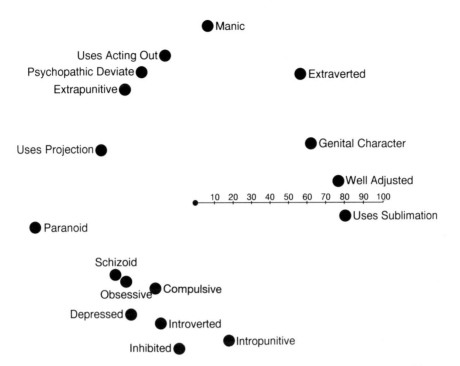

Figure 3. Circumplex organization of diagnostic constructs. From "Interrelationships of emotions, traits, and diagnostic constructs," Earl S. Schaefer and Robert Plutchik, 1966. *Psychological Reports, 18,* 408. Copyright 1966 by C. H. Ammons and R. B. Ammons, Eds., Pubs. Reprinted with permission.

four 5-item scales were developed with a median internal consistency reliability of .86 and a range from .73 to .96. A factor analysis of data on 153 students replicated three major factors of extroversion versus introversion, considerateness versus hostility, and task-orientation versus distractibility. The factor of extroversion included scales of verbal expressiveness, gregariousness, friendliness to teacher, and cheerfulness versus depression, social withdrawal, submissiveness, and self-consciousness. The factor of task-orientation included scales of perseverance, conscientiousness, attentiveness, concentration, methodicalness, academic seriousness, and achievement-orientation versus distractibility, hyperactivity, and inappropriate talkativeness. The factor of hostility was well defined by cruelty, resentfulness, quarrelsomeness, irritability, hostile dominance, covert hostility, suspiciousness, and argumentativeness, with the opposite pole defined by considerateness. The emphasis on negative rather than positive social behavior may be a result of a focus on pathology in research on social adjustment. Subsequent studies with a subset of 12 scales selected to sample the factors replicated factors of extroversion, task-orientation, and hostility.

Complementing the domain of social and emotional behavior with task-oriented versus distractible behavior resulted in a three-dimensional rather than two-dimensional model for classroom behavior.

Research on creativity motivated the development of scales with Marianna Edgerton for curiosity and creativity. Factor analysis of sets of items included in factors of extroversion versus introversion, considerateness versus hostility, and task-orientation versus distractibility, with added items for curiosity and creativity, replicated the earlier factors and revealed a fourth factor of curiosity–creativity items. The hypothesis that if general intelligence can be tested it also can be observed and rated motivated the development of an extensive set of concepts and items of intelligent behavior. The goal of this effort was to develop a brief scale for intelligence rather than to develop reliable scales for components of intelligence. Empirical analyses of ratings on a 70-item form that included marker items for earlier factors revealed a factor of verbal intelligence defined by items of vocabulary, information, comprehension, generalization, and assimilation of ideas. The factor of verbal intelligence was clearly differentiated from previous factors of task-orientation and curiosity–creativity.

A factor analysis of items for scales of extroversion versus introversion, curiosity–creativity, verbal intelligence, task-orientation versus distractibility, and considerateness versus hostility revealed the highest loadings of each item on the factor it was selected to define. Yet a clear pattern was found in item loadings on other factors. The average loading of each set of items of a scale with each of the factors was computed. Extroversion and considerateness items have zero average loadings on the other factor. An order of neighboring was found from curiosity–creativity to verbal intelligence to task-orientation. Verbal intelligence items have very low loadings on both extroversion, and considerateness. Curiosity–creativity items have loadings on extroversion and task-orientation items have loadings on considerateness. Despite the identification of five factors from item intercorrelations, the factor loadings suggest a simple three-dimensional ordered configuration.

The factor analysis motivated development of the hierarchical model for the universe of adaptive behavior of Figure 4. The universe of adaptive behavior, which also might be described as personality, includes domains of social adjustment and academic competence. Each of the domains is subdivided into factors. Each of the factors has been isolated from items describing specific behaviors. This hierarchical model suggests that the domain of social and emotional behavior, although the major focus of social and abnormal psychology, should be complemented by other constructs to yield a more comprehensive model of personality and adaptive behavior (Schaefer, 1981).

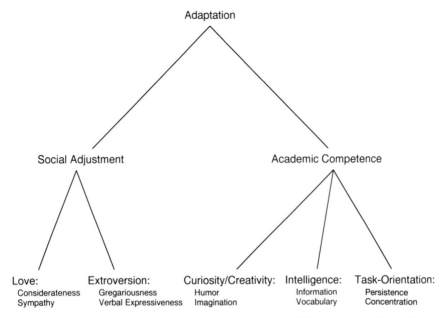

Figure 4. Hierarchical model for adaptive behavior. From "Development of adaptive behavior: Conceptual models and family correlates," Earl S. Schaefer, 1981. In N. J. Begab, H. C. Haywood, and H. L. Garber (Eds.), *Psychological influences on retarded development: Volume I. Issues and theories in development* (p. 163). Copyright by University Park Press, Baltimore, 1981.

Development of a Spherical Model for Child Adaptive Behavior

A factor analysis of scale scores for the Classroom Behavior Inventory confirmed an order of neighboring among scales with three major factors of considerateness versus hostility, extroversion versus introversion, and a factor of academic competence defined by verbal intelligence with substantial loadings for task-orientation and curiosity–creativity. Task-orientation and distractibility also shared variance with the factor of considerateness, and curiosity–creativity shared variance with the factor of extroversion. This factor analysis suggested the generalized spherical model for adaptive behavior of Figure 5 in which scales of extroversion, considerateness, and intelligence define independent dimensions of the model and scales of curiosity–creativity and task-orientation share variance with these dimensions.

The order of neighboring of the scales of the Classroom Behavior Inventory was confirmed by factor analyses of data on additional samples of kindergarten children. A two-dimensional spatial plot of a three-dimensional structure was generated by a multidimensional scaling analysis

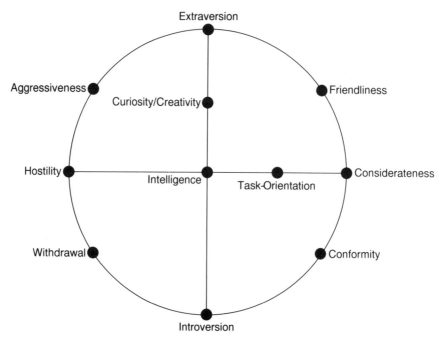

Figure 5. Spherical model of child adaptive behavior. From Earl S. Schaefer and Marianna Edgerton, 1982. "Circumplex and sperical models for child school adjustment and competence." Paper presented at the Annual Meeting of the American Psychological Association, Washington, DC.

of scale intercorrelations using a program developed by Young, Takane, and Lewyckyj (1980). Forest Young (Personal Communication, July 1980) informed me that it is possible to plot three bipolar dimensions on a two-dimensional surface after inversion of scales with negative correlations. Thus hostility, when inverted, is positively correlated with considerateness and can be plotted in that sector. A multidimensional scaling plot of the Classroom Behavior Inventory scales revealed an order of neighboring of low hostility, considerateness, low distractibility, task-orientation, instrumental independence, verbal intelligence, curiosity–creativity, low introversion, and extroversion.

Further replication was provided by a combined analysis of scales of the Classroom Behavior Inventory, a revised and extended version of Bipolar Trait Ratings (Becker & Krug, 1964); a version of Conners (1969) Teacher Rating Scales as revised by Goyette, Conners and Ulrich (1978), which included scales for conduct problems, hyperactivity, depression, anxiety, and apathy–passivity, and global ratings of competence and adjustment. Factor analyses of the 20 scales replicated three factors of considerateness, intelligence, and extroversion. The multidimensional scaling plot of these scales, after inversion of negative scales, revealed the prox-

144   EARL S. SCHAEFER

imity of the different measures of the same construct and of related positive and negative concepts (Figure 6). The proximity of considerateness and cooperativeness with low hostility and low conduct problems reveals bipolarity of positive and negative scales. The sector of academic competence reveals an order of neighboring from task-orientation, to independence, to intelligence, to curiosity–creativity. The global rating of competence has a substantial loading on the factor of academic competence. However, the global rating of adjustment shares variance with each of the three major factors, although it is most highly related to the factor of considerateness and cooperativeness.

Further replications of this three-dimensional spherical model was provided by a study that integrated scales of the Classroom Behavior Inventory and of the Child Adaptive Behavior Inventory (Schaefer, Edgerton, & Hunter, 1983) that included altruism, antisocial behavior, hyperactivity, academic competence, apathy, asocial behavior, and depression. The factor analysis clearly replicated the dimension of considerateness versus hostility including loadings for altruism and antisocial behavior (Table 1). The factor of academic competence is best defined by scales of verbal intelligence and academic competence. The extroversion versus introversion factor includes loadings on apathy, asocial behavior, and depression.

A multidimensional scaling analysis of the scale scores plus scores for the three orthogonal factors is shown in Figure 7. The sector that includes low hostility, low antisocial behavior, considerateness and altruism neigh-

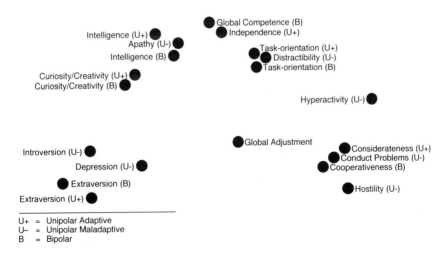

U+ = Unipolar Adaptive
U– = Unipolar Maladaptive
B = Bipolar

Figure 6. Multidimensional scaling analysis plot of multimethod ratings of child behavior. From "A unified conceptual model for academic competence, social adjustment and psychopathology," Earl S. Schaefer, Marianna Edgerton, and Wanda M. Hunter, 1983. Paper presented at the Annual Meeting of the American Psychological Association, Anaheim, CA.

TABLE 1
Factor Structure of Classroom Behavior Inventory and Child Adaptive
Behavior Inventory Scales

		Factor		
Scale	Method	I	II	III
Hostility	CBI	-81	00	-13
Antisocial behavior	CABI	-86	-06	-22
Considerateness	CBI	86	23	13
Altruism	CABI	86	27	21
Hyperactivity	CABI	-89	-34	04
Distractibility	CBI	-77	-47	06
Task-orientation	CBI	69	61	16
Independence	CBI	55	65	15
Academic competence	CABI	28	81	45
Verbal intelligence	CBI	21	84	29
Curiosity–creativity	CBI	11	78	46
Apathy	CABI	-37	-43	-70
Asocial behavior	CABI	-36	-24	-79
Extroversion–introversion	CABI	06	29	85
Depression	CABI	-10	-14	-80

Note. From "Spherical model integrating academic competence with social adjustment and psychopathology," by Earl S. Schaefer, Marianna Edgerton, and Wanda M. Hunter, 1985. Paper presented at the Biennial Meeting of the Society for Research in Child Development, Toronto, Canada. Factor I = considerateness versus hostility; Factor II = academic competence; Factor III = extroversion versus introversion. CBI = Classroom Behavior Inventory; CABI = Child Adaptive Behavior.

bors on the sector of low hyperactivity, low distractibility, task-orientation, and independence. The sector of verbal intelligence, curiosity–creativity, and academic competence also includes the factor of academic competence. Low apathy, extroversion, low asocial behavior, and low depression neighbor on the extroversion factor.

An attempt to differentiate the different sectors of the model and to integrate equivalent concepts for child behavior is shown in Table 2. The order of neighboring of concepts in the model is reflected in the vertical arrangement of concepts. The table suggests that specific combinations of cognition with different types of affect result in different types of conation or motivation. The horizontal groups of related concepts of adaptive behavior, maladaptive behavior, *DSM-III* diagnoses (American Psychiatric Association, 1980), Quay's (1979) types, and Baumrind's (1982) factors illustrate how different constructs, types, and factors might be integrated by the spherical model.

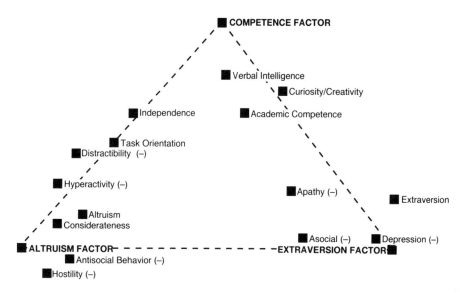

Figure 7. Multidimensional scaling analysis plot of child adaptive behavior scales and factors. From "Spherical model integrating academic competence with social adjustment and psychopathology," Earl S. Schaefer, Marianna Edgerton, and Wanda M. Hunter, 1985. Paper presented at the Biennial Meeting of the Society for Research in Child Development, Toronto, Canada.

DISCUSSION

Models of Parent–Child and Husband–Wife Relationships

Circular and spherical models for parent–child relationships reveal that love and acceptance is a major dimension throughout childhood. During adolescence lax versus firm control is differentiated from psychological control and over-involvement. An early need for relatedness is later complemented by a need for acceptance of individuality and autonomy. Similar analyses of husband–wife relationships reveal that acceptance is related to both relatedness and to respect for autonomy. During the course of development of an individual and a relationship, an initial need for loving involvement and relatedness is later complemented by a need for acceptance of individuality and autonomy. Development of measures and models for teacher–child, therapist–patient, and employer–employee relationships might explore the concepts and dimensions identified in research on family relationships.

Studies of social and emotional behavior reveal a dimension of altruism and considerateness that is similar to the dimension of love–acceptance found in research on family relationships. Very high correlations were found between a mother's perception of her child's behavior toward herself

TABLE 2
Differentiation of Major Regions of the Spherical Model and Integration of Equivalent Concepts for Child Behavior

Domain	Adaptive behavior		Maladaptive behavior	DSM-III diagnoses	Quay (1979)	Baumrind (1982)
Affect I	Considerateness Altruism	(vs.) (vs.)	Hostility Antisocial behavior	Conduct disorder	Conduct disorder	Social responsibility
Conation I	Task-Orientation	(vs.)	Hyperactivity	Attention deficit disorder with hyperactivity	Motor excess	
	Independence–Perseverance	(vs.)	Distractibility		Attention problems–immaturity	
Cognition	Academic competence	(vs.)	Academic incompetence	Mental retardation		Cognitive competence
	Verbal intelligence	(vs.)	Low verbal intelligence			
Conation	Creativity–curiosity	(vs.)	Apathy	Attention deficit disorder without hyperactivity	Attention problems–immaturity	
Affect II	Extraversion Gregariousness Cheerfulness	(vs.) (vs.) (vs.)	Introversion Asocial behavior Depression	Anxiety disorder	Anxiety–withdrawal	Social assertiveness

Note. From "Spherical model integrating academic competence with social adjustment and psychopathology," by Earl S. Schaefer, Marianna Edgerton, and Wanda M. Hunter, 1985. Paper presented at the Biennial Meeting of the Society for Research in Child Development, Toronto, Canada.

and her perception of the child's social and emotional behavior (Schaefer, Sayers, St. Clair, & Burnett, 1987). Thus a person's perception of another's personality is highly related to their perception of the other's relationship with self. An observation that a mother has a different relationship with each of her children is related to the fact that a person has different relationships with different persons. Further research on relationships and on personality that would both differentiate and integrate these domains is needed.

Integrating the Spherical Model for Adaptive Behavior With the Five-Factor Model of Personality

Research on teacher ratings of classroom behavior by Digman (1989) identified five robust trait dimensions of extroversion versus introversion, friendliness versus hostility, conscientiousness, neuroticism versus emotional stability, and intellect. Digman's (1989) first two dimensions correspond to the two dimensions of the interpersonal circle (Leary, 1957) and also to the two dimensions of the circumplex model for social and emotional behavior (Schaefer, 1961). The Digman (1989) factor of anxiety or neuroticism, defined by ratings of fearful, tense, and concerned, appears to be an intrapersonal rather than an interpersonal factor. The Big Five factors of conscientiousness and intellect are similar to factors of task-orientation and intelligence. Differentiation of curiosity–creativity from intelligence in my research may be related to variations in the definition of intellect among studies of the Big Five dimensions of personality (Digman 1990). Thus the spherical model generated by multidimensional scaling analysis integrates four of the five major factors that have been identified in personality research (Digman, 1990; Goldberg, 1993). Multidimensional scaling analyses of other empirical studies of personality are needed to confirm the integration of factors by a spherical configuration. However, Digman's (1990) observation that identical factors are found for adults and children suggests that research on adult personality would replicate the spherical model for adaptive behavior.

Toward Positive Conceptualizations of Interpersonal and Adaptive Behavior

The identification of constructs and measures of adaptive as well as maladaptive behavior in development of the spherical model and in the converging research on five major dimensions of personality supports the feasibility of a positive conceptualization of personality. Boneau's (1990) identification of major concepts in different fields of psychology reveals that abnormal and personality psychology constructs are predominantly of pathological behavior. Constructs of social and developmental psychology also emphasize negative behavior but include more positive behaviors. Behavior modification research suggests that teaching parents and teachers to respond to a child's positive behavior tends to increase the child's positive behavior and decrease negative behavior. Perhaps a shift in focus in psychology to concepts describing wellness and competence rather than pathology would contribute to mental health and competence. Examination of Boneau's (1990) lists of constructs revealed that both developmental and personality psychology tend to include concepts both for social and emotional behavior and for academic competence in contrast to the emphasis on social and emotional behavior in abnormal and social psychology. It would be useful if psychologists, teachers, parents, and policy makers would emphasize positive constructs for both interpersonal behavior and competence.

Feasibility of Further Integration of Personality Research

Success in developing reliable measures of many abstract traits by specifying observable trait–actions suggests the feasibility of further scale development. Conceptualization, measurement, and integration of a broad array of traits that complement the traits of the currently identified dimensions are needed to explore new dimensions of personality. Using multidimensional scaling analysis to integrate reliable measures for major constructs would contribute to further integrating personality research. The repeated identification of five major factors of personality and the development of circular and spherical models for interpersonal and adaptive behavior suggest the feasibility of continued integration of research on interpersonal behavior, adaptive behavior, personality, and psychopathology.

REFERENCES

Allport, G. W. (1937). *Personality: A psychological interpretation*. New York: Holt.

American Psychiatric Association. (1980). *Diagnostic and statistical manual of mental disorders* (3rd ed.). Washington, DC: Author.

Baumrind, D. (1982). Are androgynous individuals more effective persons and parents? *Child Development, 53,* 44–75.

Bayley, N. (1933). Mental growth during the first three years: A developmental study of 61 children by repeated tests. *Genetic Psychology Monographs, 14,* 1–92.

Becker, W. C. (1964). Consequences of different kinds of parental discipline. In M. L. Hoffman & L. W. Hoffman (Eds.), *Review of Child Development Research* (pp. 169–208). New York: Russell Sage Foundation.

Becker, W. C., & Krug, R. S. (1964). A circumplex model for social behavior in children. *Child Development, 35,* 371–396.

Boneau, C. A. (1990). Psychological literacy: A first approximation. *American Psychologist, 45,* 891–900.

Conners, C. K. (1969). A teacher rating scale for use in drug studies with children. *American Journal of Psychiatry, 126,* 152–156.

Digman, J. M. (1989). Five robust trait dimensions: Development, stability and utility. *Journal of Personality, 75,* 195–214.

Digman, J. M. (1990). Personality structure in emergence of the Five-Factor Model. *Annual Review of Psychology, 41,* 417–440.

Furfey, P. H. (1926). An improved rating scale technology. *Journal of Educational Psychology, 17,* 45–48.

Goldberg, L. R. (1993). The structure of phenotypic personality traits. *American Psychologist, 48,* 26–34.

Goyette, C. H., Conners, C. K., & Ulrich, R. F. (1978). Normative data on revised Conners' parent and teacher rating scales. *Journal of Abnormal Child Psychology, 6,* 221–236.

Guttman, L. (1954). A new approach to factor analysis: The radex. In P. F. Lazarsfeld (Ed.), *Mathematical thinking in the social sciences* (pp. 258–348). Glencoe, IL: Free Press.

Kruskal, J. B., & Wish, M. (1977). *Multidimensional scaling.* Sage University Paper series on quantitative applications in the social sciences, Series no. 07–011. Beverly Hills and London: Sage.

Leary, T. F. (1957). *Interpersonal diagnoses of personality: A functional theory and methodology for personality evaluation.* New York: Ronald Press.

McDonough, M. R. (1929). *The empirical study of character: Part II. Studies in psychology and psychiatry.* Washington, DC: Catholic University Press.

Osgood, C. E., Suci, G. J., & Tannenbaum, P. H. (1957). *The measurement of meaning.* Urbana: University of Illinois Press.

Plutchik, R. (1962). *The emotions: Facts, theories, and a new model.* New York: Random House.

Quay, H. C. (1979). Classification. In H. C. Quay & J. S. Werry (Eds.), *Psychopathological disorders of childhood* (pp. 3–42). New York: John Wiley.

Richards, T. W., & Simons, M. P. (1941). The Fels Child Behavior Scales. *Genetic Psychology Monographs, 24,* 259–309.

Schaefer, E. S. (1959). A circumplex model for maternal behavior. *Journal of Abnormal and Social Psychology, 59,* 226–235.

Schaefer, E. S. (1961). Converging conceptual models for maternal behavior and for child behavior. In J. C. Glidwell (Ed.), *Parental attitudes and child behavior* (pp. 124–146). Springfield, IL: Charles C. Thomas.

Schaefer, E. S. (1965a). Children's reports of parental behavior: An inventory. *Child Development, 36,* 413–424.

Schaefer, E. S. (1965b). A configurational analysis of children's reports of parental behavior. *Journal of Consulting Psychology, 29,* 552–557.

Schaefer, E. S. (1981). Development of adaptive behavior: Conceptual models and family correlates. In M. J. Begab, H. C. Heywood, & H. L. Garber (Eds.), *Psychosocial influences on retarded development: Vol. 1. Issues and theories in development* (pp. 155–178). Baltimore: University Park Press.

Schaefer, E. S., Aaronson, M. R., & Burgoon, B. (1967). *Classroom Behavior Inventory.* Unpublished form.

Schaefer, E. S., & Bayley, N. (1963). Maternal behavior, child behavior and their intercorrelations from infancy through adolescence. *Monographs of the Society for Research in Child Development, 28* (3 Whole no. 87).

Schaefer, E. S., & Bell, R. Q. (1958). Development of a parental attitude research instrument. *Child Development, 29,* 339–361.

Schaefer, E. S., Bell, R. Q., & Bayley, N. (1959). Development of a maternal behavior research instrument. *Journal of Genetic Psychology, 95,* 83–104.

Schaefer, E. S., & Burnett, C. K. (1987). Stability and predictability of women's marital relationships and demoralization. *Journal of Personality and Social Psychology, 53,* 1129–1136.

Schaefer, E. S., & Droppelman, L. (1962). *Classroom Behavior Checklist.* Unpublished form.

Schaefer, E. S., Droppelman, L. F., & Kalverboer, A. F. (1965). Development of a classroom behavior checklist and factor analyses of children's school behavior in the United States and the Netherlands. Paper presented at the meeting of the Society for Research in Child Development, Minneapolis, MN.

Schaefer, E. S., & Edgerton, M. (1979). *Marital Autonomy and Relatedness Inventory.* Unpublished form.

Schaefer, E. S., & Edgerton, M. (1982, August). *Circumplex and spherical models for child school adjustment and competence.* Paper presented at the annual meeting of the American Psychological Association, Washington, DC.

Schaefer, E. S., Edgerton, M., & Burnett, C. K. (1992). *Revised Marital Autonomy and Relatedness Inventory.* Unpublished form.

Schaefer, E. S., Edgerton, M., & Hunter, W. M. (1983, August). *Unified model for academic competence, social adjustment, and psychopathology.* Paper presented at the annual meeting of the American Psychological Association, Anaheim, CA.

Schaefer, E. S., & Plutchik, R. (1966). Interrelationships of emotions, traits, and diagnostic constructs. *Psychological Reports, 18,* 399–410.

Schaefer, E. S., Sayers, S. L., St. Clair, K. L., & Burnett, C. K. (1987, August). *Mothers' reports of child relationship with mother and of child adaptive behavior.* Paper presented at annual meeting of the American Psychological Association, New York.

Shepard, R. N., Romney, A. K., & Nerlove, S. B. (1972). *Multidimensional scaling: Theory and applications in behavior sciences* (2 vols.). New York: Seminar Press.

Thurstone, L. L. (1947). *Multiple factor analysis*. Chicago: University of Chicago Press.

Young, F. W., Takane, Y., & Lewyckyj, R. (1980). ALSCAL: A multidimesional scaling package with several individual differences options. *American Statistician, 34*, 117–118.

7

PERSONALITY SET WITHIN AN OCTAGONAL MODEL OF RELATING

JOHN BIRTCHNELL

My interest in a circumplex model grew out of a preoccupation with the relationship between clinical depression and psychological dependence (Birtchnell, 1984; Birtchnell, Deahl, & Falkowski, 1991). This led me to speculate about the nature of dependence (Birtchnell, 1988, 1991a, 1991b). I came to two important conclusions: (a) that it is necessary to distinguish between normal and pathological dependence; and (b) that dependence is made up of two separate components, one concerned with seeking closeness and one with relating from a position of needfulness. The importance of the first will become apparent later in the chapter. The importance of the second is more immediately apparent. It seemed that these two components should form the extremes of two dimensions (Birtchnell, 1987). In the light of Bowlby's (1969) attachment theory, I called the first *attachment versus detachment*. In naming the second (*directiveness versus receptiveness*) I drew on two sources: Ray's (1976) construct of directiveness, "the desire or tendency to impose one's own will on others" (p. 314), and Fromm's (1947) concept of the receptive orientation, the tendency to take what one wants "from an outside source" (p. 67).

A former colleague suggested a link between these ideas and the Interpersonal Style Inventory of Lorr and Youniss (1973). I sent the 1987 paper to Lorr who wrote, "As I view it, your system resembles Leary's and Wiggins' Interpersonal Circle. Am I correct?" (personal communication,

155

May 1987). At that time, I had not heard of the interpersonal circle but, on reading Leary's (1957) book, I readily saw the resemblance. I sent the paper to Wiggins, who wrote back, "I continue to be amazed at the number of people who have proposed similar systems quite independently of each other" (personal communication, November 1987). Argyle (1972), the British authority on interpersonal behavior, had proposed the dimensions of affiliative versus hostile and dominant versus dependent. I sent the paper to him and asked his view on the interpersonal circle. He replied, "I don't think that anyone reads the Leary book any more, but those two dimensions are very well established in social psychology, as the result of numerous factor analyses" (personal communication, May 1987). I approached Rutter, the British authority on relationships in children. He said that, in the 1960s, Schaefer had proposed similar dimensions, but they were no longer used. Blackburn (1988), a forensic psychologist, appeared to be the only British enthusiast for the circle. He considered that its circularity provides a realistic representation of the way that personality disorders merge into one another.

ALTERNATIVE TO THE INTERPERSONAL CIRCLE

Arriving at a system that resembled the interpersonal circle from this unusual starting point gave me certain advantages. Although I was reassured that the system shared certain features with the circle, I considered myself under no obligation to accept all of the principles that have come to be associated with the circle. The attachment–detachment dimension seemed to fit more comfortably into existing theory than did that of love–hate or affiliation–hostility. However, because Bowlby (1977) had defined attachment as "attaining or retaining proximity to some undifferentiated and preferred individual who is usually conceived of as stronger and/or wiser" (p. 203), I could see that it incorporated the same two components as dependence. Therefore I needed to rename the dimension *closeness–distance*. It is interesting to note that this *affiliative* dimension is always represented as the *x* axis. This is particularly appropriate, because moving toward or away from people is a horizontal activity. The second dimension is always represented as the *y* axis. I considered that this dimension required a name that reflected its verticality and selected *upperness* to describe relating from above downward and *lowerness* to describe relating from below upward (Birtchnell, 1990). Because both axes now carried a spatial connotation, I called the associated theory *spatial theory*. I have used the term *axes* rather than *dimension* because, in certain respects (see below), the axes do not behave like dimensions.

It seemed appropriate to consider human relating to be derivable from and in continuity with the relating of all other animal forms and to envisage the close and distant and upper and lower relating of humans as being extensions of similar behavior in animals (Birtchnell, 1994, 1996). It was necessary that the names I used should be simple enough to cover the relating of all animal forms and that they were sufficiently generic to incorporate the entire range of relating behaviors subsumed within them. The names of the interpersonal circle are less satisfactory from this point of view. Loving and hating are not generalizable to all animal forms and are only one aspect of being close and distant. Dominating and submitting are more appropriate to animal than to human behavior, and they are only one of many possible ways of being upper and lower. Because our inherent tendencies to relate in certain ways would not have survived had they not carried certain advantages, it was concluded that the behavior associated with each of the four positions should be considered advantageous to the individual. Therefore, being close should be neither better nor worse than being distant, and being upper should be neither better nor worse than being lower.

The benefits to animals of the four main positions have been fully described elsewhere (Birtchnell, 1994, 1996). In brief, animals stay together for more effective hunting and defence against predators; they separate to explore new environments and protect their territories. They assume an upper position in order to kill or intimidate rivals and prey and to protect their young; they assume a lower position in order to yield to those who intimidate them and to gain the protection and nourishment of parents. Although humans still do attack, defend, and yield to intimidation, it seems that most upper and lower forms of behavior have evolved from the parenting and being parented features of animal behavior, as we will see in the next section.

As with the interpersonal circle, it has proved useful to introduce intermediate positions into my system, though, to a greater extent than with the circle, the emphasis remains on the four main positions. As with the original circle, the characteristics of the intermediate positions constitute a blending of those of the positions on either side of them, and this is brought out in the naming of the positions. The arrangement of the four main positions and the four intermediate positions resembles the interpersonal circle, but because of a number of differences between spatial theory and interpersonal theory, it was deemed preferable to name the arrangement the *interpersonal octagon* (Figure 1).

There are some interesting differences between the two axes of the octagon, which to some extent have been acknowledged as applying to the dimensions of the interpersonal circle. Whereas distance undoubtedly is the opposite of closeness, lowerness is more the complement of upperness. In order for there to be closeness between two people or distance between two people, both have to occupy the same pole—both either have to be close or both have to be distant. In order for there to be an upper to lower

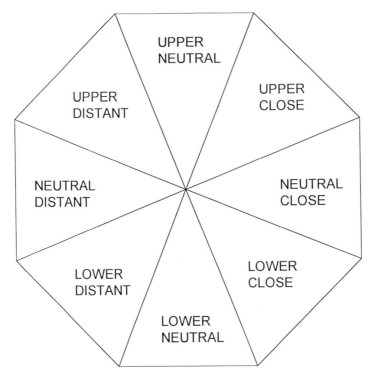

Figure 1. The interpersonal octagon. Reprinted from *How Humans Relate: A New Interpersonal Theory* (p. 59) by J. Birtchnell, 1996, Hove, England: Psychology Press. Reprinted by permission.

relationship, each person has to occupy a different pole, one the upper and one the lower. Although closeness might be conceived of as moving toward the other and distance moving away, in terms of the space between two people, there is no definable point at which a person ceases to be close and starts to be distant. However, although there can be degrees of upperness or lowerness, the distinction between them also can be a categorical one. As a person drops in status, there has to come a point when she or he ceases to be upper in relation to the other and starts to be lower.

Each octant has been given a two-word name, which can be abbreviated to two letters. The first word always refers to the vertical axis and the second to the horizontal axis. When, with the four main positions, there is no input from the second axis, the word *neutral* is inserted. On the horizontal axis it is relatively easy to define neutral closeness and neutral distance without reference to any vertical considerations. On the vertical axis it is more difficult to define a pure form of upperness or lowerness, which is clearly delineated from the intermediate positions that lie to either side of it. Upper close merges into upper neutral, which merges into upper distant, and lower close merges into lower neutral, which merges into lower distant. The dividing lines can only be arbitrary. However, the behavior of the lower close, lower neutral, and lower distant octants tends to complement that of the upper close, upper neutral, and upper distant octants. The difference results from the fact that whereas closeness can run continuously into distance, the distinction between upper and lower can be a categorical one.

One difference between spatial theory and classical interpersonal theory is concerned with motivation. Leary (1957) considered that all the social, emotional, and interpersonal activities of an individual could be understood as attempts to avoid anxiety or to establish or maintain self-esteem. This idea percolated down from Freud, via Horney (1937) and Sullivan (1953). A central feature of spatial theory is that interpersonal behavior is not based on a negative flight *from* something but rather on a positive move *toward* something. The four main positions are sometimes referred to as interpersonal objectives. They are like hungers in that people experience needs for them, and their behavior is directed toward satisfying these needs. That which is attained as a result of such behavior is called a *state of relatedness*. Unlike hungers, interpersonal objectives can be met only by interaction with another person or other people. That person, or those people, are also seeking to satisfy interpersonal needs. A consequence of this is that success or failure in attaining a state of relatedness depends on the extent to which interacting people are able to satisfy each others needs.

THE DIFFERENCE BETWEEN ADAPTIVE AND MALADAPTIVE RELATING

Although we may be born with general inclinations toward the four states, during our psychological development, we come to experience them, develop a liking for them, and acquire competencies that enable us to attain them and confidence that we can attain them. People who have a complete range of competencies are called *versatile*. As and when circumstances require it, they are able to be close, distant, upper, or lower. The relating of competent and confident people is called *positive* (adaptive). A feature of positive relating is a concern and respect for the relating needs of others. Lack of competence—or confidence—is manifest in a number of ways. People may be fearful and avoidant of a particular state and function predominantly in the opposite state (e.g., people who fear closeness remain in distance). They may feel insecure in a particular state and fear that they may not be able to hold on to it (e.g., an insecurely close person clings nervously to the person she or he is close to). They may adopt desperate and unscrupulous methods of attaining a particular state (e.g., an insecurely close person may force herself or himself on another and try to prevent the other from getting away). The relating of people who lack competence or confidence is called *negative* (maladaptive). (The distinction drawn between normal and pathological dependence in the chapter's opening paragraph is really that between positive and negative relating.) It has to be emphasised that, because of the interactional nature of relating, negative or maladaptive relating may result from the relating behavior of the other. A person may be insecurely close because the other is trying to break away, or a person may be insecurely lower because the person on whom she or he depends is unreliable.

Classical interpersonal theory offers a quite different explanation for the distinction between adaptive and maladaptive relating. Here again Leary (1957), whose view prevails to the present time, was influenced by Sullivan (1953), who considered there to be a continuity from normal interpersonal behavior to pathological. For Sullivan, the difference between adaptive and maladaptive behavior was one of extremity. The interpersonal circle was constructed to locate what Leary called *consistent moderation* at the center and *the psychiatric extremes* at the periphery. The gradient from the center to the periphery was called the *intensity*. The Interpersonal Check List (LaForge & Suczek, 1955), intended as a measure of what the circle represents, included four levels of intensity for each of the circle's 16 segments, with one item for each of the first and fourth levels and three for the second and third. The inclusion of a measure of intensity within a circular ordering conformed to what Guttman (1954) called a *radex*.

Spatial theory differs from interpersonal theory in that adaptive (positive) relating is considered to be qualitatively and not quantitatively different from maladaptive (negative) relating. Life would be boring indeed if *adaptiveness* simply meant *moderation*. However close two lovers get, their behavior need never become maladaptive. A man on a life-support machine can be extremely dependent, but such dependence is not maladaptive. For each octant there should be positive and negative forms and such forms should be measured separately, with degrees of extremity for each.

THE OCTAGON AND THE EMOTIONS

The emotions would seem to form an essential part of the processes involved in the regulation of the satisfaction of interpersonal needs. Just as with hunger, the individual would be made aware of the need for a particular state of relatedness, and her or his interpersonal behavior then would be directed toward seeking out such a state. Anticipatory excitement would be aroused at the prospects of attaining the state, and its attainment would be accompanied by contentment or euphoria. The term *bliss* could be used to describe the emotion that accompanies indulgence in a particularly desired state, and there would be a characteristic form of bliss associated with each of the four main positions. When there is danger of a state not being attained or of a state that has been attained being lost, anxiety would be experienced. The loss of a state would give rise to depression. The emotion of anger would be evoked when there was threat of a loss, or there had been an actual loss, but the person felt confident of defending it or of getting it back. Anger would more commonly be associated with the three upper octants, in which the individual has the power to defend or retrieve the state. Hate, however, would be evoked if the state was under threat or had been lost but there was little prospect of defending it or retrieving it. Depression, anger, and hate also would be experienced when the person was being forced into a state she or he did not want. Therefore, the emotions would have the function of registering failures or successes in the attainments of states, and with the possible exception of anger, no emotion would be associated with any particular octant. This approach corresponds closely with Nesse's (1990) evolutionary framework for the emotions.

It has to be acknowledged that under certain circumstances, mood changes could influence relating attitudes and behavior. Birtchnell, Falkowski, and Steffert (1992) showed that patients with a major depressive disorder had significantly higher closeness, distance, and lowerness scores than individuals in the population at large, but that on full recovery from their depression, their scores returned to the levels of individuals in the population. A similar effect has been demonstrated for measures of dependence (Hirschfeld et al., 1989), and it probably applies to personality disorders in general.

A particularly intense form of depression, which Blatt and Shichman (1983) have called *introjective depression*, would seem sometimes to be associated with lowerness. It has largely to do with feelings of guilt and self-blame. Depressed mood, and the associated low self-esteem, would be likely to increase the person's disposition to be self-critical. A particularly intense form of euphoria, frequently associated with mania, may predispose the individual to upperness, and many of the symptoms of mania could be conceived of as negative forms of upperness. It is generally acknowledged that there is a genetic determinant to the liability to swing into certain states of depression and mania (McGuffin & Katz, 1986). When such states arise in this way, it is as though the individual tries to justify experiencing them by adopting appropriate attitudes and forms of behavior.

IS THE OCTAGON A CIRCUMPLEX?

A circumplex is a set of attributes organized in a circular pattern, at regular intervals, around two orthogonal axes. Within such an arrangement, any specific attribute would have its highest correlation with the attributes on either side of it. Its correlations with its more remote neighbors would fall off monotonically to the right and to the left as a function of their sequential separation. In a correlation matrix exhibiting such an arrangement, the highest correlations would be along the principal diagonal. Along any row or column, the correlations would decrease in size until, at a quarter around the circle, there would be zero correlation, and from this point up to the mid-point around the circle, the correlations would become increasingly negative.

From a theoretical standpoint, because the concepts of closeness and distance and upperness and lowerness are simple, easily definable, abstract, and generic; because it seems unlikely that considerations of closeness and distance would be influenced by considerations of upperness and lowerness; because the four intermediate positions are defined in terms of a blending of the positions on either side of them; and because the eight octants are regularly located in a circular arrangement; the octagon should turn out to be a perfect circumplex. However, there are, a number of reasons why this may not be so.

The octagon resembles more closely the Olson circumplex (e.g., Olson, Sprengle, & Russell, 1979) than most other circular systems in that greater emphasis is placed on the four main positions than on the intermediate positions. It must be stressed, however, that the four simple constructs of closeness, distance, upperness, and lowerness contain within them a vast complexity of relating characteristics (Birtchnell, 1996). The testing of circumplexity has relied almost entirely on questionnaire studies which depend on the capacity of participants to assess their relating tendencies and to discriminate between tendencies that are similar, a capacity that may be beyond many people. It may be a fallacy to assume that greater descriptive precision can be obtained by slicing the circumplex pie into ever finer segments. Studies have revealed that the discriminatory power of respondents does not reliably extend beyond octants (Paddock & Nowicki, 1986). Within the octagon, precision is obtained, not by further slicing the pie, but by unpacking each of the four main positions and describing the many forms that each may assume (see Birtchnell, 1996). Because of the extreme complexity of these positions, even when intermediate positions are included, there are distinct limitations to representing each by a small number of items in a questionnaire. The best that can be achieved by a questionnaire approach is to focus on an attitude or form of behavior that might be considered to typify each position.

An important requirement of the circumplex is that, however finely the circumplex pie is sliced, each segment has to be the conceptual opposite of the segment that is immediately opposite it on the circle. It already has been explained that, whereas the poles of the horizontal axis undoubtedly are opposite, those of the vertical axis are more complementary. This complicates the issue of bipolarity. Furthermore, although the two poles of the two main axes of the octagon might, in certain respects, be considered conceptually opposite, it seems to be neither useful nor meaningful to consider the two pairs of opposing intermediate octants (upper close and lower distant and upper distant and lower close) as conceptually opposite. It might be said in passing that, in trying to impose this principal of bipolarity onto the interpersonal circle, a number of researchers, notably Lorr and McNair (1963), Wiggins (1979), and Kiesler (1983), have deviated from its original structure. For example, the upper right quadrant, which in the original circle was, conceptually quite correctly, concerned with teaching, giving, and supporting (a reasonable blending of dominating and loving) has become concerned with sociability.

Perhaps the most important difference between the octagon and most other circular systems is the distinction that is drawn between positive and negative relating. Whereas, in most other circular systems, adaptive and maladaptive forms of relating are considered to exist on a continuum (of intensity) from the center of the circle to the periphery, in the present system they are considered to be qualitatively distinct. Correctly, therefore, there should be a separate octagon for each (see Birtchnell, 1994). If there were an instrument that measured positive relating, the perfectly well-adjusted person would obtain maximum points on all octants, and scoring high on closeness would not be a bar to scoring high on distance also. Thus, there would be no bipolarity. Because there are positive advantages to each pole, moving away from one does not necessarily mean moving toward the other. Losing positive closeness (having satisfactory involvement with others) does not necessarily mean gaining positive distance (being secure in one's own separateness), and losing positive upperness (being in a position to be of benefit to other people) does not mean gaining positive lowerness (being in a position to benefit from the behavior of others).

There *is* an instrument that measures negative relating (see Birtchnell et al., 1992). It is called the Person's Relating to Others Questionnaire (PROQ). It is made up of 96 items, 10 negative and 2 positive for each octant. The positive items were introduced to lighten the negative tone of the questionnaire and normally are not included in the scoring. In a correlation matrix derived from 400 participants, there *were* generally high positive correlations between neighboring octants and progressively lower correlations as the distance between octants increased. In most instances, however, there were not negative correlations with octants on the opposite side. This confirms the general principle that negative relating tends to correlate with negative relating. Highly significant differences were observed between well women and women with personality disorders on octants extending from neutral distant to lower close.

It might be argued that the absence of bipolarity in both its positive and its negative versions precludes the octagon being considered a circular arrangement, though conceptually it would appear to be so. The essence of bipolarity is that scoring high on one pole of an axis has to be associated with scoring low on the opposite pole. What may cause confusion is a failure to distinguish between acts of relating and relating competencies (a term that may be synonymous with personality). In regard to acts of relating, if a person is acting in a close manner she or he cannot, at the same time, be acting in a distant manner, and if she or he is acting in an upper manner, she or he cannot at the same time be acting in a lower manner. Close and distant and upper and lower are therefore strictly bipolar. In terms of competencies, however, a good relater needs to be competent in both poles of both axes, and a bad relater can be, and sometimes is, incompetent in both poles.

It has been suggested (Birtchnell, 1994) that the structure of the classical interpersonal circle may create a false impression of bipolarity. It is considered a disadvantage that, on the horizontal dimension, loving is predominantly a positive form of relating and hating a negative form. A consequence of this, which has existed from the start (Freedman, Leary, Ossorio, & Coffey, 1951) is that the relating characteristics to the left of the circle (boast, reject, punish, hate, complain, distrust, and condemn self) are less acceptable (more negative) than those to the right (teach, give, support, love, cooperate, trust, and admire). Therefore, any bipolarity that may emerge on the horizontal axis may be a result as much of the adaptive–maladaptive dichotomy as of the love–hate dichotomy.

THE USEFULNESS OF THE OCTAGON AS A CONCEPTUAL FRAMEWORK

Relating (i.e., that which one person does to, and derives from, another) may provide the building blocks with which other behavioral constructs (such as personality) are fashioned. Therefore, there is reason to study it in its own right. The conceptual framework of the octagon has relevance for any situation in which relating occurs. Relating can range from momentary episodes to life-long dispositions. People relate in different ways toward different people and in different ways at different times toward the same person. Because of this, there should be different measures of relating that fit these different circumstances.

Containing all human relating within a simple, biaxial, conceptual framework has the effect of focusing attention upon the two axes and their characteristics. It is useful to acknowledge that the many features of the poles of each axis are united by the common theme of that pole. For example, the many forms that closeness takes are all means of attaining the commodity that is called closeness. A useful principle is that the benefits of one pole of an axis are as great as those of the opposite pole, and that excessive exposure to one pole, particularly if it is imposed, will provoke an increased desire for the other.

Understanding relating makes it easier to understand relationships. Those who fear one pole of an axis are compelled to restrict their lives in order to avoid it. This has disturbing consequences for those with whom they relate. On the horizontal axis, fear and avoidance of one pole of an axis deprives those with whom they relate of the experience of that same pole. For example, those who fear and avoid closeness, deprive those with whom they relate of closeness. On the vertical axis, fear and avoidance of one pole of an axis deprives those with whom they relate of the experience of the opposite pole. For example, those who fear and avoid lowerness, are compelled to stay upper, and force others always to be lower, thus depriving them of the experience of ever being upper.

It seems likely that the drives toward particular poles, the mental mechanisms involved in monitoring successes and failures in attaining or holding onto them, and the emotions associated with these successes and failures, are generated automatically and unconsciously. A consequence of this is that by the time we become aware of them they have already happened; so we spend much of our time producing rationalizations for why we behave the way we do.

POSITIVE AND NEGATIVE CHARACTERISTICS OF THE OCTANTS

The justification for including particular characteristics (whether positive or negative) within the various positions is, at this stage, entirely conceptual. Fuller descriptions, and more adequate justifications, with cross-referencing to other theoretical systems, are provided elsewhere (Birtchnell, 1996). Before proceeding to considerations of maladaptive (negative) forms of relating it will be necessary to provide an account of normal (positive) relating within each of the four positions of the system.

The Four Main Positions

Closeness is the condition of being physically and emotionally involved either with an individual or with a group. It is associated with the relaxation of normal interpersonal barriers and a weakening of ego boundaries. This increased intimacy and informality results in a freedom of communication. Close people develop internal representations of each other and become affectionate toward and needful of each other. They become interdependent and they collaborate to meet common objectives. They share common interests, opinions, and understandings. They exhibit the softer emotions of kindness, tenderness, and sentimentality. They have the capacity to sympathize, empathize, and identify with each other and may be prepared to make sacrifices on behalf of each other. They exhibit a curiosity about each other and a willingness to make personal revelations to each other. Under certain circumstances there also can be physical attraction, a need for increased physical contact, and sexual arousal.

Distance is the condition of being or becoming separate from others in general or from one other in particular. It may assume the form of escaping from danger or stress or of moving toward new experiences. In distance, individuals acquire the capacity to move away from parents, family, and familiar surroundings in order to experience themselves as separate beings who are capable of spending time alone, exploring their environments, and moving toward less familiar places where they may make new contacts. In this process, they develop a personal identity, acquire personal opinions, personal values, and personal standards and become self-approving. They also develop a safe and private psychic interior, establish a secure ego boundary and a sense of personal space, and protect themselves against invasion and intrusion. They are inclined to be autonomous and self-sufficient. They can be dispassionate, independent, objective, and capable of creative and original thought.

Upperness is the condition of being stronger, senior to, more able or more powerful than another or others. It is a relative concept and people acquire the experience of upperness by comparing themselves, in respect of a particular attribute, with someone else, but this can be reinforced by the acknowledgment, respect, and gratitude of others. People may gain the experience of upperness through success in competition; they may do so also by acquiring knowledge and skills that enable them to be of service to others. Such benevolent upperness assumes many forms, including taking responsibility for, setting example to, leading, commanding, judging, praising, encouraging, supporting, teaching, guiding, advising, helping, consoling, comforting, supporting, providing care for, and protecting. Many forms of upperness can be exchanged for money, which in turn, can be exchanged for possessions. By such means people can both confirm and display their upperness.

Lowerness is the condition of being weaker, junior to, less able, or less powerful than another or others. It may seem strange that lowerness should be viewed as advantageous, but upper people need to relate to lower people in order to confirm their upperness, and lower people would not permit this if they did not benefit from the relationship. It is reassuring to them that wiser, more able, and more powerful others are able to protect, take responsibility for, and provide for them. They turn to upper people for help, guidance, direction, advice, and care. They look up to, admire, respect, adore, and even worship them, and much of the appeal of religion is a result of the experience of lowerness that it affords. Lower people place themselves in the hands of upper people, and a necessary component of lowerness is trust. Upper people provide laws and give instructions that lower people obey. Lower people trust that the laws are just and the instructions are correct. In a complex society, no one can be expert at everything, so everyone needs to be, and gains from being, lower in a number of respects.

The Intermediate Positions

Upper closeness is showing concern for and being helpful and benevolent toward another. It includes protecting, supporting, providing for, nourishing, nursing, healing, soothing, rescuing, being approving, comforting, encouraging, reassuring, and consoling.

Lower closeness is seeking and receiving those things that the upper close person can provide and being accepting and appreciative of them. It includes pleading, begging, care-eliciting, feeling safely supported, cared for, and approved of, being grateful, adoring, worshiping, and praying.

Upper distance is being in charge of, setting limits to and giving direction to others. It includes assuming responsibility for and having to make decisions on behalf of others, taking control, maintaining order, issuing commands, passing judgement, imposing discipline, and, when necessary, punishing.

Lower distance is being the recipient of and accepting of the limits and controls imposed by the upper distant person. It includes accepting that person's authority, commands, judgments, discipline, and punishments, and being loyal, respectful, obedient, and dutiful.

Maladaptive (Negative) Forms of the Octants

Brief descriptions now will be provided of the maladaptive (negative) forms of the four main positions and the four intermediate positions, starting from neutral close and moving clockwise around the octagon. It is a point of some importance that the negative relating of one position is frequently a result of a lack of competence in, or fear of, the opposite position, or, in the case of an intermediate position, of the opposite positions of both its components. Thus a person who exhibits negative closeness may be doing so out of a fear or lack of competence for distance.

Neutral Close

Negatively close people are afraid of being alone and afraid of being deserted. They persistently try to attract or maintain the attention of others and are afraid that others will find other people more interesting or attractive. They experience separation anxiety (Bowlby, 1960), try to persuade others not to leave them, and when they have gone, they long for their return. They are anxious and restless when alone and try to busy or distract themselves. Such anxiety sometimes amounts to panic when they are impelled to make contact with someone by telephone or other means. They are inclined to press their attention on others, ignoring the other's needs or requests for distance, and are unable to tolerate their secrets or their privacy. They are intrusive and inquisitive. They may seek compensatory closeness by keeping dolls or pets or having fantasy friends or lovers. A different form of maladaptive closeness results from having a poorly formed identity. The person may compensate for this by trying to become fused (Bowen, 1978) to another by a process described by some as symbiosis (Taylor, 1975).

Lower Close

Laing (1965) described the condition of ontological dependence, not unlike the fusion of neutral closeness, in which a lower person so idolizes an upper person that she or he lives for and through her or him. Negatively lower close people fear that those on whom they depend will withdraw their protection, care, or affection. They demonstrate what Bowlby (1973) called *anxious attachment*. They make repeated requests for assurances that they are approved of and will not be deserted. They may weep and plead with others not to desert them, maintaining (perhaps correctly) that they cannot live without them. They may feign or exaggerate illness, disability, or hardship to play on the conscience of others. They cling so tenaciously and so try the patience of others that they risk bringing about the rejection that they dread. Fast (1967) wrote of a form of depression "involving rejection by the powerful other" and of the depressive being "helplessly dependent upon the other to reinstate him as good, acceptable, loved and part of meaningful life" (p. 262).

Lower Neutral

Just as negatively close people fear distance (i.e., being alone) so negatively lower people fear upperness (i.e., having power or responsibility). They do not consider themselves to be worthy of such a position and contrive to fail if promoted. They expect others to assume responsibility for them and require others to advise and direct them. They display what Seligman (1975) called learned helplessness. Although they may be afraid that upper others could be untrustworthy or could abuse their power by exploiting or misleading them, they have no option but to rely on them. The mentality of negatively lower neutral people is complicated by the fact that they carry within themselves the representations of past upper figures who have conditioned them to respond to upper people in certain ways. They may have been conditioned to view themselves as incompetent, clumsy, or useless.

Lower Distant

Negatively lower distant people are both afraid of having influence and afraid of being close. Therefore they remain on the periphery of life, maintaining a low profile and hoping others will not notice them. They are timid, shy, and easily intimidated. They readily submit to authority. They may be excessively deferential, self-effacing, apologetic, and accepting of criticism and blame. They lack any sense of autonomy or self-motivation and prefer only to act when instructed to do so. When they are insulted they do not retaliate and when they are attacked they back off. They are afraid to approach people for fear of rejection. They are afraid of speaking their mind for fear of retaliation. They suppress aggression and direct punishment on to themselves. As a consequence, they may be inclined to suffer from psychosomatic disorders.

Neutral Distant

Negatively neutral distant people have a limited capacity for close involvement, creating strong external barriers (high walls, locked doors, concealing clothing) and strong internal barriers (preoccupation with secrecy and privacy and the creation of an impenetrable ego boundary). They keep a safe distance from others and become anxious when others try to get close to them. They are inclined to spend long periods of time alone and may be prone to fugues or dissociation. They shun offers of help and restrict their behavior in order to manage without it. They are suspicious of the motives of others and fear that they may have the intention of doing them harm. They are clumsy in their dealings with others, say little, and keep conversation at a formal level. They are reluctant to make personal revelations and dislike it when others do so to them. They are self-centered and self-preoccupied and take little notice of the opinions of others. They may live in a world of daydreams and fantasies. They read or watch television both to escape from others and to keep them at bay. They are more interested in things or abstract ideas than in people.

Upper Distant

Negatively upper distant people use their upperness to enforce and maintain distance. They are therefore expelling and rejecting. They are self-obsessed and gain control of others in order to ensure that they get their own way. They are preoccupied by their own importance and are conceited, arrogant, pompous, and boastful. They cannot allow others to assume responsibility for them. They suppress the identity of others and dictate what should be done and how it should be done. They treat people as though they were things to be manipulated and exploited. They have no respect for the authority of others but expect others to respect and obey them. They respond with rage and indignation to disrespect and disobedience and seek revenge or retribution. They are cruel, ruthless, and unscrupulous and are prepared to resort to actual or threatened violence. They have no concern for the suffering they cause and experience no remorse. They may even derive satisfaction from humiliating others and seeing them suffer, because this confirms them in their upperness. They may employ spies and body guards to defend or protect them against rivals or enemies.

Upper Neutral

Negatively upper neutral people are not prepared to follow or to seek the advice of others, and they cannot entrust themselves to others. Therefore they try to take the lead and make decisions for them. They may become intoxicated with power, dream up ambitious plans, strive for ever higher status. They are disposed to bravado and may harbor fantasies, or even delusions, of omnipotence and grandeur. They need always to be right and will never apologize. If they do not know the answer to a problem, they will pretend they do. They take pleasure in exposing the errors and faults of others. They are inclined to resort to insult, derision, and ridicule and to look for the weak points in others in order to expose their vulnerabilities and undermine their confidence. They enjoy watching others making fools of themselves.

Upper Close

Negatively upper close people use their upperness to gain and maintain closeness. They may demand attention or force closeness on others. This may result in rape or sexual abuse. They do not like others to have friends or interests of their own and will make efforts to sabotage these. The upper close husband will insist that his wife says exactly where she has been and whom she has been with or may try to stop her looking attractive and even assault her to cause disfigurement. He may physically prevent her from leaving the house or threaten violence if she does. One form of negative upper closeness is compulsive rescuing or caregiving. People with this tendency thrive on others getting into difficulties or seeking their help. They may like to keep others weak so that the others remain needful of them, or they may continue to do things for others so that they never learn to be independent. Another form is a need to be worshiped and adored. Insecurely upper close people may love only those who love them and try to keep people interested in them by exhibiting themselves. Such public performers display themselves ever more extravagantly out of fear that their followers may lose interest in them.

FITTING THE *DSM-IV* PERSONALITY DISORDERS INTO THE OCTAGON

Personality is made up of both intrapersonal and interpersonal components. This chapter is concerned only with the latter, which are by far the more important. Interpersonal components may be defined as the persistent tendency to relate in a particular way across situations and over time. Spatial theory would have it that the four main states of relatedness are advantageous and that we need to acquire competencies in order to attain and maintain all of them. The positive forms of relating are not so much personality characteristics as the kinds of behavior that form part of the normal processes of attaining and maintaining states of relatedness. In so far as all the states are advantageous, the well-adjusted person needs to possess a complete range of competencies and to be able to draw on whichever one of them is required for any given situation. It would be difficult to ascribe to her or him any particular personality characteristic. It is conceded that some people may be more disposed toward one or more of the four main states, and such dispositions may be considered to be personality characteristics. Beyond this, it seems that what we normally consider to be personality amounts to the various ways by which people fall short of the ideal of total versatility, avoid certain forms of relating, and resort to the less than ideal negative forms of relating—namely the personality disorders.

Each *DSM-IV* personality disorder (American Psychiatric Association, 1994) comprises a cluster of behavior characteristics that are considered, by general consensus, to occur together but that have no unifying construct. There is no overall theoretical system that can explain how the disorders might be related one another. The eight octants, however, are presumed to exist on the basis of spatial theory. In the following section, I will show that most of the characteristics of the ten *DSM-IV* disorders can be described in terms of the negative forms of the eight octants, thus confirming the importance of the interpersonal components. These negative forms of the octants, were their internal consistency to be confirmed, would provide a more rational and precise basis for the classification of at least the relating characteristics of the personality disorders than the *DSM* system.

The placement of the disorders within the octagon is summarized in Figure 2, but this must be viewed in conjunction with the descriptions provided in the following section. It is disappointing that (a) six of the ten disorders extend over more than one octant, (b) the disorders are not distributed regularly around the octagon, and (c) there are few locations in which there is a one-to-one correspondence between a disorder and an octant. In some instances, more than one disorder occupies the same location. This is due (a) to the additional effect of intrapersonal factors and (b) to the fact that different disorders are concerned with different aspects

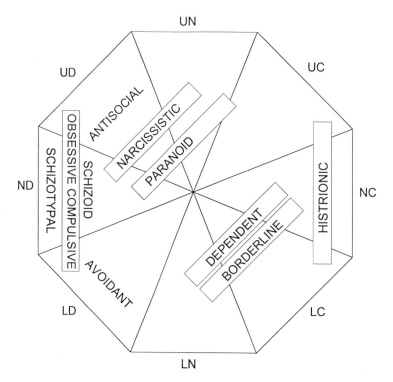

Figure 2. DSM-IV personality disorders set within the interpersonal octagon: UN = upper neutral, UC = upper close, NC = neutral close, LC = lower close, LN = lower neutral, LD = lower distant, ND = neutral distant, UD = upper distant.

of that location. The highest concentration of disorders occurs within the three distant octants, and these have been considered in detail elsewhere (Birtchnell, 1995).

The *DSM-IV* personality disorders were fitted into the octagon by the process of reading the descriptions provided in the *DSM-IV* and classifying them in terms of the maladaptive (negative) forms of relating for each octant, which were provided in the previous section. Some of the descriptions were lifted verbatim from the text of the *DSM-IV*, but some are generalizations based upon the text. Because the text for each disorder covers several pages, the selected descriptions have had to be representative. Where it seemed appropriate, descriptions provided by other authorities have also been included.

Cluster A

Individuals with Cluster A disorders are linked by the characteristic of being "odd or eccentric" (p. 629). They may be this way because they are poorly integrated with society. All three Cluster A disorders are distant, but there are distant disorders in Clusters B and C as well.

Paranoid

This is predominantly a disorder of distance. Early features are "poor peer relationships, solitariness, and social anxiety" (*DSM-IV*, p. 636). Paranoid individuals are "reluctant to confide in or become close to others" (p. 634). "They are preoccupied with unjustified doubts about the loyalty or trustworthiness of their friends and associates" (p. 634). Because they "lack trust in others" they have a "strong sense of autonomy" and an "excessive need to be self-sufficient" (p. 635). They are distant because they fear that others will do them harm. They are "hypervigilant" and ready to defend themselves and are even liable to make a preemptive strike in the anticipation of attack. They do have some involvement with others in which they may become fractious and argumentative. Although they are inclined to criticize and blame others, they have difficulty accepting criticism themselves. This is an upper characteristic. "They are often attuned to issues of power and rank, and they exhibit thinly hidden unrealistic grandiose fantasies" (p. 635). Their most pronounced upper feature is their need to keep control of people around them, and this strangely carries them into upper close territory. They need "to maintain control of their intimate relationships, questioning and challenging the whereabouts and actions of their partners and accusing them of infidelity."

Schizoid

Unlike paranoid individuals, schizoid individuals demonstrate a pure form of distance. Millon (1981) described them as lacking the need to communicate. "They show no interest in relationships with others or in sexual behavior and prefer spending time by themselves. "They have no close friends or confidants, except possibly a first-degree relative" (p. 638). Their distance-seeking is probably a result of limited tolerance of sensory stimulation, a condition described by Claridge (1987) in relation to psychotic individuals. This renders them susceptible to what Baron and Byrne (1991) called *stimulus overload*. Unlike paranoid people, schizoid individuals "are indifferent to criticism and appear not to be bothered by what others think of them" (p. 638). They are cold and aloof and seem incapable of strong emotion. "They rarely reciprocate gestures of facial expression" (p. 638). They can be useful members of society, for they are able to work, often constructively and creatively, for long periods under conditions of isolation. They live in a world of fantasies and daydreams.

Schizotypal

Schizotypal individuals are distant, like schizoid, only more so. They exhibit an "acute discomfort with, and reduced capacity for, close relationships" (p. 641). Unlike schizoid individuals, however, they are too introverted to be useful members of society. Millon (1981) described them as leading meaningless, idle, and ineffectual existences, drifting from one aimless activity to another. He observed that, "As they become progressively estranged from their social environment, they lose touch with the conventions of reality and with the checks against irrational thought and behavior that are provided by reciprocal relationship" (p. 400). They are eccentric, and their speech may include unusual or idiosyncratic phrasing and construction. The fantasies and daydreams of schizoid individuals become the illusions, ideas of reference (Millon, 1981), magical thinking (Eckbald & Chapman, 1983), and preoccupation with the paranormal (Williams & Irwin, 1991) of schizotypal individuals.

Cluster B

Individuals with Cluster B disorders are linked by the characteristics of being "dramatic, emotional, or erratic." These are not interpersonal characteristics. Therefore, it is not surprising that the four disorders in this cluster are located in different parts of the octagon.

Antisocial

Not all of the features of this disorder are contained within the octagon. Those that are not are aggressiveness (revealed by Harpur, Hare, & Hakistan, 1989, to be a distinctly separate factor), impulsiveness (considered by Blackburn, 1993, to be a component of extraversion), and the need for stimulation or proneness to boredom. The remaining features are divided between distance and upperness. The distant features are of two kinds: those that could be included under Kantor's (1993) term *commitment phobia* and those that concern a disregard for the feelings of others. In relation to the first kind, antisocial individuals *are* capable of forming close relationships (and may even get married), but they are unable to sustain them. This may be related to their proneness to boredom. In such relationships, sexuality and self-gratification tend to take precedence over affection and concern for the other. In relation to the second kind, they can be cold, callous, and brutal. The upper features belong predominantly to the upper distant octant. These individuals believe they have been badly treated by others and are set on retribution, striking back indiscriminately at the society they believe to be responsible for the harm that was done to them. They do not conform to social norms or respect the law. They exhibit a "lack of remorse, as indicated by being indifferent to or rationalizing having hurt, mistreated, or stolen from another" (p. 650).

Borderline

Borderline individuals also display certain features that are not contained within the octagon. These include impulsiveness and the need for stimulation or proneness to boredom, features also associated with antisocial individuals. In contrast to antisocial individuals, borderline individuals belong predominantly to the close and lower regions of the octagon. Their close features are an intolerance of being alone, a need to have other people with them, and intense fears of abandonment. Their perception of impending separation or rejection can lead to profound changes in affect and self-image. Their dramatic mood swings are reactions to their successes or failures in close relationships. What they seek most in close relationships is care, which places them nearer to lower close than to close. They may switch from idealizing other people to devaluing them if they believe that the other is not exhibiting enough care. They can express intense anger toward a caregiver they believe to be neglectful, but such anger may quickly switch to shame and guilt and a feeling of being evil (another aspect of lowerness). Their conviction that they are bad or evil can lead to "repeated acts of self-mutilation or attempted suicide" (p. 654).

Histrionic

The features of histrionic individuals that are not contained within the octagon are the need for novelty, immediate satisfaction, stimulation, and excitement. Like borderline individuals, histrionic individuals belong predominantly to the close and lower regions, but their behavior is quite different. What they seek out of closeness is "to be the center of attention" (p. 658). They are socially gregarious but also can be promiscuous. They are superficially charming but shallow and lacking in genuineness. "Their emotions often seem to be turned on and off too quickly to be deeply felt" (p. 655). They take a great deal of trouble over their appearance and display themselves in front of people. They thrive on being admired (which includes an element of upperness). They are seductive and dramatically over-familiar toward people, but simply to evoke a response from them. Their closeness is mainly one way—from others *to* them. In intimate relationships they often appear to be acting out a role. Their lowerness takes the form of their being highly suggestible and easily influenced by others. They may be "overly trusting, especially of strong authority figures, whom they see as magically solving their problems" (p. 655).

Narcissistic

Narcissism is almost entirely associated with upperness. Narcissistic individuals have "a grandiose sense of self-importance" (p. 658). They believe that they are superior, special, or unique and expect others to recognize them as such. They harbor fantasies of unlimited success and power. They have a sense of entitlement and expect to be given whatever they want or need. They demonstrate an unreasonable expectation of special treatment. In fact, "their self-esteem is almost invariably very fragile" (p. 658). They are boastful and pretentious, cannot tolerate criticism, and surround themselves with sycophants. They assume that their priorities are so important that they expect others to defer to them. There is a distant element to narcissism in that narcissistic individuals are entirely self-centered, discussing their own concerns in inappropriate and lengthy detail and failing to recognize that others also have feelings and needs. They show "an emotional coldness and lack of reciprocal interest" (p. 659). They take advantage of others to achieve their own ends. Blatt and Shichman (1983) considered that narcissist individuals may be defending against unconscious fears that they may be considered small and insignificant.

Cluster C

Individuals with Cluster C disorders are linked by the characteristic of being "anxious and fearful" (p. 630). This also is not an interpersonal characteristic and again, it is not surprising that the three disorders are located in different parts of the octagon.

Avoidant

Avoidant individuals belong to the lower distant octant. Although they appear to want closeness, they are afraid of attaining it for fear of the painful consequences of losing it. Millon (1981) observed that, "Desires for affection may be strong, but are self-protectively denied" (p. 303). Avoidant individuals "tend to be shy, quiet, inhibited, and 'invisible' because of the fear that any attention would be degrading or rejecting" (p. 662). They believe themselves to be "socially inept, personally unappealing, or inferior to others" (p. 662). They dread involvement with others for fear of this being confirmed. They are in a permanent state of approach-avoidant conflict. Despite their longing to be active participants in social life, they fear placing their welfare in the hands of others. They are perceptually hypersensitive, vigilantly scanning for potential threats to self, exquisitely sensitive to rejection, humiliation, and shame, devastated by the slightest hint of disapproval, and inclined to overinterpret innocuous behaviors as signs of ridicule and humiliation. They are the lower equivalent of paranoid individuals.

Dependent

Depending on the characteristics included, dependents can range from the neutral close to lower neutral positions and are most precisely located in the lower close octant. They experience the same conflicts as avoidants but are prepared to risk getting that much closer to people. At the closeness end of the range, they are afraid to be left alone and cling anxiously to the person they have chosen to entrust themselves to. At the lower end they are afraid to make even the simplest decisions and look to the trusted upper person to tell them what to do. They require constant reassurance that they are acceptable, and they are afraid to express disagreement lest this should lead to rejection. Pilkonis (1988) discovered that when raters were invited to sort dependence items into clusters, two higher-order constructs emerged—what he called *true dependence* and *borderline features*. This is of interest because borderline individuals also occupy the lower close octant.

Obsessive–Compulsive

People with obsessive–compulsive disorder are undoubtedly distant. "They have difficulty expressing tender feelings" and "express affection in a highly controlled or stilted fashion" (p. 671). "They are very uncomfortable in the presence of others who are emotionally expressive" (p. 671). "They are totally wrapped up in their own perspectives and have difficulty acknowledging the viewpoints of others" (p. 670). "They carefully hold themselves back until they are sure that whatever they say will be perfect" (p. 671). "Their everyday relationships have a formal and serious quality" (p. 671). Their behavior extends across the whole range of distant positions. They are upper distant in that they stubbornly and unreasonably insist that everything be done their way. In addition, they give detailed instructions about how things should be done. They are lower distant in that they are "rigidly deferential to authority" (p. 670) and conform totally to the rules and laws laid down by others. They have a harsh internalized upper other that causes them to "be mercilessly self-critical about their mistakes" (p. 670). When rules and established procedures do not dictate the correct answer, decision making may become a time consuming, often painful process for them.

THE CIRCULAR DISTRIBUTION OF PERSONALITY TRAITS AND DISORDERS

Detailed comparisons between the distribution of traits in spatial theory and classical interpersonal theory can be found elsewhere (Birtchnell, 1994, 1996), but it is appropriate to provide some simple comparisons here. Such comparisons are confounded by the failure of most interpersonal theorists to distinguish adequately between positive and negative relating. In this section, the octant positions will be identified using the initial letters of the octagon (see Figure 1 and the caption for Figure 2 for meaning). Taking first the octants version of the original Leary (1957) distribution, there is reasonably close correspondence between the two distributions with regard to the NC, LC, LN, UD, UN, and UC octants, but Leary's equivalent of the LD and ND octants fit more appropriately into the ND and UD positions of spatial theory. The shifted LD and ND octants extend into the Wiggins and Broughton (1985) distribution, but these authors have shifted three further octants: their equivalent of the UC, NC, and LC octants fit more appropriately into the NC, UC, and LD positions of the octagon. Kiesler (1983) retained all of Wiggins and Broughton's changes, but Strong et al. (1988) by introducing a connected–separated axis, approximating the close–distant axis, reverted to a distribution that was closer to Leary's and to that of spatial theory.

A complication of fitting personality disorders into a circular system is that the *DSM-IV* personality disorders cannot be organized into discrete and mutually exclusive categories. Livesley, West, and Tanney (1985) concluded that membership in a category of disorder is not an all-or-none phenomenon but a matter of degree. They observed that most patients show features of more than one disorder and many show some, but not all, of the features of any particular disorder. Depending on the populations studied and the instruments used, researchers have reported mean numbers of disorders per patient extending to 5.6 (Hyler, Skodol, Kellman, Oldham, & Rosnick, 1990). Dolan, Evans, and Norton (1994) concluded that multiple diagnosis is the norm rather than the exception and suggested the term *breadth* of psychopathology rather than *comorbidity* to take this into account. Observations of this kind are in keeping with the view that relating incompetence (negative relating) may extend in a number of different directions. Thus, although bipolarity may apply at a conceptual level it may be less evident in practice. Currently in progress is a project to examine, in a series of participants with confirmed personality disorder, the degree of correlation between the octant scores of the PROQ (see p. 163) and the *DSM-IV* personality disorder scores of the Personality Diagnostic Questionnaire (PDQ-IV; Hyler et al., 1990). It is anticipated that both instruments will confirm the breadth observed by Dolen and colleagues (1994) but that the locations of distribution of the two instruments will correspond.

When it comes to fitting the *DSM-III* personality disorders into circular systems (there have been no studies of *DSM-IV* disorders), the classical interpersonal theorists have been hampered by the inadequacy of their distinction between positive and negative relating. (The locations in Figure 2 were entirely in terms of negative relating.) Attempts to do this using statistical methods were reviewed by Dyce (1994), who pointed out that inconsistencies between studies may have been a result of the variation in the statistical methods used. Wiggins (1982) located compulsive at UN, histrionic at NC, dependent at LC, schizoid at LD, paranoid at ND, and narcissistic at UD. In a later study, Wiggins and Pincus (1989) located dependent at LC, avoidant and schizoid at LD, narcissistic and antisocial at UD, and histrionic at UC. Because of the pinpoint precision of these placements, comparison with the distributions in Figure 2 is not easy, but there does appear to be general agreement between the two.

CONCLUSION

My interest in the circumplex model grew out of speculation about the nature of psychological dependence. Its proposed two components became the basis for a biaxial theory of relating that resembles interpersonal theory. The axes of the theory (which is called spatial theory) are named closeness–distance and upperness–lowerness. The theory stresses a continuity between the relating of animals and humans. The four main positions plus the intermediate positions are called the interpersonal octagon. It is proposed that (a) the four main positions represent interpersonal objectives, (b) people need to develop competencies in order to attain these objectives, and (c) the emotions are responses to success or failure in attaining them. Maladaptive or negative relating is considered to be due to lack of competence, and the negative relating of one position may frequently be due to lack of competence in the opposite one. It is argued that some of the bipolarity of interpersonal theory may be due to failure to distinguish clearly between positive and negative relating. In an octagon comprising only negative relating, bipolarity would be less evident. If the characteristics of the ten *DSM-IV* personality disorders are defined in terms of the negative relating of particular octants (a) six of the disorders extend across more than one octant, (b) the disorders are not distributed evenly around the octagon, and (c) there are few locations where there is a one to one correspondence between a disorder and an octant.

REFERENCES

American Psychiatric Association. (1994). *Diagnostic and statistical manual of mental disorders* (4th ed.). Washington, DC: American Psychiatric Association.

Argyle, M. (1972). *The psychology of interpersonal behaviour.* Harmondsworth, England: Penguin Books.

Baron, R. A., & Byrne, D. (1991). *Social psychology.* London: Allyn & Bacon.

Birtchnell, J. (1984). Dependence and its relationship to depression. *British Journal of Medical Psychology, 57,* 215–225.

Birtchnell, J. (1987). Attachment–detachment, directiveness–receptiveness: A system for classifying interpersonal attitudes and behaviour. *British Journal of Medical Psychology, 60*, 17–27.

Birtchnell, J. (1988). Defining dependence. *British Journal of Medical Psychology, 61*, 111–123.

Birtchnell, J. (1990). Interpersonal theory: Criticism, modification and elaboration. *Human Relations, 43*, 1183–1201.

Birtchnell, J. (1991a). Redefining dependence: A reply to Cadbury's critique. *British Journal of Medical Psychology, 64*, 253–261.

Birtchnell, J. (1991b). The measurement of dependence by questionnaire. *Journal of Personality Disorders, 5*, 281–295.

Birtchnell, J. (1994). The interpersonal octagon: An alternative to the interpersonal circle. *Human Relations, 47*, 511–527.

Birtchnell, J. (1995). Detachment. In G. C. Costello (Ed.), *Personality characteristics of the personality disordered*. New York: Wiley.

Birtchnell, J. (1996). *How humans relate: A new interpersonal theory*. Hove, England: Psychology Press.

Birtchnell, J., Deahl, M., & Falkowski, J. (1991). Further exploration of the relationship between depression and dependence. *Journal of Affective Disorders, 22*, 221–233.

Birtchnell, J., Falkowski, J., & Steffert, B. (1992). The negative relating of depressed patients: A new approach. *Journal of Affective Disorders, 24*, 165–176.

Blackburn, R. (1988). On moral judgements and personality disorders: The myth of psychopathic personality revisited. *British Journal of Psychiatry, 153*, 505–512.

Blackburn, R. (1993). *The psychology of criminal conduct*. Chichester, England: Wiley.

Blatt, S. J., & Shichman, S. (1983). Two primary configurations of psychopathology. *Psychoanalysis and Contemporary Thought, 6*, 187–249.

Bowen, M. (1978). *Family therapy in clinical practice*. New York: Jason Aronson.

Bowlby, J. (1960). Separation anxiety. *International Journal of Psycho-Analysis, 41*, 89–113.

Bowlby, J. (1969). *Attachment and loss. Vol. 1: Attachment*. London: Hogarth Press/Institute of Psychoanalysis.

Bowlby, J. (1973). *Attachment and loss. Vol. 2: Separation, anxiety and anger*. London: Hogarth Press/Institute of Psychoanalysis.

Bowlby, J. (1977). The making and breaking of affectional bonds: I. Aetiology and psychopathology in the light of attachment theory. *British Journal of Psychiatry, 130*, 201–210.

Claridge, G. (1987). "The schizophrenias as nervous types" revisited. *British Journal of Psychiatry, 151*, 735–743.

Dolan, B., Evans, C., & Norton, K. (1994). Multiple Axis-II diagnoses of personality disorder. *British Journal of Psychiatry, 166*, 107–112.

Dyce, J. A. (1994). Personality disorders: Alternatives to the official diagnostic system. *Journal of Personality Disorders, 8*, 77–88.

Eckbald, M., & Chapman, L. J. (1983). Magical ideation as an indicator of schizotypy. *Journal of Clinical and Consulting Psychology, 52*, 215–225.

Fast, I. (1967). Some relationships of infantile self-boundary development to depression. *International Journal of Psycho-Analysis, 48*, 259–266.

Freedman, M. B., Leary, T., Ossorio, A. G., & Coffey, H. S. (1951). The interpersonal dimension of personality. *Journal of Personality, 20*, 143–161.

Fromm, E. (1947). *Man for himself.* New York: Rinehart.

Guttman, L. A. (1954). A new approach to factor analysis: The radex. In P. R. Lazarsfeld (Ed.), *Mathematical thinking in the social sciences* (pp. 258–348). Glencoe, IL: Free Press.

Harpur, T. J, Hare, R. D., & Hakistan, A. R. (1989). Two-factor conceptualization of psychopathy: Construct validity and assessment implications. *Psychological Assessment: A Journal of Consulting and Clinical Psychology, 1*, 6–17.

Hirschfeld, R. M. A., Klerman, G. L., Lavori, P., Keller, M. B., Griffith, P., & Coryell, W. (1989). Premorbid personality assessment of first onset major depression. *Archives of General Psychiatry, 46*, 345–350.

Horney, K. (1937). *The neurotic personality of our time.* New York: Norton.

Hyler, S. E., Skodol, A. E., Kellman, H. D., Oldham, J., & Rosnick, L. (1990). Validity of the Personality Diagnostic Questionnaire—Revised. Comparison with two structured interviews. *American Journal of Psychiatry, 147*, 1043–1048.

Kantor, M. (1993). *Distancing: A guide to avoidance and avoidant personality disorder.* Westport, CT: Praeger.

Kiesler, D. J. (1983). The 1982 interpersonal circle: A taxonomy for complementarity in human transactions. *Psychological Review, 90*, 185–214.

LaForge, R., & Suczek, R. (1955). The interpersonal dimension of personality. III: An interpersonal checklist. *Journal of Personality, 24*, 94–112.

Leary, T. (1957). *The interpersonal diagnosis of personality: A functional theory and methodology for personality.* New York: Ronald Press.

Livesley, W. J., West, M., & Tanney, A. (1985). Historical comment on *DSM-III* schizoid and avoidant personality disorders. *American Journal of Psychiatry, 142*, 1344–1347.

Lorr, M., & McNair, D. M. (1963). An interpersonal behavior circle. *Journal of Abnormal and Social Psychology, 67*, 68–75.

Lorr, M., & Youniss, R. P. (1973). An inventory of interpersonal style. *Journal of Personality Assessment, 37*, 165–173.

McGuffin, P., & Katz, R. (1986). Nature, nurture and affective disorder. In J. F. W. Deakin (Ed.), *The biology of depression* (pp. 26–52). London: Gaskell Psychiatry Series, Royal College of Psychiatrists.

Millon, T. (1981). *Disorders of personality: DSM-III: Axis II.* New York: Wiley.

Nesse, R. M. (1990). Evolutionary explanations of emotions. *Human Nature, 1,* 261–289.

Olson, D. H., Sprengle, D. H., & Russell, C. S. (1979). Circumplex model of marital and family systems: I. Cohesion and adaptability dimensions, family types, and clinical applications. *Family Process, 18,* 3–28.

Paddock, J. R., & Nowicki, S. (1986). An examination of the Leary circumplex through the Interpersonal Check List. *Journal of Research in Personality, 20,* 107–144.

Pilkonis, P. A. (1988). Personality prototypes among depressives: Themes of dependency and autonomy. *Journal of Personality Disorders, 2,* 144–152.

Ray, J. J. (1976). Do authoritarians hold authoritarian attitudes? *Human Relations, 29,* 307–325.

Seligman, M. E. P. (1975). *Helplessness: On depression, development and death.* San Francisco: Freeman.

Strong, S. R., Hills, H. I., Kilmartin, C. T., DeVries, H., Lanier, K., Nelson, B. N., Strickland, D., & Meyer, C. W., III. (1988). The dynamic relations among interpersonal behaviors: A test of complementarity and anticomplementarity. *Journal of Personality and Social Psychology, 54,* 798–810.

Sullivan, H. S. (1953). *The interpersonal theory of psychiatry.* New York: Norton.

Taylor, G. J. (1975). Separation–individuation in the psychotherapy of symbiotic states. *Canadian Psychiatric Association Journal, 20,* 521–526.

Wiggins, J. S. (1979). A psychological taxonomy of trait-descriptive terms: The interpersonal domain. *Journal of Personality and Social Psychology, 37,* 395–412.

Wiggins, J. S. (1982). Circumplex models of interpersonal behavior in clinical psychology. In P. S. Kendall & J. N. Butcher (Eds.), *Handbook of research methods in clinical psychology* (pp. 183–221). New York: Wiley.

Wiggins, J. S., & Broughton, R. (1985). The interpersonal circle: A structural model for the integration of personality research. In R. Hogan (Ed.), *Perspectives in personality* (Vol. 1, pp. 1–47). Greenwich, CT: JAI Press.

Wiggins, J. S., & Pincus, A. L. (1989). Conceptions of personality disorders and dimensions of personality. *Psychological Assessment: A Journal of Consulting and Clinical Psychology, 1,* 305–316.

Williams, L. M., & Irwin, H. J. (1991). A study of paranormal belief, magical ideation as an index of schizotypy and cognitive style. *Personality and Individual Differences, 12,* 1339–1348.

8

CIRCULAR STRUCTURE OF VOCATIONAL INTERESTS

TERENCE J. G. TRACEY and JAMES B. ROUNDS

The overriding models of vocational interest have been factor lists in which the focus is on the number of independent factors that exist in the vocational interest domain (e.g., Guilford, Christensen, Bond, & Sutton, 1954; Hansen, 1984; Jackson, Holden, Locklin, & Marks, 1984; Kuder, 1977; Rounds & Dawis, 1979). Although Roe introduced a circular model of interests in 1956, vocational psychology was still dominated by the factor list approach. Widespread attention to circular models of interests occurred relatively recently with Holland's (1973) description of his six vocational interest types.

Holland (1959, 1973, 1985a) proposed a theory of vocational personality and work environments that is considered the most influential in vocational psychology (Borgen, 1986; Brown & Brooks, 1990; Osipow, 1983). He proposed that there are six personality types and work environments (realistic, R; investigative, I; artistic, A; social, S; enterprising, E; and conventional, C; hereafter referred to collectively as RIASEC). Most all major interest inventories now provide scores on these six types, and these types have been used extensively to categorize occupations (e.g., Gottfredson & Holland, 1989). The six types (both personality and work environments) have been proposed to exist in a hexagonal structure with proximity being related to degree of similarity. Holland's hexagonal model is presented in Figure 1. Holland (1973, 1985a) proposed that the hexagonal

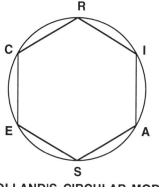

HOLLAND'S CIRCULAR MODEL

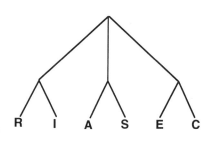

GATI'S PARTITION MODEL

Figure 1. Holland's circular representation of personality types and Gati's single partition alternative. R = realistic; I = investigative; A = artistic; S = social; E = enterprising; C = conventional. Adapted from "Evaluating Holland's and Gati's Vocational Interest Models: A Structural Meta-Analysis," T. J. G. Tracey and J. B. Rounds, 1993, *Psychological Bulletin, 113*, 229-246. Reprinted by permission from the American Psychological Association.

structure (circular arrangement with equal distances between the types) can be used to generate hypotheses regarding the stability and predictability of interests (those with interest types more proximate should demonstrate more stable interests and vocational histories), and job satisfaction (a closer match between one's interests and one's work environment will be related to greater satisfaction). Because of its simplicity and completeness, Holland's model has dominated the field of vocational psychology.

Much of this focus on Holland's model involved examinations of the extent to which Holland's model fit interest data and its invariance across different groups (i.e., age, gender, and culture). The literature on the structure of interests was dominated by equivocal results generated from studies on single samples. Even reviews of the literature (e.g., Gati, 1991; Hansen, 1984; Holland, 1985a; Prediger, 1982) offered conflicting conclusions about the adequacy of Holland's hexagonal model of interest types. We believe that focusing on Holland's model in a quantitative manner across a wide variety of studies is necessary to evaluate the structure of interests, and as such much of our work has sought to examine Holland's model in a structural meta-analytic manner.

EXAMINATION OF HOLLAND'S CIRCULAR STRUCTURE

Our work has focused almost exclusively on Holland's model, and it has served as a stimulus in our examination of the circular structure of vocational interests. We summarize work examining the circular structure of Holland's RIASEC personality types with respect to (a) specification of different circular models, (b) the relative merits of a circular model over alternative conceptions, (c) the orientation of the dimensions underlying the circular structure, (d) the generalizability of the circular arrangement of RIASEC types, and (e) the relation of the RIASEC types and hexagonal structure to other personality constructs.

Circular Arrangement of RIASEC Types

Holland's hexagonal model is really a circumplex model consisting of six types. Guttman (1954) used the term *circumplex* to refer to a pattern of relations in a matrix in which the magnitude decreased as one moved away from the main diagonal and then increased, thus representing a circular structure. As noted by Browne (1992), there are a variety of different specific definitions of a circumplex that have been presented and examined, ranging from Guttman's modified simplex definition to much more constrained ones. In our work, we have defined and examined two separate definitions of a circular structure and referred to these as the *circular order model* and the *circumplex*.

The circular order model specifies that the types can be arranged in a circle in which the distance between types represents the relative magnitude of the relations. This is perhaps one of the less restrictive representations of circular order, specifying only that the types be arranged in a circular manner. This circular order model requires that the correlations between adjacent types be greater than those between all nonadjacent types (e.g., realistic–investigative > realistic–artistic, social–enterprising > investigative–social, artistic–social > artistic–conventional), and the correlations among alternate types be greater than those between opposite types (e.g., realistic–artistic > artistic–conventional). The circular order model has been examined using Hubert and Arabie's (1987) randomization test of hypothesized order relations, which determines the probability of the specified model fitting the correlation matrix relative to a null conjecture of random relabeling of the rows and columns of the matrix. (See Rounds, Tracey, & Hubert, 1992, for a detailed example of this statistic.)

The second representation of Holland's hexagon, termed the *circumplex model*, is a more constrained version of the circular order model, wherein identical relations among the correlations are hypothesized (i.e., correlations between adjacent types are greater than those between all nonadjacent types, and correlations between alternate types are greater than those between opposite types), except the constraint of equality of correlations within set is added. Specifically, the correlations among adjacent types are viewed as being equal (i.e., realistic–investigative = investigative–artistic = artistic–social = social–enterprising = enterprising–conventional = conventional–realistic), as are the correlations among all alternate types (i.e., realistic–artistic = investigative–social = artistic–enterprising = social–conventional = enterprising–realistic = conventional–investigative), as are the correlations among all opposite types (i.e., realistic–social = investigative–enterprising = artistic–conventional). Thus the correlation matrix among the six RIASEC types with its 15 correlations can be represented using three correlations: one for adjacent between types, one between alternate types, and one between opposite types. Confirmatory factor analysis has been used as a means of examining the fit of this circumplex model to data sets.

A more restrictive representation of the circumplex model has been specified, called the *exact circumplex* (Rounds & Tracey, 1993). Instead of testing the fit of three correlations as representing the correlation matrix among RIASEC types as in the circumplex model just described, the exact circumplex model uses a single correlation. Assuming that the six RIASEC points are equidistant around the circle, it is possible to represent the magnitude of the correlations as exactly proportional to the distance on the circle; correlations between adjacent types should be three times those correlations between opposite types (e.g., realistic–investigative = 3 × realistic–social) and correlations between alternate types should be twice those correlations of opposite types (e.g., realistic–artistic = 2 × realistic–social). Thus all 15 correlations in the RIASEC correlation matrix can be represented using only one parameter—the magnitude of opposite correlations. This is obviously a restrictive model and requires that all geometric properties of the circular structure be valid. We have applied all three specifications of a circular model (i.e., circular order model, circumplex, and exact circumplex) to RIASEC data. The term *circular model* is used throughout this chapter to refer to the general circular structure. When the specific definitions of circular structure are applied, they will be identified explicitly.

Circular Versus Cluster Representations

Gati (1991) reviewed the literature on the structure of vocational interests and concluded that Holland's circular model was not appropriate and that his own single partition of the RIASEC types was superior. (The two models of RIASEC interests are presented in Figure 1.) Gati claimed that there existed only three discrete clusters, and this was the set of relations that mattered. However, Gati's examination of the data was flawed with respect to incorrectly representing the differences between his and Holland's models (Tracey & Rounds, 1993) and applying an invalid test of model data fit (Hubert & Arabie, 1987). To examine the relative merits of the two competing models in a more valid manner, a variety of statistical techniques was applied to a sample of 104 RIASEC correlation matrices garnered from the literature (Tracey & Rounds, 1993). First, Hubert and

Arabie's (1987) randomization test of hypothesized order relations was used to examine the fit of Holland's circular order model and Gati's partition model. Both models were found to fit the data significantly, but the unique relations predicted by Gati's model poorly fit the data, indicating that the unique aspects of Gati's model were not supported by the data. Second, the fit of the circumplex model and Gati's model were examined using confirmatory factor analysis, and Holland's circumplex model was the more parsimonious and adequate fit to the data. Third, an individual differences cluster analysis was conducted—because Gati's model is essentially a cluster model—and the results were not supportive of Gati's partition. In sum, Gati's conclusions regarding the flawed nature of Holland's model were wrong for both logical and empirical reasons. Holland's circular structure (as represented by both the circular order and circumplex specifications) was superior to Gati's alternative.

The fit of Holland's circular model to RIASEC data was supported with respect to both the circular order and the circumplex definitions across 104 different RIASEC correlation matrices using a wide variety of instruments (Tracey & Rounds, 1993). The exact circumplex definition of the circular model on a meta-analysis of 77 U.S. RIASEC matrices (Rounds & Tracey, 1993) also fit well, supporting the application of geometric properties to the RIASEC data, where relations among the types follow Euclidean principles (i.e., distance is directly proportional to magnitude of the relation).

Orientation of Dimensions

Hogan (1983) noted that there are two basic approaches in thinking about and approaching structural issues of personality: a factor list approach and a circumplex approach. A factor list approach, which is the more standard approach in vocational and personality psychology, attempts to understand the relations among items by defining and labeling the underlying dimensions. A clear, explicit understanding of and an estimation of the dimensions or factors themselves are the goals of a factor list approach. This typically becomes translated into the search for a simple structure in factor analysis, wherein items load only on one factor. Items that load on several factors pose conceptual and psychometric problems in this approach and thus are to be avoided because they do not result in clear scales and factors. By determining the number of factors that underlie any data set, a parsimonious grasp of the structure is generated.

A circumplex approach exists in two dimensions, and the focus is less on the specific dimensions underlying the circular structure than on the circular structure itself. The circular structure carries information about the similarity of points on the circle to other points on the circle that is not easily generated by knowing the underlying dimensions. For example, items loading highly on both dimensions are to be avoided as conceptually ambiguous but valued as representing a point on the circle. Clusters of items loading highly on both underlying dimensions would be viewed as representing a unique type, quite different from types loading highly only on one of the underlying dimensions. By examining the circular nature of items, one can generate different types that are conceptually distinct and are unable to be generated in a factor list model. Further, the placement of these types around the circle carries information about the similarity of one type to another. The circumplex approach thus is limited to two dimensions and is not as parsimonious as the factor list approach, because there are many more types generated than just two dimensions. However, the circular structure of the types carries implicit information on the relations among the types that is not as easily generated in the factor list model.

With respect to the RIASEC types, the work of Prediger (1982; Prediger & Vansickle, 1992) is the most prominent example of a factor list approach. Prediger (1982) examined the RIASEC structure across a variety of data sets and found support for the two bipolar, underlying dimensions of people–things and data–ideas. Prediger's model is depicted in Figure 2. The people–things dimension separates the social type from the realistic type; each of these scales loads highly on only this dimension. However, there is no dimensional clarity with respect to the other four types, where each loads highly on both dimensions. The data–ideas dimension differentiates enterprising and conventional types from artistic and investigative types. The dimensional approach accounts for the six types using only two dimensions and enables a quick understanding of the structure, but it does not do a good job of differentiating the types that are a blending of the dimensions.

Prediger and Vansickle (1992) claimed that the key aspects of the RIASEC structure are these two dimensions solely, not the circular nature of the types. Categorizing an individual's interest patterns and work environments on these two dimensions would provide much more useful information than knowing what types are most represented. But we have argued that although the underlying dimensions of the circumplex are important, these are less important than the circular structure itself (Rounds & Tracey, 1993). Knowing that types are arranged in a circle carries more useful information than knowing the underlying dimensions. If the data are arranged in a perfect circle, then any orientation of axes would have equal utility in accounting for data variation. The underlying dimensions could then be viewed as arbitrary, given the circular structure. To adopt an arbitrary orientation of dimensions as the basis for defining the space that exists in a circle appears less straightforward than just recognizing the primacy of the circular structure itself.

To illustrate this argument, the different possible orientations of dimensions underlying the RIASEC circumplex across 77 U.S. RIASEC matrices

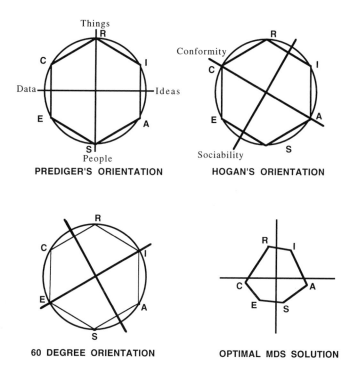

Figure 2. Three theoretical orientations of the two dimensions underlying Holland's circular structure and the empirical optimal structure yielded from three-way multidimensional scaling. Adapted from "Prediger's dimensional representation of Holland's RIASEC circumplex," J. B. Rounds and T. J. G. Tracey, 1993, *Journal of Applied Psychology, 78,* 875–890. Reprinted by permission from the American Psychological Association.

can be examined (Rounds & Tracey, 1993). The three-dimensional orientations underlying the RIASEC circle were examined: Prediger's people–things and data–ideas dimensions, Hogan's conformity (differentiating conventional from artistic) and sociability (differentiating enterprising and social from realistic and investigative) dimensions, and an alternative orientation (60° different from Prediger's) with one dimension differentiating enterprising from investigative and the other dimension differentiating conventional and realistic from social and artistic. All three-dimensional orientations equally accounted for the data (each accounted for 75% of the variance), and thus each could be argued as being the underlying dimensions. In order to determine if there was a "best" orientation, we conducted a three-way multidimensional scaling (MDS) analysis of the 77 RIASEC matrices and the optimal orientation of the underlying dimensions (depicted in Figure 2) was between those of Prediger and Hogan. However, the improvement in fit of this optimal orientation above the others was minor (variance accounted for was .79 versus .75 for the others). The orientation of the underlying dimensions of the RIASEC circle was arbitrary.

Both Prediger's factor model and Holland's circumplex model equally account for the relations among the six RIASEC types, but they differ with respect to focus, the underlying dimensions versus primacy of the circular structure. Given the arbitrary nature of the underlying dimensions, it appears more valid to focus on the circular structure itself over the underlying dimensions.

Generalizability of Holland's Circular Structure

There has been an extensive literature in vocational psychology regarding differences in RIASEC interest scores across different groups varying in gender, culture, and age (Holland, 1985a). This comparison of mean differences among groups is important only to the extent that the structure of the scales is invariant across these groups. To compare scale scores of different groups requires that the scores have the same meaning and structure. It is much less common to examine the structural invariance of interest scales than it is to examine mean differences.

The invariance of the circular order model across gender, instrument, and age was examined on 77 U.S. RIASEC samples (Tracey & Rounds, 1993). No differences in fit across gender were found. In an examination of the structural invariance of the circular order model across gender on one sample of the Strong Interest Inventory (SII), Hansen, Collins, Swanson, and Fouad (1993) concluded that the fit was different for males and females. Their result was contrary to our results, but because they examined only one instrument and our results could be confounded by different instruments, the invariance across gender for only the SII across six separate samples was evaluated (Anderson, Tracey, & Rounds, in press). No support was generated for structural differences across gender on the SII.

When the age of the respondents was divided into those between 14 and 18, those between 18 and 22, and those 22 or older, there was no difference in fit of the circular order model. Nor was there any difference in the fit of the circular model across the four major interest inventories (Vocational Preference Inventory, Self-Directed Search, American College Testing Program, and Strong Interest Inventory). Identical results were obtained when the fit of the exact circumplex was evaluated (Rounds & Tracey, 1993). Regardless of circular model examined (i.e., circular order model, circumplex, or exact circumplex), the structural invariance of the RIASEC circle across gender, age, and instrument was supported.

It is common to assess vocational interests of students in high school and college, and hence most of the studies focus on these age groups. Relatively little is known of vocational interests in people prior to these ages. A recent study by Mueller, Rounds, and Tracey (1996) examined the structure of interests in elementary school children. First an instrument of activities was developed and piloted on college students. The instrument yielded six RIASEC scales that adhered to the circular order model. The instrument was administered to fourth-grade students, and no support was found for the circular structure among the RIASEC scales. The structure of the scales for these children was unidimensional, with the realistic and investigative scales being differentiated from the other four scales. This structure represented a male–female dimension. Independent ratings of the items with respect to their gender supported this interpretation. Items that were viewed as being stereotypically associated with boys anchored one end of the dimension and items stereotypically viewed as associated with girls anchored the other end. Children in the fourth grade organized their interests according to gender role norms. Yet by the time children reached high school, they had interests that had a circular structure. The timing of this shift in structure and the variables that account for this change are exciting avenues of future investigation.

In studies of structural invariance, we did find differences in the fit of the circular order, circumplex, and exact circumplex models between U.S. and non-U.S. samples (Rounds & Tracey, 1993; Tracey & Rounds, 1993). The non-U.S. samples, however, were quite divergent with respect to country and cultural aspects, and it was hard to draw any conclusions. To better examine the cultural invariance of the RIASEC structure, we expanded our search beyond published sources to include dissertations and foreign journals. We generated 96 separate samples, 76 from 18 different countries and 20 from ethnic minority U.S. samples (Rounds & Tracey, 1996a). Relative to the fit of the circular order model obtained on the U.S. samples, the fit of both the foreign and U.S. ethnic minority samples was significantly lower. The circular order model did not account for the RIASEC structure as well for these different cultures. To assess if the structure of the RIASEC scales was related to aspects of economic development in the differing cultures, the extent to which gross domestic product was related to the fit of the circular order model was studied. We thought that more economically developed cultures would have more highly differentiated work environments, and thus individuals' interests would reflect this increased differentiation. However, there was no relation between the gross domestic product and the fit of the circular order model.

An alternative explanation of these results is that the lack of fit of the circular order model could be attributable to the format of the instrument. The U.S. instruments were developed to reflect our culture and usage in different cultures could render the scales and structure useless. Some researchers simply administered the standard inventories unchanged in their cultures, others translated the items, others adapted the scales by altering some items to reflect their own cultures, and other created their own RIASEC scales from scratch. We reasoned that instruments closer to the specific culture (i.e., own creation or adapted) would be more likely to demonstrate the circular structure; however, empirical support was not generated for this hypothesis. All types of instruments, however, demonstrated equally poor fit to the circular model. More work is needed on the different structures across culture and the possible reasons for them.

The lack of support of the circular model for the U.S. ethnic minority samples was surprising. The circular order model did not fit as well for African American, Latino/a, Asian American, or Native American samples as it did for the U.S. samples (the U.S. samples may have included ethnic minorities, but these samples were either samples of convenience or representative samples and thus the minority ethnic groups were not selected specifically nor were they large in numbers). Given the overlap of racial and cultural groups and economic status in this country, perhaps the poorer fit of the circular model in these ethnic minority samples could be attributable to restricted opportunity to act on one's interests and to witness different occupations.

With respect to the U.S. samples, Holland's circular model provides a viable structure of the relations of the RIASEC interest scales, and there are no differences in this structure across gender, age, and instrument. This circular structure was not invariant across culture. For both non-U.S. and U.S. ethnic minority samples, the circular structure fit less well than it did for U.S. samples as a whole.

Structure of High Point Codes

Almost all of the research on the structure of interests and work environments focuses on the relations among the correlations of the RIASEC scales. However, examination of correlational structure ignores differences in the levels of the scales—in other words, mean score differences. RIASEC scales typically are interpreted with respect to high point codes, the one (e.g., a high point code of realistic), two (e.g., a high point code of realistic–investigative or realistic–social), or three (e.g., a high point code of realistic–investigative–artistic or realistic–social–artistic) scales with the highest scores. An individual is informed that she or he is a realistic–investigative type for example and thus should examine occupations that demonstrate a similar pattern. However, these high point codes also should manifest the circular structure if they are to be appropriately interpreted. We examined the circumplex structure of these high point codes for both interest inventories and occupations using log-linear analysis. The results supported the presence of a circumplex structure but only after baseline information was accounted for (Tracey & Rounds, 1992). There clearly are differences in the base rates of different high point codes, and this is especially true across gender. Females have a much higher base rate on the social code as the first or second type than males. Once this general tendency for females to score highest on social (great mean differences across the scales between males and females) the data adhere to a circumplex structure. There are clear differences in the means of the different scales (males are most likely to score highest on realistic and investigative, whereas females score highest on social), but once these differences are accounted for, the structure of the data conforms to a circumplex, supporting usage of this structure with high point codes.

RIASEC Types as Personality Types

Hansen (1984) has noted that there is a long-standing hypothesis in vocational psychology about the interest–personality link. Holland (1973, 1985a) has asserted that his RIASEC interest types are personality types themselves. Hogan (1983) has argued that the two dimensions underlying the RIASEC circle are two of the Big Five personality traits: sociability and conformity. However, exploratory examinations of the correlation of RIASEC scales with personality scales have not yielded support for this contention. There is a moderate correlation between enterprising and social scales with extroversion and a moderate correlation of openness to experience with artistic scales (Bolton, 1985; Costa, McCrae, & Holland, 1984; Goh & Leong, 1993; Gottfredson, Jones, & Holland, 1993; Peraino & Willerman, 1983), but in general, the magnitude of the correlations is small (Holland, 1985a).

One problem with the existing research examining the relation of personality traits with the RIASEC scales is that the circular structure of the RIASEC scales is ignored. Most studies simply correlate the RIASEC scales to, for example, the Big Five trait scales. The Big Five are excellent examples of a factor list approach and thus have been constructed to be relatively independent. The RIASEC scales fit a circumplex model and there are implicit relations among the scales. Given this circular structure, attempts should be made to determine how different personality variables relate to the RIASEC circle itself, not the separate scales. In this vein, we recently regressed the Big Five scales (as measured by the NEO Personality Inventory) onto the RIASEC structure (Rounds & Tracey, 1996b) whereby the means of the Big Five scales for each of the RIASEC types are correlated with the RIASEC scale locations on the circle. Only one of the Big Five traits, extroversion, significantly fit the RIASEC circular structure. Extroversion was placed on the RIASEC circle in an identical manner to Hogan's underlying dimension of sociability depicted in Figure 2. Extroversion differentiated enterprising and social types from realistic and investigative types. Openness to experience had the highest single correlation to an individual scale, artistic, but openness was not related to any of the other RIASEC types in a systematic manner so as to characterize the RIASEC circle (i.e., openness was not negatively correlated with conventional, which it would need to be to serve as the other underlying dimension). There does appear to be some support for viewing extroversion as being one of the underlying dimensions in the RIASEC circle.

Another obvious personality model that may overlap with the RIASEC circle is the interpersonal circle (Kiesler, 1983; Leary, 1957; Wiggins, 1979, 1982). Foa and Foa (1974) have posited that the types of the interpersonal circle can be viewed as a set of cognitive types that form the basis of information processing. If this view of interpersonal cognitive sets is accurate, then extrapolating this idea to how vocational interests are processed may be important. Schneider (1987a, 1987b) has argued that work environments and, by extension, interests are inherently interpersonal, and differing qualities of interpersonal interactions and preferences for interpersonal interactions should be central to all vocational models. In this vein, Broughton, Trapnell, and Boyes (1991) examined the overlap between the Self-Directed Search (SDS; Holland, 1985b) and the Interpersonal Adjective Scale–Revised (IAS-R; Wiggins, Trapnell, & Phillips, 1988). They rescaled the SDS items to create eight scales arranged in a circular structure, instead of the typical six RIASEC scales. They found that the eight revised SDS scales (which they called the Interpersonal Occupation Scales; IOS) corresponded highly with the IAS-R scales, supporting the interpersonal nature of occupational interests. The IOS scales and the IAS-R scales were in agreement; however, there was less correspondence of the SDS RIASEC scales with the IAS-R. It could be that the interpersonal circle and vocational interests *do* overlap, but given the exclusion of several SDS items in the IOS, potentially important aspects of interest variation could be omitted.

Schneider, Ryan, Tracey, and Rounds (in press) examined the overlap of the Vocational Preference Inventory (VPI; Holland, 1985c) and the IAS-R. Using multidimensional scaling and scaling the two instruments together revealed that there were three underlying dimensions accounting for the two circles. The two circles shared the affiliation dimension. The affiliation dimension from the IAS-R was identical to the people–things dimension of the VPI. The IAS-R circle was defined by the underlying dimensions of power and affiliation, whereas the VPI circle was defined by data–ideas and affiliation. There was no variation of the IAS-R scales on the data–ideas dimension nor for the VPI scales on the power dimension. The presence of the same affiliation dimension in both circles caused us to reinterpret the common people–things dimension. It appeared that this dimension did not focus so much on people versus things as on a preference for others versus a lack of preference (or avoidance) of others, which fits more with the affiliation definition of the IAS-R. So types low on affiliation (i.e., realistic and to a lesser degree conventional and investigative) may not be indicating a preference for things per se but a preference for not working closely with others. Thus, recent work has yielded more overlap among RIASEC scales and personality measures than was previously assumed to exist (Holland, 1985a). However, this increased support for the overlap of vocational interest and personality data rests on the incorporation of the underlying circular structure of the RIASEC scales.

EXTENSIONS OF HOLLAND'S CIRCULAR MODEL

To this point, the focus has been on Holland's RIASEC circle, its specification, validity, underlying dimensions, invariance, and overlap with personality dimensions. Recently we have begun to explore possible extensions of Holland's RIASEC model. These extensions include the addition of a prestige dimension to Holland's model leading to a three-dimensional, spherical structure and the study of the six RIASEC types as being arbitrary abstractions of the circle of vocational interests.

Spherical Representation of Interests and Concentric Interest Circles

Prestige is typically one of the primary attributes yielded in studies in the perceptions of occupations (e.g., Goldthorpe & Hope, 1972; Hodge, Siegel, & Rossi, 1964; Plata, 1975; Rounds & Zevon, 1983). The dimension of prestige, however, is rarely invoked in studies of vocational interests. The absence of prestige in vocational interest data may be a methodological artifact attributable to research focusing primarily on scales rather than items. Typically most scales are constructed of items covering a range of prestige, and combining items into scale scores removes prestige variance. We hypothesized (Tracey & Rounds, 1996) that prestige exists in vocational interest data, especially data using occupational titles as items, and that prestige could be combined with the vocational interest circle to provide a spherical representation of interests.

In a study evaluating the prestige dimension, college students responded to their liking of 229 occupational titles that varied with respect to prestige level. The responses were examined using principal components analysis and revealed a general response factor and three substantive factors. Given that the effect of the general factor on the structure of the interest circle is negligible (Rounds & Tracey, 1993), only the three substantive factors were examined. The first two substantive factors were similar to Prediger's people–things and data–ideas dimensions, and the third substantive factor resembled prestige. As a check we correlated the loadings of this prestige factor with standard indicators of prestige and found high correlations, supporting our interpretation that it was indicative of prestige. Given that three dimensions accounted for the items, three separate circles were constructed using pairs of the three dimensions. Each circle created by the two underlying dimensions was divided into octants, and ten items were selected to represent each octant. These items were then summed and examined to see if the octant scale scores fit a circular structure. This procedure created three separate circular structures, one defined by the people–things and data–ideas dimensions, one defined by the people–things and prestige dimensions, and one defined by the data–ideas and prestige dimensions. Combining the three circles into one three-dimensional structure resulted in a sphere, and this spherical representation of interests is presented in Figure 3.

The validity of the spherical structure has been examined on separate samples of college students and high school students using the randomization test of hypothesized order relations (Hubert & Arabie, 1987; Rounds et al., 1992) and multidimensional scaling. The spherical structure was well supported in both cross-validation samples. The support provided for the spherical structure argues against the other three-dimensional structure in the literature—that of a truncated cone posited by Roe (1956). This spherical structure is valuable in that it incorporates an important and previously neglected aspect of interests, that of prestige, with the circular structure of interests. Using the globe as a metaphor with the people–things and data–ideas circle comprising the equator and the prestige dimension comprising the axis from the north to south poles, the spherical structure implies that there is maximal differentiation of the standard people–things and data–ideas circle at the equator (moderate prestige), but as prestige increases or decreases, the importance and differences among interest types decrease, and prestige alone becomes more salient.

Interests as Concentric Circles

In this study we found that an eight-type circle for vocational interests fit the data as well as the more typical six RIASEC-type circle (a result also supported by Trapnell, 1989), which stimulated us to examine (Tracey & Rounds, 1995) if the number of types comprising the interest circle was arbitrary. Could the interest circle be divided into any number of slices and still be valid? To this end, we examined if the items were uniformly distributed around the people–things and data–ideas circle and found that they were. There were no clusters of items that represent naturally occurring interest types. Given this uniform distribution of items, there is no empirical basis for selecting six types as the best means of representing the circle. Eight could serve as well as could 4 or 10 or 16 or 32. Viewing the interest circle as continuous enables one to construct scales of varying complexity to meet assessment and counseling goals. Depending on the context—for example, with someone early in the process of thinking about his or her interests—it may be desirable to represent the interest circle as only four quadrants (e.g., Prediger's [1982] people, data, things, and ideas). In other contexts—for example, someone who has very clear interests but

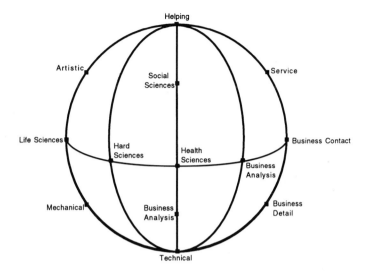

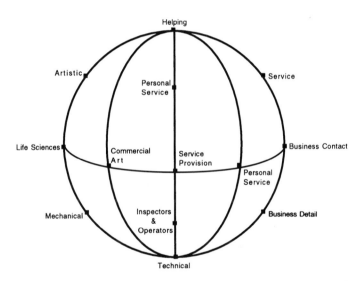

Figure 3. Spherical representation of interests. *Note*: The top half of the sphere is presented above and the bottom half of the sphere is presented below. Adapted from "The Spherical Representation of Vocational Interests," T. J. G. Tracey and J. B. Rounds, 1996, *Journal of Vocational Behavior, 41,* pp. 431–439. Reprinted by permission from Academic Press.

who wishes specific vocational information—the entire circle may not need to be represented. In this more clearly focused example, a much more finely tuned carving of the circle, such as 16 or 32 sections, might be desired. We have proposed a series of concentric circles, varying in complexity, as an alternative to the standard six RIASEC scales to represent the vocational interest circle. The level of specificity could be selected depending on the desired level of complexity of scores required. Our work in this area of variable complexity of interest representation has just begun. Research into the specific content of the different levels of specificity is needed as well as the evaluation of the utility of presenting varying levels of interest complexity to individuals. The assumption of tailoring interest representation to individual need has intuitive appeal but requires examination.

With computerized adaptive testing, it is possible to foresee applications of the spherical and concentric interest circles in interest assessment. These two models build on the circular nature of vocation interests but expand by including a third dimension and viewing the circle in multiple levels of complexity. Viewing interests as circular in nature has served as the basis of the research in vocational psychology for most of the past half century, and by further refining our conceptions about the circular nature of interests, we think that newer generation models can be developed.

REFERENCES

Anderson, M. Z., Tracey, T. J., & Rounds, J. (in press). Examining the invariance of Holland's vocational interest model across sex. *Journal of Vocational Behavior.* Manuscript submitted for publication.

Bolton, B. (1985). Discriminant analysis of Holland's occupational types using the 16 Personality Factor Questionnaire. *Journal of Vocational Behavior, 27,* 210–217.

Borgen, F. H. (1986). New approaches to the assessment of interests. In W. B. Walsh & S. H. Osipow (Eds.), *Advances in vocational psychology: Vol. 1. The assessment of interests* (pp. 31–54). Hillsdale, NJ: Lawrence Erlbaum.

Broughton, R., Trapnell, P. D., & Boyes, M. C. (1991). Classifying personality types with occupational prototypes. *Journal of Research in Personality, 25,* 302–321.

Brown, D., & Brooks, L. (1990). *Career choice and development* (2nd ed.). San Francisco: Jossey-Bass.

Browne, M. W. (1992). Circumplex models for correlation matrices. *Psychometrika, 57,* 469–497.

Costa, P. T., Jr., McCrae, R. R., & Holland, J. L. (1984). Personality and vocational interests in an adult sample. *Journal of Applied Psychology, 69,* 390–400.

Foa, U. G., & Foa, E. B. (1974). *Societal structures of the mind.* Springfield, IL: Charles C. Thomas.

Gati, I. (1991). The structure of vocational interests. *Psychological Bulletin, 109,* 309–324.

Goh, D. S., & Leong, F. T. L. (1993). The relationship between Holland's theory of vocational interests and Eysenck's model of personality. *Personality and Individual Differences, 15,* 555–562.

Goldthorpe, J. H., & Hope, K. (1972). Occupational grading and occupational prestige. In K. Hope (Ed.), *The analysis of social mobility: Methods and approaches* (pp. 131–152). Oxford: Clarendon.

Gottfredson, G. D., & Holland, J. L. (1989). *Dictionary of Holland occupational codes*. Odessa, FL: Psychological Assessment Resources.

Gottfredson, G. D., Jones, E. M., & Holland, J. L. (1993). Personality and vocational interests: The relations of Holland's six interest dimensions to five robust dimensions of personality. *Journal of Counseling Psychology, 40*, 518–524.

Guilford, J. P., Christensen, R. R., Bond, N. A., & Sutton, M. A. (1954). A factor analytic study of human interests. *Psychological Monographs, 68* (4, Whole No. 375).

Guttman, L. (1954). A new approach to factor analysis: The radex. In P. R. Lazarsfeld (Ed.), *Mathematical thinking in the social sciences* (pp. 258–348). Glencoe, IL: Free Press.

Hansen, J. C. (1984). The measurement of vocational interests: Issues and future directions. In S. D. Brown & R. W. Lent (Eds.), *Handbook of counseling psychology* (pp. 99–136). New York: Wiley.

Hansen, J. C., Collins, R. C., Swanson, J. L., & Fouad, N. A. (1993). Gender differences in the structure of interests. *Journal of Vocational Behavior, 42*, 200–211.

Hodge, R. W., Siegel, P. M., & Rossi, P. H. (1964). Occupational prestige in the United States, 1925–1963. *American Journal of Sociology, 70*, 286–302.

Hogan, R. (1983). A socioanalytic theory of personality. In M. M. Page (Ed.), *Nebraska symposium on motivation 1982. Personality: Current theory and research* (pp. 55–89). Lincoln: University of Nebraska Press.

Holland, J. L. (1959). A theory of vocational choice. *Journal of Counseling Psychology, 6*, 35–45.

Holland, J. L. (1973). *Making vocational choices: A theory of careers*. Englewood Cliffs, NJ: Prentice-Hall.

Holland, J. L. (1985a). *Making vocational choices: A theory of vocational personalities and work environments* (2nd ed.). Englewood Cliffs, NJ: Prentice-Hall.

Holland, J. L. (1985b). *Self-Directed Search manual*. Odessa, FL: Psychological Assessment Resources.

Holland, J. L. (1985c). *Vocational Preference Inventory manual* (1985 ed.). Odessa, FL: Psychological Assessment Resources.

Hubert, L., & Arabie, P. (1987). Evaluating order hypotheses within proximity matrices. *Psychological Bulletin, 102*, 172–178.

Jackson, D. N., Holden, R. R., Locklin, R. H., & Marks, E. (1984). Taxonomy of vocational interests of academic major areas. *Journal of Educational Measurement, 21*, 261–275.

Kiesler, D. J. (1983). The 1982 interpersonal circle: A taxonomy for complementarity in human transactions. *Psychological Review, 90*, 185–214.

Kuder, F. (1977). *Activity, interests, and occupational choice.* Chicago: Science Research Associates.

Leary, T. (1957). *The interpersonal diagnosis of personality: A functional theory and methodology for personality evaluation.* New York: Ronald Press.

Mueller, D., Rounds, J. B., & Tracey, T. J. G. (1996). *Structure of vocational interests in elementary school children.* Manuscript in preparation.

Osipow, S. H. (1983). *Theories of career development* (3rd ed.). Englewood Cliffs, NJ: Prentice-Hall.

Peraino, J. M., & Willerman, L. (1983). Personality correlates of occupational status according to Holland types. *Journal of Vocational Behavior, 22,* 268–277.

Plata, M. (1975). Stability and change in prestige rankings of occupations over 49 years. *Journal of Vocational Behavior, 6,* 95–99.

Prediger, D. J. (1982). Dimensions underlying Holland's hexagon: Missing link between interests and occupations? *Journal of Vocational Behavior, 21,* 259–287.

Prediger, D. J., & Vansickle, T. R. (1992). Locating occupations on Holland's hexagon: Beyond RIASEC. *Journal of Vocational Behavior, 40,* 111–128.

Roe, A. (1956). *The psychology of occupations.* New York: Wiley.

Rounds, J. B., & Dawis, R. V. (1979). Factor analysis of Strong Vocational Interest Blank items. *Journal of Applied Psychology, 64,* 132–143.

Rounds, J. B., & Tracey, T. J. G. (1993). Prediger's dimensional representation of Holland's RIASEC circumplex. *Journal of Applied Psychology, 78,* 875–890.

Rounds, J. B., & Tracey, T. J. G. (1996a). Cross-cultural structural equivalence of RIASEC models and measures. *Journal of Counseling Psychology, 43,* 310–329.

Rounds, J. B., & Tracey, T. J. G. (1996b). *Examination of personality constructs in Holland's RIASEC circumplex.* Manuscript in preparation.

Rounds, J. B., Tracey, T. J. G., & Hubert, L. (1992). Methods for evaluating vocational interest structural hypotheses. *Journal of Vocational Behavior, 40,* 239–259.

Rounds, J. B., & Zevon, M. B. (1983). Multidimensional scaling research in vocational psychology. *Applied Psychological Measurement, 7,* 491–510.

Schneider, B. (1987a). E = f(P, B): The road to a radical approach to person–environment fit. *Journal of Vocational Behavior, 31,* 353–361.

Schneider, B. (1987b). The people make the place. *Personnel Psychology, 40,* 437–453.

Schneider, P. L., Ryan, J. M., Tracey, T. J. G., & Rounds, J. B. (in press). Examining the relationship between Holland's RIASEC types and the interpersonal circle. *Measurement and Evaluation in Guidance and Development.*

Tracey, T. J. G., & Rounds, J. B. (1992). Evaluating the RIASEC circumplex using high-point codes. *Journal of Vocational Behavior, 41,* 295–311.

Tracey, T. J. G., & Rounds, J. B. (1993). Evaluating Holland's and Gati's vocational interest models: A structural meta-analysis. *Psychological Bulletin, 113,* 229–246.

Tracey, T. J. G., & Rounds, J. B. (1995). The arbitrary nature of Holland's RIASEC types. *Journal of Counseling Psychology, 41*, 431–439.

Tracey, T. J. G., & Rounds, J. B. (1996). The spherical representation of vocational interests. *Journal of Vocational Behavior, 48*, 3–41.

Trapnell, P. D. (1989). *Structural validity in the measurement of Holland's vocational typology: A measure of Holland's types scaled to an explicit circumplex model.* Unpublished master's thesis, University of British Columbia.

Wiggins, J. S. (1979). A psychological taxonomy of trait-descriptive terms: The interpersonal domain. *Journal of Personality and Social Psychology, 37*, 395–412.

Wiggins, J. S. (1982). Circumplex models of interpersonal behavior in clinical psychology. In P. C. Butcher & J. N. Butcher (Eds.), *Handbook of research methods in clinical psychology* (pp. 183–221). New York: Wiley.

Wiggins, J. S., Trapnell, P., & Phillips, N. (1988). Psychometric and geometric characteristics of the revised Interpersonal Adjective Scales (IAS-R). *Multivariate Behavioral Research, 23*, 128–143.

II

THE CIRCUMPLEX IN
RELATION TO EMOTIONS

9

HOW SHALL AN EMOTION BE CALLED?

JAMES A. RUSSELL

How do people describe the emotions they experience or witness? Descriptions come to us so easily (she's anxious, he's angry, they look bored) that many researchers assume that they already know the answer. But what *is* the answer? Do people (of all ages and all cultures) use a set of basic categories, such as anger, fear, happiness, and sadness? Or do they use a set of dimensions (how pleasant, how aroused), or do they place the emotion within a structure? And if a structure is used, is it a circumplex, a factor analytic simple structure, a hierarchy, or something else?

An understanding of emotions requires an understanding of how lay-persons describe their own emotions and those of others. Description is the basis of knowledge, both scientific and nonscientific, no less for emotion than for anything else. I use the word *emotion* here rather loosely to stand for emotional reactions, moods, affect, and related temporary affectively charged states generally. Of course, there is much more to the study of emotion than the study of lay description. Nevertheless, the lay description is always presupposed in any study of emotion. A layperson's description is an essential part of the psychologist's access to the social cognition and the experience of emotion. Indeed, in the study of emotion, we can do little without relying on lay description directly or indirectly. For instance, to assess emotion, whether in a highly formal manner or simply on the spot, we rely on someone's (perhaps even the psychologist's) description of that emotion or on an instrument that was validated against lay descriptions. Thus, in the study of mood, we ask our patients, clients, or participants in experiments to describe how they feel. Or we might use a biological index that previously had been shown to correlate with such reports. In the study of facial expressions of emotion, we ask observers how, for example, the woman shown in Figure 1 feels.

Before examining such questions, let me ask you another. What are you sitting on as you read this chapter? Let us imagine that you are sitting at your desk and that you reply, "a chair." The answer, "a chair," fails to distinguish what you are sitting on from dining room chairs, bean bag chairs, love seats, car seats, dentist's chairs, judge's benches, thrones, those portable chairs without legs used at the beach, and on and on. *Chair* is a heterogeneous category. Notice that you could have said "my old office chair," or "a dark brown oak chair," or even "a dark brown swiveling oak office chair of a nineteenth-century design." Indeed, there is no clear end to the amount of information you could have included in your description. Or you could have said "a piece of furniture," "manufactured good," "artifact," "physical object," or "thing." Your imaginary one-word answer, "chair," would be misleading if we took it to exhaust your powers of description.

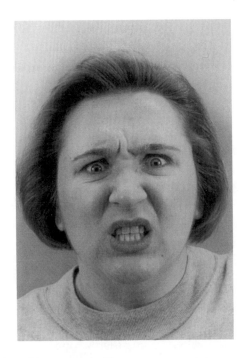

Figure 1. How does this woman feel?

As Brown (1958) observed, speakers select one word (or a very few) from their potential description of the object in question. Which few words the speaker chooses depends on the context of conversation. Speakers withhold details (such as color) that they think the listener does not want. Speakers withhold knowledge (that chairs are objects) that they assume the listener already has. Therefore most of a description remains implicit.

Now return to the woman shown in Figure 1. How is she feeling? Many readers would say "angry." Here again, you could say more. "She looks as if she has been frustrated; she is furious, determined to make herself heard." Indeed, your description could include indefinitely many details, especially if you had more information than simply a still photograph of her facial expression. Or you could have selected another single word: She is "furious," "frustrated," "determined," "attentive," "aroused," "unhappy," "awake," "upset," "emotional," and so on. The one word answer, "angry," would be misleading if we took it to be the full extent of anyone's description of the woman's emotion. The same is true when we ask our patients, clients, or participants in an experiment about their own moods or emotional reactions.

Psychologists' instruments for the description of emotion typically yield the equivalent of a one-word answer. A major roadblock to progress in the psychology of emotion is that our descriptions are too simple by an order of magnitude. To describe a particular instance of emotion as *anger* both says too much (the concept of anger suggests various features that may not be true in a particular case) and too little (much else remains unspecified). For a full account of how emotions are understood, we need to make explicit the full extent of a person's description of an emotion, much of which is omitted or only implicit in their short answers. My theme in this chapter is that all six of the following properties are required to give a complete portrait of how emotions are described. All six are invoked when someone describes any particular emotion (that is, a particular person's emotion at a specific time and place). Any one of these six properties, considered alone, provides only a partial picture and—like any partial truth—can be misleading.

1. A specific instance of an emotion is a member of a category, indeed of many categories.
2. Membership in each emotion category is a matter of degree rather than all or none.
3. Emotion categories are related to each other as described by a circumplex.
4. Emotions fall along certain continua, such as intensity, degree of pleasure or displeasure (hedonic value), and amount of arousal.

5. Emotion categories are understood in terms of a script, which is a prototypical sequence of causally connected and temporally ordered constituents.

6. Emotion categories are embedded in a fuzzy hierarchy.

Each of these properties (and others) has been offered as *the* way to describe emotions—hence controversies on categories versus dimensions, cluster analysis versus multidimensional scaling, and fuzzy categories versus the circumplex. Our instruments for assessing moods or self-reported emotions are based often on only one of these partial truths and thus fail to yield a full description. Let us consider each property in turn and then how they are related to one another.

CATEGORIES OF EMOTION

We never step into the same river twice, because we always encounter individual water molecules never encountered before. True, but it is usually more useful to ignore the uniqueness of each water molecule and simply treat all water molecules as members of the same category. Fortunately, our brain does this categorization for us, and only long philosophical reflection could lead us to see the utter novelty of everything we encounter. Probably the most important thing we do with objects and events is to categorize them. Much of the human cortex seems devoted to categorizing what the world offers (Marr, 1970). And not just in humans. The rabbit does not treat each event or object as something unique and novel but responds to it as an example of a category—a carrot, for example. In turn, Peter Rabbit, however unique to Heraclitus, is just a member of the category of rabbits to the fox. By knowing its category membership, the fox predicts how this particular rabbit, never seen before, will run away but is worth pursuing because it will make a good meal.

We never encounter or experience the same emotion twice, but we make each instance of emotion understandable by grouping it with other instances that it resembles by categorizing it. Happiness, anger, fear, jealousy—the English language provides somewhere between 500 and 2,000 labels for emotion categories. Categories of emotion are the most obvious part of the description of emotion. What has been less obvious are two additional facts.

First, happiness, anger, fear, jealousy, and our other categories seem so natural and obvious that we tend to assume that all human beings must categorize the emotions in the same way. Thus, theorists such as Ekman (1972) and Izard (1977) have assumed that, in recognizing facial expressions of emotion, all human beings rely on the same universal and innate categories. However, linguists and anthropologists have found counterexamples. The categories of emotion found in other languages and cultures often resemble the categories available in Indo-European languages, but differences can be found as well (Russell, 1991b; Wierzbicka, 1992).

Second, the same specific emotional state is a member of many different categories. See Russell (1989) for details on this second fact.

FUZZY MEMBERSHIP

Membership in a category is not either–or but rather a matter of degree. In everyday conversation, we say that the glass is full, even when it is only 90% full. We tend to round off, saying that the woman in Figure 1 is angry (rounding to 100%) and ignoring the other categories (rounding to 0%). Nevertheless, when asked, anyone can readily estimate degree of category membership. And cases exist that defy categorization: The borders of emotion categories are vague.

That categories admit their members in degrees and have fuzzy boundaries has turned out to be one of the most exciting, practical, and theoretically important ideas in a range of fields. Fuzzy logic supplements traditional two-valued (true–false) logic. The major uses so far have been in computer technology and engineering, but the impact also has been felt from linguistics (Lakoff, 1987) to psychology (Neisser, 1979; Ogden, 1977; Rosch, 1975).

Rather than forcing us to draw an arbitrary line between, for example, the category of chairs and not-chairs, fuzzy categories allow us to note degrees of chairness. Or degrees of birdness (from robins to owls to emus to penguins to pterodactyls to bats), of humanity (adult humans to newborns to Neanderthal fetuses), or of emotions (from anger to pride to boredom to serenity), or of love (from mother's love and romantic love to infatuation to love of books). The fuzziness of emotion categories now has been well established (Averill, 1980; Fehr & Russell, 1984; Fehr, Russell, & Ward, 1982; Russell, 1991a).

THE CIRCUMPLEX OF EMOTION

Once we have more than one category, the question arises how the categories are related one to another. Some order more informative than an alphabetically arranged list must be established for the emotion categories expressed in each language.

Some measuring instruments (such as the commonly used forced-choice format in which observers choose one emotion from a short list) assume that any two category labels are either synonyms or mutually exclusive. Other instruments (such as self-report mood scales) typically assume that two labels are either synonyms or independent of one another. (The typical self-report assessment scale achieved through factor analysis, for example, assumes independent clusters of alleged synonyms.) Again, we see reality forced into a Procrustean either–or mold. The obvious possibility not allowed in these traditional approaches is that different category labels are related to one another in different ways: Some are synonyms, some mutually exclusive, some independent, but most are none of these exactly. Examination of the correlations actually measured between emotion categories suggests that they can bear any degree of relationship to one another.

A structure (that is, a representation of relations among categories) that is capable of capturing a continuously varying reality—and indeed that is now well established for emotion—is the circumplex. Figure 2 shows a schematic representation of a circumplex that illustrates how emotions, feelings, moods, and related states fall in a continuous order around the perimeter of a two-dimensional space. Adjacent categories are more similar. Categories 180° apart are opposites. The center of the space establishes a neutral point or adaptation level. The shortest distance from the neutral point to the location of a particular emotion represents the *intensity* of that emotion.

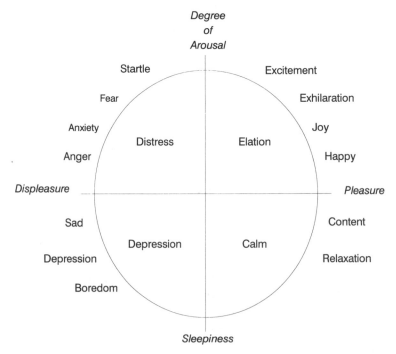

Figure 2. A circumplex for emotions.

A circumplex for emotion is being discovered more and more frequently. To my knowledge, Schlosberg's circular ordering for emotions (1941) came first; 17 years passed before Plutchik's (1958, 1962), then 22 more years before Russell's (1980). After that, only 3 years passed before Daly, Lancee, and Polivy's (1983), and another 2 years before Watson and Tellegen's (1985) and Fisher, Heise, Bohrnstedt, and Lucke's (1985). After that, the time gaps are too small to estimate accurately.

Each researcher has developed a circumplex based on somewhat different data, asking a somewhat different question. Any one representation will depend on the sample of research participants, the analytic technique, the exact domain sampled, the means of assessing the relationship between emotions, and so forth. Nevertheless, the convergence obtained despite these sources of variation is impressive. Figure 2 is an attempt to abstract across these different investigations.

To illustrate the convergence within one domain, consider the description of emotion through facial expression; Figure 3 shows a circumplex of facial expressions.

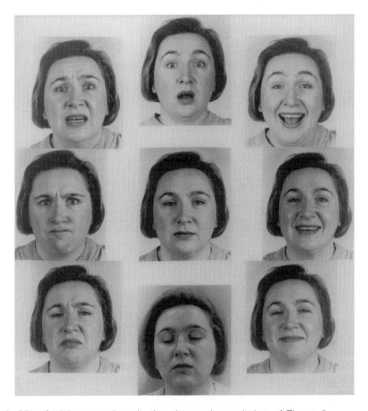

Figure 3. Nine facial expressions in the circumplex ordering of Figure 2.

Schlosberg's (1941) results were replicated by Triandis and Lambert (1958) in Greece and by Osgood (1966) in Sweden. Abelson and Sermat (1962) replicated Schlosberg's results with a different technique—multidimensional scaling. Russell did so with children and in several cultures. Even 2-year-olds judge facial expressions in a way that yields a circumplex. Indeed, a circumplex for facial expressions was found in participants even with extensive brain damage (Adolphs, Tranel, Damasio, & Damasio, 1994), the only exception being one patient with bilateral destruction of the amygdala.

A circumplex is also an appropriate structure for self-reported feelings. When people are presented with a set of mood-descriptive adjectives or sentences, their responses are structured as predicted by the circumplex. The circumplex is the most successful model in this domain. Initially, a factor-analytically simple structure (a moderate number of independent unipolar dimensions) seemed more successful (Borgatta, 1961; Izard, 1972; McNair & Lorr, 1964; Nowlis & Nowlis, 1956) but lately has been surpassed by the circumplex. When the unipolar scales are expressed as a function of the dimensions of the circumplex, plus a method factor, most of the reliable variance is accounted for (Russell & Mehrabian, 1977). The clearest success of the circumplex is in its prediction of bipolarity rather than unipolarity. Lorr and Thayer, who had earlier interpreted their results in terms of unipolar factors (McNair & Lorr, 1964; Thayer, 1967), found, on closer inspection, bipolar factors (Lorr, 1989; Thayer, 1978, 1986). Russell (1979) showed that the more method artifacts are removed, the clearer the evidence for bipolarity. The coup de grâce was given to the unipolar view by a study using confirmatory factor analysis by Green, Goldman, and Salovey (1993).

Plutchik observed that emotions can be described in various terms: emotions, behaviors, functions, defense mechanisms, personality traits. Each of these yields a meaningful circular ordering (Plutchik, 1980). In the same way, Thayer (1986) studied actual and perceived physiological arousal associated with emotion and proposed a structure similar to a circumplex.

Consider as well the range of analytic techniques that have yielded support for a circumplex: exploratory and confirmatory factor analysis, multiple regression, and multidimensional scaling have been mentioned already. In an experimental paradigm on emotion judgments, Russell and Fehr (1987) confirmed predictions derived from the circumplex. Most such techniques have relied on verbal data and thus an important question is whether the circumplex is dependent on language. Because similar results have been found across languages, certainly no one language is essential. When the circumplex is derived from observers' judgments of similarity between faces, verbal labels play no explicit role in the results (although they could play a covert role). The results with preschool children are perhaps the most telling: 2-year-olds make judgments that conform to a circumplex and yet show no signs of knowing verbal labels (anger, fear, etc.) that they might attach to the faces.

It is arbitrary for me to stop here: A circular ordering has emerged in various domains, as the other chapters in this volume attest. A circumplex structure is ubiquitous in psychology. It is an empirical finding that a circumplex emerges in all these domains. Nothing logical or mathematical forces that same structure to emerge. However, we need to develop analytic techniques for establishing when two circumplexes are the same. For example, one question worth pondering is the extent to which other domains are structured as a circumplex *because* they are related to emotion.

DIMENSIONS OF EMOTION

Figure 2 also is interpretable with dimensions. Indeed, from the beginning, the circumplex has suggested dimensions: Schlosberg's (1941) circular ordering revealed two underlying dimensions: pleasant–unpleasant and attention–rejection. Although the pleasant–unpleasant dimension has been interpreted similarly across investigators, the second dimension has not. Schlosberg himself later added a third—degree of activation (Schlosberg, 1954), but this was found to be largely redundant with attention–rejection (Abelson & Sermat, 1962)—thus leaving two interpretations of the same dimension. Still another interpretation is degree of engagement (Watson & Tellegen, 1985). With the center of the space thought of as a neutral point or adaptation level, intensity is the distance outward.

Thinking of human emotions as varying along underlying continua can be traced back as far as people have written about human feelings. Greek philosophers spoke of the essential role of pleasure and displeasure in human life. Darwin and Spencer spoke of a dimension of activation. Wundt's introspection yielded three dimensions (pleasant–unpleasant, excited–relaxed, tense–depressed). The full dimensional structure of emotion has yet to be worked out, but the outlines are clear enough.

SCRIPTS

What is the meaning of a category label, such as *anger, fear,* or *embarrassment?* Various theories of meaning have been proposed, but no successful classical theory has been defended; that is, no one has been able to state features common to all and only cases of anger, or fear, or embarrassment. Following the lead of James, Wittgenstein, Averill, Rosch, and others, Fehr and Russell (1984) suggested that nonclassical alternatives should be explored as ways to define emotion words. Their specific proposal was that an emotion word is understood as a script.

To know the meaning of a word such as anger is to know anger's prototypical sequence. Its antecedent causes, feelings, physiological changes, expressions, actions, and consequences unfold in a causally connected temporal order. No one of these features need be necessary or sufficient. Instead, a person compares the features of a particular case with the full prototypical sequence. The greater the resemblance, the greater its degree of membership in the category of anger (and hence gradedness of membership and the fuzziness of borders). As a consequence, two actual cases of anger, for example, each may resemble the prototype in different ways but share little in common with each other.

In everyday language, we sometimes say that, given an event and someone's overt reaction to it, an observer *infers* the emotion of the other. On the script hypothesis, this manner of speaking is somewhat misleading. There is no emotion other than the full script: Emotion is not an event that exists in addition to the constituents of the script, their temporal order, and causal connections. Of course, an observer often infers some of the constituents, especially the private feelings of another. Given any *one* feature of the script known to be present, and no contrary information, the observer is often willing to infer other parts of the script. (Given only a facial expression or vocal intonation, participants may label the expresser as angry. Given an antecedent event, such as an insult, the observer similarly will guess the rest of the sequence.) When more features of the script are known, then observers are more confident in their inference.

I believe that a similar story can be told when the observer and the expresser are the same person. In the case of self-observation, the observer has the advantage of better information, including memories of previous encounters and access to private information such as feelings. Nevertheless, the self-observer is still not infallible. I can deny sincerely that I am jealous or envious, and yet jealousy or envy might still be the most objective description of my state.

The script theory concerns the layperson's concept of anger (and other emotions), but researchers have developed a concept of anger per se following the same pattern. Different theorists have pointed to different features, but taken together, psychology's concepts are evolving toward the layperson's. For example, Izard (1971, 1977) pointed to feelings, physiological correlates, and expressive behaviors as the constituents of individual emotions. Frijda (1986) pointed to cognitive processing of antecedent events and subsequent actions as the constituents. Plutchik (1994) and Scherer (1992) viewed emotions as a series of steps.

The notion of scripts reveals a further ambiguity in the description of instances of emotion. Suppose that an observer labels a specific event as *anger*. From that label, we do not know precisely which features of the anger script the observer is willing to endorse and to what degree. If the event labeled anger, for instance, concerned the woman of Figure 1, the observer might infer that she is reacting to something she finds offensive but that she will be unlikely to commit an aggressive act. In another case, the observer might be uncertain about the precipitating event but be confident that aggression is sure to follow. Because no one feature of the anger script is necessary, the observer's use of the word *anger* is compatible with both of these cases.

A FUZZY HIERARCHY

Everyone knows that annoyance is a type of (a subcategory of) anger, anger is a type of being upset, upset is a type of emotion, and emotion is a type of temporary state. Such relations suggest a class-inclusion hierarchy and the method of hierarchical cluster analysis. And some writers have followed this line of thought. Yet these categories are not strict examples of set inclusion and violate the principles of a hierarchy (Russell & Fehr, 1994). There exist cases of annoyance that are not anger, cases of annoyance that are not examples of being upset, emotions that are not temporary, and so on. None of this is surprising, because natural language hierarchies in general fail as strict class-inclusion hierarchies. (A car seat is a chair, and a chair is a piece of furniture, but a car seat is not a piece of furniture.)

So we have a paradox. Emotion categories appear to form a hierarchy and yet they lack its essential feature of class inclusion. The notion of a *fuzzy hierarchy* attempts to resolve this paradox by describing how two properties of emotion categories together can simulate a class-inclusion hierarchy. First, different categories overlap (the same specific event can be a member of emotion, jealousy, and anger), and, second, categories vary in breadth (fewer events qualify as anger than as emotion, fewer still as jealousy). In this way, many (although not all) examples of jealousy are also cases of anger and many (although not all) examples of anger are also cases of emotion. Thus, many cases do fit a hierarchy (although not all), but the relations are not strict class inclusion.

RELATIONS AMONG THESE SIX PROPERTIES

A full description of a person's understanding of any emotional state requires at least the six properties I have outlined. Far from being in opposition to one another, these six are related to one another.

The most obvious fact about emotions is that we categorize them, because our words (only proper names are excepted) are associated with general categories rather than with particulars. The remaining properties elaborate on the nature of these categories (defined by scripts, the features of which are dimensions and which admit degrees of membership) or relations between two or more categories (relations specified by the circumplex and fuzzy hierarchy).

Consider the traditional dispute between categories and dimensions. The meaning of words in general is not either categorical or dimensional. *Warm* is a category that specifies a (fuzzy) region along an underlying dimension of temperature. We create categories even when we recognize that we are dealing with something that is inherently dimensional as when we break up height into *short* and *tall*. In the same way, many (but not all) uses of *happy* and *sad* capture a region along a simple bipolar dimension.

Actual instances of emotion are members of more than one category; indeed, if membership is thought of as a continuum from 0% to 100%, then there is no need to choose which categories any specific instance falls into: any actual instance is described by its membership in all categories. In using any one emotion category, it is therefore essential to recognize that membership in each category is graded, that categories are related to one another in a systematic fashion—hence the circumplex and the fuzzy hierarchy.

The proponents of the circumplex anticipated fuzzy logic by placing emotions not in separate categories but by charting their varying degrees of overlap. Indeed, the circumplex is directly derivable from fuzzy-category membership. Observers can rate facial expressions (or other emotional stimuli, such as their current mood) as to their degree of membership in various categories. If we have such ratings for a reasonable sample of facial expressions and of emotion words, the ratings can be used to derive a circumplex (Russell & Bullock, 1986). (Schlosberg's evidence showed the same result, although Schlosberg was steeped in the tradition of either–or categories and therefore referred to some judgments as *correct* and to the others as *errors*. It was the "errors" that revealed the circumplex—showing that far from being errors they were systematic.)

Let me end on an interesting new line of thought that ties the circumplex to dimensions. Feldman (1995a, 1995b) has discovered individual differences in the circumplex. She theorizes that individuals differ in the degree to which they monitor the hedonic versus arousal components of their emotional state. The result is that the circumplex varies in shape for different individuals. The perfectly round circumplex represents the group, but each individual's circumplex is an ellipse elongated along either the horizontal or the vertical dimension.

CONCLUSION

Imagine a man sitting in a movie theater absorbed in a horror movie. Is he experiencing fear? He's feeling agitated, but he does not flee; indeed, he paid money to have this state created in him. Although riveted, his face is impassive. Fear is usually unpleasant, but this man says that he thoroughly enjoys this film. He's in no real danger, and he knows it. So, is he experiencing fear? Some readers may decide yes, others no, but most recognize that the question is not easy to answer and that psychology has not agreed on a method to answer this question.

Questions of this sort plague the psychology of emotion. This very question arises in studies in which films are used to induce emotion in order that facial behavior or some physiological correlates of fear might be assessed. Similar questions arise at a conceptual level whenever a researcher or a theorist tries to state just what counts as fear or any other type of emotion.

The answer implied by the present analysis is that the original question—like "what time is it on the moon?"—has no good answer. As put, the question presupposes the traditional two-valued logic: the movie-goer is either afraid (1.0) or not (0). According to fuzzy logic, the man's state is a member of the category of fear to some intermediate degree, say, .6. According to the circumplex, he is described as belonging to a range of emotion categories. According to a dimensional analysis, the man is in a highly aroused but pleasant state. According to the script hypothesis, his state shows some features of fear (his mind is filled with danger, he is physiologically aroused, mentally agitated), but not others (no real danger, no flight, no agony).

A full description of this man's emotional state cannot be captured adequately with any one of the six properties I listed. But then few if any of our emotional states can. Fear in the movie theater exemplifies the complexity of our emotional lives. Our descriptions must come to reveal rather than conceal that complexity.

REFERENCES

Abelson, R. P., & Sermat, V. (1962). Multidimensional scaling of facial expressions. *Journal of Experimental Psychology, 63,* 546–554.

Adolphs, R., Tranel, D., Damasio, H., & Damasio, A. (1994). Impaired recognition of emotion in facial expressions following bilateral damage to the human amygdala. *Nature, 372,* 669–672.

Averill, J. R. (1980). A constructivist view of emotion. In R. Plutchik & H. Kellerman (Eds.), *Theories of emotion* (Vol. 1, pp. 305–340). New York: Academic Press.

Borgatta, E. I. (1961). Mood, personality, and interaction. *Journal of General Psychology, 64,* 105–137.

Brown, R. (1958). How shall a thing be called? *Psychological Review, 65,* 14–21.

Daly, E. M., Lancee, W. J., & Polivy, J. (1983). A conical model for the taxonomy of emotional experience. *Journal of Personality and Social Psychology, 45,* 443–457.

Ekman, P. (1972). Universals and cultural differences in facial expressions of emotion. In J. K. Cole (Ed.), *Nebraska Symposium on Motivation, 1971.* Lincoln: University of Nebraska Press.

Fehr, B., & Russell, J. A. (1984). Concept of emotion viewed from a prototype perspective. *Journal of Experimental Psychology: General, 113,* 464–486.

Fehr, B., Russell, J. A., & Ward, L. M. (1982). Prototypicality of emotions: A reaction time study. *Bulletin of the Psychonomic Society, 20,* 253–254.

Feldman, L. A. (1995a). Valence-focus and arousal-focus: Individual differences in the structure of affective experience. *Journal of Personality and Social Psychology, 69,* 153–166.

Feldman, L. A. (1995b). Variations in the circumplex structure of emotion. *Personality and Social Psychology Bulletin, 21,* 806–817.

Fisher, G. A., Heise, D. R., Bohrnstedt, G. W., & Lucke, J. I. (1985). Evidence for extending the circumplex model of personality trial language to self-reported moods. *Journal of Personality and Social Psychology, 49,* 233–242.

Frijda, N. H. (1986). *The emotions.* Cambridge: Cambridge University Press.

Green, D. P., Goldman, S. L., & Salovey, P. (1993). Measurement error masks bipolarity of affect ratings. *Journal of Personality and Social Psychology, 64,* 1029–1041.

Izard, C. E. (1971). *The face of emotion.* New York: Appleton-Century-Crofts.

Izard, C. E. (1972). *Patterns of emotions.* New York: Academic Press.

Izard, C. E. (1977). *Human emotions.* New York: Plenum Press.

Lakoff, G. (1987). *Women, fire, and dangerous things: What categories reveal about the mind.* Chicago: University of Chicago Press.

Lorr, M. (1989). Models and methods for measurement of mood. In R. Plutchik & H. Kellerman (Eds.), *Emotion: Theory, research, and experience* (Vol. 4, pp. 37–53). San Diego, CA: Academic Press.

Marr, D. (1970). A theory for cerebral neocortex. *Proceedings of the Royal Society of London* (Series B), *176,* 161.

McNair, D. M., & Lorr, M. (1964). An analysis of mood in neurotics. *Journal of Abnormal and Social Psychology, 69,* 620–627.

Neisser, U. (1979). The concept of intelligence. *Intelligence, 3,* 217–227.

Nowlis, V., & Nowlis, H. H. (1956). The description and analysis of mood. *Annals of the New York Academy of Sciences, 65,* 345–355.

Ogden, G. (1977). Fuzziness in semantic memory: Choosing exemplars of subjective categories. *Memory and Cognition, 5,* 198–204.

Osgood, C. E. (1966). Dimensionality of the semantic space for communication via facial expressions. *Scandinavian Journal of Psychology, 7,* 1–30.

Plutchik, R. (1958). Outlines of a new theory of emotion. *Transactions of the New York Academy of Sciences, 20,* 394–403.

Plutchik, R. (1962). *The emotions: Fact, theories, and a new model.* New York: Random House.

Plutchik, R. (1980). *Emotion: A psychoevolutionary synthesis.* New York: Harper & Row.

Plutchik, R. (1994). *The psychology and biology of emotion.* New York: Harper Collins.

Rosch, E. (1975). Cognitive representations of semantic categories. *Journal of Experimental Psychology: General, 104,* 192–233.

Russell, J. A. (1979). Affective space is bipolar. *Journal of Personality and Social Psychology, 37,* 345–356.

Russell, J. A. (1980). A circumplex model of affect. *Journal of Personality and Social Psychology, 39,* 1161–1178.

Russell, J. A. (1989). Culture, scripts, and children's understanding of emotion. In C. Saarni & P. Harris (Eds.), *Children's understanding of emotion* (pp. 293–318). Cambridge: Cambridge University Press.

Russell, J. A. (1991a). In defense of a prototype approach to emotion concepts. *Journal of Personality and Social Psychology, 60,* 37–47.

Russell, J. A. (1991b). Culture and the categorization of emotion. *Psychological Bulletin, 110,* 426–450.

Russell, J. A., & Bullock, M. (1986). Fuzzy concepts and the perception of emotion in facial expressions. *Social Cognition, 4,* 309–341.

Russell, J. A., & Fehr, B. (1987). Relativity in the perception of emotion in facial expressions. *Journal of Experimental Psychology: General, 116,* 223–237.

Russell, J. A., & Fehr, B. (1994). Fuzzy concepts in a fuzzy hierarchy: Varieties of anger. *Journal of Personality and Social Psychology, 67,* 186–205.

Russell, J. A., & Mehrabian, A. (1977). Evidence for a three-factor theory of emotions. *Journal of Research in Personality, 11,* 273–294.

Scherer, K. (1992). What does a facial expression express? In K. Strongman (Ed.), *International review of studies on emotion* (pp. 139–165). New York: Wiley.

Schlosberg, H. (1941). A scale for judgment of facial expressions. *Journal of Experimental Psychology, 29,* 497–510.

Schlosberg, H. (1954). Three dimensions of emotion. *Psychological Review, 61,* 81–88.

Thayer, R. E. (1967). Measurement of activation through self-report. *Psychological Reports, 20,* 663–678.

Thayer, R. E. (1978). Toward a psychological theory of multidimensional activation (arousal). *Motivation and Emotion, 2,* 1–34.

Thayer, R. E. (1986). Activation–deactivation adjective checklist: Current overview and structural analysis. *Psychological Reports, 58,* 607–614.

Triandis, H. C., & Lambert, W. W. (1958). A restatement and test of Schlosberg's theory of emotion with two kinds of subjects from Greece. *Journal of Abnormal and Social Psychology, 56,* 321–328.

Watson, D., & Tellegen, A. (1985). Toward a consensual structure of mood. *Psychological Bulletin, 98,* 219–235.

Wierzbicka, A. (1992). *Semantics, culture and cognition.* New York: Oxford University Press.

10

A CIRCUMPLEX INVENTORY OF IMPACT MESSAGES: AN OPERATIONAL BRIDGE BETWEEN EMOTION AND INTERPERSONAL BEHAVIOR

DONALD J. KIESLER, JAMES A. SCHMIDT, and
CHRISTOPHER C. WAGNER

This chapter will describe the development of a circumplex Impact Message Inventory (IMI; Kiesler, 1987a; Kiesler, Anchin, et al., 1976, 1985; Kiesler & Schmidt, 1993; Perkins et al., 1979), which was designed to measure the distinctive covert behaviors between individuals as they reciprocally interact during a particular interpersonal transaction.

We first will summarize the procedure used for development of the IMI. Then we will detail the methods of analysis we have used to demonstrate the IMI's circumplex structure. Finally, we will argue that the covert interpersonal engagements measured by the IMI, which in turn contribute toward mediation of an individual's overt reactions, can be conceptualized best as components of a transactional emotion process that is peculiarly essential to interpersonal behavior itself. We will conclude that (a) a significant class of emotional phenomena is transactional–interpersonal in nature and that (b) emotion is an essential component of the cyclical interpersonal transaction process.

PROLOGUE: SOME NECESSARY INTERPERSONAL COMMUNICATION THEORY

The original IMI was designed to measure the command or relationship messages registered covertly by therapists in reaction to their patients' verbal and nonverbal behaviors during psychotherapy sessions. It was embedded in Kiesler's evolving interpersonal communications conceptualization of personality, psychopathology, and psychotherapy (Kiesler, 1979, 1982a, 1982b, 1983, 1986a, 1986b, 1988; Kiesler, Bernstein, & Anchin, 1976). The focus was on psychotherapy phenomena referred to by Freudians as *transference–countertransference* and by Sullivan as *parataxic distortions*.

A central proposition in the conceptualization of the IMI was that a relationship is the momentary and cumulative result of the reciprocal *command messages* (Ruesch & Bateson, 1951), primarily nonverbal, exchanged between two interactants (Kiesler, 1979). One half of a relationship is the encoder to decoder (ED) *evoking message* (Beier, 1966), by which an encoder imposes a condition of emotional, cognitive, and imaginal engagement on the decoder. As a result of the ED-evoking message the decoder is "pulled" to countercommunicate or respond as the encoder wishes without the decoder's being clearly aware of his or her compliance.

The second half of a relationship consists of decoder to encoder (DE) messages registered covertly by the decoder in response to the ED messages. These emotional, cognitive, behavioral, and fantasy covert responses of the decoder were named the DE-*impact message* (Kiesler, 1979, 1982b, 1988; Kiesler, Bernstein, & Anchin, 1976). The decoder's reciprocal covert responses represent the receiving end of relationship communication. They comprise the impacts or pulls-to-respond that are a direct result of the encoder's evoking messages.

The Nature of Impact Messages

Several classes of impact messages can be distinguished (Kiesler, 1982b, 1988): (a) *direct feelings*—when Interactant B is with Person A, Person A arouses distinct feelings and pulls specific emotions from him or her (e.g., bored, angry, suspicious, competitive, cautious, etc.); (b) *action tendencies*—Interactant B also experiences definite urges or pulls to do or not to do something with Person A (e.g., I should avoid interrupting him; I should leave her alone; I should defend myself; I have to be gentle with her; I have to find some answers soon; etc.); (c) *perceived evoking messages*—when with Person A, various thoughts run through Interactant B's head about what Person A is trying to do to him or her or what he or she thinks Person A wants Interactant B to do, including thoughts about what Person A is feeling or thinking about Interactant B (e.g., this person wants me to put him on a pedestal; she thinks I can't be trusted; he would rather be left alone; she is determined to be in control of me; he wants to be the center of attention; etc.); and (d) *fantasies*—when with Person A, interactant B may experience more or less vivid images of himself or herself in concrete interactions with person A (e.g., Persons A and B on separate rafts floating out to sea; Interactant B holding Person A in her lap in a rocking chair; Persons A and B playing poker, each wearing dark glasses; Persons A and B making love on a white sand beach; etc.).

Within contemporary interpersonal theory (Anchin & Kiesler, 1982; Carson, 1969; Kiesler, 1982a, 1983, 1991; Leary, 1957; Wiggins, 1982) the ED-evoking message is equivalent to the interpersonal reflex (Leary, 1957) or interpersonal act. An interpersonal act imposes a condition or command as a result of which an interactant tends to behave as Person A signaled. At mostly automatic levels interpersonal actions are designed to push or force others to respond in ways that confirm self-definitions and self-presentations—and that make it more likely that we will act in our preferred (similar) manner again. Our interpersonal behavior serves the function of establishing distinctive kinds of relationships with others—relationships that are comfortable, anxiety-free, and that serve to confirm our conceptions of who we are as individuals. A major effect of this transactional negotiation is that we begin to restrict the covert experience of persons interacting with us in a manner that makes it more likely they will respond overtly in the ways we desire. As interpersonal acts, ED-evoking messages express relationship messages or presentational claims that fall in the two-factor space of control and affiliation as represented on the interpersonal circle.

Interpersonal Complementarity

In a similar way, in interpersonal theory the DE-impact message is equivalent to the first stage of the complementary response (Carson, 1969; Kiesler, 1983; Orford, 1986). The broadest notion of reciprocity or complementarity is that interpersonal acts are designed to invite, pull, elicit, draw, entice, or evoke restricted classes of reactions from those with whom we interact, especially from significant others. Reactions by others to these acts are not random, nor are they likely to include the entire range of possible reactions. Rather, they tend to be restricted to a relatively narrow range of interpersonal responses.

Complementarity is specifically defined in terms of interpersonal behavior as operationalized by the two-dimensional interpersonal circle (Carson, 1969; Kiesler, 1983). Complementarity occurs on the basis of (a) reciprocity in respect to the control dimension (dominance pulls submission, submission pulls dominance) and (b) correspondence in regard to the affiliation dimension (friendliness pulls friendliness, hostility pulls hostility). In other words, complementarity exists among interactants when Interactant B reacts to Person A with interpersonal acts that are reciprocal in terms of control and corresponding in terms of affiliation. Through complementary responses, Interactant B essentially confirms Person A's self-presentational bids on both the control and affiliation axes. Figure 1 pres-

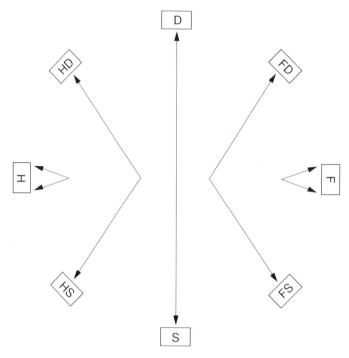

Figure 1. Complementary octants of the Interpersonal Circle (D = dominant; HD = hostile–dominant; H = hostile; HS = hostile–submissive; S = submissive; FS = friendly–submissive; F = friendly; FD = friendly–dominant).

ents the complementary octants of the interpersonal circle: D (dominant), HD (hostile–dominant), H (hostile), HS (hostile–submissive), S (submissive), FS (friendly–submissive), F (friendly), FD (friendly–dominant). It illustrates that the complementary response always occurs vertically within the circle and always within the right or left half.

A given instance of successful negotiation for the complementary response consists of a two-stage sequence occurring rapidly in Interactant B: (a) a covert response, labeled the DE *impact message*, and (b) the subsequent overt reaction, labeled the *complementary response* (Kiesler, 1983, pp. 205–206). To illustrate, Person B initiates a transaction with Person A, whose characteristic interpersonal behaviors are measured at the circle octant hostile–submissive (see Figure 1). As their transaction proceeds, B increasingly experiences the covert first stage of complementarity pull by registering covert impacts that are complementary to Person A's circle categories: direct feelings such as feeling "superior to him" and "frustrated that he won't defend his position"; action tendencies such as "I should be very gentle with him" and "I could tell him anything and he would agree";

and perceived evoking messages such as "he thinks he is inadequate" and "he would accept whatever I said." As B continues to experience these pulled-for complementary internal engagements, his actions (the second stage of the complementary response) increasingly reflect overt behaviors from the complementary circle octant, hostile–dominant.

DEVELOPMENT OF THE IMPACT MESSAGE INVENTORY

Impact messages, thus, refer to all internal events Interactant B experiences as predominantly produced or elicited by Person A during their transactions. They include direct feelings, action tendencies, perceived evoking messages, and metaphors or fantasies, all of which symbolize Interactant B's thematic covert engagements during transactions with Person A. Impact messages directly record Person A's bid for the interpersonal circle complementary response. In turn, these internal events substantially mediate Interactant B's subsequent overt reactions to Person A—reactions that may or may not correspond precisely to the pulled-for complementary response.

The Impact Message Inventory (IMI; Kiesler, 1987a; Kiesler, Anchin, et al., 1976, 1985; Kiesler & Schmidt, 1993; Perkins et al., 1979) is an interpersonal circle transactional inventory designed to measure a target person's characteristic pattern of interpersonal behavior. It was constructed on the assumption that the interpersonal or evoking style of Person A can be validly defined and measured by *assessing the covert responses or impact messages evoked within Person B* who has interacted with or observed Person A.

The IMI was designed to identify a person's distinctive pattern of interpersonal behavior by measuring the generalizable impacts self-reported by an interpersonal partner or partners. Although interactants often are not clearly aware of their internal engagements or impacts in reaction to others, these covert reactions can become available and reportable as attention is focused on them. Response to the IMI items demands a focus on these internal events, which typically occur as experential "ground" in one's transactions with others. The IMI, thus, is a self-report transactant inventory that taps the automatic, relatively preconscious sets of emotional and other covert reactions we have to others.

The essential measurement procedure of the IMI is as follows. Respondent B records on the IMI the extent to which each item accurately describes the impact a particular target person (A) produces in him or her during an interaction just completed or during their previous transactions. From an empirical keying of items derived from a standardization sample, each item describes a covert reaction characteristically elicited or pulled by a person with interpersonal behavior characteristic of one of the circle categories of interpersonal behavior. If a particular item is scored strongly by Respondent B, then target Person A receives a high score on the corresponding interpersonal circle category. The sum of the item scores for a given IMI scale indicates the relative strength of the corresponding circle category of interpersonal behaviors as experienced interpersonally by B. Each of the circle scales is comprised of three subscales of IMI items measuring direct feelings, action tendencies, and perceived evoking messages. (The IMI as yet does not measure *fantasies*, the fourth category of impact messages described previously.)

For example, following an interaction with Person A (who manifests a strong pattern of dominant interpersonal behavior) Respondent B endorses, as very descriptive of his or her covert reactions to A, empirically keyed dominant scale items such as, "he makes me feel bossed around," "I should tell him he's often quite inconsiderate," "he wants me to put him on a pedestal," and so on. Person A's dominant scale score, then, is the sum of the scores marked by Respondent B to each of the items comprising that scale. The other circle scale scores are obtained in an identical manner.

Development of the IMI (Kiesler, 1987a; Perkins et al., 1979) thus followed the strategy of empirically anchoring distinctive covert impacts to pure categories of interpersonal circle behavior. Our approach took the following steps.

1. A description of the overt interpersonal behaviors of a hypothetical person typifying each pure circle category (e.g., dominant, competitive, mistrusting, hostile, detached, etc.) was constructed in written paragraph form based on the items of Lorr and McNair's (1967) Interpersonal Behavior Inventory.

2. These paragraph descriptions of pure classes of interpersonal behaviors were used as standardized interpersonal stimuli to elicit free-response covert, internal reactions (direct feelings, action tendencies, perceived evoking messages) from samples of interactants who were instructed to imagine themselves interacting with a person who exemplified each of the pure interpersonal categories.

3. The multiple covert free-response reactions recorded by the sampled interactants were then scaled by psychometric procedures in order to align subsets of impact items with the corresponding circle category that distinctively evoked them.

4. The result was a standardized inventory that permits systematic assessment of any Person A's interpersonal behavior by measuring Respondent B's self-reported covert reactions experienced while interacting with Person A.

Table 1 presents examples of items for the later octant scale version of the IMI.

CIRCUMPLEX PROPERTIES AND ANALYSES OF THE IMPACT MESSAGE INVENTORY

Since initial development of the IMI, an appreciation of the utility and elegance of the circumplex model of emotion and personality has evolved, together with innovative strategies in garnering evidence supporting the circularity of the IMI scales. For several reasons, the original 15 IMI scales were only putatively circular in relation to one another. Lorr and McNair's (1967) Interpersonal Behavior Inventory (IBI) scales served as anchors for the original IMI items and scales. Unfortunately, the IBI scales subsequently were shown to be somewhat lacking in circularity, on both empirical and theoretical grounds (Kiesler, 1983). As a result, the original 15-scale IMI version (Kiesler, Anchin, et al., 1976, 1985) lacked desirable circle and circumplex characteristics (Kiesler, 1983, 1987a; Perkins et al., 1979; Wiggins, 1982).

An octant-scale version of the IMI (using a subset of 56 of the original 90 items) has been developed that has satisfactory internal consistency reliability and demonstrates excellent circumplex structure (Kiesler & Schmidt, 1993; Schmidt, Wagner, & Kiesler, 1994). In this section we will summarize the analyses used to examine the structure of these IMI octant scales and comment briefly on the rationale and usefulness of each method. The IMI octants are named for the region of the circle whose impacts they measure (see Figure 1). Recall that the octants, reading counterclockwise starting at the top of the circle are called dominant (D), hostile–dominant

TABLE 1
Sample Items From the Impact Message Inventory

Octant scale	Sample item: "When I am with this person, she (he) makes me feel . . ."
Dominant (D)	bossed around"
Hostile–dominant (HD)	that she thinks it's every woman for herself"
Hostile (H)	distant from her"
Hostile–submissive (HS)	that I should do something to put her at ease"
Submissive	I should tell her to stand up for herself"
Friendly–submissive (FS)	that she trusts me"
Friendly (F)	welcome with her"
Friendly–dominant (FD)	that she wants to be the charming one"

(HD), hostile (H), hostile–submissive (HS), submissive (S), friendly–submissive (FS), friendly (F), and friendly–dominant (FD).

One of the historically popular ways to evaluate the structure of circle measures is the method of principal components analysis. This approach has helped establish the circumplexity of the Interpersonal Adjectives Scales (IAS) in their various incarnations (Wiggins, 1979; Wiggins, Phillips & Trapnell, 1989; Wiggins, Trapnell, & Phillips, 1988) and the circumplex scales of the Inventory of Interpersonal Problems (IIP; Alden, Wiggins, & Pincus, 1990). Principal components analysis is particularly useful in exploring the structural properties of a set of scales because it provides an overall assessment of how strongly the interpersonal dimensions are represented in the data, offers quantitative weights of the relationship between each scale and the interpersonal factors, and generates easily plotted results for visual inspection. Rotation of the factor solution using the Procrustes method (Schonemann, 1987), which seeks to minimize the least-squares differences between the actual angular locations of the scales and their predicted locations, furnishes even more information about the adequacy of the circumplex structure.

First, it should be noted that in principal components analyses the scales are routinely ipsatized prior to analysis. Ipsatization (Cronbach, 1949), by which an individual's octant scores are each represented in terms of deviations from that individual's grand mean of octant scores, is used to control for the presence of a large first factor on which all the variables (the octant scales, in this case) load positively (Alden et al., 1990; Gurtman, 1992, 1994). The interpretation of this first factor is dependent on the measure in question. For instance, the Inventory of Interpersonal Problems (Horowitz, Rosenberg, Baer, Ureño, & Villaseñor, 1988), when subjected to principle components analysis, produces a large first factor believed to represent the overall intensity of interpersonal problems or the general level of discomfort experienced by the respondent (Alden et al., 1990; Horowitz et al., 1988). In the case of the IMI octant scales, in contrast, the general factor seems to represent the strength or clarity of the target individual's interpersonal impacts.

In any event, this general factor does not seem relevant to differences in interpersonal behavior across individuals; rather, as suggested by Wiggins, Steiger, and Gaelick (1981), it appears to represent differences in Likert scale responding *within* individuals. By ipsatizing the scales prior to principal components analysis, the effects of this noninterpersonal general factor are removed, allowing a cleaner, less obstructed view of the scales' relation to the interpersonal dimensions (Alden et al., 1990; Gurtman, 1994). For example, submitting IMI octant scores from 759 respondents (Schmidt et al., 1994) to principle components analysis yields a three-factor solution (using the 1.0 minimum eigenvalue criterion), in which case one factor may be interpreted as a general factor. Ipsatizing these same scores prior to principle components analysis yields a two-factor solution with superior circumplex structure.

Schmidt and colleagues (1994) present evidence supporting the circumplex structure of the IMI octant scales; in the section that follows, their data are combined with several unpublished IMI data sets to present additional confirmation of the circular nature of the IMI octant scales. The analyses to be presented are based on 1,109 respondents, including university undergraduates, patients in outpatient psychiatric settings, and surgery patients.

Principle Components Analysis With Procrustes Rotation

After ipsatizing the octant scores, a principle components analysis with Procrustes rotation was conducted, resulting in a two-factor solution using the minimum eigenvalue of one criterion. The factors account for 40% and 28% of the total variance, respectively. As mentioned previously, the Procrustes method is particularly useful in evaluating circumplex scales because it rotates the factor matrix as closely as possible to an a priori structure (dictated by the mathematics of the circumplex in this case; see Table 2, first two columns) and provides coefficients useful in describing the relationship among the octant scales. Among these are the angle of separation between axes of the circle and the reference structure loadings.

The primary axes of the interpersonal circle, dominance and affiliation, are predicted to be orthogonal to one another; in a two-dimensional space, then, these axes should be separated at an angle of 90°. Comparison of the observed angle to the predicted angle provides one bit of evidence regarding the circumplexity of the scales. The actual angle of separation between the IMI axes for the current sample is 89.7°, indicating that the primary interpersonal dimensions are more or less orthogonal. For comparison purposes, this angle corresponds to a correlation of .006 between axes.

Another Procrustes coefficient that allows evaluation of the scales' structure is the reference structure loading. These coefficients present the relationship between the scales and the axes correcting for any intercorrelation between them. The lower the intercorrelation between axes, the greater the correspondence between the reference structure and the more typical the factor loadings. The use of the reference structure coefficients may be problematic in some instances—for example, when the relations between the octant scales and underlying empirical factors are of interest. Yet, inasmuch as the trigonometric equations used to calculate angular placement of scales assumes orthogonal dimensions, the appropriateness of using nonorthogonal factor loadings to calculate the angular displacement of octant scales is questionable. To be clear, therefore, researchers evaluating the circumplexity of a set of scales should routinely report the inter-

TABLE 2
Characteristics of the Revised Impact Message Inventory Octant Scales

Octant	Target loadings: DOM Axis	Target loadings: LOV Axis	Reference structure loadings: DOM Axis	Reference structure loadings: LOV Axis	Angular location (in degrees)	Predicted location (in degrees)	Displacement from predicted location	Vector length
D	1.000	0.000	0.81785	-0.14554	100	90	10	.83
HD	0.707	-0.707	0.49809	-0.69952	144	135	9	.86
H	0.000	-1.000	0.00873	-0.77694	180	180	0	.78
HS	-0.707	-0.707	-0.57182	-0.62569	223	225	-2	.85
S	-1.000	0.000	-0.77947	-0.22589	254	270	-16	.81
FS	-0.707	0.707	-0.41426	0.70913	329	315	14	.82
F	0.000	1.000	-0.10923	0.86982	353	0	-7	.88
FD	0.707	0.707	0.49123	0.64675	37	45	-8	.81

Summary Statistics
Mean displacement from theoretical location (degrees) = 8.58
Mean vector length = .83
Average cosine of discrepancy (A*) .985
Chi-square test of A* 3.88*
Proportion of agreement .952

Note. * = $p < .05$. D = dominant; HD = hostile–dominant; H = hostile; HS = hostile–submissive; S = submissive; FS = friendly–submissive; F = friendly; FD = friendly–dominant; DOM = dominant; LOV = love.

axis correlation whenever factor loadings or reference structure coefficients are presented.

The reference structure loadings for the IMI octants are also presented in Table 2 and may be compared to the target loadings. Inspection of the reference structure coefficients reveals a circular pattern of relationship between the scales and the axes. The largest loadings can be found between the octants that represent the positive pole of their respective dimensions (the D octant for the dominance axis, the F octant for the affiliation axis). The magnitude of the loadings then decrease until they reach their lowest position (on the negative pole of their respective axes) at which point they begin to increase in magnitude as they again approach the positive pole.

Indices of Angular Location and Vector Length

Although the reference structure coefficients are useful in evaluating the structure of the IMI scales, two other circumplex indices are especially helpful. The angular location and vector length of the scales in two-dimensional space allow for more direct comparison between the placement of scales and their predicted location.[1] The angular locations for eight scales evenly spaced around the circle (using the positive pole of the affiliation axis to represent 0) may be found in Table 2. The actual angular location of the IMI octant scales and their displacement (in degrees) from their predicted location are presented also. As can be seen, the mean displacement of the octants from their predicted location is less than 9°. Because the region of the circle represented by each octant spans 45°, scales displaced more than 22.5° from their predicted location would fall outside the segment of the circle they purport to measure. Although both the submissive and friendly–submissive scales demonstrate more displacement than desired, the scales remain in their respective segments of the circle.

Vector length, or the variable's distance from the origin of the circle (expressed in unit scores bounded by 0 and 1), represents the extent to which a scale loads on, or is represented by, the two interpersonal factors (Gurtman, 1993; LaForge, 1977; Wiggins et al., 1989). In Table 2 vector lengths of the IMI octants range from .78 to .88, with a mean length of .83. By virtue of these values, it appears the IMI scales all show strong

---

[1]The angular location and vector length of a scale are easily calculated from the reference structure coefficients. The formula to calculate angular location is

$$\text{Angle} = \arctan \left(\frac{\text{DOM}}{\text{LOV}} \right)$$

The formula to calculate vector length is

$$VL = (\text{DOM}^2 + \text{LOV}^2)^{1/2}$$

In both formulas, DOM represents the correlation between the scale and the dominance pole of the control axis and LOV represents the correlation between the scale and the friendly pole of the affiliation axis.

relationships with the two interpersonal factors with little variation. A plot of the ipsatized octants in two-dimensional space may be seen in Figure 2.

Fisher's Proportion of Agreement Index

Fisher (Fisher, 1983; Fisher, Heise, Bohrnstedt, & Lucke, 1985; see also chapter 11, this volume) has focused on the trigonometric underpinnings of the circumplex to devise a means for calculating the proportion of agreement between the angular locations of a set of scales and their predicted locations. His method calculates the average cosine of the discrepancies between predicted and actual angular locations and converts that figure into a proportionate measure of agreement. In the case of the IMI scales in Figure 2, the average cosine of discrepancy for the actual versus predicted comparison is .985; rescaled to a proportionate measure this yields .952, signifying 95.2% agreement between the actual angular locations of the IMI scales and their predicted locations. A chi-square test of independence (Fisher, 1983), whose null hypothesis asserts no relationship between the two sets of angular locations, yields a value of 3.88, which is significant at the .05 level. It may be concluded, therefore, that the angular

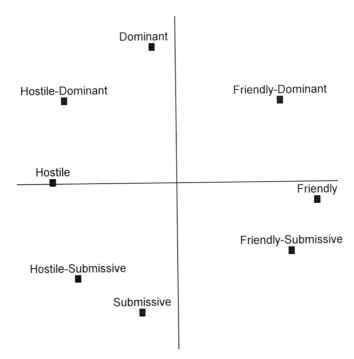

Figure 2. Reference structure of the ipsatized IMI octant scales (n = 1,109).

locations of the IMI octant scales depicted in Figure 2 are not independent of their predicted locations.

Although the existing IMI octant scales (Kiesler & Schmidt, 1993) demonstrate adequate circumplex properties, as the previous analyses have just documented, the scales are not without need of improvement. Another difficulty is that the octant version lacks scale items that are balanced numerically for the three distinct impact subscales (direct feelings, action tendencies, and perceived evoking messages).

Under current development by Kiesler and Schmidt (Schmidt, 1994) is a revised IMI (IMI-2) octant measure that will concentrate on equivalent-item subscale measures of the two most distinctive classes of interpersonal impact messages: direct feelings and action tendencies. Also scoring changes will be made so that scale scores will use labels that characterize the respective class of covert reactions of Interactant B—rather than continuing the often conceptually obfuscating practice of labeling scales according to target Person A's corresponding pattern of overt interpersonal behavior. This change in scoring will permit direct circle characterization of Interactant B's covert complementary response, which then can be compared conceptually and empirically to circle measures of Interactant B's subsequent actual overt responses—among many other exciting possibilities.

IMPACT MESSAGES AND TRANSACTIONAL EMOTION

In this final section we attempt to base the DE-impact message (the covert first stage of the complementary interpersonal response) in recent conceptualizations of human emotion. We will argue, first, that the IMI measures central covert components of the complex emotional response as recently conceptualized. Second, we will document how the IMI measures these important covert events within the context of specific interpersonal encounters. We conclude that the IMI can serve as an operational bridge between the areas of emotion and interpersonal behavior—permitting closer integration of respective conceptualizations of personality, psychopathology, and psychotherapy.

Emotion Refers to a Complex Set of Covert Reactions to an Appraised Environmental Object or Event

A recent consensus has emerged among a sizeable group of emotion theorists (Arnold, 1960a, 1960b; Averill, 1980; Frijda, 1986; Kemper, 1978; Lazarus & Averill, 1972; Lazarus & Folkman, 1984; Lazarus, Kanner, & Folkman, 1980; Plutchik, 1962, 1980, 1991). These theorists agree in substance with the definition of emotion as referring to a complex chain of covert responses that are triggered by an individual's intuitive appraisal of an environmental event or object as significant or important (that is, as desirable or undesirable, valuable or harmful). This appraisal, in turn, triggers a complex, distinctive set of covert behaviors including: (a) subjective feeling reactions, (b) urges to action (action impulses, action tendencies), (c) physiological–somatic reactions, and (d) somatic kinesthetic feedback resulting from expressive facial reactions. This set of distinctive covert reactions, in turn, serves to moderate the individual's subsequent actual overt response. Finally, each component of this emotional process (cognitive appraisal, subjective feeling, urge to action, physiological response, facial feedback, overt reaction) can be subjected to inhibitory and regulatory processes that serve as normal to abnormal defensive operations in protection of the self-system.

To illustrate, Lazarus and colleagues (1980) defined emotions as "complex, organized states . . . consisting of cognitive appraisals, action impulses, and patterned somatic reactions. Each emotion quality (e.g., anger, anxiety, joy) is distinguished by a different pattern of components" (p. 198). In the same way, Plutchik (1980) stated,

> An emotion is an inferred sequence of events set in motion by some stimulus. The components of the sequence are: an inferred cognition (e.g. danger); a subjective feeling (e.g. fear); a physiological arousal (e.g. rapid heart-beat); a motor impulse (e.g. to run); and behavior (e.g. running). (p. 333)

Several theorists add fantasy processes (Singer, 1973, 1974) and additional cognitive components (Kemper, 1978; Lazarus et al., 1980) to the complex of four inner reactions detailed previously. Singer (1973, 1974) offered the proposition that fantasy processes, dreams, and imagery provide the key link between cognition and affect; he provided extensive examples of how positive and negative emotion imagery can be used to attenuate or inhibit the other within the context of psychotherapy. Lazarus and colleagues (1980), in addition to the *primary* cognitive appraisal involved in evaluation of the environmental event or object, described *secondary* cognitive appraisals (evaluating coping resources and options that might be available in a stressful encounter) and *reappraisals* (the feedback process from the environment resulting from the individual's reactions) as additional components of the covert emotion complex. Kemper (1978) added that cognitive components other than those involved in the original appraisal of the environment can include "labels that identify the emotion, for example, 'I feel *angry*,' 'Am I ever *happy!*' or 'I feel I'm in *love*'" (p. 47); "The cognition can also arise from explicit appraisal of one's somatic state, for example, 'My hands are sweating, I must be *anxious*' (cf. Schachter and Singer, 1962)" (pp. 47–48).

This brief analysis makes clear that the four major classes of impact messages (direct feelings, action tendencies, perceived evoking message, fantasies) overlap remarkably with major components of the covert emotion process as detailed by more recent emotion theorists. Further, retention of direct feeling and action tendency items in our reconstruction of IMI-2 seems supported for several reasons. First, our own work, as well as analyses by emotion researchers (e.g., Conte & Plutchik, 1981; Russell, 1979, 1980; Watson & Tellegen, 1985), confirms that the domain of direct feelings (e.g., fear, anger, boredom, etc.) takes the form of a circumplex around two bipolar axes. For example, Russell's analyses led him to conclude that any particular affect is some combination of pleasure and arousal, best represented in a two-dimensional bipolar circular space in which affects fall in the following order: pleasure (0°), excitement (45°), arousal (90°), distress (135°), displeasure (180°), depression (225°), sleepiness (270°), and relaxation (315°). This and other circumplex models of subjective feeling reactions permit and suggest the possibility of meaningful alignments of the covert direct feeling domain with the domain of overt interpersonal behavior (also demonstrably circumplex in structure around the bipolar axes of control and affiliation).

Second, the action tendency component of the complex set of covert emotional reactions is considered by several theorists to be the criterial component of the emotion process. Arnold (1960a) stated that emotion is *felt action tendency*: "The intuitive appraisal of the situation initiates an *action tendency that is felt as emotion*, expressed in various bodily changes, and that eventually may lead to overt action" (p. 177). Emotion is

> The felt tendency toward anything intuitively appraised as good (beneficial), or away from anything intuitively appraised as bad (harmful). This attraction or aversion is accompanied by a pattern of physiological changes organized toward approach or withdrawal. The patterns differ for different emotions. (Arnold, 1960a, p. 182)

According to Frijda (1986), action tendencies are "states of readiness to execute a given kind of action," (p. 70), to execute a given class of actions having the same intent.

> One action tendency is readiness for attacking, spitting, insulting, turning one's back, or slandering, whichever of these appears possible or appropriate at a given moment; a different action tendency is readiness to approach and embrace, fondle, look at avidly, or say sweet things, again according to what the circumstances favor. (pp. 70–71)

In sum, *action readiness change* is the defining feature of emotion: "Emotional experience largely consists of experienced action readiness or unreadiness: impulse to flee or strike or embrace; lack of impulse, apathy, listlessness" (Frijda, 1986, p. 469).

Lazarus and colleagues (1980) asserted that emotions are "complex, organized states . . . consisting of cognitive appraisals, action impulses, and patterned somatic reactions" (p. 198). According to their notion of action impulse, "an action that is set in motion internally (psychophysiologically) need not be carried out or visible; it can be suppressed, denied, or transformed" (p. 198).

Plutchik (1980) noted "emotions are complex sequences of events that include impulses to action as an important part of the sequence" (p. 360). He based his analysis partly on Bull's (1951, 1952) attitude theory of emotion, which conceives emotion as

> a sequence of neuromuscular events in which postural set or preparatory motor attitude is the initial step. This preparatory attitude is both involuntary and instinctive and is the end result of a slight, tentative movement which gives a new orientation to the individual, but does not immediately go into the consummatory stage of action. (Bull, 1952, cited in Plutchik, 1980, p. 355).

Bull and her collaborators (Bull & Gidro-Frank, 1950; Pasquarelli & Bull, 1951) conducted studies using hypnotized research participants that led Bull to draw two important conclusions: (a) skeletal muscle activity as well as visceral activity is involved in emotional feelings, and (b) different emotions have different postures or impulses to action associated with them. Plutchik's own empirical studies led him to align eight classes of impulses to action with his eight primary subjective feelings (e.g., *fear*: an impulse to withdraw or get away; *anger*: an impulse to attack or hurt; *joy*: an impulse to embrace or mate). Plutchik cautioned that

> Although feelings of fear and anger are often associated with the behaviors of flight or fight, they need not necessarily result in such behaviors. This is simply because the situation may prevent the carrying out in action of the feelings. . . . However, the *impulse* to run or the *impulse* to attack may still be present. (1980, p. 353)

Consistent with these notions, our decision to drop perceived evoking message items in reconstructing IMI-2 was based partly on Wiggins' observations, as follows:

> A more precise understanding of the links of interpersonal action–reaction sequences might be achieved by developing separate and larger item pools for each of [the three] domains. The domain of perceived evoking messages, for example, would seem be closely related to, if not redundant with, [other interpersonal behavior inventories], which measure the perceived interpersonal behavior of others. (1982, p. 200)

Singer's (1973, 1974) analysis of the central link that fantasy serves between cognition and emotion suggests further that we might at some later date gain considerably from construction and addition of items that measure our fourth class of impact messages—namely, fantasies and metaphors. Especially in the psychotherapeutic context one of the safest, least threatening modes of interpersonal feedback from the therapist is in the form of fantasy or metaphor—in contrast to feedback of direct feelings, action tendencies, or perceived evoking messages (Kiesler, 1988).

The Most Important Class of Environmental Objects or Events Appraised During Emotion Is Interpersonal–Transactional

Another growing consensus among recent emotion theorists is that a central, if not ubiquitous, class of environmental objects or events that trigger the human emotion sequence is social, interpersonal, and transactional.

To illustrate, Averill (1980) detailed the necessity of understanding the social antecedents and consequents that comprise the emotional experience. According to Averill, emotion arises from social situations (e.g., anger might be caused by another person blocking one's goals) and serves social functions (e.g., expressed anger might stop the person from blocking one's goals in the future). Averill (1980) emphasized,

> As important as the physical setting may be for emotional behavior, the social environment is generally even more important. Some emotions, such as anger and love, typically demand some kind of response on the part of another person. However, the importance of social cues is not limited to emotions that involve mutual interaction between two or more persons. Many emotional roles are like soliloquies: only one actor is directly involved, but the response is played for and to an audience. Laughter, for example, is much heartier in the presence of others; embarrassment and shame do not occur in solitude; and any parent can testify how young children often await the arrival of a sympathetic audience before bursting into tears. (p. 323)

Berscheid (1983) proposed a model in which emotional interdependence is a vital component of close interpersonal relationships. Emotion is defined as autonomic arousal caused by interruptions of well-practiced, organized action sequences, coupled with cognitive appraisal of that arousal. In close relationships, members' action sequences are closely intertwined—members have frequent, strong, and diverse impacts on each other over a long period; as a consequence they are especially capable of interrupting each other's well-practiced action sequences and eliciting arousal and emotion.

Lazarus and colleagues (Lazarus et al., 1980; Lazarus & Launier, 1978) offer a transactional or relational principle of emotions. They have asserted that "emotions arise out of ongoing relationships or *transactions* ... in which the person influences and is influenced by the environment, especially the social environment. ... To understand any given encounter in which there is an emotional episode, attention must be given to the changing *relationship* between the person and environment as the encounter proceeds" (Lazarus et al., 1980, p. 195).

The strongest transactional statement to date comes from Kemper's (1978) social interactional theory of emotions and is based on his proposition that most human emotions result from outcomes of interaction in social relationships. Kemper's basic argument is that "events in the social environment instigate emotions. The most important events are the ongoing or changing patterns of social relations between actors" (Kemper, 1978, p. 26). "I do not claim that all emotion is of this [interpersonal] character, nor that any given emotion results only from social relationships" (p. 347). Kemper's general hypothesis is that

> A *very large class of emotions results from real, imagined, or anticipated outcomes in social relationships*. To account for emotions that have a social locus, we must be able to specify the full range of real, imagined, and anticipated relational outcomes. (Kemper, 1978, p. 43)

Kemper presented in detail a model of relational outcomes anchored on the two basic interpersonal dimensions, which he labels *power* (coercive control of one action by another as in domination, threat, force, control, etc.) and *status* (voluntary compliance and giving to others as in friendship, support, affection, warmth, etc.). "Whether the relationship is in equilibrium or not, I propose that each actor is either satisfied or dissatisfied in some degree with his own and the other's positions on the power and status dimensions" (Kemper, 1978, p. 49). To illustrate, (a) When Actor A appraises his or her own *power* as adequate, A feels secure; when interpreted as excessive, A feels guilty and anxious; when appraised as insufficient, A feels fear. However, when B's power is appraised by A as adequate, A feels secure; when appraised as excessive, A feels fear; when appraised as insufficient, A feels guilt. (b) When Actor A appraises his or her own *status* as adequate, A feels happy; as excessive, A feels shame; as insufficient, A feels depressed. However, when B's status is appraised by A as adequate, A feels happy; when B's status is appraised as excessive, A feels anger, contempt, and shame; when B's status is appraised as insufficient, A feels guilt–shame and anxiety.

One can conclude from these brief analyses that the interpersonal behavior of other individuals (within specific transactional episodes and over larger periods of transactional history) forms the major, most significant class of environmental events and objects that trigger the emotion sequence. This interpersonal behavior includes both that imposed by social roles and conventions (Averill, 1980) and that emerging from more enduring interpersonal dispositions and self-presentations (e.g., Carson, 1969; Kiesler, 1982a, 1983, 1988; Leary, 1957). Further, as considerable evidence documents, this interpersonal behavior—this major class of environmental stimuli—forms a domain organized on various interpersonal circumplexes (Kiesler, 1983; Wiggins, 1982) around the bipolar axes of control and affiliation. The circumplex includes such behavioral categories (counterclockwise around the 1982 circle) as dominant, competitive, mistrusting, cold, hostile, detached, inhibited, unassured, submissive, deferent, trusting, warm, friendly, sociable, exhibitionistic, and assured.

CONCLUSION

The analysis in this chapter makes it clear that the latest version of the Impact Message Inventory (Kiesler and Schmidt's upcoming IMI-2) will measure key (subjective feeling reactions, action tendencies or impulses), but not all, components of the covert emotion process defined by recent emotion theorists. Further, it will measure these covert emotion behaviors exclusively in reaction to an interactant's distinctive pattern of interpersonal behavior within a specific transaction. In other words, in the case of the IMI, the specific environmental event or object, appraisal of which activates Respondent B's set of covert emotional responses, is the overt interpersonal behavior of target Person A. The direct feelings triggered by Respondent B's appraisal include (but may not be limited to) the domain of feeling responses found to fall in a circular pattern on two-dimensional circumplexes by emotion researchers (e.g., Russell, 1979, 1980). Further, an essential concomitant of Respondent B's covert feeling responses is a distinctive set of action tendencies of at least two sorts: (a) automatic tendencies to emit a class of overt reactions that would constitute the exact interpersonal complementary response to Person A's interpersonal pattern; and (b) automatic tendencies, ranging from minimally to very intense, to emit various inhibitory or defensive behaviors (at any stage of the emotion process: appraisal, feeling, action tendency, overt reaction) that would interfere with enactment of the pulled-for overt complementary response. Whether Respondent B's resulting enactment in response to target Person A is some form of complementary or noncomplementary interpersonal behavior depends on the relative strength of these two sets of covert tendencies.

This conceptualization makes it obvious that the empirical research on interpersonal complementarity (e.g., Orford, 1986) needs to be very cautiously interpreted (Kiesler, 1987b, 1991; Schmidt, 1994). None of the research in regard to which Orford (1986) drew his mostly pessimistic conclusions regarding the principles of complementarity studied the crucial link in the interpersonal transaction cycle.

The interpersonal transactional cycle (Carson, 1969; Kiesler, 1986a; Safran, 1984) specifies four reciprocally chained links:

1. Person A's covert behaviors instigate
$\downarrow$
2. Person A's overt actions evoke
$\downarrow$
3. Person B's covert responses instigate
$\downarrow$
4. Person B's overt reactions.

Virtually every study of interpersonal complementarity summarized by Orford (1986) measured complementarity at the 2 and 4 links (correlations exclusively between A and B's *overt* behaviors). In contrast, precise theoretical tests of interpersonal complementarity *require* comparison of measurements at the 2 *and* 3 links—correlations between A's overt behavior and B's *covert* reactions (Kiesler, 1987b, 1991; Schmidt, 1994).

The reconceptualization of impact messages within the framework of emotion theory as just summarized makes the following point abundantly clear: Whether interpersonal feelings plus action tendencies that reflect the pulled-for complementary response get enacted or not depends on the presence and strength of competing inhibitory–defensive processes. These inhibitory–defensive processes arise when inconsistencies exist between Person B's characteristic style of self-definition and self-presentation and: (a) behaviors inherent in the pulled-for complementary response; (b) behaviors under the control of environmental factors such as physical setting and social–interpersonal variables (i.e., role expectations—status, gender, and other interactant factors—as Orford, 1986, articulated).

In sum, theoretical principles of interpersonal complementarity (Carson, 1969; Kiesler, 1983; Orford, 1986) can *never* be tested precisely solely by matching two interactants' patterns of overt behavior; tests at this level are one link removed in the interpersonal transaction cycle and invariably can provide only approximate confirmations. Instead, precise tests require matches of one person's pattern of *overt* behavior with an interactant's pattern of *covert* behavior. This 2. A overt action, leading to 3. B covert link in the transaction cycle represents the measurement stance of the IMI and is the essential factor that makes the inventory uniquely suited for tests of interpersonal complementarity as well as other propositions of interpersonal theory.

Finally, it seems that emotion theorists and researchers could profit considerably from use of the IMI as a key measure of covert events occurring during various instances of transactional emotion. In addition, the circumplex model of overt interpersonal behavior (e.g., Kiesler, 1983), to which the IMI is linked empirically, provides a comprehensive model both of the classes of interpersonal behavior that can define significant environmental events or objects that trigger the emotion sequence, as well as the corresponding classes of complementary overt reactions that are mediated by covert components of the emotion process.

REFERENCES

Alden, L. E., Wiggins, J. S., & Pincus, A. L. (1990). Construction of circumplex scales for the Inventory of Interpersonal Problems. *Journal of Personality Assessment, 55,* 521–536.

Anchin, J. C., & Kiesler, D. J. (Eds.). (1982). *Handbook of interpersonal psychotherapy.* Elmsford, NY: Pergamon Press.

Arnold, M. B. (1960a). *Emotion and personality: Vol. 1. Psychological aspects.* New York: Columbia University Press.

Arnold, M. B. (1960b). *Emotion and personality: Vol. 2. Neurological and physiological aspects.* New York: Columbia University Press.

Averill, J. R. (1980). A contructivist view of emotion. In R. Plutchik & H. Kellerman (Eds.), *Emotion: Theory, research, and experience* (Vol. 1: *Theories of emotion,* pp. 309–339). New York: Academic Press.

Beier, E. G. (1966). *The silent language of psychotherapy: Social reinforcement of unconscious processes.* Chicago: Aldine.

Berscheid, E. (1983). Emotion. In H. H. Kelley, E. Berscheid, A. Christensen, J. H. Harvey, T. L. Huston, G. Levinger, E. McClintock, L. A. Peplau, & D. R. Peterson (Eds.), *Close relationships* (pp. 110–168). New York: Freeman.

Bull, N. (1951). The attitude theory of emotion. *Nervous and Mental Disease Monograph* (No. 81).

Bull, N. (1952). The attitude theory of emotion. *International Record of Medicine, 165,* 216–220.

Bull, N., & Gidro-Frank, L. (1950). Emotions induced and studied in hypnotic subjects. II. *Journal of Nervous and Mental Disease, 112,* 97–120.

Carson, R. C. (1969). *Interaction concepts of personality.* Chicago: Aldine.

Conte, H. R., & Plutchik, R. (1981). A circumplex model for interpersonal personality traits. *Journal of Personality and Social Psychology, 40,* 701–711.

Cronbach, L. H. (1949). Statistical methods applied to Rorschach scores: A review. *Psychological Bulletin, 46,* 393–429.

Fisher, G. A. (1983, September). *Coefficients of agreement for circular data.* Paper presented at the meeting of the American Sociological Association, Section on Methodology, Detroit, MI.

Fisher, G. A., Heise, D. R., Bohrnstedt, G. W., & Lucke, J. F. (1985). Evidence for extending the circumplex model of personality trait language to self-reported moods. *Journal of Personality and Social Psychology, 49*, 233–242.

Frijda, N. H. (1986). *The emotions.* New York: Cambridge University Press.

Gurtman, M. B. (1992). Construct validity of interpersonal measures: The interpersonal circumplex as a nomological net. *Journal of Personality and Social Psychology, 63*, 105–118.

Gurtman, M. B. (1993). Constructing personality tests to meet a structural criterion: Application of the interpersonal circumplex. *Journal of Personality, 61*, 237–263.

Gurtman, M. B. (1994). The circumplex as a tool for studying normal and abnormal personality: A methodological primer. In S. Strack & M. Lorr (Eds.), *Differentiating normal and abnormal personality* (pp. 243–263). New York: Springer.

Horowitz, L. M., Rosenberg, S. E., Baer, B. A., Ureño, G., & Villaseñor, V. S. (1988). The Inventory of Interpersonal Problems: Psychometric properties and clinical applications. *Journal of Consulting and Clinical Psychology, 56*, 885–892.

Kemper, T. D. (1978). *A social interactional theory of emotions.* Melbourne, FL: Krieger.

Kiesler, D. J. (1979). An interpersonal communication analysis of relationship in psychotherapy. *Psychiatry, 42*, 299–311.

Kiesler, D. J. (1982a). Interpersonal theory for personality and psychotherapy. In J. C. Anchin & D. J. Kiesler (Eds.), *Handbook of interpersonal psychotherapy* (pp. 274–295). Elmsford, NY: Pergamon Press.

Kiesler, D. J. (1982b). Confronting the client–therapist relationship in psychotherapy. In J. C. Anchin & D. J. Kiesler (Eds.), *Handbook of interpersonal psychotherapy* (pp. 274–295). Elmsford, NY: Pergamon Press.

Kiesler, D. J. (1983). The 1982 Interpersonal Circle: A taxonomy for complementarity in human transactions. *Psychological Review, 90*, 185–214.

Kiesler, D. J. (1986a). Interpersonal methods of diagnosis and treatment. In J. O. Cavenar, Jr. (Ed.), *Psychiatry* (Vol. 1, pp. 1–23). Philadelphia: Lippincott.

Kiesler, D. J. (1986b). The 1982 Interpersonal Circle: An analysis of *DSM-III* personality disorders. In T. Millon & G. L. Klerman (Eds.), *Contemporary directions in psychopathology: Towards the DSM-IV* (pp. 57–59). New York: Guilford Press.

Kiesler, D. J. (1987a). *Research manual for the Impact Message Inventory.* Palo Alto, CA: Consulting Psychologists Press.

Kiesler, D. J. (1987b, October). Complementarity: Between whom and under what conditions? *Clinician's Research Digest: Supplemental Bulletin, 5*(20).

Kiesler, D. J. (1988). *Therapeutic metacommunication: Therapist impact disclosure as feedback in psychotherapy.* Palo Alto, CA: Consulting Psychologists Press.

Kiesler, D. J. (1991). Interpersonal methods of assessment and diagnosis. In C. R. Snyder & D. R. Forsyth (Eds.), *Handbook of social and clinical psychology: The health perspective* (pp. 438–468). Elmsford, NY: Pergamon Press.

Kiesler, D. J., Anchin, J. C., Perkins, M. J., Chirico, B. M., Kyle, E. M., & Federman, E. J. (1976). *The Impact Message Inventory: Form IIA*. Richmond: Virginia Commonwealth University.

Kiesler, D. J., Anchin, J. C., Perkins, M. J., Chirico, B. M., Kyle, E. M., & Federman, E. J. (1985). *The Impact Message Inventory: Form IIA*. Palo Alto, CA: Consulting Psychologists Press.

Kiesler, D. J., Bernstein, A. B., & Anchin, J. C. (1976). *Interpersonal communication, relationship, and the behavior therapies*. Richmond: Virginia Commonwealth University.

Kiesler, D. J., & Schmidt, J. A. (1993). *The Impact Message Inventory: Form IIA Octant Scale Version*. Palo Alto, CA: Mind Garden (Consulting Psychologists Press).

LaForge, R. (1977). *Using the ICL: 1976*. Unpublished manuscript.

Lazarus, R. S., & Averill, J. R. (1972). Emotion and cognition: With special reference to anxiety. In C. D. Spielberger (Ed.), *Anxiety: Contemporary theory and research* (pp. 241–283). New York: Academic Press.

Lazarus, R. S., & Folkman, S. (1984). *Stress, appraisal and coping*. New York: Springer.

Lazarus, R. S., Kanner, A. D., & Folkman, S. (1980). Emotions: A cognitive–phenomenological analysis. In R. Plutchik & H. Kellerman (Eds.), *Emotion: Theory, research, and experience* (pp. 189–217). New York: Academic Press.

Lazarus, R. S., & Launier, R. (1978). Stress-related transactions between person and environment. In L. A. Pervin & M. Lewis (Eds.), *Perspectives in interactional psychology*. New York: Plenum Press.

Leary, T. (1957). *Interpersonal diagnosis of personality: A functional theory and methodology for personality evaluation*. New York: Ronald Press.

Lorr, M., & McNair, D. M. (1967). *The Interpersonal Behavior Inventory, Form 4*. Washington, DC: Catholic University of America Press.

Orford, J. (1986). The rules of interpersonal complementarity: Does hostility beget hostility and dominance, submission? *Psychological Review, 93*, 365–377.

Pasquarelli, B., & Bull, N. (1951). Experimental investigation of the mind–body continuum in affective states. *Journal of Nervous and Mental Disease, 113*, 512–521.

Perkins, M. J., Kiesler, D. J., Anchin, J. C., Chirico, B. M., Kyle, E. M., & Federman, E. J. (1979). The Impact Message Inventory: A new measure of relationship in counseling/psychotherapy and other dyads. *Journal of Counseling Psychology, 26*, 363–367.

Plutchik, R. (1962). *The emotions: Facts, theories, and a new model*. New York: Random House.

Plutchik, R. (1980). *Emotion: A psychoevolutionary synthesis.* New York: Harper & Row.

Plutchik, R. (1991). *The emotions* (Rev ed.). Lanham, MD: University Press of America.

Ruesch, J., & Bateson, G. (1951). *Communication: The social matrix of psychiatry.* New York: Norton.

Russell, J. A. (1979). Affective space is bipolar. *Journal of Personality and Social Psychology, 37,* 345–356.

Russell, J. A. (1980). A circumplex model of affect. *Journal of Personality and Social Psychology, 39,* 1161–1178.

Safran, J. D. (1984). Assessing the cognitive interpersonal cycle. *Cognitive Therapy and Research, 8,* 333–348.

Schachter, S., & Singer, J. E. (1962). Cognitive, social, and physiological determinants of emotional states. *Psychological Review, 69,* 379–399.

Schmidt, J. A. (1994). *Revision of the Impact Message Inventory: Reconstruction to a circumplex criterion.* Unpublished doctoral dissertation, Virginia Commonwealth University, Richmond, VA.

Schmidt, J. A., Wagner, C. C., & Kiesler, D. J. (1994). *The Impact Message Inventory Octant Scales: Initial evaluation of structural and psychometric characteristics.* Unpublished manuscript

Schonemann, P. H. (1987). A generalized solution of the orthogonal Procrustes problem. *Psychometrika, 31,* 1–16.

Singer, J. L. (1973). *The child's world of make-believe: Experimental studies of imaginative play.* New York: Academic Press.

Singer, J. L. (1974). *Imagery and daydream methods of psychotherapy and behavior modification.* New York: Academic Press.

Watson, D., & Tellegen, A. (1985). Toward a consensual structure of mood. *Psychological Bulletin, 98,* 219–235.

Wiggins, J. S. (1979). A psychological taxonomy of trait-descriptive terms: The interpersonal domain. *Journal of Personality and Social Psychology, 37,* 395–412.

Wiggins, J. S. (1982). Circumplex models of interpersonal behavior in clinical psychology. In P. C. Kendall & J. N. Butcher (Eds.), *Handbook of research methods in clinical psychology* (pp. 183–221). New York: Wiley.

Wiggins, J. S., Phillips, N., & Trapnell, P. (1989). Circular reasoning about interpersonal behavior: Evidence concerning some untested assumptions underlying diagnostic classification. *Journal of Personality and Social Psychology, 56,* 296–305.

Wiggins, J. S., Steiger, J. H., & Gaelick, L. (1981). Evaluating circumplexity in personality data. *Multivariate Behavioral Research, 16,* 263–289.

Wiggins, J. S., Trapnell, P., & Phillips, N. (1988). Psychometric and geometric characteristics of the revised Interpersonal Adjective Scales (IAS-R). *Multivariate Behavioral Research, 23,* 517–530.

11

THEORETICAL AND METHODOLOGICAL ELABORATIONS OF THE CIRCUMPLEX MODEL OF PERSONALITY TRAITS AND EMOTIONS

GENE A. FISHER

I became interested in the circumplex model of personality traits in the course of a study of moods. My colleagues at Indiana University had collected data from 141 students who had rated their feelings twice a day, shortly after rising and shortly before retiring, over a period of 15 days. To represent the structure of the 33 moods that had been rated, we considered the dimensions of the semantic differential, evaluation, potency, and activation (Osgood, May, & Miron, 1975) and the two-dimensional circumplex elaborated by Plutchik and his colleagues (Conte & Plutchik, 1981; Plutchik & Platman, 1977; Schaefer & Plutchik, 1966). We found that the circumplex model fit the data best, particularly for moods and also for personality traits that arise from moods. The results of our study are reported in Fisher, Heise, Bohrnstedt, and Lucke (1985).

In this chapter I elaborate on the mood study. First, I explore the relationship between emotions and personality traits via moods. This discussion will clarify why the circumplex model should be applied with equal force to both emotions and personality traits. It also will explain why the circumplex is applied to the language of emotions and personality traits and not to the organic structures—or circuits of the brain—that generate emotional states and quite possibly personality traits. In the second section I will use the mood study to illustrate a number of methodological issues that arise in measuring, modeling, and comparing circumplexes. In our study (Fisher et al., 1985), we found that language about perceived mood states closely aligns in structure with language rating the similarity and dissimilarity in meaning of mood words. In either case, whether one rates perceived states or the meaning of terms, the hypothesis that the semantic structure forms a circumplex is a highly restrictive one, requiring several criteria be met to confirm it. Finally, in the third section I try to explain why the circumplex model arises and not some other. Because the circumplex deals with the language of emotions and personality traits, I invoke the semantic differential and suggest that evaluation and activation are the dimensions along which we classify emotions. However, in the domain of emotionally grounded language the two dimensions are not orthogonal or independent. Rather, high levels of activation or inactivation preclude evaluation, and evaluation is most intensive when activation or arousal is blocked.

LINKING EMOTIONS AND PERSONALITY TRAITS

Mood can be considered a bridge between emotions and personality traits. Mood represents an ongoing affective state that contains both feelings of emotion and disposition toward an emotional response. It is often said in the clinical literature, "Mood is to affect as climate is to weather." A particular event may throw one into a particular mood, such as angry or cheerful, but once unleashed, the mood is likely to affect a wide range of subsequent behaviors, many of which may be unrelated to the precipitating event. Conversely, one often may find oneself in a particular mood—say cheerful or depressed—with no apparent precipitating incident other than perhaps a memory of which one is dimly aware or an impression of one's situation that one has scarcely elaborated. However it arises, mood tends to color, if not direct, much of our behavior and provides the basis for the attributions of internal causality we and others make for our behavior.

In our study students were asked to rate their moods shortly after arising and shortly before retiring (exactly when was left, of course, to the students). They were asked to rate 33 words on a 5-point scale, with 0 indicating *does not describe my mood* and 4 indicating *definitely describes my mood*. Thus, in the morning one might wake up feeling cheerful and enthusiastic or nervous and depressed. One might go to bed feeling peaceful or irritable. We did not attempt in the mood study to determine the origin of these moods, but in a later study (Bohrnstedt & Fisher, 1986) we found two of the moods—self-esteem (i.e., confidence) and depression—had rather different sources. Confidence appears to reflect satisfactory role performances in the present, whereas depression is more tributary to conflicted relationships with parents during childhood and adolescence. Other sources of depression, such as recent losses and stressful life events, were not measured in this study.

In short, external events, both recent and distant, determine mood. But they are events that the individual plays a part in either to prevent, alter, or endure. How the individual responds will have an effect on other, similar events in the individual's field of experience. The reported mood, therefore, is an indicator of an ongoing process within the individual of relating and adjusting to his or her social environment. These responses may be fleeting and transitory, if the events that precipitate them occur infrequently or the response is not generalized to other, similar events. The responses also may recur frequently to the extent that the precipitating events are recurrent or that the response itself is generalized to apply to a class of events. Thus, many mood terms can be used to describe both states and traits. To the extent that it is a response to particular events, a mood is a state of mind. To the extent that the mood recurs again and again, particularly in response to different events, it is a personality trait.

To explain the link between emotion and personality traits via mood, we need to begin with a theory of emotions. Most fundamentally, emotions should be considered "circuits of the brain," as described by Panksepp (1982, 1986), who has identified four fundamental emotional responses: expectation, anger, fear, and distress. These circuits have been identified through brain stimulation studies of humans in which electrical stimulation of specific sites generates the emotional–behavioral response—for example, biting in response to an anger–generating stimulus. These circuits, however, are not sufficient to account for the role of emotions in human behavior. We need to add that the brain processes emotional responses, making them available to memory, cognition, and consciousness. When we talk of emotions as *feelings*, we are referring to a readout of our emotions that the brain provides. The perceptual–motor theory of emotion proposed by Leventhal and Mosbach (1983) places primary emphasis on the function of emotions to "reflect or meter the moment-by-moment states of the organism" (p. 356). By defining emotions as readouts they are able

> To include within the concept of emotion a broad range of states, including the typical primary emotions (fear, anger, disgust, joy, depression, etc.) as well as states such as fatigue–tiredness and pain–distress. All the labels tell us about the organism's state at a particular moment—a moment when it may be struggling with a specific, environmental problem. (Leventhal & Mosbach, 1983, p. 381)

Emotions imply some movement or behavior emanating from the organism. The movement may be expressive–communicative, as when one smiles or frowns, or it may be overt action, as when one strikes another in anger or hugs another in joy. Leventhal and Mosbach identified three somewhat independent and separate, hierarchically organized motor systems. At the lowest level, called the *expressive motor level*, are instinctual circuits that include the startle reflex and spontaneous facial expressions. The motor systems that generate facial expression are unlearned, although one can learn to display the expressions generated by this system. At the next level, called the *schematic level*, motor activity is guided by schematic structures derived from memory and perception. Images in memory and perception are frequently used to evoke emotional arousal and behavior. At the highest level, called the *conceptual level*, words and propositions are used to guide and direct the activity of the expressive and schematic motor systems.

In many instances of behavior all three motor systems are activated. For example, we see a car that we like at the dealership and make an offer to buy it, smiling at the salesperson as we shake hands and close the deal. But there are many instances when intended behavior does not match with the promptings arising from the expressive and schematic motor systems or when promptings arise from these systems before an intention is formed in the voluntary behavioral system. In these instances we *experience* an emotion as we become aware of the (thus far) unheeded promptings of the expressive and schematic motor systems. That is, "the automatic motor impulse (from the expressive and schematic systems) is felt as an emotion rather than as a movement when it is not anticipated or intended" (Leventhal & Mosbach, 1983, p. 377).

When there is no discrepancy—in other words, when the intended behavior aligns with the urges of the lower systems—we *experience* no emotion, even though the behavior may express or be driven by emotion. The behavior is experienced simply as planned movement. We might say, however, that in such cases we do experience emotion, but this is emotion of a self-referring nature. We feel ourselves as fulfilled, at peace, or effectively active, such as aggressive. I am suggesting that the self-monitoring function of emotions extends to the point of giving us a readout of how well intentional behavior has been integrated with emotional impulse.

Leventhal and Mosbach's model of emotions accords a critical role to cognitive processing of impulses welling up from the schematic and expressive motor systems. Cognitive awareness of feelings can lead to the effective suppression of emotion and the behavior it urges, and it can lead to the eliciting of emotions that are not experienced but are required by social norms. Hochschild (1983) discussed at length the cognitive devices flight attendants were taught to employ in order to have cheerful and friendly feelings toward an intoxicated and abusive passenger. The attendants were encouraged to instruct the perceptual system to imagine the bothersome passenger as a little boy throwing a tantrum in their living room. This image conjured up maternal feelings of tenderness and compassion toward the passenger that displaced the unpleasant feelings occasioned by the passenger's rude behavior. Once the emotional task was accomplished, the flight attendant could serve the passenger cheerfully and easily. Voluntary, planned behavior (serving the passenger) was accomplished without emotional resistance. Leventhal and Mosbach identify a number of the many ways the cognitive system draws on, manages, tricks, and even overrides the lower motor systems. These devices only confirm the notion that emotions are messages to the cognitive motor system to enable it to bring final, integrating order into human behavior.

The ability of the cognitive system both to elicit and suppress emotion and its role as the final fashioner of behavior suggest that habitual modes of dealing with emotions, both successfully and unsuccessfully, are stable elements of the human personality. That is, persons who express a recurrent emotional style, such as being cheerful or irascible, have particular methods of responding to classes of events and social interactions, modes that are accompanied by a characteristic emotional readout. Some interact with others by being agreeable, attuned to the other's wants, needs, and expectations. Others strive to block the demands of others by showing irritation or anger. In short, there are many facets of the personality that have an emotional character. In fact, we may hypothesize that personality traits, as styles of behavior elaborated by and unique to each individual, are necessarily characterized by emotions, because emotional readouts accompany and direct all behavior.

The view of emotion and personality I have presented gives special emphasis to cognitive assimilation of emotional experiences. Although feelings are generated by expressive motor processing, they are named, classified, understood, and evaluated in the conceptual motor system. The circumplex has been defined wisely as the structure of emotion and personality trait *language*; in other words, the circumplex describes how we name, classify, and understand emotions and personality traits. Conte and Plutchik (1981) described the similarity and dissimilarity in meaning (denotation) of personality trait terms as indicated by the proximity or distance from one another on the circumplex. Wiggins (1979) analyzed the similarity and dissimilarity of students' ratings of their personality traits and found they approximated a theoretically derived circumplex. In our study (Fisher et al., 1985) we showed that students' ratings of their diurnal moods had a circumplicial structure. That is, feelings that tended to co-occur also tended to be close to one another on the circumplex, whereas feelings that never occur together were located at opposite poles of the circumplex. Although these are three very different ways of evaluating personality traits, one by classification of words, one by assessment of one's own personality, and one by identification of one's feelings, all three entail conceptual processing of emotions. The focus of the circumplex model is on how we conceptualize the emotions that we experience.

On the one hand, restricting the circumplex model to emotion and personality trait language prevents us from making a full statement of the structure of emotion, because the focus is on only one aspect of that structure. In their core, emotions are discrete, interlinked, but somewhat independent electrochemical circuits of the brain. There may be only four such mechanisms, as Panksepp (1982, 1986) proposed, or more likely, there are several (yet to be identified by brain stimulation studies) emotion centers in the brain, as evidenced by the important role that distinct facial expression plays in emotion (Ekman, Friesen, & Ellsworth, 1972; Tomkins, 1980) and the corresponding identification of a set of primary emotions (Izard, 1977, Plutchik, 1980). A full description of emotional processing requires a complex systems model that interrelates conceptual, schematic, and expressive motor systems (Leventhal & Mosbach, 1983).

On the other hand, the circumplex model focuses on a crucial component of the emotion–motor system, viz., the readout that emotions give us regarding the state (and traits) of the organism. The circumplex describes how such readout is understood. In interpreting the meaning of the circumplex later in this chapter I will consider how the understanding we have of emotions as messages reflects the structure of emotions themselves.

METHODOLOGICAL ISSUES

In our study of moods (Fisher et al., 1985) we wanted to show that the circumplex model of personality trait language extended to self-reported moods and that the circumplex structure of self-reported moods was virtually the same as the circular structure of the meaning of trait terms reported by Conte and Plutchik (1981). We faced a number of methodological difficulties in accomplishing this task. We had to develop suitable measures of reported moods both as personality traits and emotional states. We then had to develop and apply criteria for defining circular structure. Finally, we had to show that the circumplex structure we obtained was equivalent to the structure obtained by Conte and Plutchik (1981) based on the meaning of personality trait terms.

Measuring Traits

Our first problem was to determine whether a trait measure could be developed from here-and-now experiences of feelings. Here-and-now experiences of mood refer to the *state* of the organism. It is not necessary that being in a particular emotional state at a particular time indicates a stable disposition that could be called a personality trait. It is true that moods have a dispositional quality and last longer than emotional reactions or expressions, but moods fall far short of the stability and permanence required of personality traits.

Although our respondents rated a total of 33 predesignated moods, only 17 of them were taken from Conte and Plutchik's carefully compiled list of 171 personality traits, suggesting that many moods are not generally thought of as personality traits. One item was chosen from each 21 degree interval on the circle in order to represent the entire circumplex. The 17 items are affectionate, agreeable, aggressive, calm, cheerful, confident, depressed, easygoing, enthusiastic, grouchy, helpless, impulsive, irritable, nervous, peaceful, quarrelsome, and reserved. These items clearly refer to personality traits, but they also refer to states that anyone might be in at one time or another. The items not selected are angry, afraid, apathetic, bored, burned out, frustrated, horny, insecure, lonely, optimistic, reflective, rejected, rowdy, spacey, spiritual, and worried. These terms rather clearly refer most commonly to emotional responses to situations or objects, although a few, such as optimistic, spiritual, and worried, could be used to designate personality traits. The remaining 17 items were selected from the Conte and Plutchik circumplex for the express purpose of replicating the circular structure with self-reported ratings of mood.

We resolved the trait measurement problem by averaging the respondents' ratings of their moods over the 30 time periods of the study. Zuckerman (1983, p. 1084) argued that asymptotically the average of state measures approaches the measure of trait. The more frequently one experiences a particular mood, the more likely one is to have a trait that in its operation gives rise to the mood. Such a measure is far from perfect, because one is not able to determine whether recurrence of the mood is attributable to stable features in the respondent or in the respondent's environment. For example, an exceptionally difficult roommate may lead a rather easygoing respondent to report frequently feelings of irritation and grouchiness. A second, and more serious problem, is that the measure is susceptible to systematic bias. Social desirability may prompt some respondents to underreport some feelings, such as irritable and grouchy, and overreport others, such as cheerful and confident. We found that as the study progressed over the 2-week period, respondents reported more consistently, from one period to the next, occurrences of moods rated high on social desirability. Thus, the 30-period average may overstate the extent to which respondents possess socially desirable traits and understate those that are less desirable.

The mischief done by measurement error produced a circumplex of personality traits that was far from satisfactory. The average ratings of items high or low on a bipolar social desirability scale tended to be more highly correlated with one another than the ratings of items with little or no social desirability, causing the desirable and undesirable items to appear closely bunched together on the circumplex. In our study (Fisher et al., 1985) we showed that social desirability bias was the probable cause of this result.

We were left with the problem of measuring moods as states. On the one hand, we had no lack of observations, 141 students rating each mood 30 times. But each rating reflected both the respondent's current state and any trait that may have influenced the mood. In addition, systematic measurement error, such as social desirability bias, was likely to be present. Trait influences and systematic bias induce autocorrelation among the responses, accounting for as much as 50% of the variance of some of the items.

To separate trait and state components in the data and attenuate systematic bias we regressed each of the 33 mood ratings from the 5th to the 30th time period on the first 20 principal components of the ratings of all 33 mood items over the previous four time periods. The residuals of these regressions are in effect residualized scores (cf. Bohrnstedt, 1969) that approximate the serially independent fluctuation in each rating. Then, for each period from 5 through 30 we computed the covariance matrix of the residualized scores. The resulting 26 covariance matrices were averaged to form a pooled within-period covariance matrix representing 2,020 nearly independent observations. The pooled covariance matrix was put in correlation matrix form and analyzed to determine the structure of the mood items.

Demonstrating Circular Structure

Factor analysis is commonly used to reduce a property space defined by a number of measures to a smaller space of considerably fewer underlying dimensions. In most psychometric analyses the focus is on the dimensions that define the reduced, or essential, property space. Each dimension represents a latent variable—one that is not observed but which determines the placement of the measures in the property space and accounts for their correlation with one another. The focus of factor analysis becomes that of determining first the number of dimensions in the reduced property space and second, the meaning of these dimensions. It turns out, however, that the dimensions of the space may be rather arbitrary. Factor analysis really identifies a configuration of points (variables) in a smaller space (i.e., one with fewer dimensions than the number of measures). Almost any scheme of axes can be used to locate those points. An initial factor analysis solution will choose axes that give the greatest variation (spread) in the points to the first axis, the next greatest to the second axis, and so on. This solution may not provide substantively meaningful axes. Rotation is often used to find a more interpretable or theoretically expected set of axes. Even here, however, the properties of the configuration of the measures in space are not overlooked. The goal of rotation in most cases is to arrive at *simple structure*—in other words, axes that project through clusters of points in the configuration so that each point has a high location on one axis and relatively low or zero location on the other axes.

The circumplex model envisions a reduced property space in which measures are not lumped or clustered together. The reduced space has only two dimensions, no matter how many measures are used, and these measures are arranged, not necessarily uniformly, along the circumference of a circle. It is claimed that the dimensions used to locate the circle are completely arbitrary (Conte & Plutchik, 1981, p. 70) and devoid of substantive meaning. The meaning of the circular arrangement consists in the relative position of one measure with respect to the other. Some emotions or personality traits are highly similar, placing them close together in the two-dimensional space, whereas others are quite dissimilar, placing them at opposite poles of the circle. I do not think the dimensions of the circumplex are arbitrary. The identifying characteristic of the circumplex is the configuration—points arranged along a circle—not the lack of meaningful underlying dimensions. When I discuss the meaning of the circumplex, I will suggest two theoretically meaningful underlying dimensions that are related in an interpretable, curvilinear fashion.

Factor analysis is used to estimate the configuration of points on the circumplex. In an ideal situation, one should use maximum-likelihood factor analysis, because the items (i.e., ratings of emotional states or personality traits) tend to have some unknown admixture of measurement error. Principal components analysis is more typically used, probably because it is computationally more simple. The results are typically very similar to maximum-likelihood factor analysis. Maximum-likelihood factor analysis has the advantage of providing a statistical test of the dimensionality of the reduced space (i.e., the number of factors to extract), but this advantage does not count for much when the measures have highly skewed distributions. The maximum-likelihood factor analysis model presupposes normally distributed variables. When the variables are skewed, the factor analysis tends to identify more dimensions in the data than are actually present. Principal components analysis using eigenvalues greater than 1 as the criterion for extracting factors tends to extract the same number of factors as maximum likelihood, even when the variables are skewed. Here I report the results of the principal components analysis, because this method is more generally recommended (see Wiggins, 1979). I will show that despite its limitations principle components analysis is able to provide a reasonably accurate estimate of the circular structure of mood data.

To depict a circumplex, a principal components analysis of emotion or personality trait data must show that the measures lie on or near the circumference of a circle. Although a circle necessarily entails two dimensions, it is not necessary that the reduced property space contain only two dimensions, as Wiggins (1979) suggested. The property space of emotions may require three or even four dimensions, but the configuration of points within the space may fall along a circle tilted in various ways by the additional dimensions. We find this condition when we examine the principal components of the *state matrix*—that is, the matrix of residual factor scores. The components are shown in Table 1. A plot of the first three components is shown in Figure 1. The configuration of points clearly approximates a circle with a number of fairly small deviations from the circumference. But this circle is tilted in the three-dimensional space with points in the high–high corner of the first two dimensions (peaceful and calm) being elevated in the third dimension. The elevation tapers off as we move from either side along the circle of the peaceful–calm pole and reaches its lowest level as we reach the opposite (nervous–aggressive–impulsive) side of the circle.

Skewedness in the measures may require three dimensions to represent the property space. The first component contrasts positive with negative interaction: confident, enthusiastic, cheerful, easygoing, and agreeable

TABLE 1
Principal Components of the State Matrix

Item	1	2	3	4
Impulsive	.37	.58	−.05	.19
Confident	.66	.41	.10	−.09
Enthusiastic	.65	.48	.06	.00
Affectionate	.56	.17	.28	.24
Cheerful	.77	.30	.07	−.01
Easygoing	.69	−.14	.32	.04
Agreeable	.69	.06	.16	.08
Peaceful	.55	−.39	.46	−.08
Calm	.48	−.48	.45	−.12
Reserved	−.17	−.46	.29	.13
Depressed	−.60	.07	.32	.29
Helpless	−.47	−.03	.32	.51
Nervous	−.26	.28	.01	.61
Irritable	−.69	.27	.35	−.23
Grouchy	−.68	.31	.36	−.27
Quarrelsome	−.56	.40	.38	−.24
Aggressive	.04	.64	.14	−.11
Eigenvalues	5.34	2.31	1.33	1.07
Percentage of variance explained	31.4	13.6	7.8	6.3
Cummulative percentage of variance explained	31.4	45.0	52.8	59.1

Note. Adapted from "Evidence for Extending the Circumplex Model of Personality Trait Language to Self-Reported Moods," by G. A. Fisher, D. R. Heise, G. W. Bohrnstedt, and J. F. Lucke, 1985, *Journal of Personality and Social Psychology, 49*(1), p. 238. Copyright 1985 by the American Psychological Association. Reprinted by permission.

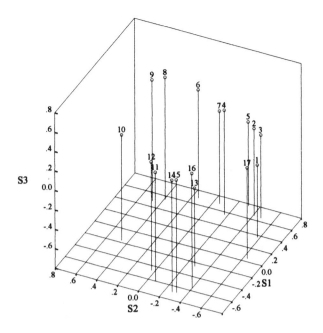

Figure 1. Plot of the first three principal components (S1, S2, S3) of the state matrix. Items are numbered as follows: 1 = impulsive, 2 = confident, 3 = enthusiastic, 4 = affectionate, 5 = cheerful, 6 = easygoing, 7 = agreeable, 8 = peaceful, 9 = calm, 10 = reserved, 11 = depressed, 12 = helpless, 13 = nervous, 14 = irritable, 15 = grouchy, 16 = quarrelsome, 17 = aggressive.

are contrasted with depressed, irritable, and grouchy. Both the second and third component contrast active with inactive poles of the circumplex, but in slightly different ways. The second component contrasts impulsive and aggressive with calm and reserved. The third component contrasts impulsive and nervous with peaceful and calm. The contrast between impulsive and calm appears in both (loadings of .58 and −.48 in the second component and loadings of −.05 and .45 in the third component), but each component contains contrasts not included in the other (aggressive and reserved in the second component with loadings of .64 and −.46, and nervous and peaceful in the third component with loadings of .01 and .46). In short, the third component can be dismissed as a methodological artifact resulting from the skewedness of the measures used.

The fourth component suggests a somewhat greater separation of helpless and nervous from irritable, grouchy, and quarrelsome than the circumplex (represented by components one and two) indicates. Again, the fourth component may have no substantive meaning but reflect skewedness in the distribution of the variables. In sum, we may expect that with different kinds of measures, correlation matrices of emotions and traits may factor into more than two dimensions. But the excess of dimensions over two probably reflect artifacts of measurement, rather than additional structural properties of emotions and traits.

Table 2 presents the principal components of the matrix of averaged ratings, which we will call the *trait matrix*. Three components have eigenvalues greater than 1, indicating that more than two dimensions are needed to represent the property space. The first component appears to represent a general factor, because all the loadings are positive, but there is a clear gradient in the loadings from a high of .91 (on enthusiastic and cheerful) to a low of .21 (on depressed). The component appears to contrast positively and negatively valued traits. The source of this component is the level or magnitude of the averaged ratings. The last column in Table 2 shows the 15-day average of the 17 mood items. Some mood items, such as confident, cheerful, and easygoing received consistently high ratings (means of 1.67, 1.59, and 1.68) compared to others such as helpless, grouchy, and quarrelsome (means of .43, .41, and .31). Respondents with high average ratings on one of the (sample) high average items, such as confident, were likely to have high average ratings on other (sample) high

TABLE 2
Principal Components of the Trait Matrix

Item	1	2	3	Mean rating
Impulsive	.67	.07	−.57	.94
Confident	.90	−.19	−.11	1.67
Enthusiastic	.91	−.20	−.16	1.34
Affectionate	.83	−.18	−.05	1.48
Cheerful	.91	−.32	−.03	1.59
Easygoing	.88	−.28	.19	1.68
Agreeable	.88	−.22	.11	1.44
Peaceful	.87	−.28	.25	1.56
Calm	.87	−.22	.31	1.64
Reserved	.56	.32	.37	.93
Depressed	.21	.81	.21	.51
Helpless	.28	.77	.16	.43
Nervous	.24	.69	.02	.53
Irritable	.26	.83	.03	.51
Grouchy	.23	.85	−.01	.41
Quarrelsome	.33	.82	−.10	.31
Aggressive	.62	.34	−.51	.74
Eigenvalues	7.76	4.52	1.05	
Percentage of variance explained	45.7	26.6	6.2	
Cummulative percentage of variance explained	45.7	72.2	78.4	

average items, such as cheerful. Thus, items with high average ratings correlated more highly with one another than did items with low average ratings. In short, the first component of the trait matrix represents the overall level of the trait in the sample. The mean ratings have a correlation of .956 with the loadings on the first principal component of the trait matrix.

We may conclude that the first principal component of the trait matrix represents differential average levels of mood within each respondent. That is, given the measures that we used (a 5-point rating scale), individuals have higher levels of some traits than others. This result is an artifact of the measuring process. It does not represent the structure of the various moods as indicators of personality traits. Although there are three components in the matrix, only the second and third are relevant to showing whether a circumplex structure is present.

Figure 2 shows a plot of the second and third principal components of the trait matrix. The points are nearly arranged around the circumference of a circle. Impulsive and aggressive are somewhat close together at

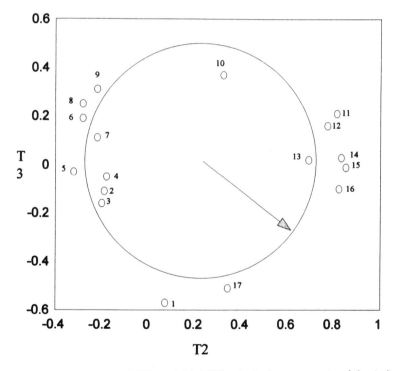

Figure 2. Plot of the second (T2) and third (T3) principal components of the trait matrix. Items are numbered as follows: 1 = impulsive, 2 = confident, 3 = enthusiastic, 4 = affectionate, 5 = cheerful, 6 = easygoing, 7 = agreeable, 8 = peaceful, 9 = calm, 10 = reserved, 11 = depressed, 12 = helpless, 13 = nervous, 14 = irritable, 15 = grouchy, 16 = quarrelsome, 17 = aggressive.

the south pole of the figure. Reserved is near the north pole, with calm and depressed at either side. The negative feelings—depressed, helpless, irritable, nervous, grouchy, and quarrelsome—are bunched somewhat close together on the east side, whereas the positive feelings—calm, peaceful, easygoing, agreeable, cheerful, affectionate, enthusiastic, and confident—are fairly well spread out on the west side. The configuration appears close to a circle, but the center of this circle appears to be shifted to the right along the axis of the second component. The problem seems to be relatively small negative loadings on the second component. The relative size of the average ratings appears to be affecting the magnitude of the loadings on the second component as well as the first. Still, I believe that the configuration itself is more representative of structure than the location of items along axes. We can translate (i.e., add a constant to) the axes of the components to get coordinates of the points on the circumplex that have their origin at the center of the circle.

Departures From Circularity

In determining whether a circumplex is present we need to estimate how far the points in the structure deviate from the circumference of a circle. If the items fall on a circle, the distance from the center of the circle to each point should be the same, because a circle is generated by a constant radius. We can easily measure the length of the vector from the origin to the item using the loadings on each of the two components in the structure as coordinates. We then find the mean length of the vectors and their standard deviation. The mean length provides an estimate of the radius of the circumplex. The standard deviation of the vectors measures the scatter around or deviation from the circumference. The larger the standard deviation is relative to the radius, the less likely the configuration is a circumplex.

In the case of the state matrix we find that the mean vector length or radius is .659 with a standard deviation of .121. The coefficient of variation (the ratio of the standard deviation to the mean) is .184. Thus, the points on this circumplex are within 20% of its radius (about 9% on each side). To determine the radius of the trait matrix, I centered the loadings of the second and third components at their means—.21 for the second component, .01 for the first—to get an estimate of the distance of each coordinate from the center of the circle. The estimated radius is .524 with a standard deviation of .086 and a coefficient of variation of .164.

Figure 3 presents a plot of the loadings of the first two components of the state matrix. A circle with a radius of .66 centered at 0,0 is also presented to show how close the items come to the estimated circumplex. Most of the items are close to the circumference, but the items numbered 10, 12, and 13 (reserved, helpless, and nervous) pull back more than one

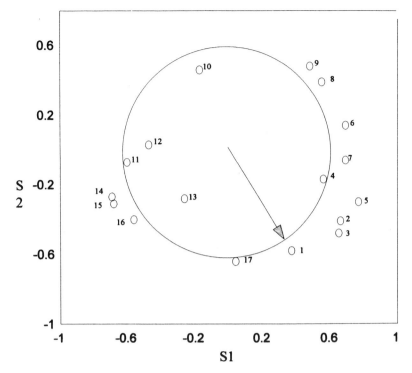

Figure 3. Plot of the first (S1) and second (S2) principal components of the state matrix. Items are numbered as follows: 1 = impulsive, 2 = confident, 3 = enthusiastic, 4 = affectionate, 5 = cheerful, 6 = easygoing, 7 = agreeable, 8 = peaceful, 9 = calm, 10 = reserved, 11 = depressed, 12 = helpless, 13 = nervous, 14 = irritable, 15 = grouchy, 16 = quarrelsome, 17 = aggressive.

standard deviation from the circumference, whereas items 3 and 5 (enthusiastic and cheerful) project out too far (i.e., more than one standard deviation). Although nearly a third of the 17 items are off target, the patterning of the remaining items is sufficiently strong to suggest that the overall structure is circular. One is led to speculate as to why three of the items fall short and two project out too far. Measurement error is a likely cause. Table 1 shows us that a fourth component is picking up variance in depressed and helpless that is not explained by the first two components. This variance could be correlated measurement error. Respondents may have found it difficult to identify feelings of being helpless or nervous. Feeling reserved also may have been hard to identify. Respondents may have had difficulty thinking of being reserved as a mood. They may have viewed it as a personality trait that might express itself in particular interactions but might not be likely to be operative at the times when the ratings were recorded (i.e., on arising and retiring).

When we compare the state circumplex with the Conte and Plutchik (1981) circumplex, we will see that cheerful and enthusiastic perhaps load too highly on the second component. A smaller loading on the second component would move each point closer to the circumplex. Greater activation is associated with these emotions, as reported moods, than semantic evaluations of them represented in the Conte and Plutchik circumplex would suggest. Respondents may overstate the intensity of pleasurable feelings.

A circle also has been drawn in Figure 2, the plot of the second and third principal components of the trait matrix, to show visually how well the items align with a circumplex. In this case four items—numbers 11, 14, 15, and 16 (depressed, irritable, grouchy, and quarrelsome)—fall far outside the circle, whereas three, items 2, 4, and 10 (confident, affectionate, and reserved), fall more than one standard deviation short of the circumference of the circle. There are somewhat more deviations from circularity in the trait matrix than in the state matrix, but overall the extent of deviation is not as great. The four negative moods—depressed, irritable, grouchy, and quarrelsome—appear to run parallel to the estimated circumplex, lying a bit outside it. The configuration of the trait items looks like a circle that has been distorted in some way. The measuring process, using averages of diurnal ratings to estimate traits, may account for the distortion, but we do not know how.

Principal components can be used to determine the presence of a circumplex, but measurement error and measurement artifacts may distort the shape of the circumplex obtained and cause more components than the required two to be extracted. Using several different measures, both of emotion and personality traits, strengthens the evidence for the circumplex model. But each replication of the model using different measures will yield a less than ideal estimate of the circumplex.

Comparing Circumplexes

If we accept that the configuration of items resulting from the principal components analysis was probably generated by a circumplex (i.e., that the distortions in the configuration are artifacts of measurement or arise from measurement error), we must next determine whether the circumplex we have found matches the circumplex found in other studies. Wiggins (1979), for example, developed eight personality rating scales that were expected theoretically to fall exactly 45° apart on the circumplex. In a study in which I developed measures of agreement for circular data (Fisher, 1983), I found quite close agreement between the circumplex generated from Wiggins' data and the theoretical standard. The eight scales were on average no more than 5.34° from their theoretically expected positions. In the study of moods (Fisher et al., 1985) we also sought to compare the circumplexes we obtained with an established standard—the circumplex of personality traits reported by Conte and Plutchik (1981). To illustrate methods of comparing circumplexes, I will repeat those comparisons here, using the circumplexes shown in Figures 2 and 3.

Figures 4 and 5 present idealized circumplexes of the state and trait matrices, respectively, together with the idealized Conte and Plutchik circumplex. The circumplexes are idealized in the sense that the points in each configuration have been projected onto the circumference of the circle by extending or shortening the vector length of each item as needed. Our concern is with the location of the items on the circle, whether each emotion or trait in the reported mood data is as far from the preferred direction (i.e., 0°) as the corresponding trait is in the Conte and Plutchik (1981) circumplex. Figures 4 and 5 allow us to make this comparison visually. The mood data are presented on the inner circle of each figure; the comparison data are presented in the outer circle. By comparing item pairs on the two circles—Item 1 on the inner circle with Item 1 on the outer

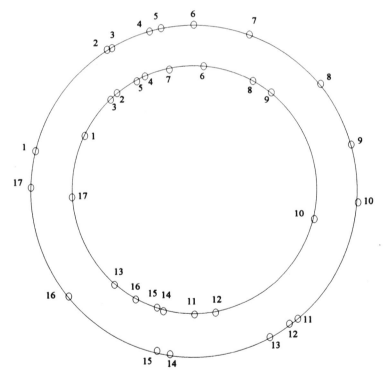

Figure 4. Plot of the Conte–Plutchik circumplex (outer circle) and the circumplex obtained from the first two principal components of the state matrix (inner circle). Loadings have been projected onto the circumference of the circle. Items are numbered as follows: 1 = impulsive, 2 = confident, 3 = enthusiastic, 4 = affectionate, 5 = cheerful, 6 = easygoing, 7 = agreeable, 8 = peaceful, 9 = calm, 10 = reserved, 11 = depressed, 12 = helpless, 13 = nervous, 14 = irritable, 15 = grouchy, 16 = quarrelsome, 17 = aggressive.

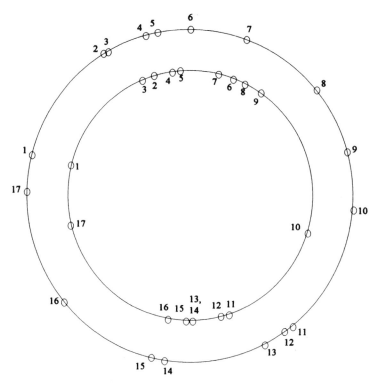

Figure 5. Plot of the Conte–Plutchik circumplex (outer circle) and the circumplex obtained from the second and third principal components of the trait matrix (inner circle). Loadings have been projected onto the circumference of the circle. Items are numbered as follows: 1 = impulsive, 2 = confident, 3 = enthusiastic, 4 = affectionate, 5 = cheerful, 6 = easygoing, 7 = agreeable, 8 = peaceful, 9 = calm, 10 = reserved, 11 = depressed, 12 = helpless, 13 = nervous, 14 = irritable, 15 = grouchy, 16 = quarrelsome, 17 = aggressive.

circle, and so forth—one can easily see how near or apart the replicated items are.

To develop a measure of the agreement in location of items on the circumplex, we need to project the items onto a common circle, pair each item on the mood circle with its corresponding item on the Conte and Plutchik (1981) circle, and measure the angle that separates the pairs. It is easiest to compute the cosine of one half the angle that separates each pair. Thus if two items, A and A,' are separated by 20° on the common circle, half the angle of separation would be 10°, and the cosine of that angle would be .985. These cosines are computed for all pairs of items. The average cosine for all pairs is then converted back to an angle. This angle, doubled, represents the average angular separation among the items. The cosine of the doubled angle provides a coefficient of agreement, which I have named A*, for the two circumplexes. The cosine is used because it provides a measure of agreement that is bounded between -1 and 1. The cosine of $0°$ is 1.0; the cosine of $180°$ is -1. Two points on a circle cannot be separated by more than $180°$. The cosine is a useful measure because the correlation coefficient, often used as a measure of agreement, is also a cosine of angular separation. It represents the separation between two variables projected as vectors into a space that has as many dimensions as observations.

In addition to computing a measure of agreement between two (or more) circumplexes, one also must arrive at a preferred direction for each configuration. The items in Figures 4 and 5 have been numbered according to the order in which they appear on the Conte and Plutchik (1981) circumplex. The numbering begins arbitrarily with impulsive as Number 1 and moves (again arbitrarily) clockwise to confident, enthusiastic, and so on. To get the same (clockwise) ordering on the state matrix, the signs of the loadings on the first component were reversed (see Figure 3). Although all the circumplexes are going in the right direction, it is not clear where $0°$ (the preferred direction) is for each circumplex. For one of the circumplexes, say the Conte and Plutchik (1981) circumplex, the starting point is arbitrary. Let us take Item 1, impulsive, as the preferred direction. But Item 1 may not be the appropriate preferred direction for the mood data circumplex. Closer agreement between the circumplexes may be obtained by choosing a different preferred direction for the mood data circumplex. Changing the preferred direction amounts to rotating the axes of one of the circumplexes.

In Fisher (1983) I presented a formula for finding the angle of rotation that ensures the closest possible agreement between the two circumplexes. In the case of the state matrix shown in Figure 4, a small rotation of $6.5°$ was required. This rotation brought the coefficient of agreement up from .903, an average angular separation of $25.4°$, to .909, an average angular separation of $24.6°$. In the case of the trait matrix, rotation was not used, because the optimal angle of rotation was less than a third of a degree $(-.32°)$. The coefficient of agreement for the trait matrix is .942, an average angular separation of $19.7°$.

The coefficients of agreement obtained for the state and trait matrices indicate a fairly high level of overall agreement with the Conte and Plutchik circumplex. For the state matrix, the average angular separation of $24.6°$ is only 14% of the maximum allowable separation of $180°$. For the trait matrix the discrepancy is an even smaller 11%. A statistical test of whether that little discrepancy could have arisen by chance leads to rejection of the hypothesis that the locations of items on the two circumplexes were generated by independent processes. The statistic, developed by Mardia (1972), multiplies the cosine of one half the average angular separation by the square root of two times the number of items being compared. This statistic has a chi-square distribution with $1°$ of freedom. The value of the statistic is 5.57 for the state matrix and 5.66 for the trait matrix. Both values are far above the critical value of 3.84 ($p = .05$).

Although agreement between the circumplexes is good, there remain several discrepancies that should be examined. In some respects the two circumplexes are not identical. We need to ascertain whether the discrepancies are the result of measurement error or whether they indicate somewhat different structures in our cognitions of emotional states and personality traits. Looking at the state circumplex in Figure 4 we find two major dislocations. The items depressed and nervous are considerably shifted (more than 25°) in the clockwise direction, compared with their location on the Conte and Plutchik (1981) circumplex. In terms of meaning (i.e., on the Conte and Plutchik circumplex), depressed, helpless, and nervous tend to be close together, removed somewhat from irritable and grouchy and separated farther still from quarrelsome. In the state circumplex these feelings all come rather close together. Although fairly different in meaning, they appear to cooccur as moods, or perhaps, respondents had difficulty distinguishing among these feelings when they reflected on their current mood. Figure 4 shows a similar, though far less severe, bunching up of the moods easygoing, agreeable, peaceful, and calm.

Three discrepancies (angular separations greater than 25°) stand out in the trait matrix shown in Figure 5. Calm and quarrelsome are displaced counterclockwise to about the same degree (39° and 40°). Nervous is displaced clockwise, but to a lesser extent (26°). As in the state matrix, calm is located too close to peaceful and easygoing, and quarrelsome is located too close to irritable and grouchy. We also see even greater bunching of depressed, helpless, nervous, irritable, grouchy, and quarrelsome than appeared in the state matrix. Overall, the separation of evaluation and activation is not as great in the mood matrices as it is in the semantic matrix.

INTERPRETING THE CIRCUMPLEX

Characterization of the discrepancies between the two sets of circumplexes requires a theory to explain what the circumplex is. Why do cognitions of emotions and personality traits tend to have a circular structure? Can this structure be expected to vary across contexts, as when one is thinking about one's self, or one's feelings, or about the meaning of emotional and personality trait terms?

Following the theory of Leventhal and Mosbach (1983), emotions are experienced when behavior is not planned or intended. When intended behavior is fully underway, little or no emotion is felt. Emotions may be felt during a lull in the execution of a task, or as a prompting to initiate a new behavior. In either case the emotion is a message to the conceptual motor processing system to initiate or modify behavior. The conceptual motor system must evaluate this message and decide whether to go along with the impulse represented in the emotion or to suppress it. In identifying (i.e., recognizing and interpreting) the emotional message the conceptual system assesses whether the feeling indicates that the present or contemplated course of behavior should not be pursued or whether the feeling indicates that the current line of behavior has been or will be successful and rewarding and should be pursued further. In other words, is the message to stop and do something different or to continue? The emotion message also may be characterized by how strongly it leans toward action or inaction. It may indicate unwillingness on the part of the lower motor systems to engage in behavior, or it may simply ratify behavior that is already fully underway. These two properties of the emotional message are readily recognized as the evaluation and act dimensions of the semantic differential (Osgood et al., 1975). In general, evaluation, potency, and act are referred to as the emotional connotation of all language. In this theory, two of the dimensions—evaluation and act—are applied to emotional connotation itself.

The two dimensions of evaluation and act are not independent. The more fully an action is underway, particularly an intentional act, the lower the emotional impulses to inhibit it or enhance it. Thus, at the peak of activation or quietude, say somewhere in the neighborhood of aggressive or calm and reserved on the Conte and Plutchik (1981) circumplex, there is no emotional movement to inhibit or foster action and as a consequence, no evaluation. In my view, being calm or aggressive is rather lacking in emotional feeling other than a sense of confirmation that the self has achieved its purposes. The extremes of evaluation, feeling cheerful on the one hand and feeling between being nervous and being irritable on the other, relate entirely to a disposition to act or withdraw from activity. They suggest no specific activity to be pursued or blocked. One who is cheerful is disposed to like everything and one who is irritable is ready to oppose everything.

As we move from the extremes of evaluation to either the active or inactive pole, the emotions on the circumplex increasingly refer to action in progress or being blocked. Feeling affectionate implies a readiness to show affection toward others and initiate behaviors related to bonding and social solidarity. Enthusiasm is more active in that it voices approval of some specific project or purpose as it is being launched. Confidence requires a similar level of activity; it too appears in the early stages of executing a plan of action. Impulsiveness, however, refers to action in the making, the carrying out of a plan without hesitation or deliberation. Aggressiveness is emotional energy directed to augmenting the intensity and vigor by which a course of action is pursued.

Going now from high evaluation to total blocking of activity, we see that easygoing is a feeling that inhibits reaction to minor irritations in social interaction. An easygoing person is tolerant and not judgmental. The actions being opposed are generally minor in intensity. Agreeableness goes a bit farther. In being agreeable one makes accommodation to others, accepting demands and to some extent sacrificing the satisfaction of one's own wishes and needs. In peacefulness, conflict is nearly resolved. Opposition in the form of demands for action or criticism that requires self-defense has been overcome. With calm, disturbances are even farther removed and unanticipated.

At the extreme of negative evaluation is an undefined feeling, perhaps one that is never experienced. With irritableness and grouchiness we see the beginnings of resistance to something aversive in our environment that we are unwilling to accept or suffer any longer. We feel quarrelsome when we have begun to engage the irritant, seeking to remove it. With aggression the battle against the irritant is fully joined. Aggressiveness is both vigor in accomplishing our purposes and intensity in overcoming opposition. The passive side of resistance is seen in the movement from nervousness to depression and helplessness. Nervousness involves the anticipation of unpleasant experience and vague calls to prevent it. Depression and helplessness refer to ongoing difficulty. Efforts are being made but they seem ineffectual. Next, though not appearing on 17 items of the Conte and Plutchik (1981) circumplex considered in this study, should be despondency and despair, in which the opposing force is quietly suffered. Only the message that nothing can be done is echoed in the feeling. Reserved is a means, where one is able, of removing oneself from the unwelcome object, and because it is effective, it falls close to calm on the circumplex, near the inactive pole.

These interpretations of the 17 emotions and traits of the mood study show how we apply the concept of activation in the identification and classification of feelings. Also, as the level of activation (or passivity) attached to an emotion increases, the intensity of evaluation decreases, because as emotions rise toward the active–inactive poles of the circumplex, their value on the evaluation axis decreases. We understand evaluation as prompting movement toward or away from some object. The more the individual is involved in moving toward or away from something, the less discrepant the intentional behavior of the organism is from the behavior prompted by the expressive and schematic motor systems, and hence the less intense the emotional message. To illustrate, the singing and happy expression of a cheerful person is manifest most commonly when the person is *not* engaged in interaction with others or dealing internally with problems of self-esteem. One may be cheerful in the presence of total strangers or even enemies, occasions in which the individual is not doing any of the behaviors that cheerfulness exhibits. A confident person, however, can see some match between his or her action and the outcome that is confidently awaited. With impulsivity there is an urge to short circuit any process of reflection and deliberation, an urge that generally is acceded to, making it difficult to distinguish between impulse as emotion and the behavior of acting on impulse.

A similar line of reasoning can be applied to the other emotions on the circumplex. As activation goes up (or down) the discrepancy between emotion as readout and actual behavior decreases. But there are two poles to activation—doing and not doing—and two poles to evaluation—urging behavior toward an object or away from it. That is, there are two modalities of activation and two modalities of evaluation. Combining these together with the tendency for evaluation to wane with increased levels of activation (or inactivation), we can represent the relationship between the two variables as a curvilinear one that keeps the sum of the two values (squared to remove the effect of modality) constant. The formula for a circle is, as we all know, $x^2 + y^2 = r^2$. In the case of the circumplex x represents evaluation, positive or negative, and y represents activation, positive or negative. However high the value of x, the value of y must be commensurately smaller to ensure that the sum of the squares of x and y is r^2. The negative relationship between the two variables appears when we solve for either x^2 or y^2: $y^2 = r^2 - x^2$.

CONCLUSION

This interpretation of the circumplex is drawn directly from two principles of Leventhal and Mosbach's (1983) perceptual-motor theory of emotion. It begins with the notion that emotions, as experience, are readouts to the conceptual motor level of states of the organism, and in particular of motivational preferences from the schematic and expressive motor systems. Then, the interpretation draws on Leventhal and Mosbach's theory that emotion registers a degree of discrepancy between intended behavior and the preferences of the schematic and expressive systems. It accounts for the observed tendency for emotions to be relatively unperceived when intentional activity is fully underway by suggesting that discrepancy necessarily must be less to the extent that activity is present.

Conte and Plutchik argued that underlying dimensions cannot explain the circumplex, because "any particular axis is arbitrary and no more basic than any other" (1981, p. 70). It is true that once points are located on a circle, their positions relative to one another will be invariant whatever the coordinates used to locate them. The metric used to determine the location of the points is indeed arbitrary. But one cannot explain the points on the circumplex unless one can show a functional relationship between the two axes on which it is measured. Whatever axes are chosen, even if arbitrarily, the relationship between x and y for a circumplex will always be $x^2 + y^2 = r^2$. The problem is to determine for what x and y that relationship makes sense. I believe that x as activation and y as evaluation are related as $x^2 + y^2 = r^2$. Activation and evaluation are the properties that we consider in identifying and classifying emotional states. They capture the structure of emotional experience.

REFERENCES

Bohrnstedt, G. W. (1969). Observations on the measurement of change. In E. F. Borgatta & G. W. Bohrnstedt (Eds.), *Sociological methodology, 1969* (pp. 113–133). San Francisco: Jossey-Bass.

Bohrnstedt, G. W., & Fisher, G. A. (1986). The effects of recalled childhood and adolescent relationships compared to current role performance in young adults' affective functioning. *Social Psychology Quarterly, 49,* 19–32.

Conte, H. R., & Plutchik, R. (1981). A circumplex model for interpersonal personality traits. *Journal of Personality and Social Psychology, 40,* 701–711.

Ekman, P., Friesen, W. V., & Ellsworth, P. C. (1972). *Emotion in the human face.* Elmsford, NY: Pergamon Press.

Fisher, G. A. (1983, August). *Coefficients of agreement for circular data with applications to circumplex models and rotation of factors.* Paper presented at the annual meeting of the American Sociological Association, Detroit, MI.

Fisher, G. A., Heise, D. R., Bohrnstedt, G. W., & Lucke, J. F. (1985). Evidence for extending the circumplex model of personality trait language to self-reported moods. *Journal of Personality and Social Psychology, 49,* 233–242.

Hochschild, A. R. (1983). *The managed heart: Commercialization of human feeling.* Berkeley: University of California Press.

Izard, C. E. (1977). *Human emotions.* New York: Plenum Press.

Leventhal, H., & Mosbach, P. A. (1983). The perceptual–motor theory of emotion. In J. T. Cacioppo & R. E. Petty (Eds.), *Social psychophysiology: A sourcebook* (pp. 353–388). New York: Guilford Press.

Mardia, K. V. (1972). *Statistics of directional data.* New York: Academic Press.

Osgood, C. E., May, W. H., & Miron, M. S. (1975). *Cross-cultural universals of affective meaning.* Urbana: University of Illinois Press.

Panksepp, J. (1982). Toward a general psychobiological theory of emotions. *Behavioral and Brain Sciences, 5,* 407–467.

Panksepp, J. (1986). The anatomy of emotions. In R. Plutchik & H. Kellerman (Eds.), *Emotion: Theory, research, and experience* (pp. 91–124). New York: Academic Press.

Plutchik, R. (1980). *Emotion: A psychoevolutionary synthesis.* New York: Harper & Row.

Plutchik, R., & Platman, S. R. (1977). Personality connotations of psychiatric diagnoses: Implications for a similarity model. *Journal of Nervous and Mental Disease, 165,* 418–422.

Schaefer, E. S., & Plutchik, R. (1966). Interrelationships of emotions, traits, and diagnostic constructs. *Psychological Reports*, *18*, 399–410.

Tomkins, S. S. (1980). Affect as amplification: Some modifications in theory. In R. Plutchik & H. Kellerman (Eds.), *Emotion: Theory, research, and experience.* New York: Academic Press.

Wiggins, J. S. (1979). A psychological taxonomy of trait descriptive terms: The interpersonal domain. *Journal of Personality and Social Psychology*, *37*, 395–412.

Zuckerman, M. (1983). The distinction between trait and state scales is *not* arbitrary: Comment on Allen and Potkay's "On the arbitrary distinction between traits and states." *Journal of Personality and Social Psychology*, *44*, 1083–1086.

12

THE INTERPERSONAL CIRCLE AND THE EMOTIONAL UNDERCURRENTS OF HUMAN SOCIABILITY

RAUNI MYLLYNIEMI

My interest in the circumplex model of interpersonal traits started when I read Leary's (1957) *Interpersonal Diagnosis of Personality* in the early 1970s. I was seeking a theoretical background to my dissertation topic, which concerned interpersonal responses given to a projective test styled after Rosenzweig's (1945) Picture Frustration Test. I was impressed—and still am—by the simultaneous richness and clarity of Leary's book: It offered a fascinatingly elaborate picture of the social side of personality and at the same time showed how the description could be derived from relatively few basic concepts and principles. Since then I have remained convinced that Leary's personality system, the *interpersonal circle*, as it is often called, carries within it some very important messages not only about personality dispositions but also about the basis of human sociability.

Since the 1950s, the interpersonal circle has, in the main, retained the substance and structure that Leary and his colleagues gave to it (Freedman, Leary, Ossorio, & Coffey, 1951; Leary, 1957), although slightly altered

The study was supported by the Social Science Research Council of the Academy of Finland. I wish to thank Ahti Jokinen for posing the photographed expressions, Raija Sassi for drawing the expression pictures, and Seppo Roponen for technical assistance.

circles have been constructed (Kiesler, 1983; Strong et al., 1988; Wiggins, 1979, 1982). The conceptual system has gained in elegance from the many empirical analyses that have shown a good fit with the circumplex model (Guttman, 1954; Wiggins, 1980). The circular plots that have emerged in factor analyses or multidimensional scaling analyses of interpersonal variables have made the fit evident to the naked eye. However, despite the theoretical refinements and the empirical circumplexes found, we must wonder what is in the substance of interpersonal behavior that generates the circular pattern and whether anything of value is gained by paying further attention to it.

In this chapter I propose an emotion-based interpretation of the interpersonal circle. To put it in simple terms, when the interpersonal circle is divided into the quadrants that are commonly called friendly–submission, friendly–dominance, hostile–submission, and hostile–dominance (Carson, 1969; Kiesler, 1983; Orford, 1986), it is actually divided into its emotionally homogeneous areas. The quadrants could as well be called trusting, nurturing, fearfulness, and aggression. This interpretation will be fitted first to the octant form of Leary's circle. The four emotional orientations proposed are described as control processes in which feelings serve an important regulatory function. The other possible way of uniting octants within quadrants produces the socially homogeneous areas of the circle, which will henceforth be called affiliation, hostility, dominance, and submission. Starting from the structure of emotional polarities, the categorical division of the circle can be systematized in a novel manner. Some new data is offered to clarify the propositions.

AN EMOTIONAL INTERPRETATION OF THE INTERPERSONAL CIRCLE

Figure 1 summarizes the contents of Leary's (1957) interpersonal octant categories and proposes their connections to four more primary emotional orientations: trusting, nurturing, aggression, and fearfulness. The figure only presents the ordinary, moderate forms of the social dispositions in Leary's system. The grades of intensity have been omitted and terms referring to the pathologically extreme forms of the behaviors have been retained only in the octant labels. Overtly normative terms (such as *stern but fair*) and terms describing likely responses (such as *helped by others*) also have been omitted. Figure 1 thus shows what kinds of dispositions or styles of behavior Leary included in each of the octants and how he arranged the octants relative to each other to form a closed circular order.

It is true that multivariate analyses of interpersonal data have not given dimensions interpretable as trusting versus aggression and nurturing versus fearfulness as the major axes of the figure, nor are the two pairs of

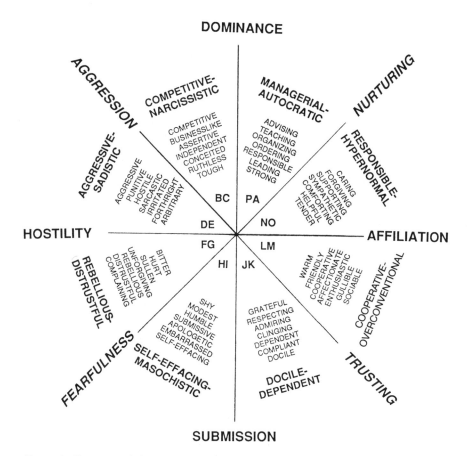

Figure 1. Contents of the octant categories of the interpersonal circle as described by Leary (1957). Social and emotional polarity axes added.

terms natural-sounding semantic opposites. The Learyan octants, as summarized in Figure 1, and the broader descriptions of the respective psychological dispositions suggest the kind of interpretation that I am presenting. Paying attention to these emotional axes will make it possible to gain a deeper understanding of the socially meaningful polarities: affiliation versus hostility and dominance versus submission.

The Nature of Emotional Orientation

What kinds of psychological entities are trusting, nurturing, aggression, and fearfulness? I already have called them emotional orientations. They may be presented as feedback-controlled processes—for instance, in the way Bowlby (1969) described attachment behavior and Plutchik (1983) described the emotions of sadness and fear. An orientation, then, is a process by which the organism first recognizes a discrepancy between its present relation to the environment or ongoing events and a more desirable relation. This recognition will activate certain system-specific types of action. If these bring about the desirable relation the process will be terminated; if not the discrepancy is fed back into the system and action continues. Among emotion theorists, at least Plutchik (1980), MacLean (1980), and Izard (1991) have systematized the fundamental emotions according to their functional consequences. The four orientations can be perceived similarly, but instead of being bound to some single emotion or feeling quality they can be presented as emotion patterns—processes in which reaching the terminal state is paralleled with a transition from unpleasant feelings to pleasant ones (cf. Kemper, 1978; Lazarus, 1991).

Perhaps the most distinctive features of an emotional process are its spontaneity and the special role that subjective experiences—feelings—play. Even the most discrepant emotion theories agree that emotions resist volitional control. An emotional control process can be conceived of as proceeding spontaneously at all of its crucial phases. The process is started spontaneously because in the organism there is a readiness to recognize particular features in the environment and to project special meanings onto them. As Frijda (1986) said, emotions arise in response to special *situational meaning structures*. Perceiving the emotion-specific meanings will lead to the spontaneous activation of action readiness and expressive behavior. An essential part of spontaneity is the onset of an emotion-specific awareness—feelings. Feelings comprise the meanings perceived in the environment, the felt desires to act in a certain way, and more generally sensed pleasure or displeasure. As Arnold (1960) wrote, the spontaneous processes by which perceptions and cognitions are coded into feelings can be called *intuitive appraisals*.

Of course, human beings can place emotionality under some control. We follow display rules and control the outward expressions according to cultural conventions (Ekman, 1980). We even follow feeling rules and try to evoke the proper kinds of inner experiences (Hochschild, 1978). Changing feelings is harder work than changing expressions. It is easier to produce, say, a smile to mask embarrassment than to get rid of the feeling. Feelings, I think, are more important parts of emotional processes than expressions. They have a twofold function; they are, at the same time, information and motivators (Frijda, Kuipers, & ter Schure, 1989; Schwarz, 1990). The information function has been expressed in many ways. Frijda (1986) called feelings *relevance signals*; Buck (1984) compared them with *progress reports*, Zajonc and Markus (1984) spoke about feelings as *soft representations*, and von Cranach, Mächler, and Steiner (1985) more simply as *representations*. What, then, do feelings signal, report, or represent? Because most of them can be categorized fairly easily as either pleasant or unpleasant, let us only consider the two hedonic qualities. It is not surprising that several authors have come to the conclusion that unpleasant feelings, such as fear or disappointment, inform us about failures or impending harm of some kind, whereas pleasant feelings, such as satisfaction and joy, tell us about successes and benefits. Feelings give us a progress report on how harmfully or beneficially things are proceeding. Thus they represent harms and benefits. An emotional organism is motivated not only to get rid of troubles and threats but also to get rid of emotional harms—the unpleasant feelings that inform us about troubles and threats. Moreover, an emotional organism is motivated not only to gain material benefits but also to gain emotional benefits—the pleasant feelings that inform of successes.

An emotional orientation, then, can be depicted as a control process in which the organism is prepared to notice harmful changes of a certain kind in its relation to ongoing events. Such harmful events will be coded intuitively into an unpleasant feeling, an emotional harm. Motivation to get rid of this harm will be evoked. Process-specific expressions will be spontaneously activated, and certain types of action will be experienced as desirable. When proper action, or some other causes, bring about the desired beneficial state of events, the unpleasant feeling will fade away. The recognition of the favorable turn of events then will be intuitively coded in a pleasant feeling, an emotional benefit.

Four Emotional Security Orientations

The emotional processes of trusting and nurturing can together be called the two attachment orientations. These orientations, it is presumed here, represent the types of contact-seeking that originate in the action readinesses and feeling qualities of the early mother–infant attachment relation. There are, of course, other sources of emotional attraction, such as interest, curiosity, and sexuality, and these types of attraction may arise together with the attachment orientations. Sexual attraction is often but not always combined with emotional attachment. It may be argued, as Eibl-Eibesfeldt (1971) did, that tenderness in human relations derives from the caregiving system, not from sexuality.

By trusting orientation, I mean the type of contact-seeking in which a childlike pattern of behavior and feelings prevails. Such a pattern can be traced down to the infant's attachment to his or her caregiver. Bowlby (1969) described early attachment behavior as a control system that works to make the infant keep close to the mother and to maintain her attention. The main functional consequence of attachment is protection, but as Sroufe and Waters (1977) pointed out, to the infant the ultimate goal of attachment is the security he or she feels. The trusting orientation of a grown-up person can be constructed as a process that starts as feelings of loneliness, dejection, or distress. The person is motivated to seek contact with and elicit protectiveness, comfort, or support from another. Some familiar, self-confident, nurturingly inviting person is preferred as the contact person. The process is terminated in a feeling of security, perhaps tinged with tears if the distress that started the process had been intensive. A more cheerful feeling, the joy of reunion, or even a mixture of joy and tears, also may terminate the process. The trusting person then loses the emotional harms of loneliness and distress and gains the emotional benefits of security and joy.

The nurturing orientation is a maternal or parental form of attachment. The biological function of parental behavior is to benefit offspring, and although nurturing refers to more generally applied and less intensely felt mothering, it still means benefiting others. Unlike the other three emotional orientations, nurturing is an altruistic orientation. The person is motivated to seek contact in order to protect, comfort, and support the other. Yet, as far as feelings go, nurturing also can be presented as an egoistic process that makes the individual seek emotional benefits. Contact-seeking of the nurturing kind may be evoked by pleasant feelings of attraction to the other, but it also may be evoked by strongly felt emotional harms: worry, compassion, or pity. Altruistic action may mitigate such feelings, and tenderness, joy, and a benevolent outward-focused self-satisfaction may be experienced instead.

Humans probably have a biologically based propensity to develop both kinds of attachment orientations. The orientations are part of our shared repertoire of sociability, universally present in all cultures. Comparisons with other species, at least with other primates, also can be made. Primatologists have shown how forms of behavior typical of mother–infant interaction (such as kissing, embracing, grooming, holding close) have been carried over to adult interaction. Behaving like a mother and infant, showing reciprocal attachment, makes it possible for adult primates to maintain relaxed proximity (Goodall, 1986; Reynolds, 1981). As Eibl-Eibesfeldt (1971) in particular showed, a similar conclusion can be made about human sociability.

The remaining two emotional orientations—fearfulness and aggression—can be called the *defensive orientations*. In social contexts they are evoked in reponse to conflicts in which people have to defend their profits or gains, or even their health and life, against others' attempts to weaken their competitive capacity. Conflict is an inevitable part of life, and humans, like other animals, must have some innate propensity to develop relevant means of coping. Emotion research has shown that similar facial expressions are recognized as communicating fear and anger in otherwise very different cultures (Ekman, 1973; Izard, 1971), and that similar antecedent events and similar behaviors and physiological symptoms are connected with these feelings in different cultures all over the world (Wallbott & Scherer, 1986). Again, however, rather than indicating some single emotions, the defensive orientations can be presented as processes directed from felt harms to felt benefits.

The functional consequence of the fearful orientation is avoidance of danger. Although as an emotional event, this orientation is essentially a process for freeing oneself of fear and insecurity, it also can be perceived as the seeking of a pleasurable feeling state to replace fear. Fear carries the message of danger, and in a competitive encounter it indicates weak chances of winning. The motivation to flee, hide, or retire from competition is evoked. If such measures then carry the person out of danger, the person experiences relaxation. This relaxation may be felt as relief, which at times is a highly pleasurable feeling.

The functional consequences of the aggressive orientation are more varied: avoiding danger, securing gains, striking down obstacles, winning in competition, correcting injustices. Although even a weak individual, if desperate, can feel extreme anger and fight fiercely, normally someone is provoked into aggression and can maintain the orientation because of an intuitive confidence in his or her superior or sufficient resources. The process may start as feelings of uncertainty and even fear, but if competitive superiority is fairly certain at the outset, irritation and anger are felt instead. An aggressive orientation need not lead to harming the opponent. Even animals mostly fight by using threatening gestures. The important thing is to show superior resources and make the other contestant give in. Various pleasant feelings, such as enjoyment from reinforced self-confidence and triumphant self-satisfaction, may follow. If the contest was close, relief is mingled with these feelings.

These four orientations all can be categorized as emotional security orientations. They far from exhaust human, socially relevant emotionality. Much of human sociability is based on what may be called *competence emotionality*—emotional harms and benefits connected to exploration, achievement, mastery, and play (cf. Buck, 1984; White, 1959). Equally important to human social life are normative social emotions—emotional harms and benefits connected to conformity, deviance, honor, and justice. Although normative feelings, such as shame and indignation, also may be counted as security concerns, they are uniquely human adaptations and more recent phenomena in evolution than the emotional attachment and defensive orientations. I propose in this chapter that the interpersonal circle can be seen as the patterning of the forms of sociability that derive their direction and meaning from the four primary emotional security orientations mentioned previously.

POLARITIES OF THE INTERPERSONAL CIRCLE AND THE EMOTIONAL AMBIVALENCIES UNDERLYING SOCIAL ORIENTATION

Figure 2 presents the emotional and social polarities of the interpersonal circle. The emotional polarities (indicated by bold lines) are the following: the overall contradiction between attachment and defensiveness; the contradiction between trusting and nurturing within the attachment orientations; and the contradiction between fearfulness and aggression within the defensive orientations. The general contradiction between attachment and defensiveness is actualized in two ways: For the more resourceful, dominant party it is that between nurturing and aggression, and for the less resourceful, submissive, party it is between trusting and fearfulness.

Thus the four social areas of the circle are defined as four types of emotional ambivalence. Contradictions among these ambivalent types of orientation show the two social polarities of contradiction between dominance and submission and between affiliation and hostility. (The latter social polarity coincides with the basic emotional polarity of attachment and defensiveness.)

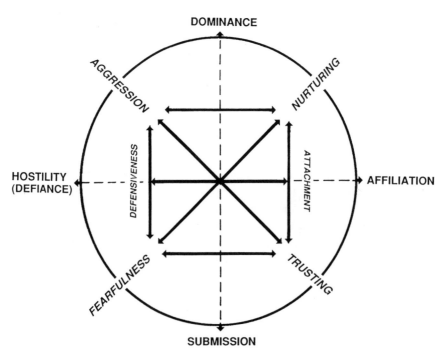

Figure 2. Polarities of the interpersonal circle: a proposal.

Hostility, if based on simultaneous experience of aggression and fear (as the Leary system suggests), might be better presented as restrained rebelliousness or defiance. In Figure 2, I have added the latter term *defiance* in parentheses alongside hostility. In the following three figures, however, *hostility* is put in parentheses instead of defiance, which is hence recommended as the more adequate interpretation of the axis pole.

The social axes of the interpersonal circle—affiliation versus hostility–defiance and dominance versus submission—both represent obvious pairs of contradictory psychological tendencies as well as natural sounding semantic opposites. The proposed emotional axes—trusting versus aggression and nurturing versus fearfulness—are different. Social life does not often put us in situations in which emotional inclinations either to nurture or to fear or either to trust or to attack a person would appear as natural alternatives, and thus these two pairs of terms do not sound like meaningful semantic opposites. It is paradoxical that it is these two semantically unlikely pairs of opposites that are presented as the fundamental polarities of the interpersonal circle.

CATEGORIES OF THE INTERPERSONAL CIRCLE

In Figure 3, the areas of the circle are labeled according to the present interpretation of the interpersonal circle. Each octant has been given a label that refers to its social meaning and the emotional meaning that is the more pronounced of the two underlying emotional orientations. The more general labels (affiliation, dominance, etc., and trusting, nurturing, etc.) can be used in two ways. First, they can be taken to denote the quadrants of the figure. The circle can be divided into quadrants in two ways: into four emotionally homogeneous areas or four socially homogeneous areas. But, instead of denoting the quadrants of the circle these more general labels can be taken to refer to special intervening categories. In this case submission, for instance, would refer to the category between trusting–submission and fearful–submission. This category would denote a submissive orientation in which the two emotional elements are in balance or submissive behavior, pure and simple, such as a ritual display of subordination. Fearfulness would refer to the category between fearful–submission and fearful–defiance. This category would denote purely fearful orienation without encompassing any submissive or defiant meaning.

THE STRUCTURE OF INTERPERSONAL LANGUAGE

The largest body of empirical evidence for the circumplex organization in the interpersonal domain comes from self-inventories or other self-

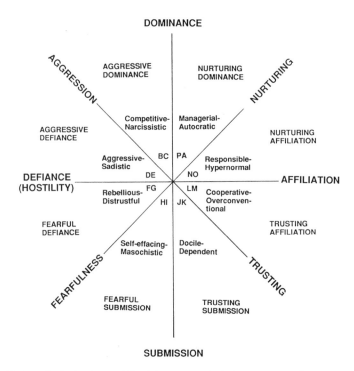

Figure 3. Categorical structure of the interpersonal circle: a proposal.

report measures. Jackson and Helmes (1979) suggested that, because of the nature of the data, the two axes might reflect response sets rather than true traits. At first sight, studies of the relevant categories in which the self-presentation part has been dropped entirely—namely, the studies of interpersonal term meanings as such—would solve the problem. Indeed, when similarities among term meanings were studied, good circumplexes appeared. However, this leads to more severe attacks on the interpersonal circle. Shweder and D'Andrade (1979) showed that there are good grounds to argue that, instead of reflecting accurately some substantial structure of interpersonal action, the interpersonal circle only reflects the structure of a set of cognitive categories. The next self-evident question is, why should the interpersonal categories then show the circumplex organization? This question is the more pertinent because we now have congruent evidence from different cultural backgrounds; whether it reflects cognitive categories or more substantial psychological tendencies, the circle might be universal.

The following analyses have shown that interpersonal terms in different cultures fit well to Leary's circle and can be represented by a two-dimensional model: Shweder's (1972; Shweder & Bourne, 1984) analysis of 81 Oriya personality descriptors (Orissa, India), White's (1980) analysis of 37 A'ara personality descriptors (Salomon Islands), Conte and Plutchik's

(1981) analysis of 40 English interpersonal terms (United States), and Lutz's (1986) study of 31 Ifalukian emotion words (Ifaluk, Micronesia); most of these were interpersonal in meaning.

In none of these studies were the terms sampled to represent a predetermined system of categories; only a predetermined domain was explored. According to the definite system of interpersonal categories put forward in this chapter, a sample of words representing just these categories should show the characteristics of the interpersonal circle. A two-dimensional figure in which the terms would appear in the theory-based order should be found. The following study was designed to investigate this.

Method

Seventy-two Finnish-language adjectives were selected to represent the 16 categories as presented in Figure 3—the 8 octant categories plus the 8 intervening categories. The categories trusting, nurturing, fearfulness, and aggression were represented by three terms each; all the other categories by five terms each. These terms are given in Table 1. The terms were assigned and agreed on by two judges acquainted with the present theory. The terms were then appraised by 20 judges—first-term students of social psychology who were not acquainted with the interpersonal theory. The terms were written on cards and the research participant was asked to sort them according to similarity of meaning into eight piles, which did not need to be equal in size. The participant was asked to rate the similarity of the piles pairwise by using a 4-point scale of similarity.

In each participant's estimations, all the terms placed in the same pile were given the similarity value of 5. Otherwise the similarity value of a pair of terms was the value of their respective piles and varied between 1 and 4. Each term was thus roughly estimated in relation to the others on a 5-point scale of similarity. Mean similarities were calculated across the participants. The final matrix was formed by correlating the columns of the 72×72 matrix of mean similarities in which the value 5 was given to each diagonal cell. The correlation matrix was then factor analyzed by the principal components method.

Results

Figure 4 shows the plot of the terms on the first two unrotated factors. These explain 92% of the variance. As can be seen, the resulting pattern is definitely a circumplex. Because the terms were preassigned on a theoretical basis to 16 ordered categories, we can find out if the theoretical order (the theory-based ordering by two judges) and the empirical order (the average ordering by 20 naive judges) correlate. Because different cor-

TABLE 1
English Translations of the 72 Finnish Interpersonal Adjectives Chosen to Represent the 16 Categories of the Interpersonal Circle (as Presented in Figure 4)

Submission	Affiliation	Dominance	Defiance
dependent	affiliating	decisive	brusque
docile	gregarious	determined	defiant
helpless	friendly	dominating	rebellious
obedient	sociable	enterprising	rejecting
submissive	warm	self-reliant	sarcastic

Trusting–submission	Nurturing–affiliation	Aggressive–dominance	Fearful–defiance
agreeable	benevolent	commanding	bitter
compliant	gentle	demanding	grudging
grateful	helpful	independent	hurt
modest	supporting	outspoken	sullen
respecting	sympathetic	scheming	unforgiving

Trusting	Nurturing	Aggression	Fearfulness
appealing	nurturing	aggressive	evasive
clinging	protecting	merciless	fearful
trusting	tender	threatening	suspicious

Trusting–affiliation	Nurturing–dominance	Aggressive–defiance	Fearful–submission
affectionate	conciliating	hurting	obliging
open-hearted	negotiating	punitive	quiet
cooperative	guiding	puffed up	reserved
gullible	responsible	ruthless	self-effacing
faithful	self-sacrificing	triumphing	servile

relations would be obtained depending on where the comparison of the two orders started, four Spearman's rank correlation coefficients were calculated. The comparison was first started from the category submission, which was given Rank 1 in the theoretical order. The adjacent categories, trusting–submission and fearful–submission, were given Rank 2, and so on, until dominance was given Rank 9. Dividing the empirical order into categories was started by taking *submissive* as the prototype term of *submission*. Submissive and the four terms closest to it were given Rank 1, the next five terms in both directions Rank 2, the next three (which corresponded with the three-term categories of trusting and fearfulness) Rank 3, and so on. Special care was taken to give extra rank points to terms that lay on

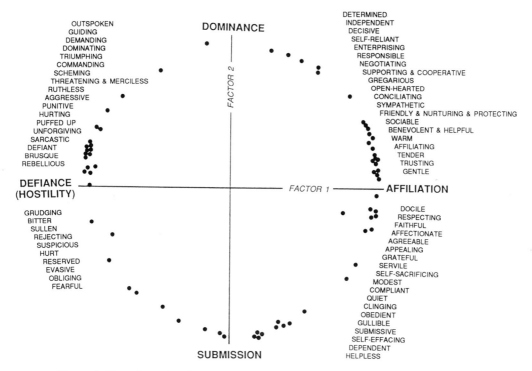

Figure 4. Two-dimensional plot of 72 Finnish-language interpersonal terms. Principal components analysis of a correlation matrix based on the method of sorting according to similarity. English translations of the terms are given in each quadrant in the order of placement. Identically placed terms are on the same line.

the "wrong" side of the start category, such as *servile*, a term preassigned to fearful–submission but lying on the trusting side of submission. The rank correlation of these two orders was 0.80. When comparisons were started from affiliation, dominance, and defiance and *affiliating, dominating,* and *defiant* were taken as the respective prototypes, rank correlation coefficients of 0.85, 0.71, and 0.91 were obtained. All these correlations are significant beyond the 0.001 level.

However, we should not be misled by the exactness of these figures of correspondence. It must be evident to anybody who starts inspecting the terms that hardly any of them applies to only one category. They are more extensive in meaning, they vary in extensiveness, and, no doubt, some other theoretical raters would have preassigned them differently. Interpersonal categories remain fuzzy, however theoretically applied. But certainly we are safe in concluding that the two fuzzy orders show fairly high correspondence.

Taken together, the studies of interpersonal terms speak for the universality of the circumplex pattern in this domain. Why should essentially the same kind of pattern be uncovered in these diverse languages? It is usual to refer to the universal semantic dimensions evaluation and potency as a possible explanation. Even though the absence of the third semantic dimension, activity, may be surprising, if the circle is merely a case of the semantics of good versus bad and strong versus weak, it would render the finding uninteresting. Something more substantial should be there to be accurately reflected. The suggestion put forward here is that what is reflected is the patterning of cooccurences among certain universally present emotional tendencies.

NONVERBAL COMMUNICATION OF INTERPERSONAL ORIENTATIONS

Leary (1957) stressed the automatic, reflex-like quality of interpersonal responses. The interpersonal meanings of overt behavior are expressed, "partly in the content of verbal meaning of the communication, but primarily in the tone of voice, gesture, carriage, and external appearance" (pp. 96–97). A circumplex of such nonverbal expressions, which would correspond in meaning with the categories of the interpersonal circle, would speak strongly for the reality of the circle.

Gifford and O'Connor (1987; Gifford, 1991) showed that certain nonverbal behaviors correlate with interpersonal traits as measured by Wiggins's (1979) Interpersonal Adjective Scales. Observed behaviors such as gestures, smiles, head orientation, nods, and object manipulation, as well as reported interpersonal distance, could be mapped on the circle as monotonically increasing and then decreasing patterns of correlation. Furthermore, many studies of nonverbal communication, which have not referred to the interpersonal circle, have mapped its polarities (e.g., Ellyson & Dovidio, 1985; Kalma, 1991).

The emotional analysis of the interpersonal circle, proposed in this chapter, leads to a fairly clear-cut hypothesis. If the emotional orientations of trusting, nurturing, fearfulness, and aggression unite in specific combinations in the social orientations of affiliation, dominance, defiance, and submission and if the emotional orientations are communicated by some typical expressive elements, the respective combinations of such elements should communicate the social orientations and, when properly analyzed, show their typical configuration, the circumplex.

Method

I tested the hypothesis earlier by using drawn face diagrams (Myllyniemi, 1982). This earlier research was replicated by using photographs of real faces.

Stimulus Material

Photographs of facial expressions posed by a professional actor were used as material. The actor posed the expressions according to the investigator's instructions: Each expression was to carry the expressive elements of either only one emotional orientation or of two orientations in combination. The choice of expressive elements was based on the descriptions of angry, fearful, and sad faces given by Ekman (1973) and Izard (1971), the taxonomies of human nonverbal behavior of Grant (1969) and Brannigan and Humphries (1972), and some findings of Eibl-Eibesfeldt (1980).

The following expressive elements of (a) the eye region and the direction of gaze, (b) the mouth, and (c) head and shoulder postures were taken to carry the meanings of the four orientations.

Trusting (T) elements: (a) keen gaze with tense eyeballs ("bright" eyes); the eyes open, but not as open as in fear, and the eyebrows not raised; or the eyebrows drawn together and raised in the middle ("sad" eyes); (b) smile with the lips parted and the upper teeth showing ("upper smiler") (Grant, 1969); (c) head thrust toward the target of the gaze.

Perhaps none of the listed elements alone can communicate trusting; they always have to appear in certain combinations. For instance, as such, "keen gaze" probably only communicates interest. When connected with some other trusting element, however, it gives the expression an appealing quality.

Nurturing (N) elements: (a) relaxed eyeballs and eyelids, the eyes open or half-closed; the eyebrows raised (a welcoming element) (cf. Eibl-Eibesfeldt, 1980); (b) wide, "flat" smile, the lips closed; (c) head tilted to one side (cf. Eibl-Eibesfeldt, 1980).

Both kinds of attachment expressions are tentative.

Aggressive (A) elements: (a) eyebrows drawn together and lowered in the middle; (b) lips pressed together with the corners straight or down; (c) straightened back and shoulders; the head lifted and drawn backwards.

Fearful (F) elements: (a) direct gaze with the eyes wide open or looking away; (b) a squared pattern of the mouth, with the lips open and drawn back; (c) the head lowered ("chin in") (cf. Grant, 1969) or drawn backwards.

These defensive expressions are less tentative. The descriptions of the expressions of fear and anger by Ekman (1973) could be followed in the (a) and (b) elements. The head and shoulder postures are more problematic. A straightened body and lifted head are displays of strength and self-confidence; but it may be that such displays are already social rituals, signs of dominance rather than pure aggression. The same applies to looking away as a sign of fear. Perhaps it can be used only socially, as an expression of submission; an individual encountering real danger cannot take the risk of not being attentive to the threatener.

Figure 5 includes drawings based on the photographs. The labeling of the expressions shows the agreement of two independent judges. Label A (aggressive), for instance, indicates that the pose contains only aggressive expression elements (one or more), and pose AF (aggressive–fearful) contains both aggressive and fearful elements.

The study set was 1 trusting (T), 2 trusting–nurturing (TN), 1 nurturing (N), 2 nurturing–aggressive (NA), 3 aggressive (A), 3 aggressive–fearful (AF), 1 fearful (F), and 3 fearful–trusting (FT) faces. The aim was to include one pose from each type of single-emotion expression and three poses from each type of double-emotion expression. Because sufficient numbers of natural looking nurturing–aggressive and trusting–nurturing combinations were not available, two extra aggressive poses were included instead. Aggressive expressions were chosen for these extras because, as previous studies had shown, gaps were most likely to appear near aggression in the dominant area.

Participants and Procedure

The expression photographs were submitted to two kinds of appraisal and analysis. In both appraisals the research participants were first-term

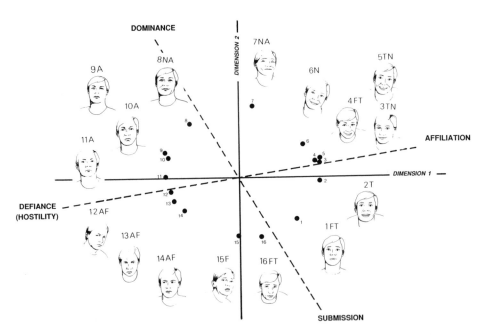

Figure 5. Two-dimensional plot of 16 photographed expressions. Multidimensional scaling of a correlation matrix based on the method of rating scale profile similarity. Variables composed of rating scales fitted as extra axes. Preassigned meanings of the expressions: T = trusting, N = nurturing, F = fearful, A = aggressive, TN = trusting–nurturing, FT = fearful–trusting, AF = aggressive–fearful, NA = nurturing–aggressive.

students of social psychology, and they participated on a voluntary basis. In the first analysis (Figure 5), 22 participants appraised the photographs on 18 five-point rating scales. The scales were worded to represent the two social polarities (dominance versus submission; affiliation versus defiance) and four of the emotional polarities (trusting versus nurturing; nurturing versus aggression; aggression versus fearfulness; fearfulness versus trusting) of the interpersonal circle as presented in Figure 2. For each expression, mean ratings of the 18 scales were calculated across the participants. The resulting profiles of 18 mean values were correlated.

In the second analysis (Figure 6) the expressions were sorted out according to mere similarity by 20 participants. Each participant was given the 16 photographs in a randomly ordered pack and asked to sort them in at least four or as many as eight piles according to the similarity of social disposition communicated by the expressions. As in the study of term meanings, the participant was asked to rate the similarity of the piles pairwise on a 4-point scale of similarity. All the expressions placed in the same pile were given the similarity value of 5. Otherwise the similarity value of a pair of expressions was the value of the respective piles and varied between 1 and 4. Each expression thus came to be estimated in relation to

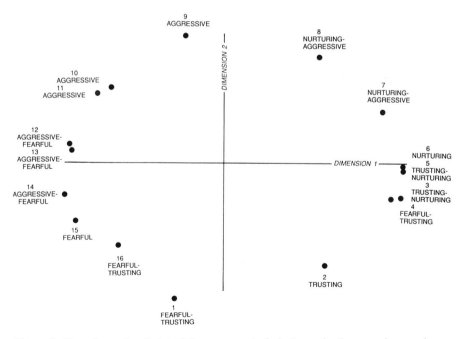

Figure 6. Two-dimensional plot of the same set of photographed expressions as in Figure 5. Multidimensional scaling of a correlation matrix based on the method of sorting according to similarity.

the others on a 5-point scale of similarity. Mean similarities were calculated across participants, and the columns of the 16×16 matrix were correlated.

Results

Both intercorrelation matrices of 16 expressions were submitted to multidimensional scaling, using the KYST-2 program of Kruskal, Young, and Seery (1973). Figure 5 shows the order of the expressions calculated from the rating scale profiles. Figure 6 shows the corresponding order of the expressions when these were sorted out according to mere similarity. Both configurations are definitely two-dimensional. The stress indices for the two-dimensional case were as low as 0.009 in the rating scale study and 0.029 in the sorting study, and little room was left for further decline in stress. Expression Number 4 is similarly misplaced in both analyses. Although preassigned as a fearful–trusting expression it is found among the affiliative ones. With the exception of this misplacement and the finding that the nurturing expression and the second of the trusting–nurturing expressions are almost identically placed in Figure 6, the order of the eight categories of expressions corresponds with the theory-based order.

Chang and Carroll (1972) developed a multiple regression procedure, PROFIT, by which interpretive extra axes can be fitted to multidimensional scaling figures. Among the 18 rating scales that were used in the rating study, three were constructed to differentiate the expressions along the social polarity affiliation versus defiance, and another three to differentiate them along dominance versus submission. The three scales were summed up in both cases, and the composite variables were fitted into the KYST-2 figure. The polarity dimensions have been added to Figure 5. These extra axes show how the participants saw social meanings in the faces, which, as it is supposed, expressed the four types of emotional meanings and their specific combinations. In this study, Dimension 1 and Dimension 2 of the multidimensional scaling analysis seem to point out the emotional polarities, whereas the extra axes point out the social polarities, more or less in accordance with theoretical expectations.

Figures 7 and 8 show corresponding plots of expressions from an earlier study in which drawn facial diagrams were used as stimulus materials (Myllyniemi, 1982). The methods of appraisal and analysis were identical with the ones applied in the two studies presented previously. Again, Figure 7 comes from a study in which the expressions were rated along verbal polarity scales and Figure 8 from a sort-out study. It was easy to combine expression elements in these artificial faces, and thus we could construct expression combinations supposedly representing the 16 categories of the interpersonal circle (as presented in Figure 3 in this chapter). So, for instance, the three types of trusting–fearful combinations included faces combining such elements in equal amounts (category: submission), faces with

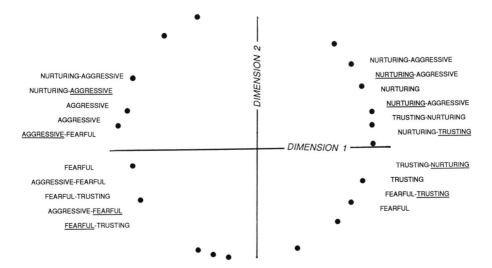

Figure 7. Two-dimensional plot of 20 drawn face diagrams. Multidimensional scaling of a correlation matrix based on the method of rating scale profile similarity. Preassigned expressive meanings of the diagrams are given in each quadrant in the order of the placement of the diagrams. More pronounced expressive meaning underlined. (Based on Figure 13 in Myllyniemi, 1982.)

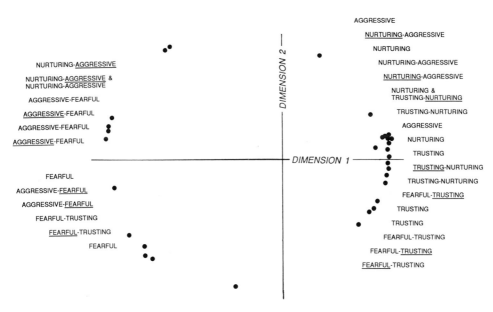

Figure 8. Two-dimensional plot of 32 drawn face diagrams. Multidimensional scaling of a correlation matrix based on the method of sorting according to similarity. Preassigned expressive meanings of the diagrams are given in each quadrant in the order of the placement of the diagrams. More pronounced expressive meaning underlined. (Based on Figure 15 in Myllyniemi, 1982.)

more trusting than fearful elements (category: trusting–submission), and faces with more fearful than trusting elements (category: fearful–submission).

These figures, too, are clear circumplexes. The stress indices for the two-dimensional case were 0.018 in the rating scale study (Figure 7) and 0.043 in the sort-out study (Figure 8). There are many minor misplacements in the two circle orders, but the division into the four emotional areas can be seen in both figures.

CONCLUSIONS

The title of this chapter includes the term *emotional undercurrents*. It is proposed that types of social orientation that we call dominance, submission, affiliation, and hostility (or defiance) are—sometimes weakly, sometimes strongly—energized and directed by underlying emotional orientations. The emotional orientations—trusting, nurturing, fearfulness, and aggression—are also ways of relating to others. The interpersonal circle, the special correlative structure of the social orientations mentioned, which first served to direct attention to the emotional orientations, however, also indicated that emotional undercurrents tend to appear in special ambivalent combinations.

The hypothetical structure of the interpersonal circle was tested using two types of empirical material: interpersonal term meanings and facial expressions. The analysis of terms differed from corresponding earlier studies in that the terms were sampled to represent the 16 categories of the circle, as they were specified in this study. A good circumplex in which the terms were found more or less in the expected order was obtained. This small-scale study indicates that, whatever the ultimate reason, the interpersonal terms show circumplexity also in Finnish. This study thus adds to the diversity of the language groups in which the interpersonal circumplex has been found.

The expression studies were conducted to determine whether expressions and expression combinations supposedly representing the emotional structure of the interpersonal circle would show circumplexity. Expression photographs and drawn face diagrams were appraised, first by rating along verbal scales that represented the polarities of the circle and second by sorting according to similarity. Clear circumplexes and more or less similar figures were obtained by both kinds of stimulus materials and by both appraisal methods. The trusting and nurturing expressions, however, were not very well differentiated from each other. Perhaps the true expression elements of attachment were not found, or perhaps attachment orientations are not as well communicated by some momentary facial expressions, or perhaps these two types of orientation are, in reality, more closely located than the two defensive types. This analysis corresponds with Masters' (1979) *behavioral triangle*, a general-level ethological analysis of social relations in a three-cornered figure of flight, attack, and bonding. We attempted to split the bonding, but perhaps the two parts cannot be separated entirely from each other.

I will conclude by commenting briefly on the following two questions: why should the proposed description represent a more basic form of the interpersonal circle? and why should hostility be relabeled defiance?

Seeking a developmental order is a worthwhile principle to be followed in any psychological explanation. In the case of the interpersonal circle, the broad evolutionary rather than the ontogenetic perspective is indicated. The fearful, aggressive, trusting, and nurturing forms of emotionality can be regarded as old in the evolutionary sense, parts of the shared mammalian behavior repertoire. If the social dispositions of the interpersonal circle really are in some essential part generated by these forms of emotionality, then a description in which they are taken into account can be called more basic. From this perspective, forms of the circle that include polarities such as extraversion versus introversion (Kiesler, 1983; Strong et al., 1988) and weak versus strong achievement motivation (Wiggins, 1980) have enriched the description with dispositions that correlate with the polarities of the basic emotional structure.

As a social disposition, the fearful–aggressive orientation can only mean rebelling against, challenging, or defying a somehow stronger interaction partner. I chose the latter—*defiance*—as the general label for this pattern of both being afraid of and yet wanting to compete with and conquer a partner. When the social orientations of the circle are listed as defiance, submission, dominance, and affiliation, it is obvious that the interpersonal circle actually summarizes the types of social behavior needed to establish social cohesion by first building a dominance hierarchy. Hierarchical organization is also an old phenomenon. It is a wide-spread form of social organization in other primates, not least in our nearest relatives, the chimpanzees (de Waal, 1987; Goodall, 1986; Vehrencamp, 1983). Descriptions of the social life of these animals show that much of the dynamics of the interindividual encounters can be summarized by using the four terms mentioned alone (Myllyniemi, 1993). If the interpersonal circle uncovers some basic structure of human sociability it is not very surprising that the structure should prove to be an arrangement of the hierarchically meaningful types of social orientation.

REFERENCES

Arnold, M. B. (1960). *Emotion and personality*, 2 vols. New York: Columbia University Press.

Bowlby, J. (1969). *Attachment and loss. Volume 1: Attachment.* New York: Basic Books.

Brannigan, C. R., & Humphries, D. A. (1972). Human non-verbal behaviour as means of communication. In N. G. Burton Jones (Ed.), *Ethological studies of child behaviour* (pp. 37–64). Cambridge: Cambridge University Press.

Buck, R. (1984). *The communication of emotion.* New York: Guilford Press.

Carson, R. C. (1969). *Interaction concepts of personality.* Chicago: Aldine.

Chang, J. J., & Carroll, J. D. (1972). *How to use PROFIT, a computer program for property fitting by optimizing nonlinear or linear correlation.* Murray Hill, NJ: Bell Laboratories.

Conte, H. R., & Plutchik, R. (1981). A circumplex model for interpersonal personality traits. *Journal of Personality and Social Psychology, 40,* 701-711.

Cranach, M. von, Mächler, E., & Steiner, V. (1985). The organization of goal-directed action: A research report. In G. P. Ginsburg, M. Brenner, & M. von Cranach (Eds.), *Discovery strategies in the psychology of action* (pp. 19–61). London: Academic Press.

de Waal, F. (1987). Dynamics of social relationships. In B. B. Smuts, D. L. Cheney, R. M. Seyfarth, R. W. Wrangham, & T. T. Struhsaker (Eds.), *Primate societies* (pp. 421–429). Chicago: Chicago University Press.

Eibl-Eibesfeldt, I. (1971). *Love and hate. The natural history of behavior patterns.* New York: Holt, Rinehart & Winston.

Eibl-Eibesfeldt, I. (1980). Strategies in social interaction. In R. Plutchik & H. Kellerman (Eds.), *Emotion. Theory, research, and experience. 1. Theories of emotion.* New York: Academic Press.

Ekman, P. (1973). Cross-cultural studies of facial expressions. In P. Ekman (Ed.), *Darwin and facial expression. A century of research in review* (pp. 169–222). New York: Academic Press.

Ekman, P. (1980). Biological and cultural contributions to body and facial movements in the expression of emotions. In A. O. Rorty (Ed.), *Explaining emotions* (pp. 73–101). Berkeley: University of California Press.

Ellyson, S. L., & Dovidio, J. F. (Eds.). (1985). *Power, dominance, and nonverbal behavior.* New York: Springer.

Freedman, M. B., Leary, T. F., Ossorio, A. G., & Coffey, H. S. (1951). The interpersonal dimension of personality. *Journal of Personality, 20,* 143–161.

Frijda, N. H. (1986). *The emotions.* Cambridge: Cambridge University Press.

Frijda, N. H., Kuipers, P., & ter Schure, E. (1989). Relations among emotion, appraisal, and emotional action readiness. *Journal of Personality and Social Psychology, 57,* 212–228.

Gifford, R. (1991). Mapping nonverbal behavior on the interpersonal circle. *Journal of Personality and Social Psychology, 61,* 279–288.

Gifford, R., & O'Connor, B. (1987). The interpersonal circumplex as a behavior map. *Journal of Personality and Social Psychology, 52,* 1019–1026.

Goodall, J. (1986). *Chimpanzees of Gombe. Patterns of behavior*. Cambridge, MA: Belknap Press, Harvard University Press.

Grant, E. C. (1969). Human facial expression. *Man, 4*, 525–536.

Guttman, L. (1954). A new approach to factor analysis: The radex. In P. F. Lazarsfelt (Ed.), *Mathematical thinking in the social sciences* (pp. 258–348). Glencoe, IL: Free Press.

Hochschild, A. R. (1978). Emotion work, feeling rules, and social structure. *American Journal of Sociology, 85*, 551–575.

Izard, C. E. (1971). *The face of emotion*. New York: Appleton-Century-Crofts.

Izard, C. E. (1991). *The psychology of emotions*. New York: Plenum Press.

Jackson, D. N., & Helmes, E. (1979). Personality structure and the circumplex. *Journal of Personality and Social Psychology, 37*, 2278–2285.

Kalma, A. (1991). Hierarchisation and dominance assessment at first glance. *European Journal of Social Psychology, 21*, 165–181.

Kemper, T. D. (1978). *A social interactional theory of emotions*. New York: Wiley.

Kiesler, D. H. (1983). The 1982 Interpersonal Circle: A taxonomy of complementarity in human transactions. *Psychological Review, 90*, 185–214.

Kruskal, J. B., Young, F. W., & Seery, J. B. (1973). *How to use KYST-2, A very flexible program to do multidimensional scaling and unfolding*. Murray Hill, NJ: Bell Laboratories.

Lazarus, R. S. (1991). *Emotion and adaptation*. New York: Oxford University Press.

Leary, T. (1957). *Interpersonal diagnosis of personality: A functional theory and methodology for personality evaluation*. New York: Ronald Press.

Lutz, C. (1986). The domain of emotion words on Ifaluk. In R. Harré (Ed.), *The social construction of emotions* (pp. 266–288). Oxford: Basil Blackwell.

MacLean, P. D. (1980). Sensory and perspective factors in emotional functions of the triune brain. In A. O. Rorty (Ed.), *Explaining emotions* (pp. 9–36). Berkeley: University of California Press.

Masters, R. D. (1979). Beyond reductionism: Five basic concepts in human ethology. In M. von Cranach, K. Foppa, W. Lepenies, & D. Ploog (Eds.), *Human ethology. Claims and limits of a new discipline* (pp. 265–284). Cambridge: Cambridge University Press.

Myllyniemi, R. (1982). Nonverbal communication of elemental social orientations—Studies with face diagrams. *Research Reports. Department of Social Psychology. University of Helsinki, 1*.

Myllyniemi, R. (1993, September). *Systemness of social interaction*. Paper presented at the Tenth General Meeting of the European Association of Experimental Social Psychology, Lisbon, Portugal. September 15–20.

Orford, J. (1986). The rules of interpersonal complementarity: Does hostility beget hostility and dominance, submission? *Psychological Review, 93*, 365-377.

Plutchik, R. (1980). *Emotion. A psychoevolutionary synthesis*. New York: Harper & Row.

Plutchik, R. (1983). Emotions in early development: A psychoevolutionary approach. In R. Plutchik & H. Kellerman (Eds.), *Emotion. Theory, research, and experience. Vol. 2. Emotions in early development* (pp. 221–257). New York: Academic Press.

Reynolds, P. (1981). *On the evolution of human behavior: The argument from animals to man.* Berkeley: University of California Press.

Rosenzweig, S. (1945). The picture-association method and its application in a study of reactions to frustration. *Journal of Personality, 14,* 3–23.

Schwarz, N. (1990). Feelings as information. Informational and motivational functions of affective states. In E. T. Higgins & R. M. Sarrentino (Eds.), *Handbook of motivation and cognition* (Vol. 2, pp. 527–561). New York: Guilford Press.

Shweder, R. A. (1972). *Semantic structures and personality assessment.* Doctoral dissertation, Harvard University. (University Microfilms No. 72–29: 584)

Shweder, R. A., & Bourne, E. J. (1984). Does the concept of the person vary cross-culturally? In R. A. Shweder & R. A. Levine (Eds.), *Culture theory. Essays on mind, self, and emotion* (pp. 159–199). Cambridge: Cambridge University Press.

Shweder, R. A., & D'Andrade, R. G. (1979). Accurate reflection or systematic distortion? A reply to Block, Weiss, and Thorne. *Journal of Personality and Social Psychology, 37,* 1075–1084.

Sroufe, L. A., & Waters, E. (1977). Attachment as an organizational construct. *Child Development, 48,* 1185–1199.

Strong, S. R., Hills, H. I., Kilmartin, C. T., DeVries, H., Lanier, K., Nelson, B. N., Strickland, D., & Meyer, C. W. III (1988). The dynamic relations among interpersonal behaviors: A test of complementarity and anticomplementarity. *Journal of Personality and Social Psychology, 54,* 798–810.

Vehrencamp, S. (1983). A model for the evolution of despotic versus egalitarian societies. *Animal Behaviour, 31,* 667–682.

Wallbott, H. G., & Scherer, K. R. (1986). How universal and specific is emotional experience? Evidence from 27 countries on five continents. *Social Science Information, 25,* 763–795.

White, J. S. (1980). Conceptual universals in interpersonal language. *American Anthropologist, 82,* 759–781.

White, R. W. (1959). Motivation reconsidered: The concept of competence. *Psychological Review, 65,* 297–333.

Wiggins, J. S. (1979). A psychological taxonomy of trait-descriptive terms: The interpersonal domain. *Journal of Personality and Social Psychology, 37,* 395–412.

Wiggins, J. S. (1980). Circumplex models in interpersonal behavior. In C. Wheeler (Ed.), *Review of personality and social psychology* (Vol. 1, pp. 265–293). Beverly Hills, CA: Sage.

Wiggins, J. S. (1982). Circumplex models of interpersonal behavior in clinical psychology. In P. C. Kendall & J. N. Butcher (Eds.), *Handbook of research methods in clinical psychology* (pp. 183–221). New York: Wiley Interscience.

Zajonc, R. B., & Markus, H. (1984). Affect and cognition: The hard interface. In C. E. Izard, J. Kagan, & R. B. Zajonc (Eds.), *Emotions, cognitions and behavior* (pp. 73–102). Cambridge: Cambridge University Press.

III

APPLICATIONS OF THE CIRCUMPLEX MODEL TO CLINICAL ISSUES

13

PERSONALITY DISORDERS AND THE INTERPERSONAL CIRCUMPLEX

THOMAS A. WIDIGER and STEVEN HAGEMOSER

The interpersonal circumplex model of personality has rich clinical (Benjamin, 1993), theoretical (Kiesler, 1983; Leary, 1957), and empirical (Wiggins, 1982) foundations. Fundamental to our understanding and description of personality is the characteristic manner of relating to others (Wiggins, 1982). No model of personality can fail to include interpersonal relatedness. In addition, "when personality traits are inflexible and maladaptive and cause significant functional impairment or subjective distress . . . they constitute Personality Disorders" (American Psychiatric Association, 1994, p. 630). It is to be expected that the personality disorders identified in the American Psychiatric Association's *Diagnostic and Statistical Manual of Mental Disorders (DSM)* would represent (at least in part) maladaptive variants of interpersonal relatedness (Widiger & Kelso, 1983).

It has in fact been suggested that personality disorders are essentially, if not entirely, disorders of interpersonal relatedness (Benjamin, 1993; Kiesler, 1986). The *DSM-IV* includes sections for disorders of anxiety, mood, sex, sleep, and other behavior patterns. The personality disorders could represent the interpersonal disorders. To the extent that personality is es-

The authors express their appreciation to Paul Costa, Jerry Wiggins, and Dan Ozer for clarification regarding the distinction (or lack thereof) between the FFM and the FFFM.

sentially interpersonal relatedness (Leary, 1957; Wiggins, 1982), disorders of personality would be disorders of interpersonal relatedness.

However, personality may involve more than one's manner of relating to others. Personality traits are defined in *DSM-IV* as "enduring patterns of perceiving, relating to, and thinking about the environment and oneself that are exhibited in a wide range of social and personal contexts" (American Psychiatric Association, 1994, p. 630). How one relates to others is indeed a major component of personality, but there may be other components that are equally significant. In this chapter we will review the extent to which most or all of the *DSM* personality disorders are adequately described by the interpersonal circumplex, compare its coverage with a complementary model, and discuss implications for the clinical treatment of personality disorders.

DSM PERSONALITY DISORDERS FROM THE PERSPECTIVE OF THE INTERPERSONAL CIRCUMPLEX

There have been many studies on the relationship of the interpersonal circumplex to personality disorders. We will confine our chapter to those studies that concerned most to all of the *DSM* personality disorders, thereby excluding those studies that were confined to just one or two personality disorders (e.g., Blackburn & Maybury, 1985; Bradlee & Emmons, 1992) or studies that concerned personality disorder nomenclatures other than the *DSM* (e.g., Millon, 1987; Strack, Lorr, & Campbell, 1990).

DSM-I

The first published presentation of the interpersonal circumplex is typically credited to Freedman, Leary, Ossorio, and Coffey (1951). Freedman and colleagues also suggested that each of the interpersonal traits would have both normal and maladaptive variants. Leary and Coffey (1955) subsequently described six personality disorders with respect to this circumplex. They administered the Minnesota Multiphasic Personality Inventory (MMPI) and an interpersonal circumplex adjective checklist to 302 consecutive psychiatric outpatients. Of the 302 patients, 102 provided uninterpretable interpersonal circumplex or MMPI profiles, a finding the authors suggested would be resolved with an improvement in scoring. Six MMPI personality profiles that could be placed along the circumplex were identified: psychopathic, schizoid, obsessive, phobic, hysteric, and psychosomatic. Table 1 and the following quotation summarize their findings.

> Patients who employ aggressive, nonconventional modes of maladustment tend to obtain the psychiatric diagnosis of psychopathic person-

TABLE 1
Leary and Coffey (1955) Interpersonal Circumplex Description of Personality Disorders

Interpersonal circumplex location	Personality disorder
Managerial, autocratic	—
Responsible, externalizing	Psychosomatic
Cooperative, overagreeable	Hysterical
Trustful, dependent	Phobic
Modest, self-punishing	Obsessive
Skeptical, distrustful	Schizoid
Critical, aggressive	Psychopathic
Competitive, exploitative	—

ality. Patients with distrustful, passively-resistant modes of adjustment tend to be called schizoids; submissive self-punishing patients tend to be called obsessives; docile dependent patients tend to be labeled phobics; bland, naive, overconforming patients tend to be diagnosed hysterics, and responsible, hypernormal patients fit the psychosomatic pattern of the MMPI. [In sum,] of the eight interpersonal modes of adjustment–maladjustment, six are related to psychiatric categories. Two interpersonal modes, however, the autocratic–managerial and the competitive–narcissistic, seem to have no psychiatric equivalent. (Leary & Coffey, 1955, p. 118)

Leary and Coffey (1955) suggested that the two gaps might reflect inadequacies within the psychiatric nomenclature. "We are led to speculate that these types have received little diagnostic attention because they do not come for help" (p. 118). They suggested that the autocratic, power-oriented interpersonal pattern might receive a diagnosis of compulsive personality disorder, a prediction that subsequently was confirmed (e.g., Wiggins, 1982). The other gap has since been filled by including the narcissistic personality disorder in the third edition of the *DSM* (American Psychiatric Association, 1980).

However, there are also some qualifications that should be noted in this initial effort by Leary and Coffey (1955). Some of the personality disorders they identified in fact may not represent valid personality disorder constructs (e.g., the psychosomatic personality) and the rationale for their placements may no longer apply (e.g., distrustful, passive–resistant persons are much more likely to be diagnosed with the passive–aggressive or perhaps the paranoid personality disorder than with the schizoid personality disorder). In addition, they did not consider many of the *DSM-I* personality disorder diagnoses that were in use at the time, such as the emotionally unstable, passive–aggressive, cyclothymic, and inadequate (American Psychiatric Association, 1952). The failure to consider the cyclothymic and inadequate diagnoses was perhaps wise, given their questionable validity and eventual deletion from the nomenclature. However, emotionally unstable personality disorder is the *DSM-I* version of borderline personality disorder.

An additional effort during the time of *DSM-I* was provided by Lorr, Bishop, and McNair (1965). Lorr and colleagues administered a peer report interpersonal circumplex scale to the therapists of 525 persons being seen within individual psychotherapy. "Approximately 48% were diagnosed psychoneurotic, 37% were labeled personality disorders, and 16% were categorized otherwise" (Lorr et al., 1965, pp. 468–469). Lorr and colleagues divided the interpersonal circumplex into four quadrants: (a) Type I was said to be inhibited, submissive, and abasive; (b) Type II was characterized by agreebleness, nurturance, affection, and sociability; (c) Type III by hostility, mistrust, and detachment; and (d) Type IV was exhibitionistic, dominant, competitive, and hostile. Lorr and colleagues found very few personality disorder diagnoses within the Type II quadrant. These persons "tend to be labeled psychoneurotic or to be left undiagnosed" (1965, p. 471). There was also little distinction among the other three types, but this was probably a result of the failure to distinguish between individual personality disorders. They did note that "Type IV members (dominant, competitive, exhibitionistic) . . . are more frequently diagnosed personality trait disturbance, that is, Passive–Aggressive, Aggressive, or Compulsive" (p. 471).

DSM-II

Plutchik and Platman (1977) continued the personality disorder research with *DSM-II* (American Psychiatric Association, 1968). They had 20 psychiatrists rate 7 of the 10 *DSM-II* personality disorders (and a category of well-adjusted) with respect to 66 bipolar combinations of 12 trait terms. Correlations among the 8 categories were submitted to a factor analysis. Two factors accounted for 91% of the variance, and the results were plotted in the form of a circumplex. One curious aspect of their findings were notable gaps in the circle, but this may have been a result of the statistical effects of including a well-adjusted category (i.e., the gaps did not necessarily correspond to any particular interpersonal style). It also should be noted that Plutchik and Platman did not include three of the ten *DSM-II* personality disorders, but the ones they excluded were subsequently deleted from the nomenclature (i.e., explosive, asthenic, and inadequate).

DSM-III

Wiggins (1982) provided the first effort at understanding the *DSM-III* personality disorders in terms of the interpersonal circumplex. "At least seven of these categories of personality disorder emphasize interpersonal behavior . . . and these categories bear a close resemblance to the octants of the interpersonal circumplex" (Wiggins, 1982, p. 211). His placement of each personality disorder is provided in Table 2. However, his effort might be notable not only for what he included within the interpersonal circumplex, but also for what he failed to include: the borderline, avoidant, antisocial, and schizotypal personality disorders. Wiggins also had a gap in the upper right (gregarious–extraverted) octant (see Table 2), which he filled with a proposed diagnosis of hypomanic personality disorder.

Morey (1985) provided the first empirical study on the relationship of the interpersonal circumplex to the *DSM-III* personality disorders. He administered the Interpersonal Check List (ICL; LaForge & Suczek, 1955) and the Millon Clinical Multiaxial Inventory (MCMI-I; Millon, 1982) to 66 psychiatric inpatients. The interpersonal circumplex accounted for 47% of the variance in the MCMI-I personality disorder scales. The correlations of the MCMI-I personality disorder scales with the ICL axes then were used to plot each of the personality disorders within the circumplex. Notable was the absence of any personality disorders in the lower-left (rebellious–distrustful) quadrant and only one (paranoid) in the upper-right (responsible–hypernormal) quadrant. Morey (1985) concluded that, "it appears that the primary differentiation among personality disorders occurs along the Control axis with little variation on the Affiliation dimensions" (p. 362). This finding was surprising, but it was probably a result of the unusual sample. Almost a third of the research participants were diagnosed with schizophrenia and 18% with a bipolar mood disorder. In addition, the

TABLE 2
Wiggins (1982) Interpersonal Circumplex Description of *DSM-III*
Personality Disorders

Interpersonal circumplex location	*DSM-III* personality disorder
Ambitious–dominant	Compulsive
Gregarious–extraverted	—
Warm–agreeable	Histrionic
Unassuming–ingenuous	Dependent
Lazy–submissive	Passive–aggressive
Aloof–introverted	Schizoid
Cold–quarrelsome	Paranoid
Arrogant–calculating	Narcissistic

mean age was 19.8 (SD = 5.8). In other words, many of the participants were probably below the minimal age of a personality disorder diagnosis and at least half had a major Axis I disorder. It is unlikely that a sufficient range of personality disorder or interpersonal circumplex symptomatology was sampled to obtain a circumplex structure.

Plutchik and Conte (1985) replicated Plutchik and Platman (1977) in two studies using the *DSM-III*. In the first study, 10 psychiatrists rated the 11 *DSM-III* personality disorders and a category of well-adjusted with respect to their similarity to three reference personality disorders: compulsive, antisocial, and histrionic. In the second study, 12 psychiatrists rated the 11 *DSM-III* personality disorders and a category of well-adjusted with respect to 20 adjectives. The two-factor solution of the correlations among the 12 categories conformed to a circular structure, and the correlation of the angular locations of the 12 categories obtained from the two studies was .91. The solutions provided by the two studies were then averaged. "Borderline, narcissistic, and antisocial cluster together opposite dependent; histrionic is opposite compulsive; and the schizoid, schizotypal, avoidant [and passive–aggressive] cluster is in the opposite side of the circle from well-adjusted" (p. 10). Plutchik and Conte concluded that the findings from their studies provided "strong evidence for the construct validity of the circumplex structure of personality disorders" (p. 11). Plutchik and Conte were clearly successful in placing all of the *DSM-III* personality disorders within a circular structure. However, it also should be noted that there was little differentiation among many of the personality disorders (e.g., the schizoid, schizotypal, avoidant, and passive–aggressive personality disorders had virtually the same location on the interpersonal circumplex, as did the borderline, narcissistic, and antisocial). In addition, a circumplex structure is likely to be obtained if the personality disorders are rated with respect to adjectives or terms that are chosen to represent the interpersonal circumplex. (One might also obtain a circular structure of animals, vegetables, and fruit assessed with respect to their similarities to adjectives chosen to represent octants of the interpersonal circumplex).

Kiesler (1986) reviewed the prior attempts at characterizing the personality disorders in terms of the interpersonal circumplex, particularly those by Leary (1957; Leary & Coffey, 1955) and Wiggins (1982) (see Tables 1 and 2). He concluded that these efforts "(a) have not succeeded in locating all 11 disorders on the Interpersonal Circle, (b) at best agree in Circle location for only 4 of the 11, and (c) at worst agree on Circle location for only 1 of the 11 disorders" (Kiesler, 1986, p. 578). He suggested that one difficulty has been the failure to recognize that some of the personality disorders provide complex interpersonal circumplex profiles rather than representing particular octants or quadrants (a concern also noted by Wiggins, 1982). Kiesler, therefore, coded individual *DSM-III* personality disorder criteria rather than an entire personality disorder diagnosis. A summary of this effort is provided in Table 3. For example, the borderline personality disorder (BPD) criterion of inappropriate anger was coded within the hostile–cold (or rancorous–sadistic) segment, whereas BDL idealization was coded in the opposite friendly–warm (or devoted–indulgent) segment. The borderline personality disorder is described by Kiesler in terms of four of the eight interpersonal circumplex octants, some of which are opposite to each other. The disorder could not be placed within any particular location of the interpersonal circumplex, but at least part of borderline personality disorder and all of the other personality disorders were described in terms of the interpersonal circumplex. The descriptions are more complex than those of Wiggins (see Table 2) but they are perhaps more realistic and accurate.

Note, however, that only two of the seven *DSM-III* personality disorders considered by Wiggins (1982) (i.e., schizoid and paranoid) are placed in the same interpersonal circumplex octants by Kiesler (1986). For example, whereas Wiggins placed the dependent personality disorder solely within the unassuming–ingenuous octant, Kiesler failed to code even one of the dependent personality disorder symptoms within this octant (trusting–deferent); Wiggins placed the *DSM-III* compulsive personality disorder solely within the ambitious–dominant octant, but Kiesler coded the compulsive personality disorder symptoms as belonging within the submissive–unassured and inhibited–detached octants (see Tables 2 and 3). In addition, it is also important to note that Kiesler apparently was unable to code many of the individual personality disorder criteria, including five of the eight borderline criteria. Borderline impulsivity, affective instability, identity disturbance, intolerance of being alone, and physically self-damaging acts were not coded in terms of the interpersonal circumplex.

TABLE 3
Kiesler (1986) Interpersonal Circumplex Description of *DSM-III* Personality Disorders

	DSM-III personality disorder										
	PRN	SZD	SZT	ATS	BDL	HST	NCS	AVD	DPD	CPS	PAG
Dominant–assured							X				
Exhibitionist–sociable						X	X				
Friendly–warm					X						
Trusting–deferent					X						
Submissive–unassured								X	X	X	
Inhibited–detached		X	X					X	X	X	X
Hostile–cold	X			X	X						X
Mistrusting–competive	X		X		X						

Note. PRN = paranoid, SZD = schizoid, SZT = schizotypal, ATS = antisocial, BDL = borderline, HST = histrionic, NCS = narcissistic, AVD = avoidant, DPD = dependent, CPS = compulsive, and PAG = passive–aggressive.

Kiesler, Van Denburg, Sikes-Nova, Larus, and Goldston (1990) sub-sequently had 240 undergraduates and 22 graduate students provide inter-personal circumplex ratings of videotaped intake interviews of eight patients diagnosed with a *DSM-III* personality disorder. The eight inter-views included 7 of the 11 *DSM-III* personality disorders (borderline, avo-idant, dependent, and paranoid were excluded for methodological issues). The interpersonal circumplex ratings significantly differentiated the seven personality disorders despite the brevity of the interviews (about 5 to 10 minutes each). Kiesler and colleagues concluded, "Patterns of overt inter-personal behavior are indeed different for patients who have various per-sonality disorders" (p. 449). However, the differences they obtained were not always consistent with expectations. "At best, our tests of Kiesler's (1986) Circle translations . . . were confirmed for only 3 cases (schizoid, narcissistic, compulsive). Predictions for the other 5 cases either were con-firmed only partially or not at all" (Kiesler et al., 1990, p. 450).

DeJong, van den Brink, Jansen, and Schippers (1989) replicated the analyses of Morey (1985). They administered the ICL (LaForge & Suczek, 1955) and the Semistructured Interview for *DSM-III* Personality Disorders (SIDP; Pfohl, 1983) to 51 alcohol-dependent inpatients of an addiction treatment center (77% male). Forty-one percent of the variance in per-sonality disorder symptomatology was accounted for by the interpersonal circumplex. All of the personality disorders were placed successfully within the interpersonal circumplex, but DeJong and colleagues (1989) noted the failure to confirm the predictions for the borderline, histrionic, and anti-social personality disorders. More importantly, the results did not conform to a circumplex structure. All of the personality disorders were within the upper-left or lower-left quadrants. In other words, the right (affiliative) side of the circumplex was entirely empty, and discrimination among the per-sonality disorders was primarily with respect to control (i.e., dominance versus submission). The authors concluded that "the convergence of the two approaches to personality taxonomy is not as high as might be ex-pected from a theoretical standpoint, and it seems that DSM–III PDs [per-sonality disorders] are not as differentiated with regard to affiliative needs as has been hypothesized" (DeJong et al., 1989, p. 145). However, it also should be noted that the effort of DeJong and colleagues to replicate Mor-ey's study also succeeded in sharing the substantial methodological limi-tation. Fifty-one inpatient alcohol-dependent patients may not provide suf-ficient variance with respect to the personality disorders or the interpersonal circumplex to adequately reproduce the circumplex structure.

Wiggins and Pincus (1989) administered to 581 college students the *DSM-III* MMPI personality disorder scales developed by Morey, Waugh, and Blashfield (1985) and Strack's (1987) Personality Adjective Check List (PACL) that assessed the personality disorders in Millon's (1981) variant of *DSM-III*. To assess the interpersonal circumplex, they administered the

Interpersonal Adjective Scales–Revised (IAS–R; Wiggins, 1979; Wiggins & Broughton, 1991). They found that "only slightly more than half of the personality disorder categories studied had interpretable projections on the interpersonal circumplex" (p. 308). These were the histrionic, dependent, schizoid, antisocial, and narcissistic personality disorders. Meaningful projections were not obtained for the borderline, avoidant, schizotypal, or compulsive personality disorders.

Romney and Bynner (1989) submitted the solutions from three previously published factor analyses of the *DSM–III* personality disorder symptomatology (Hyler & Lyons, 1988; Kass, Skodol, Charles, Spitzer, & Williams, 1985; Livesley & Jackson, 1986) to a structural equation modeling to assess their goodness of fit to the interpersonal circumplex. They found that only a subset of the personality disorders (i.e., dependent, histrionic, narcissistic, schizoid, and paranoid) could be described in terms of a circumplex. They concluded that "it is clear that Wiggins' original [1982] postulated circumplex for seven DSM–III personality disorders . . . cannot be sustained for either our nonclinical or clinical samples" (p. 533). They suggested that additional dimensions of personality would be necessary to account adequately for the other personality disorders, such as the borderline, compulsive, schizotypal, and passive–aggressive.

Sim and Romney (1990) subsequently assessed the relationship of the *DSM-III* personality disorders to the interpersonal circumplex based on their own sample of 54 inpatients diagnosed with a personality disorder. To assess the interpersonal circumplex, they administered the ICL (LaForge & Suczek, 1955) to the patients and one or more of their nurses. They correlated the ten MCMI-I personality disorder scales (Millon, 1982) and the MCMI-I hypomania scale to the ICL axes scores and plotted the results. Four of the personality disorder diagnoses could not be placed meaningfully within the interpersonal circumplex based on the nurses' ratings: borderline, passive–aggressive, avoidant, and (surprisingly) schizoid. All but one of the personality disorders were placed successfully within the circumplex based on the patients' self-ratings. The one exception was the borderline personality disorder (borderline personality disorder did have a marginal placement barely within the docile–dependent octant but only when unweighted MCMI-I scores were used).

Pincus and Wiggins (1990) administered the MMPI personality disorder scales, the PACL, and the Inventory of Interpersonal Problems (IIP; Horowitz, Rosenberg, Baer, Ureño, & Villaseñor, 1988) to 321 undergraduates. They reported that "at least one pair of PD [personality disorder] scales fell in each quadrant of the interpersonal problem checklist" (p. 349). However, not all of the personality disorders could be represented. The results were compelling for the histrionic, narcissistic, antisocial, paranoid, schizoid, avoidant, and dependent personality disorders, but no meaningful projections onto the interpersonal circumplex could be generated for the borderline, compulsive, passive–aggressive, or schizotypal personality disorders. "It may be that the central dysfunction associated with compulsive, passive–aggressive, borderline, and schizotypal PDs involves cognitive and/or emotional processes rather than interpersonal behavior" (p. 350).

DSM-III-R

No theorist provided revisions of the personality disorder placements by Kiesler (1986) and Wiggins (1982) based on the *DSM–III–R* (American Psychiatric Association, 1987) revisions to the personality disorders. Soldz, Budman, Demby, and Merry (1993), however, did cross-validate the results of Wiggins and Pincus (1989) using the *DSM–III–R* taxonomy with a sample of 102 psychiatric patients who had been referred to a study on group psychotherapy. To assess the *DSM–III–R* personality disorders, they administered the MCMI-II (Millon, 1987) and the Personality Disorder Examination (Loranger, 1988). To assess the interpersonal circumplex, they administered the Inventory of Interpersonal Problems (IIP; Horowitz et al., 1988). They found that "most of the disorders are placed in easily interpretable locations" (Soldz et al., 1993, p. 45). However, they also noted that many were near the origin of the circumplex, indicating a failure to fully or adequately describe the disorder. "Borderline scales are closer to the origin . . . because several aspects common to borderlines, such as affective instability and identity disturbance, are not conceptually represented in the interpersonal circumplex" (p. 46). The same concern was raised for the schizotypal and compulsive personality disorders. Soldz and colleagues also indicated that some personality disorders were not adequately differentiated. They noted in particular that "circumplex space does not clearly distinguish between avoidant and schizoid disorder" (1993, p. 45).

DSM-IV

Benjamin (1993) has provided interpersonal circumplex profiles for the *DSM-IV* personality disorders (American Psychiatric Association, 1994). Her interpersonal circumplex model is unique in two important respects. The first is that she disagrees with the traditional interpersonal circumplex perspective "that normality and abnormality [are] different points on the same measurement continuum" (Leary, 1957, p. 17; see also McLemore & Brokaw, 1987; Pincus, 1994). Benjamin (1994) referred to her Structural Analysis of Social Behavior (SASB) as a dimensional model, but she also emphasizes that the interpersonal circumplex and personality disorder constructs refer to discrete entities that are distinct from each other and from normal interpersonal functioning. "Normality is not a mild version of pathology, it is qualitatively different" (Benjamin, 1994, p. 286).

In addition, the SASB interpersonal circumplex contains three surfaces to include a focus on self, focus on others, and the introjection of others' treatment of self. The model is in part an integration of the different perspectives on the interpersonal circumplex of Leary (1957) and Schaefer (1965), as well as an integration of the interpersonal circumplex with psychodynamic object-relations theory. Benjamin (1993) suggested that "the more complex dimensionality of SASB permits adequate description of all of the personality disorders listed in the DSM" (p. 24).

Table 4 provides Benjamin's descriptions of each of the *DSM-IV* personality disorders in terms of the three SASB interpersonal circumplex surfaces. She uses the same approach as Kiesler (1986), recognizing that the personality disorders cannot be placed within single, specific locations. Each represents instead combinations of different facets within and across the three surfaces. In fact, as noted in Table 4, some of the SASB descriptors are said to involve complex combinations (e.g., narcissistic self-love occurs in combination with self-neglect, whereas narcissistic self-blame does not). Given the extent of the overlap and complexity (see Table 4), it is difficult to understand how these complex profiles support a position that the *DSM–IV* personality disorders involve qualitatively distinct personalities.

An additional caution is that these personality disorder descriptions have not yet been subjected to an empirical test. The only published finding has concerned 16 patients diagnosed with borderline personality disorder compared to patients diagnosed with paranoid schizophrenia ($n = 10$), bipolar mania ($n = 7$), schizoaffective disorder ($n = 6$), and other major Axis I disorders (Benjamin, 1994). Interpersonal circumplex results for borderline personality disorder would be of considerable interest, given the consistent failure to account for this disorder in terms of the interpersonal circumplex. However, the published results were rather limited, confined largely to differences among the groups with respect to their memories or impressions of their mother, father, and other relatives.

Klein and colleagues (1993) developed a self-report measure of the *DSM–III–R* personality disorders based on the SASB that obtained significant correlations with respective personality disorder scales from the MCMI-I (Millon, 1982) and the *DSM–III* Personality Diagnostic Questionnaire (Hyler et al., 1988). However, these correlations should not be interpreted as verifications of SASB hypotheses. Klein and colleagues indicated that they "used Benjamin's formulations of the interpersonal dynamics and pathogenesis of each syndrome to guide item construction" (1993, p. 287), but in fact the items are direct representations of the personality disorder diagnostic criteria; for example: (a) "I often get personal messages from the media (TV, radio, the news) that were sent especially to me" (schizotypal

TABLE 4
Benjamin's (1993) Interpersonal Circumplex Description of *DSM-IV* Personality Disorders

	PRN	SZD	SZT	ATS	BDL	HST	NCS	AVD	DPD	OBC
Focus on self										
Separate	X			X			X			
Disclose										
Reactive love						O				
Trust						O			X	O
Submit			O		X				X	
Sulk								X	X	
Recoil	X		X					X		
Wall off	X	X	O	O		O		X		O
Focus on others										
Emancipate			O		X					
Affirm				O						
Active love										
Protect	X		O	O	X	O	X			O
Control							X			
Blame	X			X	X	X	X	X		X
Attack	X			O	X		X			
Ignore		X		X			X			O
Introjection										
Self-emancipate										
Self-affirm										
Active self-love							O			
Self-protect				O	X					
Self-control	X		X					X		
Self-blame					X		X	X	X	O
Self-attack		X			X					X
Self-neglect		X	X	O		O	O			O

Note. Os within same column are considered to be in complex combinations with one another; Xs are not. PRN = Paranoid, SZD = schizoid, SZT = schizotypal, ATS = antisocial, BDL = borderline, HST = histrionic, NCS = narcissistic, AVD = avoidant, DPD = dependent, and OBC = obsessive–compulsive.

scale), (b) "I shift back and forth between strong love and strong hate for the people I am closest to" (borderline scale), and (c) "I often get so involved in making each detail of a project absolutely perfect that I never finish" (compulsive scale) (Klein et al., 1993, p. 288). The inventory appears to be a measure of the *DSM* personality disorders, not the SASB interpersonal circumplex.

In sum, research has consistently obtained a close and meaningful correspondence of the interpersonal circumplex with many of the personality disorders. Maladaptive interpersonal relatedness does appear to be a major component for some of the personality disorders, and the manner of this relatedness may be understood with respect to the interpersonal circumplex. However, it also appears that the interpersonal circumplex may not provide a complete understanding of the personality disorders. "To the extent that personality disorders involve more than interpersonal disorders the circumplex will be an inadequate model" (Widiger & Kelso, 1983, p. 499). This caution was noted earlier by Conte and Plutchik: "If other types of descriptors [are] included, such as abilities, interests, or intelligence, analysis of the data would most likely not [produce] a circumplex due to the increased dimensionality of such data" (1981, p. 707).

INTERPERSONAL CIRCUMPLEX AND THE FIVE FACTOR MODEL

The limitations of the interpersonal circumplex in accounting for the *DSM* personality disorders may reflect a limitation of the model in accounting for all of the most important dimensions of personality. Theorists and philosophers have disagreed for a long time (and may never agree) with respect to the most significant dimensions of personality. A more empirical approach to this question is to assess the frequency or extent of a trait within the language (Goldberg, 1993). Traits that people have identified as the most important naturally will be those with the greatest number of terms to characterize their various nuances, manifestations, and degrees. It is difficult to imagine a fundamental dimension of personality failing to receive a significant encoding or representation within the language, and it is compelling to at least begin with the language to identify the traits that are the most important for describing one's self and others (Saucier & Goldberg, 1996).

This lexical approach has consistently identified five dimensions of personality (Goldberg, 1993; McCrae & Costa, 1990; Wiggins & Pincus, 1992), hereafter referred to as the Five Factor Model. McCrae and Costa (1989) assessed the relationship of the Five Factor Model to the interpersonal circumplex. They administered the NEO Personality Inventory (NEO-PI; Costa & McCrae, 1985) and the IAS-R (Wiggins, 1979) to 173 adults.

A joint factor analysis yielded a five factor solution, with all eight IAS-R facets of the interpersonal circumplex loading substantially and solely on two of the dimensions of the Five Factor Model: extraversion and agreeableness. Five Factor Model extraversion and agreeableness appear to be approximately 45° rotations of the interpersonal circumplex dimensions of affiliation and power. None of the eight facets of the interpersonal circumplex loaded significantly on the other three dimensions: neuroticism, openness, and conscientiousness. McCrae and Costa (1989) concluded that, "The interpersonal circumplex and the five-factor model thus appear to be complementary models of personality [in that] the five-factor model provides a larger framework in which to orient and interpret the circumplex, and the interpersonal circumplex provides a useful elaboration about aspects of two of the five factors—Extraversion and Agreeableness—and their combinations" (p. 593).

The additional dimensions of neuroticism, conscientiousness, and openness may provide the Five Factor Model with incremental validity in accounting for the *DSM* personality disorders, as indicated in the studies by Wiggins and Pincus (1989) and Soldz and colleagues (1993). Both studies found that the interpersonal circumplex was inadequate to characterize all of the personality disorders but the personality disorders were "readily interpretable [within] the 'Big Five' factors" (Wiggins & Pincus, 1989, p. 314). Soldz and colleagues likewise concluded that their results "lend strong support to the position that the Big Five personality factors can adequately represent the distinctions among the personality disorders" (1993, p. 51). We will illustrate these conclusions with respect to the dimensions of neuroticism, conscientiousness, and openness.

Neuroticism

Neuroticism is particularly important in describing and understanding personality disorder pathology (Clark, Vorhies, & McEwen, 1994; Trull, 1992). Most of the personality disorders are defined in part by an excessive degree of neuroticism (Widiger, Trull, Clarkin, Sanderson, & Costa, 1994). Neuroticism represents the disposition to experience negative affects, including anxiety, depression, and anger. Watson and Clark (1984) in fact characterize this dimension as negative affectivity. Another label has been emotional instability (Goldberg, 1993; Wiggins & Pincus, 1992), because this dimension describes a person's characteristic level of emotional adjustment and stability, including such facets as self-consciousness, vulnerability, and impulsivity (McCrae & Costa, 1990).

Borderline personality disorder, the most prevalent of the *DSM* personality disorders and one that has failed to be accounted for in most interpersonal circumplex studies, appears to be primarily extreme neuroticism (Widiger, Trull, et al., 1994). This association has been verified in a number of studies (Widiger & Costa, 1994). Persons who are at the highest levels of negative affectivity, impulsivity, and angry hostility are likely to be diagnosed with borderline personality disorder (e.g., Bruehl, 1994). The relationship of borderline personality disorder to the Five Factor Model was itself the focus of a study by Clarkin, Hull, Cantor, and Sanderson (1993). They administered the NEO-PI to 62 female patients diagnosed with borderline personality disorder at New York Hospital–Cornell Medical Center. They concluded that this disorder is described well within the Five Factor Model, noting in particular the contribution of the facets of neuroticism.

> The [borderline] patient is characterized by extreme and distressing feelings of trait anxiety, hostility, and depression; painful self-consciousness and vulnerability in relating to others; and dyscontrol of impulses. The sense of self-consciousness and vulnerability in interpersonal situations is accompanied by a hostile and suspicious approach to others (low Agreeableness). Feelings of warmth and positive emotions are lacking (two low subscales of Extraversion). There is a lack of goal directedness and perserverance in reaching goals (low Conscientiousness). (Clarkin et al., 1993, p. 475)

Neuroticism, however, is also important to the understanding of many of the other personality disorders, including the dependent, schizotypal, and avoidant (Trull, 1992). For example, it is difficult to describe fully the avoidant personality disorder and to differentiate it from the schizoid without considering neuroticism. The avoidant and schizoid personality disorders are placed within the same octant of the interpersonal circumplex (i.e., aloof–introverted), but the schizoid personality disorder represents almost pure introversion (i.e., excessively low warmth, low gregariousness, and low emotionality) whereas the avoidant personality disorder involves introversion (low gregariousness, low assertiveness, and low excitement-seeking) and neuroticism (self-consciousness, vulnerability, and anxiousness).

Conscientiousness

The studies that assessed the association of the interpersonal circumplex with the *DSM* personality disorders also indicated a failure of the interpersonal circumplex to describe adequately the compulsive personality disorder (e.g., Romney & Bynner, 1989; Soldz et al., 1993; Wiggins & Pincus, 1989). Compulsive personality disorder appears to represent a maladaptive variant of conscientiousness. Conscientiousness involves a person's characteristic degree of organization, persistence, and motivation in goal-directed behavior (Costa & McCrae, 1992). Conscientious persons tend to be organized, reliable, hard-working, self-disciplined, and punctual.

Persons who are extremely conscientious would be excessively devoted to their work to the point that significant sacrifices are made to social relationships; perfectionistic to the point that tasks are not completed; and preoccupied with organization, rules, and details. These are traits that are central to the compulsive personality disorder (American Psychiatric Association, 1994).

Excessively low levels of conscientiousness are seen in other personality disorders, particularly the antisocial and the passive–aggressive (Widiger, Trull, et al., 1994). Antisocial persons are exploitative and aggressive (i.e., antagonism), but they also tend to be hedonistic and irresponsible (i.e., low conscientiousness). Likewise, passive–aggressive persons are oppositional (i.e., antagonism), but they also are lax, negligent, and irresponsible (i.e., low conscientiousness).

Openness

The relationship of the Five Factor Model dimension of openness to the DSM personality disorders has been more problematic than the others (Widiger & Costa, 1994). There also has been more disagreement concerning how best to characterize this factor (Goldberg, 1993; Wiggins & Pincus, 1992; Wiggins & Trapnell, 1996). Costa and McCrae (1992) suggested that it involves the active seeking and appreciation of experiences. Extreme openness would be associated with flexibility in thinking, and even personal growth, self-actualization, and self-realization. Tellegen (Tellegen & Waller, in press), however, described this dimension as involving the degree of conventionality in one's attitudes, beliefs, behaviors, and perceptions. Highly unconventional persons would include the open, creative, and reflective persons described by Costa and McCrae (1992) but also the odd, eccentric, peculiar, and aberrant persons diagnosed with a schizotypal personality disorder.

There is less disagreement regarding excessively low openness (or closedness). Persons who are very low in openness tend to be dogmatic, rigid, and closed-minded. Such traits are included within the DSM-IV diagnostic criteria for the paranoid and compulsive personality disorders (American Psychiatric Association, 1994). They are also central to personality disorders that were proposed (then rejected) for DSM-IV, such as racism and sexism (Widiger & Chat, 1994).

FACETS OF THE INTERPERSONAL CIRCUMPLEX AND THE FIVE FACTOR MODEL

As suggested earlier, the extraversion and agreeableness dimensions of the Five Factor Model appear to be approximately 45° rotations of the interpersonal circumplex dimensions of affiliation and power (McCrae & Costa, 1989; Wiggins & Broughton, 1991). However, the characterization of extraversion and agreeableness by Costa and McCrae (1992) is not in the form of a circumplex. Table 5 presents the facets of extraversion and agreeableness identified by Costa and McCrae (1995). It is apparent that the six facets of extraversion are located largely within the ambitious–dominant, gregarious–extraverted, and warm–agreeableness octants of the interpersonal circumplex, and the six facets of agreeableness are located largely within the warm–agreeable, unassuming–ingenuous, and lazy–submissive octants. These locations have been verified empirically by McCrae and Costa (1989). Note that all of these facets are then on the affiliative side of the interpersonal circumplex (the side on which relatively few personality disorders have been placed; DeJong et al., 1989; Morey, 1985). However, extraversion and agreeableness are bipolar dimensions, and the facets for introversion and antagonism would be located on the other side of the circumplex. For example, the respective facets of antagonism might be exploitation (versus altruism), oppositionalism (versus compliance), arrogance (versus modesty), deception (versus straightforwardness), tough-mindedness (versus tender-mindedness), and suspicion (versus trust) that would be located within the arrogant–calculating and cold–quarrelsome octants of the interpersonal circumplex.

The Five Factor Model facets for extraversion and agreeableness were selected largely on the basis of their loading primarily on either extraversion or agreeableness (i.e., simple structure; Costa & McCrae, 1995), whereas the facets of the interpersonal circumplex were selected to represent equidistant locations around the circumplex (e.g., Wiggins, 1979). As a result, the 12 facets of extraversion and agreeableness are not equivalant to the 8 octants of the interpersonal circumplex. They represent instead somewhat different slices along the circumplex. In addition, the unique nature of the circumplex structuring of interpersonal traits is not readily apparent in the simple structure facets of extraversion and agreeableness, whereas the facets of the interpersonal circumplex facilitate the generation

TABLE 5
Costa and McCrae (1995) Facets of Extraversion and Agreeableness

Extraversion	Agreeableness
Activity	Altruism
Assertiveness	Compliance
Excitement-seeking	Modesty
Gregariousness	Straightfowardness
Positive emotions	Tender-mindedness
Warmth	Trust

and testing of hypotheses that follow from the circumplex structure (e.g., Kiesler, 1983; Orford, 1986). The emphasis given to identifying facets that are equidistant from each other by Benjamin (1993), Kiesler (1983), Leary (1957), and Wiggins (1979) facilitates the generation of hypotheses or predictions concerning complementarity, opposites, and antitheses (Orford, 1986) that are substantially more difficult to generate using the facets of the Five Factor Model identified by Costa and McCrae (1995).

McCrae and Costa (1989), however, suggested that the Five Factor Model emphasis on simple structure will be more successful in identifying underlying etiology (and perhaps pathology): "Simple structure factors identify relatively tight clusters of covarying traits, and it may be hypothesized that their covariation is due to a common underlying cause" (McCrae & Costa, 1989, p. 592). To the extent that there is a specific etiology for introversion or its facets, McCrae and Costa might be correct. However, the etiology for most to all of the pervasive and enduring patterns of human behavior will likely be multifactorial and complex, rather than specific. Simple structure then may provide no such advantages.

McCrae and Costa (1989), however, also suggested that the Five Factor Model structure is preferable to the circumplex structure because the interpersonal circumplex has been limited to interpersonal relatedness. "Extraversion and Agreeableness define the plane of interpersonal behavior, but [these] are not merely interpersonal dimensions" (McCrae & Costa, 1989, p. 592). The interpersonal circumplexes of Benjamin (1993), Kiesler (1983), Leary (1957), and Wiggins (1979) fail to include affective and attitudinal components and are perhaps then limited and incomplete. Watson and Clark (1984), for example, documented the importance of positive affectivity within the dimension of extraversion. Affective components are certainly needed for any complete description of the DSM-IV personality disorders. The interpersonal circumplexes noted previously fail to include the emotionality of the histrionic personality disorder, which is central to the understanding of this disorder (American Psychiatric Association, 1994) and is represented in part by positive emotionality of Five Factor Model extraversion. Likewise, the interpersonal circumplexes noted previously fail to include the anhedonia of the schizoid personality disorder, which is represented well by excessively low positive emotionality (Widiger et al., 1994).

However, the failure to include affective components may be an arbitrary result of interpersonal circumplex facet selections. The affective components of personality also may conform to a circumplex structure that is closely related to the interpersonal circumplex (Plutchik, 1980; Schaefer & Plutchik, 1966; Watson & Tellegen, 1985). The original interpersonal circumplex study of the DSM-II personality disorders by Plutchik and Platman (1977) concerned emotional trait terms. Perhaps the interpersonal circumplex could be expanded to include the affective as well as the interpersonal symptoms of the personality disorders.

Saucier (1992) indicated as well how neuroticism (or negative affectivity) may be on a circumplex with extraversion (or positive affectivity), extraversion with agreeableness (the interpersonal circumplex), and neuroticism with agreeableness. The circumplex structure is not unique to interpersonal functioning. It simply may reflect the presence of dimensions of personality that are on a continuum with each other and lack simple structure. "In a perfect circumplex, as many variables inhabit the interstitial regions as inhabit the regions where the factor axes are placed" (Saucier, 1992, p. 1027). This may occur for many important dimensions of personality. One then would be able to construct a variety of circumplexes. The placement of the anchor or defining dimensions within these circumplexes (e.g., extraversion–introversion versus dominance–submission) would be statistically arbitrary.

However, even if the placement of the anchor dimensions is statistically arbitrary, their locations can have conceptual and theoretical significance. For example, the preference for the Five Factor Model versus the interpersonal circumplex rotations and facets may reflect in part the particular needs or interests of the clinician, theorist, or researcher. McCrae and Costa (1989) do note that the interpersonal circumplex dimensions of love (or affiliation) and status (or power) "are essentially interactional concepts that describe the relationships between two individuals . . . [As such,] these dimensions would seem to be the obvious choice of social psychologists" (p. 591) or, we would add, clinical psychologists with an interpersonal systems theoretical orientation (e.g., Benjamin, 1993). As we noted earlier, complementarity, antithesis, and other interpersonal system concepts are readily derived from the interpersonal circumplex version of these dimensions but not as easily from the Five Factor Model facets.

A CLINICAL ILLUSTRATION

We do find the interpersonal circumplex principles of complementarity to be of use in our clinical practice, although not in all of the ways that have been suggested. We find the principles to be particularly helpful in anticipating and understanding reactions to persons with various personality disorders (and in understanding the development and maintenance of pathological relationships), but we have not relied on the principles to effect change in the behavior of persons with personality disorders, as suggested by Benjamin (1993), McLemore and Brokaw (1987), and others.

The principle of complementarity, for example, suggests the occurrence of reciprocity with respect to power and correspondence with respect to affiliation (Carson, 1969). In other words, hostility begets hostility, warmth begets warmth, dominance begets submission, and submission begets dominance. However, empirical support for this principle has been mixed. Research has provided support for correspondence along affiliation but not reciprocity along power (Orford, 1986). One explanation for the inconsistent results has been the failure to consider adequately the contributions of individual differences (Bluhm, Widiger, & Miele, 1990). The interpersonal circumplex has been used both to predict the effect of a situational press on behavior and to characterize the predispositions that persons bring to the situation. To the extent that behavior is largely the result of the interpersonal press, persons cannot be said to have a characteristic manner of relating to others that is consistent across situations; and to the extent that behavior is the result of a personality disposition, the interpersonal context will not be influential.

One might expect that the behavior of persons with a personality disorder will be determined largely by their personality, rather than by the situational context. Their inflexibility in response to situational cues is in part why they are thought to have a personality disorder. Persons with a personality disorder are precisely those persons who are most likely to be unresponsive to the interpersonal context in which they are functioning. Complementarity is less likely to be evident within the population of individuals with personality disorders.

This in fact has been our clinical experience. Behaving submissively or passively with a dependent person does not tend to evoke more assertive or dominant behavior. It can evoke anxiety and insecurity as the dependent person is often seeking the other person to take control. Behaving assertively with a compulsive person tends not to evoke cooperativeness. It can escalate oppositionalism, because the compulsive person is often quite competitive and needs to feel in control.

Likewise, we have not found that warmth necessarily begets warmth in an aggressive, hostile person with an antisocial personality disorder. Persons with an antisocial personality disorder often will perceive warmth to be sappy, untrustworthy, naive, and a sign of weakness. The antagonism of persons with antisocial personality disorder may have resulted in part from an intense and sustained hostile environment. Perhaps this disposition could be reversed with an equally intense and sustained friendly environment (Benjamin, 1993; McLemore & Brokaw, 1987), but no such environment is present nor realistically available. The warm, friendly environment provided within a therapeutic relationship or therapeutic community is too limited in intensity, scope, and duration to have a significant effect in most cases.

However, we do find the interpersonal circumplex to be very useful in anticipating and understanding the reactions of others (including ourselves) to persons with a personality disorder. It has been our experience that patients will attempt to recreate interpersonal circumplex complementarity within the therapeutic relationship. For example, dependent (or submissive) persons often are seeking a dominant therapist. As noted within the *DSM-IV* diagnostic criteria, they prefer that others make their decisions for them and to take responsibility for their lives (American Psychiatric Association, 1994). This interpersonal pull often will convey a transferential recreation of an earlier significant relationship, consistent with the psychodynamic model of personality development (Stone, 1993). It may at times be useful or even necessary to accept this interpersonal pull. A supportive treatment that does not seek fundamental personality change often will work with the predominant interpersonal manner of relatedness (Choca, Shanley, & Van Denburg, 1992; Stone, 1993). However, often one's manner of relating to a client is not well planned or controlled. Young therapists in particular are often swept into a complementary relationship that only further affirms the patient's personality disorder.

Likewise, compulsive (or dominant) patients often will prefer a more deferential therapist. Persons with a compulsive personality disorder may need to feel in command. Their desire to have persons be within a submissive relationship to them is again evident within the *DSM-IV* diagnostic criteria (e.g., "reluctant to delegate tasks or to work with others unless they submit to exactly his or her way of doing things," American Psychiatric Association, 1994, p. 673). They often will reject suggestions, advice, and insights in part to maintain their sense of control and authority. Therapists who are themselves dominant often will perceive compulsive persons to be stubborn, defiant, resistant, and even combative, whereas more neutral or inexperienced therapists often will find themselves drifting into a passive, submissive stance.

The interpersonal circumplex complementarity of the histrionic (affiliative) personality disorder is also evident within the *DSM-IV* personality disorder criteria. The "interaction [of histrionic persons] is often characterized by inappropriate sexually seductive or provocative behavior" (American Psychiatric Association, 1994, p. 657). One should be sensitive to their pull for warmth, friendship, intimacy, and affection. Therapists often will find themselves drawn into a personal relationship with their histrionic patients (Stone, 1993). The pull often will be subtle, as in the form of seemingly innocent remarks or gestures. It is courteous to be friendly and responsive but it is usually countertherapeutic to become more personal than professional.

Finally, the person with an antisocial personality disorder often will provoke hostility. It is not unusual for therapists to develop strong feelings of animosity, resentment, irritation, and contempt for the antisocial person. It can be quite difficult to maintain feelings of warmth or (unconditional) positive regard for the person with an antisocial personality disorder. Hostility begets hostility. Immediate, active, and forceful confrontation of antisocial behavior is often therapeutic and even necessary, but confrontation that is simply in reaction to hostility is usually countertherapeutic.

CONCLUSION

The theory of personality and personality disorders that we prefer is the Five Factor Model, but the interpersonal circumplex does provide a particularly elegant and enriching embellishment of two of its dimensions. The interpersonal circumplex does provide a richly informative description of interpersonal relatedness but also may provide a limited description. For example, we believe that most interpersonal circumplex formulations fail to include affective components of extraversion that are central to the personality disorders that involve this dimension of personality. The interpersonal circumplexes of Benjamin (1993), Kiesler (1983), Leary (1957), and Wiggins (1979) do include the gregariousness and warmth of the histrionic personality disorder but not the excitement-seeking and emotionality that are important in its description and understanding. In addition, the interpersonal circumplex does not include additional dimensions of personality (e.g., neuroticism) that are central to many of the personality disorders (e.g., borderline).

The Five Factor Model dimensions themselves may be placed on a circumplex with respect to each other. Just as extraversion can be placed on a circumplex with agreeableness, extraversion (or positive affectivity) also may be placed on a circumplex with neuroticism (or negative affectivity) as indicated by Watson and Tellegen (1985); and perhaps neuroticism also can be placed on a circumplex with agreeableness, as indicated by Saucier (1992). However, none of these alternative formulations are inconsistent with the importance of these dimensions for describing and understanding the DSM-IV personality disorders as maladaptive variants of common personality traits. The domains of personality functioning identified by each approach are congruent with and complement one another. The rotations and facets that are selected depend primarily on the particular emphasis or focus that is desired.

In sum, the interpersonal circumplex and the Five Factor Model are not incompatible or contradictory models of personality. They complement rather than contradict one another. The interpersonal circumplex provides a particular understanding of the interactional nature of the dimensions of extraversion and agreeableness that can have considerable theoretical interest and clinical relevance, and their inclusion within the Five Factor Model provides a more complete understanding of their placement within and relationship to other important dimensions of personality.

REFERENCES

American Psychiatric Association. (1952). *Diagnostic and statistical manual. Mental disorders.* Washington, DC: Author.

American Psychiatric Association. (1968). *Diagnostic and statistical manual of mental disorders* (2nd ed.). Washington, DC: Author.

American Psychiatric Association. (1980). *Diagnostic and statistical manual of mental disorders* (3rd ed.). Washington, DC: Author.

American Psychiatric Association. (1987). *Diagnostic and statistical manual of mental disorders* (3rd ed., rev.). Washington, DC: Author.

American Psychiatric Association. (1994). *Diagnostic and statistical manual of mental disorders* (4th ed.). Washington, DC: Author.

Benjamin, L. S. (1993). *Interpersonal diagnosis and treatment of personality disorders.* New York: Guilford Press.

Benjamin, L. S. (1994). SASB: A bridge between personality theory and clinical psychology. *Psychological Inquiry, 5,* 273–316.

Blackburn, R., & Maybury, C. (1985). Identifying the psychopath: The relation of Cleckley's criteria to the interpersonal domain. *Personality and Individual Differences, 6,* 375–386.

Bluhm, C., Widiger, T. A., & Miele, G. M. (1990). Interpersonal complementarity and individual differences. *Journal of Personality and Social Psychology, 58,* 464–471.

Bradlee, P. M., & Emmons, R. A. (1992). Locating narcissism within the interpersonal circumplex and the Five-Factor Model. *Personality and Individual Differences, 13,* 821–830.

Bruehl, S. (1994). A case of borderline personality disorder. In P. T. Costa & T. A. Widiger (Eds.), *Personality disorders and the Five-Factor Model of personality* (pp. 189–197). Washington, DC: American Psychological Association.

Carson, R. C. (1969). *Interaction concepts of personality.* Chicago: Aldine.

Choca, J. P., Shanley, L. A., & Van Denburg, E. (1992). *Interpretive guide to the Millon Clinical Multiaxial Inventory.* Washington, DC: American Psychological Association.

Clark, L. A., Vorhies, L., & McEwen, J. L. (1994). Personality disorder symptomatology from the Five-Factor perspective. In P. T. Costa & T. A. Widiger (Eds.), *Personality disorders and the Five-Factor Model of personality* (pp. 95–115). Washington, DC: American Psychological Association.

Clarkin, J. F., Hull, J. W., Cantor, J., & Sanderson, C. J. (1993). Borderline personality disorder and personality traits: A comparison of SCID-II BPD and NEO-PI. *Psychological Assessment, 5,* 472–476.

Conte, H., & Plutchik, R. (1981). A circumplex model for interpersonal personality traits. *Journal of Personality and Social Psychology, 40,* 701–711.

Costa, P. T., & McCrae, R. R. (1985). *The NEO Personality Inventory manual.* Odessa, FL: Psychological Assessment Resources.

Costa, P. T., & McCrae, R. R. (1992). *Revised NEO Personality Inventory (NEO-PI-R) and NEO Five-Factor Inventory (NEO-FFI) professional manual.* Odessa, FL: Psychological Assessment Resources.

Costa, P. T., & McCrae, R. R. (1995). Domains and facets: Hierarchical personality assessment using the Revised NEO Personality Inventory. *Journal of Personality Assessment, 64,* 21–50.

DeJong, C. A. J., van den Brink, W., Jansen, J. A. M., & Schippers, G. M. (1989). Interpersonal aspects of *DSM-III* Axis II: Theoretical hypotheses and empirical findings. *Journal of Personality Disorders, 3,* 135–146.

Freedman, M. B., Leary, T. F., Ossorio, A. G., & Coffey, H. S. (1951). The interpersonal dimension of personality. *Journal of Personality, 20,* 143–161.

Goldberg, L. R. (1993). The structure of phenotypic personality traits. *American Psychologist, 48,* 26–34.

Horowitz, L. M., Rosenberg, S. E., Baer, B. A., Ureño, G., & Villaseñor, V. S. (1988). Inventory of Interpersonal Problems: Psychometric properties and clinical applications. *Journal of Consulting and Clinical Psychology, 56,* 885–892.

Hyler, S. E., & Lyons, M. (1988). Factor analysis of the *DSM-III* personality disorder clusters: A replication. *Comprehensive Psychiatry, 29,* 304–308.

Hyler, S. E., Reider, R. O., Williams, J. B. W., Spitzer, R. L., Hendler, J., & Lyons, M. (1988). The Personality Diagnostic Questionnaire: Development and preliminary results. *Journal of Personality Disorders, 2,* 229–237.

Kass, F., Skodol, A. E., Charles, E., Spitzer, R. L., & Williams, J. B. W. (1985). Scaled ratings of *DSM-III* personality disorders. *American Journal of Psychiatry, 142,* 627–630.

Kiesler, D. J. (1983). The 1982 interpersonal circle: A taxonomy for complementarity in human transactions. *Psychological Review, 90,* 185–214.

Kiesler, D. J. (1986). The 1982 interpersonal circle: An analysis of *DSM-III* personality disorders. In T. Millon & G. Klerman (Eds.), *Contemporary directions in psychopathology: Toward DSM-IV* (pp. 571–597). New York: Guilford Press.

Kiesler, D. J., Van Denburg, T. F., Sikes-Nova, V. E., Larus, J. P., & Goldston, C. S. (1990). Interpersonal behavior profiles of eight cases of *DSM-III* personality disorders. *Journal of Clinical Psychology, 46,* 440–453.

Klein, M. H., Benjamin, L. S., Rosenfeld, R., Treece, C., Justed, J., & Greist, J. H. (1993). The Wisconsin Personality Disorders Inventory: Development, reliability, and validity. *Journal of Personality Disorders, 7,* 285–303.

LaForge, R., & Suczek, R. F. (1955). The interpersonal dimensions of personality: III. An interpersonal check list. *Journal of Personality, 24,* 94–112.

Leary, T. (1957). *Interpersonal diagnosis of personality: A functional theory and methodology for personality evaluation.* New York: Ronald Press.

Leary, T., & Coffey, H. S. (1955). Interpersonal diagnosis: Some problems of methodology and validation. *Journal of Abnormal and Social Psychology, 50,* 110–124.

Livesley, W. J., & Jackson, D. N. (1986). The internal consistency and factorial structure of behaviors judged to be associated with *DSM-III* personality disorders. *American Journal of Psychiatry, 143,* 1473–1474.

Loranger, A. W. (1988). *Personality Disorder Examination* (PDE) *manual.* Yonkers, NY: D.V. Communications.

Lorr, M., Bishop, P. F., & McNair, D. M. (1965). Interpersonal types among psychiatric patients. *Journal of Abnormal Psychology, 70,* 468–472.

McCrae, R. R., & Costa, P. T. (1989). The structure of interpersonal traits: Wiggins's circumplex and the Five-Factor Model. *Journal of Personality and Social Psychology, 56,* 586–595.

McCrae, R. R., & Costa, P. T. (1990). *Personality in adulthood.* New York: Guilford.

McLemore, C. W., & Brokaw, D. W. (1987). Personality disorders as dysfunctional interpersonal behavior. *Journal of Personality Disorders, 1,* 270–285.

Millon, T. (1981). *Disorders of personality. DSM-III: Axis II.* New York: Wiley.

Millon, T. (1982). *Millon Clinical Multiaxial Inventory manual* (2nd ed.). Minneapolis, MN: National Computer Systems.

Millon, T. (1987). *Manual for the Millon Clinical Multiaxial Inventory-II* (MCMI-II). Minneapolis, MN: National Computer Systems.

Morey, L. C. (1985). An empirical comparison of interpersonal and *DSM-III* approaches to classification of personality disorders. *Psychiatry, 48,* 358–364.

Morey, L. C., Waugh, M. H., & Blashfield, R. K. (1985). MMPI scales for *DSM-III* personality disorders: Their derivation and correlates. *Journal of Personality Assessment, 49,* 245–251.

Orford, J. (1986). The rules of interpersonal complementarity: Does hostility beget hostility and dominance, submission? *Psychological Review, 93,* 365–377.

Pfohl, B. (1983). *Structured interview for DSM–III personality disorders (SIDP).* Iowa City: University of Iowa Medical Center.

Pincus, A. L. (1994). The interpersonal circumplex and the interpersonal theory: Perspectives on personality and its pathology. In S. Strack & M. Lorr (Eds.), *Differentiating normal and abnormal personality* (pp. 114–136). New York: Springer.

Pincus, A. L., & Wiggins, J. S. (1990). Interpersonal problems and conceptions of personality disorders. *Journal of Personality Disorders, 4,* 342–352.

Plutchik, R. (1980). A general psychoevolutionary theory of emotion. In R. Plutchik & H. Kellerman (Eds.), *Emotion: Theory, Research, and Experience: Vol. 1. Theories of Emotion* (pp. 3–33). New York: Academic Press.

Plutchik, R., & Conte, H. R. (1985). Quantitative assessment of personality disorders. In R. Michels (Ed.), *Psychiatry* (Vol. 1, chap. 15, pp. 1–13). Philadelphia: J. B. Lippincott.

Plutchik, R., & Platman, S. (1977). Personality connotations of psychiatric diagnoses. *Journal of Nervous and Mental Disease*, 165, 418–422.

Romney, D. M., & Bynner, J. M. (1989). Evaluation of a circumplex model of *DSM-III* personality disorders. *Journal of Research in Personality*, 23, 525–538.

Saucier, G. (1992). Benchmarks: Integrating affective and interpersonal circles with the Big-Five personality factors. *Journal of Personality and Social Psychology*, 62, 1025–1035.

Saucier, G., & Goldberg, L. R. (1996). The language of personality: Lexical perspectives on the Five-Factor Model. In J. S. Wiggins (Ed.), *Theoretical perspectives for the Five-Factor Model* (pp. 21–50). New York: Guilford Press.

Schaefer, E. S. (1965). Configurational analysis of children's reports of parent behavior. *Journal of Consulting Psychology*, 29, 552–557.

Schaefer, E. S., & Plutchik, R. (1966). Interrelationships of emotions, traits, and diagnostic constructs. *Psychological Reports*, 18, 399–410.

Sim, J. P., & Romney, D. M. (1990). The relationship between a circumplex model of interpersonal behaviors and personality disorders. *Journal of Personality Disorders*, 4, 329–341.

Soldz, S., Budman, S., Demby, A., & Merry, J. (1993). Representation of personality disorders in circumplex and Five-Factor space: Explorations with a clinical sample. *Psychological Assessment*, 5, 41–52.

Stone, M. (1993). *Abnormalities of personality. Within and beyond the realm of treatment.* New York: W. W. Norton.

Strack, S. (1987). Development and validation of an adjective checklist to assess the Millon personality types in a normal population. *Journal of Personality Assessment*, 51, 572–587.

Strack, S., Lorr, M., & Campbell, L. (1990). An evaluation of Millon's circular model of personality disorders. *Journal of Personality Disorders*, 4, 353–361.

Trull, T. J. (1992). *DSM-III-R* personality disorders and the Five-Factor Model of personality: An empirical comparison. *Journal of Abnormal Psychology*, 101, 553–560.

Watson, D., & Clark, L. A. (1984). Negative affectivity: The disposition to experience aversive emotional states. *Psychological Bulletin*, 96, 465–490.

Watson, D., & Tellegen, A. (1985). Toward a consensual structure of mood. *Psychological Bulletin*, 98, 219–235.

Widiger, T. A., & Chat, L. (1994). The *DSM-IV* personality disorders: Changes from *DSM-III-R*. In R. Michels (Ed.), *Psychiatry* (chap. 14.2, pp. 1–13). Philadelphia: J. B. Lippincott.

Widiger, T. A., & Costa, P. T. (1994). Personality and personality disorders. *Journal of Abnormal Psychology*, 103, 78–91.

Widiger, T. A., & Kelso, K. (1983). Psychodiagnosis of Axis II. *Clinical Psychology Review*, 3, 491–510.

Widiger, T. A., Trull, T. J., Clarkin, J. F., Sanderson, C. J., & Costa, P. T. (1994). A description of the *DSM-III-R* and *DSM-IV* personality disorders with the

Five-Factor Model of personality. In P. T. Costa & T. A. Widiger (Eds.), *Personality disorders and the Five-Factor Model of personality* (pp. 41–56). Washington, DC: American Psychological Association.

Wiggins, J. S. (1979). A psychological taxonomy of trait-descriptive terms: The interpersonal domain. *Journal of Personality and Social Psychology, 37,* 395–412.

Wiggins, J. S. (1982). Circumplex models of interpersonal behavior in clinical psychology. In P. Kendall & J. Butcher (Eds.), *Handbook of research methods in clinical psychology* (pp. 183–221). New York: Wiley.

Wiggins, J. S., & Broughton, R. (1991). A geometric taxonomy of personality scales. *European Journal of Personality, 5,* 343–365.

Wiggins, J. S., & Pincus, A. L. (1989). Conceptions of personality disorders and dimensions of personality. *Psychological Assessment, 1,* 305–316.

Wiggins, J. S., & Pincus, A. L. (1992). Personality: Structure and assessment. *Annual Review of Psychology, 43,* 473–504.

Wiggins, J. S., & Trapnell, P. D. (1996). A dyadic–interactional perspective on the Five-Factor Model. In J. S. Wiggins (Ed.), *The Five-Factor Model of personality: Theoretical perspectives* (pp. 88–162). New York: Guilford Press.

14

EVALUATING A CIRCUMPLEX MODEL OF PERSONALITY DISORDERS WITH STRUCTURAL EQUATION MODELING

DAVID M. ROMNEY and JOHN M. BYNNER

Our interest in the circumplex model arose from a concern about methodology as much as theory. Over a period of 20 years we have been carrying out analyses of personal characteristics data motivated by dissatisfaction with the hierarchical models favored by the dominant personality theorists who work in the psychometric tradition. Through Guttman's work on the radex representation of ability test data as an alternative to factors (Guttman, 1954) and the advent of Jöreskog's confirmatory factor analysis (CFA) and subsequently structural equation modeling (SEM; Jöreskog, 1974), we became aware of the much wider range of models open to theorists other than the hierarchical factor model. There were compelling indications that the routinely established hierarchical theory of personal characteristics data (e.g., Eysenck, 1970) was influenced strongly by the statistical methodology available at the time to support it—namely, exploratory factor analysis (EFA).

EXPLORATORY VERSUS CONFIRMATORY FACTOR ANALYSIS

The purpose of EFA is to determine the minimum number of factors that are needed to sufficiently explain the covariance of a set of variables. Should these factors be intercorrelated, another EFA could be carried out

327

on the factors themselves, resulting in a lesser number of secondary factors. And if these secondary factors are also intercorrelated, yet another factor analysis could be performed, and so on, to produce a hierarchical arrangement of factors—with the most general factors at the top of the hierarchy and the most specific factors at the bottom. CFA, however, is used, as its name suggests, to test an a priori hypothesis about the number and nature of predetermined factors that account for a given correlation matrix. CFA is concerned only with the measurement component of SEM—the other component being strictly structural (i.e., the tracing of causal pathways between factors). Thus SEM is sometimes referred to loosely as a combination of factor analysis and path analysis.

From Galton through Pearson, Spearman, Thompson, Thurstone, and Burt, an important data source for the study of personal characteristics has been the correlations among the item responses obtained through inventories and tests. EFA applied to such data imposes a particular structure, one of underlying factors that can be identified theoretically with latent traits. Inherent in this approach is the problem of indeterminancy, because there is a variety of ways of determining the number of factors and the relations that should hold between them. When a factor solution conforms to Thurstone's oblique simple structure (i.e., factors are permitted to correlate), then factor analysis can be applied to identify the second-order factors underlying them. The process can be continued to a third or even fourth level until only one, two, or three underlying factors emerge from the analysis. It is at this stage that major theoretical constructs such as Eysenck's extraversion (E) and neuroticism (N), Spearman's general intelligence (G), and so on, are identified with the factors and great theoretical edifices are built around them. This is not to deny the wide range of other empirical evidence that can be amassed in support of the significance of such latent traits as neuroticism, extraversion, and intelligence in the explanation of behavior. Rather, what is meant is that EFA repeatedly applied to the correlations between relevant test items is bound to end up with factors like them. More recently, for instance, a Five Factor Model of personality has emerged as the most popular model (Digman, 1990).

Unlike EFA, the attractions of SEM, as applied through such software programs as LISREL and EQS (Bentler, 1985; Jöreskog & Sörbom, 1984; McDonald, 1980) is that it offers possibilities of liberating theory in more dynamic directions because we can determine how changing the magnitude of one factor might affect others. It also gives precise methods for testing the goodness-of-fit of a variety of different models to the observed data. Through the use of these programs to test alternative models to the traditional hierarchical factor models derived from EFA, we soon discovered that these alternative models not only frequently fitted the data better but also made more sense theoretically and held greater promise for therapeutic intervention.

There are many ways of modeling correlations that disregard factors. Functional relationships between the variables involved, for example, reflect the situation in which one variable is a function of, and therefore may be seen to be influenced by, another. Such relationships may be either nonreciprocal (recursive) in form, as is typical in path models, or reciprocal (nonrecursive) in form in which variables mutually influence each other. A dynamic set of relationships among a set of continually changing variables is just as plausible as the factorial one, but can never be assessed through the application of EFA. The great attraction of SEM is that it allows the researcher to model, under certain conditions, such possibilities directly, alongside or as an alternative to the factor model, which is a special case. In early work in SEM with a self-image inventory, for example, one of us concluded using LISREL that five oblique, first-order factors were needed to summarize data from 15 self-image rating scales. Attempts to fit a second-order factor model to the correlations among the factors using CFA failed. A causal model, in which one factor was represented as a function of the others, not only fitted the data but had much more heuristic value (Bynner, 1981).

Drawing examples from our work on cognitive abilities, personality disorders, and social attitudes, our book *The Structure of Personal Characteristics* (Romney & Bynner, 1992a) demonstrates that applying this methodology to personal characteristics data opens up theoretical and practical possibilities that simple factor models derived from EFA effectively deny. In this scenario the main role of exploratory factor analysis is to help construct and measure scales with higher reliability than the individual items that comprise them (Bynner, 1988). To test a theory properly we need statistical methods, such as SEM, that allow for developmental and dynamic relationships among variables as well as hierarchical ones.

THE SIMPLEX AND THE CIRCUMPLEX

For cognitive abilities and self-attitudes we discovered simplex models (probabilistic sequences of variables) that fitted the data better than the traditional factor models and had clear implications for both theory and intervention. These simplex models indicated how one variable or factor could lead to (and influence) another sequentially so that changing one variable in the chain would result in a change in all those that followed. However, although the simplex model could be applied nicely to abilities and attitudes, it did not seem to have much relevance for personality traits. In the literature, the closest rival to the traditional hierarchical structure was the circumplex model. The general circumplex model was first proposed by Guttman (1954) to apply to any variables that formed a circular order, and Leary (1957) was the first to apply the model to personality traits.

Individuals with personality disorders manifest traits to an extreme degree and are unable to adjust their behavior to prevailing circumstances. As a consequence, they cannot adapt properly to social and occupational situations in which they may function inadequately and experience subjective distress. In the circumplex model of personality disorders, the disorders are considered to be intense and rigid manifestations of particular personality traits and are arranged around the periphery of a circle in such a way that those disorders resembling each other are close together and those that are different are far apart. In other words, the distance between the personality disorders on the circle depends on their degree of similarity to each another, with the most similar being adjacent and the most different being diametrically opposite. For example, paranoid personality disorder, a combination of cold and quarrelsome traits, can be placed on the circle next to narcissistic personality disorder, arrogant and calculating, but placed opposite to histrionic personality disorder exemplified by warm and agreeable traits. It is important to note that the circumplex of personality (disorders) is regarded as an *interpersonal* circumplex. This implies that not all personality traits and disorders would necessarily occupy a place on the circle.

CONFIRMING THE CIRCUMPLEX

If a set of variables is arranged around a circle, then the variables closer together would have stronger intercorrelations than those further apart. This means that the correlation matrix should conform to a definite (circumplex) pattern so that the correlations decline to a minimum as we move away from the main diagonal toward the corner and then start to increase. This specific pattern is exemplified for seven variables in Table 1.

TABLE 1
Representation of a Circumplex Correlation Matrix

Variables	V1	V2	V3	V4	V5	V6	V7
Variable 1	1						
Variable 2	ρ_1	1					
Variable 3	ρ_2	ρ_1	1				
Variable 4	ρ_3	ρ_2	ρ_1	1			
Variable 5	ρ_4	ρ_3	ρ_2	ρ_1	1		
Variable 6	ρ_3	ρ_4	ρ_3	ρ_2	ρ_1	1	
Variable 7	ρ_2	ρ_3	ρ_4	ρ_3	ρ_2	ρ_1	1

Note. $\rho_1 > \rho_2 > \rho_3 > \rho_4$.

Note, however, that the pattern is order-dependent. Arbitrary reordering of the variables will destroy the pattern. Note also that the correlations are symbolized by the Greek letter ρ to indicate that they are *population parameters*, free from sampling error. As the variables are arranged equidistantly around the circle, correlations between them will be equal also. (Equal correlations are represented by those having the same subscript in Table 1.)

Jöreskog (1974) described the analytical procedure for fitting a circumplex pattern to a correlation matrix. He assumed that corresponding to each variable on the circle there is an underlying factor. For seven variables, therefore, there would be seven factors, which are analogous to *prototypes*—pure or ideal forms of the characteristics that are being measured (cf. Cantor, Smith, French, & Mezzich, 1980). These factors are orthogonal (i.e., uncorrelated with one another) so that the fuzziness or overlap that occurs among the manifest personality traits does not occur among them. Hence, although the variables themselves may be represented on a circle in two-dimensional space, the underlying factors occupy seven dimensions. As a consequence, the factor matrix is referred to as a *circulant* (i.e., circle-producing) factor matrix rather than a circumplex factor matrix.

Jöreskog made the assumption that half the variables are always loaded on the same factors when the number of variables is even and half the variables plus one when the number of variables is odd. This means that for seven variables each factor would correlate with four—and only four—variables. Thus, Variable 1 would load, say, on Factors I, II, III, and IV; Variable 2 would load on Factors II, III, IV, and V; Variable 3 would load on Factors III, IV, V, and VI, and so on. Note that each variable has four factors in common with a neighboring variable. This would produce the factor matrix shown in Table 2. Different factor loadings (λ) are designated by different subscripts in the table in order to distinguish them from one another. Note that loadings represented by the same subscripts

TABLE 2
Representation of a Circulant Factor Matrix With Only Positive
Correlations

Variables	I	II	III	IV	V	VI	VII
Variable 1	λ_1	λ_1	λ_1	λ_1	0	0	0
Variable 2	0	λ_2	λ_2	λ_2	λ_2	0	0
Variable 3	0	0	λ_3	λ_3	λ_3	λ_3	0
Variable 4	0	0	0	λ_4	λ_4	λ_4	λ_4
Variable 5	λ_3	0	0	0	λ_3	λ_3	λ_3
Variable 6	λ_2	λ_2	0	0	0	λ_2	λ_2
Variable 7	λ_1	λ_1	λ_1	0	0	0	λ_1

Note. λ represents factor loadings.

are constrained to be equal (i.e., all the λ_1s are equal, all the λ_2s are equal, all the λ_3s are equal, etc.).

The limitation of Jöreskog's factor solution is that it only applies to matrices in which all the correlations are zero or above; however, when there are negative correlations (as happens between contrasting personality traits) this solution does not work. It was Cudeck (1986) who first suggested a factor solution for matrices containing negative correlations (see Table 3). As before, all the loadings constrained to be equal are represented by the same subscript.

From a technical standpoint SEM is far superior to EFA, which is the usual method employed to identify the principal axes on which the circumplex is based. Following the latter procedure, personality traits and disorders are plotted on these axes and the circularity of their distribution typically is assessed qualitatively by visual inspection. With SEM, however, the circularity can be tested directly and quantitatively for goodness-of-fit. If a model fits the data well, the correlation or covariance matrix that can be derived from the model should match the correlation or covariance matrix used as input for the model. If, however, the discrepancy between the original matrix and the derived matrix is more than negligible, the model does not fit the data well. This, then, is a quantitative measure of goodness-of-fit; but it should be noted that there are many other measures of goodness-of-fit, some of which are described later in the chapter.

PROPOSED MODEL

As has been discussed throughout this book, circumplex personality theorists believe that personality traits lie on a continuum and that maladaptive exaggerations of these traits constitute the basis of personality disorders. This hypothesis was verified in a study by Sim and Romney

TABLE 3
Representation of a Circulant Factor Matrix With Some Negative Correlations

Variables	I	II	III	IV	V	VI	VII
Variable 1	λ_1	λ_2	λ_3	λ_4	0	0	0
Variable 2	0	λ_1	λ_2	λ_3	λ_4	0	0
Variable 3	0	0	λ_1	λ_2	λ_3	λ_4	0
Variable 4	0	0	0	λ_1	λ_2	λ_3	λ_4
Variable 5	λ_4	0	0	0	λ_1	λ_2	λ_3
Variable 6	λ_3	λ_4	0	0	0	λ_1	λ_2
Variable 7	λ_2	λ_3	λ_4	0	0	0	λ_1

Note. λ represents factor loadings.

(1990) who gave the Interpersonal Check List (LaForge, 1977) to 90 patients diagnosed clinically by psychiatrists as personality disordered and to a control group of 97 university students. The patients produced higher (more intense) and more restricted (more rigid) scores than the students. Similar findings had been reported previously by Wiggins, Phillips, and Trapnell (1989) on a sample of exclusively normal individuals. The authors argued, incidentally, that they were justified in using normal (instead of clinical) individuals because,

> The personality traits that are maladaptively expressed in personality disorders are assumed to be represented in a normal population. . . . Also responses of undergraduates to items assessing psychopathology yield endorsement rates and variability sufficient for psychometric studies and patterns of relationships similar to those obtained from clinical populations. (p. 306).

In an earlier theoretical formulation, Wiggins (1982) speculated how the circumplex model might be applied to *DSM-III* personality disorders. He selected seven of these disorders, added hypomanic personality disorder (a *DSM-II* diagnosis that was discarded in *DSM-III*) to fill what otherwise would have been a gap, and ordered them around the circle in positions that corresponded with their matching personality traits (see Figure 1). Hypomanic personality disorder, Wiggins argued, "represents an exaggeration of gregarious–extraverted behavior . . . and seemed to provide a close fit" (p. 213).

Although other circumplex models of personality have been proposed (e.g., Kiesler, 1983), we felt that the Wiggins model was the most plausible because he did not attempt to place every personality disorder on the interpersonal circle. Because at least five dimensions (the Big Five) are needed to cover all personality traits and the circle is defined by only two, control and affiliation, he recognized that those personality disorders that are not primarily interpersonal should not be on the circle. What is questionnable about his model, however, is that he included on the circle hypomanic personality disorder, which does not officially exist as a personality disorder but as a transitory state (hypomanic state). This meant that recent studies of personality disorder would not have included such a disorder in their investigations. As a consequence, there would be no extant data against which the proposed model could be tested in its entirety and there would always be a gap left on the circle by the (alleged) missing hypomanic personality disorder.

DATA SOURCES

The data we chose for our SEM came from two separate studies, the second (Hyler & Lyons, 1988) being a replication of the first (Kass, Skodol,

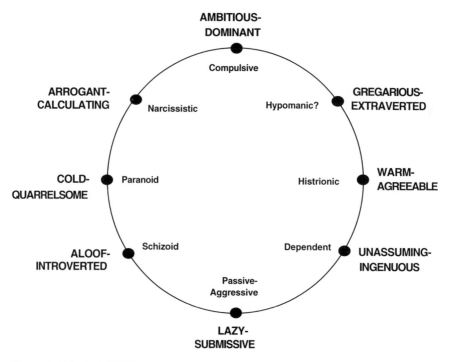

Figure 1. Wiggins' (1982) Interpersonal Types (Outside Perimeter) and Corresponding Diagnoses (Inside Perimeter). From "Structural Approaches to Classification," by R. K. Blashfield, 1986, in T. Millon and G. L. Klerman (Eds.), *Contemporary directions in psychopathology: Toward the DSM-IV* (p. 389). New York: Guilford Press. Copyright 1986 the Guilford Press. Adapted with permission.

Charles, Spitzer, & Williams, 1985) on a sample from a different population. In the earlier study, 609 mainly lower-income outpatients were assessed for personality disorder by 35 psychology and psychiatry residents who had been trained to make *DSM-III* diagnoses. The residents were required to rate patients on each of the 11 personality disorders on a 4-point scale according to whether the patient (a) exhibited none or very few traits, (b) exhibited some traits, (c) almost met *DSM-III* criteria, or (d) met *DSM-III* criteria completely. The later study was similar to the first except that it was a national study with 287 psychiatrists and a usable sample of 358 patients who were predominantly middle-income.

METHOD

The results of both studies were published as correlation matrices among all 11 *DSM-III* personality disorders. We extracted a submatrix from each data set that was based just on the seven personality disorders in Wiggins' circumplex model (Romney & Bynner, 1989). We used the computer program EQS (Bentler, 1985) to test the model under two conditions: one exactly as formulated by Wiggins in which there was no measurement error (Model 1a), and the other in which measurement error was included (Model 1b, a quasi-circumplex). The reason we had to use EQS rather than LISREL was because at the time the LISREL algorithms were based on Guttman's circumplex models of abilities that did not allow for the *negative* correlation coefficients that occur among personality traits.

EQS comes with a number of measures of goodness-of-fit that indicate the extent to which the model fits the data. The most familiar of these measures is χ^2, which is an indication of the probability that the matrix derived from the model departs from the original matrix. Unfortunately, χ^2 is a function of sample size, so that with a large sample a very minor discrepancy between the two matrices could be statistically significant. The magnitude of χ^2 is also a function of the number of degrees of freedom; the more degrees of freedom available (i.e., the more parsimonious the model) the larger the value of χ^2. This is why it has been suggested by Wheaton, Muthén, Alwin, and Summers (1977) that in comparing (nested) models the ratio χ^2/df should be used rather than the χ^2 value alone; otherwise, the fit of the model could be improved merely by relaxing some constraints. Another measure of goodness-of-fit is the Normed Fit Index (NFI), which indicates how much of the variance and covariance in the correlation matrix is explained by the model. The value of this index varies from 1, where all the variance is explained, to 0 where none of it is explained. Another measure is the Non-Normed Fit Index (NNFI), which is the NFI corrected for capitalization on chance by taking degrees of freedom into account. Finally, there is the average absolute standardized residual (AASR) obtained by subtracting the implied matrix from the actual matrix. The closer this value is to zero, the better the model fits the data. (For a discussion of newer goodness-of-fit indices, such as the Comparative Fit Index, which were not available for EQS when our analyses were carried out, see Bentler, 1989. For a more general discussion of goodness-of-fit indices in confirmatory factor analysis, see Marsh, Balla, & McDonald, 1988.)

FINAL MODEL

Testing Wiggins' model with the 1985 data resulted in a poor fit. The fit indices for this model (designated Model 1a) are given in Table 4. When the error variances were set free (Model 1b), the iterative estimates of the parameters failed to converge, indicating an even worse fit.

TABLE 4
Goodness-of-fit Values for Circumplex Models

Model	χ^2	df	NNFI	AASR
		1985 data		
1a	130.62	18	.958	.089
1b	—	—	—	—
4a	37.60	8	.983	.055
4b	7.59	3	.993	.021
		1988 data		
1a	113.62	18	.955	.096
1b	72.01	1	.953	.086
4a	46.06	8	.971	.100
4b	6.74	3	.992	.029

Note. NNFI = Non-normed Fit Index; AASR = Average Absolute Square Residual.

In view of the fact that the legitimacy of placing compulsive personality disorder on an interpersonal circle had been questioned by Frances and Widiger (1986) on the grounds that the disorder had a strong cognitive component and, in addition, there was empirical evidence from EFA that the disorder tapped a different factor (Blashfield, Sprock, Pinkston, & Hodgin, 1985), we reanalyzed the correlation matrix with this particular disorder omitted. But this second model (both 2a and 2b) was unacceptable, either because the certain factors were (artificially) constrained by the computer program at zero (2a) or because of a failure of the iterative process to converge (2b).

We tried a third model, with the factors preloaded on three instead of four variables. Model 3a was a slight improvement over Model 1a, but Model 3b was quite inappropriate because of its poor fit. We decided to take a closer look at the correlation matrix. Our eyes told us that passive–aggressive personality, which lay on the opposite pole to the already discarded compulsive personality disorder, did not fit the circumplex pattern. We tried the model once again with this disorder omitted, too (i.e., the model now comprised only five of the original seven disorders). Model 4a fitted the data fairly well and Model 4b fit the data extremely well (see Table 4).

Having established a good fitting model for the 1985 data, we ran through the same steps for the 1988 data and evaluated the fit of the same series of models. The results, which are given in the bottom half of Table 4, clearly show that the last model (4b) fitted the data very well, far better than any of the other models.

In Figure 2, the five personality disorders surrounding the circle—histrionic, dependent, schizoid, paranoid, and narcissistic—are joined by the hypothetical hypomanic personality disorder to fill the gap between narcissistic and histrionic personality disorders and to preserve the symmetry of the arrangement, but the vertical axis from compulsive to passive–aggressive, which figures in Wiggins' model, has been eliminated. We have commented already on the unlikelihood of a disorder with a primary cognitive dysfunction such as compulsive personality disorder being on an interpersonal circle. However, aside from the fact that passive–aggressive disorder lies on the opposite pole from compulsive personality disorder, the rationale for not placing it on an interpersonal circle is not immediately obvious. It is interesting to note that in a more recent version of Wiggins' interpersonal circle both compulsive and passive–aggressive personality disorders have been removed (Wiggins & Pincus, 1989).

Although there is no hard evidence for hypomanic personality disorder to exist as a disorder on the circle, the fact that it would be located directly opposite schizoid personality disorder, exhibiting contrasting traits, suggests strongly that it should occupy that spot. Nevertheless, one might take the view that hypomanic personality disorder is more like the opposite

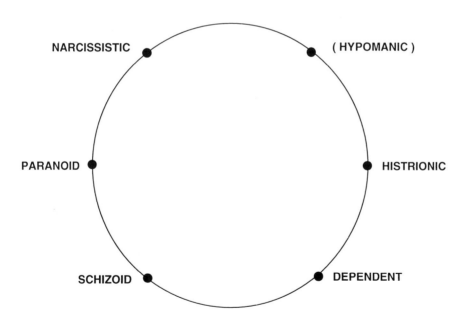

Figure 2. A five- or six-variable circumplex model of personality disorders. From "Evaluation of a Circumplex Model of *DSM-III* Personality Disorders," by D. M. Romney and J. M. Bynner, 1989, *Journal of Research in Personality, 23,* p. 534. Copyright 1989 by Academic Press. Reprinted with permission.

of (a putative) dysthymic or depressive personality disorder than schizoid personality disorder.

Finally, it should be pointed out that the arrangement of the personality disorders on the circle is consistent with their grouping in *DSM-III-R* (American Psychiatric Association, 1987, p. 337), which classified them into three clusters (A, B, and C) according to which salient traits they had in common. Paranoid and schizoid are adjacent and both lie in Cluster A and so are narcissistic and histrionic, both lying in Cluster B. Dependent stays by itself in Cluster C. This consistency with *DSM-III-R* increases our confidence in the validity of the circumplex model.

OTHER PERSONALITY DISORDERS

We have demonstrated using SEM that 5 out of the 11 *DSM-III* personality disorders lie on a circumplex. In these disorders the primary problem is caused by interpersonal factors. But what of the other seven disorders that do not fall on the circumplex? Compulsive personality disorder was eliminated from the circumplex because of its strong cognitive component. Could it be that the other personality disorders also possessed a cognitive component that barred their admission to the interpersonal circumplex?

In a study on cognitive abilities Bynner and Romney (1986) found that the abilities could be ordered in a sequence with one ability leading to the next. If the remaining personality disorders all had a cognitive component, perhaps they too could be arranged so that they would fall in a definite order on a straight line (i.e., form a simplex). The pattern of correlations expected for a simplex is shown in Table 5. Note that correlations are equal within a diagonal and increase progressively from the corner to the main diagonal. The simplex is in fact a special (limiting) case of the circumplex "when one of the parameters increases towards infinity" (Browne, 1992, p. 471). The difference, therefore, between the circumplex and the simplex is that the latter is open-ended so that the correlations

TABLE 5
Representation of a Simplex Correlation Matrix

Variables	V1	V2	V3	V4	V5
Variable 1	1				
Variable 2	ρ_1	1			
Variable 3	ρ_2	ρ_1	1		
Variable 4	ρ_3	ρ_2	ρ_1	1	
Variable 5	ρ_4	ρ_3	ρ_2	ρ_1	1

Note. $\rho_1 > \rho_2 > \rho_3 > \rho_4$.

just continue to increase with increasing distance between the variables, never reaching a maximum as they do on the circumplex, after which they start to decrease. As with the circumplex, however, any arbitrary reordering of the variables will destroy the simplex pattern.

The correlations among antisocial, borderline, avoidant, passive–aggressive, and compulsive disorders were taken from Kass and colleagues (1985) and from Hyler and Lyons (1988). Schizotypal personality disorder was omitted a priori from the matrix because we felt that it overlapped unduly with schizoid personality disorder, which already had been mapped on the circumplex.

To test how well the data fitted the simplex model, the two correlation matrices were analyzed using the LISREL VI computer program (Jöreskog & Sörbom, 1984). (For details, see Romney & Bynner, 1992a.) The fit indices in LISREL are χ^2 which is the same as in EQS; the goodness-of-fit index (GFI), which is similar to NFI in EQS; the adjusted goodness-of-fit index (AGFI), which is similar to NNFI in EQS; and the root mean square residual (RMSR), which is similar to AASR in EQS except that the residuals are squared. As with the circumplex, the simplex was tested under two conditions: (a) a model in which it was assumed that the disorders were measured perfectly reliably and (b) a quasi-simplex model in which the correlations were corrected for attenuation (measurement error).

The 1985 data fit the simplex very well, but only after some fine tuning, which involved correcting just one of the variables (avoidant personality disorder) for attenuation. (This differs from the circumplex in which *all* the variables were corrected for attenuation to achieve the best fitting model.) The model did not fit the 1988 data quite as well, even after the same fine tuning, but it fitted the data better than any other ordering of the variables. A single-factor model also was tested on both sets of data; however, this model fitted the data much worse. See Table 6 for goodness-of-fit indices.

The quasi-simplex model shows how the five personality disorders fall on a continuum running from antisocial at one end to compulsive at the other, with borderline, avoidant and passive–aggressive in between. This model is illustrated in Figure 3. Note that the squares represent the observed personality traits or variables that are being (fallibly) measured and the circles represent the corresponding latent variables or factors free from measurement error.

The dimension being measured seems to correspond to one of the personality dimensions proposed by Cloninger (1987)—namely, the novelty-seeking dimension.

> Individuals who are higher than average in novelty seeking . . . are characterized as impulsive, fickle, excitable, quick-tempered, extravagant and disorderly. . . . They are said to neglect details and are quickly

TABLE 6
Goodness-of-fit Values for Simplex and Factor Models

1985 data				
Model	χ^2	df	AGFI	RMSR
Simplex	11.54	5	.974	.036
Factor	37.90	5	.963	.077
1988 data				
Simplex	29.23	5	.921	.074
Factor	43.51	5	.927	.101

Note. AGFI = Adjusted Goodness of Fit Index; RMSR = Root Mean Square Residual.

distracted or bored. In contrast, individuals who are lower than average in novelty seeking . . . often become preoccupied with narrowly defined focused details and require considerable thought before making decisions. (p. 575)

Thus, at one end of the continuum are people with antisocial personalities who are easily bored and are notorious for seeking thrills and other distractions whereas at the other end are people with compulsive disorders who insist on sameness and cannot bear to have their routine disturbed. People with borderline, avoidant, and passive–aggressive personality disorders are in between these two extremes on the continuum so that their levels of novelty seeking should be intermediate, with borderline ranking higher than avoidant and avoidant ranking higher than passive–aggressive.

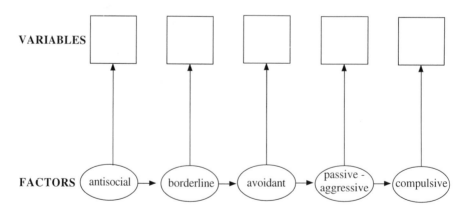

Figure 3. A quasi-simplex model of five personality disorders.

RELATIONSHIP TO THE FIVE FACTOR MODEL

Much has been written about the Five Factor Model theory of personality that currently holds sway over the psychological community and how these five dimensions relate to personality disorders (e.g., Costa & Widiger, 1994). But the question then arises: How do these five dimensions relate to the circumplex and simplex models previously described?

Two of the Big Five dimensions—extraversion and agreeableness—are interpersonal dimensions that seem to correspond to the dominance and affiliation axes defining the circumplex. Indeed there is empirical evidence for this supposition (e.g., Soldz, Budman, Demby, & Merry, 1993). However, two of the other five dimensions—conscientiousness and neuroticism—seem to reflect the continuum on which the simplex is based. The continuum may be thought of as representing a *blend* of the two factors. As we move from left to right along the continuum, individuals become more conscientious and more neurotic. In psychodynamic terms the continuum stretches from the id to the superego. At one end of the continuum we have the undersocialized individuals with antisocial personality disorder who have little sense of responsibility and are only marginally affected by anxiety; in contrast, at the other end we have the overly socialized individuals with compulsive personality disorder who tend to be unduly conscientious and are often racked with anxiety. As we move from left to right along the continuum, conscientiousness and anxiety should increase progressively.

The last of the Big Five, openness to experience, is represented on neither the circumplex nor the simplex. But a study by Wiggins and Pincus (1989) has shown that only schizotypal personality disorder loaded on this factor (i.e., it seems to stand alone). As schizotypal personality disorder was intentionally omitted from our analyses, because of its apparent undue overlap with schizoid personality disorder, we did not have to reckon with this specific factor. However, we may be criticized for omitting this personality disorder from our analyses because it is an official psychiatric diagnosis.

CLINICAL IMPLICATIONS

The separation of the personality disorders into two groups—those on the circumplex and those on the simplex—suggests that although the primary deficit in the former is interpersonal, the primary deficit in the latter is cognitive. However, the primary cognitive deficits in the latter then lead to secondary deficits that are interpersonal in nature. In other words, because of their aberrant cognitive styles, people with personality disorders on the simplex have difficulties relating to and interacting with others. For example, people with compulsive personality disorder have a rigid conceptual framework that prevents them from compromising; antisocial personalities have no moral sense and act impulsively and hedonistically; those with borderline personality disorders tend to construe people as either good or bad, keep changing their minds about them, and struggle with confused emotions; those with avoidant personality disorders see other people as threatening or potential sources of embarrassment; and passive–aggressive people are concerned that they will be taken advantage of and react accordingly by being obstructive.

If it is true that only 5 out of the 11 *DSM-III-R* personality disorders (plus a hypothesized hypomanic personality disorder) fall on the interpersonal circumplex, then this would have implications for classification and assessment as well as for treatment. What it means is that for the purposes of classification, hypomanic personality disorder should be reinstated as an official diagnosis, as it was in *DSM-II*. However, this is a vain hope, and hypomanic personality disorder did not make a comeback in *DSM-IV* (American Psychiatric Association, 1994). Moreover, passive–aggressive personality disorder (also known now as negativistic personality disorder), one of the links in our simplex chain of personality disorders, has been relegated to an appendix in *DSM-IV* "on the grounds that there was insufficient information to warrant [its] inclusion" as an official category (p. 703). In future, therefore, we cannot expect individuals to be diagnosed with this disorder, which will make replication of our results more difficult.

With regard to the assessment of personality disorders, our findings suggest that interpersonal circumplex inventories should restrict their scope to the six interpersonal personality disorders that have been found to lie on the circle. Another set of scales should be devised for the personality disorders on the simplex and items should be weighted toward the cognitive aspects of these disorders. Schizotypal personality disorder could have its own special scale, as it does already (cf. Claridge & Beech, 1995; Claridge & Broks, 1984).

With respect to treatment, the implications are very different depending on whether the personality disorder in question lies on the circumplex or on the simplex. If it lies on the circumplex and the primary deficit is therefore interpersonal, the treatment of choice would appear to be also some form of interpersonal psychotherapy (Horowitz & Vitkus, 1986). Thus patients who are diagnosed as dependent would be trained to become more autonomous and self-assertive. Treatment for the personality disorders on the simplex, however, should be more cognitive than interpersonal. Thus antisocial personalities should be trained in moral development and impulse-control in keeping with the notion that their primary deficit is cognitive rather than interpersonal.

CONCLUSION

We started this chapter with a point about methodology and it is fitting to end with one. The advances in statistical analysis, as represented by SEM, have opened up new ways of looking at personality disorders from which we are only just beginning to reap the full benefit. The discovery that two of the Big Five dimensions of personality—extraversion and agreeableness—can be accounted for by the circumplex and two—conscientiousness and neuroticism—by the simplex has not only enabled apparently competing (interpersonal versus cognitive) conceptions of personality disorders and appropriate therapy for them to be resolved but also has pointed to exciting new directions for theory and practice.

There is no question that these advances would have been much more difficult to achieve without the assistance of the LISREL and EQS computer programs. Their great value is in providing direct answers simultaneously to the two questions with which science is fundamentally concerned: Does this way of conceptualizing the key variables in a study and the relations between them stand up empirically? When the model fails to fit and the theory clearly does not work, then the theorist is forced to go back to first principles and reconceptualize both.

Our experience with many different data sets has convinced us how rewarding this process can be. In the case of the personality disorders data, we would never have had any idea that a simplex would be needed to represent the relations among the variables not forming the circumplex, if first, other representations had not failed to fit the data, and second if we had not already recognized the value of simplex models in our work on cognitive abilities.

As with any statistical modeling technique applied to survey data we acknowledge the need to interpret our confirmed models with a degree of caution. This is especially the case in drawing causal inferences from them, which as Cliff (1983) pointed out, can never be established unequivocally without experimental controls. However, we agree with Hoyle and Smith (1994) who stated that "directionality can be inferred from data generated by cross-sectional studies in which a clear, logical, theoretical or empirically based cause-effect sequence can be proposed" (p. 439). Therefore, Cliff's caveat need not be taken to mean that we should reserve all theoretical judgment and postpone all therapeutic action. The challenge is to recognize the case SEM advances for new theoretical formulations and then subject these to every kind of empirical test to see how well they survive. In the case of personality disorders, this includes trying out the new therapeutic strategies implied by them in the widest possible variety of clinical settings.

As we have illustrated, SEM by itself cannot provide the alternatives to prevailing theory and practice. It can help provide new ways of thinking, from which theoretical and practical advances are most likely to arise.

REFERENCES

American Psychiatric Association. (1987). *Diagnostic and statistical manual of mental disorders* (3rd ed., rev.). Washington, DC: Author.

American Psychiatric Association. (1994). *Diagnostic and statistical manual of mental disorders* (4th ed.). Washington, DC: Author.

Bentler, P. M. (1985). *Theory and implementation of EQS: A structural equation program.* Los Angeles: University of California Press.

Bentler, P. M. (1989). *EQS structural equations program manual.* Los Angeles: BMDP Statistical Software.

Blashfield, R., Sprock, J., Pinkston, K., & Hodgin, J. (1985). Exemplar prototypes of personality disorder diagnoses. *Comprehensive Psychiatry, 26,* 11–21.

Browne, M. W. (1992). Circumplex models for correlation matrices. *Psychometrika, 57,* 469–497.

Bynner, J. M. (1981). Use of LISREL in the solution to a higher order factor problem in a study of adolescent self image. *Quality and Quantity, 15,* 523–540.

Bynner, J. M. (1988). Factor analysis and the construct indicator relationship. *Human Relations, 41,* 389–405.

Bynner, J. M., & Romney, D. M. (1986). Intelligence, fact or artefact: Alternative structures for cognitive abilities. *British Journal of Educational Psychology, 56,* 12–23.

Cantor, N., Smith, E. E., French, R. D., & Mezzich, J. (1980). Psychiatric diagnosis as prototype categorization. *Journal of Abnormal Psychology, 89,* 181–193.

Claridge, G., & Beech, A. R. (1995). Fully and quasi-dimensional constructions of schizotypy. In A. Raine, T. Lencz, & S. A. Mednick (Eds.), *Schizotypal Personality* (pp. 192–216). Cambridge: Cambridge University Press.

Claridge, G., & Broks, P. (1984). Schizotypy and hemisphere functions: I. Theoretical considerations and the measurement of schizotypy. *Personality and Individual Differences, 8,* 633–648.

Cliff, N. (1983). Some cautions regarding the applications of causal-modeling methods. *Multivariate Behavioral Methods, 18,* 115–126.

Cloninger, R. (1987). A systematic method for clinical description and classification of personality variants: A proposal. *Archives of General Psychiatry, 44,* 573–588.

Costa, P. T., Jr., & Widiger, T. A. (1994). *Personality disorders and the Five-Factor Model of personality.* Washington, DC: American Psychological Association.

Cudeck, R. (1986). A note on structural models for the circumplex. *Psychometrika, 15,* 143–147.

Digman, J. M. (1990). Personality structure: Emergence of the Five-Factor Model. *Annual Review of Psychology, 50,* 116–123.

Eysenck, H. J. (1970). *The structure of human personality* (3rd ed.). London: Methuen.

Frances, A., & Widiger, T. A. (1986). Methodological issues in personality disorder diagnosis. In T. Millon & G. L. Klerman (Eds.), *Contemporary directions in psychopathology: Towards the DSM-IV* (pp. 381–400). New York: Guilford Press.

Guttman, L. A. (1954). A new approach to factor analysis: The radex. In P. F. Lazarsfeld (Ed.), *Mathematical thinking in the social sciences* (pp. 258–348). Glencoe, IL: Free Press.

Horowitz, L. M., & Vitkus, J. (1986). The interpersonal basis of psychiatric symptoms. *Clinical Psychology Review, 6,* 443–469.

Hoyle, R. H., & Smith, G. T. (1994). Formulating clinical research hypotheses as structural equation models: A conceptual overview. *Journal of Clinical and Consulting Psychology, 62,* 429–440.

Hyler, S. E., & Lyons, M. (1988). Factor analysis of the *DSM-III* personality disorder clusters: A replication. *Comprehensive Psychiatric, 29,* 304–308.

Jöreskog, K. G. (1974). Analyzing psychological data by structural analysis of covariance matrices. In D. H. Krantz, R. C. Atkinson, R. D. Luce, & P. Suppes (Eds.), *Contemporary developments in mathematical psychology* (Vol. 2, pp. 1–56). San Francisco: Freeman.

Jöreskog, K. G., & Sörbom, D. (1979). *Advancing in factor analysis and structural equation models.* Cambridge, MA: Abt Associates.

Jöreskog, K. G., & Sörbom, D. (1984). LISREL VI: Analysis of linear structural relationships by maximum likelihood, instrumental variables, and least squares methods (3rd ed.). Mooresville, IN: Scientific Software.

Jöreskog, K. G., & Sörbom, D. (1989). LISREL 7: A guide to the program and applications (2nd ed.). Chicago: SPSS.

Kass, F., Skodol, A. E., Charles, E., Spitzer, R. L., & Williams, J. B. W. (1985). Scaled ratings of *DSM-III* personality disorders. *American Journal of Psychiatry, 142,* 627–630.

Kiesler, D. J. (1983). The 1982 interpersonal circle: A taxonomy for complementarity in human transactions. *Psychological Review, 90,* 185–214.

LaForge, R. (1977). The Interpersonal Check List. In J. E. Jones & J. W. Pfeiffer (Eds.), *The 1977 handbook for group facilitators* (pp. 89–96). La Jolla, CA: University Associates.

Leary, T. F. (1957). *Interpersonal diagnosis of personality: A functional theory and methodology for personality evaluation.* New York: Ronald Press.

Marsh, H. W., Balla, J. R., & McDonald, R. P. (1988). Goodness of fit indices in confirmatory factor analysis. *Psychological Bulletin, 103,* 391–411.

McDonald, R. P. (1980). A simple comprehensive model for the analysis of covariate structures. *British Journal of Mathematical and Statistical Psychology, 33,* 161–183.

Romney, D. M., & Bynner, J. M. (1989). Evaluation of a circumplex model of *DSM-III* personality disorders. *Journal of Research in Personality, 23,* 525–538.

Romney, D. M., & Bynner, J. M. (1992a). A simplex model of five *DSM-III* personality disorders. *Journal of Personality Disorders, 6,* 34–39.

Romney, D. M., & Bynner, J. M. (1992b). *The structure of personal characteristics.* New York: Praeger.

Sim, J. P., & Romney, D. M. (1990). The relationship between a circumplex model of interpersonal behaviors and personality disorders. *Journal of Personality Disorders, 4,* 329–341.

Soldz, S., Budman, S., Demby, A., & Merry, J. (1993). Representation of personality disorders in circumplex and Five-Factor space: Explorations with a clinical sample. *Psychological Assessment, 5,* 41–52.

Wheaton, B., Muthén, B., Alwin, D. E., & Summers, G. F. (1977). Assessing reliability and stability in panel models. In D. Heise (Ed.), *Sociological methodology 1977* (pp. 84–136). San Francisco: Jossey-Bass.

Wiggins, J. S. (1982). Circumplex models of interpersonal behavior in clinical psychology. In P. C. Kendall & J. N. Butcher (Eds)., *Handbook of research methods in clinical psychology* (pp. 183–221). New York: Wiley.

Wiggins, J. S., Phillips, N., & Trapnell, P. (1989). Circular reasoning about interpersonal behavior: Evidence concerning some untested assumptions underlying diagnostic classification. *Journal of Personality and Social Psychology, 56,* 296–305.

Wiggins, J. S., & Pincus, A. L. (1989). Conceptions of personality disorders and dimensions of personality. *Psychological Assessment: Journal of Consulting and Counseling Psychology, 1,* 305–316.

15

THE CIRCUMPLEX STRUCTURE OF INTERPERSONAL PROBLEMS

LEONARD M. HOROWITZ, D. CHRISTOPHER DRYER, and
ELENA N. KRASNOPEROVA

This chapter summarizes our thinking about the nature and organization of interpersonal problems. Interpersonal problems, like interpersonal behaviors, can be organized graphically in a two-dimensional circumplex. In this chapter we propose a theory to explain why interpersonal problems can be organized in this way and the conditions under which interpersonal problems arise. Our theory assumes that every interpersonal behavior invites a person to respond with some particular other behavior (its complement), and the relationship between a behavior and its invited complement is also best described in terms of the two-dimensional circumplex. We begin our account descriptively, enumerating the interpersonal problems that people mention most frequently, citing evidence that they meet the criteria for a two-dimensional circumplex, and applying the results to clinical assessment. After that, we present our theory and some of its implications.

THE ORGANIZATION OF INTERPERSONAL PROBLEMS

When people begin psychotherapy, they frequently mention interpersonal problems that they have observed in themselves. Even if the person begins the interview by describing uncomfortable feelings (e.g., depression), a large number of interpersonal problems get mentioned as well—for example, difficulties in getting close to other people, difficulties being assertive, difficulties being too competitive, and so on. To examine the variety of interpersonal problems, Horowitz (1979) and Horowitz, Weckler, and Doren (1983) studied a large sample of initial interviews and identified the interpersonal problems that people expressed during that initial interview. From the problems that were identified, Horowitz, Rosenberg, Baer, Ureño, and Villaseñor (1988) constructed an inventory, called the Inventory of Interpersonal Problems (IIP).

The Inventory of Interpersonal Problems (IIP)

The IIP contains 127 statements of problems (see Figure 1 for an example of a portion of the IIP). The statements are in two forms. Some begin, "It is hard for me to. . . ." Others are in the form, "These are things I do too much." The person is asked to consider each statement and circle

INVENTORY OF INTERPERSONAL PROBLEMS

Here is a list of problems that people report in relating to other people. Please read the list below, and for each item, consider whether that problem has been a problem for you with respect to *any* significant person in your life. Then select the number that describes how distressing that problem has been, and circle that number.

EXAMPLE					
How much have you been distressed by this problem?					
It is hard for me to:	Not at all	A little bit	Moderately	Quite a bit	Extremely
00. get along with my relatives.	0	1	2	3	4

Parl I. The following are things you find hard to do with other people.

It is hard for me to:	Not at all	A little bit	Moderately	Quite a bit	Extremely
1. trust other people.	0	1	2	3	4
2. say "no" to other people.	0	1	2	3	4
3. join in on groups.	0	1	2	3	4
4. keep things private from other people.	0	1	2	3	4
5. let other people know what I want.	0	1	2	3	4
6. tell a person to stop bothering me.	0	1	2	3	4

Figure 1. A fragment of the Inventory of Interpersonal Problems (IIP).

a number from 0 to 4 to indicate the amount of distress that he or she has experienced from that problem. To study the organization of the problems empirically, the IIP was administered to 200 patients at an outpatient clinic (Horowitz et al., 1988), and a factor analysis was performed to examine the interrelationships among the items. The first two factors were interpreted to be two interpersonal dimensions, a dimension of affiliation, nurturance, or communion (ranging from friendly or warm behavior to hostile or cold behavior) and a dimension of control, dominance, or influence (ranging from dominating or controlling behavior to yielding or relinquishing control). If an item's loadings on these two factors are used as coordinates, the items can be plotted graphically, as shown in Figure 2. Different items fell in different regions of the space, and no region of the space was without items.

We also can divide the space into octants to examine problems in each narrow region of the space. When we say that the organization of items within this two-dimensional space forms a *circumplex*, we mean that every region of the two-dimensional space contains some interpersonal problems that were mentioned in the initial psychiatric interview. Thus, problems exist that correspond to every combination of the two underlying factors: Some problems reflect too much friendliness (or too much

Figure 2. Illustrative items from each circumplex subscale of the IIP.

hostility); others reflect too much dominance (or too much submissiveness). Some reflect too much friendly-dominance; others reflect too much friendly–submissiveness. There are no empty regions of the space.

Furthermore, items that are close to one another in the graph are correlated positively because they both reflect similar amounts of the two underlying dimensions. However, items that are diametrically opposed to each other on the graph are, in general, negatively correlated because they reflect opposite amounts of the two underlying dimensions. Finally, items that are separated by 90° (e.g., problems in being too friendly versus problems in being too dominating) are uncorrelated (orthogonal), because one is determined primarily by the horizontal factor whereas the other is determined primarily by the vertical factor.

Alden, Wiggins, and Pincus (1990) divided the graph of Figure 2 into octants and identified eight items from each octant that best represented that region of the space. In this way they constructed eight 8-item subscales, one for each octant of the two-dimensional space. Each subscale is so named that we can describe the content of problems in each particular octant. The subscales are labeled (too) domineering, vindictive, cold, socially avoidant, nonassertive, exploitable, over-nurturant, and intrusive.

Together the subscales meet the criteria for a circumplex described previously (Guttman, 1954). Subscales in adjacent octants are correlated positively, subscales that are diametrically opposed are correlated negatively, and subscales that are separated by 90° are uncorrelated. The smaller the angle separating two subscales, the higher the correlation between them. If a person has his or her most severe problems in a particular region of the graph, the person is likely to have other noteworthy problems in adjacent regions of the space. It is possible for a person to have problems in diametrically opposite octants, but statistically, that is not probable: People who complain that they cannot be assertive rarely complain as well of being too domineering. Implications of this statistical organization of the problems will be examined later.

APPLICATIONS OF THE INVENTORY OF INTERPERSONAL PROBLEMS

The eight subscales can be plotted graphically to describe any one patient's pattern of responses. Figure 3 shows one patient's responses. This patient, Ms A, was a single woman in her late 30s, who complained of difficulties getting into a committed relationship. Although she was very intelligent, attractive, and successful in her career, she had never had a relationship with a man that lasted more than 6 months. She was approaching 40 and wanted to be married and have children, and she was feeling frustrated, lonely, and desperate. As shown in Figure 3, her problems

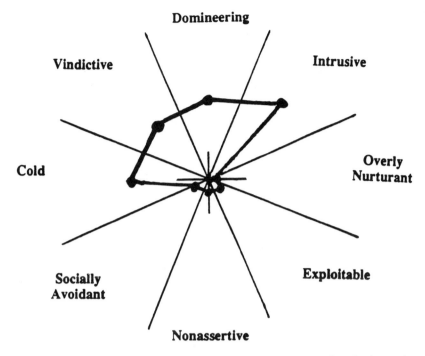

Figure 3. Mean amount of distress reported by Ms A to items of each circumplex subscale of the IIP.

were mainly problems in the octants labeled cold, vindictive, domineering, and intrusive.

The Inventory of Interpersonal Problems (IIP) also has been used to study the psychotherapeutic process. Horowitz and colleagues (1988) determined what kinds of problems are discussed most often in a brief dynamic psychotherapy and what kinds of problems are most likely to change. The patients in the study were 50 men and women who were receiving a 20-session dynamic psychotherapy. The majority of problems that got discussed were problems of friendly submissiveness. For example, many of those problems described the patient's being too exploitable. Problems of being too domineering or being too competitive or being too cold got discussed much less frequently. The investigators also found that problems of friendly submissiveness had a very high rate of improvement, whereas problems of hostile dominance had a much lower rate of improvement. Indeed, Ms A, the woman who had difficulty forming a committed relationship, was a person with many of these difficult-to-treat problems. Her problems were primarily in the region of hostile dominance, and not surprisingly, she showed very little improvement during the treatment.

In addition to describing people and their problems, the IIP has been used to compare different instruments and clarify what a given instrument is measuring. For example, if an instrument claims to be measuring dependency (or assertiveness or mistrust), we should be able to locate the construct in question within the interpersonal space. It should correlate most strongly with the circumplex subscale that it most closely resembles, and it should correlate less well with other circumplex subscales. Gurtman (1991, 1992a, 1992b) has used the IIP in this way to locate different instruments in the interpersonal space. In particular, he has shown that two different measures of trust or two different measures of dependency can differ substantially in their location in the interpersonal space, so they are measuring substantially different constructs.

The work of psychotherapy, to a large extent, addresses interpersonal problems. In order to understand what is being treated, however, we need to understand what an interpersonal problem is. A person with an interpersonal problem desires a particular type of interpersonal interaction (that is, the person has a particular interpersonal goal or wish), but that goal often gets frustrated. To understand the problem, we therefore need to assess people's interpersonal goals as well as their actual interpersonal behaviors. We also need to understand how (and why) an interpersonal goal gets frustrated so that we can devise appropriate interventions. These issues are considered in our theory, which is described in the following section.

AN INTERPERSONAL MODEL

Interpersonal models began emerging in the 1940s and 1950s, typically as a reaction against prevailing theories such as classical psychoanalysis and behavioral theories of learning (e.g., Horney, 1945; Leary, 1957; Sullivan, 1953). The behavioral theories, for example, had reduced interpersonal events to discrete stimuli and responses, as though one person's action is a stimulus that mechanically elicits the partner's response. However, Leary emphasized that people do not merely emit responses in each other's presence; a person who boasts to another person, for example, "is doing something *to* that other person" (1957, p. 91). Boasting communicates a variety of messages, including an invitation to the other person to acknowledge the boaster's superiority. Principles of interpersonal theorists have been summarized by various authors (e.g., Benjamin, 1974, 1986; Horowitz & Vitkus, 1986; Kiesler, 1983; Orford, 1986; Wiggins, 1982). Our own model contains four principal postulates, which are described in the following sections and applied to interpersonal problems.

Interpersonal Behaviors Can Be Described in Terms of Two Dimensions

Interpersonal behaviors, like interpersonal problems, can be described along two principal dimensions—a dimension of affiliation, nurturance, or communion that ranges from hostile behavior to friendly behavior and a dimension of control, dominance, or influence that ranges from yielding behavior to dominating behavior. One example is shown in Figure 4. In this example, *advise* lies in the quadrant that connotes friendly–dominating behavior, *scold* in the quadrant that connotes hostile–dominating behavior, *defer* in the quadrant that connotes friendly–yielding behavior, and *sulk* in the quadrant that connotes hostile–yielding behavior.

Empirical Evidence

Several reviews exist of research showing this organization of interpersonal content—for example, Berzins (1977), Bierman (1969), Carson (1969), DeVoge and Beck (1978), and Wiggins (1982). Since the original work of LaForge and Suczek (1955) and Leary (1957), numerous investigators have applied factor analysis and other statistical methods to identify two major interpersonal dimensions. The two interpersonal dimensions have sometimes been related to two fundamental human needs, which initially may be interconnected but later diverge: (a) a need to maintain an image of other people that enables the person to relate to others in a satisfying way and (b) a need to maintain an image of the self that permits the person to behave autonomously. In other words, human development

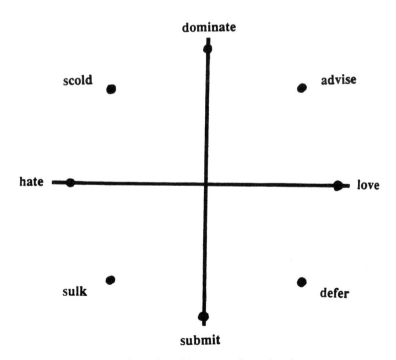

Figure 4. Interpersonal behaviors placed in a two-dimensional space.

seems to pose two tasks for each person—that of interpersonal relatedness (connectedness) and that of self-definition (individuation). A similar distinction has been proposed by other theorists—identity versus intimacy (Erikson, 1963), agency versus communion (Bakan, 1966), and autonomy versus homonomy (Angyal, 1941). Interpersonal difficulties are thought to arise because of problems with either.

Blatt (1990) has written that personality develops as an interplay between two fundamental developmental lines, one that ideally leads to a stable, realistic, and essentially positive identity and one that ideally leads to satisfying, intimate interpersonal relationships. Development along either line is, of course, reciprocally influenced by development along the other. A normal development of the self-concept, for example, requires a backlog of satisfying interpersonal experiences, and maintenance of satisfying interpersonal experiences requires an acceptable self-concept. Psychopathology usually reflects a major problem in one or the other, and Blatt and Schichman (1983) have postulated two primary configurations of psychopathology that correspond to problems along each of these developmental lines. Psychopathologies that they call *anaclitic*, such as the histrionic personality disorder, are distorted and exaggerated attempts to maintain satisfying interpersonal experiences, whereas psychopathologies that they call *introjective*, such as the obsessive–compulsive personality disorder, are distorted and exaggerated attempts to establish an acceptable self-definition. Whereas one reflects a preoccupation with closeness, intimacy, and love (at the expense of self-definition), the other reflects a preoccupation with self-definition, self-control, and self-worth (at the expense of satisfying interpersonal relationships).

Application to Attachment Style

Why should the two dimensions of the interpersonal space correspond to affiliation and dominance? According to Bowlby (1973) and Bartholomew (1990; Bartholomew & Horowitz, 1991), people have two important classes of mental representations that affect their interpersonal behavior: One describes a person's generalized image of other people; the other describes the person's generalized image of the self. If the person's image of other people is generally negative, the person will not trust other people, hence will avoid intimacy. If the person's image of the self is negative, the person will have low self-efficacy expectations (Bandura, 1977, 1978, 1982), hence will refrain from displaying initiative and autonomy.

Bartholomew (1990; Bartholomew & Horowitz, 1991) formed a 2 × 2 matrix, crossing image of the self with image of others, to yield four prototypic styles of attachment. Figure 5 shows the four resulting attachment patterns. Cell I describes a secure person—a person with a sense of self-worth plus an expectation that other people are generally friendly. Pre-

	Positive	Negative
Positive **MODEL OF OTHER**	CELL I **SECURE** Comfortable with intimacy and autonomy	CELL II **PREOCCUPIED** Preoccupied with relationships
Negative	CELL IV **DISMISSING** Dismissing of intimacy Counter-dependent	CELL III **FEARFUL** Fearful of intimacy Socially avoidant

Figure 5. Four theoretical attachment styles.

occupied people (Cell II) have a negative image of the self and a positive image of other people, whereas dismissing people (Cell IV) have just the opposite pattern—a positive image of the self and a negative image of other people. Fearful people (Cell III) have a negative image of the self and a negative image of other people. According to this model, preoccupied people should exhibit friendly behavior toward other people, but their deficient sense of autonomy or control should leave them helplessly unassertive (or defensively exercising exaggerated control). Dismissing people should exhibit problems with hostility or coldness; and fearful people should exhibit both kinds of problems—hostility toward other people and a deficient sense of autonomy. Most people have had multiple experiences with different attachment figures, so most people's mental representations reflect an amalgam of these four prototypic styles. Therefore, each person could be described in terms of the person's degree of approximation to each of the four prototypic styles.

Bartholomew (1990) developed a semistructured interview in which people were asked about their close relationships. From their responses to the interview, they each could be rated for their degree of approximation to the four attachment styles. The participants also completed various questionnaires, including the IIP, so interpersonal problems could be related to attachment style. A friend of each participant also used the IIP to rate that participant's interpersonal problems. Figure 6 shows typical interpersonal problems of people in each attachment category, as reported by the participants themselves and separately, by their friends. Interpersonal problems of the secure people were evenly distributed; no one subscale of problems characterized that group as a whole. However, each of the other groups had a characteristic type of problem. Problems of preoccupied people (pos-

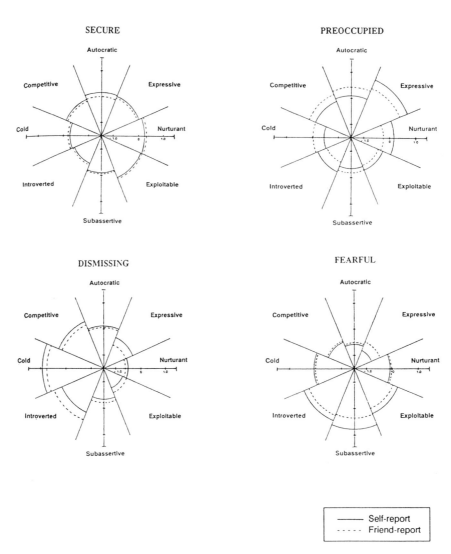

Figure 6. Mean rating of distress (by self and by friend) on each subscale of IIP for participants in each attachment style category.

itive image of others, negative image of the self) reflected friendliness toward other people with an exaggerated need to exercise control. Problems of dismissing people primarily reflected excessive hostility, and problems of fearful people primarily reflected problems of hostile submissiveness.

An Interpersonal Behavior Invites a Complementary Reaction

Our second postulate is that each interpersonal behavior invites some particular reaction from the partner (Carson, 1969; Leary, 1957). To say that one behavior invites a particular reaction implies an implicit communication between partners, a communication about the sender's wishes (which the receiver may or may not choose to gratify). When Person 1 brags to Person 2, for example, Person 1 is not merely reciting his or her achievements but rather is communicating a request inviting Person 2 to "admire me, exhibit respect, envy me." If the communication is clear, both parties perceive it, even if the receiver chooses not to gratify it. The important point is that Person 1's interpersonal action invites a particular class of reactions from Person 2, and the invited reaction may or may not be granted.

An action and the reaction that it invites are said to be complementary. According to the model, the relationship between a pair of complementary behaviors is defined by the circumplex: Complementary behaviors are assumed to be the same with respect to affiliation and reciprocal with respect to dominance. For example, as Person 1 scolds Person 2 (hostile dominance), Person 2 is invited to respond with hostile submissiveness; as Person 1 helplessly discloses some personal problem to Person 2 (friendly submissiveness), Person 2 is invited to offer friendly advice (friendly dominance). Even if Person 2 chooses not to grant the invited complement, both partners may note the communication from one to the other.

Empirical Research on Complementarity

A number of studies relating to this principle have been summarized by Bluhm, Widiger, and Miele (1990), Horowitz and Vitkus (1986), Kiesler (1983), and Orford (1986). Some of these studies have tested a strictly behavioral interpretation of the principle, as though one partner's behavior is expected to *elicit* (mechanically and automatically) a fixed action pattern from the other. The literature clearly does not support this kind of interpretation. For example, people who are engaged in a group discussion do not necessarily or automatically respond to one member's hostile dominance with hostile submissiveness. Instead, they frequently refuse the invitation and fight back. That is, when one partner criticizes, blames, or scolds, the other is quite likely to criticize, blame, or scold in return, rather than squirm, justify the self, or sulk. This result does not refute the principle of complementarity, however, because an invitation never guarantees a complementary reaction. (The consequence of noncomplementarity will be discussed later.)

The clearest study refuting the mechanistic behavioral interpretation of complementarity is one by Strong and colleagues (1988). In this study 80 female students (the research participants) each interacted with a female confederate actress (also a student) who had been trained to enact a particular role that corresponded to one of the eight categories (octants) in the interpersonal space. The participant and the confederate were asked to create a story together about pictures from the Thematic Apperception Test (TAT); during this interaction the confederate enacted her pre-assigned role. Each interaction was videotaped, and each partner's utterances were transcribed verbatim.

For every category of confederate behaviors, the investigators examined the participants' reactions. For example, consider how participants typically reacted to a confederate who successfully enacted a leading (friendly dominant) behavior. The complementary reaction to leading in Strong and Hills' (1986) system is docile (leading behavior invites docile behavior), so the investigators expected a fairly high frequency of docile reactions. The single most frequent reactions were indeed behaviors in the docile category (comprising 31.2% of the responses); other frequent behaviors were other forms of friendly submissiveness, so for this and several other categories the participants did frequently accept the invitation and responded with the complement. Although many participants did not accept the invitation at all, a majority did, responding with friendly submissiveness.

However, the participants' reactions to other behavioral categories were not as predictable. Reactions to behaviors on the hostile side of the interpersonal space were less often complementary. Self-enhancing (e.g., bragging) behavior, for example, rarely led to the invited complement (self-effacing behavior). Instead, the participants were more apt to react to a self-enhancing confederate with cooperative behavior—as though the participant were trying to move the interaction onto friendlier interpersonal terrain. Although a self-enhancing confederate is inviting a partner to exhibit inferiority, partners rarely accepted that invitation; instead, they frequently responded with some other interpersonal behavior. The important point is that an interpersonal behavior conveys an invitation to the partner, and the invited reaction is by no means inevitable.

Problematic Interpersonal Complementarity: The Maintenance of Depression

In everyday interactions people do at times behave in noncomplementary ways, refusing to provide the invited interpersonal reaction. Sometimes, however, people find it very difficult *not* to fulfill a partner's apparent wishes. As a result, complementary patterns occur that at first seem natural, comfortable, or satisfying, but in time both partners come to feel stuck and personally dissatisfied. One example occurs in interactions involving a depressed person. The interaction sequence seems to involve four steps.

To begin with, many depressed people feel incompetent, helpless, and powerless. A depressed person typically exhibits a number of related symptoms that include passivity, unassertiveness, a sense of helplessness, and negative judgments about the self (including a sense of incompetence and a lack of efficacy).

Second, the depressed person's display of helplessness, incompetence, and unassertiveness invites other people to take charge. Coyne, Aldwin, and Lazarus (1981) interviewed depressed and nondepressed people seven times at 4-week intervals to determine how depressed and nondepressed people typically cope with stress. The participants were asked about the most stressful events that had occurred during the previous month—what happened and how they had coped. Although depressed and nondepressed people reported approximately the same number of stressful events, depressed people more often reported that they had tried to talk to other people to obtain advice and information.

Then, when other people do take charge, they invite the depressed person to react submissively, thereby confirming the depressed person's passive, incompetent, and helpless self-image. As a result of this behavior, depressed people think self-derogating thoughts and anticipate future failure, reducing their motivation, effort, and energy level. Investigators (e.g., Altman & Wittenborn, 1980; Beck, 1967; Blumberg & Hokanson, 1983; Cofer & Wittenborn, 1980; Gotlib & Robinson, 1982; Hokanson, Sacco, Blumberg, & Landrum, 1980) have observed that depressed people often express self-derogations to others to obtain help in coping with their stress. As they utter these self-derogations, their verbal content generally conveys to the listener a further sense of helplessness, incompetence, and unassertiveness.

Horowitz and colleagues (1991) examined self-derogations. Male and female research participants each interacted with a confederate actor of the same gender. The partners of each dyad were presented with different lists of topics (e.g., "the kind of people I find it easy/hard to talk to"), and they were asked to select and speak about eight different topics from the list. They talked in turns; first the confederate spoke about a topic, then the participant, then the confederate, and so on. The confederate's topics were all predetermined, and the script was varied to produce three different experimental conditions, corresponding to a self-derogating, other-derogating, or nonderogating self-disclosure from the confederate. Participants were assigned to a condition at random. They were asked to indicate their degree of satisfaction with the conversation after each round of monologues. Those who interacted with a self-derogating confederate became progressively less satisfied as the interaction continued. In addition, they themselves selected a larger number of self-derogating topics to speak about than participants in the other two conditions.

Finally, other people in many cases react to the depressed person's self-derogations by trying to change, control, or influence the depressed person. The participants also had an opportunity to react to their partner's monologues. The interactions were videotaped, and the participants' reactions to the confederates' monologues were classified into broad categories. Two of these broad categories were (a) telling the person to think, feel, or behave differently and (b) simply acknowledging the partner's remarks. As expected, reactions of the first type occurred significantly more often toward a self-derogating confederate, and those of the second type occurred significantly less often toward a self-derogating confederate. Even raters who viewed the participants' videotaped reactions without knowing what the confederate had said judged the participants to be more dominating toward a self-derogating confederate than toward a nonderogating confederate.

A number of investigators have reported that people initially react to a depressed person's comments with genuine concern and a wish to help the person (Coates & Wortman, 1980; Lowenstein, 1984). Coyne (1976a, 1976b) and Hinchcliffe, Hooper, and Roberts (1978) have described people's efforts to reduce the depressed person's discomfort by direct action. For example, people report that they actively try to avoid the depressing topic, distract the person from that topic, offer advice to the person, or offer words of encouragement (Blumberg & Hokanson, 1983; Coyne, 1976a, 1976b; Grinker, 1964).

Krasnoperova and Horowitz (1995) had students describe experiences that involved an achievement failure, a romantic breakup, or a difficulty with a friend. These verbatim descriptions were then presented to other listeners who were asked how they would respond. The resulting responses were classified, and each category was rated for the degree of control that it reflected. *Controlling responses* were defined as responses designed to influence or alter the speaker's behavior or experience; *noncontrolling responses* were defined as responses that contained no such intent. Raters rated each response along a scale from 0 (not at all controlling) to 4 (extremely controlling). Here are some types of responses that were identified; the mean rating of control is shown in parentheses.

1. Scold the person for being depressed (3.44)
2. Give advice (3.06)
3. Change the way the person feels about the situation; tell the person not to be upset (3.06)
4. Tell the person what you would do in his or her place (2.94)
5. Tell the person to go distract himself or herself, to cheer up (2.81)
6. Encourage the person to examine and express his or her feelings (2.63)
7. Direct the person's thinking toward other problem-free areas or topics (2.56)
8. Distract or cheer the person up (2.50)
9. Change the way the person thinks about the situation; convince the person that things are not that bad (2.19)
10. Side with the person; agree with the person's course of action; say that the other person was wrong (1.69)

11. Decide whose fault it is (1.69)
12. Try to make sense of the motivation and behavior of the people involved; examine and explain the situation (1.56)
13. Reassure the person that the future will be better (1.44)
14. Reassure the person that he or she is still a person of worth (1.25)
15. Tell the person about your own similar experience (0.81)
16. Make a reflective comment about people in general or about situations in general (0.63)
17. Indicate that you understand how the person feels (0.56)
18. Be there for the person—listen, comfort the person, show that you like and care about him or her (0.50)
19. Tell the person that you are sorry and feel bad for him or her (0.44)
20. Express sympathetic commiseration (0.38)

Bagdanoff (1995) had female students interact with a depressed confederate partner. The partner seemed like another female student, but she was actually an actress enacting a standardized script portraying a depressed student. Each participant was told that her partner had been feeling down about something so she should "be a good person for your partner to talk to." The interaction, which was videotaped, lasted 15 minutes. Every statement that the participant uttered was classified into one of the categories listed in the previous list. Responses 1 through 9 were said to be *controlling* (the ones that occurred most frequently were 2, 3, 5, and 9); responses 12 through 20 were said to be *noncontrolling* (the ones that occurred most frequently were 12, 15, 16, and 19). Overall, the noncontrolling responses were about twice as frequent as the controlling responses, but the controlling responses became increasingly more frequent as the interaction progressed. The 15-minute period was divided into three successive 5-minute periods. The mean number of controlling responses per participant during each period was 0.6, 1.7, and 2.6. The mean number of noncontrolling responses in each period was 3.5, 3.8, and 3.4. The participants were then classified into controlling participants, who produced a relatively large number of controlling responses, and noncontrolling participants, who did not. Among the controlling participants, the mean number of controlling responses in each period was 1.3, 3.9, and 4.3; the mean number of noncontrolling responses was 3.6, 3.5, and 3.2. The corresponding means for the noncontrolling participants were 0.2, 0.2, and 1.5 controlling responses and 3.4, 4.0, and 3.6 noncontrolling responses. Thus, all participants, but especially the controlling participants, came to produce an increasing number of controlling responses.

Other writers also have commented on the controlling nature of people's reactions to a depressed person. For example, Coates and Wortman

(1980) remarked that "the depressed are likely to feel that others' kindness is not meant for them as they are, but rather . . . for the positive image they are (supposed to be) presenting" (p. 172). Watzlawick, Weakland, and Fisch (1974) commented that the other person's attempts to cheer up the depressed person amount to a "demand that the patient have certain feelings (joy, optimism, etc.) and not others (sadness, pessimism, etc.)" (p. 34).

Thus, the depressed person's unassertiveness seems to invite the other person to take charge, and many partners do accept that invitation. The dominance in turn invites the depressed person to continue feeling incompetent and helpless, which in turn invites the dominating person to continue taking charge. Thus, we see a vicious circle develop in which both participants are doomed by their own methods. The depressed person, by openly displaying discomfort, makes an inadvertent bid for the other person to take charge; and the other person, by trying to cheer, support, change, distract, or coerce the depressed person into nondepression, elicits more unassertive behavior, thereby sustaining the depressed person's depression. To overcome depression, the person must find partners who will not take charge, or the person must stop communicating an invitation for others to take charge.

Troubles-Telling Versus Service Encounters

Sociolinguists Jefferson and Lee (1992) differentiate between two kinds of interactions that are relevant to the depressed person's difficulty. They taped audio dyadic conversations that occurred naturally in the workplace. Among the conversations that they observed, two subsets were called *troubles-telling* and *service encounters*. In a troubles-telling, the speaker approaches a listener to describe some form of distress. The speaker apparently wants the partner merely to listen and empathize; there is no wish for the listener to offer advice or attempt to influence the speaker. In a service encounter, on the other hand, the speaker presents a problem for the listener to help solve. The speaker is apparently receptive to influence and implicitly seeks help or advice.

Difficulties arise, however, when the speaker and listener fail to understand each other. The speaker, for example, may intend to engage in troubles-telling, but the listener may interpret it as a service encounter. In that case the troubles-teller might indicate his or her dissatisfaction with the listener's response—for example, by rejecting the advice with a statement that might begin "Yes, but . . . ." Jefferson and Lee (1992) provided examples that illustrate such miscommunications. Apparently, depressed people are not very successful at rejecting unwanted advice, and they respond instead with complementary compliance, which then exacerbates their problems.

Troubles-telling may be viewed as a request for friendly listening that maintains equality along the vertical dimension; the speaker does not want the listener to serve as an expert bent on solving the speaker's problem. In other circumstances, however, the speaker may want a service encounter and would be equally dissatisfied with a friendly listener who only listened and empathized. In a service encounter we happily submit ourselves to a higher authority who (we hope) has expertise for solving our problem. The distinction thus highlights the importance of a speaker's wishes (goals), which themselves can be organized by a circumplex. In a later section we will return to a description of interpersonal goals.

Noncomplementarity Creates an Interpersonal Tension Between Partners

When a partner's response is *noncomplementary*, a palpable tension arises between the two people. Suppose Person A, in displaying a particular behavior, communicates a wish to Person B for a particular reaction, and suppose Person B frustrates that wish by failing to provide the desired reaction. Person A may try again (and yet again) to obtain the desired reaction, but after successive failures, the interactants have to accept their dissatisfaction and leave the field. Person A, for example, might scold Person B by saying, "I find you very irritating" (hostile dominance), and Person B, instead of responding with the invited complement ("I'm very sorry") responds with hostile dominance: "Well, I find *you* very irritating!" The interaction would seem unfinished to an outside observer, who would expect further negotiation until the two partners achieved a sense of closure. An episode cannot comfortably end at a point of tension. Further interacting is needed to produce a sense of closure.

An Illustration of Noncomplementarity

Writers of drama deliberately create this kind of tension to arouse our curiosity about the ensuing resolution. In Tennessee Williams' play *A Streetcar Named Desire*, there are a number of scenes that first show a tension, then further struggle (negotiation), and finally an eventual resolution that relieves the tension. The play involves a young married couple, Stella and Stanley, who receive a visit from Stella's sister, Blanche. Stanley and Blanche, however, do not hit it off; their personalities clash from their earliest encounters. Stanley, a tough, macho truck-driver, refuses to be woman-dominated by his sister-in-law, and Blanche, a lively, flirtatious, and somewhat flamboyant Southern belle, keeps trying in subtle ways to manipulate him with her feminine charms. The two get into repeated power struggles.

Exhibit 1 presents a fragment of an early scene in which Stanley and Blanche confront each other. We asked students to examine each utterance in the script (before they knew about the interpersonal theory) and to rate it along each interpersonal dimension. Each student rated one character or the other, first along a dimension of affiliation from −1 (hostile) through 0 (neutral) to +1 (friendly) and then along a dimension of control from −1 (submissive) through 0 (neutral) to +1 (dominant). The mean rating of each utterance in the script was computed. In the early lines of the scene, the statements were not complementary. The mean ratings of Blanche described her comments as friendly dominant (0.4, 0.6). In one line, for example, she says to Stanley, "I'm going to ask a favor of you in a moment;" and Stanley generally responded with hostility, as when he said, "What could that be, I wonder?" (−.3, 0). This noncomplementarity creates the dramatic tension. Throughout successive utterances their interactions are noncomplementary, and by the final set of utterances, the power struggle is clear and overt: Both exhibit hostile dominance—(−.3, .7) for Blanche and (−.2, .7) for Stanley. Finally, in the next to last line of the scene, Stanley booms out his very hostile, dominating remark (−1.0, −1.0), which Blanche complements with her clear hostile submissiveness (−.3, −.9). This complementary submission reduces the tension, producing a momentary feeling of relief and closure. Scenes of this type occur throughout the play, building up to a final crescendo in a much later scene in which Stanley actually rapes Blanche (hostile dominance), and Blanche responds with a "nervous breakdown" (hostile submissiveness)— over-powered, withdrawn, and unable to continue the struggle. Although the play does not have a happy ending, the tension of noncomplementarity is resolved, and one at least feels a sense of closure.

Problematic Noncomplementarity: Tension in Distressed Marriages

People typically minimize the tension of noncomplementarity by negotiating and eventually establishing complementarity or by leaving the relationship altogether. In some cases, however, the interpersonal tension is not resolved. Rather than seeking new partners, each person stays in the relationship and endures the tension.

Noncomplementarity of this kind seems to occur between spouses in a distressed marriage. Gottman (1979) studied distressed and nondistressed couples as they talked to each other under laboratory conditions. The husband and wife were asked to name several types of problems that they had encountered in their marriage. In the course of the session, they discussed some of their more disturbing problems. The couple was videotaped, and their interaction was transcribed and coded. One way of coding the data was to record the number of times the husband and wife disagreed with each other. For the nondistressed wives, the mean proportion of agreements

Exhibit 1. Fragment of a scene from *A Streetcar Named Desire*.

SCENE TWO

BLANCHE:
I'm going to ask a favor of you in a moment.
STANLEY:
What could that be, I wonder?
BLANCHE:
Some buttons in back! You may enter!
[*He crosses through drapes with a smoldering look.*]
How do I look?
STANLEY:
You look all right.
BLANCHE:
Many thanks! Now the buttons!
STANLEY:
I can't do nothing with them.
BLANCHE:
You men with your big clumsy fingers. May I have a drag on your cig?
STANLEY:
Have one for yourself.
BLANCHE:
Why, thanks! . . . It looks like my trunk has exploded.
STANLEY:
Me an' Stella were helping you unpack.
BLANCHE:
Well, you certainly did a fast and thorough job of it!
STANLEY:
It looks like you raided some stylish shops in Paris.
BLANCHE:
Ha-ha! Yes—clothes are my passion!
STANLEY:
What does it cost for a string of fur-pieces like that?
BLANCHE:
Why, those were a tribute from an admirer of mine!
STANLEY:
He must have had a lot of—admiration!
BLANCHE:
Oh, in my youth I excited some admiration. But look at me now! [*She smiles at him radiantly.*] Would you think it possible that I was once considered to be—attractive?
STANLEY:
Your looks are okay.

BLANCHE:

I was fishing for a compliment, Stanley.

STANLEY:

I don't go in for that stuff.

BLANCHE:

What—stuff?

STANLEY:

Compliments to women about their looks. I never met a woman that didn't know if she was good-looking or not without being told, and some of them give themselves credit for more than they've got. I once went out with a doll who said to me, "I am the glamorous type, I am the glamorous type!" I said, "So what?"

BLANCHE:

And what did she say then?

STANLEY:

She didn't say nothing. That shut her up like a clam.

BLANCHE:

Did it end the romance?

STANLEY:

It ended the conversation—that was all. Some men are took in by this Hollywood glamor stuff and some men are not.

BLANCHE:

I'm sure you belong in the second category.

STANLEY:

That's right.

BLANCHE:

I cannot imagine any witch of a woman casting a spell over you.

STANLEY:

That's—right.

BLANCHE:

You're simple, straightforward and honest, a little bit on the primitive side I should think. To interest you a woman would have to—[*She pauses with an indefinite gesture.*]

STANLEY [*slowly*]:

Lay . . . her cards on the table.

BLANCHE [*smiling*]:

Well, I never cared for wishy-washy people. That was why, when you walked in here last night, I said to myself—"My sister has married a man!"—Of course that was all that I could tell about you.

STANLEY [*booming*]:

Now let's cut the re-bop!

BLANCHE [*pressing hands to her ears*]:

Ouuuuu!

was .76 (more agreements than disagreements), whereas the corresponding mean for the distressed wives was .39. The corresponding proportion for the nondistressed husbands was .66, and for the distressed husbands it was .46. A disagreement usually indicates that an assertion by one partner has been challenged by the other partner—in other words, an assertive act by one was followed by a noncomplementary counterassertion by the other. If the counterassertion is perceived as unfriendly, it would be noncomplementary with respect to affiliation as well as dominance. Gottman's results showed that distressed couples displayed (a) more hostile behavior in general and (b) more hostile reactions in response to friendly actions. Similar findings have been reported by Birchler, Weiss, and Vincent (1975), Gottman (1980), and Margolin and Wampold (1981).

People Learn Complete Interpersonal Sequences Rather Than Isolated, Individual Responses to Particular Stimuli

Early in life, people participate in numerous complementary interactional patterns, observing and overlearning both parts of familiar complementary sequences. Each part of the sequence constitutes a role—the two complementary roles are similar in affiliation and reciprocal in dominance—and the sequence as a whole forms a social script. According to this proposition, a person who regularly performs just one role of a familiar complementary sequence (e.g., the dominant role in a dominance–submission script) also has acquired the capacity to perform the other role as well. For example, suppose a child (Person B) is scolded by a parent (Person A) at every provocation. The frequently scolded child regularly exhibits the complementary reaction (sulking), not the dominating action. Nonetheless, we assume that the child has learned the role of the scolder as well as that of the scoldee. Because the child acquires the potential to perform either role, he or she can extend the original learning to new situations in two different ways.

In Paradigm 1, the child B who has participated regularly in the A–B (scolder–scoldee) social script now can reproduce that pattern by finding other people who will also scold him or her. If we call these people A*, the paradigm generalizes the earlier "A scolds B" to "A* now scolds B." For example, a woman (B) who has been scolded by her mother (A) often might now find herself frequently scolded by her husband, by her friends, and by her boss (A*).

In Paradigm 2, the child B who has participated regularly in the A–B (scolder–scoldee) social script also can reproduce that pattern by enacting the role of *scolder* toward new scoldees call them B*); the paradigm thus extends the earlier "A scolds B" to "B now scolds B*." Because we assume that the person has learned both roles, the person can now *initiate* sequences instead of merely reacting. This paradigm resembles the behaviorist's modeling, but the postulate emphasizes the coherence of the two roles in forming a unitary social script. For this reason, a child who has been verbally, physically, or sexually abused learns to be a *victimizer* as well as a victim. The more often the person has been victimized, the more strongly the person also would have learned the role of victimizer. Naturally, the person may enact the dominating role only when it is safe to do so (e.g., toward a doll), but once all threat has been removed, the latent capacity easily manifests itself.

The complementary relationship between the behavior of A and the behavior of B in these paradigms is described by the circumplex. In many cases, however, the person only permits himself or herself to perform one of the two roles. Person B, for example, might exhibit only the behavior of the scoldee, not that of the scolder (Paradigm 1). If a social script rather than a response has been learned, though, the scoldee of Paradigm 1 also should have acquired the capacity to scold, the complement described by the circumplex. Presumably some inhibition or interference keeps the behavior from manifesting itself. If this inhibition were lifted, however, the person's capacity to enact the latent complement should now manifest itself.

The theoretical issue can be posed as follows. Suppose a person in everyday interactions performed just one role of a familiar complementary sequence, and suppose the person complained of an interpersonal problem. For example, a person who found it hard to behave assertively might report being assertive in dreams or in interactions with a pet or a child, but in everyday interactions the person could not bring himself or herself to be assertive. Should we ascribe problems like these (a) to the person's not knowing appropriate assertiveness responses (i.e., lacking the competence or skill) or (b) to some process of inhibition or interference that keeps the skill from manifesting itself behaviorally?

The term *skill deficit* implies a lack of know-how: The person does not know how to produce the necessary motor patterns, just as a person might not know how to cook, swim, or speak Swahili. The term *social skill deficit* thus implies that the person never learned the social skill, is now socially inept, and needs to be shown—step by step—how to produce appropriate social behaviors. An alternate explanation for the deficit is that the person possesses the skill (i.e., has learned the social script), but other processes currently interfere with the person's performance (e.g., the person becomes too anxious to perform). In that case, the skill would exist as a latent capacity.

A number of investigators have documented the poor social performance of lonely people (Brennan, 1982; Chelune, Sultan, & Williams, 1980; French, 1981; Gerson & Perlman, 1979; Hansson & Jones, 1981; Horowitz & French, 1979; Horowitz, French, & Anderson, 1982; Jones, Freeman, & Goswick, 1981; Jones, Hobbs, & Hockenbury, 1982; Solano, Batten, &

Parish, 1982), and many writers have ascribed the behavioral differences between lonely and nonlonely people to a lack of skill. In a review of the behavior modification literature, Bellack and Morrison (1982) concluded that "interpersonal behavior consists of a set of learned performance abilities" and that social skills deficits are due to "deficient learning histories resulting in limited or faulty repertoires" (p. 719).

If lonely people really lack social skills, they should not, without further training, be able to produce appropriate social responses because they lack the essential raw material of elementary skills. However, the terms *inhibition* or *interference* imply processes that impair the enactment of one or the other complementary role in a well-practiced social script. For example, lonely people may *expect* to perform poorly, and these expectations may reduce their activity level, thereby mimicing a deficient response repertoire. Then interpersonal sequences that follow further sustain the person's poor social performance.

Vitkus and Horowitz (1987) hypothesized that some lonely people assume passive interpersonal roles that invite complementary reactions from others (which then sustain their passivity). If this hypothesis is correct, it should be possible to construct a situation that removes this source of interference and exposes the person's latent capacity. For example, if a lonely person were *assigned* a particular interpersonal role, an active role that connoted competence, that role might help expose the person's capacity and enhance the person's social performance. However, if the person were assigned a passive role, the person should exhibit the deficits reported in the literature on loneliness.

In the study of Vitkus and Horowitz (1987) participants were told that they would be discussing a common, everyday problem with another student. (The other student was a confederate who was not aware of the experimental hypothesis.) When the participant and the confederate arrived for the experimental session, they were told that they each would be assigned different roles to play in order to make the problem seem more realistic but that their task was to work together in generating actual solutions to the problem.

Lonely and nonlonely participants, selected by their high or low scores on the UCLA Loneliness Scale, were randomly assigned to one of two conditions. In one condition, the participants were asked to play the role of a listener or counselor; in that role they were to listen to their partner describe the problem. In the other condition, the participants were asked to play the role of a person with a problem; in that role they were to imagine that they actually had the problem and were to describe it to their partner. Although the term *listener* sounds passive and inactive, it connotes (in this context) a wiser counselor, advisor, or confidant; the term *person with a problem*, on the other hand, connotes a troubled person who is stuck with a problem.

The interaction was audiotaped, and a number of behavioral measures were assessed—the number of solutions the participant generated, the number of unsolicited remarks (questions, opinions), the number of direct partner references, and so on. The total amount of time in the interaction was recorded as well. The results showed that the participants' behavior differed greatly according to the role assignment. In the role of *expert listener*, the participants generated more solutions to hypothetical problems, made more direct partner references, produced more unsolicited remarks, and conversed for a longer time with the confederate. Lonely or not, as *expert listeners*, they generally became more active (and interactive) than they did when assigned the role of *a person with a problem*.

These results are consistent with other results in the research literature. Schwartz and Gottman (1976) demonstrated that nonassertive people have a greater capacity to respond assertively than is sometimes evident. They compared nonassertive, moderately assertive, and highly assertive people in their ability to produce assertive responses under three experimental conditions. In each condition, the participants were asked to produce responses to a set of unreasonable demands. In the first (least threatening) condition, the participants were asked simply to *write* possible refusal responses; the task was impersonal and conducted entirely in writing. In the second condition, the participants were asked to imagine that a friend was being confronted by a set of unreasonable demands, and they were to respond orally on behalf of that friend. In the third (most threatening) condition participants were asked to imagine that the situations were real and that they themselves were being confronted with a set of unreasonable demands. The results showed that nonassertive participants were just as competent as assertive people in responding to the first two (less stressful) conditions, but they produced significantly fewer responses in the third condition. The investigators concluded that the participants' responses in the first two tasks reflected a competence to perform socially, but the stress induced by the third task interfered with their performance. Arkowitz and his colleagues (e. g., Arkowitz, Lichtenstein, McGovern, & Hines, 1975; Glasgow & Arkowitz, 1975) reported similar results comparing males who dated frequently with males who dated infrequently. When the two groups interacted with a friendly, passive, nonthreatening female partner, the difference between the groups' social behavior disappeared.

Thus, poor social performers do not necessarily lack social skills. Under special laboratory conditions they can produce the complement to their more usual behavior, and this complement is identified by the circumplex. Therefore, whenever we assess a person's interpersonal problem, we need to determine whether processes exist that are impairing an otherwise adequate performance, preventing the person from enacting the desired but unaccustomed role.

THE NATURE OF AN INTERPERSONAL PROBLEM

The Inventory of Interpersonal Problems enumerates the most common interpersonal complaints and organizes them thematically in the form of a circumplex. But what does it mean to say that a person suffers distress from this or that problem? One interpretation is that the behavior of Person A regularly clashes in some way with the behavior of Person B. For example, Person B may repeatedly dominate Person A, and Person A may feel compelled to submit, so Person A feels stuck in an intolerable complementary behavioral pattern. Or Person A may find it *difficult* to react with the complement—for example, Person B repeatedly dominates, and Person A reacts by rebelling and fighting Person B. As a result, Person A consistently experiences the tension due to noncomplementarity and therefore feels stuck in a noncomplementary pattern.

However, we cannot define an interpersonal problem as a relationship between two people's behaviors. A pattern of complementary behaviors may constitute a distressing problem for one dyad of partners but a happy state of affairs for another dyad, depending on each partner's wishes. Some people want partners who will take charge, and other people want partners who will not take charge. Therefore, any account of an interpersonal *problem* has to consider the troubled person's wishes or goals in interpersonal interactions.

Interpersonal Goals

Dryer (1993; Dryer & Horowitz, in press) regards an interpersonal problem as a discrepancy—a discrepancy between the role in a social script that Person A *would like to enact* with Person B and the role that Person A typically does enact. A person who wants friendliness but repeatedly experiences hostility is a person with an interpersonal problem. For this reason an interaction may reflect a problem from the perspective of one participant but a nonproblem from the perspective of the other.

Different reasons exist to explain why the person does not succeed in enacting the social scripts he or she wants with other people. As described previously. one possible reason is a lack of skill or know-how; the person may not know how to behave to produce the desired behavior in others. The person, for example, unwittingly may convey signals to other people that systematically invite the wrong kind of behavior. That is, the person systematically may miscommunicate his or her wishes—for example, intending to be friendly but being perceived as hostile. A second possible reason would involve a conflict: The person has the capacity to produce the desired effect (and perhaps does so with ease in his or her dreams), but in everyday life the person finds it too anxiety-arousing to behave in ways that would produce the desired behavior. A third possible reason is that the person, out of habit, keeps entering the same familiar role in a social script and routinely observes the same familiar (but undesired) outcome.

Whatever the reason for the problem, the person's goals or wishes would seem to be at odds with the social script that plays itself out. For this reason we can understand a person's interpersonal problems only if we first assess the person's interpersonal goals or wishes and determine whether the behavior of the person's partner fulfills those goals.

The Inventory of Interpersonal Goals

We therefore developed a new measure, the Inventory of Interpersonal Goals (IIG), to assess a person's interpersonal goals. In developing this instrument, we first identified a sample of items that spanned the interpersonal domain, using other interpersonal measures as a guide (Horowitz et al., 1988; Kiesler, 1983; Strong & Hills, 1986). Items were considered acceptable only if they were endorsed by many people on pilot versions and "clearly and unambiguously [described] just one major goal" (Ford & Nichols, 1991, p. 72). The resulting 51 items were presented as a questionnaire that asked respondents to "imagine that you are working with another person on a task that is important to you." Each item had the stem: "It would be important to me to . . . ." Respondents indicated their agreement with each item by circling one of five numbers from 0 to 4, with 0 indicating "No, definitely not," 2 indicating "Hard to say; it depends," and 4 indicating "Yes, definitely." The format of the questionnaire and the wording of the items were based on the Assessment of Personal Goals (APG: Ford & Nichols, 1991). The questionnaire was administered to 205 Stanford undergraduate students as part of a battery of questionnaires. We followed the procedure used by other investigators (e.g., Alden et al., 1990) to generate eight 4-item subscales that met the criteria of a circumplex: Participants' responses to the items were ipsatized and standardized, and the item intercorrelations were subjected to a principal components analysis. The first principal component was interpreted as dominance goals and the second principal component as affiliation goals. Next, each of each 51 items was plotted in a two-dimensional space, using each item's loadings on each of the first two principal components. The four items having the highest communality within each 45° octant of the resulting plot formed a subscale. The items in each of the eight subscales are listed in Table 1. Subscale scores were calculated for each respondent by adding together the scores of the four items in each of the eight subscales.

We also computed, for each participant, a composite score for the dominance goals by weighting each subscale score by its theoretical coor-

TABLE 1
Subscales of the Interpersonal Goals Inventory

When I am working on a task with someone, it is important to me to:

(PA) Dominant goals	be self-confident be firm when I need to be say "no" to the other person when appropriate be aggressive when the situation calls for it
(BC) Hostile–dominant goals	not try to please the other person too much not be too gullible be assertive with the other person be aggressive without worrying about hurting the other person's feelings
(DE) Hostile goals	not trust the other person too much not be overly generous in helping the other person not put the other person's needs before my own work with the person in a way that supports my own interests
(FG) Hostile–submissive goals	not be noticed too much keep some things private from the other person not open up to my partner too much not tell personal things to my partner
(HI) Submissive goals	not fight with the other person too much not be too aggressive with the other person not argue with the other person too much allow the other person to take control
(JK) Friendly–submissive goals	put the other person's needs before my own not be too independent not be too suspicious of the other person work with the other person in a way that protects or supports the other person's interests
(LM) Friendly goals	share openly my thoughts and ideas not keep the other person at a distance too much be supportive of the other person's goals not be too cold
(NO) Friendly–dominant goals	let the other person know when I am angry confront the other person with problems that come up express my feelings to the other person directly let the other person know what I want

dinate along the dominance dimension. Following conventional procedures (e.g., Gurtman, 1991), a composite *dominance goals score* (DGS) was defined as the sum of the subscale scores each weighted by the cosine of its angular location on the interpersonal circle:

$$\text{DGS} = \text{PA} + .7\text{BC} - .7\text{FG} - \text{HI} - .7\text{JK} + .7\text{NO}$$

The value of Cronbach's alpha for these scores was 0.80, and the test–retest reliability across two testings (a 2- to 5-week interval) was 0.79. A high DGS indicates that taking charge of interactions is important to the respondent, and a low DGS indicates that yielding to the partner is important to the respondent. Some people are quite clear in wanting to feel in charge, whereas others are quite clear in wanting other people to take charge.

Dryer (1993) selected female participants who had high or low dominance goals and paired them randomly. The participants worked together in dyads on a laboratory problem-solving task, the Desert Survival Problem (Lafferty & Eady, 1974), which requires participants to imagine themselves in the following situation: Their airplane has crash-landed in the middle of a desert, and several items may be rescued from the plane before it is consumed in flames (e.g., a mirror, a map, two raincoats). The participants must rank-order the items such that the item most important to survival is ranked first, the second most important item is ranked second, and so on. First the participants completed the task separately and then they worked on the task together. They were told that an optimal solution to the problem existed and that any partners who produced this optimal solution would receive a $100 bonus. (None did.)

During their interaction, a prerecorded voice periodically instructed the participants to rate their satisfaction with the interaction. To indicate their ratings, they pressed buttons built into the table in front of them. Each participant could see her own but not her partner's buttons. They had 16 minutes to solve the problem, and the prerecorded voice instructed them to rate their satisfaction at the beginning of the problem and then every 4 minutes. The voice also indicated how much time was remaining.

Three research assistants, who were aware neither of the hypotheses nor of the participants' self-rated goals, later viewed the videotapes and rated the dominance of the participants' behaviors. They were instructed to consider certain specific behaviors as evidence of dominance (advice-giving, criticizing, focusing on one's own beliefs, expressing self-confidence) and other specific behaviors as evidence of submissiveness (self-criticizing, deferring, focusing on their partner's beliefs, expressing self-doubt).

Then a 2 × 2 matrix was prepared, classifying each participant according to her own interaction goals (dominant or submissive) and her partner's actual behavior (dominant or submissive). The interaction between the two factors was the only significant source of variance. Participants with dominant goals interacting with (behaviorally) submissive partners and participants with submissive goals interacting with (behaviorally) dominant partners both expressed satisfaction with the interaction, whereas participants in the other conditions expressed dissatisfaction.

These results demonstrate the importance of the match between the goals of one partner and the behavior of the other in determining their satisfaction. When they match, the partners are more satisfied with the interaction. Perhaps satisfaction could be predicted just as well from other interpretations of complementarity—that is, from the complementarity between the two partners' behaviors or from the complementarity between their goals. To test these alternate interpretations, we first examined the complementarity of the participants' goals. A 2×2 matrix was prepared, classifying each participant according to her own interaction goals (dominant or submissive) and her partner's interaction goals (dominant or submissive). An analysis of variance performed on the satisfaction scores showed that all effects were nonsignificant. Then we examined the complementarity of the participants' behaviors. A 2×2 matrix was prepared, classifying each participant according to her own behavior (dominant or submissive) and her partner's behavior (dominant or submissive). The interaction effect was only marginally significant. Thus, the clearest predictor of satisfaction was the match between a participant's goals and her partner's behavior. For example, there were highly satisfied dyads in which both participants said that they wanted their partner to take charge, and both partners did (behaviorally) take charge. Although their motives seemed to have clashed (and their behaviors also seemed to have clashed), both partners were satisfied and happy with the interaction. The important match was between the stated *wishes* of one and the behavior of the other.

An Example of a Mismatch: The Rejection of Depressed Others

Over time people may become frustrated by their interactions with depressed others. Gotlib and Robinson (1982) noted that within the first 3 minutes of interacting with a depressed person, research participants came to smile less and fidget more than they did with a nondepressed person; their speech became more monotonous, and the content of their conversation became more negative. We believe that these changes arise from the incongruence between the interpersonal goals of one and the actual behavior of the other when depressed and nondepressed partners interact. If the goals of one partner (described by a circumplex) are not compatible with the behavior of the other partner (also described by a circumplex), a mismatch occurs, and the partner whose goals are frustrated will be dissatisfied. To use the terminology of Jefferson and Lee (1992), people would be dissatisfied if they wanted a troubles-telling exchange (implying equality along the vertical axis) but found their partner engaged in a service encounter (implying contrasting positions along the vertical axis). (And when the service-provider observed the partner's dissatisfaction and rejection of the service, he or she would become dissatisfied as well.)

Many researchers have examined a depressed person's impact on a nondepressed partner. Notarius and Herrick (1988), for example, had female participants interact with a female confederate partner, telling each participant beforehand that her partner had been feeling down and blue, so she should be a good person for her partner to talk to. During the conversation the confederate described her unhappiness over having been rejected by her boyfriend. The interaction lasted 15 minutes, and the participant also rated her own mood and reaction. Each response that the participant produced during the conversation was identified and coded. Reactions were classified as: (a) advice-giving (e.g., "If you call your boyfriend, you'll feel better."); (b) distraction (the participants changed the topic, joked, or engaged in irrelevant chit-chat); (c) supportive listening (e.g., "That must have been rough."); (d) sympathetic commiseration (e.g., "I've had that experience myself."); (e) reflective comments regarding the depressed person's cognitions and affects (e.g., "Everyone feels badly when they break up."). The relative frequencies of these reactions, respectively, were: .43, .13, .10, .13, and .20.

Each participant's most salient type of reaction was noted, and the participants were classified into two groups. These who generated the controlling reactions described by categories (a) and (b) comprised one group [Group C (for "controlling")], and those who generated the noncontrolling reactions of categories (c), (d), and (e) comprised another group (Group N). The results showed that the participants in Group C reported more negative affect after the interaction and expressed less willingness to interact further with their partners.

We believe that a person who offers advice to a depressed partner (friendly–dominance) is providing a service encounter that initially invites the depressed partner to respond with *friendly* yielding. If the partner does not, then the advice-giver's goals are frustrated. This frustration may explain why dominating others often find interactions with depressed partners aversive and why they reject depressed people as partners (Coyne, 1976a, 1976b; Gotlib & Beatty, 1985; Hammen & Peters, 1978; Hinchcliffe et al., 1978; Howes & Hokanson, 1979; Lowenstein, 1984; Robbins, Strack, & Coyne, 1979; Salzman, 1975; Strack & Coyne, 1983; Winer, Bonner, Blaney, & Murray, 1981).

The interpersonal goals of nondepressed people apparently are not fulfilled by a depressed partner. However, a depressed partner still might satisfy the interpersonal goals of other depressed people. Locke and Horowitz (1990) studied same-gender dyads in which the two partners were (a) both dysphoric, (b) both nondysphoric, or (c) mixed. The participants received a list of self-relevant topics of conversation—half were positive (e.g., "things I like about my mother") and half were negative (e.g., "what I am most afraid of"). They had to talk on different topics for about 90 seconds each. First, one partner spoke, then the other, then the first, and so on. After each turn, the participants rated their degree of satisfaction with the interaction. All interactions were recorded on videotape. The results showed that participants were far more satisfied with the interaction when their partners were like themselves (both were dysphoric, or both were nondysphoric). Mixed dyads were less satisfied. Participants in the homogeneous dyads also rated their partners as warmer. Furthermore, as the interaction progressed, dysphoric participants in the mixed (less satisfied) dyads came to select more negative topics (e.g., "how often I have spells of the blues and what they are about"). A dysphoric person's interpersonal wishes (e.g., not to be dominated) apparently are better satisfied by another dysphoric person than by a nondysphoric person.

These findings highlight the subtlety contained in comments that are offered as social support for a person in distress. Goldsmith (1994) has related the communications that we call social support to Brown and Levinson's (1987) theory of *politeness*. According to this theory, two interacting partners want each other (a) to accept the self-image that they are each trying to project and (b) to allow each other freedom of action and freedom from imposition—conditions that are relevant to the two interpersonal dimensions of friendliness and dominance. Thus, for example, when one partner makes a request of the other, that request puts an imposition on the other partner. In the same way, when one partner criticizes the other partner, the criticism implies a nonacceptance as well as an imposition to change. When one partner gives advice to the other partner, the advice-giving also implies nonacceptance and an imposition to change. Therefore, to help a partner save face, conventional linguistic forms exist that either emphasize positive esteem for the listener (friendliness) or deny an intent to dominate (or both). A "bald on record" piece of advice (Brown & Levinson, 1987) is advice without any face-saving elements. For example, a speaker might say to a person who failed an examination, "Go talk to your professor about the exam you failed" (Message M). The advice is clear, direct, and efficient; it implies that the addressee should change, and it imposes a directive on the person toward action. However, the same message (M) could be embedded in various verbal frames that would help the person save face. Some examples are, "You are an excellent student and this experience is atypical, so (do M)"; "I don't know if this would work, but maybe you could (do M)"; and "I know someone else in your position who found it helpful to (do M)."

Goldsmith (1994) has described a procedure for examining the impact of different frames in helping the listener save face. Her results suggest that frames like these clearly influence the impact of a message. Goldsmith's procedure varied the message (M) as well as the linguistic frame unsystematically, but the procedure could be modified to keep M constant, while the frame alone was varied. Then the resulting communications could be rated and located within a two-dimensional interpersonal circumplex to characterize the impact of each frame. That is a goal of our future research.

CONCLUSION

Interpersonal problems are best understood by comparing the person's interpersonal wishes (goals) with the person's interpersonal behaviors. All three of these constructs—interpersonal problems, interpersonal goals, and interpersonal behaviors—can be described succinctly in terms of a two-dimensional circumplex. To clarify their relationship to each other, our chapter has proposed four propositions. The first is that the two underlying dimensions of each circumplex can be characterized as (a) affiliation, nurturance, or communion and (b) dominance, influence, or control. The second proposition is that each interpersonal behavior invites a particular class of reactions (the complement), and the relationship between an interpersonal action and its complement is also defined by the circumplex: Complementary behaviors are similar with respect to affiliation but reciprocal with respect to dominance. The third proposition is that noncomplementarity creates a palpable interpersonal tension between the two interacting partners.

To determine whether a familiar sequence is problematic for a person, we need to consider the person's interpersonal goals. If the person's interpersonal goals are satisfied, the behavioral sequence (complementary or not) is nonproblematic. Goals fail to be satisfied for two general reasons. At times the person produces the invited complement too readily (e.g., to avoid the tension of noncomplementarity); in that case the person is dissatisfied because the complementary behavior is not congruent with the person's interpersonal goals. At other times the person produces noncomplementary reactions too readily, generating the unpleasant tension of non-complementarity (e.g., in distressed marriages).

Various reasons exist to explain why people are unsuccessful in satisfying their interpersonal goals. One possibility is that the person lacks some form of social skill or know-how. Although people do sometimes lack a particular social skill that results in an interpersonal problem, a more common reason is that the person experiences an inhibition over manifesting an existing skill. For example, the person may be uncomfortable enacting one of the roles in a well-learned interpersonal sequence. According to our final proposition, a person who regularly performs one role in a well-learned script has acquired the competence to perform the other role as well, though the person may fear the consequences of his or her behavior and therefore may refrain from exercising that competence. In such a case the person would need help in overcoming an inhibition rather than overcoming a skill deficit. Together, these propositions may clarify the meaning of an interpersonal problem so that future research can systematize therapeutic interventions and coordinate them with each patient's individual needs.

REFERENCES

Alden, L. E., Wiggins, J. S., & Pincus, A. L. (1990). Construction of circumplex scales for the Inventory of Interpersonal Problems. *Journal of Personality Assessment, 55*, 521–536.

Altman, J. H., & Wittenborn, J. R. (1980). Depression-prone personality in women. *Journal of Abnormal Psychology, 89*, 303–308.

Angyal, A. (1941). *Foundations for a science of personality.* New York: Commonwealth Fund and Harvard University Press.

Arkowitz, H., Lichtenstein, E., McGovern, K., & Hines, P. (1975). The behavioral assessment of social competence in males. *Behavior Therapy, 6*, 3–13.

Bagdanoff, J. (1995). *Listener response style and affect in interactions with a depressed other.* Senior Honor's Thesis, Stanford University, Stanford, CA.

Bakan, D. (1966). *The duality of human existence.* Boston: Beacon Press.

Bandura, A. (1977). Self-efficacy: Toward a unifying theory of behavioral change. *Psychological Review, 84*, 191–215.

Bandura, A. (1978). The self system in reciprocal determinism. *American Psychologist, 33*, 344–358.

Bandura, A. (1982). Self-efficacy mechanism in human agency. *American Psychologist, 37*, 122–147.

Bartholomew, K. (1990). Avoidance of intimacy: An attachment perspective. *Journal of Social and Personal Relationships, 7*, 147–178.

Bartholomew, K., & Horowitz, L. M. (1991). Attachment styles among young adults: A test of a model. *Journal of Personality and Social Psychology, 61*, 226–244.

Beck, A. T. (1967). *Depression: Clinical, experimental, and theoretical aspects.* New York: Hoeber.

Bellack, A. S., & Morrison, R. L. (1982). Interpersonal dysfunction. In A. S. Bellack, M. Hersen, & A. E. Kazdin (Ed.), *International handbook of behavior modification and therapy* (pp. 717–747). New York: Plenum Press.

Benjamin, L. S. (1974). Structural analysis of social behavior. *Psychological Review, 81*, 392–425.

Benjamin, L. S. (1986). Adding social and intrapsychic descriptors to Axis I of *DSM-III.* In T. Millon & G. Klerman (Eds.), *Contemporary issues in psychopathology* (pp. 599–638). New York: Guilford Press.

Berzins, J. I. (1977). Therapist–patient matching. In A. S. Gurman & A. M. Razin (Eds.), *Effective psychotherapy* (pp. 221–251). New York: Pergamon Press.

Bierman, R. (1969). Dimensions of interpersonal facilitation in psychotherapy and child development. *Psychological Bulletin, 72*, 338–352.

Birchler, G., Weiss, R., & Vincent, J. (1975). Multimethod analysis of social reinforcement exchange between maritally distressed and nondistressed spouse and stranger dyads. *Journal of Personality and Social Psychology, 31*, 349–360.

Blatt, S. J. (1990). Interpersonal relatedness and self-definition: Two personality configurations and their implications for psychopathology and psychotherapy. In J. L. Singer (Ed.), *Repression and dissociation*. Chicago: University of Chicago Press.

Blatt, S. J., & Schichman, S. (1983). Two primary configurations of psychopathology. *Psychoanalysis and Contemporary Thought, 6,* 187–254.

Bluhm, C., Widiger, T. A., & Miele, G. M. (1990). Interpersonal complementarity and individual differences. *Journal of Personality and Social Psychology, 58,* 464–471.

Blumberg, S. R., & Hokanson, J. E. (1983). The effects of another person's response style on interpersonal behavior in depression. *Journal of Abnormal Psychology, 92,* 196–209.

Bowlby, J. (1973). *Attachment and loss, Vol. 2: Separation.* New York: Basic Books.

Brennan, T. (1982). Loneliness at adolescence. In L. A. Peplau & D. Perlman (Eds.), *Loneliness: A sourcebook of current theory, research and therapy*. New York: Wiley.

Brown, P., & Levinson, S. (1987). *Politeness: Some universals in language usage.* New York: Cambridge University Press.

Carson, R. C. (1969). *Interaction concepts of personality.* Chicago: Aldine.

Chelune, G. J., Sultan, F. E., & Williams, C. L. (1980). Loneliness, self-disclosure, and interpersonal effectiveness. *Journal of Counseling Psychology, 27,* 462–468.

Coates, D., & Wortman, C. B. (1980). Depression maintenance and interpersonal control. In A. Baum & J. E. Singer (Eds.), *Advances in environmental psychology* (pp. 149–182). Hillsdale, NJ: Lawrence Erlbaum.

Cofer, D. H., & Wittenborn, J. R. (1980). Personality characteristics of formerly depressed women. *Journal of Abnormal Psychology, 89,* 309–314.

Coyne, J. (1976a). Depression and the response of others. *Journal of Abnormal Psychology, 85,* 186–193.

Coyne, J. (1976b). Toward an interactional description of depression. *Psychiatry, 39,* 28–39.

Coyne, J. C., Aldwin, C., & Lazarus, R. S. (1981). Depression and coping in stressful episodes. *Journal of Abnormal Psychology, 90,* 439–447.

DeVoge, J., & Beck, S. (1978). The therapist–client relationship in behavior therapy. In M. Hersen, R. M. Eisler, & P. M. Miller (Eds.), *Progress in behavior modification* (Vol. 6, pp. 204–248). New York: Academic Press.

Dryer, D. C. (1993). *Interpersonal goals and satisfaction with interactions.* Unpublished doctoral dissertation, Stanford University, Stanford, CA.

Dryer, D. C., & Horowitz, L. M. (in press). When do opposites attract? Interpersonal complementarity versus similarity. *Journal of Personality and Social Psychology*.

Erikson, E. H. (1963). *Childhood and Society* (2nd ed.). New York: W. W. Norton.

Ford, M. E., & Nichols, C. W. (1991). Using goal assessments to identify motivational patterns and facilitate behavioral regulation and achievement. *Advances in Motivation and Achievement, 7*, 51–85.

French, R. deS. (1981). *Interpersonal problem-solving skill in lonely people.* Unpublished doctoral dissertation, Stanford University, Stanford, CA.

Gerson, A. C., & Perlman, D. (1979). Loneliness and expressive communication. *Journal of Abnormal Psychology, 88*, 258–261.

Glasgow, R. E., & Arkowitz, H. (1975). The behavioral assessment of male and female social competence in dyadic heterosexual interactions. *Behavior Therapy, 6*, 488–498.

Goldsmith, D. J. (1994). The role of facework in supportive communication. In B. R. Burleson, T. L. Albrecht, & I. G. Sarason (Eds.), *Communication of social support* (pp. 29–49). Thousand Oaks, CA: Sage.

Gotlib, I. H., & Beatty, M. (1985). Negative responses to depression: The role of attributional style. *Cognitive Therapy and Research, 9*, 91–103.

Gotlib, I. H., & Robinson, L. A. (1982). Responses to depressed individuals: Discrepancies between self-report and observer-rated behavior. *Journal of Abnormal Psychology, 91*, 231–240.

Gottman, J. M. (1979). *Marital interaction: Experimental investigations.* New York: Academic Press.

Gottman, J. M. (1980). Consistency of nonverbal affect and affect reciprocity in marital interaction. *Journal of Consulting and Clinical Psychology, 48*, 711–717.

Grinker, R. R. (1964). Communications by patients in depressive states. *Archives of General Psychiatry, 10*, 576–580.

Gurtman, M. B. (1991). Evaluating the interpersonalness of personality scales. *Personality and Social Psychology Bulletin, 17*, 670–677.

Gurtman, M. B. (1992a). Construct validity of interpersonal personality measures: The interpersonal circumplex as a nomological net. *Journal of Personality and Social Psychology, 63*, 105–118.

Gurtman, M. B. (1992b). Trust, distrust, and interpersonal problems: A circumplex analysis. *Journal of Personality and Social Psychology, 62*, 989–1002.

Guttman, L. (1954). A new approach to factor analysis: The radex. In P. R. Lazarsfeld, *Mathematical thinking in the social sciences* (pp. 258–348). Glencoe, IL: Free Press.

Hammen, C., & Peters, S. D. (1978). Interpersonal consequences of depression: Responses to men and women enacting a depressed role. *Journal of Abnormal Psychology, 87*, 322–332.

Hansson, R. O., & Jones, W. H. (1981). Loneliness, cooperation, and conformity among American undergraduates. *Journal of Social Psychology, 115*, 103–108.

Hinchcliffe, M. K., Hooper, D., & Roberts, J. F. (1978). *The melancholy marriage: Depression in marriage and psychosocial approaches to therapy.* New York: Wiley.

Hokanson, J. E., Sacco, W. P., Blumberg, S. R., & Landrum, G. C. (1980). Interpersonal behavior of depressive individuals in a mixed-motive game. *Journal of Abnormal Psychology, 89,* 320–332.

Horney, K. (1945). *Our inner conflicts.* New York: Norton.

Horowitz, L. M. (1979). On the cognitive structure of interpersonal problems treated in psychotherapy. *Journal of Consulting and Clinical Psychology, 47, 1,* 5–15.

Horowitz, L. M., & French, R. deS. (1979). Interpersonal problems of people who describe themselves as lonely. *Journal of Consulting and Clinical Psychology, 57,* 762–764.

Horowitz, L. M., French, R. deS., & Anderson, C. A. (1982). The prototype of a lonely person. In L. Peplau & D. Perlman (Eds.), *Loneliness: A sourcebook of current theory, research, and therapy* (pp. 183–205). New York: Wiley Interscience.

Horowitz, L. M., Locke, K. D., Morse, M. B., Waikar, S. V., Dryer, D. C., Tarnow, E., & Ghannam, J. (1991). Self-derogations and the interpersonal theory. *Journal of Personality and Social Psychology, 61,* 68–79.

Horowitz, L. M., Rosenberg, S. E., Baer, B. A., Ureño, G., & Villaseñor, V. S. (1988). Inventory of interpersonal problems: Psychometric properties and clinical applications. *Journal of Consulting and Clinical Psychology, 56,* 885–892.

Horowitz, L. M., & Vitkus, J. (1986). The interpersonal basis of psychiatric symptoms. *Clinical Psychology Review, 6,* 443–469.

Horowitz, L. M., Weckler, D. A., & Doren, R. (1983). Interpersonal problems and symptoms: A cognitive approach. In P. Kendall (Ed.), *Advances in cognitive–behavioral research and therapy* (pp. 81–125). London: Academic Press.

Howes, M. J., & Hokanson, J. E. (1979). Conversational and social responses to depressive interpersonal behavior. *Journal of Abnormal Psychology, 88,* 625–634.

Jefferson, G., & Lee, J. R. E. (1992). The rejection of advice: Managing the problematic convergence of a "troubles-telling" and a "service encounter." In P. Drew & J. Heritage (Eds.), *Talk at work* (pp. 521–571). Cambridge: Cambridge University Press.

Jones, W. H., Freeman, J. W., & Goswick, R. A. (1981). The persistence of loneliness: Self and other determinants. *Journal of Personality, 49,* 27–48.

Jones, W. H., Hobbs, S. A., & Hockenbury, D. (1982). Loneliness and social skill deficits. *Journal of Personality and Social Psychology, 42,* 682–689.

Kiesler, D. J. (1983). The 1982 interpersonal circle: A taxonomy for complementarity in human transactions. *Psychological Review, 90,* 185–214.

Krasnoperova, E. N., & Horowitz, L. M. (1995). *Responses to men's and women's troubles-telling: Effects of type of trouble and the gender of the recipient.* Stanford–Berkeley Talks, Berkeley, CA.

Lafferty, J., & Eady, P. (1974). *The desert survival problem*. Plymouth, MI: Experimental Learning Methods.

LaForge, R., & Suczek, R. F. (1955). The interpersonal domain of personality: 3. An interpersonal check list. *Journal of Personality, 24*, 94–112.

Leary, T. F. (1957). *Interpersonal diagnosis of personality: A functional theory and methodology for personality evaluation*. New York: Ronald Press.

Locke, K. D., & Horowitz, L. M. (1990). Satisfaction in interpersonal interactions as a function of similarity in level of dysphoria. *Journal of Personality and Social Psychology, 58*, 823–831.

Lowenstein, E. (1984). *Social perceptions of the depressed person: The effects of perceived responsibility and response to advice*. Unpublished doctoral dissertation, Stanford University, Stanford, CA.

Margolin, G., & Wampold, B. E. (1981). Sequential analysis of conflict and accord in distressed and nondistressed marital partners. *Journal of Consulting and Clinical Psychology, 47*, 554–567.

Notarius, C. I., & Herrick, L. R. (1988). Listener response strategies to a distressed other. *Journal of Social and Personal Relationships, 5*, 97–108.

Orford, J. (1986). The rules of interpersonal complementarity: Does hostility beget hostility and dominance, submission? *Psychological Review, 93*, 365–377.

Robbins, B., Strack, S., & Coyne, J. (1979). Willingness to provide feedback to depressed persons. *Social Behavior and Personality, 7*, 199–203.

Salzman, L. (1975). Interpersonal factors in depression. In F. F. Flack & S. C. Draghi (Eds.), *The nature and treatment of depression* (pp. 43–56). New York: Wiley.

Schwartz, R. M., & Gottman, J. M. (1976). Toward a task analysis of assertive behavior. *Journal of Consulting and Clinical Psychology, 44*, 910–920.

Solano, C. H., Batten, P. G., & Parish, E. A. (1982). Loneliness and patterns of self-disclosure. *Journal of Personality and Social Psychology, 43*, 524–531.

Strack, S., & Coyne, J. C. (1983). Social confirmation of dysphoria: Shared and private reactions to depression. *Journal of Personality and Social Psychology, 44*, 798–806.

Strong, S. R., & Hills, H. I. (1986). *Interpersonal Communication Rating Scale*. Richmond: Virginia Commonwealth University.

Strong, S. R., Hills, H. I., Kilmartin, C. T., DeVries, H., Lanier, K., Nelson, B. N., Strickland, D., III, & Meyer, C. W. (1988). The dynamic relations among interpersonal behaviors: A test of complementarity and anticomplementarity. *Journal of Personality and Social Psychology, 54*, 798–810.

Sullivan, H. S. (1953). *The interpersonal theory of psychiatry*. New York: Norton.

Vitkus, J., & Horowitz, L. M. (1987). Poor social performance of lonely people: Lacking a skill or adopting a role? *Journal of Personality and Social Psychology, 52*, 1266–1273.

Watzlawick, P., Weakland, J., & Fisch, R. (1974). *Change: Principles of problem formation and problem resolution*. New York: Norton.

Wiggins, J. S. (1982). Circumplex models of interpersonal behavior in clinical psychology. In P. C. Kendall & J. N. Butcher (Eds.), *Handbook of research methods in clinical psychology* (pp. 183–221). New York: Wiley.

Winer, D. L., Bonner, T. O., Blaney, P. H., & Murray, E. J. (1981). Depression and social attraction. *Motivation and Emotion, 5*, 153–166.

16

THE CIRCUMPLEX IN
PSYCHOTHERAPY RESEARCH

WILLIAM P. HENRY

I became acquainted with circumplex models after I joined Dr. Hans Strupp's psychotherapy research team at Vanderbilt in 1982 in pursuit of my PhD in clinical psychology. At the time, the team was preparing a large grant, which came to be known as the Vanderbilt II project (Henry, Strupp, Butler, Schacht, & Binder, 1993; Henry, Schacht, Strupp, Butler, & Binder, 1993; Strupp, 1993)—the study of the effects of manual-guided training on the process and outcome of time-limited dynamic psychotherapy (TLDP; Strupp & Binder, 1984). While planning this project, we had many debates about the state of psychodynamic research and how it might be improved. Two themes seemed to recur. The first was the problem that most research groups tended to develop and use their own in-house measures for key constructs (such as the alliance, psychodynamic techniques, etc.). Although similar, there was often enough difference in both content and procedure among these measures to make direct aggregation of research results across studies difficult. The second was that despite the field's historical emphasis on theoretical depth and coherence (going back to Freud, who frequently revised his theories to retain internal consistency), psychodynamic treatment research itself often seemed to lack the same level of integration. For example, problems might be defined as certain *DSM* diagnoses, process measures might reflect simple frequency counts of categorical interventions (such as transference interpretations), and outcomes might be measured in terms of changes on certain Minnesota Multiphasic Personality Inventory (MMPI) scales. Why should this mixed bag of variables, representing different levels of abstraction, measurement operations, and sources, necessarily relate to one another in a patterned way?

Thus we came to focus increasingly on the idea of problem–treatment–outcome congruence (Strupp, Schacht, & Henry, 1988) as a guiding principle for research. This relatively simple idea that a patient's problems, the treatment processes, and the clinical outcomes ideally should be measured in a common, theoretically meaningful metric had long been a standard in behavioral (and some cognitive) research. However, the more abstract and intrapsychic nature of psychodynamic variables made this goal much more difficult to realize. We decided to tackle this problem by adopting Benjamin's Structural Analysis of Social Behavior system (Benjamin, 1974) as a central measure of each of the three problem–treatment–outcome phases. Structural Analysis of Social Behavior (SASB) (described in greater detail in a following section) is a three surface circumplex system that measures transitive interpersonal actions toward another, intransitive interpersonal reactions to another, and introjected acts (behaviors by the self toward the self). It seemed ideal for our purposes because: (a) it provided an interpersonal theoretical framework that was consistent with psychotherapy the interpersonal focus, and (b) it offered a set of precise, concretely operationalized measurement operations encompassing both independent and self-report perspectives. Specifically, SASB held the promise of problem–treatment–outcome congruence by providing a common, unified metric with which to conceptualize, describe, and measure a patient's cyclic maladaptive patterns (CMP), the dyadic process in therapy (a chief focus of time–limited dynamic psychotherapy training), and the interpersonal and intrapsychic outcomes of primary interest to a psychodynamic therapy that was not aimed solely at symptom reduction. Most importantly, SASB, and the circumplex tradition on which it was based, enabled a set of hypotheses to link theoretically a patient's historical experiences with contemporary interpersonal problems and intrapsychic structure. In short, the SASB circumplex provided a type of operational rigor and theoretical coherence that I had been looking for.

In this chapter I would like to summarize some of my own research history with the circumplex—SASB in this case—and attempt to show how the use of the circumplex has (a) provided a common measurement metric allowing problem–treatment–outcome congruence, (b) encouraged the more meaningful aggregation of research results over time, (c) enabled the emergence of theoretical models of psychopathology and psychotherapy, and (d) been the basis for new measurement instruments to test and refine these theories. To me, one of the most important arguments in favor of the circumplex has to do with the issue of description versus explanation versus prediction; although often confused (at least tacitly) in the empirical literature on personality and psychotherapy, they are not the same thing. It is not a difficult matter, statistically speaking, to *describe* one set of constructs in terms of another—particularly when the constructs compared are sufficiently broad (such as *neuroticism*). For example, there are certainly no dearth of studies that indicate significant modest correlations between the Big Five factor of Neuroticism and the diagnosis of neuroticism (e.g., Trull, 1992). However, I believe that circumplex models (SASB in particular) hold promise not only for description but also for *explanation* and *prediction*. I will begin with a brief description of the SASB model on which much of my research rests.

THE STRUCTURAL ANALYSIS OF SOCIAL BEHAVIOR

The Structural Analysis of Social Behavior (SASB) is an interpersonal circumplex system that is based on, but expands, Leary's original interpersonal circumplex (Leary, 1957). The traditional interpersonal circumplex contains two orthogonal axes—a horizontal affiliation axis that runs from hate on the left to love on the right and a vertical control axis that runs from control to submission. Benjamin (1974) reasoned that the control–submission axis was only one form of the overall control or interdependence construct in interpersonal behavior (e.g., enmeshment). To describe fully interpersonal behavior, one also must consider behaviors involving not only enmeshment but also differentiation (autonomy-granting and autonomy-taking). In other words, autonomy is not simply the neutral point between control and submission but a separate dimension. To incorporate the two interdependence dimensions (enmeshment and differentiation) required the creation of two separate interpersonal circumplexes. In SASB, Surface 1 (focus on other) represents transitive actions by one person toward another, whereas Surface 2 (focus on self) describes intransitive or reactive behaviors by an individual. Both surfaces contain the same horizontal affiliation axis, which, like Leary's, moves from hostile disaffiliation on the left to friendly affiliation on the right. When the focus is on actions toward another the vertical interdependence dimension moves from autonomy-granting at the top to controlling behavior at the bottom. When the focus is on the self, the reactive interdependence axis moves from autonomy-taking or separation at the top to submission at the bottom. Benjamin also added a third surface—the introject, which theoretically represents Surface 1 actions by early important others transformed to become actions by the self toward the self (e.g., self-acceptance, self-criticism, self-control, etc.). This three-surface circumplex is illustrated in figure 1.

The three-surface circumplex structure enables precise explanation and predictions of both interpersonal and intrapsychic behavior as well as theoretically linking historical and ongoing interpersonal transactions to

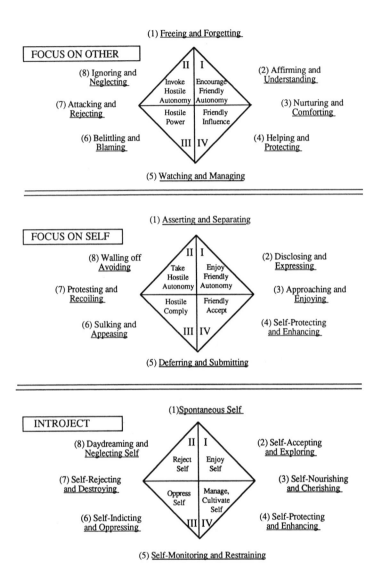

Figure 1. The SASB circumplex system. Adapted from "An Interpersonal Approach," by L. Banjamin, 1987, Journal of Personality Disorders, Vol. 1, No. 4, p. 335. Copyright 1987 by the Guilford Press. Adapted by permission.

self-concept and symptom presentation. The explanatory and predictive principles drawn from interpersonal theory include the concepts of introjection, complementarity, and antithesis. *Introjection* refers to Sullivan's (1953) basic postulate that the self is comprised of the reflective appraisals of others. That is, our self-concept and manner of acting toward ourselves mirrors how we have been treated by important figures during our development. Thus, a history of being blamed extensively becomes a pattern of introjected self-blame. The introject, though thought to be formed relatively early, is not immutable. However, it tends to remain relatively stable over time via the mechanism of interpersonal complementarity. The principle of *complementarity* states that interpersonal actions tend to pull for responses that are similar on each axis. In the case of SASB, friendliness pulls for friendliness, hostility pulls for hostility, dominance pulls for submission, and autonomy-granting pulls for autonomy-taking. The adult with a long history of being criticized as a child comes to expect it and acts in a manner that pulls for it, creating a self-fulfilling prophecy that confirms a stable introject. The principles of introjection and complementarity combined help theoretically to explain how early experiences transform into adult behavioral patterns (adaptive as well as maladaptive) and enable prediction of future behavior. The antithesis of a behavior is the opposite of its complement, located directly across from (at 180° to) the complement on the circumplex. In other words, the antithesis is opposite on both the affiliation and interdependence dimensions. In theory, responding with antithetical behavior to any given interpersonal action or reaction by another produces the maximum pull for behavior change in the other person.

The SASB system may be used in different methodological ways and at varying levels of measurement specificity. It may be used by independent raters to code ongoing interpersonal process between or among individuals or to code the interpersonal content of the spoken dialogue. There is also a self-report version, the Intrex Questionnaire (Benjamin, 1983), which allows individuals to make ratings of any relationship (such as a current significant other, mother during childhood, or the introject—how the person acts toward himself or herself). These relationships may be rated twice—in the perceived best and worst state of the relationship. The SASB system itself, regardless of the use to which it is put, may be employed at varying levels of specificity. The full model contains 36 points around each circumplex surface, whereas the cluster model (the one typically used) collapses these 36 points into eight clusters. The simplest form of the model contains four quadrants on each surface. In short, the SASB system is quite flexible in terms of what can be measured, the perspective of the ratings, and the specificity of the codes.

Using the Circumplex to Measure Therapeutic Process

I initially used SASB as a purely descriptive system in an effort to study more precisely the therapeutic alliance (Henry, Schacht, & Strupp, 1986). At the time, there was general consensus that alliance or relationship factors were major predictors of successful therapeutic outcome. However, existing research procedures consisted primarily of global ratings of broadly defined variables such as "therapist warmth," summarizing fairly long time intervals (15 to 20 minutes up to an entire session). Although these methods were sufficient to establish the general importance of the therapeutic relationship, they suffered from a number of inherent weaknesses: (a) general lack of a rigorous theoretical base; (b) patient and therapist behaviors typically were rated separately, relatively free of the momentary, reciprocal dyadic context; (c) because of the large rating units and global judgments, the measures tended to require high inference and have low specificity; and (d) they did not isolate specific therapist actions or statements that might contribute to a poor alliance.

SASB was able to overcome these limitations because rating units were small—consisting of a sentence or less—which permitted lower summary inference and higher behavioral specificity. This in turn allowed specific therapist statements to be isolated and studied. In addition, the interpersonal behavior of one participant could not be judged free of its momentary contextual relevance to the other participant. Finally, SASB was based on an interpersonal theory that permitted specific theoretical predictions, such as those based on the idea of interpersonal complementarity. That is, the behavior of one person theoretically pulls for a complementary response in another (correspondence on the affiliation dimension—hostility pulls for hostility—and complementarity on the interdependence dimension—dominance pulls for submission and autonomy-granting pulls for autonomy-taking).

Henry and colleagues (1986) explored an initial, and quite simple, question: Do therapists engage in different interpersonal behaviors in their good and poor outcome cases, despite using similar techniques? Four therapists were studied, each seeing a case with a clear-cut positive and negative outcome (drawn from a relatively homogeneous patient population of college-age men with 2-7-0 MMPI profiles [depression=psychasthenia=social introversion]). Despite the fact that a relatively small sample of dyadic interpersonal behavior was sampled (the first 15 minutes of the third of approximately 25 sessions), large, statistically significant differences in interpersonal process emerged. The results indicated that even well-trained, seasoned, doctoral-level dynamic therapists were surprisingly vulnerable to potentially damaging interpersonal process in their poor outcome cases, whereas these processes were virtually absent in the good outcome cases. In their poor outcome cases, therapists were significantly more likely to engage in hostile control (SASB Cluster 6: blaming and belittling), and less likely to offer friendly autonomy (SASB Cluster 2: affirming and understanding) or friendly control (SASB Cluster 4: helping and protecting). Patients in the low change cases were significantly more likely to take a position of hostile autonomy relative to the therapist (SASB Cluster 8: walling off and avoiding).

The preceding study provided evidence that differential outcome was correlated with differential interpersonal behavior. Because of its reliance on existing data, however, the measures of outcome (such as MMPI change) could not be directly articulated theoretically with the interpersonal process measure. Henry, Schacht, and Strupp (1990) attempted to provide a stricter test of interpersonal theory by defining outcome solely in terms of introject change as measured by the SASB Intrex questionnaire. The basic premise was provided by Sullivan (1953) who stated that the self is comprised of the *reflective appraisals* of others. That is, we tend to act toward ourselves (introjectively) as early significant others acted toward us. For example, blame is introjected as self-blame. In theory, the introject is malleable, being constantly recreated through our ongoing interpersonal transactions. However, the introject tends to remain stable, because early experiences set up strong expectancies regarding the acts of others, and these expectancies may result in perceptual distortions (i.e., transferential reactions) that create self-fulfilling prophecies via the principle of interpersonal complementarity. In other words, others are induced to behave in a way that confirms the feared expectancies, and these behaviors entrench the rigid and maladaptive introject structure. In theory, introjection of the interpersonal process of the therapist would serve to either entrench or ameliorate the patient's introject structure. This framework, operationalized by the circumplex, provided a specific theoretical rationale for the importance of the therapeutic relationship (defined directly in terms of momentary interpersonal process coded with SASB) as a *direct* change mechanism.

Henry and colleagues (1990) examined seven positive outcome cases (based on amount and direction of introject change) and seven negative outcome cases (defined as no introject change or actual deterioration). Results of the earlier study were replicated. Therapists in the bad outcome cases tended to engage in interpersonal processes that confirmed the patients' negative, self-hostile introjects, whereas therapists in the good outcome cases rarely did (instead offering almost constant ameliorative process). Although one cannot infer direct causation from these data, they are highly consistent with predictions drawn from an interpersonal theory of the alliance. It is interesting to note that the therapists' own introject predicted their interpersonal process. Therapists who were self-critical tended to be more critical toward their patients, and in turn, their patients responded with higher levels of self-criticism, completing the cycle that would be predicted theoretically.

In both studies, sequential analyses supported the principle of interpersonal complementarity as patients and therapists alike tended to respond in complementary fashion. This is noteworthy, not only theoretically but also because therapists (and in particular dynamic therapists) are traditionally schooled in the importance of *not* responding in kind to patient provocations. The data suggest that therapists do, however, and also actually initiate many of the negative sequences themselves. Finally, the high level of complex communication in poor outcome cases across both studies was notable. A complex communication is one that simultaneously communicates different (and usually contradictory) interpersonal messages. The most typical type of complex communication for therapists might be termed the *blaming interpretation*—that is, a therapist statement that was on the surface friendly–teaching (SASB Cluster 4: nurturing and protecting) but that carried a clearly blaming or critical undertone. In the case manifesting the worst clinical deterioration, more than 50% of the therapist statements were complex. The ability to measure this type of complex communication precisely is one of the great strengths of the SASB circumplex system as compared to other methodologies. On the circumplex, both parts of the interpersonal message may be plotted separately, but a global rating system would be forced to make a distinction purely along more or less affiliative lines—losing the information of the specific nature of the transaction.

In these process studies, the SASB circumplex: (a) enabled the identification of specific types of therapist statements that were likely countertherapeutic; (b) provided a theoretical rationale and supporting evidence for a mechanism by which the therapeutic relationship serves as a direct change mechanism or common factor; and (c) demonstrated the pervasiveness of negative complementary interpersonal process, even in a context that is supposedly created to provide just the opposite experience for the patient. By using an interpersonal circumplex approach to measurement, these studies were able to provide a level of description, explanation, and prediction. The interested reader is referred to Henry and Strupp (1994), which details a complete common factors model of psychotherapy process and outcome based on the crucial direct and mediating mechanisms of the alliance defined as interpersonal process.

Using the Circumplex to Measure Therapeutic Outcome

The traditional, single-surface Leary-based interpersonal circumplex is usually used in a somewhat static fashion as a personality trait typology. An individual is located at a certain point in the circumplex space that is thought of as defining the central tendency of his or her personality. The distance of this point from the origin (i.e., vector length) is used to gauge the individual's degree of rigidity on a continuum of normal expression of a trait through an extreme pathological variant of that same trait. Because the SASB is comprised of separate surfaces for interpersonal actions, reactions, and introjections, it tends to pull for a more process-oriented, and less trait-like approach.[1] In addition, the Intrex battery (Benjamin, 1983),

---

[1] Admittedly, any process that occurs with sufficient rigid regularity certainly can be seen in trait terms. Indeed, Eysenck (1990) defined traits in terms of highly correlated habits, which are themselves correlated behaviors of interpersonal transactions as measured by in this case SASB.

the chief self-report instrument based on the SASB, requires separate sets of ratings for a research participant's introject (in both best and worst states), a current significant other relationship (again, rated twice in best and worst states), the relationship with each parent when the participant was age 5 to 10, and the relationship between the two parents. The rating of each relationship (except for the introject) is actually comprised of four sets of ratings: the other's actions toward the patient, the other's reactions to the patient, the patient's actions toward the other, and the patient's reactions to the other. Although central tendencies or patterns of ratings can and do emerge across these sets of ratings, the procedure is ideally suited for measuring very specific changes in interpersonal process, without losing the overall theoretical parsimony of the underlying circumplex structure and theory. This is an important feature for clinical applications, because regardless of one's theoretical approach to therapy, a crucial marker of change is always behavioral: Patients act and react differently in their daily interpersonal environments.

From the standpoint of general interpersonal theory (Horowitz & Vitkus, 1986), a patient's presenting symptomatic complaints typically are embedded in repetitive, self-sustaining, and maladaptive interpersonal patterns. The patient's problematic interpersonal actions and reactions are seen as the result of: (a) an unconscious repetition of the wish to please and secure the love of early important others who presented pathological conditions for acceptance (Benjamin, 1993); and (b) perceptions and expectancies of others that, although currently distorted, were at one point in history likely to be true. These forces tend to guide an individual's actions and reactions in ways that confirm their feared expectancies. For example, an individual who expects others to be very critical will perceive criticism (where perhaps none originally existed) and react in a hostile submissive manner (SASB Cluster 2-6: sulk–appease). By the principle of complementarity, this tends to pull over time for actual criticism by the other person (SASB Cluster 1-6: blame), which in turn is introjected, confirming the self-critical introject structure (SASB Cluster 3-6: self-blame–indictment). Such a self-indicting stance has been implicated in the etiology of depression both from the standpoint of the criteria set for dysthymic personality in *DSM-IV* (American Psychiatric Association, 1994) as well as in the theoretical writings of any number of authors (Beck, 1983; Blatt, 1991).

The structure of the SASB system has proven to be quite theoretically consistent with these general interpersonal ideas about self-sustaining problem patterns, permitting more precise assessment of changes in specific elements of the cyclic system. Schacht and Henry (1995) proposed a methodology for using the SASB Intrex battery to formulate a patient's central cyclic maladaptive pattern (the SASB-CMP), as well as to measure changes in it. This format (see Table 1) also permits the inclusion of non-self-report

TABLE 1
Categories of the SASB-CMP

Interpersonal Acts	Introjective Acts	Expectancies: Predictions, Wishes, Fears

Acts by patient
  Patient acts on
  other
    Best state
    Worst state
  Patient reacts
  to other
    Best state
    Worst state
	Acts by patient
	  Best state
	  Worst state
		Fantasies of patient regarding
		  How patient will act and react to
		  others
		
		How others will act and react to
		patient
		How patient and other will act
		introjectively

Acts by Others
  Other acts on
  patient
    Best state
    Worst state
  Other reacts to
  patient
    Best state
    Worst state
	Acts by Others	

data obtained through interview and observation. The data are grouped into interpersonal acts, introjective acts, and expectancies. In contrast to other systems that use narrative descriptive labels (such as wish for acceptance, fear of failure, expectation of abandonment, etc.), all elements in the SASB-CMP format are translated into the same SASB codes. For example, abandonment fear would be coded "fear of 1-8," fear of failure might be coded "fear of 1-6," whereas a wish to depend on a powerful other might be coded "wish for 2-4." It is true that a narrative-based system (even one with standardized categories) and the SASB codes are often describing the same underlying phenomena. However, I believe that the uniform, circumplex-based metric into which all elements of the problem cycle are translated permits patterns to be seen more clearly. In addition, as noted earlier, the use of SASB not only permits an interpersonal problem cycle to be precisely *described*, but the dynamics of the cycle also can be *explained* and *predicted* via such principles as complementarity, introjection, and so forth. The ultimate clinical purposes of the SASB-CMP are threefold: (a) to use the structured, SASB-coded data to develop a hypothesis that explains the dynamics of the patient's self-sustaining problems, (b) to pinpoint specific interpersonal actions and reactions as targets of change, and (c) to measure outcome defined as changes in the presenting CMP.

Emergent Theoretical Models Implied by the Circumplex

The interpersonal circumplex in general, and the SASB in particular, present something of a paradox. On the one hand, the circumplex provides a theoretical model, quite distinct from purely factor-derived psychometric systems. It proposes two fundamental underlying dimensions or axes of behavior,[2] and provides a set of explanatory and predictive principles regarding interpersonal behavior and its internalization as a self-structure. On the other hand, SASB may be seen or used as a more theory-neutral language for simply describing behavior, a language capable of incorporation into other theories. The SASB-CMP format provides a procedure for structuring data in a uniform metric and explaining the cyclic dynamics of an interpersonal–intrapsychic system. I consider it to have a good degree of clinical utility as well as being a refined measure of change. However, this procedure stops just short of providing a more overarching theory of personality pathology per se, one that would permit the development of a theory-based nosology that might serve as an alternative to the more atheoretical *DSM* Axis II.

My use of the SASB circumplex has evolved from being an operational tool for measurement and a heuristic structure for defining clinical problems to being one of the bases of a more comprehensive general theoretical model of abnormal personality. (Henry, 1994).[3] This model is achieved by combining basic motivational drive postulates drawn from attachment theory, with interpersonal theory as operationalized by the SASB. The result is a model quite different from earlier circumplex-based definitions of pathology, in which pathology was seen *quantitatively* as a matter of degree of a certain trait expression. In the model described next I propose a *qualitative* definition for differentiating abnormal from normal personality.

Bowlby (1977, 1988), drawing on earlier animal research (Harlow, 1958; Lorenz, 1955), posited that the human infant engages in two primary, normative behaviors—attachment-seeking and exploration. The fact that these were seen as primary motivational forces was a break with past tradition, because these behaviors were regarded as innate despite the absence of immediate reinforcement through primary drive reduction. In a psychologically healthy infant–caretaker system, the child seeks and achieves a primary attachment (what Bowlby termed a *secure base*) and is thus free to

---

[2]Although factor analysis has been used to substantiate the centrality of these two dimensions, the dimensions themselves were conceived originally along theoretical lines as a result of a number of studies, including early primate research (Harlow, 1958).

[3]A major share of the credit for this expansion in my thinking about the use of SASB must go to its creator, Lorna Benjamin, and her groundbreaking work on translating *DSM* Axis II descriptors into SASB language and proposing specific interpersonal hypotheses to explain the etiology of each of the personality disorders. To my knowledge, she has provided the most specific, the most theoretically consistent, and the most testable model of Axis II disorders to date.

explore the environment. Typically attachment-seeking and exploratory behaviors alternate in a balanced fashion. Attachment and exploration are behaviors that translate directly into the SASB-circumplex patterns of friendly enmeshment (sequences of nurturant, protective control by the parent, and loving trust and submission by the infant) and friendly differentiation (autonomy-granting and autonomy-taking). Relatively normal development is defined in terms of a parent who facilitates bonding or attachment by being sufficiently available and empathic to the infant's needs while also being flexible enough to tolerate and encourage a degree of separation or autonomy.

Personality may be defined interpersonally as "the mental operations associated with internal representations of self and other in interaction, and made manifest in interpersonal behavior" (Henry, 1994, p. 324; see also Benjamin, 1994). The early interpersonal transactions with significant others, organized around the twin drives of attachment and differentiation, form these internalized representations that are the basis of personality.[4] Three basic processes are proposed by which a child's early interactions are copied to produce mental representations or schema that guide the manifest behavior we label *personality*: (a) the process of directly copying or imitating the behavior of significant others is termed *identification*; (b) the process by which repeated similar interpersonal cycles result in an abstract representation of the other that generates expectancies is termed *internalization*; and (c) the process by which a child comes to treat himself or herself as they have been treated by others is referred to as *introjection*. This framework for defining personality and its interpersonal etiology provides yet another compelling example of how the circumplex makes sense. That is, not only are the underlying circumplex dimensions consistent with basic primate and infant research, as well as having been validated over and over psychometrically (Wiggins, 1982), the three surfaces of the SASB circumplex also correspond to the three basic developmental processes just described.

The primary behavior of parent figures toward others, the actions that are identified with and thus imitated in the form of the child's (or adult's) transitive interpersonal actions, may be charted on SASB Surface 1. Internalized representations of important others create expectancies that shape perception and hence guide an individual's interpersonal reactions, as measured on SASB Surface 2. The Surface 1 actions by important others toward the child are introjected or replicated in the behavior of the child (or adult) toward himself or herself as represented on SASB Surface 3. The

---

[4]There are also obviously biological or temperamental determinants of personality that both shape interpersonal behavior and are in turn shaped by it (the idea of acquired biology). For the purposes of the present chapter, however, I am focusing exclusively on the social learning component of personality defined as internalized and externalized interpersonal process behaviors.

way in which these three processes sustain a stable self-concept and similar cyclic interpersonal patterns is depicted in Figure 2.

The basic motivations for attachment and differentiation, and the processes by which early interpersonal experiences form the basis of what we call personality, are considered to be universal. The qualitative distinction between normal and abnormal personality rests on what *type* of parenting behaviors provide the experiential baseline for identification, internalization, and introjection. "Normal" personality is thought to result when this early experiential baseline comes primarily from Clusters 2 (affirmation), 3 (active love), and 4 (nurturant protection). This 2-3-4 baseline (referred to as the attachment group or AG; Benjamin, 1994; Henry, 1994) can be defended as a definition of normalcy because it corresponds to the successful satisfaction of basic needs or drives as proposed by attachment theory. The AG baseline represents a balanced blend of moderate, friendly enmeshment (permitting bonding) and moderate, friendly autonomy or differentiation (permitting exploration). By contrast, individuals with abnormal personality more typically have experienced and also display a baseline of interpersonal behaviors drawn from the disrupted attachment group (DAG: SASB Clusters 6: blame, 7: attack, and 8: abandonment). In short, abnormal personality is defined qualitatively as a pattern of interpersonal transactions that are too submissive (overly enmeshed), too distant (overly differentiated), or too hostile (overly attacking). It is interesting to note that these three general trends correspond almost exactly to the three basic interpersonal coping styles in response to an un-

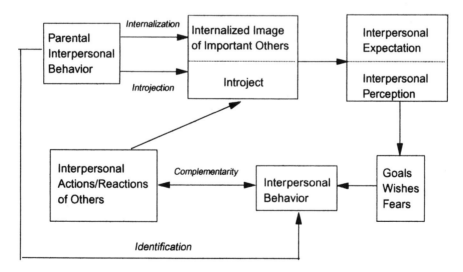

Figure 2. Interpersonal Model of Cyclic Psychopathology. Reprinted from *Differentiating Normal and Abnormal Personality* (p. 330) edited by S. Strack and M. Lorr, 1994, New York: Springer Publishing Co., Inc. Reprinted by permission.

healthy early environment as proposed by Horney (1945): moving toward, moving away, and moving against. These three forms of interpersonal imbalance, which define abnormal personality, also tie directly to various categorical systems drawn from other traditions that have been used to describe parenting style (for example, authoritarian—too enmeshed; abandoning—too distant, etc. See Tyber, 1989).

The paradox of this model is the fact that the same basic processes are responsible for both normal and abnormal personality development. This is so not only because of shared drives and copy processes but also because all individuals share the same general wishes and fears that serve to organize ongoing behavior. Namely, all people are thought to wish for the interpersonal conditions of the attachment group (affirmation, love, and protection), and fear behaviors from the disrupted attachment group (blame, attack, and abandonment). Again, the qualitative distinction between normal and abnormal rests on early social learning. Individuals raised in a toxic interpersonal environment may come to fixate exclusively on specific wishes and fears that correspond to early parenting excesses and deficits. The central fixation on single, specific wishes and fears (such as the wish for acceptance or the fear of abandonment) produces a motivational prominence that is too narrow and rigid for balanced, healthy interpersonal behavior because it tends to propel the individual toward over-enmeshment, over-differentiation, or attack. In short, although there is nothing necessarily pathological about any given individual's motivational drives and associated wishes and fears per se, certain early experiences create rigid fixations and negative internalizations that result in maladaptive attachment-seeking behaviors, which we define as abnormal.

The importance of the circumplex to both the theoretical construction and operational measurement of these ideas can be seen easily. Fundamental or innate drives, early experience, parenting styles, salient wishes and fears (and wish–fear conflicts), intrapsychic structure (the introject), and manifest interpersonal behavior and problem patterns all can be described in the same measurement metric and explained via the same set of underlying principles. This permits problem–treatment–outcome congruence, and a host of specific, testable (i.e., refutable) hypotheses coherently linking general definitions and theories of human motivation, personality pathology, early experience, and adult disorder with direct implications for the mechanisms of therapeutic change processes and outcome measurement. It is no accident that theory and research as diverse as Harlow's primate research, Bowlby's attachment theory, Horney's categorization of interpersonal coping styles, Sullivan's theory of personality as interpersonal introjection, and the major set of findings in contemporary psychotherapy research on the importance of the therapeutic relationship all can be brought together into an emergent, unified model linking pathology and its treatment. This is made possible because of the strengths of circumplex models in general and SASB in particular. It permits description, explanation, and prediction.

USE OF THE CIRCUMPLEX TO GENERATE NEW MEASURES

Because the SASB circumplex enables true, descriptive problem–treatment–outcome congruence, as well as theoretical problem–treatment–outcome unity, it provides an ideal base for the development of new instruments designed to articulate coherently with one another. That is, instruments that measure such things as early interpersonal history, current relationships with significant others, generalized interpersonal expectations and sense of self-efficacy with others, central interpersonal wishes and fears, and so on all can be related directly to one another via the same underlying dimensions of affiliation and interdependence. In this section I will describe briefly several new SASB-based instruments I have developed in order to: (a) test the underlying theory of etiology of personality dysfunction, (b) provide useful tools for clinical assessment and case formulation, and (c) measure therapeutic changes in a precise manner. These measures are currently undergoing initial pilot testing.

INTERPERSONAL HISTORY DURING EARLY DEVELOPMENT

Benjamin (1993), in her book on the interpersonal diagnosis and treatment of personality disorders, summarizes a major etiological hypothesis to account for adult Axis II disorders. The guiding principle is that the most salient interpersonal dimensionality (as measured by the SASB axes of affiliation and interdependence) of early experience matches the interpersonal dimensionality of the adult disorders or presenting complaints. This is a fundamentally different approach to the study of etiology that the circumplex allows. In more traditional approaches, categorically defined events (such as abuse or abandonment, etc.) are used as predictors of adult, categorical syndromes (i.e., major depression, borderline personality disorder, etc.). Unfortunately, such attempts (often broadly labeled *symptom specificity hypotheses*) typically have failed to uncover specific early events that are strongly tied to specific adult disorders. An alternative strategy, based on the circumplex dimensions, assumes that similar categorically defined developmental events may nonetheless differ significantly in terms of interpersonal process and context. For example, abuse might denote constant criticism (SASB Cluster 1-6), physical assault (SASB Cluster 1-7), or inappropriate abandonment (SASB Cluster 1-8). Complex variants are also possible, such as certain forms of incest in which attack is mixed with the profession of love by the abuser (SASB complex Clusters 1-3 and 1-7).

By employing the three-surface circumplex, SASB is able to provide a much higher level of specificity to the description of early events more typically referred to in global, categorical terms.

To completely test Benjamin's SASB-based etiological hypothesis, however, requires a further refinement in the specificity of measurement of early history than that offered solely by the existing Intrex battery. For example, although many individuals no doubt felt abused because of perceived abandonment by their parents, the situations in which abandonment occurred and the type of abandonment is hypothesized to be different for different personality disorders. Although the SASB Intrex battery provides a general index of perceived abandonment (SASB Cluster 1-8), it does not tap more specific contextual features. The Early Experiences Questionnaire (EEQ; Henry, 1995a) was designed to fill this gap by measuring very specific early events that are hypothesized to be related etiologically to the differential development of individual Axis II disorders. In addition, the EEQ measures the individual's perceptions of early experience separately for each parent, to reflect situations in which one parent was nurturant and the other critical, and so on.

As an example, Benjamin (1993) posited that the interpersonal history of patients with both avoidant personality disorder and borderline personality disorder is marked by repeated abandonment experiences. However, the nature of the abandonment is thought to differ significantly. An EEQ item designed to tap the abandonment experiences of the avoidant person reads, "When my parents were mad at me or ashamed of me for something, they would often just leave me out while the rest of the family did things together." A similar, abandonment-related item on the EEQ borderline scale reads, "When I was growing up, I was often left alone, not knowing when someone was coming back to take care of me." The EEQ also measures central wishes and fears related to each parental figure. For instance, one fear item relates to SASB Cluster 1-5 (watching and managing) and reads, "I worried or feared that my mother/father would try to control my actions and/or thoughts too much," and the related wish item reads, "I wished that my mother/father would have given me a lot more freedom and autonomy." The understanding of these early wishes and fears is seen as important, because rigid adult maladaptive patterns are thought to represents attempts (however maladaptive or unsuccessful) to fulfill archaic wishes and avoid feared states. It is important from a methodologic standpoint to note that these wishes and fears can be placed into the same circumplex structure used to measure early interpersonal events, current significant relationships, and the SASB-CMP format for defining a clinical problem.

Measuring Perceived Interpersonal Control

The SASB-CMP, like other psychodynamic formulation schemes, describes central interpersonal problem patterns in terms of their processes (i.e., what are the elements and how they are linked sequentially or causally). Clinical experience gained both from being a therapist as well as having interviewed a large number of patients pre- and posttherapy for research purposes suggests to me that there is another important variable to consider in addition to the nature of the CMP per se. Namely, patients with similar surface patterns nonetheless vary considerably in their degree of perceived control over different elements of the pattern. Following therapy, it is common for patients to report that they continue to experience some of the same problems or patterns but that they now feel a greater sense of personal control over these problems (i.e., enhanced self-efficacy). Although the general construct of locus of control has enjoyed a long and fruitful research heritage (Lefcourt, 1991), there is a dearth of specific, theoretically based measures of perceived interpersonal control.

The 24-item SASB-Interpersonal Locus of Control Scale (SASB-ILCS; Henry & Cheuvront, 1995)[5] combines Levenson's three-factor locus of control construct (internal control, control by powerful others, and control by chance or fate; Levenson, 1973) with the eight SASB clusters. It is based on the idea that individuals differ in their degree of perceived control over the actions of others toward them, a major factor in the definition of interpersonal pathology because it relates directly to a person's sense of helplessness versus interpersonal efficacy. Scores may be summed across clusters to yield a general index of perceived control for each of the three locus of control dimensions, or the dimensions may be summed to yield a combined index of perceived control over each SASB cluster. Individual items rate specific control beliefs, such as an individual's belief that powerful others control whether they will be abandoned (SASB Cluster 1-8), the extent to which chance controls whether or not they will be loved (SASB Cluster 1-3), and so forth.

Preliminary analyses of the SASB-ILCS (Henry & Cheuvront, 1995) indicate large, but very specific, differences between a normal and a clinical adult sample in degree of perceived interpersonal control. In general terms, as expected, the clinical sample reported significantly less interpersonal control. It is interesting to note, however, that the two groups seem to have about the same level of perceived internal control. The large overall difference between the sample is based largely on the fact that the clinical sample accords much greater control to powerful others and to chance. In other words, patients and nonpatients differ not in their sense of relative

---

[5]An earlier version of this instrument was named the Vanderbilt International Locus of Control Scale (Schacht & Henry, 1984).

personal control but rather individuals in the clinical group see external forces out of their control as much more powerful determinants of the nature of their relations. This offsets the relative equality in personal efficacy between the two groups. The pattern shows up most markedly when it involves patients' reduced sense of control over interpersonal exchanges involving friendly differentiation, affirmation, and acceptance (SASB Cluster 1-2). Preliminary results also suggest that specific control expectancies and deficits differ significantly across each of the Axis II personality disorders.

Measuring Current Interpersonal Wishes, Fears, and Power Tactics

Another instrument that has been developed based on the underlying SASB metric is the Attitudes about Significant Relationships (ASR; Henry, 1995b). It is designed to complement the SASB-CMP and the SASB-ILCS as a measure to aid in efficient interpersonal–dynamic case formulation for the purpose of treatment planning, as well as to function as a change measure. Like the EEQ, the ASR also taps interpersonal wishes and fears in circumplex form but in this case in relation to current intimate or other significant relationships. It includes a section that measures (again, in circumplex form) an individual's typical interpersonal power tactics or ways a person tries to influence important others in order to get what he or she needs or desires from the relationship. These interpersonal tactics all can be SASB-coded, range from more to less adaptive, and articulate with the underlying theory of personality pathology described earlier. For example, an adaptive tactic drawn from the attachment group (AG) reads, "I use reason and argue my point in a friendly and logical way" (Cluster 2-2: disclose and express), whereas an example representing the disrupted attachment group (DAG) states, "I blame him/her for not meeting my needs" (Cluster 1-6: blame). In addition, some items tap complex interpersonal maneuvers such as, "I try to make him/her jealous by talking to or about other people" (Clusters 2-8 and 1-5: wall-off and manage–control).

These three instruments (Intrex, SASB-ILCS, and ASR), when combined, yield overall dimensional information in the same circumplex space relevant to: (a) interpersonal transaction patterns and the resultant introject, (b) specific clusters of the circumplex over which a person does or does not feel they have control and why, and (c) central wishes and fears in current relationships and the behaviors used to express the needs and avoid the feared conditions. The fact that all of these instruments yield data in the form of the same SASB cluster codes makes the integration and patterning of diverse clinical information easier and more directly relevant theoretically. In addition, the SASB-ILCS and ASR provide contextual information, which adds specificity to the overall circumplex dimensions. Finally, the formulation derived can be compared directly, in the same metric, to early developmental experiences as measured by the EEQ. This permits specific etiological hypotheses to be tested.

THE RELEVANCE OF THE CIRCUMPLEX TO CLINICAL ISSUES AND QUESTIONS

The SASB-circumplex is of direct clinical as well as research utility, as I have argued. First, it provides a heuristic structure that aids in the relatively quick and precise description of interpersonal problem cycles for the purpose of systematic, replicable case formulation. Second, it provides a set of behavioral principles that help explain the maintenance of the interpersonal cycle (such as the principle of complementarity), as well as the effect of these interpersonal transactions on the self-concept or introject. Third, it suggests specific interpersonal behaviors that would interrupt the cycle (i.e., noncomplementary or antithetical actions). Fourth, it gives a straightforward procedure for understanding the link between early events and presenting problems in a way that is readily teachable to therapists— and that, from personal experience, makes immediate sense to patients. Fifth, it encourages the clinician to think in terms of specific interpersonal behaviors that can be targeted for change, as contrasted to more abstract concepts such as repressed anger or ungratified dependency wishes, which do not necessarily carry specific therapeutic implications for action. Sixth, by emphasizing observable interpersonal behavior patterns, the SASB heuristic does not pull as strongly for the use of trait labels (such as manipulative, paranoid, obsessive, etc.), which may be not only less meaningful or offensive to the patient but also may lead to more inadvertent blaming on the part of the therapist (see Henry et al., 1986). Seventh, it permits problem–treatment–outcome congruence—the process and content of therapy, a patient's early history, presenting problems, and outcomes to be viewed within the framework of a common metric that encourages more precise and theoretically driven thinking and empirical measurement. Eighth, and most important, this degree of operationalization and measurement specificity can be accomplished within the context of basic psychodynamic and object relational theory. The baby need not be thrown out with the bathwater for the sake of concrete empirical operationalization of the underlying theory.

In this era of managed care and strict session limits, heuristics and associated assessment procedures that are time efficient, identify more precise formulations and change targets, make sense to patients (increasing compliance and satisfaction), and provide for meaningful outcome measurement are valuable indeed. In addition to the SASB-based assessments already described, Florsheim, Henry, and Benjamin (in press) have outlined a procedure for combining attachment theory with SASB to yield relational diagnoses as opposed to the more customary individual-centered diagnosis. This procedure uses attachment-style categories as drawn from the attachment theory literature and SASB cluster codes to operationalize the interpersonal behaviors comprising the dyadic system that results from the interaction of a two-person attachment system.

INTEGRATIVE UTILITY OF THE CIRCUMPLEX

As noted, the circumplex is paradoxical in the sense that it is on the one hand highly theoretical and on the other hand provides a precise descriptive language that can be seen as theory-neutral. In recent years there clearly has been increasing emphasis on common therapeutic factors and cross-theory integration (Prochaska & Norcross, 1994). However, integration has been hampered, in part, by the lack of a comprehensive meta-framework that describes how techniques drawn from differing theoretical orientations may be seen through a shared theory of therapeutic change process that is consistent with, but more comprehensive than, existing individual theories. I believe that it is possible to understand how cognitive, behavioral, client-centered, psychodynamic, and others approaches work to promote change in different ways, but with similar results and for similar reasons in terms of an overarching circumplex–interpersonal theory of pathology and therapy. The circumplex provides a basis for the integration of theories of psychopathology and psychotherapy for two main reasons: (a) the behaviors, cognitions, and emotions[6] that are the stuff of problem definition and change measurement can be translated into the same theory-neutral language, regardless of one's primary theoretical orientation; and (b) the behavioral principles that accompany the circumplex (introjection, antithesis, complementarity, etc.) can be used to explain the efficacy of many different types of therapeutic interventions.

For example, regardless of one's accustomed interventions, the patient's presenting problems may be translated into the same behaviorally-based SASB patterns, without any required assumptions about etiology or treatment strategies. Ultimately, the successful outcome of any therapy involves (a) changes in observable behavior (SASB Surfaces 1 and 2) and (b) differences in self-perception or concept (SASB Surface 3). From the standpoint of interpersonal theory, actions (by self and others), reactions, and introjective acts are all part of a connected cycle, and to intervene at any point in the cycle should cause changes in the other parts over time (as well as in the affects embedded in a given interpersonal pattern). It is my view that therapies differ in their relative emphasis on: (a) different parts

---

[6]The translation of emotional experience into circumplex form is not touched on in this chapter, but considerable work has been done in this area (see, for example, Plutchik, 1994).

of the cycle (CMP) and (b) different components or subprocesses that maintain the cycle (surface behaviors, cognitions, wishes and fears, defenses, secondary gains or reinforcement, etc.). In the end, however, I believe that most therapies are more alike than not and simply use different explanatory heuristics and varying surface means to produce similar underlying changes in perception and behavior that interrupt the problem cycle.[7]

I propose that all therapies that are effective combine some blend of the following common processes that all can be measured and understood through the framework of the interpersonal circumplex:

1. The direct ameliorative action of the therapeutic relationship via the principle of introjection of therapist-offered interpersonal process.
2. The indirect change of interpersonal actions and reactions of the patient caused by the manipulation of expectancies of the actions and reactions of others. This might occur by means of the psychodynamically based corrective emotional experience, the cognitive challenge to distorted explanatory styles, or any of a variety of other means.
3. The direct interruption of complementary interpersonal cycles via the initiation of new patient behaviors that evoke different responses in others. These changed responses of others may serve to strengthen tentatively altered expectancies and perceptions and also lead to the reintrojection of new, more adaptive interpersonal styles. New behaviors may be encouraged through any number of mechanisms—insight, changed response contingencies, the affective bond to the therapist, behavioral skills training, cognitive restructuring through collaborative empiricism, and so on.

A behavior therapist, for example, might be more comfortable conceptualizing the therapeutic relationship as an opportunity for modeling rather than reintrojection, a more intrapsychic concept. Nonetheless, the crucial point is that it is *possible* to use the circumplex as a common language for description and explanation to integrate across different theoretical traditions.

To fully appreciate the integrative theoretical and clinical utility of circumplex-based methodology, let me compare briefly the preceding SASB-based assessment formats to at least one popular alternative methodology for describing personality pathology—the Five Factor Model (McCrae & Costa, 1985). Again, I come to the issues of description versus explanation and the extent and ease of theoretical linkage among conceptualizations

---

[7]This belief in underlying similarities does not rule out the very real possibility that some patients and some problem types may benefit differentialy from differing surface–level techniques.

of psychopathology, etiology, and treatment. I believe that for purposes of general theories of psychopathology, etiology, and treatment, the SASB-circumplex enjoys advantages over atheoretical, psychometrically derived dimensional factor structures such as the Five Factor Model:

1. SASB describes all phenomena related to etiology and types of pathology as a variable mixture of the *same* two underlying structural dimensions (affiliation and interdependence). There is no corresponding general structure within which to contextualize or understand each of the five factors.

2. The Five Factor Model ultimately may be articulated with various developmental theories of psychopathology (both psychosocial and biological), but in and of itself, the model is not directly generative of research because it is purely descriptive and carries with it no necessary theories of etiology. SASB, however, is grounded in basic primate research (Benjamin, 1974), consistent with evolutionary biology and articulates with infant studies of primary attachment behaviors (Henry, 1994). Most important, it proposes distinct, testable hypotheses linking early experiences and adult disorders (see Benjamin, 1993).

3. The Five Factor Model is essentially a trait model and as such pulls for the conceptualization of problems as profiles of relative elevations on each of the factors. It is paradoxical that the Five Factor Model thus may ultimately tend to be reduced to categories, despite its dimensional basis, and as such is more static and insensitive to context. SASB tends to pull for the description of problems in terms of process that is context sensitive and transactional and hence more functionally amenable to case formulation and treatment planning.

4. In this vein, the Five Factor Model provides information in terms of labels (be it higher-order factors or lower-order facets) that are somewhat isolated or abstracted from the individual possessing them. In addition, although these labels may *imply* certain behaviors, they do not directly articulate them. SASB, however, directly and concretely describes the specific behaviors that constitute the problem, suggests where they came from and why, and proposes specific behavioral principles for change. In short, SASB is capable of description, prediction, and explanation, whereas the Five Factor Model is a purely descriptive system.

CONCLUSION

In terms of Axis II personality disorders we are in an era that is lively and challenging. Although most theorists, researchers, and clinicians recognize the general folk wisdom of the *DSM* disorders (i.e., we *do* see people who more or less fit a number of the descriptive *DSM* categories), there is a widespread yearning for a more comprehensive, theoretically based, unifying dimensional structure to serve as the foundation for a new nosology of personality disorder. In other words, as scientists we are looking for core pathologies rather than surface correlations, and as clinicians we are looking for more precise guides to case formulation and treatment planning. There are many dimensional models ranging from biological to psychosocial and from purely psychometric to theoretical, vying to fulfill these needs for a unified theory. I tend to view these models as complementary and interactive rather than necessarily competing for the distinction of single truth. All of these approaches ultimately may contribute some unique pieces to the puzzle of understanding psychopathology—its causes and its cures.

In this chapter, I have attempted to sketch what I believe to be the unique strengths or inherent superiorities of a circumplex-based approach—SASB in particular—to the unified understanding and study of clinical problems, treatment processes, and therapeutic outcomes. I believe that the interpersonal circumplex is unique in that it permits a broader theoretical understanding of psychotherapy, without *necessarily* contradicting or requiring abandonment of many current, more specific systems or theories of treatment. In the comparatively brief history of psychotherapy research, longevity of a system or approach is a relative matter. The utility and fundamental theoretical soundness of the interpersonal circumplex has been an enduring tradition that has gathered momentum slowly since its introduction in the 1950s. I feel that the interpersonal principles embodied in the circumplex approach are now poised to move out of a more specific interpersonal niche toward application as a cross-theoretical common language. If I am correct, the circumplex is on the verge of reaching maturity as a theoretical platform that encourages the development of new, emergent integrative theory (not simply the translation of one theory's language into that of another). If this happens, researchers in the area of psychodynamics finally might achieve an elusive goal—operational rigor without sacrificing the meaningful essence of complex constructs.

REFERENCES

American Psychiatric Association. (1994). *Diagnostic and statistical manual of mental disorders* (4th ed.). Washington, DC: Author.

Beck, A. T. (1983). Cognitive therapy of depression: New perspectives. In P. J. Clayton & J. E. Barrett (Eds.), *Treatment of depression: Old controversies and new approaches* (pp. 265–284). New York: Raven Press.

Benjamin, L. S. (1974). Structural Analysis of Social Behavior. *Psychological Review, 81*, 392–425.

Benjamin, L. S. (1983). *The Intrex user's manual: Parts I and II*. Salt Lake City, UT: Department of Psychology, University of Utah.

Benjamin, L. S. (1993). *Interpersonal diagnosis and treatment of personality disorders*. New York: Guilford Press.

Benjamin, L. S. (1994). Good defenses make good neighbors. In H. R. Conte & R. Plutchik (Eds.), *Ego defenses: Theory and measurement*. New York: Wiley.

Blatt, S. J. (1991). A cognitive morphology of psychopathology. *The Journal of Nervous and Mental Disease, 179*, 449–458.

Bowlby, J. (1977). The making and breaking of affectional bonds: I. Aetiology and psychopathology in the light of attachment theory. *British Journal of Psychiatry, 130*, 201–210.

Bowlby, J. (1988). *A secure base: Parent–child attachment and healthy human development*. New York: Basic Books.

Eysenck, H. J. (1990). Biological dimensions of personality. In L. A. Pervin (Ed.), *Handbook of personality: Theory and research*. New York: Guilford Press.

Florsheim, P., Henry, W. P., & Benjamin, L. S. (in press). Integrating individual and interpersonal approaches to diagnosis: The Structural Analysis of Social Behavior and attachment theory. In F. Kaslow (Ed.), *Handbook of Relational Diagnosis*. New York: Wiley.

Harlow, H. F. (1958). The nature of love. *American Journal of Psychology, 13*, 673–685.

Henry, W. P. (1994). Differentiating normal and abnormal personality: An interpersonal approach based on the Structural Analysis of Social Behavior. In S. Strack and M. Lorr (Eds.), *Differentiating normal and abnormal personality*. New York: Springer.

Henry, W. P. (1995a). *Early Experiences Questionnaire*. Unpublished manuscript, University of Utah, Salt Lake City, UT.

Henry, W. P. (1995b). *Attitudes about significant relationships*. Unpublished manuscript, University of Utah, Salt Lake City, UT.

Henry, W. P., & Cheuvront, C. (1995, June). *The measurement of interpersonal control*. Paper presented at the annual convention of the Society for Psychotherapy Research, Vancouver, Canada.

Henry, W. P., Schacht, T. E., & Strupp, H. H. (1986). Structural analysis of social behavior: Application to a study of interpersonal process in differential psychotherapeutic outcome. *Journal of Consulting and Clinical Psychology, 54*, 27–31. Reprinted in A. Kazdin (Ed.), (1992). *Methodological issues in clinical research*. Washington, DC: American Psychological Association.

Henry, W. P., Schacht, T. E., & Strupp, H. H. (1990). Patient and therapist introject, interpersonal process and differential psychotherapy outcome. *Journal of Consulting and Clinical Psychology, 58*, 768–774.

Henry, W. P., Schacht, T. E., Strupp, H. H., Butler, S. F., & Binder, J. L. (1993). The effects of training in time-limited dynamic psychotherapy: Mediators of therapist's response to training. *Journal of Consulting and Clinical Psychology, 61*, 441–447.

Henry, W. P., & Strupp, H. H. (1994). The therapeutic alliance as interpersonal process. In A. O. Horvath & L. S. Greenberg (Eds.), *The working alliance: Theory, research and practice*. New York: Wiley.

Henry, W. P., Strupp, H. H., Butler, S. F., Schacht, T. E., & Binder, J. L. (1993). The effects of training in time-limited dynamic psychotherapy: Changes in therapist behavior. *Journal of Consulting and Clinical Psychology, 61*, 434–440.

Horney, K. (1945). *Our inner conflicts*. New York: Norton.

Horowitz, L. M., & Vitkus, J. (1986). The interpersonal basis of psychiatric symptoms. *Clinical Psychology Review, 6*(5), 443–469.

Leary, T. (1957). *Interpersonal diagnosis of personality: A functional theory and methodology for personality evaluation*. New York: Ronald Press.

Lefcourt, H. M. (1991). Locus of control. In J. P. Robinson, P. R. Shaver, & L. S. Wrightsman (Eds.), *Measures of personality and social psychological attitudes* (pp. 412–499). San Diego, CA: Academic Press.

Levenson, H. (1973). Multidimensional locus of control in psychiatric patients. *Journal of Consulting and Clinical Psychology, 41*, 397–404.

Lorenz, K. (1955). Morphology and behavior patterns in closely allied species. In B. Schaffner (Ed.), *Group processes*. New York: Macy Foundation.

McCrae, R. R., & Costa, P. T. (1985). Updating Norman's adequate taxonomy: Intelligence and personality dimensions in natural language and in questionnaires. *Journal of Personality and Social Psychology, 49*, 710–721.

Plutchik, R. (1994). *The psychology and biology of emotion*. New York: HarperCollins

Prochaska, J. O., & Norcross, J. C. (1994). *Systems of psychotherapy*. Pacific Grove, CA: Brooks/Cole.

Schacht, T. E., & Henry, W. P. (1984). *Vanderbilt Interpersonal Locus of Control Scale*. Unpublished manuscript, Vanderbilt University, Nashville, TN.

Schacht, T. E., & Henry, W. P. (1995). Modeling recurrent relationship patterns with Structural Analysis of Social Behavior: The SASB-CMP. *Psychotherapy Research, 4*, 208–221.

Strupp, H. H. (1993). The Vanderbilt psychotherapy studies: Synopsis. *Journal of Consulting and Clinical Psychology, 61*, 431–433.

Strupp, H. H., & Binder, J. L. (1984). *Psychotherapy in a new key: A guide to time-limited dynamic psychotherapy*. New York: Basic Books.

Strupp, H. H., Schacht, T. E., & Henry, W. P. (1988). Problem–treatment–outcome congruence: A principle whose time has come. In H. Dahl & H.

Kachele (Eds.), *Psychoanalytic Process Research Strategies* (pp. 1–19). New York: Springer.

Sullivan, H. S. (1953). *The interpersonal theory of psychiatry*. New York: Norton.

Trull, T. J. (1992). *DSM-III-R* personality disorders and the Five-Factor Model of personality: An empirical comparison. *Journal of Abnormal Psychology, 101,* 553–560.

Tyber, E. (1989). *Interpersonal process in psychotherapy: A guide for clinical training.* Pacific Grove, CA: Brooks/Cole.

Wiggins, J. S. (1982). Circumplex models of interpersonal behavior in clinical psychology. In P. C. Kendall & J. N. Butcher (Eds.), *Handbook of research methods in clinical psychology* (pp. 183–221). New York: Wiley.

17

THE INTERPERSONAL CIRCUMPLEX AS A STRUCTURAL MODEL IN CLINICAL RESEARCH: EXAMPLES FROM GROUP PSYCHOTHERAPY, INTERPERSONAL PROBLEMS, AND PERSONALITY DISORDERS

STEPHEN SOLDZ

I entered psychology with a strong background in natural sciences and mathematics. I also have a skeptical personality. I, therefore, gradually noticed the lack of consensual agreement between therapists facing the same clinical material. Two experts facing the same patient at a case conference often disagreed radically about the nature of the patient's difficulties. Such experiences, repeated many times, led me to feel that research was essential to clarify the nature of the therapeutic endeavor.

As a newcomer to psychotherapy research with a psychoanalytic bent, personality change was at the core of my thinking about therapy. I was interested in the therapeutic change that occurs with longer-term psychotherapies; it seemed that a major claim of these therapies was that they could lead to changes in personality that were unlikely to occur without therapy. Three approaches to personality appealed to the mathematical side of my personality. Kelly's (1955) personal construct psychology helped elucidate personality as an individual's processes of the construction of reality while providing an axiomatic account of the structure of personality and an appealing account of the nature of personality change. Kelly thus transcended the idiographic–nomothetic split in psychology. From a very different perspective, both the interpersonal circumplex (Leary, 1957; Wiggins, 1982; Wiggins & Broughton, 1985) and the Five Factor Model (Digman, 1989; Goldberg, 1992; John, 1990; McCrae, 1992; McCrae & Costa,

411

1987, 1990) provided models of aspects of personality that were replicable and whose structural nature appealed to my sensibilities.

Kelly (1955) pointed out that an individual can construe reality in various, sometimes contradictory, ways. In the Kellyan spirit, I have continued to pursue work in all of these theoretical traditions, trying to build bridges between them wherever possible. In this chapter I will discuss briefly some of the attractions of the interpersonal circumplex and will present those aspects of my work that were based on it.[1]

ATTRACTION OF THE INTERPERSONAL CIRCUMPLEX

The interpersonal circumplex is a model of interpersonal functioning that, as currently developed, encompasses three related aspects of this functioning, namely interpersonal *behavior* (e.g., Kiesler, 1983; Tracey, 1994), interpersonal *dispositions* (e.g., Wiggins, 1982; Wiggins & Broughton, 1985), and interpersonal *problems* (e.g., Alden, Wiggins, & Pincus, 1990). The interpersonal circumplex supplies a consistent structure to these domains (Gurtman, 1992, 1993). It posits that the interpersonal domain can be conceptualized usefully in terms of two dimensions—dominance (DOM) and affiliation (LOV)—and that individual behaviors, dispositions, and problems can be arrayed in a circle around the origin of the space marked by these two axes. The interpersonal circumplex thus draws on the factor analytic tradition of personality measurement while giving greater attention than do most other models to off-axes locations that form combinations of the two primary dimensions.

One of the primary attractions of the interpersonal circumplex is that it is replicable across instruments (Alden et al., 1990), types of interpersonal functioning (namely behaviors, dispositions, or problems), and study populations. Furthermore, the interpersonal circumplex can be found to underlie instruments assessing interpersonal functioning that were originally developed based on theoretical orientations independent of the circumplex. For example, Horowitz, Rosenberg, Baer, Ureño, and Villaseñor (1988) developed the Inventory of Interpersonal Problems (IIP) to measure difficulties in interpersonal functioning of patients entering psychotherapy. The IIP was constructed through a systematic examination of the presenting problems of patients seeking outpatient therapy. Horowitz (1979) noticed that the overwhelming majority of these problems were interpersonal in

---

[1]In my work, *circumplex* always refers to the *interpersonal circumplex*. Although I have experimented with Benjamin's Structural Analysis of Social Behavior (Benjamin, 1974), I have not engaged in any completed projects using her three-circumplex model. Nonetheless, the Structural Analysis of Social Behavior has an attraction to the psychoanalytically inclined part of me, and work such as that of Benjamin herself (1974, 1994) and Henry, Schacht, and Strupp (1986), which use this alternative circumplex approach, is very interesting (Soldz, 1990).

nature and based the IIP on the most common of these problems. The original paper on the IIP proposed a factor structure that bears no direct relation to the interpersonal circumplex. Nonetheless, from this 128-item instrument, Alden and colleagues (1990) were able to select eight items that measure problems in each of the circumplex octants, resulting in the Inventory of Interpersonal Problems Circumplex Scales (IIP-C). By the very fact that the IIP systematically covered the domain of problematic interpersonal behaviors, the interpersonal circumplex was contained within the instrument.

This robustness of the circumplex is one of its special attractions; it makes it one of the few concepts in "soft" psychology that hold out the possibility of forming the basis for cumulative knowledge. As the statistician de Leeuw (1994) recently commented, "This is one of the peculiar things about the social sciences. They do not seem to accumulate knowledge, there are very few giants, and every once in a while the midgets destroy the heaps" (p. 13). The interpersonal circumplex, and the related structural model of personality, the Five Factor Model, have the potential for forming the basis for accumulating knowledge.

My personal contributions to the use of circumplex models have focused on the structural aspects of the circumplex as a model of the interpersonal domain. I so far have neglected the more dynamic aspects of the circumplex, such as the notion of behavioral complementarity (Tracey, 1994). This work has focused on five areas that exemplify its use as a structural model: (a) the finding of the interpersonal circumplex in analyses of ratings of patient process in group psychotherapy; (b) the exploration of the relation of personality disorders to circumplex space; (c) replicating and extending our understanding of the relationship of the interpersonal circumplex to the Five Factor Model; (d) developing a short form of the IIP-C—the Inventory of Interpersonal Problems–Short Circumplex Scale (IIP-SC)—that could be used in settings in which extreme brevity was needed; and (e) exploring personality as manifest in group psychotherapy from the perspective of the self, therapists, and other group members.

THE CIRCUMPLEX IN GROUP PSYCHOTHERAPY

As part of a long-term study of process–outcome relationships in group psychotherapy, the Mental Health Research Program of Harvard Community Health Plan developed an instrument to measure individual member process in groups, the Individual Group Member Interpersonal Process Scale (IGIPS-I; Budman, Rothberg, & Davis, 1989). This instrument consists of 42 items, 38 of which are rated at the level of individual patient statements (e.g., "insensitive to other group members," "demonstrates self-awareness," "makes connections between own experiences and those of other group members," "highlights similarities between own behavior in the group and outside the group") and 4 of which involve global ratings of patient behavior over an entire half-hour group segment (e.g., "presents issues in a manner that engages others," "expresses affect"). This instrument was the culmination of our efforts to explore group process at the level of the individual patient (Soldz, Budman, & Demby, 1992; Soldz, Budman, Demby, & Feldstein, 1990) and at the level of the cohesion of the group as a whole (Budman, Soldz, Demby, Davis, & Merry, 1993; Budman, Soldz, Demby, Feldstein, & Springer, 1989).

In order to study group process through the IGIPS-I, we used videotapes from seven time-limited groups that ran for 15 sessions each. There were a total of 52 patients in these groups. We trained raters in the meaning of the IGIPS-I items until they obtained a minimum level of reliability. We then had these raters rate the patient behaviors in the first four sessions of these seven groups. Each patient *turn of speech* (a period of speech bounded before and after by speech from others) was rated on each of the 38 IGIPS-I items (Soldz, Budman, Davis, & Demby, 1993). The four more global items received ratings for each patient for each half hour segment. For each patient, we formed an overall score for each of the 38 turn-of-speech level IGIPS-I items by averaging the ratings for that item over all the times that patient had spoken during the 12 half hours (4 sessions $\times$ 3 half hours per session) that had been rated (the four global items were averaged over the 12-half hour segments). As the distributions of most of these items were dramatically skewed (for most of them, 0 was the most common rating and high ratings occurred infrequently), we combined the 42 items into 12 scales by combining theoretically related items. For example, a self-esteem scale was created by subtracting the sum of the "makes self-deprecating comments" ratings from the sum of the "makes self-appreciative comments" ratings and dividing by the number of times the patient discussed his or her own issues, feelings, or behavior.

A principal component analysis of these 12 scales was then performed. When we extracted two components, they clearly represented the two interpersonal circumplex dimensions, rotated slightly to resemble the locations of extraversion and agreeableness in the Five Factor Model (McCrae & Costa, 1989; Soldz, Budman, Demby, & Merry, 1993a; Trapnell & Wiggins, 1990). In fact, when five components were extracted, they bore a striking resemblance to the Five Factor Model. Of greatest interest are the first two components of the five component solution (which strongly resemble the two-component solution). The first, activity, had high loadings (> .50) on "how often patient spoke," "discloses personal material," and "expresses affect." The second component, interpersonal sensitivity, had high loadings on "makes connections with other group members," "sensitivity when addressing other group members," and "positive sentiment" (Soldz, Budman, Davis, & Demby, 1993). It seems reasonable to identify the first dimension with the Five Factor Model extraversion factor and the second with the agreeableness factor. As has been shown by Mc-Crae and Costa (1989), Soldz, Budman, Demby, and Merry (1993a), and Trapnell and Wiggins (1990), these two dimensions mark out the same space as do the circumplex axes, though with a rotation of about 45° (see discussion that follows). Thus, our results demonstrate that interpersonal behavior in the therapeutic group setting can be represented in circumplex space even when the instrument used to measure this behavior was not designed explicitly on circumplex principles.

The other three components that we obtained were better understood as representing personality dimensions that were not primarily interpersonal in nature, namely comfort with self, self-focused, and psychologically minded. These results present further support for the position that the interpersonal circumplex dimensions represent the interpersonal aspects of personality, whereas more dimensions are needed if less interpersonal aspects of personality are to be encompassed also.

It is interesting to note that, when we examined the relationship of these two dimensions to outcome, we found that those patients who were moderate on interpersonal sensitivity did *worse* than those who were at either extreme. It appeared that those who were extreme on this dimension, in either direction, were taking greater risks in the group setting than those who were more moderate on this variable; these patients "neither reach out to and make connections with others nor reveal hostile, negative behaviors in such a way that they can be worked on by the group" (Soldz, Budman, Davis, & Demby, 1993, p. 561). In fact, it turned out that those low on interpersonal sensitivity had the best outcome, perhaps because they were more willing to take the opportunity provided by group therapy to experiment with hostile behaviors and thus work on problematic interpersonal patterns. The activity dimension did not reveal any connection to outcome, whereas for two of the noninterpersonal dimensions, comfort with self and self-focused, being moderate was positively related to good outcome.

RELATION OF PERSONALITY DISORDERS TO THE INTERPERSONAL CIRCUMPLEX

As the researchers at the Mental Health Research Program of the Harvard Community Health Plan continued our studies of group therapy, we turned to personality disorders. One side effect of this work was the generation of a rather large set of data on patients presumed by their therapists to have personality disorders (Budman, Demby, Soldz, & Merry, in press). This data set included personality disorder diagnoses derived from the Personality Disorder Examination, a structured clinical interview (PDE; Loranger, 1988), the personality disorder scales of the Millon Clinical Multiaxial Inventory, version II (MCMI-II; Millon, 1980), and the Inventory of Interpersonal Problems (IIP; Horowitz et al., 1988), from which we extracted the IIP-C, a circumplex measure of interpersonal problems. Our first interesting finding was the "extremely close convergence between the theoretical and empirical placement of the [octant] scales" (Soldz, Budman, Demby, & Merry, 1993a, p. 44). This finding is of particular importance because the IIP-C was constructed using a college student population, and our results indicated that the circumplex structure of this instrument was replicable in our patient sample, strengthening the case that personality structure is similar in normal and clinical populations[2] (e.g., Wiggins, 1994).

We then were able to plot the various personality disorders in circumplex space by correlating the number of *DSM-III-R* (American Psychiatric Association, 1987) criteria met (from the PDE) or the MCMI-II Personality Disorder Base Rate scores with the circumplex dimensions of LOV (affiliation) and DOM (dominance). The result (Figure 1) indicated that there were very interpretable relations between personality disorders and the circumplex model, as has been found with other samples and instruments by other researchers (DeJong, van den Brink, Jansen, & Schippers, 1989; Kiesler, Van Denburg, Sikes-Nove, Larus, & Goldston, 1990; Morey, 1985; Pincus & Wiggins, 1990; Sim & Romney, 1990; Wiggins & Pincus, 1989). Many of the disorders fell near the line that runs from intrusive (NO) to socially avoidant (FG). Individuals diagnosed as histrionic were at the high end of the NO line, whereas individuals diagnosed as avoidant and schizoid were at the FG end. MCMI-II dependents were high on the exploitable (JK) octant, whereas PDE dependent individuals were slightly in this direction. Several of the MCMI-II scales clustered near domineering (PA), including narcissistic, antisocial, and sadistic—with the latter halfway between domineering and vindictive (BC), as would be expected. Thus, circumplex space indicated meaningful distinctions between these disorders that is consistent with the conceptualization of the disorders. Histrionic individuals, for example, would be expected to be intrusive, whereas avoidant and schizoid individuals are socially avoidant.

It is of interest that none of the disorders well represented in circumplex space was near the cold–overly–nurturant axis. It would seem that *DSM-III-R* personality disorders do not reflect pure extremes on either pole of affiliation. All disorders appear to involve either dominance or submis-

---

[2]We obtained a similar result with our measure of the Five Factor Model, the 50-Bipolar Self-Rating Scales (Goldberg, 1992), in which a principal components analysis revealed that 49 out of 50 items had their highest loading on the dimension to which they were assigned, whereas the holdout had a trivially higher loading on another dimension. These results strengthen the argument that participant structure is continuous between normal and pathological populations.

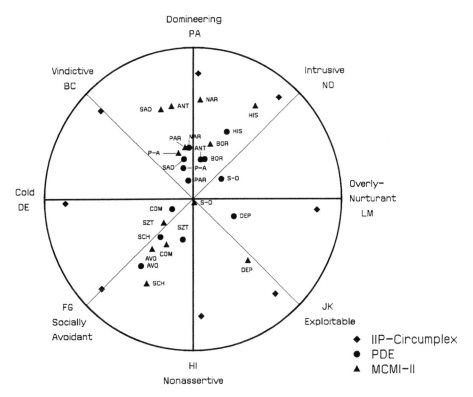

Figure 1. Location of Personality Disorder Examination and Millon Clinical Multiaxial Inventory II personality disorder scales in Inventory of Interpersonal Problems circumplex space. NAR = narcissistic; HIS = histrionic; BOR = borderline; ANT = antisocial; PA = passive–aggressive; PAR = paranoid; S-D = self-defeating; DEP = dependent; SAD = sadistic; COM = obsessive–compulsive (PDE) or compulsive (MCMI-II); SZT = schizotypal; AVO = avoidant; SCH = schizoid. From Soldz, Budman, Demby, and Merry (1993a).

siveness. It is unclear if the absence of disorders representing pure affiliation represents a lack of *DSM-III-R* representation of such problems or a fact about the nature of personality pathology. Certainly, those who feel that sadomasochism plays a large role is personality pathology (e.g., Kernberg, 1975) would not find such a result surprising.

This analysis, along with related results from other researchers (De-Jong et al., 1989; Kiesler et al., 1990; Morey, 1985; Pincus & Wiggins, 1990; Sim & Romney, 1990; Wiggins & Pincus, 1989), support the position that the circumplex model can represent meaningful and important aspects of the interpersonal functioning of personality disordered patients. However, the MCMI-II personality disorder scales were, in most cases, better represented in circumplex space than were the number of *DSM-III-R* criteria met, as represented by the PDE. If we look only at the PDE scales, only avoidant and histrionic disorders were well represented in this space.

Given the low concordance between the MCMI-II and the PDE (Soldz, Budman, Demby, & Merry, 1993b), these results present modest support for the strength of the circumplex model in representing personality pathology, as diagnosed by MCMI-II self-report questionnaire data. In fact, one of the reasons for the better representation of the MCMI-II in circumplex space in this study probably has to do with method variance, as both the MCMI-II and the IIP-C are self-report inventories. It appears that self-report inventories are more representable in the IIP-C circumplex space than are structured clinical interviews.

Another problem with this representation of personality disorders in circumplex space is that many of the disorders are not distinguished from each other. For example, borderline, paranoid, passive–aggressive, antisocial, and narcissistic all were grouped together just above the origin toward domineering (PA), between intrusive (NO) and vindictive (BC). Thus, the circumplex model, at least as operationalized by the IIP-C, did not distinguish the particular characteristics of each of these disorders. To some degree, this lack of distinction between disorders is a result of the comorbidity that is common when structured clinical interviews are used for diagnosis (Perry, 1992; Soldz et al., 1993b). Nonetheless, we were interested in whether other structural representations of personality could better distinguish these disorders.

FIVE FACTOR MODEL AND THE CIRCUMPLEX

The most popular alternative structural model of personality is the Five Factor Model, also known as the Big Five. The Five Factor Model postulates that personality can be encompassed in a five-dimensional space, the axes of which are extraversion, agreeableness, neuroticism (or emotional stability, if labeled from the other direction), conscientiousness, and openness to experience. Much evidence suggests that many aspects of personality can be encompassed within this framework (Digman, 1989; Goldberg, 1992; John, 1990; McCrae, 1992; McCrae & Costa, 1987, 1990). It appears that the Five Factor Model is replicable whether one looks at self-report or other report, and over a wide variety of instruments, tasks, and even languages and cultures.

Given the evidence for the Five Factor Model as a representation of personality, the question naturally arises as to the relation between it and circumplex models. As indicated previously, McCrae and Costa (1989) and Trapnell and Wiggins (1990) had explored this question previously. These authors conjectured that the interpersonal dimensions of the circumplex can be identified with the extraversion and agreeableness dimensions of the Five Factor Model, though with the axes rotated approximately 45°, so that extraversion went from intrusive to socially avoidant, and agreeable went from exploitable to vindictive. The data presented in their samples of normal individuals supported this conjecture.

We examined this issue with data from our personality disordered sample. The interpersonal circumplex was represented by the IIP-C. The Five Factor Model was represented by the 50 Bipolar Self-Rating Scales (50-BSRS; Goldberg, 1992). When we correlated extraversion with the circumplex dimensions of affiliation and dominance, we indeed found that it correlated almost identically, indicating that it could be located in circumplex space, with a 43° rotation from the dominance axis toward intrusive (NO), in almost perfect agreement with the previous findings from nonclinical samples. Agreeableness had a somewhat higher correlation with affiliation than dominance, leading it to be rotated only 20° from the affiliation axis toward exploitable (JK), leading to some divergence from its theoretical location. Nonetheless, our findings provide strong support for the position that the Five Factor Model dimensions include the interpersonal circumplex dimensions as a subset of a more comprehensive model.

Because this book is on circumplex models and not the Five Factor Model, I will not discuss in detail our findings on the relation between the Five Factor Model and personality pathology. We did find that each of the non-interpersonal circumplex dimensions contributed to understanding the personality disorders. Neuroticism, for example, was related to at least one of the measures for each of the disorders. It had its highest relationship with borderline, supporting the position of Widiger (1993) that this disorder can be conceptualized as an extreme of neuroticism. This finding helps explain why the studies of the relation of borderline pathology to the interpersonal circumplex had led to inconsistent results (Soldz et al., 1993a), because the essence of this disorder is not primarily interpersonal, though it may find expression in erratic interpersonal behavior.

The Five Factor Model also can shed light on another phenomenon involving the interpersonal circumplex. It is frequently asserted that circumplexity can best be brought out in measures when they are ipsatized before analysis by subtracting the participant's mean score from each item (Wiggins, Steiger, & Gaelick, 1981). But why is this? Ipsatizing is often conceptualized as removing an overall tendency of some people to complain. Wiggins, Steiger, and Gaelick (1981) expressed this line of reasoning:

> Many workers regard the general component found in interpersonal data as a "nuisance factor" peculiar to a given method of measurement, rather than as a substantive dimension of personality. Whether it is called a "checking factor," an "acquiescence factor" or an "intensity factor," the component is thought to reflect individual differences in

the use of the response format rather than differences in the perception of self or others. (p. 283)

This nuisance factor so far has remained rather mysterious. By examining the relationship between the interpersonal circumplex and the Five Factor Model, we were able to shed some light on this matter. When the IIP mean was correlated with the Big Five factors we found that it had its highest correlation with the neuroticism factor (.55 versus $-.37$ with extraversion and $-.21$ with agreeableness). Thus, the IIP essentially measures three of the Big Five factors, not just the two represented in the interpersonal circumplex. Examination of the correlation of the individual IIP items revealed a similar pattern: There were numerous correlations with each of these three factors from the Five Factor Model. Ipsatizing essentially removes the relationship with Neuroticism, thus allowing the circumplex qualities of the instrument to shine through. The mysterious tendency to complain thus can be conceptualized as being identical to neuroticism from the Five Factor Model. I suspect that this finding will generalize to other circumplex instruments, thus illuminating why ipsatizing helps bring out circumplex properties.

SHORT IIP-C

Another excursion into the circumplex involved the construction of a short form of the IIP-C, the IIP-SC (Soldz, Budman, Demby, & Merry, 1995b). As was noted previously, Alden, Wiggins, and Pincus (1990) took the 128-item IIP and constructed a 64-item shorter version, the IIP-C, which has eight items representing each of the eight interpersonal circumplex octants. This instrument has been found to have excellent psychometric properties and is currently in wide use. The fact that the IIP-C reduces the number of items in the IIP by half makes it more usable in situations in which patient time is limited or in which the instrument is part of a larger battery. However, there are situations in which even 64 items is a lot. For example, in one study, we wanted to have each patient in therapy groups complete a version of the IIP on every other member. In such a situation, in which an individual may be completing the same instrument between five and ten times, every item that can be eliminated makes it more likely that the measures will be completed. In another study, we were screening patients in the waiting room 5 minutes before their therapy sessions; again, this is a situation in which brevity is extremely important.

In order to meet the need for a version of the IIP that is even briefer than the IIP-C, we constructed the IIP-SC (Soldz, Budman, Demby, and Merry, 1995a) by taking the four items that had the highest correlations with each IIP-C octant score in a sample of 143 time-limited group therapy patients as shown in Table 1. We then examined the properties of this short instrument in two other samples—one sample consisted of a group of 107 patients referred for a study of personality disorders and the other sample was a set of 105 patients (all those who agreed to participate) seen by therapists in a training seminar at an outpatient clinic of the Harvard Community Health Plan.

We found that the IIP-SC had excellent psychometric properties in all three samples. The circumplex scales all were located near the hypothesized circumplex location. The mean absolute angular deviations from the the-

TABLE 1
The 32 Inventory of Interpersonal Problems Items in the IIP-SC

IIP item	Octant
It is hard for me to understand another person's point of view	PA
I am too aggressive toward other people	PA
I try to control other people too much	PA
I argue with other people too much	PA
It is hard for me to be supportive of another person's goals in life	BC
It is hard for me to feel good about another person's happiness	BC
I am too suspicious of other people	BC
I want to get revenge against people too much	BC
It is hard for me to show affection to people	DE
It is hard for me to experience a feeling of love for another person	DE
It is hard for me to feel close to other people	DE
I keep other people at a distance too much	DE
It is hard for me to join in groups	FG
It is hard for me to introduce myself to new people	FG
It is hard for me to socialize with other people	FG
It is hard for me to ask other people to get together socially with me	FG
It is hard for me to tell a person to stop bothering me	HI
It is hard for me to confront people with problems that come up	HI
It is hard for me to be assertive with another person	HI
It is hard for me to be firm when I need to be	HI
It is hard for me to let other people know when I am angry	JK
It is hard for me to be assertive without worrying about hurting the other person's feelings	JK
I am too easily persuaded by other people	JK
I let other people take advantage of me too much	JK
It is hard for me to attend to my own welfare when somebody else is needy	LM
I try to please other people too much	LM
I put other people's needs before my own too much	LM
I am affected by another person's misery too much	LM
It is hard for me to keep things private from other people	NO
I open up to people too much	NO
I want to be noticed too much	NO
I tell personal things to other people too much	NO

Note. PA = domineering; BC = vindictive; DE = cold–hearted; FG = socially avoidant; HI = unassured–submissive; JK = exploitable; LM = warm–agreeable; NO = intrusive.

oretical locations were 11.37° for the short-term group sample, 6.90° for the personality disorder sample, and 5.72° for the patients of therapist-trainees (see Figure 2). Coefficient alphas for the octants, measuring internal consistency reliability, were extremely high for such short scales; they ranged from .68 to .84. We reasoned that the correlations over several months could be seen as a lower bound for the test–retest reliability of the scales, since changes because of treatment could have reduced the correlations. In the short-term group sample, the median 4-month test–retest correlation was .66. For the personality disorder patients the median 3-month test–retest correlation was .83, whereas for the general outpatient sample it was .72. Thus, the octant scores exhibited good internal consistency and test–retest ordinal stability.

We also examined the sensitivity of the IIP-SC for measuring change as a result of treatment. We found that it did indeed change in the expected direction over the course of treatment for both group samples. In the short-term group, the median octant effect size r was marginally lower and in the personality disorder sample marginally higher than the corresponding

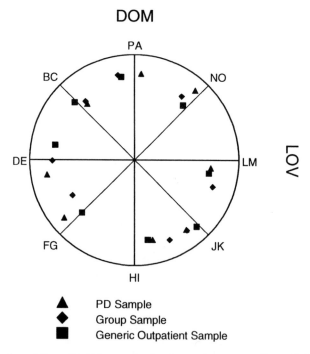

Figure 2. Location of three IIP-SC samples in circumplex space. (From Soldz, Budman, Demby, & Merry, 1995b. Reprinted by special permission of the publisher, Psychological Assessment Resources, Inc., Odessa, FL 33556, from *Assessment*, Volume 2, Number 1, Copyright 1995 by PAR, Inc. Further reproduction is prohibited without permission from PAR, Inc.).

effect sizes for the longer IIP-C. Thus, the IIP-SC appeared to be about as responsive to change as a result of treatment as the larger IIP-C. In fact, the overall mean of the IIP-SC, as a general measure of interpersonal problems, was as treatment responsive as the mean of the 128-item IIP.

Thus, in constructing the IIP-SC, we have developed a brief measure of the circumplex representation of interpersonal problems. This measure can be used in situations in which time pressure argues against the use of longer instruments. If one's primary interest is in the structural placement of an individual in circumplex space, then the IIP-SC probably can be used safely. If one is interested in more fine-grained analyses, such as analyses of individual items, then one would have to weigh carefully the trade-off between brevity and comprehensiveness.

THE INTERPERSONAL CIRCUMPLEX FROM THE PERSPECTIVE OF SELF AND OTHERS

One difficulty with the application of the interpersonal circumplex and of the Five Factor Model is that they depend on the point of view of the individual making the ratings. The interpersonal circumplex has been shown to arise whether interpersonal behavior is assessed from the perspective of the self or of others rating the self. However, although the same structure may arise no matter the perspective of the observer, this does not mean that different observers will necessarily agree on the placement of a given individual in circumplex space. So far this issue has not been explored much. A similar issue arises with the Five Factor Model. McCrae and Costa (1987) have shown convergence between self-report and ratings of spouses and close friends on their Five Factor Model measure for a nonclinical sample of individuals without disorders. There is, in fact, an extensive literature in personality theory regarding deteminates of self–other convergence and divergence in personality trait ratings (Funder & West, 1993).

We have less knowledge of these issues for clinical populations, however. In most cases, the issue appears to have been largely ignored. For example, as pointed out by Van Denburg, Kiesler, Wagner, and Schmidt (1994), all studies of the relation of personality disorders to the Five Factor Model have used self-report to determine patient location in Five Factor space (e.g., Costa & McCrae, 1990; Costa & Widiger, 1994; Soldz et al., 1995a; Wiggins & Pincus, 1989), and only one small-scale examination of the interpersonal circumplex and personality disorders has used ratings of interpersonal behavior to determine circumplex location (Kiesler et al., 1990).

We have started to make a dent in this area by investigating convergences between self, therapist, and other group members ratings of personality in group psychotherapy for personality disorders (Soldz, Budman, Demby, & Merry, 1995b). In particular, we had group patients fill out the 50-Bipolar Self-Rating Scales on themselves and on every other member in the group. We also had the therapist fill out this instrument for each member of her or his group. We found reasonable agreement among the other group members, with intraclass correlations ranging from .59 to .90. For the two dimensions that span circumplex space, namely extraversion and agreeableness, the intraclass correlations were .86 and .72, respectively. Other group members thus tended to have greater agreement on a given target patient's extraversion than on his or her agreeableness. When we compared the mean of the other group member ratings with those of the therapist, the correlations were .70 for extraversion and .65 for agreeableness, indicating strong agreement between the therapists and other group members on patients' personality traits in the interpersonal domain. (Results were similar for the three noninterpersonal dimensions.)

When we examined the correlation between other group members and therapists and the patients themselves, we found something quite different. Only for the extraversion factor was there significant agreement between the patients and those who rated them (self–other group member: $r = .66$; self–therapist: $r = .65$). For agreeableness and for the three noninterpersonal dimensions, the correlations were small and nonsignificant.

We further speculated that patients with more personality disturbance would have higher levels of disagreement between self and others, reasoning that personality pathology involves nonconsensual views of oneself, among other things. The results were exactly the opposite. The more DSM-III-R Axis II symptoms a patient possessed, the more agreement existed among therapists and other group members about that patient's personality profile. Thus, more disturbed patients saw themselves in more consensual ways.

This result may be artifactual, however. In two previous studies (Soldz et al., 1990; Soldz et al., 1992), we had shown that more disturbed patients talked more in group therapy and that they talked more about themselves, in particular. Thus, more disturbed patients provide more opportunity for other patients to observe how they view themselves. Furthermore, in our personality disorder study, we screened patients for the presence of personality pathology by means of a structured clinical interview. Those who either were not aware of or were unwilling to admit to their problematic personality characteristics may not have received a personality disorder diagnosis and thus may have tended to be screened out of our study. This latter artifact may be one that bedevils much research on personality disorders based on self-report.

Although our study of self–other agreement on personality traits was based on a small number of participants, it is one of very few to explore this important area. In general, clinical researchers do not take enough account of these issues in their research. If we assume that pathology involves disturbances in construal of self and others, as most clinicians implicitly do, then we cannot assume that patient self-report is comparable to the views of others who know the patient well. However, it is important to note that no viewpoint is privileged. Until we understand more about these issues, clinical researchers should strive to measure key variables from as many perspectives as is practicable.

CONCLUSION

The results of these studies support the utility of the interpersonal circumplex model for understanding clinical phenomena. The interpersonal circumplex can be located in many situations in which interpersonal behavior is being investigated. In some sense, one could argue that the revealing of the circumplex in a study of a given domain is an indication that the domain under investigation is indeed interpersonal in nature (Gurtman, 1992, 1993).

The interpersonal circumplex provides us with an indication of the structure of the interpersonal domain. There appear to be two underlying dimensions. Of course, although the number of dimensions is invariant, the location of the axes is underdetermined. The interpersonal circumplex and the Five Factor Model place these axes in different locations, rotated about 45° from each other. However, we currently have no objective criteria for determining the optimal location of axes. The choice ultimately rests on pragmatic grounds, such as agreement with common sense or other theories. If one truly has a circumplex structure in one's data, then the axes are not determinable from traditional factor analytic criteria for simple structure. The fact that many personality disorders are located on the interpersonal circumplex line from gregarious–extraverted to aloof–introverted, which is where the Five Factor Model extraversion axis lies, suggests that the Five Factor location may have some advantages for clinical uses.

Of course, one of the primary advantages of the interpersonal circumplex, and of circumplex models in general, is that they are as concerned with modeling the off-axis behavior of individuals as they are with the placement on the axes. Thus, with the interpersonal circumplex, one can get a profile of an individual's placement for each octant. This type of profile allows us to examine a number of questions that are theoretically and clinically fascinating. For example, is psychic health related to being well-rounded, rather than extreme in one area (Wiggins, Phillips, & Trapnell, 1989)? Do profiles with peaks at noncontiguous points on the circumplex indicate the presence of psychological conflict? Questions like these go far beyond the structural issues on which my research has concentrated so far. Yet it is precisely these types of questions, along with issues regarding the nature of interpersonal complementarity (Orford, 1986; Tracey, 1994) and the issues raised previously regarding self–other convergence and divergence in personality assessment, that make the interpersonal circumplex so exciting and so much more than a mere structural model. Confirmation of the robustness of the interpersonal circumplex as a structural model strengthens the exploration of these more dynamic questions regarding interpersonal behavior.

REFERENCES

Alden, L. E., Wiggins J. S., & Pincus, A. L. (1990). Construction of circumplex scales for the Inventory of Interpersonal Problems. *Journal of Personality Assessment, 55,* 521–536.

American Psychiatric Association. (1987). *Diagnostic and statistical manual of mental disorders* (3rd rev. ed.). Washington, DC: Author.

Benjamin, L. S. (1974). Structural analysis of social behavior. *Psychological Review, 81,* 392–425.

Benjamin, L. S. (1994). SASB: A bridge between personality theory and clinical psychology. *Psychological Inquiry, 5,* 273–316.

Budman, S. H., Demby, A., Soldz, S., & Merry, J. (in press). Group therapy for patients with personality disorders: Outcomes and dropouts. *International Journal of Group Psychotherapy.*

Budman, S. H., Rothberg, P., & Davis, M. (1989). *The Individual Group Member Interpersonal Process Scale (IGIPS).* Boston: Harvard Community Health Plan, Mental Health Research Program.

Budman, S. H., Soldz, S., Demby, A. Davis, M., & Merry, J. (1993). What is cohesiveness? An empirical examination. *Small Group Behavior, 24,* 199–216.

Budman, S. H., Soldz, S., Demby, A., Feldstein, M., & Springer, T. (1989). Cohesion, alliance and outcome in group psychotherapy: An empirical examination. *Psychiatry, 52,* 339–350.

Costa, P. T., & McCrae, R. R. (1990). Personality disorders and the Five-Factor Model of personality. *Journal of Personality Disorders, 4,* 362–371.

Costa, P. T., & Widiger, T. A. (1994). *Personality disorders and the Five-Factor Model of personality.* Washington, DC: American Psychological Association.

DeJong, C. A. J., van den Brink, W., Jansen, J. A. M., & Schippers, G. M. (1989). Interpersonal aspects of *DSM-III* Axis-II: Theoretical hypotheses and empirical findings. *Journal of Personality Disorders, 3,* 135–146.

Digman, J. M. (1989). Five robust trait dimensions: Development, stability, and utility. *Journal of Personality, 57,* 195–214.

Funder, D. C., & West, S. G. (Eds.). (1993). Viewpoints on personality: Consensus, self–other agreement, and accuracy in personality judgement (Special issue). *Journal of Personality, 61*(4).

Goldberg, L. R. (1992). The development of markers for the Big-Five Factor structure. *Psychological Assessment, 4,* 26–42.

Gurtman, M. B. (1992). Construct validity of interpersonal personality measures: The interpersonal circumplex as a nomological net. *Journal of Personality and Social Psychology, 63,* 105–118.

Gurtman, M. B. (1993). Constructing personality tests to meet a structural criterion: Application of the interpersonal circumplex. *Journal of Personality, 61,* 237–263.

Henry, W. P., Schacht, T. E., & Strupp, H. H. (1986). Structural analysis of social behavior: Application to a study of interpersonal process in differential psychotherapeutic outcome. *Journal of Consulting and Clinical Psychology, 54,* 27–31.

Horowitz, L. M. (1979). On the cognitive structure of interpersonal problems treated in psychotherapy. *Journal of Consulting and Clinical Psychology, 47,* 5–15.

Horowitz, L. M., Rosenberg, S. E., Baer, B. A., Ureño, G., & Villaseñor, V. S. (1988). Inventory of Interpersonal Problems: Psychometric properties and clinical applications. *Journal of Consulting and Clinical Psychology, 56,* 885–892.

John, O. P. (1990). The "Big Five" factor taxonomy: Dimensions of personality in the natural language and in questionnaires. In L. A. Pervin (Ed.), *Handbook of personality: Theory and research* (pp. 66–100). New York: Guilford Press.

Kelly, G. (1955). *The psychology of personal constructs: A theory of personality.* New York: Norton.

Kernberg, O. (1975). *Borderline conditions and pathological narcissism.* New York: Jason Aronson.

Kiesler, D. J. (1983). The 1982 interpersonal circle: A taxonomy for complementarity in human transactions. *Psychological Review, 90,* 185–214.

Kiesler, D. J., Van Denburg, T. F., Sikes-Nova, V. E., Larus, J. P., & Goldston, C. S. (1990). Interpersonal behavior profiles of eight cases of *DSM-III* personality disorders. *Journal of Clinical Psychology, 46,* 440–453.

Leary, T. (1957). *Interpersonal diagnosis of personality: A functional theory and methodology for personality evaluation.* New York: Ronald Press.

de Leeuw, J. (1994). *Statistics and the Sciences.* Unpublished manuscript.

Loranger, A. W. (1988). *Personality Disorder Examination* (PDE) *Manual.* Yonkers, NY: DV Communications.

McCrae, R. R. (Ed.). (1992). The Five-Factor Model: Issues and applications (Special issue). *Journal of Personality, 60*(2).

McCrae, R. R., & Costa, P. T. (1987). Validation of the Five-Factor Model of personality across instruments and observers. *Journal of Personality and Social Psychology, 52,* 81–90.

McCrae, R. R., & Costa, P. T. (1989) The structure of interpersonal traits: Wiggins' circumplex and the Five-Factor Model. *Journal of Personality and Social Psychology, 56,* 586–595.

McCrae, R. R., & Costa, P. T. (1990). *Personality in adulthood.* New York: Guilford Press.

Millon, T. (1980). *Manual for the Millon Clinical Multiaxial Inventory II (MCMI-II).* Minneapolis, MN: National Computer Systems.

Morey, L. C. (1985). An empirical comparison of interpersonal and *DSM-III* approaches to classification of personality disorders. *Psychiatry, 48,* 358–364.

Orford, J. (1986). The rules of interpersonal complementarity: Does hostility beget hostility and dominance, submission? *Psychological Review, 93,* 365–377.

Perry, J. C. (1992). Problems and considerations in the valid assessment of personality disorders. *American Journal of Psychiatry, 149,* 1645–1653.

Pincus, A. L., & Wiggins, J. S. (1990). Interpersonal problems and conceptions of personality disorders. *Journal of Personality Disorders, 4,* 342–352.

Sim, J. P., & Romney, D. M. (1990). The relationship between a circumplex model of interpersonal behaviors and personality disorders. *Journal of Personality Disorders, 4,* 329–341.

Soldz, S. (1990). The therapeutic interaction: Research perspectives. In R. A. Wells & V. J. Giannetti, (Eds.), *Handbook of the brief psychotherapies* (pp. 22–53). New York: Plenum Press.

Soldz, S., Budman, S. H., Davis, M., & Demby, A. (1993). Beyond the interpersonal circumplex in group psychotherapy: The structure and relationship to outcome of The Individual Group Member Interpersonal Process Scale. *Journal of Clinical Psychology, 49,* 551–563.

Soldz, S., Budman, S. H., & Demby, A. (1992). The relationship between Main Actor behaviors and treatment outcome in group psychotherapy. *Psychotherapy Research, 2,* 52–62.

Soldz, S., Budman, S. H., Demby, A., & Feldstein, M. (1990). Patient activity and outcome in group psychotherapy: New findings. *International Journal of Group Psychotherapy, 40,* 53–62.

Soldz, S., Budman, S. H., Demby, A., & Merry, J. (1993a). Representation of personality disorders in circumplex and Five-Factor space: Explorations with a clinical sample. *Psychological Assessment, 5,* 41–52.

Soldz, S., Budman, S. H., Demby, A., & Merry, J. (1993b). Diagnostic agreement between the Personality Disorder Examination and the MCMI-II. *Journal of Personality Assessment, 60,* 486–499.

Soldz, S., Budman, S. H., Demby, A., & Merry, J. (1995a). Personality traits as seen by patients, therapists and other group members: The Big Five in personality disorder groups. *Psychotherapy: Theory, Research and Practice, 32,* 678–687.

Soldz, S., Budman, S. H., Demby, A., & Merry, J. (1995b). A short form of the Inventory of Interpersonal Problems Circumplex Scales. *Assessment, 2,* 53–63.

Tracey, T. J. (1994). An examination of the complementarity of interpersonal behavior. *Journal of Personality and Social Psychology, 67,* 864–878.

Trapnell, P. D., & Wiggins, J. S. (1990). Extension of the Interpersonal Adjective Scales to include the Big Five dimensions of personality. *Journal of Personality and Social Psychology, 59*, 781–790.

Van Denburg, T. F., Kiesler, D. J., Wagner, C. C., & Schmidt, J. A. (1994). Not a completed bridge, but several solid spans. *Psychological Inquiry, 5*, 326–329.

Widiger, T. A. (1993). The *DSM-III-R* categorical personality disorder diagnoses: A critique and an alternative. *Psychological Inquiry, 4*, 75–90.

Wiggins, J. S. (1982). Circumplex models of interpersonal behavior in clinical psychology. In P. C. Kendall & J. N. Butcher (Eds.), *Handbook of research methods in clinical psychology* (pp. 183–221). New York: Wiley.

Wiggins, J. S. (1994). Shoring up the SASB bridge between personality theory and clinical psychology. *Psychological Issues, 5*, 329–332.

Wiggins, J. S., & Broughton, R. (1985). The interpersonal circle: A structural model for the integration of personality research. In R. Hogan & W. H. Jones (Eds.), *Perspectives in personality* (Vol. 1. pp. 1–47). Greenwich, CT: JAI Press.

Wiggins, J. S., Phillips, N., & Trapnell, P. (1989). Circular reasoning about interpersonal behavior: Evidence concerning some untested assumptions underlying diagnostic classification. *Journal of Personality and Social Psychology, 56*, 296–305.

Wiggins, J. S., & Pincus, A. L. (1989). Conceptions of personality disorders and dimensions of personality. *Psychological Assessment, 1*, 305–316.

Wiggins, J. S., Steiger, J. H., & Gaelick, L. (1981). Evaluating circumplexity in personality data. *Multivariate Behavioral Research, 16*, 263–289.

18

INTERPERSONAL ASSESSMENT AND THERAPY OF EATING DISORDERS: A CLINICAL APPLICATION OF A CIRCUMPLEX MODEL

JAMES K. MADISON

This chapter focuses on the application of a circumplex model of personality to the evaluation and treatment of persons with eating disorders. The particular model applied is a two-dimensional circumplex advanced by Leary (1957) and further developed by others (e.g., Kiesler, 1983; Wiggins, 1979). The model is used to derive expected diagnostic patterns, to empirically validate these expected patterns, and to discuss implications for clinical work with the population of individuals with eating disorders.

Interpersonal theories of anorexia and bulimia have lagged behind other approaches to conceptualizing treatment for eating disorders. Psychodynamic and cognitive theorists have been responsible for most of the conceptual and therapeutic tools used in the area. Although the importance of body image, food preoccupations, and weight are readily evident to anyone working with eating-disordered clients, psychodynamically oriented theorists such as Bruch (1973) have emphasized other characteristics such as ineffectiveness, interpersonal distrust, perfectionism, and fears of maturity. Deficits in self-regulation also have been postulated (Geist, 1985). Although the incorporation of measures of some of these variables into the Eating Disorders Inventory (Garner, 1991) has made possible a more operational definition of these variables, these theories have not spawned the kind of specific treatment protocols that have resulted from cognitive–behavioral approaches.

Cognitive–behavioral theorists view individuals with eating disorders as sharing a set of distorted and dysfunctional attitudes, behaviors, and beliefs about food, body size, and weight (Fairburn, 1985; Mizes, 1985). Treatment strategies have been adapted from cognitive–behavioral interventions in other domains and applied to the treatment of eating disorders. The focus of these interventions is to help clients disrupt, challenge, and reframe their dysfunctional behaviors and beliefs. Cognitive–behavioral approaches to anorexia and bulimia have resulted in specific treatment protocols that have been successful, particularly in the treatment of bulimia. Clients treated with these procedures show changes in both their thinking about weight and food issues and in their actual dysfunctional behaviors (Fairburn, 1985; Garner & Bemis, 1982; Pyle, Mitchell, Eckert, Hatzukami, & Goff, 1984).

Interpersonal strategies for evaluating and treating eating disorders that have reached the literature have not been systematically derived from interpersonal theory. The most definitive trial of an explicitly interpersonal therapy for eating disorders resulted from the selection of treatment modeled after Klerman, Weissman, Rounsaville, and Chevron's (1984) interpersonal therapy for depression as a control treatment in a study of cognitive behavioral treatment of bulimia (Jones, Peveler, Hope, & Fairburn, 1993). In follow-up studies, the group receiving interpersonal therapy has not differed from the cognitive–behavioral treatment group, with both groups showing substantial success in recovery from bulimia (Fairburn, Peveler, Jones, Hope, & Doll, 1993). Because this treatment was not expected to have a significant impact on bulimia, there was no explicit theoretical rationale for its use. The outcome measures were the same as those used for assessment of cognitive–behavioral and behavioral treatments in the same study. Although this particular study was well done in its use of multiple dependent variables, none of the measures selected explicitly evaluated variables related to theories of interpersonal style.

Only two studies to date have employed an interpersonal assessment model in evaluating clients with eating disorders. Humphrey (1989, 1994) studied families of bulimic clients using the three-dimensional circumplex Structural Analysis of Social Behavior (SASB) model (Benjamin, 1974) to examine the patterns of interaction among members of these families. This work has allowed operationalization and study of some of the family dynamics that have been postulated in studies of eating disorders. In addition, the use of this model may allow development of explicit therapy strategies for populations or subpopulations of these bulimic clients, parallel to Benjamin's (1994) recommendations for personality disorders.

In the realm of connecting therapy to explicitly interpersonal assessment, Wilfley's (1994) recent work stands alone. She has begun to look specifically at the interpersonal effects of group therapy with bulimic patients using Horowitz's Inventory of Interpersonal Problems (IIP; Horowitz, Rosenberg, Baer, Ureño, & Villaseñor, 1988). At the time of this writing, circumplex models have not been applied to either the analysis of the outcome or to the development of interventions in this research project. However, the availability of circumplex scores from IIP protocols would allow circumplex analysis in the future.

THE INTERPERSONAL DESCRIPTION OF PEOPLE WITH EATING DISORDERS

One goal of this chapter is to present hypotheses about eating-disordered clients in terms of a two-dimensional circumplex. Descriptions furnished in the literature about anorexia and bulimia were used as a starting point. For this purpose, the descriptors of eating behavior and cognitive distortions relating to weight and food are not directly useful. However, some of the descriptors of eating-disordered clients readily lend themselves to interpersonal descriptors. Interpersonal mistrust (Bruch, 1973), avoidance, and withdrawal (Garfinkel & Garner, 1982) can be translated into terms of the interpersonal circumplex. Informal descriptions by family members and others who deal with eating-disordered patients on a daily basis often include words that clearly describe interpersonal aspects of eating-disordered clients. A final set of descriptors includes the observation that individuals with both bulimia (Johnson & Connors, 1987) and anorexia (Garfinkel & Garner, 1982) show strong self-doubt and a sense of ineffectiveness. These descriptors, although not exhaustive, are fairly representative of interpersonal descriptions in the literature and were taken as the starting point for this analysis.

The present study employed the circumplex model articulated by Wiggins (1979) to develop initial hypotheses and to evaluate empirically those expectations. Wiggins' model has several advantages for the present study. First, the model remains firmly tied to prior interpersonal concepts and theory. Its relationship to other two-dimensional circumplexes (e.g., Kiesler, 1983; Leary, 1957) is well articulated, both conceptually and methodologically. Second, the Interpersonal Adjective Scales (IAS) that were developed to operationalize the model have demonstrated adequate psychometric properties including the circumplex ordering of its variables. Third, the conceptual connection of Wiggins' circumplex to interpersonal theory allows access to concepts that can be used to generate treatment expectations based on results of the present study. The circumplex is depicted in Figure 1.

To develop the initial expectations for an interpersonal diagnostic description of eating-disordered clients, the terms drawn from descriptions

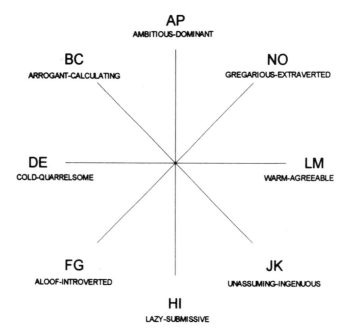

Figure 1. The interpersonal circumplex, modeled after Wiggins (1979).

of these clients were placed on the two-dimensional circumplex. Withdrawal and avoidance fit readily into the lower-left quadrant. Specifically, the aloof–introverted octant appears to be an appropriate placement for this aspect of client behavior. Interpersonal characteristics in the aloof–introverted octant include introversion, distance, impersonal, and undemonstrative.

The interpersonal mistrust and manipulative behaviors of eating-disordered clients also was viewed as implying a degree of hostility in relating to others, but it appears to reflect a more active or controlling orientation in this hostility. For this reason, the arrogant–calculating octant was chosen to depict this range of behavior. The interpersonal attributes of this octant include being conceited, tricky, and calculating.

Finally, the inconsistent–self-doubting octant was added to accommodate the passivity and self-deprecation inherent in some descriptions of eating disorders. Individuals whose interpersonal styles are best characterized by this octant can be seen as inconsistent, self-doubting, and meek.

This examination suggests that the interpersonal style of clients with eating disorders can be described best as a complex admixture of characteristics from the aloof–introverted, arrogant–calculating, and inconsistent–self-doubting octants of the Wiggins circumplex. Thus, in planning treatment for individuals in this population, one would anticipate that the typical client would present a largely hostile interpersonal style.

She or he would be expected to show this hostility both in terms of submissive self-deprecation and withdrawal, and at the same time seeking control through manipulation and expressions of resentment.

Validation of the Hypothesis in a Clinical Sample

The next step was to attempt to validate this expectation using clinical data. Two questions were regarded as central. First, are the expectations based on general descriptors of eating-disordered patients supported by scores on an actual measure of interpersonal style? Specifically, do clients with eating disorders show elevations in the three octants described earlier? In addition, do these scores show a meaningful relationship with the actual eating disorder diagnosed? Humphrey (1989) was able to demonstrate some differences in family interaction patterns between anorexic and bulimic families based on Structural Analysis of Social Behavior codings that have clear implications for family therapy. Parallel findings in this context would have implications for differential therapy for eating-disordered subgroups.

The second question is whether the use of interpersonal measures can reveal meaningful subgroups within an eating-disordered population, regardless of specific eating disorder diagnosis. This is a different way of addressing the issue of treatment selection. Treatment decisions for this clinical group typically are based on the manner in which the client deals with food rather than the manner in which the client deals with other people. Such an approach is highly consistent with behavioral and cognitive behavioral frameworks but is not consistent with interpersonal theory.

Method

To evaluate the initial interpersonal circumplex analysis of eating disorders, the records of 101 clients of the University of Nebraska Eating Disorders Program were selected at random from those of clients entering the program between 1991 and 1994. As part of a comprehensive, interdisciplinary evaluation of their eating disorders, these clients had completed the Interpersonal Adjective Scales (IAS) along with other more traditional psychometric instruments and the Eating Disorders Inventory (EDI; Garner, 1991).

The clients whose test results were analyzed were diagnostically heterogeneous. They had all come to the clinical setting either seeking treatment for themselves or had been sent by others for treatment of an eating disorder. As the only comprehensive treatment program in its region, the University of Nebraska attracts complicated and difficult patients who are not easily managed in other settings. Many individuals had concomitant Axis I and Axis II disorders and were suffering from the physical and emotional consequences of starvation and dietary chaos. This particular sample ranged in age from 14 to 44 years, with a mean age of 21.8 years. Chart reviews were done to assign clients diagnosed under the *DSM-III-R* criteria to the new *DSM-IV* subtypes. Of the sample, 60% were diagnosed with bulimia nervosa, purging subtype; 17% with anorexia nervosa, restricting subtype; 12% with anorexia nervosa, bulimic subtype; and the rest with atypical eating disorders. The latter group was composed primarily of individuals showing anorexic symptoms who had not reached explicit *DSM-IV* criteria for anorexia—in other words, their weight had not reached 85% of ideal body weight but was low and dropping lower. Of these clients 52% were also diagnosed with an affective disorder and 27% with an anxiety disorder. It is acknowledged that the heterogeneity of this sample could mask findings specific to eating disorders. However, it is likely that few emotional disorders appear in uncontaminated or pure form but rather appear as prototypic clusters. Further, the typical clinician is confronted with heterogeneous symptoms and client populations day to day. The purpose of these investigations is to provide insights that may prove useful in a clinical setting. It is hoped that what may have been lost by eschewing pure prototypes may be compensated by gains in clinical utility.

Analysis of Data Based on the Wiggins Circumplex

The initial analysis of data was straightforward. The numbers of clients showing one or a combination of the three octants identified previously was assessed. The data were scanned for seven possible profiles. Three possible single octant codes were examined—arrogant–calculating, aloof–introverted, and lazy–submissive. Three two point codes also were evaluated—arrogant–calculating + aloof–introverted, arrogant–calculating + lazy–submissive, and aloof–introverted + lazy–submissive. The other possibility includes individuals having all three identified octants as their three highest scores. A client was counted as having a single high point code for a given octant if that scale was the highest scaled score among the eight octant scales. Scores were transformed to *t*-scores based on Wiggins' (1979) college-age norms to provide a common metric for these comparisons.

Analysis of Interpersonal Adjective Scales Octant Scores

The high point analysis was only partially supportive of the a priori assignments of clients to octants. The three suggested octants—lazy–submissive, aloof–introverted, and arrogant–calculating—each accounted for 9.57% of the one-point codes. The three most frequent octant high points were warm–agreeable, gregarious–extraverted, and cold–quarrelsome, respectively accounting for 22.5%, 19.1%, and 17% of the profiles. The relatively high frequency of the cold–quarrelsome octant is consistent with the literature-based descriptors in that it is in the same half of the circumplex as the three octants originally anticipated. It is actually bordered by two of the octants aloof–introverted and arrogant–calculating—suggested by the analysis of descriptors. However, the strong presence of the warm–agreeable and gregarious–outgoing octants was not suggested by the initial approach to anticipating interpersonal styles of eating-disordered clients. These octants emphasize a nurturant and affiliative interpersonal style very different from the more predominantly hostile styles identified in the literature and different from the cold–quarrelsome octant identified in the present analysis.

Analysis of Interpersonal Adjective Scales Profile Data

In order to evaluate more complex profiles within the client data, individuals were grouped according to the two octants in which their highest t-scores were obtained. For example, clients having their two highest scores in octants PA and NO would be said to have a two point code of ambitious–dominant + gregarious–extraverted.

The two-point coding of IAS profiles presents a similar picture to the high-point or single-octant coding of the data. The most common two-point code is warm–agreeable + gregarious–extraverted with 13%, followed by arrogant–calculating + cold–quarrelsome with 12%, and cold–quarrelsome + aloof–introverted with 10%. Of the two-point pairings initially suggested, only aloof–introverted + lazy–submissive was among the five most frequent profiles. Unassuming–ingenuous + warm–agreeable and gregarious–extraverted + arrogant–calculating each accounted for 6% of the profiles.

As a whole, the results suggest that there is a hostile, cold group of eating-disordered clients, some of whom also show withdrawal or calculated manipulativeness. This coldness was not fully appreciated in the descriptions employed to develop the content analysis. However, it is consistent with such clinical experiences as having one member of a group break down in tears while talking about a particular issue only to have the rest of the group members sit by impassively. The existence of the inhibited, self-abasing style also received some support from the analysis. The most surprising finding from the standpoint of the initial octant assignments was the clear indication of another group or groups of eating-disordered patients with a markedly different style. There appears to be a substantial group of clients who demonstrate preferred interpersonal styles in the warm–agreeable and gregarious–extraverted octants of the circumplex. This interpersonal analysis might suggest that different interventions and treatment goals would be applicable to this more stylistically affiliative group than to the group showing stronger hostility in their style.

Cross-Validation of Results

Given the exploratory nature of this study, it was particularly important to cross-validate the results using a second sample. For this purpose, a separate sample of 101 eating-disordered clients were drawn from clients of the Eating Disorders Program. There were no differences between the two samples on age, diagnosis, or most IAS variables. Only the IAS, ambitious–dominant octant scores differed significantly with the second group showing a mean score of 40.4 ($SD = 11.52$) compared to a mean of 36.4 ($SD = 12.74$) in the first group. In the context of the number of tests run, such a result would be expected as a chance difference.

Analysis proceeded in the same manner for the second as for the first sample of clients. Again, the most common octant high point was in warm–agreeable (23.6%). The four remaining octant high points were cold–quarrelsome (18%), aloof–introverted (12.4%), and gregarious–extraverted (12.4%). For two-point codes, warm–agreeable + gregarious–extraverted was again the highest with 19% of the sample. Unassuming–ingenuous + warm–agreeable was more heavily represented in the second sample with 9% of the clients. Cold–quarrelsome + aloof–introverted was again the second most common two-point code with 10%. The three originally hypothesized codes showed the same frequencies in the second sample as in the first.

Implications

The results of the second study supported the conclusions reached in the first set of analyses. Although there are some differences in detail, the analyses suggest the existence of two subgroups of eating-disordered clients with the cold–quarrelsome octant characterizing one group and the warm–agreeable octant characterizing the other. The interpersonal styles of the two groups suggested by this finding are highly dissimilar—indeed, opposite each other in interpersonal style—and call for very different therapeutic approaches. If treatment for eating-disordered clients is based on some assumption of uniformity among these clients, serious disservice could be done to them. Although eating-disordered clients may show significant similarities in their tendency to distort body size, overvalue thinness, and to focus on food and weight issues, this study indicates that this similarity does not extend to interpersonal styles. In pursuing the promising results of Fairburn and his colleagues (1993) using interpersonal methods, this will be an important added dimension.

CLUSTER ANALYSIS OF INTERPERSONAL ADJECTIVE SCALES SCORES

To further validate the idea of two underlying interpersonal subgroups among eating-disordered clients, the data were subjected to cluster analysis. The goal of the more formal statistical procedure was to answer the question of whether the proposed groupings could be derived from a method other than that used in the preceding analyses. Specifically, cluster analysis was used to determine the extent to which two groupings resembling those derived from the high-point analysis described earlier could be derived by a systematic multivariate method. The K-means method was chosen because it compares favorably with other clustering techniques (Andreasen & Grove, 1982) and is particularly well suited to situations in which there is a rationale for anticipating that participants might be classified into a specific number of groups.

An initial analysis was performed using the first sample of 100 clients selected for the first high-point analysis. Results are shown graphically in Figure 2. The first cluster clearly conforms to the expectation of a warm–agreeable pattern. The second cluster, dominated by high-points in cold–quarrelsome, aloof–introverted, and lazy–submissive, corresponds to the more hostile, detached pattern evident in the previous analysis. The presence of lazy–submissive in this profile conforms to descriptions of passivity and self-doubt from the original content analysis but suggests that these elements are mixed with more specifically hostile elements.

The cross-validation sample was subjected to the same analysis. The profiles from this analysis are highly similar to those generated from the initial clustering. Again, the mean profile for the first cluster is dominated by octants warm–agreeable and gregarious–extraverted. The profile for the second cluster shows an even more marked relative elevation for the cold–quarrelsome octant than did the first analysis. However, the same three scales remain the most elevated in this analysis. The mean profiles for this analysis are shown in Figure 3.

Both the relatively simple approach of evaluating the frequency of occurrence of octant high points and the more complex cluster analysis approach support the existence of two distinct subgroups within this client sample. The greatest deviation from expectations developed from interpersonal descriptors in the literature was the existence of the warm, outgoing subgroup. However, the empirical results from the IAS indicated that this subgrouping is reliable and that it includes a large number of the clients sampled. The next stage of the investigation was to determine the relationship of these interpersonally based groups of gregarious–extraverted and pathology-specific to eating disorders.

The similarity of the cluster analysis between the original sample and the cross-validation sample warranted combining the two client samples

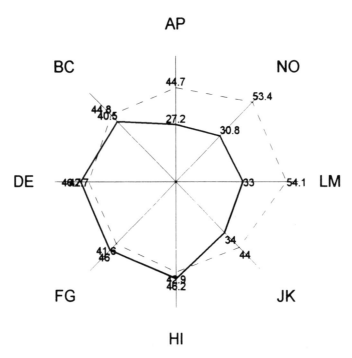

Figure 2. Mean *t*-scores of groups identified through cluster analysis. The group with the more hostile style is represented by the solid line, the more affiliative group by the dashed line. (AP = ambitious–dominant; BC = arrogant–calculating; DE = cold–quarrelsome; FG = aloof–introverted; HI = lazy–submissive; JK = unassuming–ingenuous; LM = warm–agreeable; NO = gregarious–extraverted.)

for this stage of the study. To determine the relationship between assigned diagnosis and membership in either the cold, aloof group or the warm, outgoing group, a chi-square analysis was conducted. In the absence of any a priori construction relating these two categories, expected frequencies were assigned based on row and column totals. There was no support for the general hypotheses of differences between the two groups in diagnosed eating disorder ($\chi^2 = 28.64$, *df* = 35, *p* = .68).

INTERPERSONAL STYLE AND EATING-DISORDERED PATHOLOGY

To evaluate the relationship of specific eating-disordered pathology to the interpersonally derived groups, client scores on the Eating Disorders Inventory (EDI) were used. This inventory is unique among measures designed specifically for use with this client population. It includes three scales measuring attitudes and beliefs specifically related to eating and body image—drive for thinness, bulimia, and body dissatisfaction. It also in-

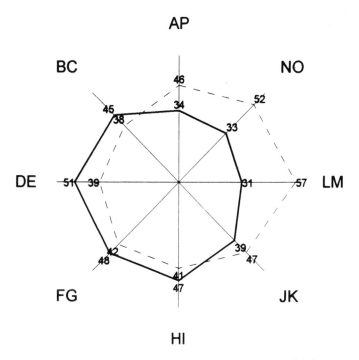

Figure 3. Mean *t*-scores from the cluster analysis of the cross-validation sample. The group with the more hostile style is represented by the solid line, the more affiliative group by the dashed line. (AP = ambitious–dominant; BC = arrogant–calculating; DE = cold–quarrelsome; FG = aloof–introverted; HI = lazy–submissive; JK = unassuming–ingenuous; LM = warm–agreeable; NO = gregarious–extraverted.)

cludes scales measuring other aspects of eating-disordered behavior and beliefs, including some with interpersonal referents—interpersonal distrust, interoceptive awareness, ineffectiveness, perfectionism, and maturity fears. (The newest version of the EDI has three additional scales that were not included in the analysis because some clients had been assessed with the original version.) There was no reason to expect that specific distortions regarding food or weight should be related to the distinct interpersonal styles identified in this study. However, those variables more directly related to interpersonal issues might be expected to show such a relationship. Discriminant function analysis was employed to address this question. EDI variables were entered into the analysis in a stepwise manner. The analysis was halted when the *p* value of the *F* ratio to enter exceeded .05.

None of the eating-specific EDI scales met the criteria for entry into the analysis. Only ineffectiveness and perfectionism reached significance in the analysis. The equation based on these two variables was significant beyond the .05 level [*F* (1,132) = 12.41, *p* = .0006]. Classification into assigned groups was successful for 65.7% of the cases. The next variable that could have been entered in the analysis was the B scale. When the effect of its addition to the analysis was explored, the classification accuracy was unaffected.

IMPLICATIONS

By applying an analysis of these clients from the perspective of an interpersonal circumplex, distinct and markedly different subgoups have been identified. These groups have opposite styles for relating to others—one distant and hostile and the other nurturant and overtly valuing contact with other people. Further, these groupings do not show a systematic relationship to specific disturbances in eating per se, either in terms of diagnosis or in terms of assessed attitudes and beliefs. This implies that an analysis of interpersonal issues can proceed in parallel with more traditional cognitive–behavioral evaluation of these clients. Without getting into disputes about the primacy of one domain or the other, it appears that the two represent relatively independent ways of approaching the assessment task. Cognitive approaches emphasize beliefs and distortions common among these clients. Interpersonal analysis suggests that there also may be substantial differences among them.

Interpersonal theory (Benjamin, 1979; Kiesler, 1983) and the two-dimensional circumplex also can be used to postulate therapeutic strategies for the two groups of eating-disordered clients identified in this study. Before proceeding, it is important to emphasize that what has been identified at this point is interpersonal style. It is inferred that the styles that were displayed in the IAS are indeed related to the problems these individuals experienced that contributed to their eating disorder. In other words, it is assumed that problems in interpersonal relations, not problems relating to food itself, have propelled these clients into treatment and that these interpersonal problems are represented by their position on the circumplex. It is readily acknowledged that this is a working assumption on which the following therapy strategies are based. Much work is needed to validate this empirically.

The hostile group is the most straightforward to analyze. It is assumed that the style of these individuals is dominated by the cold distance and hostility of the cold–quarrelsome quadrant. Interpersonal theory suggests a possible deficit in their ability to deal with others in a warm and agreeable manner. This impression is further reinforced by examination of the circumplex mapping of this group in Figures 2 and 3. The shape of the score plot indicates that the cold group is not so much characterized by extreme elevations in the hostile octants as by relatively low scores in the affiliative octants.

The goal of therapy could be conceptualized as enhancing these individuals' abilities to relate to others using behaviors from the opposite octant in which their preferred style is demonstrated. Because the analysis suggests that the interpersonal style of this group is likely to be a complex combination of other cold and submissive octants (e.g., aloof–introverted and lazy–submissive), the therapist will have to select specific goals depending on the specific combination of behaviors shown by the client. In general, the complementarity principle generates the expectation that clients in this group are likely to draw both hostility and control from their treatment team. Particularly in the early stages of treatment, these clients may be regarded with mistrust and treated in a distant and cold manner. An interpersonal analysis may warn the therapists against emitting these behaviors and instead suggest exerting pressure on the client by moving to the anticomplementary or opposite position on the circle.

The nurturant, sociable subgroup is in some ways more problematic, though other studies suggest that they may be more treatable than the first group. This is most obvious in the plot of this group in Figure 3. Interpersonal theory suggests that these individuals have difficulty presenting behaviors from the opposite octants—cold–quarrelsome and aloof–introverted. They are the real life anticomplements of the first group. They tend to evoke cooperative and trusting responses from their treatment staff members. However, interpersonal theory warns that this could be an error, confirming a dysfunctional style rather than promoting change. The data also suggest that this group may not suffer so much from an extreme style but rather from a deficit in behaviors that are relevant to conflict and setting interpersonal boundaries or distance.

Based on this conceptualization, the treatment goal for this group might be to increase the ability of these clients to maintain appropriate interpersonal distance and to express anger or hostility when appropriate. This group was characterized as problematic partly as a result of the reluctance of therapists who typically are viewed as friendly–dominant in style to move to an octant that has negative cultural connotations in dealing with their clients. Yet, this is one of the recommendations that can be derived from circumplex models. If the client needs to develop skills in this area, the therapist must present the appropriately complementary behaviors to allow this skill development to occur. To compound matters further, the therapist dealing with eating-disordered clients is generally dealing with women. By addressing these issues, this approach explicitly invites clients to violate cultural stereotypes of female role behavior (Wiggins & Holzmuller, 1978).

In this context, Kiesler's (1983) emphasis on levels and intensity of interpersonal behavior may be particularly useful. The therapeutic issue is whether the client's warm and accommodating style is dysfunctional. Has it become a rigid and inflexible way of dealing with people such that she is having serious boundary problems and enmeshment with others in her environment? If the answer is yes, then the therapist is obliged to use the most effective tools to help change those behaviors. The circumplex and interpersonal theory can point the way, but the therapist must use careful judgement about the intensity of anticomplementary behavior used to move the client out of her rigid style. Techniques such as role play and fixed role therapy may allow the therapist and client to experience hostile transactions while preserving the therapeutic alliance and protecting self-esteem.

CONCLUSION

This chapter demonstrated the potential of an interpersonal circumplex model of personality for assessing and developing treatment recommendations for individuals with eating disorders. Except for family therapy, conceptualizations of eating disorder treatment have emphasized either psychodynamic or cognitive behavioral constructs. Treatments centered on altering distorted beliefs about food, weight, and body image consistently have demonstrated effectiveness, particularly with bulimia. However, recent work has indicated that interpersonal therapy strategies may be as effective with the same clinical population. The two-dimensional circumplex model of personality presented by Wiggins (1979) was used to develop initial expectations based on interpersonal descriptions of eating disordered clients and to assess the validity of these expectations.

The findings of this study indicate that there are two significant subgroups of eating disorder clients with substantially different interpersonal styles. Concepts derived from theories of the interpersonal circumplex indicate that these groups may have substantially different treatment needs. One group of individuals show a largely distant and hostile way of relating to others. For this group, techniques that promote more comfort and warmth in relating to others appear particularly relevant. Strategies to assist them in taking a more active role with others are also appropriate. Therapeutic traps include a tendency to distance these clients or exercise some forms of subtle hostile control. The second group shows a more friendly and nurturing style. It is possible that they experience deficits in their ability to tolerate conflict and set appropriate boundaries in relationships. A potential therapeutic trap could be the inadvertent reinforcement of their lopsided style due to their likability and apparent willingness to cooperate with the therapist. Naturally, these results require further investigation with other groups of eating-disordered clients and with other related circumplex measures. The further application of this model to understanding eating disorders holds much potential for improved therapeutic targeting of interpersonal interventions with this population, enhancing a treatment approach that has already begun to show efficacy.

REFERENCES

Andreasen, N. C., & Grove, W. M. (1982). The classification of depression: A comparison of traditional and mathematically derived approaches. *American Journal of Psychiatry, 139,* 45–52.

Benjamin, L. S. (1974). Structural analysis of social behavior. *Psychological Review, 81,* 392–425.

Benjamin, L. S. (1979). Structural analysis of differentiation failure. *Psychiatry, 42,* 1–23.

Benjamin, L. S. (1994). *Interpersonal diagnosis and treatment of personality disorders.* New York: Guilford Press.

Bruch, H. (1973). *Eating disorders.* New York: Basic Books.

Fairburn, C. G. (1985). Cognitive–behavioral treatment for bulimia. In D. M. Garner & P. E. Garfinkel (Eds.), *Handbook of psychotherapy for anorexia nervosa and bulimia* (pp. 160–192). New York: Guilford Press.

Fairburn, C. G., Peveler, R. C., Jones, R., Hope, R. A., & Doll, H. A. (1993). Predictors of 12-month outcome in bulimia nervosa and the influence of attitudes to shape and weight. *Journal of Consulting and Clinical Psychology, 61,* 696–698.

Garfinkel, P. E., & Garner, D. M. (1982). *Anorexia nervosa: A multidimensional perspective.* New York: Brunner/Mazel.

Garner, D. M. (1991). *The Eating Disorder Inventory-2 professional manual.* Odessa, FL: Psychological Assessment Resources.

Garner, D. M., & Bemis, K. M. (1982). A cognitive–behavioral approach to anorexia nervosa. *Cognitive Therapy and Research, 6,* 123–150.

Geist, R. A. (1985). Therapeutic dilemmas in the treatment of anorexia nervosa: A self-psychological perspective. In S. W. Emmett (Ed.), *Theory and treatment of anorexia nervosa and bulimia* (pp. 268–288). New York: Brunner/Mazel.

Horowitz, L. M., Rosenberg, S. E., Baer, B. A., Ureño, G., & Villaseñor, V. S. (1988). Inventory of Interpersonal Problems: Psychometric properties and clinical applications. *Journal of Consulting and Clinical Psychology, 56,* 885–892.

Humphrey, L. L. (1989). Observed family interactions among subtypes of eating disorders using structural analysis of social behavior. *Journal of Consulting and Clinical Psychology, 57,* 206–214.

Humphrey, L. L. (1994, October). *Family process in anorexia and bulimia.* Address to the Thirteenth National Conference on Eating Disorders, Columbus, OH.

Johnson, C., & Connors, M. E. (1987). *The etiology and treatment of bulimia nervosa.* New York: Basic Books.

Jones, R., Peveler, R. C., Hope, R. A., & Fairburn, C. G. (1993). Changes during treatment for bulimia nervosa: A comparison of three psychosocial treatments. *Behavior Research and Therapy, 31,* 479–485.

Kiesler, D. J. (1983). The 1982 interpersonal circle: A taxonomy for complementarity in human transactions. *Psychological Review, 90*, 185–214.

Klerman, G. L., Weissman, M. M., Rounsaville, B. J., & Chevron, E. S. (1984). *Interpersonal therapy of depression.* New York: Basic Books.

Leary, T. (1957). *Interpersonal diagnosis of personality: A functional theory and methodology for personality evaluation.* New York: Ronald Press.

Mizes, J. S. (1985). Bulimia: A review of its symptomatology and treatment. *Advances in Behavior Research and Therapy, 7*, 91–142.

Pyle, R. L., Mitchell, J. E., Eckert, E. D., Hatzukami, D. E., & Goff, G. M. (1984). The interruption of bulimic behaviors: A review of three treatment programs. *Psychiatric Clinics of North America, 7*, 275–286.

Wiggins, J. S. (1979). A psychological taxonomy of trait-descriptive terms: The interpersonal domain. *Journal of Personality and Social Psychology, 37*, 395–412.

Wiggins, J. S., & Holzmuller, A. (1978). Psychological androgyny and interpersonal behavior. *Journal of Consulting and Clinical Psychology, 46*, 40–52.

Wilfley, D. E. (1994, October). *Interpersonal psychotherapy adapted for group and for the treatment of binge eating disorder.* Paper presented at the Thirteenth National Conference on Eating Disorders, Columbus, OH.

EPILOGUE: THE FUTURE OF THE CIRCUMPLEX

ROBERT PLUTCHIK and HOPE R. CONTE

The contributors to this book have shown that the circumplex model has relevance to understanding the structure of both personality and emotions. The chapters have explored the issues of how a circumplex may be constructed, what the elements of the circumplex consist of, how the circumplex may apply to other related domains such as personality disorders and psychotherapy, and how the circumplex is related to the more traditional factor analytic models. In this epilogue, we will examine and review these and other issues concerning the future role of the circumplex model in psychology. We will cite its strengths and some of its weaknesses and we will suggest ideas for future research.

ISSUE 1: THE DIVERSITY OF CIRCUMPLEX MODELS

A number of different methods have been proposed for identifying a circumplex structure of basic elements. The circumplex is basically a description of the similarity structure of the components of a domain. Such components may consist of personality traits, broad personality dimensions, emotions, personality disorder labels, ego defenses, vocational interests and choices, interpersonal styles, and psychiatric symptoms, to name a few. This wide potential application of the circumplex model does not mean that it applies to all aspects of psychology. For example, intellectual functions do not fit readily into a circumplex structure, nor do the subscales of many psychological tests such as the Minnesota Multiphasic Personality Inventory.

The domains in which the circumplex appears to fit most readily are those that relate to interpersonal relations—that is, how people interact with each other. Implicit in such interactions are the ideas of degree of similarity of elements and the idea of polarity of elements. When present, these ideas of similarity and polarity generally lead to an overlapping circular structure of the interacting elements; the concept of conflict is often implicit in the structure.

In the preceding pages many suggestions have been given on how to determine the degree to which a circumplex structure exists for a given domain. Most depend on establishing a matrix of distances between each element of the domain and every other element. As has been illustrated, this can be done by means of correlation coefficients, multidimensional scaling, smallest-space analysis, direct similarity scaling, semantic differential methods, sinusoidal plotting of correlational matrices, and a variety of lesser known methods.

Given this diversity of starting points and methods it is not surprising that not all circumplex structures that have been published look similar. Besides the variety of methods used, there also have been great differences in the elements used to describe the circumplex. In the domain of affect, for example, some researchers have used such terms as *fatigue, lethargy*, and *low activation* to describe emotions. Other investigators have assumed that such terms do not describe the qualities of emotions per se but only their intensity levels. Instead they have chosen terms like *disgust, guilt*, and *depression*. It is evident that a circumplex that incorporates one set of terms will not look exactly like a circumplex that incorporates a partially non-overlapping set.

The same reasoning applies to the area of personality. A circumplex that uses such terms as *arrogant, ingenuous* and *unassured* (Wiggins) will appear different from one that uses terms such as *exploitable, cold, overly nurturant*, or *intrusive* (Horowitz), or one that uses such terms as *pessimistic, belligerent, passive*, or *curious* (Plutchik). The Kiesler Interpersonal Circle uses such terms as *self-reliant, aloof, punitive*, and *dependent* and also creates a circumplex. Despite these apparent differences, all these circumplexes are based on samples of terms from the same universe of personality and affect languages. In the same way, when the Structural Analysis of Social Behavior (SASB) model developed by Benjamin uses transitive verbs for one set of interpersonal relations (focus on other), intransitive verbs (focus on self) for another set, and self-introjects for a third, the result is three different circumplex structures—yet each clearly related to the other by theoretical constructs.

Another possible reason for the discrepancies among different circumplex models is the total number of elements included in the analyses. For example, if a dozen terms are selected for use in a circumplex analysis the chances of low overlap is obviously greater than if hundreds of terms are used. With large numbers of terms the overlap of meanings are more obvious and the chances of discrete breaks in the circumplex are much less. With large numbers of trait or affect terms, the seamless character of the circumplex structure becomes more evident. This has been demonstrated by such investigators as Conte and Plutchik (1981), Fisher (chapter 11, this volume), Hofstee, de Raad, and Goldberg (1992), McCormick and Goldberg (chapter 5, this volume) Plutchik (1980), and Saucier (1992). Fisher (chapter 11, this volume), McCormick and Goldberg (chapter 5, this volume), and Wiggins and Trobst (chapter 3, this volume) particularly have shown that the circular order of personality traits and emotions appear to be quite consistent over different samples of individuals and analytic procedures.

ISSUE 2: THE QUESTION OF AXES

The tradition has grown up in factor analytic studies to attribute theory-based names to the smaller number of factors derived from a larger number of intercorrelated variables. This seems like a reasonable procedure until one discovers the diversity of names given to the factors that are identified even in similar domains of study. Factor analytic studies of personality have produced such labels as extroversion, neuroticism, surgency, planfulness, intelligence, openness to experience, culture, love, hostility, control, thoughtful, tired–inert, spontaneous, expressive, impassive, and composed, to name a few. It hardly seems likely that all these dimensions are basic factors of personality. The choices of labels undoubtedly depend on the initial choices of items, on the personal predilections of the investigators, and on the actual degree of overlap of the traits found in each cluster. As one increases the factor weights used to select the defining terms for a given factor, different possibilities of labeling the factor become apparent. As factor weights are reduced in size for selection of factors, there is generally an increasing degree of overlap of the elements that are used to define the factors.

This simple, well-known reality is one of the reasons that has been given by some of the contributors to this book for looking for a circumplexical structure rather than a hierarchical-factor model. In all studies of personality and emotions, a large number of items (elements, traits, affects) load sometimes heavily on two or more factors. Thus there is sometimes considerable overlap of the elements of these domains; such overlap implies the possibility of a similarity structure that may be represented by a circumplex.

These observations have implications for how we conceive of axes. In a factor analytic model, anywhere from 2 to 16 or more axes may be selected as fundamental axes and given labels. These labels usually are used as the reified dimensions of the scales of a personality test. However, if the elements of a domain of study overlap as much as it appears on the basis of evidence from many studies, one may raise questions about the true nature of the labeled axes. To what extent are the labeled axes arbitrary? To what extent do they depend on the arbitrary weights used in defining factors? To what extent are clusters of terms dependent on accidents of sampling of items or on the use of small samples of terms? To what extent are factors a reflection of response biases related to such things as social desirability or lack of ipsatizing and standardization (chapter 15, this volume).

Although there is some agreement among different personality theorists as to what the true axes are, there is disagreement as well. Some claim that the basic dimensions are affiliation or nurturance and control or dominance. Others have described the basic axes as dominance–submission versus love–hate; some have called the axes emotional stability versus neuroticism; others have labeled them autonomy versus friendly–loving; and others have called them pleasure–displeasure versus attention–rejection, cheerful–depression versus aroused–tired, extraverted versus introverted, or conservative versus radical. Although some theorists prefer to consider the basic dimensions as unipolar, many others believe them to be bipolar (chapter 2, this volume), particularly when extreme bias scores are partialled out.

In a circular configuration it is unnecessary to look for any particular pair of axes as basic. The axes are arbitrary reference points that simply help us plot the positions of the variables relative to one another. The axes may be removed or ignored, and all relationships among the variables are expressed through the circular network.

An important feature of a circular structure is that it may reveal empty sectors that might be filled systematically in subsequent research. In theory, adding variables should not change the relative configuration of the original ones but would result in a more complete mapping of the universe being studied. The goal of a circumplex analysis is to sample all sectors of an interpersonal domain equally, which, if accomplished, would have the effect of showing the arbitrary nature of statistically computed factors.

The points that have been made suggest that so-called basic personality or emotion axes are fundamentally arbitrary. For example, in Kiesler's 1982 interpersonal circle in which all the trait terms are equally distributed around a circle, no one axis is any more basic than any other. In the same way, in Wiggins' octant circumplex, arrogant–unassuming is no less basic than assured–unassured.

An alternative way of saying this is that in any true or nearly true circle the positions of all points (or elements) on the circle relative to one another will be invariant whatever the coordinates used to locate them. Assumed underlying dimensions cannot explain the circumplex because any particular axis is arbitrary and no more basic than any other. In a relatively seamless circle of elements, any rotation of axes does not change the relations among the elements.

It is important to emphasize that there is nothing objectionable about the arbitrary labeling of preferred axes. They may be thought of, in a sense, as somewhat arbitrary selections of class-intervals. This makes it easier to discuss points of interest, and to create psychometric instruments that are useful. But, from a descriptive point of view, it does appear inappropriate to reify certain axes or labels as more fundamental than others.

ISSUE 3: IMPLICATIONS OF THE CIRCUMPLEX FOR TEST CONSTRUCTION AND MEASUREMENT

Factor analytic models have been used frequently to identify factors that may become the bases for psychometric tests or scales. This characteristic has been true also for circumplex models. As early as 1955, LaForge and Suczek developed an interpersonal checklist based on the Leary system of 16 interpersonal mechanisms. In 1958, Stern developed a circumplex-based test of 30 scales to measure such dimensions as achievement, aggression, deference, dominance, and impulsion. In 1959, Schaefer showed that ratings of social–emotional bahavior of mothers toward their children could be described by means of a circumplex. In 1965, Lorr and McNair analyzed self-report data to create a "hypothetical interpersonal behavior circle" that included 14 dimensions labeled by such terms as dominance, sociability, deference, abasement, mistrust, and detachment.

In 1974, Plutchik and Kellerman published the Emotions Profile Index, which is a circumplex-based test for measuring both emotions and personality based on eight scales. The scales were given such labels as gregariousness, trust, dyscontrol, and timidity. In this same year, Benjamin described her Structural Analysis of Social Behavior (SASB) system based on a circular model of interpersonal relations and has elaborated it since then into three interrelated circumplexes. This system has become a widely used test instrument, particularly in relation to psychotherapy research.

At the end of the 1970s, Wiggins developed the Interpersonal Adjective Scales (IAS; Wiggins, 1979), which is a clear circumplex representation of interpersonal space. Profiles based on this scale are used to assess personality dispositions. And in 1979, Horowitz and his colleagues identified interpersonal problems of people who had entered psychotherapy. The resulting test was called the Inventory of Interpersonal Problems (IIP) and has been used extensively in the past few years. In chapter 15 of this volume, Horowitz and Dryer describe the development of a new Inventory of Interpersonal Goals (IIG) based on the circumplex, and Kiesler, Schmidt, and Wagner (chapter 10, this volume) present a new circumplex Inventory of Impact Messages designed to measure interactants' covert experiences as they reciprocally interact in interpersonal encounters. Chapter 10 also demonstrates the intimate relationship between personality and emotions as they relate to transactional interpersonal processes. It is thus evident that the circumplex model has provided a potent basis for the creation of new psychometric instruments.

There is another important characteristic that the circumplex has in this context—to help clarify or reinterpret existing tests or scales by measuring more precisely their properties through secondary analyses. Two examples will be given.

The California Q-Set developed by Block (1961/1978) consists of 100 statements about personality traits that may be rated by judges, observers, or peers. It has been used widely in personality research. Gurtman (chapter 4, this volume) has reexamined California Q-Set data from a study published by Lanning (1994) based on 940 individuals rated by experts. Gurtman found that only 40 items had single-factor loadings (of .30 or more), whereas all but 1 of the remaining 60 items loaded significantly on two, three, or four factors. This kind of overlap is characteristic of the circumplex structure rather than simple structure. Plotting of the Q-Set data revealed at least two circumplexes—an interpersonal circumplex and an affective circumplex, both of which bear obvious resemblances to the Wiggins and Kiesler circles as well as those proposed by others. Further statistical tests showed a quite uniform distribution of the items of the test around a circle. Gurtman also has shown how to determine the thematic quality of a trait (that is—its predominant descriptive content), its breadth of coverage (fidelity or bandwidth), and its factorial saturation (shared variance with other traits of the particular domain being studied).

Using these statistical tools, Gurtman has shown how the "optimally adjusted personality" fits into the circumplex pattern. He also has demonstrated how the narcissistic personality pattern fits into a circumplex structure. He has argued that this method of analysis of published or archival data provide insights that are not fully seen by other methods.

A second illustration of a psychometrically useful function of the circumplex is seen in the chapter by McCormick and Goldberg (chapter 5, this volume). It is evident that items that fall near one another on a circumplex have similar meanings. However, it is possible to show that items that are clockwise to a given point of reference have different connotations than those that are counterclockwise. For example, in the Big Five factor structure, McCormick and Goldberg noted that "items located in the counter clockwise direction from 'dominance' turn out to be blends of Agreeableness (e.g., friendliness) and Extraversion, whereas items located in the clockwise direction are blends of Disagreeableness (e.g., hostility) and Extraversion." These authors also demonstrate that the scales of the Interpersonal Checklist (ICL) of the Leary system are not equally spaced around the circumference of a circle but that by a reanalysis of the density distribution of all the items, a much closer approximation to an ideal circumplex may be obtained. Wiggins (1979) also found that the use of item locations based on self-descriptions enabled him to cross-validate on different samples nearly perfect circumplex structures of his Interpersonal Adjective Scales (IAS).

A scaling of items of the ICL revealed interesting individual differences in the interpretation of items. Most judges considered the item "able to give orders" as similar in meaning to "managerial," whereas some defined it as "responsible." Two participants even placed this item in the docile category. Such internal item analyses can be used to identify both deviant raters and ambiguous items (McCormick & Goldberg, chapter 5, this volume).

ISSUE 4: RELATIONS BETWEEN THE CIRCUMPLEX AND THE FIVE FACTOR MODEL

The Five Factor Model has emerged from the factor analytic tradition based on two fundamental assumptions: (a) that some variables, items, or scales are strongly connected with each particular factor and no others (the criterion of simple structure or factorial univocality), and (b) that the items or components of a factor are largely equivalent and interchangeable. Based on these assumptions, extensive research, particularly in recent years, has led many researchers to conclude that a great deal of personality rating and self-report data may be subsumed under five broad, relatively independent factors that have been usually labeled by the following terms:

I. Extraversion
II. Agreeableness
III. Conscientiousness
IV. Emotional stability
V. Intellect/openness

This model has been interpreted from at least four different theoretical perspectives (Wiggins & Pincus, 1992). The enduring–dispositional perspective has been based on longitudinal studies of personality and aging and has led to the development of an assessment instrument in which each of the five broad factors is measured by six facets each (Costa & McCrae, 1989). The dyadic–interactional perspective stemmed largely from studies of dyadic interaction in psychotherapeutic settings, and has generated a set of eight circumplex scales (the Interpersonal Adjective Scales Revised that can provide scores for the five factors (Trapnell & Wiggins, 1990). The social competency perspective came out of studies of effective performance in work and social settings and has led to the development of scales designed to measure some but not all the five factors (Hogan, 1983). And the lexical perspective has been based on the study of personality descriptive terms in the natural language and has led to the development of domain scores for the five factors based on sets of adjectives (Goldberg, 1981). All these perspectives continue to stimulate research at the present time.

Despite this general interest in, and support for, the general Five Factor Model, a number of investigators have raised questions about the model and proposed an alternative way of conceptualizing the meaning of *personality structure*. As McCormick and Goldberg (chapter 5, this volume) pointed out,

> In a perfectly simple-structured world, each item would be associated with one and only one factor, and all of its loadings on other factors would be near zero. In the real world, most items are factorially complex rather than factorially univocal, and most items have substantial loadings on two or more factors ... an item ... is in fact a multidimensional package. (pp. 105)

This statement clearly applies to many of the complex constructs studied by psychologists, constructs related to personality disorders, psychopathology, authoritarianism, social adjustment, and work functioning.

That these issues are not merely theoretical has been demonstrated by various authors. For example, the study by Saucier (1992) examined the extent to which the Big Five dimensions were clearly discrete axes in contrast to the degree to which interstitial variables were located in the spaces between axes. "In a perfect simple structure, there are no interstitial variables .... In a perfect circumplex, as many variables inhabit the interstitial regions as inhabit the regions where the factor axes are placed." (Saucier, 1992, p. 1027)

Saucier's data were based on self- and peer ratings made by 320 students on 394 trait adjectives. Using several indices of the presence of interstitial variables (e.g., second highest loading is large compared to highest loading), he showed that three of the Big Five factors showed high levels of interstitial variables. These three were extraversion (I), agreeableness (II), and emotional stability (IV). In other words when Axis I data were plotted against Axis II or Axis IV data, fairly complete circumplex similarity structures were formed. When pairs were plotted involving conscientiousness (III) or intellect (V), circumplex patterns were not evident. These findings are interpreted as implying the existence of a three-dimensional, circumplex-ordered emotion–personality space defining interpersonal relations. Similar results have been reported by Hofstee, de Raad, and Goldberg (1992).

Although the question of the relation between the Five Factor Model and the circumplex model is far from settled, it is likely that some preliminary observations can be made. The Five Factor Model appears to provide a reasonable approximation to the broad, omnibus conception of personality, which focuses on many classes of individual differences. For some of the pairs of dimensions, however, there are considerable interstitial distributions of trait characteristics, with variables loading on multiple factors, so that a circumplex structure fits the data reasonably well. The axes for which this is most true are those that relate to interpersonal relations, which includes both personality traits and emotions. It may be tentatively concluded that the Five Factor Model and the circumplex model are complementary, but with each having a different focus of interest. For a broad look at personality dispositions the Five Factor Model may be of most use, whereas an interest in specific traits, blends, and interpersonal interactions may suggest the need to focus on the circumplex model. Future research should clarify these issues.

ISSUE 5: THE IMPORTANCE OF THE CIRCUMPLEX MODEL

A close examination of the theory and data presented in this book will show that there are often inconsistencies in the terms and labels given for different aspects of the circumplex. We have noted already that this at least in part reflects the proclivities, interests, and backgrounds of the different investigators; their different methods of approach; as well as the size of the samples of concepts used. However, it should be kept in mind that there is nothing unusual in finding disagreements among scientific investigators. This fact is certainly true of the many attempts by earlier personality and emotion researchers to identify basic factors or dimensions, relevant variables, and comprehensive theories. This is also true of all other areas of psychology. The study of the circumplex is relatively new and new methods and concepts are currently being developed. Creative thinking about possible applications is apparent and sometimes marked disagreements become evident. To the extent that this occurs this should be thought of as a positive development. It represents the ferment associated with new ideas.

However, it may be concluded that the contributors to this volume have shown how the circumplex idea can be applied to a wide variety of problems in the psychology of personality and emotions. The model has relevance for understanding personality traits, personality disorders, emotions, psychiatric symptoms, psychotherapy interactions, adaptive functioning, vocational preferences, and goal-setting. Investigators interested in the model have demonstrated a number of mostly unfamiliar ways of mathematically and psychometrically dealing with circular configurations so that future research can be both more sophisticated and informative. The focus on items or components rather than factors has revealed some interesting things about existing personality scales and has helped eliminate certain ambiguities in test results. Of great importance is the fact that the circumplex model has stimulated the development of new tests and scales that will provide the raw material for much future research.

Finally, it should be emphasized that the circumplex model has led to many testable hypotheses that have become the basis of ongoing research programs. The work of Kiesler and his associates (chapter 10, this volume) on the interpersonal circle has led to specific hypotheses about interpersonal interactions. This has been followed up by Horowitz and Dryer (chapter 15, this volume) who have made specific proposals about psychotherapeutic interventions based on the model. The work of Benjamin and her colleagues (Henry, chapter 16, this volume) on the SASB circumplex has led to relatively precise ways to describe interpersonal problems and has provided a set of principles to help explain the persistence of negative interpersonal cycles. It has focused the clinician's attention on fairly specific interpersonal behaviors that might be targeted for change. And, in making sense of a patient's history, problems, affects, process of therapy, and outcomes, it has incorporated aspects of psychodynamic theory into a general view of interpersonal interactions. It would appear that the circumplex model of interpersonal interactions has both descriptive and dynamic aspects; it has stimulated the development of new measuring instruments and has provided substantive hypotheses that are likely to provide the basis for much future research as well as theory.

REFERENCES

Benjamin, L. S. (1974). Structural Analysis of Social Behavior. *Psychological Review, 81*, 392–425.

Block, J. (1961/1978). *The Q-Sort method in personality assessment and psychiatric research.* Palo Alto, CA: Consulting Psychologists Press.

Conte, H. R., & Plutchik, R. (1981). A circumplex model for interpersonal personality traits. *Journal of Personality and Social Psychology, 40*, 710–711.

Costa, P. T., & McCrae, R. R. (1989). *The NEO-PI/FFI Manual Supplement.* Odessa, FL: Psychological Assessment Resources.

Goldberg, L. R. (1981). Language and individual differences: The search for universals in personality lexicons. In L. Wheeler (Ed.), *Review of personality and social psychology* (Vol. 2, pp. 141–165). Beverly Hills, CA: Sage.

Hofstee, W. K. B., de Raad, B., & Goldberg, L. R. (1992). Integration of the Big Five and circumplex approaches to trait structure. *Journal of Personality and Social Psychology, 63*, 146–163.

Hogan, R. (1983). A socioanalytic theory of personality. In M. Page (Ed.), *1982 Nebraska Symposium on Motivation: Personality—current theory and research* (pp. 55–89). Lincoln: University of Nebraska Press.

Horowitz, L. M. (1979). On the cognitive structure of interpersonal problems treated in psychotherapy. *Journal of Consulting and Clinical Psychology, 47*(1), 5–15.

LaForge, R., & Suczek, R. F. (1955). The interpersonal dimension of personality: III. An interpersonal checklist. *Journal of Personality, 24,* 94–112.

Lanning, K. (1994). Dimensionality of observer ratings on the California Adult Q-Set. *Journal of Personality and Social Psychology, 67,* 151–160.

Lorr, M., & McNair, D. M. (1965). Expansion of the interpersonal behavior circle. *Journal of Personality and Social Psychology, 2,* 823–830.

Plutchik, R. (1980). *Emotion: A psychoevolutionary synthesis.* New York: Harper & Row.

Plutchik, R., & Kellerman, H. (1974). *Manual of the Emotions Profile Index.* Los Angeles: Western Psychological Services.

Saucier, G. (1992). Benchmarks: Integrating affective and interpersonal circles with the Big-Five personality factors. *Journal of Personality and Social Psychology, 62,* 1025–1035.

Schaefer, E. S. (1959). A circumplex model for maternal behavior. *Journal of Abnormal and Social Psychology, 59,* 226–235.

Stern, G. G. (1958). *Activities Index.* Syracuse, NY: Syracuse University Research Center.

Trapnell, P. D., & Wiggins, J. S. (1990). Extension of the Interpersonal Adjective Scales to include the Big Five dimensions of personality. *Journal of Personality and Social Psychology, 59,* 781–790.

Wiggins, J. S. (1979). A psychological toxonomy of trait descriptive terms: The interpersonal domain. *Journal of Personality and Social Psychology, 37,* 395–412.

Wiggins, J. S., & Pincus, A. L. (1992). Personality: Structure and assessment. *Annual Review of Psychology, 43,* 473–504.

AUTHOR INDEX

Numbers in italics refer to listings in reference sections.

Aaronson, B. S., 27, *42*
Aaronson, M. R., 140, *152*
Abelson, R. P., 212, 213, *217*
Adolphs, R., 212, *217*
Alden, L. E., 62, 73, *77*, 228, *241*, 350, 372, *379*, 412, 413, 420, *426*
Aldwin, C., 359, *380*
Allen, B., 18, *41*
Allport, G. W., 25, *41*, 139, *150*
Altman, J. H., 359, *379*
Alwin, D. E., 335, *346*
American Psychiatric Association, 146, *150*, 171, *179*, 299, 300, 301, 302, 308, 314, 316, 319, *321*, 338, 342, *344*, 393, *407*, 416, *426*
Anchin, J. C., 222, 223, *241*, *243*
Anderson, C. A., 368, *382*
Anderson, M. Z., 190, *198*
Andreasen, N. C., 439, *445*
Angyal, A., 354, *379*
Apter, A., 40, *42*
Arabie, P., 185, 186, 187, 196, *199*
Archer, D., 97, *102*
Argyle, M., 156, *179*
Arkowitz, H., 370, *379*, *381*
Arnold, M. B., 233, 235, *241*, 274, *291*
Averill, J. R., 209, *217*, 233, 237, 239, *241*, *243*

Baer, B. A., 47, *54*, 62, 78, 228, *242*, 307, *322*, 348, *382*, 412, 427, 433, *445*
Bagdanoff, J., 361, *379*
Bakan, D., 58, *77*, 354, *379*
Bales, R. F., 58, *79*
Balla, J. R., 335, *345*
Bandura, A., 354, *379*
Baron, R. A., 173, *179*
Bartholomew, K., 82, *101*, 355, *379*
Bateson, G., 222, *244*
Batschelet, E., 109, 112, 120, *128*
Batten, P. G., 369, *383*
Baumrind, D., 146, *150*

Bayley, N., 27, *41*, 134, 136, 140, *150*, *152*
Beatty, M., 376, *381*
Beck, A. T., 359, *379*, 393, *408*
Beck, S., 353, *380*
Becker, W. C., 137, 139, 144, *150*, *151*
Beech, A. R., 342, *344*
Beier, E. G., 222, *241*
Bell, R. Q., 134, 136, *152*
Bellack, A. S., 369, *379*
Bemis, K. M., 432, *445*
Benjamin, L. S., 11, *14*, 49, 50, 54, *54*, 75, *77*, 299, 308, 309, 310, 316, 317, 318, 320, *321*, *322*, 352, *379*, 386, 387, 389, 392, 393, 396, 397, 399, 400, 403, 406, 408, *412n1*, *426*, 432, 442, *445*, 451, *456*
Bentler, D. M., 51, *54*
Bentler, P. M., 328, 335, *344*
Bernstein, A. B., 222, *243*
Berscheid, E., 237, *241*
Berzins, J. I., 353, *379*
Bierman, R., 353, *379*
Binder, J. P., 385, *409*
Birchler, G., 367, *379*
Birtchnell, J., 155, 156, 157, *158*, 161, 162, 163, 164, 165, 172, 177, *179*, *180*
Bishop, P. F., 302, *323*
Blackburn, R., 156, 174, *180*, 300, *321*
Blaney, P. H., 376, *384*
Blashfield, R., 336, *344*
Blashfield, R. K., 306, *323*, 334
Blatt, S. J., 161, 176, *180*, 354, *380*, 393, *408*
Block, J., 24, *42*, 82, 83, 86, 87, 88, 94, 99, *452*, *451*
Bluhm, C., 318, *321*, 357, *380*
Blumberg, S. R., 359, 360, *380*, *382*
Bohrnstedt, G. W., 49, *54*, 87, *100*, 112, *129*, 211, *218*, 232, *242*, *245*, 246, 252, *254*, 268
Bolton, B., 193, *198*

Hope, K., 195, *199*
Hope, R. A., 432, *445*
Horney, K., 159, *181*, 352, *382*, 398, *409*
Horowitz, L. M., 47, *54*, 62, 78, 82, *101*,
    228, *242*, 307, 308, *322*, 342,
    345, 348, 349, 351, 352, 354,
    357, 359, 360, 368, 371, 372,
    376, *379*, *380*, *382*, *383*, *393*,
    409, 412, 416, *427*, 433, *445*,
    451, *457*
Horowitz, M. J., 29, *42*
Howes, M. J., 376, *382*
Hoyle, R. H., 343, *345*
Hubert, L., 185, 186, 196, *199*, *200*
Hull, J. W., 313, *321*
Humphrey, L. L., 432, 435, *445*
Humphries, D. A., 285, *292*
Hunter, W. M., 145, *145*, 146, *147*, *148*,
    152
Hyler, S. E., 178, *181*, 307, 309, *322*,
    333, 339, *345*

Irwin, H. J., 174, *182*
Izard, C. E., 208, 212, 214, *218*, 250,
    268, 274, 276, 285, *293*

Jackson, D. N., 50, *54*, 183, *199*, 280,
    293, 307, *323*
Jansen, J. A. M., 306, *322*, 416, *426*
Jefferson, G., 362, 375, *382*
John, O. P., 81, 84, 85, *101*, 411, 418,
    427
Johnson, C., 433, *445*
Johnson, D. M., 75, *79*
Johnson, J. A., 82, 84, 98, *101*
Jones, E. M., 193, *199*
Jones, R., 432, *445*
Jones, W. H., 368, *381*, *382*
Jöreskog, K. G., 327, 328, 331, 339, *345*
Justed, J., *322*

Kalma, A., 284, *293*
Kalverboer, A. F., 140, *152*
Kanner, A. D., 233, *243*
Kantor, M., 174, *181*
Kass, F., 307, *322*, 333, 339, *345*
Katz, R., 161, *181*
Kavanagh, J. A., 114, 122, 127, *130*
Keller, M. B., *181*
Kellerman, H., 38, 40, *42*, 44, 451, *457*
Kellman, H. D., 178, *181*
Kelly, G., 411, 412, *427*
Kelso, K., 299, 311, *324*

Kemper, T. D., 233, 234, 238, *242*, 274,
    293
Kernberg, O., 417, *427*
Kiesler, D. J., 27, *42*, 62, 78, 86, 89, 94,
    95, 98, *101*, 163, 178, *181*, 194,
    199, 221, 222, 223, 224, 225,
    226, 227, 233, 237, 239, 240,
    241, *241*, *242*, 243, 244, 272,
    291, *293*, 299, 304, 305, 306,
    308, 309, 316, 320, *322*, 333,
    345, 352, 357, 372, *382*, 412,
    416, 417, 423, *427*, 429, 431,
    433, 442, 443, *446*
Kilmartin, C. T., *182*, 294, *383*
Klein, M. H., 309, 311, *322*
Klerman, G. L., *181*, 432, *446*
Klett, C. J., 52, 53, *55*
Krantz, D. H., 107, *130*
Krasnoperova, E. N., 360, *382*
Krug, R. S., 139, 144, *151*
Kruskal, J. B., 135, *151*, 288, *293*
Kuder, F., 183, *200*
Kuipers, P., 274, *292*
Kyle, E. M., *243*

Lafferty, J., 374, *383*
LaForge, R., 26, *42*, 48, 53, *54*, 109, 111,
    115, 116, *130*, 160, *181*, 231,
    243, 303, 306, 307, *322*, 333,
    345, 353, *383*, 451, *457*
Laing, R. D., 62, 78
Lakoff, G., 209, *218*
Lambert, W. W., 212, *220*
Lancee, W. J., 211, *218*
Landrum, G. C., 359, *382*
Lanier, K., *182*, 294, *383*
Lanning, K., 83, 84, 85, *101*, 452, *457*
Larus, J. P., 306, *322*, 416, *427*
Lasky, J. J., 52, 53, *55*
Launier, R., 238, *243*
Lavori, P., *181*
Lazarus, R. S., 233, 234, 236, 238, *243*,
    274, *293*, 359, *380*
Leary, T., 26, *42*, 48, 53, *54*, *55*, 60n2,
    63, *77*, 78, 89, *101*, 109, 115,
    116, 122, *129*, *130*, 139, 149,
    151, 156, 159, 160, 164, 178,
    181, 194, *200*, 223, 239, *243*,
    271, 272, 273, 284, *292*, *293*,
    299, 300, 301, 304, 308, 309,
    316, 320, *323*, 330, *345*, 352,

Storm, C., 17, *45*
Storm, T., 17, *45*
Strack, S., 31, 37, *45*, 48, *55*, 71, *79*,
    300, 306, *324*, 376, *383*
Strickland, D., *182*, *294*, *383*
Strong, S. R., 178, *182*, 272, 291, *294*,
    357, 358, 372, *383*
Strupp, H. H., 385, 386, 389, 391, 392,
    408, 409, 412n1, *427*
Suci, G. J., 49, *55*, 139, *151*
Suczek, R. F., 26, *42*, 48, 53, 54, 111,
    115, 116, *130*, 160, *181*, 303,
    306, 307, *322*, 353, *383*, 451,
    457
Sullivan, H. S., 59, *79*, 159, 160, *182*,
    352, *383*, 388, 391, *410*
Sultan, F. E., 368, *380*
Summers, G. F., 335, *346*
Suppes, P., 107, *130*
Sutton, M. A., 183, *199*
Swanson, J. L., 190, *199*

Takane, Y., 144, *153*
Tannenbaum, P. H., 49, *55*,139, *151*
Tanney, A., 178, *181*
Tarnow, E., *382*
Taylor, G. J., 168, *182*
Taylor, S. E., 66, *77*
Tellegen, A., 84, 86, *102*, 211, 213, *220*,
    235, *244*, 316, *320*
ter Schure, E., 274, *292*
Thayer, R. E., 212, *219*
Thissen, D., 82, 87, *102*
Thurstone, L. L., 104, *131*, 133, 135, *153*
Tomkins, S. S., 250, *269*
Tomlinson-Keasey, C., 83, *100*
Torgerson, W. S., 107, *131*
Tracey, T. J., 62, *79*, 113, *131*, *184*, *185*,
    186, 187, 188, 189, 190, 191,
    192, 193, 194, 195, *197*, 198,
    200, 412, 413, 426, *428*
Tracey, T. J. G., 186, 187, 190, 191, 195,
    196, *200*, *201*
Tranel, D., 212, *217*
Trapnell, P., 48, 56, 57, 64, *80*, 109, *132*,
    194, *201*, 228, *244*, 333, *346*,
    425, *429*
Trapnell, P. D., 48, *55*, 59, 62, 65, 73,
    80, 194, 196, *198*, *201*, 314, *325*,
    414, 415, 418, *429*, 453, *457*
Treece, C., *322*
Triandis, H. C., 58, 63, *79*, 212, *220*

Trobst, K. K., 66, 67, *80*
Trower, P., *22*, *45*
Trull, T. J., 312, 313, *324*, 387, *410*
Tversky, A., 107, *130*
Tyber, E., 398, *410*

Ulrich, R. F., 144, *151*
Upton, G. J. G., 87, *102*, 112, *131*
Ureño, G., 47, 54, 62, 78, 228, 242, 307,
    322, 348, *382*, 412, *427*, 433,
    445

Vaillant, G. E., 38, *45*
van den Brink, W., 306, *322*, 416, *426*
Van Denburg, E., 319, *321*
Van Denburg, T. F., 306, *322*, 416, 423,
    427, *429*
Vansickle, T. R., 188, *200*
Vehrencamp, S., 291, *294*
Villaseñor, V. S., 47, 54, 62, 78, 228,
    242, 307, *322*, 348, *382*, 412,
    427, 433, *445*
Vincent, J., 367, *379*
Vitkus, J., 342, *345*, 352, 357, 369, *382*,
    383, 393, *409*
Vorhies, L., 312, *321*

Wagner, C. C., 227, *244*, 423, *429*
Waikar, S. V., *382*
Wainer, H., 82, 87, *102*
Wallbott, H. G., 276, *294*
Wampold, B. E., 367, *383*
Ward, L. M., 209, *218*
Waters, E., 275, *294*
Watson, D., 84, 86, *102*, 211, 213, *220*,
    235, *244*, 312, 316, *320*, *324*
Watson, G. S., 112, 121, *131*
Watzlawick, P., 362, *383*
Waugh, M. H., 306, *323*
Weakland, J., 362, *383*
Weckler, D. A., 62, 78, 348, *382*
Weiss, R., 367, *379*
Weissman, M. M., 432, *446*
West, M., 178, *181*
West, S. G., 423, *426*
Wheaton, B., 335, *346*
Wherry, R. J., Sr., 104, *131*
White, J. S., 280, *294*
White, R. W., 277, *294*
Widaman, K., 83, *100*
Widiger, T. A., 299, 311, 312, 313, 314,
    316, 318, *321*, *324*, 336, 341,

SUBJECT INDEX

Anorexia nervosa, 431–445
    complementarity principle application, 443
    Eating Disorders Inventory scores, 440–442
    Interpersonal Adjective Scale scores, 436–440
    interpersonal description of, 433–438
    subgroups, clinical applications, 442–444
Antisocial personality disorder
    complementarity principle, clinical application, 318–319

    conscientiousness levels, 314
    interpersonal circumplex model, 31–37, 416–418
    novelty-seeking dimension, 339–341
    octagonal model, 172, 174
    Personality Disorder Examination and MCMI-II, 416–418
    quasi-simplex model, 339–341
    and therapeutic relationship, 319
Anxious attachment, 168
Anxiousness, 22
Arousal, 234–235
Assertiveness capacity, 370
Assessment of Personal Goals, 372
Attachment relationship
    in abnormal personality development, 396–398
    biologically based propensity, 276
    and emotions, 275–276
    facial expression, 285–290
    and interpersonal behavior, 354–356
    interpersonal circle polarities, 278–279
    and interpersonal octagon, 155–156
    personality development model, 395–398
    and relational diagnoses, 403–404
    and self-image, 354–356
Attitude theory, 236
Attitudes about Significant Relationships, 402
Autonomy and Relatedness Inventory, 138
Average absolute standardized residual, 335
Avoidant personality disorder

interpersonal circumplex model, 31–37, 416–417
neuroticism relationship, 313
octagon model, 172, 176
Personality Disorder Examination and MCMI-II, 416–417
quasi-simplex model, 339–340
Axes conception, 449–450

Bandwidth of traits, 91–92
Behavior therapy, 405
Behavioral scale measures, 134–135
Behavioral triangle, 291
Big Five. *See* Five Factor Model
Bipolar Self-Rating Scale, 419
Borderline personality disorder
    interpersonal circumplex, 31–37, 304–310, 417–418
    and neuroticism, 312–313, 419
    novelty-seeking dimension, 339–341
    octagon model, 172, 175
    Personality Disorder Examination and MCMI-II, 417–418
    quasi-simplex model, 339–341
Breath of trait coverage, 91–94
Bulimia nervosa, 431–445
    complementarity principle application, 443
    Eating Disorders Inventory scores, 440–442
    Interpersonal Adjective Scale scores, 436–440
    interpersonal description, 433–438
    subgroups of, clinical implications, 442–444

California Q-Set
    affective circumplex, 84–89
    circumplex structure, 84–89, 93–99, 452
    factor loadings, 83
    interpersonal circumplex, 84–89
    overview, 82–83
Categorical–dimensional dispute. *See also* Hierarchical model
    emotions, 216
    personality disorders, 34
Child abuse, 368
Child Adaptive Behavior Inventory, 145–146
Child behavior
    circumplex model development, 138–143

and interpersonal circumplex, 312,
314–315, 341, 414–415, 418–420
self versus other ratings, 424
vocational interests correlation,
193–194

Facet theory, 58–59
Facial expressions
children's judgements of, 212–213
circumplex of, 211–212
interpersonal circle emotional analysis, 284–291
judgements of, color wheel analogy, 23
Factor analysis. *See also* Confirmatory factor analysis; Exploratory factor analysis; Five Factor Model
and axes conception, 449–450
in conceptual model development, 135–136
Interpersonal Checklist, 116–119
mood states-traits, 252–258
Factor list approach
circular structure comparison, 187–189
vocational interests, 187–189
Factorial saturation, 92–93
Fantasy, 234–235, 237
Fearfulness orientation
and defensiveness, 276–277
facial expressions, 285–290
functional consequences, 277
interpersonal circle interpretation, 272–273, 278–291
Feelings, 274–275
Fidelity versus bandwidth distinction, 91–92
Five Factor Model
AB5C structure, item analysis, 114
affective circumplex relationship, 83–84
circumplex operationalization, 114
group psychotherapy analysis, 414–415
interpersonal circumplex relationship, 48, 54, 83–84, 311–321, 418–420, 453–455
and personality disorders, 311–321
and self versus other ratings, 423–425
simple structure emphasis, 316
simplex model relationship, 341

Structural Analysis of Social Behavior comparison, 405–406
structure of, 48
vocational interests correlation, 193–195
Fusion, 168
Fuzzy categories, emotion, 209, 215

Gap tests, 87, 89
Gati's partition model, 184, 196–187
Gender roles, and vocational interests, 191–193
Goodness-of-fit
measures, 335, 339
structural equation modeling, 332, 339
Group psychotherapy
Five Factor Model, 414–415
interpersonal circumplex analysis, 413–415
interpersonal sensitivity in, 415
outcome factors, 415
speech analysis in, 414
Guttman's model, 106–107

Helping behavior. *See* Social support transactions
Hierarchical model
assumptions in, 104
and axes conceptions, 449–450
child adaptive behavior, 142
exploratory factor analysis, 327–329
limitations, 104–105, 327–329, 449–450
High point codes, 192–193
Histrionic personality disorder
complementarity principle, 319
interpersonal circumplex, 31–37, 303–310, 316, 337, 416–417
and emotionality, 316
octagonal model, 172, 175
Personality Disorder Examination and MCMI-II, 416, 417
structural equation modeling, 337
and therapeutic relationship, 319
Holland's occupational model, 183–201
generalizability, 190–192
and personality types, 193–195
structure, 184–195
Hyperkinetic behavior, 140–141
Hypnosis, 236
Hypomanic personality disorder, 333, 337, 342

ABOUT THE EDITORS

Robert Plutchik, PhD, is Professor Emeritus of Psychiatry and Psychology at the Albert Einstein College of Medicine, and Associate Director of the Psychiatry Department at the Bronx Municipal Hospital Center. Earlier in his career he was involved in psychiatric research at the New York State Psychiatric Institute. Subsequently, he was Director of Program Development and Clinical Research at the Bronx Psychiatric Center. He also spent several years as a Fellow at the National Institute of Mental Health conducting brain stimulation research in primates. He has taught at Columbia, Yeshiva, Hofstra and Long Island Universities as well as at SUNY Purchase and the New School for Social Research. His main areas of current interest include the study of emotions, psychotherapy, suicide and violence.

Dr. Plutchik has served as a consultant to the National Institute of Mental Health and to AT&T, as well as other agencies and companies. He had lectured widely at medical schools and universities throughout the United States and in a number of foreign countries, including New Zealand, China, and Japan. He is author or co-author of over 250 publications, has written five books and coedited six books. His work on emotion is internationally recognized. He has been invited to contribute articles on emotion to the *World Book Encyclopedia*, the *Academic American Encyclopedia*, *Blackwell's Encyclopedic Dictionary of Psychology*, and the *International Encyclopedia of Neurology, Psychiatry, Psychoanalysis and Psychology*. He is the author of *The Emotions: Facts, Theories and a New Model* (Random

House, 1962), *Foundations of Experimental Research* (Harper and Row, 1968), *Emotion: A Psychoevolutionary Synthesis* (Harper and Row, 1980), and *The Psychology and Biology of Emotion* (HarperCollins, 1994).

Hope R. Conte, PhD, is Professor of Psychiatry and Psychology at the Albert Einstein College of Medicine and Director of the Psychodynamic Psychotherapy Research Fellowship Program of the Psychiatry Department at the Bronx Municipal Hospital Center. She is the author or coauthor of over 100 publications in peer reviewed journals, with major interests in the areas of personality and psychotherapy research and psychometrics. Some of her articles that are considered seminal include the following: "A Circumplex Model for Interpersonal Personality Traits," published in the *Journal of Personality and Social Psychology* in 1981; "Combined Psychotherapy and Pharmacotherapy in the Treatment of Depression: A Systematic Analysis of the Evidence," 1986, in the *Archives of General Psychiatry*; and "Interrelations Among Ego Functions and Personality Traits: Their Relation to Psychotherapy Outcome," published in the *American Journal of Psychotherapy* in 1991.

Most recently, Dr. Conte has contributed two chapters to volumes dealing with ego defenses that describe recent work with a self-report scale for the measurement of ego defense mechanisms that she helped to develop. She is senior editor of a book now in press titled *Ego Defenses: Theory and Measurement*.